Celebrate
Our Daughters

Celebrate
Our Daughters

150 Years of Women in Wesleyan Ministry

Maxine L. Haines and Lee M. Haines

wesleyan
publishing
house

Indianapolis, Indiana

Copyright © 2004 by The Wesleyan Church
Published by Wesleyan Publishing House
Indianapolis, Indiana 46250
Printed in the United States of America

ISBN 0-89827-282-3

Library of Congress Cataloging-in-Publication Data

Haines, Maxine L.
    Celebrate our daughters : 150 years of women in Wesleyan ministry / Maxine L. Haines ; completed and
edited by Lee M. Haines.
        p. cm.
    ISBN 0-89827-282-3 (pbk.)
    1. Wesleyan Church--Clergy--Biography. 2. Women clergy--Biography. I. Haines, Lee M., 1927- II. Title.
    BX9995.W48H35 2004
    287'.1'0922--dc22

                                                                                            2004009377

Front cover photo: Rev. Vera Close leading singing at a regional youth convention, Colorado Springs, Colo., 1949.
Back cover photo: Maxine L. Shockey (Haines), college graduation photo, 1948.

Dedicated to Our Granddaughters

Nicole Rene Haines, age twenty-two, and

Kristen Suzanne Haines, age twenty,

Both of whom are already called and preparing for the ministry

and

Katherine Elizabeth Haines (Katie Beth), age twelve,

who is waiting for the Lord's instruction

Maxine L. Shockey (Haines)
1925—2002

THE WESLEYAN CHURCH AND ITS PRECEDING ORGANIZATIONS

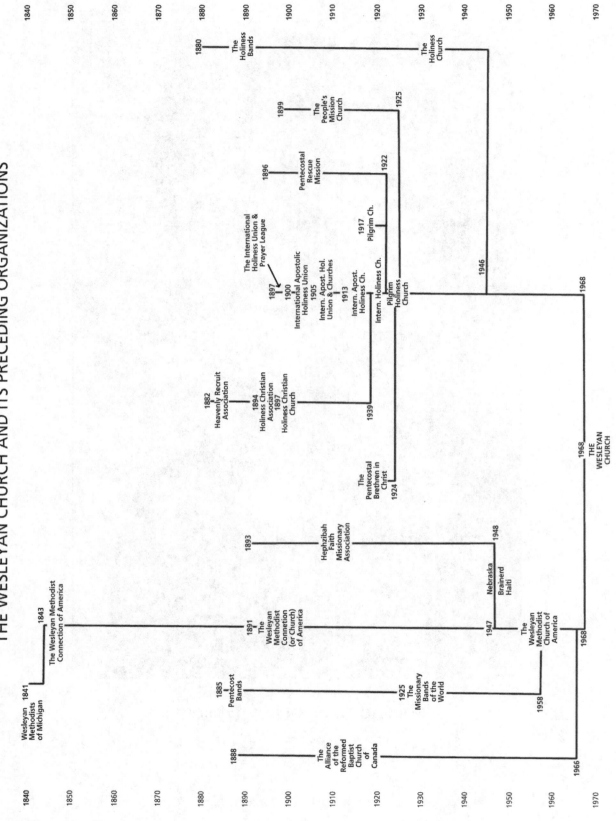

Contents

Preface

Rev. Maxine L. Haines was the lady I began sharing my life with through two and one-half years of courtship, and then more fully through fifty-four years of marriage. Even before that, I have memories of her leadership in our home church during her teen years, teaching, preaching, and singing. We preached together in our home church, were ordained together in 1950, and had a team ministry through our entire marriage.

Both of us have had deep concern over women being called into the ministry and investing time, energy, and money in preparation only to find that there are few opportunities to fully serve in that capacity. About six years ago, Maxine came to the conclusion that perhaps eyes could be opened if the Church only knew how God has worked through women in the past. She became convinced that she should research and write such a book—to preserve the history of what has indeed been a glorious miracle of divine grace and human service. She did not want these women to be forgotten or for the Church to fail to appreciate their amazing contributions.

Maxine did enormous research, primarily at the Archives and Historical Library of The Wesleyan Church. She examined all the district and conference journals from the fourteen organizations that have been known by at least twenty-five different names, all now merged as The Wesleyan Church. She concentrated her research on the period from 1841, when abolitionists in Michigan organized as Wesleyan Methodists, to 1968, when the Wesleyan Methodist and the Pilgrim Holiness Churches became one. In addition, she contacted district superintendents, past and present, and other church leaders, for leads and information on Wesleyan women ministers. She also contacted women ministers still living and families and friends of those who had passed on. She collected an unbelievable amount of data. We both were surprised when she identified nearly two thousand Wesleyan women ministers who began their ministry before 1968. She was forced by the sheer volume to limit the group about whom she would write. She laid aside hundreds of files of women who had been licensed only. Nearly all of the approximately one thousand she selected for inclusion were ordained. She included a few non-ordained women who had unusual prominence, had pastored extensively, or had preached widely across the churches.

In the fall of 2000, Maxine developed cancer. Surgeries, chemotherapy sessions, and series of radiation treatments followed through 2001 and into 2002. But on September 16, 2002, she went home to be with her Savior. By that time she had completed her research and had written about half of the stories that would eventually fill almost two-thirds of the pages of this book. She also jotted down ideas that have contributed to the writing of the conclusion. As I saw her slipping from us, I knew that this project must be completed as her final gift to the Church she loved and served. She had consulted and shared with me through those years. But I still found it to be a large challenge to immerse myself in what she had already written and then continue with her purpose and design. It has been a service of love and has brought tremendous inspiration and blessing to me at the same time. I offer this work in the hope that God may use it to inspire His Church to continue affirming and using our daughters in His service.

LEE M. HAINES

October 2003

Introduction

Celebrate our daughters—God's servants!

The culture of the current day has blinded our eyes to the achievements of many noble, courageous, and sacrificial women who served to advance the kingdom of God in The Wesleyan Church. This book is written to encourage all Wesleyans to recall and remember the women who served in ordained ministry in the past and to anticipate the future contribution of ordained women both to our fellowship and to the Church of Jesus Christ.

Women were the founding pastors of what have become some of our largest congregations. While we rejoice that these churches have grown in size and have become influential in their communities, we should also remember those who planted them. Over the years, daring women—single, married, and widowed—have pioneered churches, assisted struggling churches, and revived dying churches. They have gone into the ghettos where men feared to walk and pulled the "brands" from the fire. They fearlessly entered the red light districts and snatched prostitutes from their surroundings. They established homes for unwed mothers and refuges for homeless and degraded persons. They even ventured to assist in housing for the worn, weary, and aged workers of the Church. Much of their work took them from their familiar surroundings into the mountains, the slums, the strongholds of slavery, and the battlegrounds of drugs, tobacco, and alcohol. They felt the call of God to take the gospel not only to all races and educational and economical levels in North America but also across the oceans to every nation. This book honors and celebrates these women, our daughters, who were God's servants.

This book may be unlike any other you have read. It is not a single story with a few major characters whose exploits are traced through the entire book. Rather, the book comprises many stories with many characters, sometimes changing its course several times on a single page. Yet it *is* one story, almost kaleidoscopic in nature, that tells how God has called "our daughters," guided them, and empowered them to do great exploits in His service.

An earnest attempt has been made to identify all of the women who began their ministry in The Wesleyan Church and its antecedent bodies by 1968, a limit imposed in order to keep the work manageable. District minutes and other records, however, are incomplete; some ordained women may not be identified here. The hundreds of other Wesleyan women preachers who served the Church as pastors and evangelists but were not ordained have not been included because of limited space.

Of the seven chapters, the first includes the women who began their ministry prior to 1900. The second chapter covers the two decades from 1900 to 1919 and includes the women who began their ministry in those years. Chapters 3 through 7 each deal with a single decade, and the last chapter leads up to 1968. Inasmuch as some of the women served for thirty or forty or even more years, each chapter overlaps with the following chapters because each woman's story is completed in the chapter that records the beginning of her ministry. Within each chapter, a chronological sequence is followed. For example, chapter 4, dealing with the 1930s, begins with the women who began ministry in 1931. The entries are arranged in alphabetical order for each year.

The reader will notice that the title *Mrs.* appears before the woman's name in some of the story headings. That title is included for married women in any of four cases: (1) when only the last name of the woman is known, (2) when the woman's first name is unknown but her husband's first name or initials are known, (3) when only initials are known and it is unclear whether they are the woman's or her husband's, or (4) when it is known that the woman was married but that fact is not obvious in the story itself.

The stories vary in length from several hundred words to a single sentence—all that's known in some cases. A few stories deal with more than one woman in situations in which two or three ladies teamed up for an extended period. Many of the stories stop at 1968, a limit placed on the book by the authors in order to keep it manageable. For some women, information extending beyond 1968 and as far as the twenty-first century was readily available and was included.

On page 8 of this book, there is a chart of The Wesleyan Church's "family tree," showing dates of origin, name changes and dates of the respective mergers. Many stories, particularly in the early chapters, will be clarified a bit by referencing the chart.

Few will read this book through from front to back. A better approach would be to read the introduction and the introductory section of each of the seven chapters, then to go back and sample one or more of the longer stories from each chapter. Proceed as you feel comfortable, but be sure to read the conclusion at some point.

We suggest that you be aware of the following as you read.

First, try to get a feel of the magnitude of this part of our history, the sheer number of women involved, the groups and areas in which they served, and the cumulative significance of their contributions to the Church.

Second, notice that all branches of our family tree are represented. Women in ministry comprise a common heritage that all our Holiness groups share.

Third, observe the variety of ways in which women have followed God's call to the ministry over obstacles and opposition.

Finally, reflect upon the contributions of ordained women in leadership, in pastoring, in evangelism, in planting new churches, in reviving dead churches, in compassion ministries, in service on mission fields, and in training workers. Recognize how greatly reduced would be The Wesleyan Church if these women had not served.

Call, Vision, and Compassion

Women have held a place of respect and dignity from the earliest days of the Wesleyan-Holiness Movement. The Wesleyan Methodist Connection (referred to in these stories by its later name, the Wesleyan Methodist Church) was founded in 1843, but two years earlier the Michigan Conference (District) had already been organized.[1] It is well known that the Wesleyan Methodist Church was among the earliest religious groups who fought for the freedom of black slaves. However, their involvement in the women's rights movement has not been well publicized. In July 1848 the Wesleyan Methodist Church in Seneca Falls, New York, was host to the first Woman's Rights Convention. This convention called for fairer treatment of women and for their right to vote.[2]

In 1867 the Seventh General Conference of the Wesleyan Methodist Church voted its approval of the desire of the state of Kansas to give women the right to vote, with the hope that other states would follow.[3] In 1864 and 1875, the General Conference refused to take any action on the licensing and ordination of women as ministers. The General Conference of 1879 voted to license women to preach but not to ordain them.[4] The General Conference of 1891 removed the 1879 section from the *Discipline*, leaving the whole matter to the annual conferences (districts). By 1891 several conferences began to ordain women. This was not without controversy and debate.[5] In 1912 Iva E. Crofford was elected the

first woman conference president.[6] (She married Clayton H. Hyde in 1936.)

According to Luke 22:24–29, Jesus' disciples began raising the question as to which one of them was the greatest soon after they had eaten their last meal with Jesus. He answered the dispute by declaring that whoever sees or finds a need in humanity and serves to meet that need is given a kingdom. The ruler of the kingdom is the one who yields himself or herself to meet the needs of others. Jesus then declared that this kind of service is evidence of real fellowship with Himself.

From the beginning, Wesleyan women ministers have served God and the Church unselfishly in many areas. Some of these women never sought ordination. They were busy fulfilling God's call to advance the Kingdom by preaching, evangelizing, and helping the needy. They were women filled with courage—courage to endure under the pressure of ridicule. They possessed courage to bear patiently the hardships of survival during periods of hunger and lack of clothing and warm shelter. Their courage enabled them to bear the burden for lost humanity in the vilest places. This God-given courage caused them to be true to the Lord's command, "Go into all the world and preach the good news to all creation" (Mark 16:15).

Some of the stories that follow will refer to organizations by names no longer familiar. Groups organized during this period that eventually came together in what is now The Wesleyan Church include The Wesleyan Methodist Connection of America (1843), later renamed The Wesleyan Methodist Connection (or Church) of America (1891); the Holiness Bands (1880), later known as the Holiness Church (of California); the Heavenly Recruit Association (1882), later renamed the Holiness Christian Association (1894) and still later the Holiness Christian Church (1897); the Pentecost Bands (1885), later renamed the Missionary Bands of the World (1925); the Alliance of the Reformed Baptist Church of Canada (1888); Hephzibah Faith Missionary Association (1893); Pentecostal Rescue Mission (1896); International Holiness Union and Prayer League (1897), which was the mainstream of what later became the Pilgrim Holiness Church; and the People's Mission Church (1899).

The records in these early days are incomplete. Many times ordained women were listed but not given an appointment. Yet there are evidences that they were pastors or evangelists, or were engaged in other ministerial duties. For some women, more complete stories are given because more materials about them were available. Others have very brief stories or none at all because there was no further information about them in the records. All these women, and perhaps many more whose stories were not found, left their footprints on the sands of time and the fingerprints of God's grace on congregations in North America and around the world.

Mary was chosen because God needed a woman to mother and nourish the Son of God, who would become the Son of Man. She was chosen because she was spiritually prepared. She was chosen because she was a willing and obedient maiden. She didn't say, "I can't do this because I'm a woman."

From 1841 to 1899 the following women were chosen to become part of God's plan in advancing His kingdom on earth. It was during this period that holiness revivals swept the churches. In 1844 the first General Conference of the Wesleyan Methodist Church had adopted an article titled "Sanctification."[7] There followed several years of controversy over terminology. While some of the leaders were busy defining terminology, women evangelists, some unlicensed and almost none

ordained, were filling pulpits proclaiming the "full gospel" of repentance and heart purity.

Here are some of the heartwarming and inspiring stories of women preachers from the period of 1841 to 1899.

Laura Smith Haviland

"I was hungry and you gave me something to eat, I was thirsty and you gave me something to drink, I was a stranger and you invited me in, I needed clothes and you clothed me, I was sick and you looked after me, I was in prison and you came to visit me" (Matt. 25:35–36). These words summarize the life of Laura Smith Haviland. She took her relationship with Christ to mean she must minister to the needs of all people groups.

Laura was born in Canada in 1808. Her parents were committed Quakers. When she was seven they moved to New York, and when she became seventeen she married Charles Haviland, who was also a very committed Quaker. Her parents moved in 1826 to Michigan, near Adrian. Charles and Laura with their two children followed in 1829. This became the home base for all her ministerial activities.

Memorial statue of Rev. Laura Smith Haviland, Adrian, Mich.

Laura received all her education as a child from her mother and a neighbor lady. She became an avid reader and often read books on slavery and other social evils of that day. She became the mother of eight children. It is not surprising that she became the teacher for her children. But she also saw the educational needs of orphans and neglected children of her county. She would not tolerate sexual discrimination, racial boundaries, or religious barriers and established the Raisin Institute in 1836. The school was open to all children regardless of gender, race, or creed. Much later she started a school for refugees and former slaves who had fled the South and were living in Kansas. She presented to Congress the need for funding and obtained financial help for this school.

Laura's spiritual hunger found satisfaction when she moved to Michigan. The Quakers were an anti-slavery group, but they did not believe in getting "excited" about the issue. Soon after they arrived in Michigan, she and Charles established the first station on the Underground Railroad in Michigan. This cooperative system among some anti-slavery people enabled fugitive slaves to reach freedom in Canada secretly. The Havilands' daring experiences in the abolition movement caused them to withdraw from the Quakers. In 1841 they joined in the organization of Wolf Creek, the first Wesleyan Methodist church in Lenawee County, Michigan. In this group Laura found the warm spiritual experience for which she had longed.

She often endangered her life by arousing the wrath of some slaveholders who were seeking their runaway slaves. They placed a bounty of three thousand dollars on her head, dead or alive. But she continued to make trips into the South and personally escorted bands of escapees to Canada and freedom. Her courageous efforts to help the black slaves led the Michigan Annual Conference to recognize her work among the slaves as a conference appointment—on the same level as a pastor or evangelist.

Laura expressed compassion for the sick by using nursing skills to aid her sick neighbors. After the Civil War, she obtained permission to use these skills for the wounded soldiers and slaves. Her daring courage resulted in the firing of a supervisor in a military hospital because of his neglect and cruelty to patients.

Education of children, breaking racial barriers, freeing slaves, and nursing the ill were not enough for her. She gave her energy also to a prison ministry. She pled with President Andrew Jackson for the life of a convict. Her compassion knew no boundaries. She visited to encourage those who were imprisoned for assisting slaves and who spoke out against slavery. She was successful in pleading for three thousand Union soldiers who were imprisoned on islands in the Gulf of Mexico.

A very dark time came for Laura during an epidemic of erysipelas in 1845. Death entered her home. Her husband, her infant child, her mother, her father, and her sister all died within six weeks. She also became very ill but recovered. She was a widow at age thirty-six with seven children and a huge debt of seven hundred dollars, but she trusted God. With His help she overcame the prejudices of local businessmen against women in the workplace, took charge of her husband's business, and became a successful businessperson.

Laura Smith Haviland answered God's call and used her gift of helps to advance His kingdom until her death in 1898.[8]

Mrs. Mary A. Will

Mary A. Will was the first woman to be ordained as a minister of the Wesleyan Methodist Connection (later Wesleyan Methodist Church). By October 1860, she was a licensed minister and the pastor of the Nora Circuit in the Illinois Conference. She was very much involved with the emerging holiness revival. She reported on this part of her work in January, February, and March 1861. Her circuit had seen 130 converted, and believers were being sanctified—although holiness preaching was meeting opposition. She reported the laying-off of gold ornaments and superfluous apparel, the burning of novels, and the breaking of the tobacco habit: "They are endeavoring to be Christians in earnest, going on to full salvation." She also reported that in meetings in Wisconsin, manifestations that "bore a striking resemblance to the day of Pentecost, save the speaking in tongues" were taking place.

In June 1861 a layperson, S. A. Stock, corrected a misunderstanding that Mary Will was a "joint pastor" with her husband. He insisted that *she* was the pastor. "We are glad to say, that our church never has been so well governed under any pastor, as it has been under sister Will." At the 1861 session of the Illinois Conference, Mary A. Will was ordained.

When the General Conference of the Wesleyan Methodist Connection met in 1864, the Committee on Conference Records reported the action of the Illinois Conference to the General

Conference. By a split vote, with the chair casting the deciding vote, the committee declared that ordaining a female was unscriptural. The committee's report, however, was amended on the floor of General Conference by a 38 to 8 vote so as to decline to take any action on the subject and leave it to the annual conference (district). As amended, the report was adopted. Also brought before this General Conference were opposing resolutions, one forbidding ordination of women and one approving their ordination. Neither was adopted.

At some point following the 1864 General Conference, the Illinois Conference deposed Mary A. Will from the ordained ministry. Apparently this was the result of the General Conference debate. Mary Will's friend and fellow minister, Mrs. H. E. Hayden, in November 1876 said that Illinois had led the way in ordaining women but then had backslidden. The records are unclear as to whether Mary Will was allowed to continue ministry as a licensed minister. In October 1870 she was reported to be ill. In 1875 her deposition was appealed to the General Conference. The committee to which the appeal was referred declared Illinois's action of deposing Mary Will from the ministry was irregular and illegal. But the General Conference did not adopt the committee's report. In 1879 the General Conference voted to license women as ministers but not ordain them. It was not until 1891 that the General Conference struck out the 1879 action and left the matter of ordination once again up to the annual conferences (districts).[9]

Mrs. H. E. Hayden

While Mrs. H. E. Hayden apparently began preaching in 1862, the first record of her was in the minutes of the 1864 General Conference. She was listed as a coauthor of a resolution proposing that the General Conference approve the recognition and ordination of women preachers. By October 1870 she had apparently spoken at the session of the Illinois Conference of the Wesleyan Methodist Church in a Sunday evening service. In June 1871 she reported on her labors as pastor at Warren, Illinois, where several had

sought after holiness. There is no record of her ordination, so she may well have fallen victim to the controversy over Mary A. Will. In commenting in November 1876 on Mary A. Will's treatment by the Illinois Conference, Mrs. Hayden cited the ordination of women in the Champlain and Michigan Conferences. In September 1879, Mrs. Hayden said that she had started preaching seventeen years before. She wrote various articles on women and the ministry for the columns of the denominational periodical as late as December 1879.[10]

Mary E. Kinney Depew

The woman who would influence the Wesleyan Methodist Church in a holiness revival was born Mary E. Kinney on July 2, 1836, in Ohio.[11] Her family was one of contrasts. Her father was an intense abolitionist with strong convictions. Her mother, while a firm believer and promoter of the abolition movement, was quiet, meek, gentle, and

warm. Her older brother, D. S. Kinney, would become a strong leader as the denominational publisher.

Mary was converted in 1849 at age thirteen. Soon she discovered something in her heart that rebelled against God. She was told that was normal. She soon died spiritually. But she kept up her religious front, and she and others considered her a Christian.

Mary was twenty-nine when she married J. W. Depew. A son was born to them but died in infancy. Illness struck Mary the next year, and death seemed imminent. She was again awakened to her need of a Savior, sought God, and repented. God forgave her sins and healed her body.

Once again Mary struggled with the carnal nature. The Holy Spirit drew her on to seek a higher way of living for God. Three years later at the Allegheny Annual Conference, she was led into the experience of heart purity. She came to believe that God could cleanse her heart from all unrighteousness and fill her with a love for Him that would end the civil war within. She forsook earthly ambitions, possessions, and the love for others' approval. She chose to be entirely the possession of the Lord Jesus Christ.

Immediately Mary E. Depew became a witness of the work of the second great event—sanctification. That witness would be her work for the Lord until her death. God called her to warn others who were deceived by empty, fruitless profession of religion and to call them to be cleansed and filled with His Holy Spirit.

For her, that witness meant to preach the full gospel. She met with opposition from friends, family members, and hearers. One woman declared it was sacrilegious and boastful for a woman to preach. Even the Wesleyan Methodist Church was divided on this question. In 1864 the issue was fervently debated in General Conference, which refused to approve or disapprove licensing and ordaining women. The issue was before the people during her entire ministry. In 1879 the General Conference decided to license but not ordain women. Shortly before her death, the rule against ordination of women was repealed. While Mary Depew was probably the most influential Wesleyan Methodist preacher of her time, male or female, she apparently was never licensed or ordained. The official minutes of the 1887 General Conference list her as a *lay* delegate from the Lockport (Western New York) Conference.

Mary was called, gifted, and used of God. She would do nothing but obey the inner urge to preach the message. The denominational periodical recorded account after account of revivals in Indiana, Illinois, Michigan, and New York and of her many converts. She was in Indiana in 1876 during the annual conference conducted in the Union Chapel (now Blue River) Church and preached. From that time on, she received invitations from many churches all over the conference (district). She accepted those invitations. Many pastors, church leaders, and laypersons were led into the experience of heart purity under her preaching. In a meeting at Plymouth, Indiana, the pastor, Jacob Hester, a church planter, evangelist, and

pastor, led the way to the altar under her preaching. His entire congregation followed.[12] Often her salary was a "collection to defray her expenses."[13]

Clara Tear, who later became Clara Tear Williams and wrote the song "All My Life Long I Had Panted," was often Mary's traveling companion. Clara started her ministry as a song evangelist but later became a holiness preacher, evangelist, and pastor. Mary had a great influence upon her.

Not only did Mary live the experience of heart holiness, but her husband also lived this same experience. In 1885 Mary was invited to supervise the women students and give them weekly lectures at Houghton Seminary in Houghton, New York. J. W. Depew sold the family farm in Ohio and moved with her to Houghton. There he built a home. It would take a life dedicated completely to the Lord to give up his plans in order for his wife to be obedient to God's will and call. At Houghton, Mary conducted a daily 4 A.M. prayer meeting, which not only the women students but also the men students attended. Many of the future pastors and missionaries of the Wesleyan Methodist Church were either saved or sanctified—or both— under her ministry at the school. She later changed the time of those meetings to 8 A.M.

Mary E. Depew departed this earthly life in 1892.

Mary M. Talbert

Mary Talbert was born in Carmel, Indiana, on May 9, 1849. During her childhood she lived on a farm near Noblesville, Indiana. On November 16, 1866, at the age of seventeen, she married William Talbert.

When she was twenty-five (1874) she received the call of God to be a preacher in the Wesleyan Methodist Church. God gave her the gift of "pastor." The Talberts' first pastorate was the Cherry Valley circuit in the Illinois Conference. Later they served as pastors of four churches in the Indiana Conference. Those churches were Boxley, New Castle, Mt. Etna, and the Albion circuit. They retired from the pastorate in 1886. She was the mother of seven children. She spent her later years as an invalid.

Mary was also interested in the temperance movement and helped to organize the local Women's Christian Temperance Union. The local union was later named after her. After her retirement she made her home in Albion, Indiana, and lived there until her death July 14, 1931.[14]

Jennie Woodman Ayres

Jennie Woodman was born in Chester, Michigan, June 21, 1851.[15] She married Josiah Ayres November 6, 1875.[16] Josiah was some fifteen years her senior and had migrated from Prince Edward Island, Canada, to Kansas. He was a charter member of the Kansas Wesleyan Methodist Conference. As soon as they were married, they entered pastoral work (1875-76) at Hall Church in Kansas. Josiah had been a missionary in Kansas, and his work had resulted in the organization of four circuits. Some of their years in Kansas were spent doing this kind of missionary work. During the 1883–84 year, they pastored the Ames (or Morgan Chapel) work. During the winter of 1885–86, the couple held a meeting in the Excelsior schoolhouse. This meeting was successful, and a Wesleyan class (church) was organized there April 1, 1886. They stayed as pastors during the next conference year.

Jennie was the mother of four children. One son, John, and his wife were early pioneer Wesleyan Methodist missionaries in Sierra Leone, West Africa. John was smitten with an illness that took his life a short time after they arrived there.

About 1889, the Ayres family moved to Michigan, and they were assigned to the Coopersville charge. The following year they served the Holland and Olive charges. They purchased a farm near Allendale. On this farm Josiah was killed by a falling tree on March 1, 1895.

After Josiah's death, Jennie became the pastor of Barry and Hickory Corners charge from 1896 to 1899. She also served the Hastings and Rives Junction churches for one year each.

In 1903 she moved to Houghton, New York, and was pastor of the Houghton church. Her sons were students in the seminary there at that time.

She transferred her membership to the Lockport Conference on March 30, 1904, but she returned her membership to the Michigan Conference before June 1, 1905, and was assigned as pastor of the Romulus charge. Her son John had left this charge when he departed for Africa that year.

Jennie served as the president of the Michigan Conference Woman's Home and Foreign Missionary Society (WH&FMS) from 1900 to 1903. She was the lady who in 1902 suggested the possibility of a denominational women's missionary organization. In 1903 the WH&FMS was organized by the General Conference. During the years she was president of the Michigan WH&FMS, she was the acting organizer of the general conference WH&FMS and traveled to several conference sites in Ohio, South Carolina, North Carolina, northern Michigan, Kansas, New York, Wisconsin, and her own Michigan Conference. She was an able speaker and an excellent fund-raiser. Often she would speak one or two times during the conference sessions, giving "splendid addresses" and raising "liberal" offerings for missions at home and on the foreign fields.

In September 1906 Jennie became the first matron of the girls' dormitory at Houghton. She served here for three years. In 1914 she was assigned to pastor Bird Lake but did not accept the church. Traveling became difficult for her as she became older. She served Michigan pastorates at Gun Lake and Ohio Corners, Diamond Springs, and a few months as supply at Allegan. She was appointed missionary at large from 1915 to 1917. During the conference year of 1917, Rev. S. A. Manwell became ill and was unable to fill the pulpit at Rives Junction, Michigan. Jennie took over the pastorate for three months.

She lived and died victoriously. She went to be with the Lord December 16, 1918.[17]

A. S. A. Pixley

This lady was known only as "Sister A. S. A. Pixley," leaving open the question as to whether the initials were her own or those of her husband. She was an "elder" (ordained minister) in the Michigan Conference of the Wesleyan Methodist

Church. Prior to February 1879, she tried to transfer to the Kansas Conference as an elder but was not accepted.[18]

------∞∞∞------

Fanny M. Wike

Fanny M. Wike was a woman of prayer. She was born in 1850 and did not become a Christian until she was thirty years old (1880). She was obedient to the Lord and soon afterward was sanctified. She joined the Wesleyan Methodist Church in Canton, Ohio, in 1880.

Fanny was a minister in the Allegheny Conference. She was the pastor of the Pleasant Valley charge for five years and the Middlefield church for two years.

Fanny's concern and burden were for the women and girls who lived reckless and sinful lives in the worst red light district (area where prostitutes walked the streets and plied their trade) in Canton, Ohio. She visited these women and pled with them to leave these places of debauchery. She wanted to open a "home of rest" for them. After spending an entire night in prayer, God led her into a new venture—the establishment of the "House of Rest," Bethshan Rescue Home. The home opened in the spring of 1911 as a maternity hospital and home for unwed mothers.

When Bethshan opened, alcoholic women and girls, prostitutes, unwed expectant mothers, and juvenile delinquents came. Almost immediately the house was filled to capacity. Women came faster than the money. Often there wasn't enough food or even enough flatware to set the table for all of them. Everyone in the home prayed for God to "give . . . daily bread"—and He did. The home provided shelter and met physical needs, but Fanny Wike's first desire was for women to be instructed in the way of salvation. Many of the women found forgiveness for their sins here.

Bethshan Home was in operation for about thirty years. In 1941 government regulations made it impossible to keep it open.

Fanny M. Wike died November 18, 1936. A memorial fund was established in her honor called the Fanny Wike Memorial Fund. This fund enabled the board of managers to purchase a double-oven gas stove, cabinets, and sink for the kitchen. This was a fitting memorial for the woman who prayed a "house of rest" into existence and by prayer and the grace of God kept it in operation.[19]

------∞∞∞------

Anna M. Kirk Folger

Anna M. Kirk was born June 13, 1851, in York, Ohio. She was converted in 1879 and sanctified March 15, 1880, at her family altar. She joined the Wesleyan Methodist Church in 1881 in Damascus, Ohio. She became the church class leader (similar to a Bible study leader) in 1882 and received her license to preach in 1887. The North Carolina Conference held at Kings Mountain in 1901 ordained her. The officiating minister was Eber Teter, general missionary secretary of the Church.[20]

Anna Kirk likely engaged in tent evangelistic meetings. She was the owner of a large tent. In 1892 and 1893 the H. S. Abbotts and S. J. "Jack" Cowan were conducting meetings in South Carolina. Word of this reached the denominational headquarters, and General Missionary Secretary W. H. Kennedy requested L. L. Folger, president of the North Carolina Conference, to check out the report. Folger was so impressed with this evangelistic effort that he sent for Anna Kirk's tent. The tent was used in a meeting at Central, South Carolina. Central (now Central First) Wesleyan Church was organized after that tent meeting.[21]

Anna Kirk came into the North Carolina Conference under President Sechrest, who served from 1880 to 1890. Roy S. Nicholson stated that she was received in 1888 and would become a great leader in the conference. She was the pastor of a circuit in 1888.[22] That circuit may have been the Neighbors Grove church in Asheboro.

L. L. Folger's first wife had died. Anna was pastoring in the North Carolina Conference, where he also worked. The two united in marriage March 28, 1894.[23]

Together L. L. and Anna pastored Shady Grove (1901–02) and Long Shoals (1904–05) in the North Carolina Conference. L. L. served as president of the North Carolina Conference for two terms of four years each. L. L. and Anna were the camp meeting evangelists at the South Carolina camp in 1904 and shared the pulpit from service to service.[24]

The Folgers were not people of one conference. They served as pastors at the Fargo church in the Ohio Conference beginning in 1909.[25] Their next move took them to South Carolina to be the pastors of Central Church (now Central First Church). One year during this pastorate, Anna also served as the pastor of the Walhalla church. Central Wesleyan College (now Southern Wesleyan University) had been established in Central, South Carolina, in 1906. The Central church was moved to a new location nearer to the college during this pastorate.[26]

In October 1914 the Folgers felt led to work in the Illinois Conference. However, they returned in 1918–20 to again pastor Central First. Anna did her part in sharing the burdens and work of these churches. In 1920, at the end of the conference year, the Folgers moved to the Indiana Conference and became the pastors of the Huntington Wesleyan Methodist church.[27] The call to move on took them next to the Ohio Conference, where they pastored together the Africa (1922–24) and Harrison Chapel (1925–27) churches.[28] After these pastorates they returned to the Indiana conference, where Anna was listed as a general evangelist from 1927 to 1930.[29]

Anna Kirk Folger loved the Lord and His work both in the homeland and on the foreign fields. Evidence of her love for mission work is seen in her missionary activities. She was vice president of the general Woman's Home and Foreign Missionary Society (WH&FMS) and was general organizer. The duties of the organizer included organization of new societies, both conference and local, to strengthen in any way possible those groups already organized, to deliver missionary messages and to raise money for missions. This involved much travel. The salary was "fixed at not less than one dollar per day and expenses." Later it was raised to $1.25 per day of employment. She served as the general organizer for four years. It was during these years that she was instrumental in creating the WH&FMS district organizers.[30]

Anna also served as the Southern District (Area) organizer, which involved visiting all her five or six conferences (districts) and as many as possible of the local societies, organizing more societies and bands, raising missionary funds, holding missionary conventions, and strengthening the work in general.

She held conference positions as vice president of the WH&FMS in South Carolina, president of the Ohio Conference WH&FMS, and one year as treasurer in the Ohio Conference. Her interests extended to home missions also. She was a member of the Cambridge Rescue Mission for some years and also the Ohio Conference missionary board.

Anna Kirk Folger was a model in sacrifice and devotion for the cause of missions at home and abroad. She was deeply spiritual, modest, kind, dependable, and of the highest Christian character. She completed a useful and dedicated life and ministry of over fifty years to her Lord and the Wesleyan Methodist Church when she died at her home in Fairmount, Indiana, March 3, 1931.[31]

Ida M. Abbott

H. S. Abbott was born in Illinois and had served in the Civil War under the Union flag. He was known as the "one-legged Civil War veteran." Ida M. was his wife. They were an evangelistic team with the Free Methodist Church in southern California. They held a meeting in Ennis, Texas, for a Wesleyan Methodist pastor and after that meeting transferred their membership to the Wesleyan Methodist Church. H. S. was regarded as a great preacher, and his wife, Ida M., was a very capable preacher and singer. They were mightily used by God in evangelistic work.

The General Conference of 1891 elected W. H. Kennedy to be the first general missionary secretary. He was responsible for extending the work of the Church both at home and overseas. Kennedy contacted the Abbotts and asked them to assist him in revivals in the South. Their first assignment was to be in North Carolina in the winter of 1892. On their way, they stopped at Seneca, South Carolina, to visit with Rev. Warren

Parker. While there, they discovered the work in North Carolina that they had been assigned to had been postponed. Therefore, they began work in the South Carolina area.

For the next two or three years the couple conducted meetings in South Carolina. They first rented a town hall in Seneca for two dollars a night and held a meeting that lasted nine days. In March 1893 they held meetings at Townville, in Anderson County. Both of these meetings resulted in the organization of churches.

The Abbotts kept moving on. Their next meeting was in the Oakway community and began April 12, 1893. On April 30, 1893, the Oakway church was organized with thirty-four members.

Their success caught the attention of the general Church, and L. L. Folger, superintendent of the North Carolina Conference (district), was sent to check out their activities. He was greatly impressed and joined in their efforts by sending for the tent of Anna Kirk to be used in the meetings.

The Abbotts continued to hold meetings during the summer and fall, and churches were organized at Denver and Anderson in Anderson County. Ida M. became the first pastor of the Anderson church, which was organized October 18, 1893. The services were first held in the Abbotts' home and later moved to the Anderson Courthouse.

The work in the South Carolina area mushroomed. It became evident that the group should be organized into a conference. W. H. Kennedy organized this conference November 1, 1893, and H. S. Abbott was elected the president. The Abbotts were enabled by God to establish eleven churches with 399 members during this short period of time. Nearly four hundred people were saved and joined the Wesleyan Methodist Church. However, their work was not always easy, for they were often persecuted for preaching the holiness message.[32]

During this fast-growing time, there were few holiness preachers to fill the pulpits. In 1894 during the second district conference, three ministers were ordained who had not finished their studies. Ida M. Abbott was one of the three. They all promised that they would complete their studies.[33]

H. S. Abbott was reelected president in 1894, but he resigned sometime during the year, and the couple moved to Oregon. They felt the conference (district) was established and that they should move on.

The Annual Session Minutes of the South Carolina Conference recorded the death of Ida M. Abbott in 1896.

Belle Slayton McClure
Louke Hodson

Belle Slayton was born November 30, 1869, in Ohio. She was converted June 6, 1886, and joined the Methodist Episcopal Church in Elwood, Indiana, in December 1886. At age eighteen she began her Christian ministry, which lasted over sixty years. She attended a service in the Hartford City Wesleyan Methodist Church in 1890 and was sanctified in her home after that service. She joined the Wesleyan Methodist Church in May 1891. In July of that year she felt God's call to preach. She preached her first sermon in Salem Chapel (later known as South Salem). From that time, she sought to enter every open door as an evangelist or pastor.

Belle married L. C. McClure, a minister in the Indiana Conference of the Wesleyan Methodist Church, on August 20, 1893. One daughter, Stella, was born to them but died at age five. L. C. McClure died April 23, 1908.

Belle would remarry later but was better known as Belle McClure. She was ordained at Fairmount, Indiana, August 29, 1900. She pastored the following Indiana churches: Greenwood, Hamlet, Kirklin, Bluffton, Huntington, Miami, Mt. Olive, Cicero, and Laketon.[34]

She and L. C. McClure joined the North Carolina Conference of the Wesleyan Methodist Church in 1902. She became the pastor of First Wesleyan Methodist Church in Gastonia, North Carolina, and served there from 1902 to 1905. During her pastorate, an annual camp meeting was started on the church property. Initially the camp was held in a tent. Much later it was replaced by a wooden tabernacle. Eventually the camp meeting was moved to Colfax, North Carolina.[35]

Belle returned to the Indiana Conference in 1906. She conducted a revival meeting in the Elwood, Indiana, area that year and organized a new church of eight members there. She was appointed the pastor of this new work and served there for two years.[36]

Belle's husband, L. C. McClure, was appointed pastor of the Kirland, Georgia, church, in 1908, and when he died in April of that year, she finished the conference year there as pastor. She also served two other churches in Georgia, the Asburn and Bethel churches. She returned to the Indiana Conference about 1911. She spent several years as a general evangelist. She held meetings in the Indiana and Michigan Conferences and in the South, as well as six months in California.

Belle married Nelson Louke of Elwood, Indiana, September 18, 1917. He died September 9, 1920. She lived alone for thirteen years and then married Harley Hodson of Bakers Corner, Indiana, in 1933. He died December 21, 1938.

From her first appointment in 1893 to her last in 1946, fifty-three years, Belle upheld the doctrines of the Wesleyan Methodist Church. She had an earnest, zealous, and fruitful ministry, although she experienced a measure of misunderstandings, losses, sorrow, and loneliness. She died April 9, 1947.[37]

Clara Tear Williams

Clara Tear was born near Painesville, Ohio, September 22, 1858.[38] Her parents were devout, and their home was well stocked with the spiritual writings of the Wesleys, John Fletcher, Hester Ann Rogers, and Phoebe Palmer. She had a great spiritual awakening at age thirteen and was sanctified in a holiness meeting at age seventeen. She had planned to be a schoolteacher but during her second year of teaching, she was called of God to "public" service. At first the call was for evangelistic singing, but later she became a Spirit-filled holiness evangelist and pastor.

During her teaching years she had contracted tuberculosis. Since God had called her to the ministry, she believed He would heal her—and He did. After her cleansing experience of holiness, a request was made for those who had been sanctified to stand. She arose, and the girl who previously could never pray in public began to talk! All fear of people was gone. "I felt like a bird in the air. Oh, it was wonderful."

During a revival meeting in Troy, Ohio, with Professor Ralph E. Hudson as the evangelist, she was asked to write a hymn for a hymnal that Hudson was preparing for publication. That night she went to her room, prayed, and then composed four verses and the chorus of a song she called "Satisfied." She wrote the song on the back of an old envelope.

The next morning she gave the song to Professor Hudson. He was greatly moved by the words and he composed the music for it immediately. That song has survived for over a century and can still be found in many hymnals today by both the titles "Satisfied" and "All My Life Long I Had Panted."

In the fall of 1882, when she was twenty-four, she began a ministry with Mary Depew, a very successful holiness evangelist. She accompanied Mary in meetings in Indiana, Illinois, Michigan, and Ohio. In the winter of 1885–86, she worked alone in Indiana, because Mary had accepted a position at Houghton College. One of her tent meetings, held in Bryant, Indiana, resulted in a Wesleyan Methodist church being organized there in October 1884.[39]

Clara Tear had been sanctified under the Free Methodist ministry, but most of her meetings were with the Wesleyan Methodist people, and she transferred her membership to the Wesleyan Methodist Church. In the spring of 1888 she attended the Allegheny Conference and went from there to the Lockport Conference (Western New York). Here she became acquainted with Bertha Grange. They formed a team that lasted the rest of their lives. They sang together, and Clara preached. Later Bertha would become a nanny to Clara's children.

In 1889 Clara Tear served on a committee to compile the church hymnal *Sacred Hymns and Tunes*.[40] The following year she served as a delegate to the General Conference.[41]

Clara conducted meetings in Indiana, Michigan, Ohio, Vermont, New York, and

Pennsylvania. Many people at this time were "holiness fighters," who were opposed to the message. Her meetings were sometimes boycotted, and church doors were often locked. But wherever she went, people were converted and sanctified. In the tent meetings at that time several preachers would preach one after another. Many times she would not know what she was going to preach, for no message seemed appropriate. One time she was very burdened for the congregation but did not feel clear about any message. When she went to the platform, the text came: "Have ye received the Holy Ghost since ye believed"? After the service she wrote in her diary, "When I spoke, the message came. It was as fresh to me as to the people."

Sometimes there would be unusual manifestations of the power of God in her services. Clara reflected on these times: "I am not sure the later results were better than from many less spectacular meetings."

In 1894 she accepted the Middlefield, Ohio, pastorate. It was during this time that she became acquainted with W. H. Williams, a lay preacher and Sunday school worker. It was a simple friendly acquaintance. But one night she had a "revelation" that he would become her husband. She loved the work of evangelist and being free "from temporal cares." Her first reaction was, "Oh, dear—I thought I was done with the subject of marriage." She received two letters from Mr. Williams, the second one a proposal of marriage. In May 1895 they were married. She was thirty-seven, and he was forty.

Clara pastored several churches before her marriage, which included Salineville, Ohio; Chichester and Willow churches (predecessors to the current Phoenicia and Shokan congregations), in the Champlain Conference (now Eastern New York/New England District); Middlefield, Ohio, and Windsor Mills, in the Allegheny Conference. After their marriage, Clara and W. H. together pastored Indiana and the Pine Grove circuit in Pennsylvania and Canton and Massillon in Ohio. They then returned to serve a second time at the Pine Grove circuit.

The occasion of the couple's coming to the Pine Grove circuit is worth mentioning here. In 1901, when Clara was attending the Allegheny annual conference, she learned that this circuit, a group of four appointments (churches) was open. The conference requested her to take the charge. Her husband was not present nor could he be consulted. She felt compelled to accept and did so. William was "startlingly surprised" and "it was a heavy burden for him, but he bore it bravely." They had no horse and buggy, and the circuit was twenty miles from one end to the other. When the wagons arrived to take their possessions, God had also provided a good horse and buggy for them to take to their new home in Dixonville, Pennsylvania.

The churches, Dixonville and Hillsdale at one end and Rich Hill and Spruce at the other end, had services on alternate Sundays. There was a good group of young people at Hillsdale. A member, Cy Rnak, purchased a large hack (horse drawn carriage) so he could take the young people to meetings held at a distance from home. On Sunday afternoons, Cy with his hack full of youth and the Williamses in their buggy would go to Wilgus, a mining town, halfway between the two preaching points. Clara would conduct street meetings at Wilgus on Sunday afternoons. The Williamses served this circuit for five years.

Clara usually did the preaching. At Dixonville a Lutheran lad came to the Wesleyan church on Sunday evenings to hear Clara preach. That boy would become the father of Rev. James Bence, who became a district superintendent and the father of Drs. Clarence (Bud) and Phil Bence and their sisters. Her influence upon that young lad has resulted in many blessings for The Wesleyan Church.[42]

Clara and her husband moved next to the Canton, Ohio, church, where they worked for three years. Clara had a profound influence on Clara McLeister who would later become the general president of the Woman's Home and Foreign Missionary Society. By this time Clara had become a seasoned Christian. Her life as a Spirit-filled holiness evangelist and pastor had resulted in a mature and great soul winner. She delighted in leading persons into the way of holiness. She was a very gifted and talented speaker. Her great wisdom in soul winning obviously came from God. Clara McLeister considered Clara Tear Williams her mentor.

The Williamses became the parents of three children, Grace Evangeline (1896), Beulah (1898), and Mary (1902). Two ladies helped Clara care for the children so she would be free to work in the church. They were "Auntie Beede" and Bertha Grange.

In the early 1920s Mr. Williams's health had declined and made it necessary for them to leave the pastorate. He did janitorial work at Houghton College for about five years. He suffered a paralyzing stroke and died in 1934.

Clara spent her last days at Houghton. People of the church remembered her as a very plain and modestly dressed woman. She usually wore a plain dark dress with high neck, long sleeves, and white lace collar and cuffs. She spent time on her porch or at a window of her home watching the students as they passed her home. She prayed for every one of them. She often carried a white handkerchief in her hand, and when she got blessed, she would stand and wave her hankie, giving silent praise to God.[43]

Clara Tear Williams entered her heavenly rest July 1, 1937.[44]

Alice J. Ingalls Whiting

Workers in the Holiness Church of California began their service records in 1880. Histories and memories do not make clear whether the women who preached were ordained. Churches could invite any member or members from any holiness church to become their pastor(s). A man and his wife were often appointed as pastors. There may have been some significance in women being called "sister" or the fact that when a man and his wife were listed, her given name was also listed. From the very beginning of this group of churches, women were given places of great responsibility. Several women served on the committee that drafted the rules, regulations, constitution, and articles of incorporation. These women were Alice J. Whiting (Mrs. A. J.),[45] Mrs. Georgia Letchworth (often listed as G. W.), and Mrs. Emma Brand.[46]

James Washburn, one of the early leaders of the Holiness Church of California, describes Alice J. Whiting, saying she "seemed quick of perception, and early in the organization of the Holiness churches, rendered effective service in establishing many of the saints by her clear teaching, backed by scriptures which were given her in great abundance. . . . [She] declares this truth, to the glory of God, and encouragement of the church."

Alice J. Ingalls was born April 25, 1862, in Jefferson County, Wisconsin. When she was about fifteen, she heard messages on holiness but was really never converted, though she joined the Wesleyan Methodist Church. After her marriage to A. J. Whiting, they moved to South Dakota. However, because of her husband's poor health, they moved to California in 1884. She was converted at home and presented herself wholly to the Lord. Soon after this, she and her husband united with the Holiness Church in Redlands, California.

God approved of her efforts and work for Him, although she felt she had not been successful. Because of her influence, her husband and all her children were saved.

The couple entered the gospel work in 1892. In December 1894 they held meetings in a hall at Perris but soon moved into a German Methodist Episcopal church, which they rented. The next year they served as pastors at Las Bolsas, California. Alice shared the pulpit at Burbank with C. H. Stanton for one year, but the following year she was the solo pastor there. She also served as pastor at the Norwalk and Redlands churches. In the early days of the organization, she often spoke one or two times during the annual camp meeting.

In 1894 Alice was given a certificate of recognition as a minister. This was the equivalent of ordination papers. She was the only ordained woman chosen to serve on the first Board of Elders in 1896.

By 1900 A. J.'s lung condition became worse, and they were forced to move to a higher, drier climate. They had faced difficult conditions in the church as well as his failing health. Alice wrote, "It would be no small trial for us to quit the work; pray for us."

A. J. again joined Alice in 1905 in pastoring the Ontario, California, church. Alice was elected editor of *The Pentecost,* the official paper of the Holiness Church, in 1909. She improved the paper and made it a weekly rather than a semi-monthly paper. She resigned from this office in April 1917 but was again elected editor in 1925. She served two more years in this capacity.

The last recorded entry on Alice was November 1925. She pastored the Boyles Heights, California, church with L. A. Clark.

Georgia W. Letchworth

It was difficult to understand all the workings of the Holiness Church of California. Members were active in tent meetings, mission work, jail services, and other areas of ministry. Georgia W. Letchworth, often referred to as "Mrs. G. W.," was involved in all these areas at some point in her life.

After July 25, 1885, she and Lizzie Broadie were the workers at a church in San Bernardino. In September of that year she was one of the regular workers on the J. F. Washburn team. They conducted a very successful tent meeting in Pasadena from September 23 to October 26.[47]

These bands of workers were diligent and full of zeal for the Lord. Nothing was too hard for them to do. No place was inaccessible. They always went out "by faith," trusting the Lord to supply the needs for the grounds, for the tents, and for all their physical needs.

In 1887 the Washburn team held a meeting at Oceanside in San Diego County. Interest among the people was so great that it was evident that they needed to build a house of worship. They had no money to buy supplies or food. A man who was a mason by trade but was now operating a bakery offered to lay the bricks for the building. Washburn's son went to the bakery and learned enough to help run the bakery while the man laid bricks. The women cooked whatever food was donated to them. Georgia Letchworth, along with each of the other women, also laid bricks. When the money ran out, they went to prayer, and God always answered by sending in the necessary funds.[48]

Georgia reported in November 1891 that she had assisted in organizing the First Holiness Church in Los Angeles in the city proper.[49] In 1892 she was elected recorder of the Association and served in that office for at least three years.[50] In 1893 she and Sister Spohn worked in the Los Angeles Holiness Mission Number 1.

At the Fifteenth Annual Camp Meeting (1894), Georgia W. Letchworth was recognized as a person called to the ministry (ordained).[51] The Holiness Church was not limited to the California and Arizona area for service. That year Georgia was in Lexington, Missouri, and held two jail services each Sunday morning. At least one person was converted on one Sunday. Her audience was composed of both black and white persons.

When health prevented her service in the tent meetings and other physically difficult work, she simply found other ways to gather in a harvest of souls. She gave this report at one annual assembly meeting: "I am not in the tented field, but the Master lets me gather some handfuls of grain in the great harvest." At this time she reported that twenty-five had been saved under her ministry and twelve had been sanctified. These converts came in "peculiar and unexpected ways"—by her personal witness along the streets, visiting with persons on their porches and in other ways.[52]

Another year she reported that eighty were saved and thirty-two were sanctified. In one little room, ten people had gathered. She preached, and seven persons were sanctified. She then was invited to visit a lady who was in a room upstairs in that home. She also was saved. On another day, she walked past the old courthouse, where about 150 people were sitting on the steps. She asked to speak and showed them the way of salvation. They listened and thanked her for the message.

The last recorded event of Georgia W. Letchworth was in 1910. She attended the Thirty-First Annual Camp Meeting and General Assembly and gave her testimony.[53]

Nellie Clark Moyle

Nellie Clark and her husband and family moved to what became known as Vineland,

California, in 1880. They began attending camp meetings being held near there at El Monte and Azusa by holiness evangelist Hardin Wallace, one of the founders of the Holiness Church of California. Nellie was not a Christian, but her husband, J. H. (James), was a member of the Congregational Church and had been an active church and Sunday school worker. His Christian life was not satisfying to himself or Nellie.

October 8, 1884, their youngest child died. Nellie's heart was broken. Kind friends did what they could and directed her to God. Soon after the boy's death, a cottage meeting (similar to a Bible study) was held at the home of their next-door neighbor. Nellie was converted that day. She then had the joy and comfort she needed in her sorrow. On November 30, 1884, her husband was sanctified. The couple became acquainted with the J. F. Washburn family. Washburn had conducted the funeral of their child.

In 1885 they attended the camp meeting held at Artesia by Washburn's groups and saw many people saved and sanctified. Two years later, Washburn held a tent meeting at Oceanside, and the Clarks were among the workers. Nellie recalled how they would make a circle around a seeker and pray until he or she "came through victoriously." The young boys at these meetings said that if anyone knelt and the workers gathered in a circle around him or her, that person was a "goner."[54]

J. H. and Nellie Clark became regular workers in the J. F. Washburn team. The workers were singers, exhorters, preachers, evangelists, and common laborers. They usually traveled by a buggy or wagon drawn by a team of horses. They carried their songbooks, lanterns or lamps, and other objects necessary to conduct a meeting. The largest items were the tents they lived in and the large meeting tent. The Holiness Association would assign a tent to a man who was responsible for taking it from place to place and conducting tent meetings. They also used "gospel wagons," drawn by a team of horses. J. H. and Nellie Clark were in charge of Gospel Wagon Number 1. Little is known about the contents of such wagons, but they must have carried all the personal needs of the workers and the properties needed for holding tent meetings.[55] A set of double harnesses and two blan-

kets were donated at one time to be used in the gospel wagon ministry.[56]

After working on the J. F. Washburn team for a time, the Clarks began their own tent work July 1885 and continued in this sort of work until 1887, when J. H. became the pastor of the Pasadena church for several years.[57]

After leaving the pastorate at Pasadena, they took up the Gospel Wagon Number 1 work. They held a street meeting on New Year's Eve at the corner of Fair Oaks and Colorado Streets in Pasadena. When the street meeting ended, they went to the tabernacle on the corner of Fair Oaks Avenue and Peoria Street. Here they conducted a watch night service.[58]

J. F. Washburn and his group took Tent Number 5, and the Clarks with Gospel Wagon Number 1 held a meeting that lasted for six weeks at Santa Ana in 1892. Their tent meetings were successful in gaining converts. At Santa Ana there were seventy-five professions, including those being sanctified, justified, and reclaimed. The congregation was made up of Quakers, German Methodists, Baptists, Episcopalians, and Adventists. A number of these joined the Holiness Church after the tent meeting.

These people firmly believed in modeling Jesus' ministry and preaching, teaching, and healing. Frequently many people were healed in their meetings. On New Year's Day, after the meeting in Pasadena, a physician's wife was healed in her home. They came to her and prayed with her, and God healed. That night an aged sick lady was prayed for, after which her pain ceased and she quietly and peacefully died. A physician was healed and testified to the power of God to heal the body and save from a terrible habit of using morphine. A father who had a cancerous tumor, with no hope of getting well, was healed.[59]

Were they financially successful? Nellie said their wagon was paid for before the wheels made a single revolution on the road. They never asked for money. They just prayed. Then God told people what He wanted them to give toward keeping it on the road. The Lord kept the wagon going. The persons who failed to do their part are the losers, she declared.

There were many unpleasant circumstances in those tent meetings. They lived in small tents. They contended with dust, flies, and worst of all, at Oceanside, California, fleas. They could have been comfortable in their home. But the inner fire burning in their hearts to get people saved and sanctified would not let them rest. They were compelled by the love of God to take the gospel to lost humanity.

J. H. died suddenly and unexpectedly January 31, 1896. In the last few months of his life, his favorite way of saying goodbye was "If the chariot comes, I am ready."[60] Nellie Clark married W. E. Moyle, a home missionary worker, some time after J. H.'s death.[61]

Mrs. S. J. Hutchinson

The History of the Holiness, Pilgrim and Pilgrim Holiness Churches of California records on page 54 that Mrs. S. J. Hutchinson was the pastor of the East Los Angeles Holiness Church from June 21, 1894 to August 1895.

Lizzie Snow

The Holiness Church of California recommended (ordained) as a minister of the gospel Lizzie Snow in 1895. As soon as this meeting was over, she and her husband, O. L. Snow, left California and went to Illinois, where they were engaged in tent meetings. They wrote from Ashland, Illinois, that they had put up the tent, taken it down because of a bad storm with heavy rain, and put it up again. However, ten people had been converted; five of them united with the church.[62]

Lizzie preached at the annual camp meeting that was held at Riverside, California.[63]

Mrs. Mary Foster

Mary Foster was installed on May 1, 1895, as the pastor of the Garvanza Holiness church. That church was organized during the year. Mary was considered a church planter.[64]

Eva Wyatt

Eva Wyatt was another of the women who was a regular worker with the J. F. Washburn group in the Holiness Church of California. In 1888 they held a tent meeting at Elsinore, California. On May 23 they pitched the tents by the lakeshore. They did not know anyone in the area, but a man had told them there would be lumber they could get for nothing and that there would be ground for them to use for the camp. That was all they needed to know, and they put up the big tent. The men went for a load of wild hay, which they used to feed the horses and used for covering the ground under the tent. In the first meeting, which lasted six weeks, two women were sanctified. Enough people were saved to start a church. After the tent meeting, they held their church meetings in a building that had been a billiard saloon.[65]

Eva worked with W. E. Shepard in another group, which conducted a meeting at Santa Rosa. Here twelve persons were converted.[66] She again joined the J. F. Washburn team for another tent meeting. They spent six weeks in worship in the valley and mountains and held two services each day. Eva reported, "It meant something to travel and camp in the dirt, and hot sun without shade. Money could not tempt us to do it, but the love of God constrains us. Therefore we carry on."[67]

Eva traveled with the Washburn team to Santa Paula. Once they arrived, the men departed to get straw, chairs, lumber, and other things for the meeting. A group of curious people watched and wondered if they were a band of wandering gypsies. However, when they listened to the music, they became convinced that this group of people loved them. Thirty professions were made in less than a month. During that meeting they had endured heavy rains and hard winds.[68]

Eva worked with another group in 1900 led by Alfred Adams Sr. at San Luis Obispo. The meeting lasted fourteen days. The had traveled in a wagon pulled by a team of horses for 450 miles. Adams had started out for that meeting with nothing in his pocket, but when they returned, he had sixty-five cents.

Only God knows the courage of the women who traveled in these groups. They did not expect to receive financial gain, but they were rewarded with people finding peace with God and seeing Him work many miracles of divine healing.

Josephine M. Washburn

J. F. Washburn was the leader of a corps of workers in the Holiness Church of California who used gospel tents Numbers 2 and 5. His wife, Josephine, was his partner in this "tenting" adventure. They held tent meetings all across California. Often the meetings were held in schoolhouses. In 1886 they held a meeting in the schoolhouse in Marietta for two weeks, and a number of people were saved. From this core group a church was organized, and a church building was erected.[69]

Josephine endured many hardships when they were involved in tent meetings. The following incidents happened during the 1886 year. They started off with less than one dollar on a 120-mile trip with the regular workers in the two-horse buggy. They arrived at their destination, where a woman was burdened for souls. They worked and held services for three weeks with no visible results. One of the workers became very ill. They believed strongly in divine healing and prayed—and God performed a healing miracle. This stirred the people. Many were for them and others were against them. But sixty persons made a profession, and most of these were soon sanctified. A church was organized with thirty-three members. It became necessary to build a house of worship, so a building was erected. Another miracle occurred—the building was constructed debt free. The weather was intensely hot and there was virtually no shade. In order to get relief from the heat, the workers would sit under the water tank with all their clothing on day after day. The sweating tank made their clothing damp, and they were slightly cooled in this manner. One day a terrific storm of wind, hail, thunder, and lightning came. All the tents, the large one for services, and the smaller ones in which they lived, were blown from over their heads. Papers and books were scattered for over a block.

One year they made a trip to visit all the places where they had preached. Everywhere they went they saw remarkable healings.[70] On January 29, 1895, they left their home in Glendor. The horses pulled the wagons through one to twelve inches of wet sand and water. Josephine never complained about the bad housing or travel.[71]

From 1895 to 1919 she spoke at the assembly meetings. Once she spoke on the duties of the husbands to their wives and the duties of fathers to their children. There was much confession and a great "season of prayer" for more love, consideration, and consistency in these relationships.

The association gave Josephine a certificate of recognition as a minister (ordination) in 1895. She was overcome with emotions when she received it, thoroughly surprised that the Church had given her this honor and privilege. She had spent her life going with her father and her husband as a worker, praying, singing, testifying, and preaching. But she never felt that she was to be a minister. As she held the certificate, a small white paper with a red seal, she felt like every word was written in the blood of Jesus. It was dated August 12, 1895. She held it for two years as a minister and then requested that it be changed to authorize her as an evangelist and pastor. (Research did not reveal what the differences were in the categories.)[72]

The Washburns experienced the coldest winter ever known in Phoenix in 1896. Ice stayed in the tent all day. Each morning they found one and one-half inches of ice outside the tent. She said, "I tell you it takes grit as well as grace and stick-to-itiveness to spread the holiness message in Arizona!"[73]

Sometimes she would speak with a melted heart and with great tenderness, and the people would refuse to yield. At other times when she spoke there would be many seekers. She was a regular speaker at the annual camp meetings. Josephine was the author of the book *History and Reminiscences of the Holiness Church Work in Southern California and Arizona.*

Mrs. George A. Goings

Some of the ministers of the Holiness Church of California were black. Two prominent black ministers were George A. Goings and his wife. She was always referred to as Mrs. George A. or Mrs. G. A. Goings. They felt that God was calling them to preach to their own people in the South in 1897.

The first report of their ministry in the South was at Nebo, Kentucky. When they arrived, no one had made arrangements for them. They finally were able to find a widow who took them in. The next day they conducted three services in her home. They reported, "People here have been much imposed upon by many sharks, so they will not receive anybody as they should, and all the preachers holding authority here are opposed to the doctrine of holiness." They were not willing to concede this work among Blacks to the enemy of souls.[74]

A Christian teacher invited Mrs. Goings to come to her neighborhood. Mr. Goings took her to Madisonville and then left. She walked one mile to the teacher's boarding house in dark and stormy conditions. The teacher was not there. The meeting place, a house, was six miles away, and Mrs. Goings was to preach at seven. Finally a neighbor offered to take her there in his lumber wagon. They drove over the roughest, darkest road she had ever been on, but she felt safe because God was with her. When she arrived at the house, they provided her with biscuits cooked in a three-legged, long-handled skillet on the hearth before a big log fireplace. The creek was overflowing, so the meeting was cancelled for that night. The next morning they left early and traveled over low marshy land. They came to a swiftly flowing creek, and the horses drew them safely across. These people had never seen a woman preacher, and there was real excitement in the meeting. The next morning when she left, she crossed that swiftly flowing creek by walking on a log.

The city of Nebo, located on the Ohio River, was home to several railroads, many churches, and fifty large tobacco houses. Mrs. Goings had never seen so many saloons. They were all over the town. The people lived from hand to mouth in very poor houses. Children were poorly clad. They were ill with fever in the summer and pneumonia in the winter. At that time thousands of black people and many whites lived there. Nearly every man and woman used snuff/tobacco, and many were enslaved to strong drink. Every pulpit was furnished with two spittoons for the preacher to spit tobacco juice into. Christmas was a time for everyone to get drunk, even for those professing to be Christians.

The Goings had no financial support. God used people to meet their needs for food. A man gave George $73.20 toward purchasing a tent. They used the tent for holding meetings in several cities, including a four-week meeting in New Albany, Indiana. There they saw three converted and eight sanctified. On the last night the tent was filled, and two hundred people had to stand during the entire service.

Sometimes a pastor would give them room and board when they held meetings in his town. These pastors often allowed them to use their churches for meetings.

The couple then visited Manual Labor College, where the president's seventy-five-year-old mother had worked four years as cook and had received only five dollars for all her work. She was born a slave and was deprived of an education, but she was proud and honored to be the mother of two preachers.

Their street meetings aroused much interest. As many as eleven would be kneeling at one time on the sidewalk for prayer. On Sunday three hundred persons stood and listened for ninety minutes. The Goings declared this area was in "dark heathenism as any found in the Congo."

Mrs. Goings had charge of a crusading band of women in Nashville in 1899. They went house to house each afternoon singing and praying. There were good results from this crusade.[75]

Mrs. Goings attended and preached at the Methodist Episcopal Conference. Most of this group was not interested in the holiness message, and there were only a few converts. The clergymen were opposed to women preachers.[76]

Mrs. Goings described what it meant to be a "peculiar people." It was not the way a person acted nor was it the way he or she dressed.

"Peculiar" meant the person had quit sinning. Not to use snuff was being peculiar![77]

She traveled from Nashville to California in 1902 and stopped to see relatives along the way. In St. Louis she visited a tent meeting conducted by the Church of God. That group did not believe in women saying anything in church. She wrote, "I did not stay very long!" Some churches welcomed and encouraged her. She spoke at the African Methodist Episcopal church on Sunday in Keokuk Iowa, to a large and attentive audience, which "immediately produced fruit." At Keosauqua, she spoke at a Baptist church on the two works of grace, and several, including a deacon of the church, raised their hands for prayer. In Ottawa, Iowa, her hometown, she found "saloons on every hand, and the town had become a noisy, rough, whiskey-soaked city sold out to the devil." She preached at the Salvation Army barracks, and a woman who didn't have any confidence in the "colored folks' religion" was touched by God. That woman invited her to the Free Methodist Church for services on the next Sunday. There Mrs. Goings exhorted, and the woman testified, shouted, and confessed that she now loved Mrs. Goings! At a Baptist church she was invited to "say a few words." She did, and the pastor asked her to preach that evening. When she arrived, the church was filled.

At the Annual Assembly Meeting in California, Mrs. Goings preached on the judgment.[78] Another time at this same assembly she spoke and told how she had preached against the saloons in the town of Sebree, Kentucky. As a result, the men voted to close all the saloons. She became known as "the woman that preached whiskey out of this town."[79]

In 1910 Mrs. Goings became the superintendent of the Missionary Training School.[80]

Flora Burger Buck

Flora Burger was born March 20, 1865, in Strausburg, Pennsylvania. She married A. D. Buck May 2, 1886, and was converted July 10 of the same year. They were the parents of one daughter.

Flora had every advantage of education and culture that money could give. She had a surpassingly lovely trained voice. God used her voice in leading thousands of worshipers in song.

Her husband, A. D. Buck, was the presiding elder for nine years in the Holiness Christian Church in Indiana, Kentucky, Ohio, and Michigan. Flora became known as the "mother" of the Holiness Christian Church in Indiana before her death at age fifty-seven on November 23, 1922.

Both A. D. and Flora Buck enlisted in the service of God around 1886. Both were used mightily to advance God's kingdom. He survived her by many years and was instrumental in building eight churches and helped about 165 men into the ministry and some into missionary work on the foreign fields.

Flora Burger Buck was also used greatly by God and preached to scores of people. Her ministry included three years as matron of a rescue home, four years as a pastor, and nineteen as an evangelist. The reports show that no fewer that ten thousand persons were saved under her ministry. She loved to work for the Lord. God graciously rewarded her loyalty and faithfulness to her family with all her brothers and sisters finding a saving relationship with God through her ministry. Three of her brothers became ministers of the gospel.

Flora's gospel preaching was "no uncertain sound" and uncompromising in spirit. She was a staunch defender and aggressive warrior of the cause of holiness.[81]

Mrs. Dews

In 1889 a small group of people were under the leadership of Rev. and Mrs. Dews (first names unknown), who were both preachers. Meetings were held on the land belonging to Moses Oakley in a chestnut grove. The grove was adequate during the summer months, but later they moved into a hoop shop. In 1890 the group decided it was time to build a chapel, and they were organized as a Wesleyan Methodist Church in the Champlain Conference (now Eastern New York-New England District). The Dews continued to pastor the church until 1892. The church became known as Acorn Hill.[82]

The Chichester, New York church was built in 1886. Mrs. Dews was one of the early pastors there.[83]

Mrs. A. J. Rose

Little is known about Mrs. A. J. Rose, who pastored and was an ordained minister in the Wisconsin Conference of the Wesleyan Methodist Church. The records begin with her preaching at the Burr Circuit in 1888. This circuit finally consisted of four churches: Burr, Valley, Oak Ridge, and Billings Creek. She would preach at services held alternate Sundays at Burr and Valley and Oak Ridge and Billings Creek.

The history of the Burr church records that Mrs. Rose, known as "Auntie Rose," drove a spirited pony team named Bird and Pet. This was likely the way she traveled from one church to another.

Oak Ridge church was started by a revival Auntie Rose conducted in the home of Oliver Schermerhorn. Seven persons were converted in the meeting, and in January 1893 the Oak Ridge church was organized and became a part of the Burr Circuit. They did not have a church building, so the services were held in the schoolhouse until 1896, when a church building was constructed.

The records show she pastored the Burr/Valley circuit from 1888 to 1890, and in 1890–94 the Oak Ridge/Billings Creek churches were apparently added. She pastored the Baraboo church for two years and the Valton church three years. She returned to Burr Valley/Oak Ridge/Billings Creek circuit in 1899 and continued there until 1902.

A new dining hall was completed on the Burr Campgrounds in 1959. The Woman's Missionary Society used the old dining hall for their meetings. They called it the "Rose Room" in memory of Auntie Rose, "a pioneer preacher who pastored many of the churches around the campground."[84]

Mary Everett Pierce

One of the early women preachers of the Reformed Baptist Church of Canada was Mary Everett. She was born near Fredericton, New Brunswick, March 17, 1869 and was converted at age fourteen in the Baptist church. She was sanctified two years later. Shortly after her sanctification, the family moved into Fredericton, and her father became the manager of Long's Hotel.

Mary craved the things of God. She attended as many as five different church services on Sunday. She was an avid reader of all the holiness literature she could buy or borrow. As a child, while her playmates were playing, she could be seen under a tree with the Bible in her lap. After her death, one childhood friend said "she was as one set apart," even as a child.

During the summer of 1890, Mary attended Beulah Camp Meeting. This camp, located on the St. John River at Brown's Flat, was the camp of the Reformed Baptists. There she met Ella Kinney, daughter of Rev. Aaron Kinney. They became united in spirit and effort to advance the kingdom of God. They were young and inexperienced and often met with the opposition to "women preachers." All these factors drove them to their knees and into a deeper relationship with God. These two young girls preached in all the churches of that denomination. They encouraged believers and proclaimed the full message of the gospel. Many people were saved, and several of them were called into the ministry as missionaries as well as preachers. This powerful team was broken when Ella married Herbert Sanders. Ella and Herbert were preparing for missionary work under the Reformed Baptists in South Africa.

Mary continued her ministry with the Reformed Baptist Church alone. Her fame leaped the bounds of her native province in Canada and crossed into the United States before she married D. Rand Pierce, a Methodist Episcopal pastor in Maine. Following her marriage, she became co-pastor with her husband on all their pastorates. Sometime after her marriage they united with the Church of the Nazarene. Mary rose to her peak of powers in the pulpit during their ministry at Lynn and Fitchburg, Massachusetts, and Providence, Rhode Island. When she preached she seldom failed to lift her congregations "into realms of exalted vision and blessing." She was described as a "woman of tears," for both she and her hearers were melted under the power of her preaching.

Mary Everett Pierce went home to be with her Lord August 14, 1932.[85]

Mrs. M. J. Bonney

Sometimes the journals did not provide a woman's given name, essentially identifying her as simply the wife of her husband. However, sometimes a woman was listed by her initials. Such was the case of M. J. Bonney. Her husband was known as L. O. Bonney. They were from the Michigan Conference of the Wesleyan Methodist Church. The records are sketchy, but they both were stationed as pastors at the Campbell church in Michigan in 1891. She was listed as "unemployed" for two years. They pastored the Ganges, Ada, and Cambia churches. For a number of years she was listed as a "missionary at large." Her name appeared on the list of the honored dead of the Michigan Conference. She must have been a woman of compassion and strong persuasion, for at conference time in 1896 she pled with the conference to purchase an artificial "limb," a leg, for John Wilder. The conference responded by raising an offering of $70 for that purpose. She died in 1902.[86]

Alice Dellinger and Ida A. Scoggin

One of the pioneer pastors in the Kansas Conference of the Wesleyan Methodist Church was Alice Dellinger. The conference minutes show that she entered the conference in 1892. She and Ida A. Scoggin were a pastoral team who served as evangelists and pastors together.

Alice's first pastorate was at Hall Church in 1892–93.[87] Then she served as the pastor at Wesley Chapel (also known as North Branch).[88] During the summer of 1895 "Brother and Sister Beeson," Alice Dellinger, and Ida Scoggin took the conference tent to Norton, Kansas, and held a series of meetings there. The meetings were successful, and a class (church) was organized and church building erected.[89]

Alice Dellinger and Ida Scoggin pastored at Raymond, Kansas, from 1895 to 1897.[90] The following year Alice was listed as the pastor of the Lawrence Creek Church.[91] She apparently attended Houghton College in Houghton, New York, for in 1900 the conference received an offering of $52.50 for her schooling there.

She was ordained in 1901, according to the conference minutes, but T. J. Pomeroy gives her ordination date as 1896 in his *History of the Kansas Conference*. She was appointed to evangelistic work by the conference in 1903–06. She died in 1907 or 1908.[92]

No other references were found to Ida A. Scoggin.

Elsie M. Hazeltine Richards

Elsie M. Hazeltine was born June 4, 1854, near Kingsville, Ohio. She married Charles D. Richards, a farmer, November 30, 1873. She became the mother of seven children. One daughter, Bertha, became a well-known Wesleyan Methodist pastor (Bertha Richards Ketch).

Elsie was thirty-nine years old when she was converted. She had been invited to a revival meeting held in a schoolhouse. On her second visit she gave her heart to the Lord.

Her gifts became evident immediately. She was given a local preacher's license and became the class leader and Sunday school superintendent. Soon she was assisting in evangelistic meetings and preaching in schoolhouses. Then the Allegheny Conference of the Wesleyan Methodist Church licensed her as a conference preacher (licensed minister).

She was the pastor at the Mt. Pleasant and Meadville charge. She was forced to resign this pastorate because of failing health. She died July 10, 1936.[93]

Sallie Barnes Carter

Sallie Barnes Carter[94] preached her first sermon in 1894. Seven girls from the one-room schoolhouse (grades 1–8) she was attending were playing church during the noon hour on the schoolhouse yard. Sallie was chosen as the preacher. She used John 3:16 as her text. When the altar call was given, five of the girls got saved. They were so happy that some boys were sent home to bring their parents to the school. There was no school for the rest of the day! However, the teacher instructed them that they were not to play "church" again during school hours. Twenty-five years later, Sallie met two of these girls at a place where she was preaching, and they both were still serving the Lord.

Sallie was born April 25, 1882, near Advance, North Carolina. Her parents were godly people. Her mother died when Sallie was six years old. The day of her mother's funeral, Sallie asked Jesus to be her mother and to help her to be a good girl.

Sallie began to work in the fields with her father at age ten. She plowed the fields. She bound wheat for her father, and when their own work was done, she would bind wheat for the neighbors for fifty cents a day. She early learned that "godliness with contentment is great gain" (1 Tim. 6:6, KJV). After working in the fields all day, she would walk a mile to attend prayer meeting.

Sallie often took part in the local Sunday church services. When she was twelve, she made the introductory speech at a Children's Day program. The superintendent of schools in Davie County, North Carolina, was present and was so impressed with her speech that he told her father that he would pay for Sallie's expenses through school and college if her father would provide for her clothing. Mr. Barnes talked it over with Sallie's stepmother. She was a good woman but spoke firmly against the plan. Sallie was not permitted to accept the offer.

She began teaching Sunday school at age fourteen. At fifteen, she would sometimes have charge of the services. But Sallie had not yet been born again. In September 1898, at age sixteen, she found the wonderful satisfying relationship with God. One night soon after this, she laid her hand on the shoulder of her cousin and asked him to go to church and give his heart to the Lord. He laughed at her, for he loved to play music for dances. She said she would be praying for him. He could not get away from the weight of her hand on his shoulder and the words "I will pray for you." He came to the revival meeting the next

night and was saved. Frank Hellard, her cousin, became a preacher of the gospel.

Sallie Barnes and Charlie Baker Carter were married July 24, 1899, when she was seventeen. They moved into a small two-room log house. Sallie started a family altar and kept it going the rest of her life. To this union twelve children were born in twenty-four years.

The family lived two miles from the church. Sallie would carry the smallest child in her arms, Charlie carried the next smallest, and they led the others by the hand. When they arrived, Sallie would teach a class. They would return home and eat lunch. After a short rest, they would walk one mile to a three o'clock Sunday school in a schoolhouse. There Sallie would again teach a class. Those were happy days. After devotions with the family and the children were all in bed, Sallie would sit up and study her Bible by lamplight. During those study hours, she saw that the Bible taught sanctification. She didn't understand what that was. She had never heard it preached. But her heart was hungry for something more than what she had. When people were unkind to her or said evil things about her, she would pray and ask God to help her love these people. God cleansed her heart from inbred sin.

Sallie began having prayer meetings in their home on Saturday nights. She and the children would take down the bed and set the bedstead outdoors against the house. The little room would be packed with people every Saturday night. Charlie would lead the singing, and Sallie was in charge of the services. Many people were saved in the meetings.

They still went to Sunday school and church. Her cousin, Frank Hellard, came for a revival. The people built a brush arbor, and he preached. After the revival, C. G. Bailey, the owner of the farm where they lived, was concerned about people going so far to church. He told Sallie that if she wanted a church nearer home, he would give a lot. He owned many large trees. He offered to furnish the logs and pay for having the trees sawed if she would get men to volunteer to build a church. Sallie got busy. In one week's time the men from several denominations were cutting trees and began building a church. It was then used for Sunday school and prayer meetings. The new building was just one block from their home!

Sallie served the church for six years. She later would have the privilege of holding four revivals in that church and preaching at five homecomings. She was helping in a revival there when the church was organized by the Methodist conference.

The Lord used Sallie to bring people into restored health. She often prayed for people who were ill, and they would be healed. One of her children was healed, and Sallie herself was healed of cancer.

In 1922 Charlie and Sallie moved to Hanes, North Carolina, where they could earn more money to care for their large family. They lived here for five years. Sallie taught a Sunday school class in the Methodist auditorium and led prayer meetings at the Moravian church on Sunday nights. She never called this preaching. But God had been calling her to preach for many years.

In 1922 they moved to High Point, North Carolina. The day they arrived, a lady asked her to hold a prayer meeting that Saturday night at their home. Two women were saved that night. She continued with the prayer meetings, and the crowds became very large. More people were being saved. For ten years she had been teaching and holding prayer meetings, but God continued to call her to preach, and she was under conviction because of this. One night she completely surrendered to God and in a public meeting testified of her call to preach. Her husband thought she was losing her mind and tried to reason with her, but at last he told her that she must do what God wanted. He always cooperated with her. He took her to her revivals and would come and get her when the meetings closed.

Many requests came for her to hold revivals, and many people were converted. She preached in churches and under brush arbors. Sallie was a Methodist, but her services were nondenominational.

When the family moved to High Point, Sallie soon noticed that many children in their neighborhood did not attend Sunday school or church. She became burdened for them and began offering Sunday school in her home. Some adults came with the children. The Sunday school was organized with officers. At Christmas the children performed in a Christmas program. Eventually there was a Sunday school class in each room of their seven-room home.

In 1929, during the Great Depression, God called Sallie to build a church in High Point. All she had was eighty dollars from the Sunday school offerings. The group elected three trustees. Using the eighty dollars, they made a down payment on a lot and began building. Each day money would come in to pay for the expenses of that day. Soon the little church was finished. She pastored there for two years before the Lord led her to join the Wesleyan Methodist Church. The conference president, J. A. Clement, organized the church and appointed her as pastor. She served four more years. The average annual salary during those six years was twenty-five dollars. But Sallie did not preach for money; she preached for the salvation of souls. She eventually resigned from the church when she felt God was calling her into evangelism again.[95]

Sallie's revivals usually lasted two weeks. She preached two times each day, and many gave their hearts to the Lord. Sometimes there would be from thirty-five to seventy-five people at the altar during a revival. She never took an offering, but often at the close of a meeting, people would leave money in her hand as they shook hands. Farmers would bring in food. One time a pickup truck loaded with a country ham, one hundred pounds of flour, cabbage to make a barrel of kraut, green beans, corn, tomatoes and beets came to her house. She was busy canning for over a week!

In 1937 the family moved to Thomasville, North Carolina. Here Sallie did practical nursing in homes and in hospitals until her husband suffered a stroke. In order to care for him, she managed a twelve-room boarding house with twenty roomers. She often fed sixty people a day. Her husband died in January 1945. After his death, she lived with her children, but she longed for a home of her own. In the fall of 1945 she started keeping house for her youngest son, who was home from the Navy.

Sallie had a big red-letter year in 1947, when she received her practical nurse's license in October. She finished the ministerial course of study and was ordained as a minister in the North Carolina Wesleyan Methodist Conference at Colfax, North Carolina.

Sallie invited some widows into her home for a Thanksgiving social hour in November 1953. She was now seventy-one years old. These women enjoyed the time together so much that they decided to meet each month. They organized a "Widow's Club" with fifteen members. She became the president. They helped each other but extended their care to handicapped children. They sent baskets of food, flowers, and cheery messages to the sick. She was active until the very end of her life.

Sallie Barnes Carter died May 12, 1961, after spending her life in the service of her Lord. She was the founder (church planter) of two churches, Baily's Chapel Methodist Church near Advance and Ennis Street Wesleyan Methodist Church in High Point.[96]

Ethel McKinley

Home missionary work was the burden and calling of Miss Ethel McKinley, who served the Pilgrim Holiness Church. She labored with Miss Nellie Cunnins in a mission in Pocahontas, Virginia. This was a needy coal mining section of Virginia. She lived a sacrificial and self-denying life wherever she worked. She was remembered for her house-to-house visits to talk with people. She ministered in homes, Sunday schools, and the pulpit. Her messages contained "deep truths." She probably began ministerial work in 1896. She was a graduate of Union Bible Seminary in Westfield, Indiana, where she also taught for a time.

After working for a while in Virginia, she felt led of God to do tent meeting work in West Virginia. She walked with and served God for forty-three years. She died September 13, 1937.[97]

Estella Gaines

Estella Gaines was a very cultured and devout person. She entered the South Carolina Conference of the Wesleyan Methodist Church in

1896 as a dedicated layperson. She took a leading part in the work and was faithful to the principles of the conference. She was a very loyal supporter of the conference.[98]

She was an anointed, gifted, consecrated worker and it is not surprising that she soon entered the home missionary work in the Blue Ridge Mountains. The mission work at Glenville was located in the bounds of the North Carolina Conference but it was organized with the understanding it would be a part of the South Carolina Conference. Estella Gaines served as an assistant to W. F. Stamey at the Glenville church during the conference year 1916–17.[99] The next year she supplied the Gender and Glenville mountain work under the supervision of the South Carolina Woman's Home and Foreign Missionary Society.

She was elected conference secretary of the South Carolina Conference in 1897. Her interest in missions and children led to her election as the Young Missionary Workers Band (now Wesleyan Kids for Missions) conference superintendent from 1913–1919. She served the Lord and her conference with honor. She died in 1920.[100]

Maria Matilda "Mattie" Worth Moore

Maria Matilda was called "Mattie" and was often referred to as "M. M. Worth" in the conference minutes. Mattie was born December 12, 1851, in Rush County, Indiana. She was converted and joined the Union Chapel (now Blue River) Wesleyan Methodist Church in 1875. Under the ministry of Mary E. Depew and Elmira Elliott, she learned about heart purity/holiness. She was sanctified in 1880.

Mattie ran a millinery store in Carthage, Indiana, for over fifty years. During her early years at the store, God called her to go to North Carolina. The North Carolina Conference was struggling with many issues at that time. There was tension in the Church and outside the Church caused by the mistreatment of the black slaves. They were now free, and many of them were retaliating with like abuse to the whites. A former conference leader threatened to leave the conference, and he headed up a movement to take many other ministers with him. The workers and pastors were discouraged from the troubles in the churches and the chaos outside. A fervent call for workers to come and help rescue the conference went out across the denomination.[101]

Mattie Worth, a niece of Daniel Worth, who had preached and worked in the North Carolina Conference, answered that call. She and another woman traveled across the conference. They went to every church and tried to reconcile the alienated ones. It is difficult to understand all the handicaps, dangers, and impossible labors they endured. These women made sacrifices and faced dangers but the results of their work lasted for a number of years. Mattie's real concern was for the spiritual life of the workers and pastors.[102] Sometime during that period she also pastored the Asheboro Neighbors Grove Church.[103]

During this time Mattie was working on the course of study and was preparing for ordination. She was ordained August 21, 1895, in the Wesleyan Methodist Church, apparently by the North Carolina Conference.[104] During the 1883 year, she was a licensed minister stationed at Sheridan, Indiana. She served as an associate pastor of the Blue River circuit and also pastored at Fairmount, Larwill, the Fowler circuit and Fountain City. All these churches were in the Indiana Conference. She also spent a number of years in evangelism.

On October 10, 1907, she married Cornelius Moore of New Castle, Indiana. After her marriage she served at the Fowler church and later conducted a mission in New Castle. She was on the superannuated list in 1929.[105] Even near her death, she was intensely interested in the depth of spiritual conditions of people and the church. Often she had given money to lift the financial burden of a local church or a person. In her final illness when her mind wandered, she preached to an invisible congregation. It was reported that those messages were "worthwhile." Her death occurred April 29, 1935, in the home of a niece, Eva McMichael Miller.[106]

Melvina "Mina" Jane Cretsinger Johnson

Melvina Jane Cretsinger was born July 7, 1857. She married Albert Johnson in 1887. She became the mother of seven children. She was converted, joined the Wesleyan Methodist Church in 1889, and sometime later was sanctified and called to preach. During her lifetime she was a great soul winner.[107]

In the Iowa Conference president's report of January 4, 1897, Mrs. (Albert) Mina Johnson was appointed assistant pastor of the Manona Mission. No reason was given, but that part of the report was not adopted. Her husband apparently was the pastor. He was an ordained minister. The Itinerary and Elders Orders Committee (now Board of Ministerial Development) recommended that she work under the direction of the conference. The minutes that year answered the question "How is the work supplied this year?" Manona Mission— Albert Johnson and Mina Johnson.

The *Minutes* of 1901 reported, "Albert Johnson and wife, Mina, of the Albaton charge exchanged [churches] with L. True and wife of Guthrie circuit. The exchange was approved November 2, 1900." The following year they were assigned to the West Union, Homer, and Iona, Nebraska, charge.

Questions seemed to arise often about Albert and Mina's service. The 1910 *Minutes* of the Iowa Conference stated that Albert Johnson had joined with the Apostolic Holiness Union (later to be known as the Pilgrim Holiness Church) and was participating in their activities. The Iowa Conference gave them the opportunity "to leave the Apostolic Holiness Union and remain on the Iowa Conference roll or be dismissed." No mention was made about their decision.

In December 1914 Albert Johnson and wife, Mina, held a revival meeting in the Seely schoolhouse, which was located seven miles north of Guthrie Center. A number of people were saved. A Wesleyan Methodist church was organized on August 5, 1915, after a three-week tent meeting. They had fourteen members and were known as the Seely Wesleyan Methodist Church.

On January 13, 1916, Albert and Mina were appointed supply pastors of the Guthrie Center charge. They continued to pastor there until December 11, 1922, at which time they were released from Guthrie Center and appointed pastors of the Emmual and Pleasant Hill charge. Mina was ordained in 1924. They served the Emmual and Pleasant Hill charge until 1928. They moved to the Bethel church in 1929 and remained there until 1935.

Mina Johnson died April 22, 1936.[108]

Mrs. H. Jennie Taliaferro

A church was organized in 1897 at Eskridge, Kansas. Mrs. George Crump had witnessed to her neighbors and held prayer meetings in her home. Soon a meeting was held by V. A. Taliaferro, a Wesleyan Methodist evangelist. Mrs. Crump's prayer meeting group joined the Wesleyan Methodist Church. In the fall after the organization of the Church, H. Jennie Taliaferro[109] was sent by the conference to be the first pastor. She stayed one year.[110] No records could be found for a number of years after this, but she was listed in the Kansas Conference Minutes in 1903 as an ordained minister.

Her name occurs two times as one of two conference evangelists. These conference evangelists held quarterly meetings at various local churches over the entire conference. She was elected to this position in 1903 and 1905.[111]

She served as the Woman's Home and Foreign Missionary Society president on the conference level 1902–1907.

She spent several years in evangelistic work but was on the unstationed (without appointment) list 1912–16. In 1917 her name was dropped from the conference roll because she was not a member of any local Wesleyan Methodist church.

Sarah C. Wilcox

Sarah C. Wilcox served one term as a missionary to Africa under the Methodist Board,

but her health prevented her return. She served as a pastor in the Lockport Conference of the Wesleyan Methodist Church at Ramsonville, East Leon, and Ellicott (now Hamburg).

A revival began in September 1892 and lasted for three months. One hundred twenty persons sought the Lord during that meeting. The church was organized October 31, 1892, and was known as the Ellicott church, located near Orchard Park, New York. Sometime in the late 1800s Sarah C. Wilcox was the pastor of the Ellicott (Hamburg) church. She pastored the East Leon church near Cattaraugus, New York, from 1901 to 1903.[112]

There was no report of her work in the Lockport Conference for a number of years following her appointment at East Leon.

However, Sarah C. Wilcox was received by the Iowa Conference by letter in 1907. She pastored the Guthrie Center Wesleyan Methodist church in Guthrie Center, Iowa, from 1907 through 1908.[113]

Sarah C. Wilcox, sometimes referred to as S. C. Wilcox, was introduced to the Lockport Conference in 1915. She was from the Forestville charge. The conference appointed her as the pastor of the Short Track church, which she served from 1915 to 1918. Her name did not appear on the conference roll again until 1928. That year the conference read a letter from her as a former member and pastor in the conference. She requested membership in the conference and was granted it. She remained on the conference roll until 1932.[114]

Sarah Wilcox died March 3, 1953. She was remembered for her patience, faith, and sweet spirit. She was an inspiration to all who knew her.[115]

Martha Elizabeth Fox Shelton

Martha Elizabeth Fox was born May 14, 1879. She was converted at an early age and soon felt called to the ministry. She married John H. Shelton and became the mother of six children.

Martha was ordained by the Pilgrim Holiness Church, and she was actively engaged in the work for thirty-five years. Ill health forced her to retire from the Lord's work. Her greatest desire was to be in the Lord's work. She often declared she hoped it could be said of her after her death, "She hath done what she could." She died November 17, 1950.[116]

⸺⸻⸺

Myrtle Jane Webster Brown

Myrtle Jane Webster Brown[117] was born December 23, 1874, in Decatur County, Indiana. She was converted in the Finley Methodist Church in 1897 and sanctified later that same year. Myrtle became a charter member of the Holiness Christian Church at Gaynorsville, Indiana.

After Myrtle and her sister, Adda, were converted, their brothers observed their changed lives. This transformation in the sisters brought conviction to the brothers, and they were also converted. One brother, Will Webster, became a pioneer minister of the Church in the West. The fruit of Myrtle's godly life lived on in her family. More than twelve members of her family became active in the ministry.

Myrtle received her first ministerial license in 1898 and was ordained in 1907 at Frankfort, Indiana, in the Indiana Conference of the Holiness Christian Church. This group later merged with what became the Pilgrim Holiness Church.

She was mightily used of God in the beginning of several churches during her early ministry in home missionary and evangelistic work. During this time she served churches in Wabash, Marion, and Lawrenceburg, Indiana; Auburn, Illinois; and Kingswood, Kentucky. The church in Marion was pioneered/planted by her.[118]

Myrtle was united in marriage to Charles C. Brown, December 31, 1901, and to this union two sons, Nathaniel and Joseph, and five daughters, including triplets, Mrs. E. O. Howell, Mary Hylton O'Sullivan, Mrs. John Cordier, Josephine Brown and one stepdaughter, Mrs. Earl Rager. One daughter, Anna, died in infancy.

Her husband, C. C. Brown, was a great spiritual leader in the Holiness Christian Church. He was elected presiding elder of the Southern Indiana District in 1900. In 1910 he was elected presiding elder of the Illinois/Missouri District of the Holiness Christian Church and served as general superintendent of the Holiness Christian Church from 1917 to 1919. After merger of the Holiness Christian Church with the International Apostolic Holiness Church, C. C. Brown served as the assistant general superintendent of the now named International Holiness Church. He was the presiding officer when the Pilgrim Church of California united with the International Holiness Church in 1922, and the name of the church became the Pilgrim Holiness Church.[119] Through the years Myrtle helped carry the load with her husband while he served in many administrative positions as well as preaching with him in revival, tent and camp meetings.

About 1905 C. C. and Myrtle went to Carlinville, Illinois, and opened a mission. They bought a building and organized a Holiness Christian Church. This church was probably the first organized church in the Illinois District. They opened the Holiness Bible School and later the Bethel Holiness Orphanage. The orphanage was started in a three-room house with three children. More children came and they were forced to obtain a larger building. In about a year or two they purchased a nice large house with three acres of ground. The orphanage was later moved to Kingswood, Kentucky, but long before this move, the orphanage was debt-free.

They also had a small printing business on the Bible School grounds and printed a magazine similar to the *Wesleyan Advocate*. The magazine was called *The Voice of Canaan*.[120]

They were under appointment in several districts and served under several branches of the Church. They served in the Indiana Holiness Christian Church, the International Holiness Church of Kentucky, Kentucky District Pilgrim Holiness Church, Tennessee-Alabama Pilgrim Holiness Church, Tennessee District Pilgrim Holiness, Louisiana-Mississippi District, Gulf States District, and the Indiana North Pilgrim Holiness District.[121]

After their marriage, the Browns served as pastors at Frankfort, Indiana; Auburn, Kingswood, and Carlinville, Illinois; Chattanooga and Jamestown, Tennessee. In the summer of 1929 they felt led of the Lord to minister in Elizabethtown, Kentucky. They did mission work, which began with a tent meeting. A Sunday school was organized in September 1929. At first they used a rented hall for services, and the two rooms in the back of the hall were used as a parsonage. They were forced to leave after six months because of ill health.

Myrtle Brown departed this earthly life May 14, 1963. She is still remembered for her dedication to the needs of others. Her deep devotion, strong courage, and consistent faith in God through her active life and long illness were blessings to all who knew her.

Cornelia Adams

Cornelia Adams was received by the North Michigan Conference of the Wesleyan Methodist Church in 1898. The next year she was assigned to assist her husband, J. A., as pastor at Mecosta, Michigan. They served the following two years as the pastors at Meridian. In 1903 she was listed as a conference evangelist. No mention is made of her again until 1916, when the conference president appointed her as pastor of the Lilly circuit.[122]

Abbie Ayling

In 1899 Abbie Ayling and her husband, J. W., came into the Michigan Conference of the Wesleyan Methodist Church by transfer from the Crusaders. They apparently lived or pastored at Bedford. In 1900 they were assigned to the Coldwater church and the next two years they pastored the Berlin church. In 1903 they withdrew from the Wesleyan Methodist Church.[123]

Mrs. Lorinda A. Bishop

Lorinda A. Bishop began her ministry in the Iowa Conference of the Wesleyan Methodist Church in 1899. She completed her work on the course of study with a "general average of 94.5 percent." She was ordained in 1901 in the morning service of conference.

She had been assigned as the pastor of the Des Moines work in the conference year of 1900, but she resigned October 20 in order to accept the appointment to be the pastor of the College Springs work. No records were found for the years 1902–04.

She was the first president of the Woman's Home and Foreign Missionary Society of the Iowa Conference and held this office from 1901 to 1911. A tribute was given to her after her death that stated she by "word and deed always manifested her deep interest in the cause of missions."

Other pastorates she served included Dundee and Masonville charge, Albaton, and the Union Ridge and Bennezette charge. The Bennezette church was near Bristow, Iowa, and was one of the oldest churches in the Iowa Conference. It was organized in 1885. She served this charge from 1906 to 1908.

Lorinda was elected conference evangelist in 1910. Her duties included traveling the conference and conducting many meetings. Even after she was placed on the superannuated list in 1911, she remained very active in the conference. On May 5, 1912, she requested the president of the conference to visit the Maple Street Christian Church. They wanted to join a "spiritual denomination." On June 14 a church of ten members was organized. On June 21 the property of the Christian Church was deeded to the Wesleyan Methodist Church. By this time there were thirteen families in membership, and many of them "owned homes."

While she was on the superannuated list, she was again assigned to serve the Des Moines church, from July 1, 1912, until conference. She kept that charge until she resigned in April 19, 1913. She must have died soon after this, for she was listed on the Roll of the Honored Dead in 1914.[124]

Harriet A. Kelly

Harriet A. Kelly had a burden for "worn-out" workers. A deed for about eight acres of land was given to W. M. Kelly, and a deed covering an artesian well was given to Harriet A. Kelly. They in turn gave the deeds for this acreage and well to the Holiness Church of California on September 5, 1899. Harriet wanted this land to be used for a home for worn-out workers. The land was located at Santa Fe Springs. There was also a large two-story house ready for use.

The house and land were placed in the hands of W. M. and Harriet Kelly. They received donations of fruit, vegetables, chickens, rabbits, and quilts. They made straw ticks and comforts for the beds, but they received little in cash to meet other bills. However, Harriet declared, "We have received $8.45 in cash, a sack of clothes, a case of coal oil . . . and blessings innumerable." She stayed at this home through June 1902.

In 1909 Harriet met with the Board of Elders on a proposed site for a mission on East First Street in Los Angeles. The board decided she was a proper person for mission work for the Holiness Church and asked the churches and others to assist her as they could. She was enabled to open this mission on October 14, 1909. Immediately, four persons found pardon for their sins. Harriet's street ministry brought the gospel story to Russians, Jews, Mexicans, and Japanese. She also ministered to many children. Hospital visitation and jail work were also included in her ministry.

Harriet carried on her ministry "by faith." No one connected with the mission was able to pay its expenses. On April 8, 1910, the semi-annual camp meeting gave her an offering of $20.75.[125]

Hulda Johnson Rees and Frida Marie Stromberg Rees

Hulda Johnson Rees, first wife of Seth C. Rees, was gifted supernaturally and empowered to be a minister. She almost always accompanied her husband in his public ministry. They shared the pulpit ministry from the beginning of their marriage, conducting meetings across the nation, in the slums, in churches, and in the open air. Thousands responded to their preaching ministry. Hulda became known as the "Pentecostal prophetess," and they were in great demand for meetings. Hulda became ill and died triumphantly June 3, 1898. She was the mother of two sons, Loring and Byron.[126] Hulda was Seth C. Rees's wife when he helped organize the International Holiness Union and Prayer League in 1897 (which eventually became the Pilgrim Holiness Church). He served as its first president.

After Hulda's death, Seth C. Rees married Frida Marie Stromberg November 9, 1899, in Providence, Rhode Island. Frida was born in Sweden February 3, 1872. She was a devoted Christian worker and was accustomed to the public life of the Christian ministry. She immediately took her place on the platform with Seth.

Their wedding trip took them to a great tent meeting in Laurens, South Carolina. The meeting began in a large tent that would seat one thousand persons, and it was almost full the first night. The next day a tent seating five hundred was pitched and joined to the big tent so that everyone could see and hear. The white people sat in the main tent, and the black people sat in a smaller tent. When the altar service was given in the big tent, Frida went to the smaller tent and conducted the altar service there. The people gathered around her, fell on their faces, and a great number were saved and sanctified. Mrs. Rees preached in a morning service, and fifty persons fell at the altar. During their "honeymoon tent meeting," about one thousand persons received a "definite blessing."[127]

Their first child, Paul, was born in 1900. They moved to Chicago, and here Seth conducted outstanding meetings with thousands of converts, and later in Boston. The Rees trio, Frida, Seth, and infant Paul, went west for revivals in Salem and Newburg, Oregon. Again many were saved.

While they lived in Chicago, Seth conducted tent meetings, established a rest home for prostitute women and girls, and worked in the slums in city missions and in open-air meetings. Their family increased to include Russell (1903), Evangeline (1905), and Seth Cook Jr. (1909). They moved to Southern California in the Pasadena area in 1908.

For part of this time Frida remained at home with the children. Seth, knowing how much she must have been missing the pulpit ministry and also how much he longed for her to be with him, wrote, "Thou, my precious wife, will reap a far greater share of glory than I. Thine with the 'stuff' and the little ones do the harder place, and thine will be the richer reward."[128]

After leaving the Pentecostal Church of the Nazarene and Pasadena College in June 1917, they organized an independent church, the Pilgrim Tabernacle of Pasadena. Seth was the pastor there until 1925, and Frida served as assistant pastor.[129] This church became a small denomination and then merged in 1922 with the International Holiness Church to become the Pilgrim Holiness Church. The local church was finally called Rees Memorial Tabernacle.

Seth, Frida, Evangeline, and Seth Jr. went on a worldwide evangelism crusade in 1925. Some or all of them were sick most of the time. In England, Seth, Seth Jr., and Evangeline were ill with the flu, and Frida took care of them. Sickness stalked them also in Palestine and Japan. But there were seekers in all the countries, and over one thousand seekers were reported in Shanghai.[130]

Frida knew the sorrows of this world. Death came to claim her two stepsons, Loring in 1913, Byron in 1918, and her own son, Seth Jr. in 1926 at the age of seventeen.[131]

Seth was elected general superintendent of the Pilgrim Holiness Church in 1926. Frida was listed by district appointment as an evangelist from 1923 to 1932.

Seth and Frida set out for their last evangelistic trip in 1932. This time they would go to the West Indies and South America. She almost always accompanied him in travel these last years of his life. His health had been declining for a number of years, and he returned home very ill. Before he died he told Frida, "Thee must take up the work which I am laying down. Preach the gospel." Seth died in 1933. Frida again revealed her faith and courage as she intoned at his gravesite,

Sleep on, beloved, sleep, and take thy rest;
Lay down thy heart upon thy Saviour's breast,
We love well, but Jesus loves thee best—
Good night! Good night![132]

Frida preached the great gospel. She believed and taught that God can deliver people, old, and young, from the curse of committed sins and the "inbeing" of sin itself. She was ordained by the California District and lived a beautiful and consistent Christian life. She ended her journey and ministry July 28, 1958. She had been a "queenly companion," a godly mother, and a faithful minister of the gospel.[133]

Mrs. A. A. Van Curen

Mrs. A. A. Van Curen served as pastor of the Nordhoff Chapel on Topa Topa and Signal Sreets in Ojai, California, from 1899 to 1901. This was one of the congregations of the Holiness Church of California. The church was known also as the Ojai Church.[134]

Lorena E. Hartnal

Lorena E. Hartnal was given credentials as a minister on August 26, 1899.[135] During that year she was the pastor of Los Angeles First Church, located on East 9th Street at that time. This was one of the Holiness Churches of California.[136]

Margaret Smith Hunt

Margaret Smith was born February 15, 1873. She was converted at the age of twenty-four (1897) at Cumberland Presbyterian Church in Concord, Tennessee. She preached her first sermon in 1899. Margaret joined what became the Pilgrim Holiness Church in 1914. She and Robert H. Hunt were married May 21, 1919. Mr. Hunt died in 1933. Margaret received her ministerial education at God's Bible School in Cincinnati, Ohio.[137]

She began her ministerial work by doing personal evangelism and rescue and orphanage work. This was followed by pastoral and Sunday school work. She spent a number of years working in Canada under the Ontario District of the Pilgrim Holiness Church and was the pastor at Patton and Deyer's Bay in Canada.

She also worked for a time on the Spanish Reservation in Canada.

Margaret also served as a nurse for several years in rescue homes in the Terre Haute, Indiana, area and in Cincinnati. The last seventeen years of her life were spent as an invalid, but she always maintained a cheerful attitude. She died October 27, 1965.[138]

Phebe Farmer

At the General Conference of the Wesleyan Methodist Church in 1899, "elders [ordained ministers] J. P. and Phebe Farmer, of the Miami Conference," were introduced to the body. No records of Phebe Farmer's ministry have survived.

Tents and Storefronts

At the turn of the twentieth century, the emphasis among holiness churches shifted from starting many new church groups to merger and name changes. There would be a change from major reforms in church governments and social issues toward evangelism, holiness revivals and camp meetings, and opening of new foreign mission fields. There were, however, other subtle changes in the church world outside the holiness bodies that would influence the holiness groups.

Liberalism was getting a solid foothold. The social gospel was being accepted by the mainline churches. This would result in a reaction by evangelical churches, leading to the slow ebbing-away of compassion ministries of the churches. What would become the National Council of Churches was born in 1908. The nation became involved in World War I. The issue of the right of women to vote their convictions in the temperance movement and prohibition increased in vocal endorsement. The issues of women's dress, length of hair, worldly amusements, divorce, and observance of the Lord's Day became topics of heated discussions and preaching.

The organization that was eventually to become the Pilgrim Holiness Church underwent a transition from a loose union to a denomination during this period: in 1900 the International Holiness Union and Prayer League became the International Apostolic Holiness Union, in 1905 the International

Apostolic Holiness Union and Churches, and in 1913 the International Apostolic Holiness Church (IAHC). When the Holiness Christian Church merged with the IAHC in 1919, the name was shortened to International Holiness Church. Also during this period, two groups that would eventually merge with what became the Pilgrim Holiness Church were established. One was in Pasadena, California. Seth C. Rees, who had been the first president of the International Holiness Union and Prayer League, founded the Pentecostal Pilgrim Church in 1917. The name was later shortened to the Pilgrim Church. About the same time, a group separated from the Brethren in Christ in Ohio and took the name Pentecostal Brethren in Christ.

During this period the Wesleyan Methodists established two auxiliaries that would provide many avenues of ministry for women: the Young Missionary Workers Band in 1902, and the Woman's Home and Foreign Missionary Society in 1903. In 1919 a denominational department of Sunday schools was established.

Women, loyal to the call of God, continued to evangelize and pastor churches, using tents, storefronts, and other means. Here are stories of women who as near as can be determined started their ministerial work during the 1900–1919 period.

Anna L. Kuykendal Bane

Anna L. Kuykendal was born April 4, 1879. She was converted at an early age and joined a Baptist church. In 1893 she was joined in marriage to A. A. Bane. He was not a minister. She joined the Wesleyan Methodist church in Spartanburg, South Carolina, about 1900. The family moved, and she then joined the Tracy Grove Holiness Baptist church. That church gave her a license to preach. She was faithful to the ministry, preaching and conducting meetings in various parts of North and South Carolina. A number of people were saved under her ministry.

She later joined the Bethel Wesleyan Methodist Church, and that church also granted her a license to preach. She ministered and preached faithfully until her health failed. Her death occurred March 12, 1934.[1]

Mary L. Smith

The Minutes of the Annual Convention of the Apostolic Holiness Church of Pennsylvania listed Mary L. Smith as an ordained minister in 1900. No service record could be found.

Eliza Gillock Burge

Eliza Gillock was born September 11, 1871, near Bloomfield, Indiana. She moved to Kansas and then on to Oklahoma. She was converted in her own home while washing dishes and later was sanctified in a mission hall in Alva under holiness workers who came to work in Oklahoma. She was united in marriage to P. C. Burge in 1892, and they settled near Hopeton, Oklahoma, in 1894. They adopted two children, Rowland and May.

Eliza Burge made a great contribution to the kingdom of God in many ways. She lived a pioneer life on the frontier. She was concerned about the education of her children and taught school in her house until a schoolhouse was built.

Eliza served what became the Pilgrim Holiness Church in many capacities. She was

ordained in 1926 by the Eastern Kansas and Oklahoma District and also served in the following districts: Oklahoma, Oklahoma and Texas, and Oklahoma-Texas-Louisiana. Much of her work involved helping to maintain Sunday schools and church services. She lived to be eighty-one and died May 16, 1953.[2]

Sarah Theresa Reid Harvey

Sarah Theresa Reid was born May 19, 1853, in North Carolina. She married Mills A. Harvey November 25, 1875, at age twenty-two and became the mother of nine children.

Sarah had been converted at age thirteen. While in her secret place of prayer, she was called to preach. She immediately started a family altar in her father's home. This habit of the family altar was carried into her own home, and as a result, all her children and grandchildren established family altars in their home. This was the practice of gathering the entire family together, reading from the Bible, and usually each member of the family praying. Her godly life won her husband and all her children to the Lord. She became an ardent worker in the church and especially in revivals.

In 1898 Mattie Perry, founder and superintendent of Elhanan Bible Training School, came to Old Fort, North Carolina. Perry preached the cleansed-heart holiness message. Both Sarah and her husband were sanctified. She taught her husband to read and write, and he began preparing for the ministry. He became a fearless preacher of the holiness message. Soon the authorities of the Baptist/Friends Church called for a church trial to put him out of the church. Sarah was present at the trial. When questioned about his preaching on holiness, he declared, "I preach what is in the Bible." The officials replied, "It does not matter what the Bible teaches—it is against the church doctrine." Sarah couldn't sit still any longer and rose to her feet to declare, "I have experienced holiness also, and I request to be dropped also." The officials did not want to lose her, but she insisted that she was a preacher of holiness.

Therefore, they both were dropped.

In 1913, Mills and Sarah both became members of the Wesleyan Methodist Church. She may have had a license to preach in the former church, but when they joined the Wesleyan Methodist Church, she was given a license to exhort. Because of her witness, her husband, four sons, one son-in-law, a daughter-in-law, a grandson, and a granddaughter all entered the ministry. The four sons became Wesleyan Methodist preachers. All the daughters were active in church work. Sarah died April 23, 1935.[3]

Harriett "Hattie" Louise Randall Livingston

The September 21, 1933, issue of *The Pilgrim Holiness Advocate* on page 12 contained the obituary of Rev. Hattie Livingston, a pioneer woman preacher. Hattie was born February 21, 1859, in Shopiere, Wisconsin. She married Edward Livingston December 16, 1876, and was the mother of three children. No service record for her was found.

T. A. Moses

T. A. and her husband, A. E. Moses, were a ministerial team in the Champlain Conference of the Wesleyan Methodist Church. T. A.'s given name was never mentioned in the records. She was born March 15, 1851, in Horicon, New York, and was converted at an early age. She entered the teaching profession and was well known in that field.

T. A. Moses was ordained in 1900 by the Champlain Conference. She was a preacher of "more than ordinary ability."

T. A. married Ambrose E. Moses in 1877. They had one daughter, Belle, and became known as the "most loyal and devoted family in the Wesleyan Methodist Church." They served together for fifty-six years. She was known for her undaunted faith in God and His Word.

In 1901 the couple was assigned to the Chester and Horicon, New York, charge and served there until 1906.[4] During this time a parsonage was purchased. They were appointed

to the Acorn Hill and Krumsville Churches in 1906. This was their last pastorate. T. A. also pastored the Lisbon church for a time.

The couple retired in 1911, and were cared for by their daughter, Belle, in her home at Houghton, New York. The students at Houghton remembered her faith, encouragement, and the "run over" of her holy joy and laughter. Her face shone with the glory of God.

Both A. E. and T. A. died in 1933. He died September 22, and she died three months later, on December 19.[5]

Retta Baughman

Retta Baughman was ordained by the Indiana District of the International Holiness Church in 1922. She was born April 10, 1871, and was converted in Anderson, Indiana, in 1892. She was sanctified in 1901. It was during that year that she preached her first sermon in a mission in Anderson, Indiana. She transferred her membership to one of the branches that later became the Pilgrim Holiness Church in Indiana in 1915. Her first pastorate was at what became the Pilgrim Holiness Church in Huntington, Indiana. She served there two years. She also was in charge of a mission in Anderson, Indiana, for one year. Her closing years were spent active in the Anderson First Pilgrim Holiness Church as president of the missionary society and teacher of the women's Bible class. She died September 25, 1961.[6]

Emma C. Johnston

One recorded entry was made for Emma C. Johnston, an ordained minister, in the Iowa Conference of the Wesleyan Methodist Church. That entry was found in the *Minutes of the Annual Session of the Iowa Conference of the Wesleyan Methodist Connection of America* in 1901. She was listed as a conference missionary and had been elected secretary of the conference tithing roll. The conference raised a sum of eight hundred dollars to "enable Sister Emma C. Johnson to make herself self-supporting."

Ella Kinney Sanders

Ella Kinney Sanders[7] was called to be a missionary before she was converted. She was convicted of her sins while listening to her father, Rev. Aaron Kinney, preach. She was eleven years old. She was baptized on Easter Sunday. The snow was piled high, and her father had to push aside chunks of ice in the stream. With tears in his eyes and a tremble in his voice, he declared, "I baptize thee, Ella, my daughter and sister in Jesus. . . ."

Ella spent her childhood in Canadian parsonages. When the weather was bad, her mother taught the children at home on Sundays. Ella's mother died when she was thirteen. There were ten children in the family, and eight of them were scattered after the mother's death. Ella and her oldest brother remained with their father and traveled to Nova Scotia for revival meetings.

Her father held a revival meeting at Port Maitland, Nova Scotia. In this meeting two very important people to Ella were converted, Mrs. John H. Sanders and her son, Herbert. Mrs. Sanders was a very godly woman and became a real mother to Ella. Herbert would become Ella's husband.

Before she was sanctified, Ella struggled with giving up her ambitions and answering God's call to Africa. She was fearful to tell her father of her missionary call. She had been assisting him in revivals, singing, playing the organ, teaching Sunday school classes, and leading people to Christ. She had been teaching Sunday school classes since she was fourteen. Her father affirmed her missionary call by saying, "Before you were born, your mother and I dedicated you as a missionary."

In 1890 she met Mary Everett. They formed a home missionary team and went without salary to preach in homes, schoolhouses, churches, and other places where preachers seldom went. They traveled by horse and carriage and preached in all of their denominational churches, spending from two to six weeks in each place. They were met with scoffing and were even locked out of some churches. This ministry lasted for two years, but during that time many people were saved. Several were called to become missionaries. Among them was Ida Morgan, who later would come to help with the work that the Sanders founded in Altoona, South Africa.

Herbert and Ella were engaged in 1890. He left for Brooklyn, New York, for further training and to study the Zulu language. Ella decided to apply for admission for nurse's training in Boston, but she did not receive her acceptance for a time. Herbert became very ill, and after that crisis they decided to get married immediately. They were married at the close of a holiness camp meeting, September 4, 1893. The couple completed further training and went to South Africa.

They pioneered the Alliance of the Reformed Baptist Church of Canada work in Altoona, which grew to include a missionary compound, Bible school, and hospital. The couple worked and served the people of South Africa from 1901 to 1927. Ella was ordained in 1901 and became the first woman minister to be ordained in Canada. After their return from Africa, Ella pastored churches in Canada. Herbert died in 1941. Ella died in April 1962.[8]

Olive Kyle

Olive Kyle was a minister in the Holiness Church of California. The record of her work is very incomplete. She preached at the annual assembly of the Holiness Church during camp meeting in 1901 and 1902. She also received her credentials (ordination) as a minister at the camp meeting in 1901. She and her husband, E. P., were appointed pastors of the Azusa Valley church and served there one year.[9]

Florence B. Wheeler

According to the *Minutes of the Annual Sessions of the Michigan Conference of the Wesleyan Methodist Connection (or Church) of America*

1901–1906, Florence B. Wheeler joined that conference by transfer from the Willamette Conference in 1901. She was an ordained minister. For four years of that time frame, she was listed as a general evangelist. Her husband, E. W., was elected financial agent and chief evangelist of the conference in 1901. She was invited to accompany him on his visits to each charge and to sing. She was active in the conference sessions and served one year as assistant secretary for the conference Woman's Home and Foreign Missionary Society. On February 13, 1906, she withdrew from the conference.

Mary Berg

The Pentecostal Rescue Mission of New York was served by many outstanding and gifted young women. Some of them came to Binghamton, New York to find a place of employment. Others were burdened for the lost of the big city and came to work for the mission. The mission provided rooms for girls seeking employment and those who worked at the mission home. Some were converted and then became heavily involved in the rescue mission work. These women took the gospel to the lost where they lived and worked. They went into the "dives," "barrel houses," "joints" and "brothels." These dens of vice were the gambling halls, saloons, and houses of prostitution in the large cities.

These women conducted gospel meetings daily in the home. They were the instructors in the Bible studies and attended workers' meetings each day as well as daily noon prayer meetings. Their meetings often attracted large crowds who came to see what was "going on." Sometimes the crowds were so large that the police had to scatter the crowd so the streetcars could pass.

On Saturday nights after the street meetings, the girls would go to the "dens of vice," facing the perils of the slums, exposing themselves to all kinds of "vermin," lice, fleas, flies, and rats, and various kinds of contagious diseases as well as evil persons who could do them bodily harm. These women came from good homes and often had gainful employment, but they willingly and gladly denied their ambitions for the cause of Christ in

these places. They considered themselves expendable for the purpose of rescuing the lost.

One of these outstanding young women was Mary Berg.[10] She was born in northern Pennsylvania October 24, 1869. Sometime during 1901 or 1902, she left her home and went to Binghamton, New York, in search of work. She started attending the meetings held by the Pentecostal Rescue Mission and was converted in November 1902. She was the first member of her family to receive salvation, but she became the instrument God used to lead her entire family into the saving grace of God.

God called her to the work of rescuing immoral, disgraced prostitutes who were homeless and living in the slums. Mary remained faithful to that calling all her life. Her goal was to see God transform their lives.

The mission provided a home for young women who were employed by the mission and those who worked at other jobs in the city. But they also provided rooms in another area for homeless derelicts. Mary was the first young woman to come to the home to work. She became the first matron of the home for prostitutes at Binghamton and remained there until 1907, when she was transferred to Albany, another very wicked city at the time, to do rescue work.

A home was given the mission in Albany to provide a home for the gospel workers and a shelter for the prostitutes. Mary sought untiringly to find persons with blasted hopes and wrecked lives in Albany.

In Schenectady, Mary operated a rescue mission home for prostitutes upstairs and held gospel services on the lower level of a house. She served as pastor of this group for five years.

During her years of service, Mary served as rescue/refuge and slum worker and rescue home matron wherever God led and called. This included the New York cities of Binghamton, Albany, Schenectady, Cortland, Utica, and North Troy. She pastored the church in Cortland three and one-half years, North Troy three years, Schenectady five years, and a mission in Middletown for five years. After thirty-five years of active service in these areas, she turned to caring for her sister, Ellen, for three years.

At the age of seventy-one Mary retired to become a layperson in a local church. She died May 23, 1960, only a few months before her ninety-first birthday.[11]

Nellie Churchford

Nellie Churchford went to Holland, Michigan, in 1902, where she made plans to conduct a series of tent meetings in several different locations. However, the people of Holland wanted her to stay with them and continue conducting services in their city.

Nellie's work was strongly opposed, because she taught definite and strong doctrinal messages on regeneration, sanctification, healing, and the second coming of Christ. Nevertheless, she experienced marvelous success in her meetings. Scores of people were saved, and then they were scattered to many different states to preach the gospel. Her work was mostly among the poor and unfortunate peoples.

Nellie was a graduate of the Scofield Bible School in Holland, Michigan. She was ordained by what became the Pilgrim Holiness Church at Battle Creek, Michigan.

Her work began in a tent. But as the work increased, various buildings were added until a beautiful mission was built in her honor and dedicated October 16, 1927. About four years later, December 6, 1931, God called her to her heavenly home.[12]

Maggie Case Hull

Maggie Case was born June 8, 1870, in Centralia, Kansas. She married James R. Hull March 28, 1889, and was the mother of three sons. Maggie received her call to preach in 1902. She joined the Holiness Christian Church, was granted an evangelistic license, and in September 1913 was ordained as a minister. Her pastorates included Pleasant Hill, Pleasant View, and Hopeton, Kansas. She proclaimed the story of the Cross in many successful evangelistic revivals. Her husband died in 1940. Maggie entered her

eternal rest January 24, 1947, in Alva, Oklahoma.[13]

Alma Rosella Shearer

Alma Rosella Shearer began her ministerial service with the Holiness Christian Church in Indiana.[14] She was stationed at Calvary (no mention of where this was) and served the Calvary Church. Later she was appointed to the Lawrenceburg, Indiana, church in 1910. She was ordained a minister by the Indiana Conference of the Holiness Christian Church in 1913.

Alma Rosella was born March 25, 1875. She married D. C. Shearer, and together they pastored the Nelsonville and Marion, Ohio, churches. She was both a minister and a minister's wife. When D. C. Shearer served as a district superintendent in Indiana for five years and in Illinois for five years, she either served as pastor by herself or assisted him with his official duties. She always had a burning desire to worship in church and camp meeting.[15]

Alma was the pastor of the Dow, Illinois, church in 1924 and 1925. She followed R. A. Beltz as pastor of the Lawrenceville, Illinois, church in 1926. During this pastorate she led in the building of a parsonage. She served that church for four years.[16]

Alma was elected a delegate to the General Assembly of the Pilgrim Holiness Church in 1926 and 1930. Her husband died February 16, 1940, after forty-two years of service to the Church. Alma remained active in the Church until 1961. At that time she retired. She died January 17, 1964, at age eighty-eight.

Mrs. Lydia H. Smith

Lydia H. Smith was the first conference secretary of the Oklahoma Conference of the Wesleyan Methodist Church. She planted two churches in that conference, the first being in Carevile about 1902 or 1903. It became a flourishing church early in the conference.

Lydia was a schoolteacher. Her second church plant was organized at Etna in 1907. The church began with seventeen members, and services were first held in the Hopewell schoolhouse where she taught.[17]

L. M. Warner

The Minutes of the Annual Sessions of the Champlain Conference of the Wesleyan Methodist Connection of America from 1902 to 1917 reveal that L. M. Warner, an ordained minister from the New York Conference, was received in 1902. That year the Champlain Conference assigned her with S. A. Warner to the Macomb, New York, church. They served together there until the conference year 1905. For the next eleven years they served at the Pitcarin and Fowler, New York, churches. L. M. Warner was on the superannuated list in 1916. She died in 1917.

Anabel Adams

Anabel Adams of the Holiness Church of California was given a ministerial credential (ordination papers) at the semiannual camp meeting at Redlands, California, in 1903. She often sang solos. She and her sister, Cora May Adams, often sang together. A poem was dedicated to her and the other young people who had consecrated their talents to God's work in the Holiness Church.[18]

Mrs. Esther L. Mow Dickey

Esther L. Dickey, also called E. L. Dickey, is first mentioned in the records of the Indiana Conference of the Wesleyan Methodist Church in 1903. She was already ordained as a minister at that time. She and her sister, Emma E. Martindale, conducted an "old fashion" revival at the Tipton, Indiana, church in 1900. She served several churches with Emma E. Martindale as co-pastor.

Esther was a church planter. She organized a new church of twenty-six members near Silver Lake, Indiana, in 1903 and became the first pastor of that church. Emma also helped her at this church. Esther had the spirit of a true church planter in her heart. She also organized and became the first pastor of a new church of thirteen members near Argos, Indiana. This church was called Union. The *Minutes* reveal that she pastored Silver Lake, Sheridan, Union, and a church called Franklin, located near Argos. She also served for a time as a general evangelist.

In 1913 she was unstationed and in 1916 was granted a letter of standing.[19]

Sarah A. Dilts

Sarah A. Dilts, also referred to as S. A. Dilts, came into the Indiana Conference of the Wesleyan Methodist Church in 1903 after serving as an ordained minister in the Church of God. Sarah and her husband, C. P., and B. L. Couch were assigned to the Roseburg circuit in 1904. Apparently sometime during the year she was appointed to the Hartford City charge, for records show that she resigned from that charge in 1905. She then was put in charge of a new work in Madison County by the conference president. The next year, C. P. and Sarah were the pastors at Hamilton.[20]

Anna Griggs

The semiannual camp meeting at Redlands, California, in 1903 gave ministerial credentials (ordination) to Anna Griggs.[21]

Rita "Etta" Gibson Hoffman

Etta Gibson was born July 6, 1881, on Tilghman Island, Maryland.[22] She was converted at an early age and sanctified soon after. She became a charter member of the Tilghman Pilgrim Holiness Church.

She entered God's Bible School to prepare for God's work in 1903. She also studied at Darby Bible School, in Darby, Pennsylvania.

Etta was ordained in 1906 by what became the Eastern District of the Pilgrim Holiness

Church. Seth C. Rees was the officiating minister. She worked for a time in the slums of Chicago, but most of her work for the Lord was in the field of evangelism.

God had given Etta a marvelous singing voice, and she sang with inspiration and for the glory of God. Etta served as soloist for William Jennings Bryan's Sunday school class in Florida and was heard a block away without a public address system. She served as song leader/choir director at Denton Camp, in Denton, Maryland, for over forty years. Each year she trained and directed a large choir. During those years, one of the highlights of the annual camp was the singing of "Hail Immanuel" by her choir. The sound and sight were forever etched in the memories of the campers. She was elected "Lifetime Honorary Music Director" of the Denton camp at an annual conference.

Etta liked to tell stories about going to Denton Camp. Tilghman Island was the starting point of the boat ride that took travelers down the Choptank River to the camp. After passengers embarked, services were held on the boat. The people testified, prayed, sang, and exhorted until they reached the town of Denton. Horse-drawn carts were awaiting their arrival and took them with their trunks and suitcases to the camp-ground, which was a mile away.

At the close of the ten-day camp, the service aboard the boat picked up where it had left off. The happy camp crowd sang and held services for miles down the river. Etta believed she was blessed to be able to take in the whole affair. She embarked as one of the first passengers and was one of the last to leave.

She was the author of several good hymns and poems, and many of her songs were published in a songbook. One of her poems, "The Old Camp Meeting Days," described in detail the events, persons, and "glory" of early camp meetings.

Etta worked with Seth C. Rees, George B. Kulp, and Edward Fergueson, founders and early leaders of the Pilgrim Holiness Church. Many persons sought and found the Lord under her preaching. She also worked with Bessie Jones (later Mitchell) for two years.

She was interested in all the areas of church work. Her special interests included foreign and home missionary work and the education of young people at Allentown Bible Institute, in Allentown, Pennsylvania (later Eastern Pilgrim College/United Wesleyan College).

She married Jacob Hoffman of Philadelphia in 1909. Together they traveled and ministered throughout the United States. They were used extensively in the eastern camp meetings for many years. They also served in Palestine and England in the Lord's work.[23]

Etta was very active in the Eastern District of the Pilgrim Holiness Church and was loved and respected by everyone. Both Etta Clough and Etta Mitchell, evangelists, church planters and pastors, were named after her.

Etta was known as a good and great woman, loyal to God and the Church. She was a woman of vision and strong convictions. She died March 28, 1952.[24]

Cerena Jay

Cerena Jay, whose first name was also spelled "Serena," began her ministerial service in 1903. She was from the Sheridan Wesleyan Methodist Church in Indiana. She attended Fairmount Bible School, Fairmount, Indiana (later merged into what became Indiana Wesleyan University, Marion, Indiana) and graduated from that institution in 1910.[25] She was ordained in 1909. That year she was appointed to the Strawtown charge and she also preached and pastored the Cicero church at that time. The Blue River charge was her next appointment, and she served there from 1910 to 1912. She resigned from the Elwood work in 1913 and was listed as a general evangelist in 1914.

Cerena Jay was given a letter of transfer to the Pentecostal Church of the Nazarene in 1914. She was described as a noble Christian character. She was earnest, sincere, and deeply spiritual.[26]

Imogene "Imo" Jones

Imogene "Imo" Jones was accepted to go to Africa in 1902.[27] The following year she was introduced to the Kansas Conference of the

Wesleyan Methodist Church as a prospective missionary to a foreign field (Sierra Leone, West Africa) and was given the hand of fellowship.[28] She served two terms in Africa, 1903–1905 and 1910–1913. She desired to be more useful on the mission field. So between her two terms of service she took a nursing course.

Imo was a woman of compassion. With her own meager funds, she redeemed a number of African boys from slavery. One of these boys, Sappri Turray, became an outstanding evangelist and later was elected to the highest office on the mission field.[29]

Imo was born in El Paso, Illinois, September 17, 1875 and was converted at an early age. She joined the Wesleyan Methodist Church and became very active in her local church.

In 1910 she was given a vote of thanks for working as conference tithing secretary and for her faithful service. She had prepared an attractive chart, and it was on display. She held this office for a number of years.

Imo was given the pastoral supervision of the Gospel Mission in Concordia, Kansas, in 1928. She served the mission until 1933. The mission was then closed, and the building was sold. Also during this time, from 1928 to 1932, she cared for her aged parents.

In 1934 Imo became an ordained minister and served the Kansas Conference as an evangelist for a number of years. She often was elected to conference committees. She served as the conference superintendent of the Young Missionary Workers Band (now Wesleyan Kids for Missions) from 1917 to 1919.

Imo Jones died October 24, 1949, at the age of seventy-four.

Sarah Kennedy

The Minutes of the Annual Session of the Indiana Conference of the Wesleyan Methodist Connection (or Church) of America in 1903–1904 listed Sarah Kennedy as an ordained minister. The following year she was granted a letter of standing. No service record could be found for her.

Anna Linville

Anna Linville began her association with the Indiana Conference of the Wesleyan Methodist Church in 1903.[30] From that time until 1909 she worked under the direction of the conference. The records were not clear, but apparently she was elected to become an ordained minister in 1910, although this action was referred to the annual conference for a ruling and a decision. She was appointed the pastor of Mt. Olive that year and remained through 1911, the year she was ordained.

Anna served several years as a general evangelist as well as a pastor. She pastored the Miami church 1913, Thorntown 1916–17, Greentown 1928, and Fountain City 1934–36.

During those years of being a general evangelist, she served as the pastor of a newly organized church in Atlanta, Georgia, in 1925. The church had been started as the result of the efforts of an evangelist, Rev. J. M. Hames. It was organized with twenty-two members. She did commendable work there.[31]

Anna Linville died in 1952.

Emma Mow Martindale

Records of the Indiana Conference of the Wesleyan Methodist Church first record the activities of Emma Martindale in 1903.[32] However, she and her sister, Esther Dickey, were the evangelists in an "old fashion" revival held in 1900 at the Tipton church. Her first appointment may have been the Franklin charge in 1903.

Emma was born August 6, 1864, one of a set of triplets. At the time of her death in 1941, they were the oldest living triplets in the United States. She married H. A. Martindale in 1884. He died in 1925.

Emma was converted in 1897 in the Old Gospel Hill United Brethren Church near Silver Lake, Indiana. She joined the Wesleyan Methodist Church at Laketon in 1898 and entered the ministry soon after.

Emma was appointed pastor with her sister, Esther L. Dickey, at Silver Lake in 1904. They moved to the pastorate at Sheridan in 1906 and served there two years. The next year, she was the assistant pastor to Esther at Union, near Argos.

She served for a number of years with her brother, Rev. S. A. Mow, in evangelistic work. They held services at Mt. Etna, Monument City, Bluffton, Lancaster, Warren, Plummer's Chapel, South Salem, Plymouth, Shiloh, Marion, Wabash, Elkhart, South Bend, Hamlet, and Westfield.

In 1925 Emma moved her membership to the South Bend church and was a member there at the time of her death, April 11, 1941. Her last years were spent in intercessory prayer. She always helped wherever help was needed.

She told those who were with her at her deathbed, "The voice that calls me now is not a strange voice. It is the voice I have followed and whose gospel I have proclaimed."[33]

Lydia E. Murphy

No biographical information was found on Lydia Murphy.[34] She was already married to A. U. Murphy in 1903. She was his third wife.[35] She had a license to preach in 1903, and together they were the pastors at Hamlet in the Indiana Conference of the Wesleyan Methodist Church. They lived in Kirklin in 1904 and were appointed the pastors there that year. The following year they became the pastors of the Lewis Creek work. That year, 1906, Lydia became an ordained minister. A. U. Murphy was already an ordained minister.

Between 1907 and 1913, they served as co-pastors at Hartford City, Boxley, Huntington, and Bluffton. They resigned from the Huntington work to accept the pastorate at Ferry, Michigan. They transferred their conference membership from the Indiana Conference to the North Michigan Conference. However, they transferred back to Indiana to become the pastors at Albion in 1915.

Lydia served as a general evangelist from 1916 to 1918, when she transferred to the Illinois Conference. Some time during that 1918 conference year, she and her husband were appointed as the supply pastors at the Mt. Etna circuit in the

Indiana Conference. The stay in Illinois must have been extremely short. From 1920 to 1922 they were the pastors at Kirklin. Lydia again entered the field of general evangelism for two or three years. At the close of this time she was granted a letter of standing and apparently united with the Church of the Nazarene.

She returned to the Indiana Conference as a minister on probation in 1930. It was a common practice to be on probation for one year when transferring from another denomination. She was to "choose her own field" of labor. Her husband died in 1936. She was listed as superannuated in 1941, and she died that year.

Sarah E. Schulty

A mimeographed booklet edited by Josephine Rickard entitled, *Our Heritage, Ten Years Supplement, 1960–1970* gives the following information of Sarah E. Schulty. The Falconer, New York, church was organized September 30, 1903 by the Allegheny Conference of the Wesleyan Methodist Church. Sarah E. Schulty was the first pastor and remained there as pastor from 1903 to 1911. The first church building was constructed in 1904. The church was known as the Lyndon Park Wesleyan Methodist Church.

The booklet was printed by the Western New York District of The Wesleyan Church.

Nellie B. Seely

Nellie B. Seely was given credentials as a minister (ordained) in 1903 by the Holiness Church of California. The only other information on her revealed that she was called to pastor the Murriette Church in California in 1909. She was from the Riverside Holiness Church.[36]

Mrs. Emma Phares Swisher

Emma Phares Swisher was born in 1861. She was converted as a youth and sanctified some time later. She was given a license to preach by the Church of the United Brethren in Christ, of which she was a member, in January 1890.

In September 1893 she was received into the White River Annual Conference of the United Brethren Church. She transferred her membership to the Indiana Conference of the Wesleyan Methodist Church in 1895. The annual conference session of 1896 ratified her transfer. She was ordained by the Wesleyan Methodist Church in 1904.

Emma labored faithfully until her death April 24, 1909. She served as pastor at Kirklin and the Blue River charge. Most of her labors for the Lord were in the field of evangelism. She was a good evangelist and an excellent helper in revival meetings.

The clear, radical word of the Wesleyan Methodist Church upon doctrine and reform appealed strongly to her. She was an ardent and faithful advocate of the Church's standard of Christian life and experience. She was a woman of strong Christian character. She died at age forty-eight. She was the mother of one daughter.[37]

Mary Ella Roof Graham

The engraving on a tombstone in the Wesley Chapel Cemetery near Greensboro, Georgia, records the following:

Ella Roof Graham
January 22, 1871
May 8, 1952
"She hath done what she could"

Ella Roof Graham lived a sacrificial life.[38] Her love for suffering humanity was manifested in various ways. That love for people and her obedience to God's call meant that she must preach the Word of God or go to hell. She met with opposition when it came time for her ordination. The Wesleyan Methodist Church had passed a resolution in 1891 to remove from the *Discipline* its prohibition against ordaining women. However, when her name was presented as a candidate for ordination in 1902, many objections were raised, and declarations were made that "it was not scriptural." The

opposition lost. The South Carolina Conference ordained her October 18, 1902, and she became the first woman to be ordained in that conference.[39]

Ella was the oldest of thirteen children born in her family. They were a poor farm family who lived in Lexington County, South Carolina. She spent many weary hours working in the fields to help make a living for the large family. She was small of stature but wiry and strong. She possessed a strong determination and a great ambition. That ambition and a thirst for knowledge drove her to get a college education, and she graduated first in her class. She worked as a cook and janitor to meet her financial obligations while in college and walked the hot and dusty roads selling books in the summer. She endured the sneers and scoffing of those who were better clothed than she.

Ella taught school for seven school terms in South Carolina after her graduation. But at the age of thirty she exchanged the schoolbooks for the Bible and began her ministerial labors. She worked as a home missionary in the city missions of Columbia, South Carolina, for eight months. But people began to urge her to assist in revival meetings. Her work with the young people was very effective. Her beautiful alto voice was used in solos and groups. She turned down the opportunity to work with a Chatauqua group that was touring the country and attracting multitudes in order to serve her Master as a despised holiness woman preacher who was often ignored and abused for being a preacher.

Ella Roof was teaching school in Glendale, South Carolina, and attending evening services. She was introduced to Frank M. Graham, the sweet singer from the North who had come to direct the music for the pastor, George Nally. They were attracted to each other, and after an acquaintance of two and one-half years, they were married. In this team Ella became the preacher and Frank the musician. He sang and played the organ, and the couple often sang together. She was an ordained minister, and he was a licensed minister.

In November 1904 Ella was called to be the pastor of Wesley Chapel Church located near Greensboro, Georgia, with Frank as her assistant. There was no parsonage at that time, so these preachers with their two small children lived in homes with their church members. One day a prominent citizen of the community, J. L. Wright, donated three acres of land for a parsonage. Community people donated their work and time, and the building of a five-room house was begun. The parsonage family moved in as soon as one room was in a livable condition. Frank Graham bought the sixteen acres of land adjoining the parsonage. He farmed the land to add a measure of financial help to support the family. Later, he also paid for an addition to the house—and he paid the taxes on the house as well. Finally the members of the church decided that the Grahams had invested so much in the property that they deeded the house to them.

Ella and Frank worked together in this church until Frank's death on August 25, 1931. Ella continued to pastor Wesley Chapel Church until she retired in 1948. She had served there for forty-three years and had seen many people come to the Lord. Among them was John Frank Childs, who later became president of Central Wesleyan College, in Central, South Carolina (now Southern Wesleyan University). Frank Graham's ministry in song will long be remembered. He composed many songs, among them the well-known "The Old Account Was Settled Long Ago." He never obtained a copyright for any of his songs, desiring that they all be used for the glory of God. He also published several songbooks.

Besides their work at Wesley Chapel, the Grahams did pioneer work in the North Georgia Conference and were heavily engaged in evangelistic work in other states as well. During the pastorate at Wesley Chapel they also served the Winder, Rebecca, and Union Chapel churches. Ella organized the Woman's Missionary Society at Wesley Chapel and served as president for many years. She was active in the conference work also and served on many important committees.[40]

After Frank's death, Ella was very instrumental in establishing the Union Point Wesleyan Methodist Campground in Georgia.

At one time Ella prayed for the removal of a dance hall, commonly called "Juke Joint," that was located just two miles from the church. A few weeks later the building burned to the ground! Ella never imposed dress standards on her church members, but she always wore her dresses with skirts to her ankles. Her dresses always had long sleeves. She wore high-topped laced shoes to give her ankles support and always wore a hat in the pulpit. She was very modest and strict with her appearance but was loved not only by her congregations and family but by the entire community.[41]

Mrs. Maggie Hull

Maggie Hull was a pioneer holiness preacher. She was instrumentally used of God in the conversion of Nora Dell, a fourteen-year-old girl. Two years later she led Nora into the experience of holiness. That young girl became her daughter-in-law.

Maggie was under appointment by the Indiana Conference of the Holiness Christian Church from 1904 to 1915. She was ordained by this group in 1913.

She did pastoral work under the International Holiness Church and the Pilgrim Holiness Church. Her pastorates included Hopeton and Alva, Oklahoma; and Plainview, Texas. She lived in Hopeton for forty-five years and was a woman of great faith. Maggie was used to establish churches and preaching points in the early day of the holiness movement in Oklahoma.[42]

Estelle Reid Lienard

Estelle Reid was born in Jewett, Ohio.[43] Her family later moved to Kansas. She and her younger sister, Jennie Reid (Clawson), graduated from the University of Kansas, and Estelle graduated from law school in 1898. She was the first woman to pass both the Missouri and Kansas bar examinations. She worked as a reporter for the *Kansas City Times* before the merger with *The Star* in 1901. She later served as a reporter for the *Denver Post*.

Estelle began her ministerial service in the Kansas Conference of the Wesleyan Methodist Church in 1904 and was appointed to evangelistic work in 1907. She was ordained by the Kansas conference in 1911 and served that year as a quarterly meeting evangelist.[44]

Two attempts were made to organize a Wesleyan Methodist Church at the Oakland School building, located eight miles southwest of Miltonvale, Kansas, but at neither time was it successful. Estelle was sent to pastor the first attempt in 1912. She stayed for only one year.[45]

On July 12, 1914, she was granted a letter of standing. She and her husband pastored in the Church of the Nazarene for a time.

When the Lord called Estelle into His work, she taught music for a time at Houghton College, Houghton, New York. After her marriage to Millard F. Lienard, they pastored in Nazarene churches in Kansas.

In August 1931 Estelle was called to become the pastor of a newly organized group of Wesleyan Methodists at Rice Lake, Wisconsin, with fourteen members. The group had been worshiping in various rented facilities. She found a property for sale on the corner of West Marshall Street and Wilson Avenue and led her flock in purchasing this property. The front rooms were remodeled into a neat little chapel, and the group worshiped there for several years. Part of the time her husband assisted her. While pastoring there, they also did missionary work in the surrounding territory.

The couple had charge of a missionary group in Spooner, Wisconsin, and were assisted in this work by two members of their congregation, Wilma and Charles Bakke, a brother-and-sister team. In 1936 the Spooner group organized with twenty members. The Lienards continued to pastor both Spooner and Rice Lake until M. F. Lienard died. Soon after this, Estelle's health broke, and her work at Rice Lake came to a close.[46]

Estelle had a great influence upon the lives of others. She had the gift of encouragement and the ability to help develop God-given talents and abilities in others. Two ladies from the Rice Lake Church congregation became ordained ministers, Wilma Bakke and Esther Johnson.

Estelle returned to Kansas City, Kansas, to live with her two children, Burke and Margaret. At that time she transferred her church and ministerial membership to the Church of the Nazarene. She died December 30, 1965. A memorial scholarship was established at Nazarene Theological Seminary in Kansas City in her name to help young ministers get their education. One of her favorite verses was "Study to show thyself approved" (2 Tim. 2:15, KJV).

She claimed a special promise from 2 Tim. 1:7—"God hath not given us the spirit of fear; but of power, and of love, and of a sound mind." She kept claiming that promise of a "sound mind," and God honored her prayers. Her mind was keen and alert up to her last illness. Shortly before her death, she returned to consciousness and in a very firm, clear voice she said, "This thing I know, that I shall dwell in the house of the Lord forever."

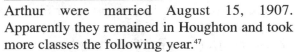

Della Mae Hunter Osborne

Della Mae Hunter was born February 28, 1881, in Jewell County, Kansas. Her father was born in England and became a United States citizen May 1, 1871. He was a homesteader in Kansas and lived in a sod house.

Della had five brothers. A sister died before Della was born.

At the age of nineteen, in 1900, she traveled by train to Houghton Seminary, Houghton, New York (later Houghton College). She was unable to get back to Kansas for two years because of a lack of funds. While at Houghton she met many of the early missionaries from Sierra Leone. Mary Lane Clarke was one of her teachers. Della  graduated from Houghton in 1905.

At Houghton Della met Arthur D. Osborne, a birthright Quaker from the Gilead-Fargo, Ohio area. The Fargo Wesleyan Methodist Church was started in his mother's home. Della and Arthur were married August 15, 1907. Apparently they remained in Houghton and took more classes the following year.[47]

According to the *Minutes* of the Kansas Conference of the Wesleyan Methodist Church, Della Hunter was licensed to preach in 1904. She pastored the Lovewell, Kansas, Church from 1905 to 1907.[48] This group met at the Lovewell Schoolhouse. When the class was organized as a church, it moved to the Pavonia Schoolhouse.[49] Della had a horse and buggy. That horse knew the way home from the places where she preached and held revival meetings. (Not all the dates given above, found from records, agree. She did pastor the Lovewell Church and go to Houghton, however.)

After Della and Arthur were married, they moved to Ohio and became the pastors of churches at Greenville, Greer, and Harrison Chapel. They served the Greer and Harrison Chapel churches two different times each. Arthur served as the president of the Ohio Conference from 1912 to 1916. During this time their two daughters, Florence and Mildred, were born.

Both Della and Arthur were ordained in 1910 by the Ohio Conference.

The couple did their ministerial work as a team. Arthur would preach Sunday morning, and Della preached each Sunday night.[50] They both were dynamic preachers, Della probably was more so than her husband. In 1917 a big change came in their ministerial service. Della's parents were in very poor health, and Della felt it was her duty and responsibility to return to Kansas to care for them. They moved to Concordia and remained there for twelve years. During this time they attended the United Brethren Church until Concordia Wesleyan Church was organized. They then became charter members of the Concordia church.

The founding pastor, W. A. Smith, of Concordia Wesleyan Church stayed in the Osborne home for one year. Evangelist William Hotchkiss stayed with them while conducting a revival meeting. Their house accommodated the traveling ministers.

After Della's parents died, the Osbornes moved to Marion, Indiana, in order for Florence to attend Marion College (now Indiana Wesleyan University). Then they returned to Harrison Chapel for a second time and served this church for seven years (1933–39). The next three years were spent as pastors of the Greer church a second time. Arthur's health began to fail, and they moved to Don and Mildred Fisher's parsonage home in Norwood, Ohio. Mildred was the couple's daughter. Arthur died August 4, 1954.

In 1963 Della moved to Phoenix, Arizona, and made her home with her other daughter, Florence. Della died May 6, 1970 at age eighty-nine.

A granddaughter, Roberta Fisher, remembers her grandmother quoting scripture, including entire psalms. Della lived with the Fishers when their children were born and were growing up. She never complained that they were too noisy, cried too much, or got on her nerves. She never criticized them or their parents. She always expressed interest in their activities.

Mrs. Clara R. Pence

The Kansas Conference assigned Clara R. Pence to be the pastor of the Oklahoma City mission in 1900. She continued to work there under appointment through 1902. No church was established there until forty years later.[51]

She was the pastor of the Beaver County Mission of the Oklahoma Conference in 1904.[52]

Bertha Cleho Cochren Schoeff

Bertha Cochren was born October 20, 1886, in Jonesboro, Indiana. She was converted December 24, 1899, and sanctified two days later. She was a charter member of the Wabash, Indiana, Holiness Christian Church and married Michael Edward Schoeff September 25, 1902. They were the parents of seven children.[53]

Bertha Schoeff was a wise and gifted minister. She was active fifty years in the ministry of what became the Pilgrim Holiness Church. Most of those years were in a team ministry with her husband, Edward Schoeff. They began their ministerial service in a mission in Peru, Indiana.

That fall they were sent to the church in Michigan City, Indiana.

They also pastored the following churches in Indiana: Tyner, Bass Lake, Wabash, Logansport, Elwood, Indianapolis First, Lawrenceburg (two times), West Terre Haute, Muncie First, Kokomo, Columbus, Richmond, Shelbyville, and Clarksburg. Edward died while they were pastoring at Clarksburg, on March 16, 1947. Bertha continued to pastor the church for another four years.

Bertha then pastored the Rising Sun Church for two years (1950–52). She also pastored the Onargo and Effingham, Illinois, churches.

Bertha preached her first sermon in 1903. She was ordained August 23, 1928.[54]

Rev. Ernest Batman, former district superintendent of the Indiana Central District of The Wesleyan Church, paid this tribute to Bertha Schoeff:

> When Ada [the lady who became his wife] and I started dating, Sister Schoeff was the pastor at her church. She received me into the Pilgrim Holiness Church. She gave me my first local preacher's license. She assisted when we were married. I esteemed her very highly, and respected her as a choice saint of God.

Bertha Schoeff entered her heavenly rest October 25, 1963.[55]

Maude E. Simmons Slater

Maude E. Simmons was born in 1883. At the age of seventeen, while she was attending God's Bible School in Cincinnati, Ohio, God called her to be a missionary. She met Charles L. Slater at this school. They were married and left immediately to do home missionary work in the state of Washington.

In 1909 Charles and Maude were accompanied to South Africa by Fred and Lelia DeWeerd. This trip by boat, train, and mule-drawn covered wagon lasted six months. Maude kept house in a wagon while their mud house with an iron roof was being built. She experienced the anxiety of a mother when their eight-month-old son, Charles Livingston, contracted a fatal eye disease and died January 17, 1911.

Maude made the adjustments of working with the white European people of South Africa and accepting whatever duties befell her on the mission field. Health problems arose, and they were forced to return to the United States after five years.

Possessing a true missionary heart, when World War I restrictions prevented their return to Africa, they volunteered to go to British Guiana, South America, to release ill missionaries to come home. They served a short eighteen months in Barbados, but again ill health forced them to return home.[56] While at home they served as pastors and evangelists. Charles Slater served as assistant general superintendent of the Pilgrim Holiness Church from 1926 to 1930. He died in South Africa May 24, 1950. Maude died March 9, 1973.

As is so often the case, Maude's achievements and activities were overshadowed by the grandeur and successful work of her husband. Much has been written about his work, but little is found about hers. She was the mother of five daughters: Flora Belle, Mary, Dorothea, Bessie, and Virginia. She was known for her courage and uncomplaining spirit; she was a woman of devotion to Christ and a loyal and devoted mother as well as a strong supporter of her husband and his labors for the Lord.[57]

Setta Mary Caldwell Folger

Setta (sometimes spelled "Zetta") Caldwell was a graduate in 1909 of Fairmount Bible School, Fairmount, Indiana (later merged into what became Indiana Wesleyan University, Marion, Indiana). She was described as a conscientious and studious woman. She was full of faith. Her gifts and spiritual devotion to God and the church placed her among the chosen few.[58]

Setta began her ministerial activities in the Indiana Conference of the Wesleyan Methodist Church in 1905. She was assigned the pastorate at Atlanta Mission in 1907–08 and was ordained in 1908. She spent one year in general evangelism after her graduation from Bible school. She was an effective pastor and spent over twenty-two years in pastorates. Setta often stayed longer than the proverbial two years. Her pastorates included Elwood, three years; Cicero, five years; Thorntown, two times—one year the first time and nine years the second time; Center, one year; Warsaw, two years; and Kirklin, two years. While she was pastoring the Thorntown church the second time, W. G. Bogue was her assistant from 1929 to 1930.[59]

Setta resigned her pastorate at Kirklin and married Rev. L. L. Folger.[60] Afterward she was always listed as Mary L. Folger. She was his third wife. He was buried in the Blue River Wesleyan Church cemetery. His second wife, Anna, and his third wife, Setta, are buried one on each side of him. Setta transferred her ministerial credentials to the Ohio Conference at the time of her marriage in 1933.

L. L. and Setta Folger shared pastoral duties after their marriage. Setta served the Indiana Conference a total of twenty-eight years as a single woman. She joined the Church Triumphant January 2, 1947.

Bertha Betzer Ellis

At the time of her death, in December 1968, Bertha Betzer Ellis was the oldest ordained minister in the Iowa District. She married G. Edwin Ellis, a member of the Friends Society, in 1907 and was the mother of Paul, Philip, Leola Rosson, and Helen Fookes.[61]

Bertha began her ministerial service in 1905 as the pastor of the Hoover Wesleyan Methodist Church near Walker, Iowa. Apparently this was a circuit, for West Union was also listed as her responsibility.[62] She was active in the conference/district work. She often conducted devotions at conference and also led the singing. She served on many conference committees and also had charge of the love feast one year at conference. A large loaf of bread was broken with designated persons who in turn shared with others; these would share with others until everyone had a good size piece of bread. The object of the meeting was to affirm one another and "straighten up" any break in the fellowship

of the entire group. The love feast was usually a time of singing and rejoicing and often repentance between persons who were at "odds" with each other.

Bertha was listed as an evangelist from 1907 to 1909. She returned to the pastorate at Hoover in 1910. She was the pastor and her husband, Edwin, was her assistant.

May 8, 1912, she was appointed to serve the Albaton church, and again Edwin was her assistant. By conference time in 1914, she had completed all the requirements for ordination and would be ordained whenever she chose. She chose to be ordained in 1916.

This pastoral team, Bertha as pastor and Edwin as assistant, served the Guthrie Center church in 1915. From 1916 to 1927 Bertha was listed as a general evangelist. The following seven years she worked as a missionary to the Hebrews (Jews). She was appointed as the temporary supply pastor with Edwin at the Marengo church. They continued in this relationship at Marengo for the next three years as well as working with the Jews.

Bertha pastored two other churches, West Berrean and Waterloo First, in the time period of 1938–41. She returned to evangelistic work from 1943 to 1951. She was superannuated (retired) in 1952.[63]

Carrie Mae Crumpton Hoos

Carrie Mae Crumpton Hoos was born June 10, 1883, at Richmond, Illinois, and departed this life June 13, 1955. She was baptized in the church and instructed by a devout Catholic grandmother. She was converted at age eighteen in a Methodist church.

She attended the Salvation Army training schools in Chicago and New York City and was ordained an officer. She married Captain Thomas H. Hoos August 7, 1905. After serving a number of years with the Salvation Army Corps, they joined the Michigan District of the International Holiness Church (later renamed the Pilgrim Holiness Church) in 1917. Carrie actively assisted her husband in his pastoral duties, including Applegate, Jeddo, "Soo," Hastings, Lansing, Flint, and Kalamazoo.

She was the mother of four children. Her husband's death occurred June 27, 1951. They completed thirty-six years of preaching ministry in the Pilgrim Holiness Church.

The following material was printed in the Michigan District *Journal* after her death. It gives an insight into her godly character. The paper was discovered in her belongings soon after her death. It was dated July 5, 1951.

My dear husband's watch, his pen and his purse came from Ann Arbor today.

They are of great value to me because he used them. But now he doesn't need his watch to mark time, for the glories of the eternal world are endless, he has met his Lord face to face and realized a complete and perfect bliss that only the blood washed inherit and which can never be fully comprehended while in this earthly body.

His pen, used to convey his thoughts to others, to record his comments on the Word of God he loved so well, and express his last dear thoughts of love to me, is not needed any longer. He finished the work God gave him to do.

His purse with a little money in it to purchase those things necessary for the sustenance of physical life, and also to disburse for the furtherance of the gospel, he no longer handles. He never loved money, nor hesitated to perform a task because the remuneration was too small. He now lives in a land of abundance, in a profusion of beauty where he laid up treasures in Heaven where moth and rust doth not corrupt nor thieves break through and steal.[64]

M. Victoria Sears

In the early days of her ministerial labors, Victoria Sears worked in the Indiana and North Carolina Conferences (1906–09) of the Wesleyan Methodist Church. She became an ordained minister in 1906, apparently under the Indiana Conference. Her ministry was in the field of evangelism, and she was listed as a general evangelist from 1913 to 1923. At that time she was on the superannuated (retired) list. She died during the 1926 conference year.[65]

May Lord Sprague

May Lord was born in 1880. She lived to be ninety-three years old. She entered her eternal home from Intercession City, Florida, October 26, 1973.

May began her first of five terms of missionary service under the Wesleyan Methodists in Sierra Leone, West Africa, in 1906. She served as the pastor of Bethel Church between the second and third terms. She often spoke at conference time when she was home on furlough. In August 1919 she married G. H. Sprague. She was his second wife. The last two terms in Africa she was Mrs. G. H. Sprague.

Her home conference, Iowa, was faithful in supporting her. In 1905 while she was a missionary-elect, they gave an initial offering of fifty-eight dollars for her support at Houghton College, in Houghton, New York, as a student. She was indebted to them for their kindness.

Here are her thoughts about the financial support, written during her declining years. This letter was written to the Iowa Conference in 1967.

Sixty-seven years ago the Iowa Conference raised money to start me in school at Houghton College, New York. . . . As I think of the Iowa Conference and what it did for me, I feel I should try to pay back the money they raised for me. It was not a loan. They gave it to me. The amount was $455. I made it do for the whole six years I was at Houghton. I did all I could to work my way through. I know I cannot pay interest but I would like to begin the middle of September 1967 to pay twenty-five dollars a month until I have paid five hundred dollars. I would like the money to go for church extension, perhaps the Marshalltown work. I'll be eighty-six in October.[66]

Sadie Kulp Strong

The Pilgrim Holiness Advocate dated April 1, 1943, on pages 4 and 5 provides the following information on Sadie Kulp Strong. Her death occurred February 5, 1943.

Sadie, the daughter of Rev. George B. Kulp, one of the general superintendents of what became the Pilgrim Holiness Church, was born

December 2, 1876, in Philadelphia, Pennsylvania. She was ordained in the Immanuel Pilgrim Holiness Church in Battle Creek, Michigan, of which her father was the founder. He preached her ordination sermon. Sadie's preaching resulted in many persons being led to the Lord. She had faith in the mighty God, and He enabled her to surmount many difficulties. Under her anointed preaching in a Methodist church in Michigan, the entire choir came to the altar to be saved.

Sadie was appointed the assistant pastor to her father in Battle Creek in 1911. She held that position for over thirty years under her father and Rev. M. L. Goodman. She also assisted her father during the time when he was general superintendent of what became the Pilgrim Holiness Church. The people loved to hear her preach under the anointing of God with a contagious and buoyant spirit.

Under Pastor M. L. Goodman, she served as assistant pastor, class leader, teacher of the ladies' Bible class, secretary of the church board, and assistant church treasurer. Whatever the task, it was done well.

On January 2, 1914, she was united to Rev. J. E. Strong in marriage. J. E. Strong died in November 1931. During their married life, she assisted her husband in revivals. They refused to accept any remuneration for these meetings. The following are two examples of their kind and generous spirits. In the early days of the Muskegon Church, when it was struggling to get started, the Strongs held a revival at the church. They returned the offering of $135 to the treasurer and added their personal check of an equal amount. At another meeting at Merrill they refused to accept anything for their work and then paid the pastor's wife for their room and board for the entire meeting.

Sadie's first interest was always for others. She lived a self-crucified life for Christ. After her mother's death, she cared for her father until his death in July 21, 1939. Her heart's desire was to be deeply spiritual. Her stepson said she was "as near perfect as a human being can be." She possessed a humble and unassuming spirit.

She also had a keen sense of discerning the needs of a struggling church or a worker. When she saw a need, she gave to meet the need. She always took a firm and uncompromising stand for the right in district affairs and insisted upon the direct leadership of the Holy Spirit in all matters of church polity and practice.

She was a woman of prayer with a burning zeal for the cause of holiness.

Ethel Grace McCrory

Ethel Grace McCrory was known as Grace. She was born March 14, 1886, at Tyner, Indiana. She chose education as her career and entered Valparaiso College. In 1903 she attended a tent meeting at Tyner and was soundly converted. Shortly after her conversion, she felt called to preach and received her local minister's license in 1905. She preached her first sermon in a Wesleyan Methodist church near North Liberty, Indiana, in the fall of 1904 and continued preaching at that church during the winter months. According to the *Minutes of the Annual Assembly of the Pilgrim Holiness Church Indiana Conference* of 1923–52, her first assigned pastorate was Bass Lake, Indiana, where she filled out the unexpired term of the pastor.

On February 16, 1934, she was married to Rev. James McCrory. Together they pastored the Clark's Hill, Rushville, Hartsville, Tyner, College Corner, Concord, Connersville, Clarksburg, and Noblesville Pilgrim Holiness churches. Grace was also instrumental in the organizing of the Walkerton and South Bend Pilgrim Holiness churches. She died May 10, 1952.

Gertrude F. Preston Clocksin

Gertrude F. Preston was born January 18, 1881. She was received into the Lockport Conference (Western New York) of the Wesleyan Methodist Church in 1905.

Gertrude was the pastor of the Ellicott church, later called the Hamburg, New York, church, from 1906 to 1908. She was ordained in 1909 by the Lockport Conference. That year she became pastor of the Olean Mission. Isabelle Willshan was her assistant.[67] She sailed to Sierra Leone, West Africa, and served as a missionary there from 1911 to 1914.

When she returned home from Africa, she transferred her membership to the Dakota Conference. Her appointment from 1914 to 1917 was the Richland, South Dakota church. The church had been organized in 1909 in the Insley schoolhouse. The first parsonage was built in 1916 under her leadership.[68]

Her next appointment was as the first pastor of the Medicine Lake, Montana, church. This church was the result of a tent meeting. The tent was filled every night, and people were converted. During this pastorate she married Elllis Clocksin, and she continued to pastor the church until the end of the 1918 conference year.[69] Her stay in the Dakota Conference lasted for nineteen years. She also pastored the Aberdeen and Mowbridge, South Dakota, churches.

In 1934 she returned to the Lockport Conference and became affiliated with the Houghton College staff for fourteen years. She was listed on the superannuated (retired) list from 1948 to 1953. Her death occurred June 5, 1953.

The Lockport Conference paid tribute to her by saying she "manifested most excellent wisdom, courage and faith."

Former District Superintendent James Bence gave this tribute: "Gertrude Clocksin was a pioneer missionary to Sierra Leone. I did not know her in her ministerial days, but I was her pastor in her retirement and final days. She would have been a great spiritual asset to any church or community. She was a real prayer warrior."

Elizabeth "Lizzie" Feltar

Lizzie Feltar gave a touching report of her experience in being called to preach at the annual session of the Kansas Conference of the Wesleyan Methodist Church in 1906. That year she was the pastor of the Easton, Kansas, church and remained there for two years. In 1908 she gave a short exhortation at conference. She pastored the Hall church for the next three years. From 1911 to 1912 her appointment was the Hollis church.

She was appointed the chair of the Second District Holiness Convention and pastored the Union Valley and Excelsior churches. The orders of the day at conference in 1915 called for her to preach a message. Following that message, she was ordained by the Kansas Conference. She spent some years as a general evangelist. Her last pastorate was at Norton, Kansas. She was granted a letter of standing on May 17, 1921.[70]

Anna E. Hines

Anna E. Hines was born January 13, 1873. She was converted August 5, 1900, in the morning and sanctified that afternoon. She began her ministerial work in the Indiana Conference of the Holiness Christian Church in 1906. She was ordained by that Church in 1914.

Anna pastored her home church in 1910 for one year. Except for that one year, her ministry was in the field of evangelism. That ministry covered twenty years. She was instrumental in bringing the Indianapolis First Church into the Indiana District of the Pilgrim Holiness Church. Her earthly labors ended September 18, 1961.[71]

Lillian Rodgers

According to the *Minutes of the Annual Session of the Indiana Conference of the Holiness Christian Church,* 1906–19, Lillian Rodgers was under that group's appointment for service. She may have served in Logansport, Indiana, and Springfield, Ohio; the records are not clear. She was ordained by this group in 1914. She was not listed after 1919 on their roll.

Josephine Akright

Josephine Akright was received as an ordained minister from the Radical United Brethren Church by the Indiana Conference of the Wesleyan Methodist Church in 1907. That year and the year following, she was assigned with her husband, also an ordained minister, to pastor the Bryant charge. They served together as pastors of the Hamlet church for two years, and the next two years she was engaged in evangelism. In the following years they pastored at North Webster (two years) and North Liberty (two years). From 1918 through 1920 she pastored the Cicero and Sheridan churches. She was again listed as a general evangelist for the next seven years. In 1929 she retired and was listed as superannuated until 1937. Her husband, H. A. Akright, died in 1934.[72]

Josephine was described as a consecrated woman who lived a godly life. She was of a cheerful and happy disposition. She was born November 13, 1851, and died January 1, 1938, at the age of eighty-seven.[73]

Grace B. Sloan

Grace Sloan, a woman with unusual ability, graduated from Fairmount Bible School, Fairmount, Indiana (later merged into what is now Indiana Wesleyan University, Marion, Indiana), in 1909. She had a prominent place in all the school activities. She believed in the power of Christ's blood to save. Her preaching was striking and very effective.[74]

Grace B. Sloan became a ministerial member of the Indiana Conference of the Wesleyan Methodist Church in 1906. She was the pastor of the Sheridan church in 1909, and the following year she was a Bible school teacher. She was ordained by the conference in 1911 and entered the field of evangelism the same years as a general evangelist. Her name did not appear on the conference roll after 1912.[75]

Nancy Anne Barts Willis

Nancy Anne Barts was born August 24, 1872, in South Bend, Indiana. She was saved March 19, 1895, the day her mother died. She was sanctified the next day. Soon after that she felt called to be a missionary to Africa. She went to Houghton Seminary, Houghton, New York (later Houghton College) to prepare for that service. She served three terms in Africa, from 1906 to 1920.

She received her license to preach from the Indiana Conference of the Wesleyan Methodist Church in 1906. While home on furlough in 1909–10 she served as the organizer of the conference Young Missionary Workers Band (now Wesleyan Kids for Missions) and the Woman's Home and Foreign Missionary Society. She spent a total of twelve years as the organizer in the Southern and West Coast Districts.

Nancy was ordained in 1917 between her second and third terms of service in Sierra Leone. She was well known throughout the Church. Those who knew her best characterized her as a woman yielded to God and Spirit-filled. She lived a devoted and useful life. The nationals of Sierra Leone declared, "She never soiled the Word of God." She preached the truth as found in the Bible.[76]

After she came home from Africa in 1920, she married Rev. J. M. Willis, a minister in the Georgia Conference. They worked together as a team in the Lord's work in Georgia until 1929. At that time they transferred to the Oregon Conference and served together on the pastorate in Portland for five years and at the Cramfordsville church for two years.

Nancy Barts Willis lived a life of continuous victory. She entered into her eternal rest September 19, 1936, in Portland, Oregon.[77]

Dinah "Effie" Reynolds Bean

Dinah, often referred to as "Effie," Reynolds was born January 20, 1891, in Troy, North Carolina. She was ordained December 28, 1907, in North Carolina. She married P. F. Bean September 30, 1909. She became mother to two sons and one daughter. P. F. joined her in the pastorate of the three churches she was serving when they got married, at Mocksville, Kernersville, and Benefit, North Carolina. They served there for three years.[78] These churches were in what would eventually be the North Carolina District of the Pilgrim Holiness Church.

She was a good preacher and a woman of great faith in God. She carried a deep concern for the lost, and her groans and intercession were remembered by those who heard her pray.[79]

They accepted the pastorate of the Hurlock charge in Maryland in June 1912 and served this charge until 1916. In October 1916 they moved to Cambridge, Maryland, to successfully pastor that church for thirteen and one-half years. They also served the Crisfield, Maryland, church for three years; Melton, Delaware, church for one year; and Demar, Delaware, church for five years. These churches were all in the Eastern District of the Pilgrim Holiness Church. She was in home missionary evangelism for one year after these pastorates.

Effie and P. F. accepted the call of the Bloxom, Viriginia, charge and faithfully served there until her health failed. Among her last words were "I'm going home to die no more." Her home-going was December 24, 1945.[80]

Anna Griffith Daley

It was not unusual for preachers and laypersons to be expelled from a church when they accepted and experienced the cleansing work of the Holy Spirit in sanctification. Such was the case of Anna Griffith. She was born March 7, 1866, in Fowler, Pennsylvania. She married John Daley February 22, 1887. Anna experienced the saving grace of God in conversion in 1898. After she was sanctified (she did not know what to call this experience until much later), her sole aim was to promote holiness. Not long after she experienced sanctification, the church where she was a member became displeased with her and others who also had been sanctified and expelled them for upholding this doctrine of holiness.[81]

The *Minutes of the Annual Session of the Lockport Conference of the Wesleyan Methodist Connection* reported that Anna was the pastor at Hazelhurst in 1907. In 1908 she was appointed the pastor of the Comes charge. Also that year she became the superintendent of a mission in Mahaffey, Pennsylvania. These two may have been the same.[82]

She transferred to the Allegheny Conference in 1909 and became the pastor of the Templeton church. She was powerful in prayer and carried a burden for the work in Pittsburgh. She personally won many persons to the Lord and discipled these new believers in the faith. She was a blessing and an enabler to all those she touched, both sinner and saint.[83]

Anna Daley's earthly life ended May 27, 1938.

Fannie Dunbar

Fannie Dunbar was given a preacher's license in 1907 by the Kansas Conference of the Wesleyan Methodist Church. That year, she and her husband were the pastors of the Hall Church in Kansas. By 1908 she had completed all of her course work and was eligible to be ordained, except she lacked one year of practical experience that was required. Her husband, I. C., was slated to be ordained in 1908, but he declined, for they desired to be ordained at the same time. That year they were stationed at Aurora, Colorado. They were ordained in 1909 by the Kansas Conference and served as the pastors at Beeler. They remained there until 1912.

I. C. and Fannie transferred from the Kansas Conference to the North Carolina Conference during the 1912 year and worked in that district for one year. They returned to Kansas in 1913. They served as evangelists for a number of years under the Kansas Conference. Their last pastorate was at the Hollis church. On January 2, 1922, they were granted letters of standing.[84]

Lucinda F. Smith

Lucinda F. Smith[85] died December 3, 1983, just seventeen days before her one-hundredth birthday. She joined the Wesleyan Methodist Church in 1907 and was given a license to preach in 1908.[86] She graduated in 1912 from Fairmount Bible School, Fairmount, Indiana (later merged into what became Indiana Wesleyan University, Marion, Indiana). She lived a Christlike life and was remembered for her pleasant smile.[87]

Lucinda was ordained by the Indiana Conference in 1923. She began her pastoral work at the Waveland, Indiana church. She lived in Kirklin and traveled by train two weekends each month to pastor the church and had the longest tenure of any pastor of that congregation. She was the pastor of the Greenwood church for two years.

She gave up pastoral work in order to care for her mother but she was faithful in serving the Lord in the local Kirklin church. She was president of the Woman's Home and Foreign Missionary Society of her church for thirty years. She also served as the class leader, a Sunday school teacher, and the quarterly meeting secretary.[88]

Ada White Ramsey

The Alabama Conference of the Wesleyan Methodist Church was started by the assistance of a woman, Ada White. She was from Alabama but had moved to North Carolina. Here she came in contact with the Wesleyan Methodist people of Kings Mountain. She was converted and began preaching. However, the Lord eventually led her back to Alabama. She preached a "strange doctrine," the possibility of freedom from sin in this life. She was also the first woman preacher many of these people had ever seen or heard. Out of her preaching and work came requests for a church. The first Wesleyan Methodist church was named in honor of her and was called Ada's Chapel. This church was organized in 1907.[89]

The first regular session of the Alabama Conference met November 10, 1910. Ada White Ramsey was ordained at that first session.[90] Her service record revealed that she was the pastor of the Friendship station in 1910 and served as conference missionary evangelist in 1911. No other service record was found.[91]

Mary Cynthia Robinson Whitney

Another one of God's servants was Mary Robinson Whitney.[92] She had a long life of useful service in Kingdom building. She was born October 15, 1855, at Prescott, Ontario. Her parents were old-fashioned Methodists who often entertained traveling evangelists in their home. She married a farmer, George Whitney, at age

twenty. After attending an old-time Methodist revival, she was converted in her home that year, 1875. Sometime after her conversion she entered into the wonderful experience of heart holiness. The "grace of holiness" became her life's theme. Mary and George soon felt led of the Lord to hold prayer meetings in their home, schoolhouses, and other persons' homes. They were instruments used of God in seeing many souls saved. Soon they were engaged in revival meetings, which resulted in the establishment of several churches in the Canada Conference of the Wesleyan Methodist Church. The Canada Conference *Minutes* were not to be found; therefore, the names of these churches could not be included here. Her husband's task became so great that, as a minister's wife, she found it "necessary and a privilege to assist him with the preaching."[93]

Summer camp was held in Shawville, Quebec, at the fairgrounds July 6–15, 1907. The evangelists were A. J. Shea, Mary Whitney's son-in-law, and Mary Whitney. There were twenty-five conversions, and eleven persons joined the Shawville Wesleyan Methodist church.[94]

George and Mary joined the Syracuse Conference in 1909. They came by recommendation from the Canada Conference and were appointed supply pastors at the East Randolph and Blatehley charge (may have been called Great Bend, Pennsylvania) until 1911.

The next year they were the song evangelists at the Iowa Conference camp meeting with A. J. Shea, of Winchester, Ontario, as the evangelist. They transferred from the Syracuse Conference to the Iowa Conference. The Itineracy and Orders Committee (now District Board of Ministerial Development) received them as conference preachers. Because of their age, the number of years of service, and their familiarity with the course of study, the committee recommended that they be ordained whenever their quarterly conference desired. Mary was ordained by the Iowa Conference in 1913.

By invitation of the Marengo, Iowa, charge, George spent several weeks preaching there. They enjoyed him as pastor, and he returned on March 1, 1912, with his family to pastor. He died sometime that year or early in 1913. Mary stayed on as pastor for another conference year and was then granted a letter of transfer July 31, 1913, to the Canada Conference.

Mary served as associate pastor at Winchester, Ontario, for two years. She often worked with her daughter, Marion, an ordained minister in the Church, in revivals. One two-week meeting was held at the Cornwell Church in Canada in 1928 with Rev. J. Scobie, a former prizefighter, as preacher and Mary and Marion as the singers. Many people attended the meeting, and the hall was filled the last night of the meeting.[95]

Mary and her daughter went to Houghton, New York, where they were engaged in evangelistic work. Revival engagements followed at Ottawa and in Jersey City. Mary transferred from the Canada Conference to the Middle Atlantic States Mission Conference May 10, 1930. She was appointed the superintendent of the Tuesday afternoon holiness prayer meetings in Jersey City. She and Marion became the founding pastors of the Willow Grove Church (Hatsboro, Pennsylvania) near Philadelphia. During their stay of about fourteen years, they built a new church building. H. Willard Ortlip, family friend and scholarship student at the Pennsylvania Academy of Fine Arts, painted a mural on the chapel wall.[96] This church grew steadily. Mary was called "Mother Whitney" by the people. Before her retirement in 1943 at the age of eighty-seven, she was known as "the oldest woman preacher in the world."[97]

Mary Whitney was loved and admired by all. She often gave the devotions, preached, or exhorted at conference. In 1938 after she had spoken, many words of deep appreciation were expressed in gratitude for the spiritual nature and God-blessed life of "Mother Whitney" and her influence on the spiritual life of the conference. In 1939 she delivered a "powerful" ordination message. Also during that conference session she was impressed of the Lord to lead the conference

in a special prayer for the healing of W. L. Thompson, home missionary secretary. In 1942 she gave a fitting address of appreciation for the longtime treasurer of the conference, F. L. Keith. After she gave her pastoral report in 1943 (she had resigned effective at the close of this conference) she was honored with these words: "This year has also brought to a close the labors of Mother Whitney within the bounds of the conference. We shall miss her shouts of praise, her testimonies, and exhortations at our gatherings. We pray God's rich blessings on her life in these days of well-earned rest."

But Mary Whitney did not completely retire. She was very active in prayer and praise. Noted ministers and workers counted it a high honor to have her pray for them. Among these were Paul S. Rees, Billy Graham, and Redd Harper, the converted cowboy. She participated in the Billy Graham London revival services by transatlantic radio and newspaper. Her grandson, George Beverly Shea, was a vocalist with the Billy Graham campaign.[98]

After her retirement she kept on spreading the gospel. She addressed a Women's Christian Temperance Union meeting in the Syracuse YWCA. During World War II she said, "We've had such a period of prosperity that it seems as if the people have forgotten God, and that something has to bring them back to a sense of their dependence upon Him. Prayer will help to solve our problems."[99]

She preached her last sermon in Rochester, New York, at the age of ninety. Among her treasured photographs is one showing her baptizing her own great-grandson.

Mary Whitney was the mother of six children. She left this earthly life May 27, 1954, at the age of ninety-eight. Two funeral services were held at Syracuse, New York, and Prescott, Ontario, where friends gathered in the little country churchyard near the old homestead where she was born to pay their final respects.[100]

—⚬⚬⚬—

Aurie L. Bodenhorn

Aurie Bodenhorn, often referred to in conference minutes as A. L., began studying for the ministry in 1908. She graduated in 1909 from

Fairmount Bible School, Fairmount, Indiana (later merged into what became Indiana Wesleyan University, Marion, Indiana). She was the chapel organist at the Bible school. She often favored the students with thoughts in rhyme since she was poetically inclined.[101] During 1909 she was the assistant pastor of the Roseburg charge. She assisted her husband, T. M. Bodenhorn, in pastoring the following churches: Laketon, Santa Fe, Bryant, Whitehall charge, Gunkle Zion, Fountain City, Mt. Zion in Howard County, Mt. Olive, and Gas City.

President W. L. Thompson read the following at the Conference in 1912. "On account of convictions and physical disabilities, Sister Aurie L. Bodenhorn desired to be relieved of the responsibilities of the Eldership (ordination) and tendered to me her parchments." It is not clear what happened. She continued to assist her husband on pastorates and was listed as an ordained minister in the conference journals.

T. M. Bodenhorn died in 1949. Aurie went on the retirement list that year and remained there until her death in 1953.[102]

Amy Brenemann

On November 23, 1908, Amy Brenemann was assigned to the Emmanual work of the Iowa Conference of the Wesleyan Methodist Church. In 1910 her husband, Austin P., was assigned to the Emmanual work also, and they pastored together there for another two years. In 1912 they were stationed at Bennezette, Iowa. The next year Union Ridge was added to the work at Bennezette, and they pastored both the churches. Union Ridge was dropped the next year from the charge. She was granted a letter of standing and joined another denomination on April 23, 1916.

During her years in the Iowa conference, Amy was active in conference work. In 1910 she was elected to the conference Sunday school board and became the conference Sunday school secretary, serving until 1914. She often led the singing for the conference sessions. She served as president of the conference Woman's Home and Foreign Missionary Society from 1911 to 1912.[103]

Dollie R. Goble Eddy

Dollie R. Goble graduated in 1909 from Fairmount Bible School, Fairmount, Indiana (later merged into what became Indiana Wesleyan University, Marion, Indiana). She was described as an eloquent speaker. She often encouraged the students at Bible school with her readings.[104] She was engaged in evangelistic work for a time. During 1909 she was the pastor of the Fountain City, Indiana, church. She resigned from this church in order to marry Birch I. Eddy in 1910 and was also ordained that year. Her husband took her to Africa for a "delayed honeymoon," and they served five terms in Sierra Leone, West Africa, from 1910 to 1928, when they were forced to return home because of ill health. Their two sons, Edward and Sherwood, were born in Africa, and both became ministers of the gospel, Edward serving as a missionary to Sierra Leone. B. I. and Dollie pioneered the work in Kamakwie and Gbendembu. Between terms in Africa, they pastored the Greensboro church and served as evangelists in the Indiana Conference.[105]

Dollie Eddy was a woman of undaunted faith in God. Her life was lived in loving concern for people. She was a devoted wife and mother. In her retirement, when failing health gripped her, she developed a great prayer ministry. She died at the age of eighty-five on January 5, 1973. Her husband, B. I. Eddy, died September 3, 1980, at the age of ninety-three.[106]

Cordelia Rebecca "Delia" Howlett

Delia Howlett began working for the Kingdom in 1908 in the Iowa Conference of the Wesleyan Methodist Church. She was born October 7, 1878, in Marengo, Iowa. She was converted at an early age. She saw a vision of the heathen in Africa and felt called of God to enter missionary work. After receiving her education at Houghton College,[107] she sailed for Africa for her first term of service in April 1908. She served four terms. Delia opened the new field in Kamabai, Sierra Leone, West Africa. She had a great deal of influence on Brahma Turay, who became the president of the West Africa Conference. He heard the gospel at the Kamakwie dispensary when he came for treatment for tropical ulcers. He was also enrolled in the Binkola Boys' School. He was sanctified there and received his call to preach there also.[108]

Delia returned home before her fourth term was completed because of failing health. She served under the Iowa Conference from 1908 to 1952. Her death occurred March 2, 1952, in Marion, Indiana.[109]

Lucinda McNew Rhoads

Lucinda Rhoads (sometimes spelled "Rhoades") began her ministerial work under the direction of the Indiana Conference of the Holiness Christian Church in 1908. She was ordained in 1913. She lived through two mergers—when the Holiness Christian Church merged with the International Apostolic Holiness Church to form the International Holiness Church, and when that group merged with the Pilgrim Church to form the Pilgrim Holiness Church.[110]

Lucinda was born September 18, 1849, in Ripley County, Indiana. She married Enoch C. Rhoads in 1871 and was the mother of four children; two of them preceded her in death. She was a woman of beautiful Christian character. She had the gift of "helps," always ready to help everyone in need. Her last earthly words were "It is well."[111]

Hedvig Melinda Peterson

Hedvig Melinda Peterson was born April 17, 1869, in Sweden. She came to the United States in 1891 and lived in Chicago. She was converted in 1893 and sanctified one week later. She spent most of her life as a gospel worker.

Hedvig went to Colorado in 1908 by the invitation of Rev. W. H. Lee of the People's Mission

Church and immediately began her labors with this group. She remained with the People's Mission Church when it merged with the Pilgrim Holiness Church and continued as a minister of that denomination until her death. She was ordained.

She served the Collins, Grand Junction, and Rocky Ford churches in Colorado and the Junction City and Wichita churches in Kansas. She also served as the matron of Pilgrim Bible College in Colorado Springs. She died at the age of eighty-four July 11, 1953.[112]

Mrs. A. E. Belk

Mrs. A. E. Belk was born April 18, 1872, in Cleveland, Ohio. She was ordained by the North Carolina Conference of the Wesleyan Methodist Church. She and her husband were both ordained ministers, and she actively assisted him in pastoring several churches.[113]

Mrs. Belk was interested in the Woman's Home and Foreign Missionary Society (WH&FMS) and served two years as vice president of the district WH&FMS. Both the Belks were involved in higher education, and they established an annuity to Central Wesleyan College, in Central, South Carolina (now Southern Wesleyan University). The annuity was to go toward campus improvements.

Mrs. Belk served as the secretary of the North Carolina Conference from 1910 to 1915 and again in 1919 and 1920.

The Belks served for a number of years in the field of evangelism. During their ministry they were instrumental in organizing and building ten churches in the North Carolina Conference.[114] They jointly served the following churches: Knoxville, Tennessee; and Hendersonville, West Asheville, Mt. Hebron, Gastonia, Loray (now Firestone), West Durham, Kings Mountain First, Long Shoals, Mt. Moriah, and Old Fort, all in North Carolina. They served Rock Hill, Glendale and Spartanburg First in South Carolina.

She preceded her husband in death on January 27, 1957, at the age of eighty-four. He died July 21, 1965.[115]

Grace E. Chadwick

Little is known about Grace Chadwick. However the influence she had on one lady, Stella Wood, merits an entry in this chapter. Grace E. Chadwick was the pastor of the Barberton, Ohio, Wesleyan Methodist Church in 1909.[116] Her influence and wise advice given to Stella Wood when it seemed impossible for her to go to India kept Stella steady. Her encouragement to be patient kept Stella from giving up. Grace Chadwick spoke at the annual missionary meeting at the Stoneboro camp meeting on the needs of India. An offering of three hundred dollars was received and used for the work in that country. Stella set sail for India in 1910.[117] Grace Chadwick's vision and burden for the lost of India continued beyond sending Stella to India. Floyd and Hazel Banker in their book *From Famine to Fruitage,* on page 60, reported that her prayer and financial support resulted in the operating of the station at Vapi, located halfway between Sanjan and Pardi.

Sarah Plunkett

The first record of ministerial service for Sarah Plunkett appeared in 1908. She was already married at that time and was serving under the Indiana Conference of the Holiness Christian Church. She was ordained by that group in 1914. She was listed as pastor at New London, Indiana; Lawrenceburg, Illinois; Shernonan, Kentucky; and Leisure, Indiana. The records are not clear about her relationship as pastor. Sometimes she served with her husband, Arthur H., in a local church, but at other times she was the solo pastor of a church near a larger church where her husband was the pastor.[118]

When the Holiness Christian Church merged with the International Apostolic Holiness Church to form the International Holiness Church in 1919, she served under them.[119] After this group merged with the Pilgrim Church to form the Pilgrim Holiness Church, she served under the Pilgrim Holiness Church, from 1923 to 1961.[120]

Rev. Ernest Batman, her pastor in her declining years, wrote this note about her:

Sister Plunkett was a member of the church when I pastored in Indianapolis. She was a very quiet, sincere lady who could become very emotional. She surprised me one Sunday morning when she got blessed and rattled the pew in front of her. Her husband was probably one of the better-educated ministers of the conference during his time of service. He was the pastor of the Frankfort, Indiana, First Church, and during his pastorate there, Sarah was the pastor of the Forrest, Indiana, church.

Lelia Zay Benedict DeWeerd

The writer recalls Lelia DeWeerd in the 1940s. She lived in retirement in Fairmount, Indiana. Lelia took special interest in all the youth of the local church. She penned a special message (almost like a prophecy) on the card of my wedding shower gift. It read, "I feel sure God is going to use your united efforts for His glory." Lelia was a special friend to all of us.

Lelia Zay Benedict married Fred DeWeerd July 14, 1905. They became the parents of seven children: Paul, Eunice, Faith, Ruth, Lelia, Miriam, and James.

Lelia and Fred DeWeerd and Charles and Maude Slater and their families arrived in Africa February 19, 1909, and served as a great and effective team there. They were used in evangelistic meetings among the European peoples, the English and Dutch, as well as the Hottentots and Kaffirs in South Africa. Fred DeWeerd became the editor of holiness tracts, books, and the "African Revivalist," which this group published. They had brought a printing press with them. A bookstore was opened in Port Elizabeth, where they sold Bibles and gospel literature. They also operated a reading room. The Slaters went into the interior, but apparently the DeWeerds stayed in the city.[121]

Little is told about Lelia's work in Africa. In 1917 Lelia was received from the International Apostolic Holiness Church into the Indiana Conference of the Wesleyan Methodist Church. She served for a number of years in general evangelism. In 1923 she was ordained by the Indiana

Conference. In 1933 she was assigned the pastorate at Gaston, Indiana. Her younger son, James, was her assistant. Lelia died in 1955.[122]

―∞∞∞―

Hattie Crosby Manyon

Hattie Crosby, the first of seven children, was born September 18, 1877, in Illinois.[123] Three years later, her family went by "prairie schooner" to the Dakota Territory and homesteaded near Mellette, South Dakota, in the same area as the Sioux Indians.

Hattie was homeschooled by her mother, who also gave her music lessons on a little organ that had been shipped from Illinois. Her father made her desk and chair. She was converted at age six and sanctified at age twenty-one. In 1887, at age nine, she became convinced that God had a work for her to do. Her mother died when Hattie was thirteen, and Hattie then became "mother" to her six younger brothers and sisters, the youngest two months old, and aided her grieving father. These experiences became excellent preparations for the work God was calling her to do.

Hattie was a prayer warrior. She prayed until all her brothers and sisters were established in the Lord. The youngest sister became the mother of Arthur Calhoon, a missionary to India and Haiti. A younger brother became the father of Robert Crosby, a missionary to South America and Puerto Rico. When she was sixteen, her father became ill and was not expected to live. Hattie prayed for God to spare his life, and He did. It was during this period that Hattie and her father knew that God was calling her to serve in Africa.

She completed her schooling and attended Redfield College and Dakota State University in Madison, South Dakota. She taught school for five years. She then attended Houghton College, in Houghton, New York, for four years and also took one year of medical instruction.

In 1904 Hattie assisted her father in moving the family to Houghton so her brothers and sisters could attend a Christian college. Then on October 5, 1905, Hattie left for Africa.

She arrived in Africa at a tragic time. Sickness and death were stalking all the missionaries. Mary Lane Clarke and Cora Cutshall were ordered home in December. Cora died soon after she reached her home. Elizabeth Ayres was pregnant and was also stricken with illness. Imo Jones accompanied her home in December. John Ayres, Elizabeth's husband, was seriously ill and died December 31, 1905. The next day, January 1, 1906, Marie Stephens died. George Clarke was also very ill. Hattie cared for the sick ones, going from room to room for ten days and nights with only one hour of rest per day. She watched as the nationals carried the dead to the Kunso Cemetery. George Clarke lingered between life and death and was sent home as soon as he was able to travel.

Hattie was left alone. She prayed, studied the language, taught, did pastoral calling, and preached. After five months, new recruits came to help, and Hattie went to Masumbo to care for the Girls' School. She was mother, matron, doctor, preacher, translator, and caretaker. She preached morning and night on Sundays. She traveled thirty-five miles to towns and hamlets to pray and speak to the people before they went to their farms to work each morning.

God gave Hattie the "gift of languages," and she quickly learned the native language. Often when the translator couldn't keep up with her preaching, Hattie would slip back and forth from English to the native language. She was used of God to bring the people to repentance.

Hattie spent four terms in Sierra Leone between 1905 and 1921. In 1908 she entered the ministry in the Dakota Conference on probation. Her successful service in Africa was a result of her prayer life. She passed her probation.[124] By 1921 her health had broken, and the last year she could work only a half day at a time and was forced to rest the other half. She asked and was given permission to go farther into the interior to open a new field to the Loko people at Bendembu. She was alone, isolated, and in a new and difficult field—but she declared those days the "happiest of my life." She opened the field where the Bible school would be established.

On one of her trips home, a young pregnant missionary wife was being sent home. The child was born on the ship, but the mother died. Hattie conducted the funeral and buried the mother at sea.

She cared for the tiny baby and took it through customs. She handed the child to the grieving grandparents in Canada. God always provided grace and love, but Hattie provided the "grit" to be God's instrument in many different difficulties.

Ill health prevented her return to Africa. In 1922 she married Raymond Boyd Manyon, and they moved to California. With other Wesleyans in the area, she and her family were helpful in launching a new church plant in Los Angeles.

Hattie Crosby Manyon became a member of the Kansas Conference in 1949, and that conference ordained her July 17, 1949.[125] Under the Kansas Conference she served both Wesleyan Methodist and Free Methodist churches in Kansas and Colorado. She spent her last days in intercessory prayer, praying by name for the African workers and all the missionaries on every field. She circled the globe with her prayers and also wrote letters of encouragement to all of them.

The Africans said, "Her face reflects the great Light that she follows." Her husband passed away in 1960. Hattie Crosby Manyon's earthly life ended December 26, 1966. She was eighty-nine years old.

Mrs. M. V. Wicks-Eggo

The *Minutes of the Annual Session of the Georgia Conference of the Wesleyan Methodist Connection, or Church, of America* of 1909 listed Mrs. M. V. Wicks-Eggo as an ordained minister. She was not assigned to any place of service and never appeared again in the *Minutes*.

Mrs. Lillian M. Elliott

Lillian M. Elliott was born in 1889 in West Virginia. She was converted in 1905 at age sixteen in a Methodist church. Shortly afterward she was led into holiness of heart by George B. Kulp. She then joined the Huntington, West Virginia, Pilgrim Holiness church and faithfully worked there until 1931. She then moved to Hopewell, Virginia, and became a charter member of the church there. She held a ministerial license for

many years. She was ordained by the Virginia District in 1954.

Lillian was the mother of five children. Her pastor made this comment concerning her spiritual walk: "I never have known Lillian Elliott to do anything that was inconsistent with her profession as a Spirit-filled child of God. . . . Her uncompromising allegiance to right and opposition to wrong was very unusual." She died June 16, 1956.[126]

Sarah A. Green

Sarah A. Green was born April 2, 1862, in New York and died October 31, 1935. She had been a minister in the Wesleyan Methodist Church for twenty-nine years. She was ordained in 1911, according to the Syracuse Conference *Minutes*. She was a supply pastor for the Free Methodist Church at North Pharsalia, New York, and had served the Wesleyan Methodist Church as a general evangelist. No other service record was found for her.[127]

Alice M. Hart

The first service record found on Alice M. Hart was in 1909 with the Indiana Conference of the Holiness Christian Church. She was ordained by that group in 1913 and pastored the Carlisle and Linton churches. She served under the Indiana District of the International Holiness Church for two years. In 1923, when that group merged with the Pilgrim Church and the merged body became the Pilgrim Holiness Church, she continued her service with them. She was elected a delegate to the General Assembly of the Pilgrim Holiness Church in 1924.

Alice was born in Carlisle, Indiana, July 3, 1865. She married William Hart in 1883. He died May 15, 1940. Alice was converted at age thirteen. She received her first license to preach in 1902. She was active in the ministry until 1951. She served as pastor at Sullivan (she bought and dedicated the church at that time), Linton, Carlisle, Pleasantville, Jasonville, and Grange Ridge. All these churches were in Indiana. The Grange Ridge church was later moved to Oaktown.

Alice served as the treasurer of the Indiana District of the Holiness Christian Church for several years. She also served on the district educational board for twenty years and was the chairperson of the board for a large part of that time. In 1927 she canvassed the entire Indiana District of the Pilgrim Holiness Church in the interest of foreign missions. She served as the district foreign missionary treasurer.

Alice M. Hart's fruitful life on this earth ended at age eighty-nine, on December 15, 1954.[128]

Iva Esther Hammon
Crofford Hyde

Iva Esther Hammon was born August 16, 1867. She married Jacob V. Crofford December 31, 1890. When the Cherokee Strip (Indian Territory) opened in 1890, the Croffords were a part of the drive across the border from Kansas when thousands stood in line to dart across the state line to get homestead land in what would later become Oklahoma. In 1893 they moved to Grant County, Oklahoma, and made their home there for several years.[129]

Records are scarce during these early years, but Jacob and Iva worked together in several early church projects of the Oklahoma Conference of the Wesleyan Methodist Church. According to the *Minutes,* she was a licensed preacher in 1909 and was assigned to evangelistic work. Sometime after this, she was ordained and was so listed in 1923. She was the pastor at Springdale in 1931, but most of the time records show her to be in evangelistic work, sometimes limited to the bounds of the Oklahoma Conference.

Iva was involved in the conference activities and often served on conference committees and boards. She was an excellent preacher. She was also involved in the organization of several churches in the Alva area. Jacob V. and Iva, along with C. L. Moore, were the first pastors of Enid Wesleyan Methodist Church in 1915. The period from 1912 to 1919 was a difficult time for the conference. But during this period ten new churches were started. It

was the beginning of the conference movement to establish new churches in the urban rather than rural areas. Iva E. Crofford served as conference president of Oklahoma for seven or so months in 1912. She was elected again in 1915 and served until 1919 as president (district superintendent).[130]

In 1910 the Oklahoma Conference Woman's Home and Foreign Missionary Society was organized, with Iva as president. Before her ordination she had served as a lay delegate to General Conference.

Jacob V. died in 1926. Iva married Clayton H. Hyde in 1936. They lived just outside Alva, Oklahoma. Iva died May 29, 1943, at the age of seventy-five.[131]

Sarah M. Jones

Josephine Washburn in her book *History and Reminiscences of the Holiness Church Work in Southern California and Arizona,* stated on page 433 that credentials as a minister (ordination) were given to Sarah M. Jones in Nashville in 1909. There was no service record for her. Also at that same meeting two other women were given credentials of evangelists. There was a difference in these categories. These women were Mattie Barnett and Martha E. Louck.

Mary E. Kuhl

Mary E. Kuhl was listed as a clergyperson in 1909 in the *Minutes of the Annual Session of the Illinois Conference of the Wesleyan Methodist Connection, or Church, of America.* Her assignment was to be the state president of the Women's Christian Temperance Union. There was no indication that she was or was not an ordained minister.

Francene McMillan

Francene McMillan[132] attended Houghton College. After her marriage, she and her husband, also a minister, moved to Ohio and were the pastors of two charges. While pastoring the Harrison Chapel work in 1906, Mr. McMillan died. Francene continued to be the pastor there until 1910. She was the pastor at West View charge in 1912.[133] She and her family moved to Houghton, and during the four years there, Francene served as the postmistress. It became necessary for her to return to Ohio to care for her mother. She was a very capable preacher and was described as a woman of sterling character.

Francene McMillan served as general president of the Woman's Home and Foreign Missionary Society from 1911 to 1919. She served on many conference committees and was assistant conference secretary for a time. Her earthly service ended in 1942.

Mary V. Meyers

Mary V. Meyers was born October 2, 1875, in Saverton, Missouri. The *Minutes of the Annual Session of the Indiana Conference of the Holiness Christian Church* showed her working under their direction in 1909. She and her husband, Ora C. Meyers, were both ordained in 1913. She preached in the Eastern and Central states for many years. She was in charge of the orphanage in Carlinville, Illinois, for over ten years. She also worked in St. Louis, as the assistant pastor in the rescue work with Rev. Melvin Pratt. The *Minutes of the Annual Assembly of the Illinois and Missouri District Pilgrim Holiness Church* recorded her activities from 1923 to 1932. She was stationed at both Jerseyville and Charleston, Illinois.

In 1930 Mary moved to Monterey Park, California. She was the president of the Women's Christian Temperance Union of Monterey Park for two years. She preached in many of the area churches and served as pastor of the Pilgrim Holiness Church at Riverside. She was the pastor of the East Los Angeles Pilgrim Holiness church at the time of her death, December 3, 1950.

Mary had been in ill health for nine years and was blind. However, she could recognize her husband, who faithfully cared for her every need. They had no biological children but adopted eight children. She was a loyal and capable leader.[134]

Grace Daugherty Sweet Nelson

Grace Jellet Daugherty was born August 8, 1886, in Carlinville, Illinois.[135] She was born into a very poor, rural, non-Christian family. When she was nine years old she was sent to live with a wealthy family in Carlinville, whom she served as a housemaid. In return, she was able to attend school. She did not object to getting up early and working late, because she now was able to learn to read and write.

While living in this home, she was allowed to attend church with the family and for the first time heard about Jesus Christ. One night during a revival the Lord spoke to her in convicting power. In her room that night she prayed *Dear God, if You are really real, and if You really love me, let me know You.* She testified later that her room lit up, and God's presence was so real that she never again doubted that God was real. She was twelve years old. She believed her mother would also be glad to come to know Jesus, but when Grace told her about her experience with God, she looked at her as if she had lost her mind.

After graduating from public school, Grace attended the Bible college in Carlinville. She worked in the kitchen to help pay her expenses. She was interested in music and asked God to help her learn to play the piano so she could help in church services. She had a very good voice and was an excellent congregational song leader.

Minutes of the Indiana Holiness Christian Church reveal that Grace pastored the Michigan City and Three Oaks charge and the Noblesville church from 1909 to 1911. At this time, Rev. and Mrs. William Webster asked her to accompany them out West to open new preaching points in Kansas and Oklahoma. Her sister, Phoebe, joined her. They helped with the music and preaching for many tent meetings and revival services in this area. She was appointed to the El Dorado, Kansas, work in 1911 and Pleasant View, Oklahoma, in 1912. She was ordained in 1914 while she was pastoring Pleasant View.

In 1915 Grace met and married Frank Sweet. They moved to Campo, Colorado, where they bought a homestead farm. During the daytime they both worked hard on the farm, and at night they held revival services in a nearby school-house. A daughter, Frances Grace (Hofen), was born in 1918. The flu epidemic raged that winter, and many people died. Grace conducted many graveside funerals, but neither she nor her infant daughter caught the flu. She pastored in and around Campo for several years.

Grace accepted a call to return to Dacoma, Oklahoma, and to pastor the rural church, Pleasant View. She was a very caring pastor and made house calls all through that rural area in her buggy pulled by her faithful horse, Victor. If there was any kind of need in the community homes day or night, they would contact Pastor Grace.

In April 1923 the family was involved in a car accident that took the life of Frank Sweet. He was a wonderful husband and father and was very supportive of Grace's ministry, which he felt was also his ministry.

Grace pastored a short time at Osawatomie, Kansas. She married Matthew G. Nelson, a farmer, August 10, 1924. Matthew respected Grace's call to be a minister and would jokingly call himself the "pastor's wife." They became the parents of a daughter, Caroline (Nelson) Lewis.

Grace's last pastorate was at the church in Hopeton, Oklahoma. During this pastorate, one Sunday morning the church building burned to the ground. The community declared, "We have to have a church in town," They began to give money to rebuild the church. A bigger and better church was built and dedicated debt free.

Grace was known for her graciousness, prayer life, love for people, hospitality, home visitation, song leading, preaching, and delicious meals. Many of her family members have and are following in her footsteps. Her daughter, Caroline, has been involved in Christian service for over fifty years with her husband, Loren Lewis. Two granddaughters, Ernestine (Lewis)

Atkinson and Francie (Lewis) Emery, are pastors' wives. One grandson, Loren Lewis, is a minister of music. Two great-grandsons, Chris Emery and Derek Atkinson, are also in the ministry. Another daughter, Frances, has also been a blessing in her community and inherited her mother's gift of caring for people.

The International Holiness Church and Pilgrim Holiness Church issued ordination certificates each year. Some of Grace's certificates were signed by church leaders George A. Kulp, Winfred L. Cox, and W. L. Surbrook.

Grace went to be with the Lord June 22, 1953.[136]

Lillie Oliver

Lillie (sometimes spelled "Lily") Oliver was under appointment with the Indiana Conference of the Holiness Christian Church from 1909 to 1915. She was ordained in 1913. No record was found for her again until 1923, when she was listed as an evangelist under the Illinois and Missouri District of the Pilgrim Holiness Church.[137]

Ethel M. Bolles
Ovenshire McCost

Ethel Bolles and J. C. Ovenshire met at Taylor University, in Upland, Indiana, while studying for the ministry. They married. In 1909 they joined the Wesleyan Methodist Church in the Michigan Conference. They served the Romulus and Martindale churches for one year. They were both ordained on the Sunday of the annual conference that year and sailed for Sierra Leone, West Africa, November 14, 1909. They served a little over one term.[138] J. C. died January 9, 1912, at the young age of thirty-two. He had been suddenly stricken with pernicious malarial fever and died within four days. He suffered intensely but without complaining. He said, "God buries his workman, but the work goes on." Ethel's strong faith and courage were revealed in this sad experience. At the midnight hour in the Kunso Cemetery B. I. Eddy and Mary Lord (Sprague) conducted the graveside funeral.[139]

Ethel came home March 12, 1912, somewhat broken in health and served in deputation work for some time. She later married Mr. McCost (first name unkown), and they lived in Marshall, Michigan.

Mae Kierstead Shaffer Moore

Mae Kierstead Shaffer served as co-pastor with her husband, Noah, in the Allegheny and Lockport (Western New York) Conferences of the Wesleyan Methodist Church.[140] She also co-pastored with him at the Centerville, New York, Methodist church from 1945 to 1946. She continued on as pastor after his death in November 26, 1946, until she retired in 1956.

Mae Kierstead was born July 31, 1881, in Marion, Indiana. She married Noah Shaffer September 4, 1908. They were the parents of four daughters.

Mae and Noah co-pastored the Delevan and Machias charge in the Lockport Conference in 1909. They transferred to the Allegheny Conference in 1910 and served as pastors at New Castle, Pennsylvania, for one year; Akron, Ohio, for three years; and Franklin, Pennsylvania for two years. She was ordained during this period by the Allegheny Conference.

They returned to the Lockport Conference in 1916 and served as pastors of the Forestville charge for three and a half years, Ashwood charge for four years, and Fillmore for five years. They again transferred to the Allegheny Conference in 1929 and pastored the Dixonsville church for four years and the Erie church for three years. These churches were in Pennsylvania.

They were the pastors at Forrestville for four years, Hess Road for one year, Higgins charge for three years, and Cattaraugus charge for five years in New York under the Lockport Conference.

Mae was active in the conference work of both conferences. She served on many committees and boards. She was the conference president of the Woman's Home and Foreign Missionary Society in Lockport from 1925 to 1928. She often was in charge of the love feast at conference time also.

She married Clinton Moore August 1957. Mae's labors ended October 17, 1958.[141]

Carrie Beebe Warburton

Former district superintendent James Bence described Carrie Warburton as "the leader" of the ministerial team of Merton D. and Carrie B. Warburton.[142] She was a woman of unusual energy. When she saw a need, she took care of it. Her grandson Ivan Kellogg describes her as a prayer warrior and a woman of great faith and obedience to God.

Paul H. Yager, Jr. in *A Flame Burning: A History of the Central New York District of The Wesleyan Church* reported that her ministry must have started in 1906. However, no record of activity exists until 1909.[143]

Carrie Beebe was born December 11, 1875, in Odessa, New York. She died January 12, 1968, at the age of ninety-two. She was married to a young minister in the Wesleyan Methodist Church, Merton D. Warburton, December 24, 1894. Three daughters were born to them: Edith (Pocock), Mary (Kellogg), and Ruth (Chamberlain). Carrie was extremely interested in the welfare of her daughters. She moved to Houghton, New York, so the girls could attend school there. They served the Delevan, Machias, and Holland churches until the girls graduated in 1916.[144]

Merton and Carrie did not always serve the same church. When she was pastor at Groton, New York, he drove the ponies a distance of sixty-five miles and supplied the Herrickville, Pennsylvania, church. She returned to the Taylor church for another five years. This time Merton drove the "Model T" to supply the Blatchley and then Berrytown, Pennsylvania, churches. (The Taylor church had been her first pastorate, in 1909.)

In 1920 a tent meeting was held at Chambers, New York. This town was a train depot with six daily passenger trains. It seemed like a good place for a Wesleyan camp. Carrie was never too busy or too high on the social ladder to do menial tasks. A "lean-to" with a cook stove served as the kitchen. Carrie and her daughter Mary Kellogg were among the ladies who worked in this kitchen in the early days.[145]

Carrie was also a church planter. She was instrumental in the organization of the Elmira church in 1925. She carried on the vision of the preceding minister at Shady Grove and planted, built, and dedicated the Riverside Church, now known as Victory Highway Wesleyan Church, one of the larger churches in the Central New York District.

There was no church in Corning, and Carrie was challenged to get a church in this town. She rented a church building in Corning for a time and then moved the small congregation to Riverside, where she rented any building that was available—a grade school and a voting booth. She held tent meetings on the main street that connected Painted Post and Corning. Guest evangelists and special musicians were invited to improve the quality of the tent meetings. Midweek prayer meetings were held in the parishioners' homes. Shady Grove had their prayer meeting on Wednesday nights, Riverside's on Thursday.

On one prayer meeting night Carrie suggested that they needed to think about purchasing a building. The country was in the middle of the Great Depression. People did not have employment, and those who were employed worked only a few hours each day. But the people prayed—and when the vote was taken, it was unanimous to build a permanent church. But how could they finance a new church? An eleven-year old girl, Reva Lane, held up a dime and offered it as the beginning donation. A lady donated five small city lots. People were happy to work on the construction of the building even though they were not paid. The basement was dug with a horse scoop pulled by a homemade tractor.

The exterior walls were laid of tile blocks that cost ten cents each. Old theater seats were purchased for twenty dollars. Carrie was "dead set against" movie theaters, but she could use those seats! A local electric company donated lighting fixtures. Carrie conducted special services in the uncompleted church with the ceiling open to the rafters. The new church building was dedicated May 22, 1932. The impossible task during the Depression was led to completion by a woman minister.

Carrie's extraordinary energy is revealed in this paragraph from her grandson Ivan Kellogg:

It amazes me that Grandma managed to mop the kitchen floor on Saturday nights, get dinner started, preach on Sunday morning at the Shady Grove morning worship, and invite guests from the congregation to dinner at the parsonage. After dinner, Carrie and her dinner guests would travel to Riverside for 2:30 and 7:00 P.M. services. Grandpa [Merton] would hold the evening worship service at Shady Grove.

It was during this period in her life that she felt she must learn to drive a car so that she could adequately care for her churches. She was fifty-four (1929) when she got her driver's license.

Carrie was a pioneer in the Woman's Suffrage Movement, which had originated in Seneca Falls, New York. She was proud of her privilege to vote and use that privilege in the national elections. In the 1950s she wrote to President Dwight Eisenhower and informed him that she was praying for him as he led our country. A letter personally written and signed by Mamie Eisenhower was sent back. Carrie was always very active in the Loyal Temperance Union. She was in charge of youth meetings that were held in the church and the schools. She was involved in the "release time" classes for public school students. She conducted these classes, which were based on religious values and attended by students on a volunteer basis. Even after retirement in 1944, she was active in church work and continued her work with the Loyal Temperance Union and classes in the schools.

Both Merton and Carrie solved many problems in their lives and the lives of their children and grandchildren by prayer. Ivan Kellogg believes God spared his life during World War II when almost all his company was killed—because his grandmother was awakened from her sleep in the night and was urged to pray for him.

Carrie served as the pastor of the following New York churches: Taylor, Groton, Holland, Delevan and Manchia, Berrytown, Elmira, Hornley and Corning, Shady Grove, Riverside (now Victory Highway), Chambers, Westfield, Manfield and Amania Mountain, Belleville, and South Bradford. In some of these churches she was the assistant to Merton, and in others he was her assistant. She was the solo pastor at many of them. Merton died while they were pastoring the Odessa church, on February 22, 1944.[146]

Carrie and Merton Warburton left a legacy of obedience to God, models of prayer life, and giving their all to the disposal of God for His use. The pattern left impressions on their children, grand-children, and great-grandchildren as they have followed God in Christian education, ministry, local church work, and foreign mission fields.

Maude White

Maude White was converted and joined the Wesleyan Methodist Church in Mechanicsburg, Pennsylvania, on November 25, 1905. She was granted a license to preach by the following spring. She had held four revivals in Meigo County, Ohio, and fifty persons were saved. She held meetings at three different points, conducting three Sunday schools and three prayer meetings in each place.[147]

In 1909 she was under appointment in the Ohio Conference and was assigned the pastorate at White's Chapel. She had previously aided in the building of this chapel, located at Coolville, Ohio. The chapel was named in honor of her family.

Much of the time she was engaged in evangel-istic work. In 1942 she was ordained by the Ohio Conference. Her death occurred March 16, 1947.[148]

Belle Bradt Burns

Paul Pierpoint in his *The Pentecostal Rescue Mission,* a mimeographed booklet celebrating seventy-five years of the Pilgrim Holiness Church in New York, recorded that Belle Bradt, an ordained minister, was pastor of the Albany Rescue Mission from 1910 to 1913. She was probably the first pastor after the mission became a church.

She was stationed at Schenectady as pastor in 1914–15. She married Mr. Burns (first name unknown), who was also a minister, during this time. She preached in Brooky Hollow mission for a time. She also served for a time in Pittsfield, Massachusetts, and Allentown, Pennsylvania.

The last record of her service was in 1920, when she was in the West Indies.[149]

Vernelia Happy Dennison Carry

Vernelia Dennison met Earl J. Carry in 1903 at the Bible college in Eskridge, Kansas (a school maintained for a short time by the Kansas Conference of the Wesleyan Methodist Church).[150] They were married in 1911. Their ministerial duties began immediately. She was ordained by the Kansas Conference. Vernelia was the mother of two children, Gerald Carry and Rosalee (Mrs. Ronald) Brannon. Earl J. Carry died November 4, 1967.[151]

Rosalee relates her mother's story as follows:

Mother and father were two distinct personalities, but I can picture them only as a team. They met as students at Eskridge Bible College. Much of their passion for ministry was influ-enced by the French influence on Eskridge Bible College. Daddy had been converted from a Roman Catholic back-ground. Mother's mother was fiercely independ-ent in a Protestant fundamental style. Her mother operated an independent orphanage in Missouri. Daddy was from Oklahoma, and Mother was from Missouri. They were fully supportive of each other, and each of their ministries comple-mented the other's.

For a period of time (1943–1950) Daddy trav-eled full-time as vice president of the Kansas Conference. His assignment was to locate promis-ing situations, lay groundwork, and begin ministries before turning the fledgling work to a more perma-nent pastor. Those labors included the initial begin-nings for what today is Scott City, Missouri, Wesleyan Church; Mountain View (Colorado Springs); a church in St. Louis, that could be today's Restoration Word Church; and another one that did not fare so well. Also, while pastoring at Kansas City First Church, they guided that group in the "mothering" process, which resulted in the development of Kansas City Immanuel, which recently merged with Overland Park.

Mother was fervent in her commitment and practice of prayer. Family devotions were a constant at our house. It was not uncommon to arrive home to discover the window blinds drawn and mother seated flat on the floor in the burden of prayer_with evidence she had devoted the entire day to such discipline. Home visitation, which included praying for the sick, was a prominent part of her/their ministry. She and Daddy alternated (frequently) in the leadership of prayer services. While she taught Sunday school classes in many settings after their ministries began, perhaps her classes of college-age young ladies during the eight years Daddy pastored the college church in Miltonvale, Kansas, were the most impacting. Recently Mrs. Loretta (Charles) Wilson voluntarily expressed appreciation for the value of the insights gained during some of those years.

Mother was intensely engaged in evangelism. Her role was seldom that of the preaching evangelist. However, she ministered as song leader and/or soloist. She loved music and was at her happiest when serving in that capacity. She had a strong soprano voice.

Mother believed that shouting was one way the Holy Spirit manifested Himself in such services. She "practiced what she believed," so it was not uncommon to witness mother, white hanky waving aloft, expressing her joy in the Lord.

Mother was fervent in her labors as an altar counselor and in the ministry of intercessory prayer. She was explicit in her instructions to "repent" (to those seeking salvation) or to "die out" (to those seeking sanctification).

The places for evangelistic labors were in church buildings or tents. Pay for the evangelist was never an issue, nor was the comfort of the housing accommodations. Even "advanced bookings" were not of major importance. I remember once we were vacationing in the Arkansas Ozarks when a pastor found out about my folks and asked them, on the spur of the moment, to conduct a revival meeting. We spent the next week with mother leading the singing and singing specials (I accompanied at the piano) while Daddy did the preaching.

Mother seldom knew a stranger. Her ability to engage others in discussion, along with her incisive ability to get quickly to the point of need, brought many persons to acknowledge their spiritual hungerings. She loved the outdoors with animal life and her flower beds, and she used those loves as a bridge to other people. She was famous for her fried chicken and fruit cobblers. The hospitality of her home was used as a tool for ministry.

Mother's preaching occurred primarily in the churches where daddy pastored and was occasioned by his absence for other ministries. Her style was exhortatory and was both evangelistic and didactic. Her most frequent themes would be holiness, prayer, faith/healing, and the authority of the Word.

My parents devoted nearly all of their adult lives in ministries to assignments in Kansas, which included Miltonvale, Salina, Ottawa, Abilene, Kansas City, and Eskridge. In addition, they served a short time as pastors in Los Angeles, California. One of my most testing childhood experiences took place in Los Angeles. As a lover of things beautiful, I yearned to see the Rose Parade. As a lover of holiness, Mother insisted that we all attend the New Year's Day County Holiness Association meeting, where my brother and I would be the only children. Mother won out. I might still be struggling to accept that decision had Daddy not had compassion and taken my brother and me to see the wilting floats after the parade and after the holiness meeting ended.

Mrs. Josiah (Leah) Smith (Kansas City) attributes her very life to the prayers of my mother and father. She was critically ill, and many despaired for her life. My parents were called. They anointed her and prayed for her healing. God answered in a rapid and dramatic way. During the years my folks served the College Church in Miltonvale, Kansas, the village was served by one medical doctor. Dr. Kimball was noted for his crusty personality and seeming disrespect for the Christians in the community. It was reported that at the restaurant one day he announced for all to hear that he was disgusted with that Wesleyan preacher and his wife. When asked what they had done, he explained they were ruining his reputation. He said. "Every time someone on College Hill gets really sick and I announce that they're going to die, someone calls that preacher and his wife. They pray for them, and the sick get well. They're ruining my reputation."

My parents traveled almost exclusively by car. Had they not been a team, this might have been forcefully changed because mother never learned to drive. She always occupied the passenger seat. We were not strangers to mechanical delays as daddy sought remedies for those old cars. We had our share of flat tires, especially during the Depression and World War II years. The cars had inadequate heaters, and rather than glass windows, the frigid Kansas winds were kept out (partially) by isinglass. In spite of difficulties and discomforts in travel and the dust and Depression of the 30s, I have no recall of mother ever murmuring or complaining. She counted it a joy to serve the Lord and to labor in His kingdom.

Mother had a love and heart for young people. While they would not likely be listed as "her converts," she certainly discipled scores of college students who were in her Sunday school class or who would come to the home for counsel and prayer.

Among those greatly influenced by her/their ministry were Mr. And Mrs. Ira Cox at Langley, Kansas, and later at Miltonvale, Kansas. As I recall, the Coxes were Christians when my parents first met them. As several younger children were born into this home, however, my parents continued to pastor the family and minister to each of the children. While several of the Cox family would possibly name my mother and father as being instrumental in their conversions, I think particularly of Martin. He and my brother were the same age and were close buddies. Martin was a frequent guest at our home, where mother tutored, encouraged, counseled, and guided both of them to be surrendered to God.

Another convert of my parents' early years was a man named Ross Mahin. Under their combined ministries, he was saved, sanctified, and ultimately called to preach. His family members also came to know the Lord. One of his daughters was Leila, who became the bride of Martin Cox, and in later years, the widowed Leila married Dr. Leo G. Cox.

It is difficult to "sort it all out" and know where mother's influence began and where daddy's entered in. They have given me a great and godly heritage. It has been a stabilizer throughout my life. I am grateful.

Leota Clark

Leota Clark was converted at Stone's Crossing, Indiana, in 1898. She was sanctified in 1910 and preached her first sermon that year at Ray Street Mission. She joined the International Apostolic Holiness Church in Indiana in 1916.

This group became the International Holiness Church in 1919, and when it merged with the Pilgrim Church in 1922, it took the name of "Pilgrim Holiness Church." Leota was granted a license to preach in 1916. Some time later she was ordained at God's Bible School in Cincinnati.

With her husband, Elmer, she pastored churches in Bluffton, Forrest, Orleans, and Seymour. All these churches were in Indiana. Several churches were started during their ministry because of their evangelistic labors. Most of her twenty-five years of ministerial work was in the field of evangelism.

Leota entered her heavenly rest in 1957.[152]

Ina Doty

Ina Doty is first mentioned in the records of the Kansas Conference of the Wesleyan Methodist Church in 1910. She was a licensed minister at that time and served with her husband, George H., as pastor of the Hollis Church. She was granted a letter of transfer to the Iowa Conference on January 13, 1914.

During her stay in the Iowa Conference, they pastored jointly the Albaton, Bethel, and Pleasant Hill churches. They were assigned to the Pleasant Hill Church in 1919 but did not complete the conference year. In 1920 they were residing in Atlanta and were engaged as general evangelists.

They were granted letters of transfer to the Alabama Conference during the conference session in 1921. No record was found of her labors in the Alabama Conference nor of the date when she was ordained. She was listed as an ordained minister in 1942.

Her husband died in 1942. She was then a member of the South Georgia Conference and served as pastor of the Tifton, Crossroads, Ashburn, and Mt. Pleasant charge after his death.

Ina was active in the South Georgia Conference until it merged with the North Georgia Conference to form the Georgia Conference in 1959. At that time she was listed as superannuated (retired). She served faithfully on the conference camp meeting and moral reform committees and was also the district Sunday school secretary for a time. Ina served as president of the conference Woman's Home and Foreign Missionary Society for several years. She was still listed as superannuated in 1967.[153]

Lenora Pendell DeWaters Rolfe

Lenora Pendell was born July 11, 1862, during the Civil War. Her mother died within twenty-four hours of her birth. In a few weeks her father was forced into military service. He placed his baby daughter in the care of relatives. When she was eighteen months old she was placed in the home of an aunt and uncle. They were godly people, and she was reared under their godly influence.

Lenora was converted and sanctified by age seventeen at the Eaton Rapids (Michigan) Holiness Camp. At that time she felt called to preach, but she struggled with the call and did not accept the challenge. On August 16, 1881, at age nineteen, she married Fred W. DeWaters. A daughter and son were welcomed into their home. Her husband, Fred, died March 31, 1895. A little later her daughter died of typhoid at the age of fifteen. Her daughter's death revived the sense of God's call upon her, Lenora's, life. She began to study for the ministry under the Crusaders and worked under their ranks until they disbanded.

Later she joined the Wesleyan Methodist Church in the North Michigan Conference. After the conference session in 1910, she was appointed pastor of the Grant Church. She served as assistant pastor with L. C. Hawkins at the Melita and County Line churches. She also was the pastor of the Hobart and Mecosta churches. She completed the course of study while she was pastoring and was ordained in 1914.[154] She was involved in mission work in Cadillac, Michigan, and from this mission a Wesleyan Methodist Church was later organized, in July 1918.[155]

During the years she was pastoring, Lenora was active in the conference and served on many conference committees. She served as vice president of the Woman's Home and Foreign Missionary Society on the conference level also.

Lenora retired from the ministry, but soon afterward she met Lyman Rolfe. They were married August 1, 1920. Together they pastored the Cobmoosa charge for two years. For two years they walked the sand hills of that area. Lyman's health began to fail, and they were forced to retire. He died July 12, 1925.

After Lyman's death, Lenora moved to Lansing. Here she kept boarders and roomers until the Depression made it financially impossible for her to keep going. She was now seventy years old. Alone and penniless, she returned to Cadillac. At no time during her ministerial career did she receive more than $155 a year. When questioned about this, her reply was "I have no regrets. Some years I received nothing. I have sacrificed and toiled, but it has all been for the cause of Christ, who is precious to me."

Lenora DeWaters Rolfe died March 23, 1947.

Minnie Wilhelmina Beisner

The Brethren in Christ, under which Minnie Beisner served as an outstanding preacher, was a denomination with churches located in Ohio. Around 1917–18 a group split from this church and became the Pentecostal Brethren in Christ. The Pentecostal Brethren merged with the Pilgrim Holiness Church in 1924. The only *Minutes* available for these two groups were from 1908–23, and they are very incomplete.

Minnie became listed as "Wilhelmina" in 1918, but she was actively involved long before this time. She gave her report at conference in 1909 as a worker at the Lighthouse Mission in Dayton, Ohio. Each following year, her reports were full of meetings, pastoral calls and visitations, works of compassion, and prison ministry.

She conducted children's meetings and reported that many were saved and sanctified. Her compassionate ministry included caring for the sick—Brother G. W. Tevis's wife for nine weeks and Miss Charlotte Chapman for two months. During this time of caring for Miss Chapman, she saw her wonderfully healed. She was a coworker of G. W. Tevis in tent and revival meetings. These meetings lasted from two to six weeks. Miss Chapman was a coworker in mission work with Minnie.

In the 1910 session, the conference gave Minnie a fifty-dollar "subscription to be raised in fifteen days" to start a new mission on the west side of Dayton. She was to be the superintendent. She opened that mission, Star of Hope, November 1, 1910. Her report the following year revealed that all the mission needs had been met, the rent paid, and two revivals held. Many had been saved and sanctified. She was conducting Sunday school each Sunday afternoon and was helping the needy by giving clothing to them. Charlotte Chapman and Emma McQuay were workers with her in this venture.

No task was too menial for Minnie. She spent about seven months at Eliado Orphanage in Asheville, North Carolina. All but one month was spent as a cook for the orphanage, the other month working in the laundry. But doing menial work did not stop her from doing personal work on a one-on-one basis.

While attending school in Greensboro, North Carolina, from 1915 to 1917, she conducted street and mission meetings and did prison work. After school, she was the matron of the Rest Cottage Rescue Home. Her work also included preaching to the chain gang prisoners on Sunday afternoon during the summer months. During this time she also spent several weeks in Virginia conducting revival services. She served as the preacher in these meetings.

Minnie usually preached at the ministerial meeting just before conference. She was elected secretary of the conference in 1917 and continued in that office until 1923, after which records are no longer available. On June 5, 1917, she took charge of the Samaria Rescue Home in Springfield, Ohio. Apparently this was a home for wayward girls. She conducted prayer meetings and Bible study classes and preached. That year she received $18.67.

The year of 1917 was a special one for her. She was ordained after camp meeting at conference time.

In 1918 she became listed as Wilhelmina Beisner. She spent three months in evangelistic and pastoral work in Pennsylvania, helped in a revival at

Sugar Grove and in a camp meeting at Bainbridge, Ohio, and preached in several churches. She always conducted children's meetings whenever she was engaged in revivals. She was the pastor at West Harmony for at least three years.

In 1922 Minnie helped Miss Atrim with office work in Indianapolis, Indiana. She returned to Springfield, Ohio, and continued in mission and revival work as well as hospital visitation and singing.[156]

Louella Teague Gallimore

Louella Teague was born June 7, 1883, in Climax, North Carolina. She married William Stephen Gallimore and was the mother of four sons.

Louella was converted under Seth C. Rees and Charles F. Weigle in Greensboro, North Carolina. She attended God's Bible School and received instruction there from Seth Rees, George Kulp, and other leaders. In 1907–08 she attended Greensboro Bible School.

She was one of the first workers to help plant the Pilgrim Holiness Church in North Carolina. She was known as a flaming soul with a burning message. She spent much time in revival work. She played the organ for great evangelists like Fred Deweerd, Sam Nelson, Daniel Hodgin, and Dinna Reynold Bean. She was a charter member of the first Pilgrim Holiness church in Greensboro. The first Pilgrim Holiness church established in Greensboro was among the first in the entire state. She was ordained by the North Carolina District and traveled over the district and elsewhere doing whatever she could to help.

She worked at Kernersville, the location of Pilgrim Bible College (later merged into United Wesleyan College, Allentown, Pennsylvania). She gave unselfishly of her time and means to help young students both financially and in the use of their talents. She often obtained places for the students to serve in the Church, especially those attending Greensboro Bible College.

Her husband was not active in the ministry, but he gave financially in order to carry on the work.

Louella was a woman with a radiant face. She lived a spotless life and possessed a beautiful spirit that manifested kindness and sympathy. She had uncompromising convictions but always displayed a gentle spirit.[157]

Sallie Gordon Hanks

W. W. Hanks was an ordained minister from Willard, Kentucky. He began his ministry under the International Apostolic Holiness Union of Kentucky. He was first married to Sally (Sallie) Hampton. She "died long ago," according to the records. He later married Mrs. Sallie (Sally) Gordon. This Sallie Hanks began to be listed among the ordained ministers of the Kentucky District of the Pilgrim Holiness Church in 1945. Sallie served as an evangelist for many years and co-pastored with W. W. Hanks at Ashland Heights, Willard, and Maysville.[158]

Bessie Jones Mitchell

Bessie Mitchell was a committed soul with a very limited education, no theological training, and a physical body that experienced great pain and suffering. She suffered with epilepsy from the time she was twenty until her death. This illness did not prevent her active participation in ministry as an evangelist and pastor.

She was a dynamic minister of the Word. She was enabled by God's help to grasp and express biblical truths and spiritual insights in a marvelous way. Bessie lived in the Word. When she was to preach, she would take her Bible and retreat to the woods, the barn, or her bedroom and ask God to give her a message. She fed on the Word until she was "so full" she had to share the Word with others. Her son, Roland, has scores of her outlines of sermons that reveal a grasp of biblical truth and Christian experience that is amazing.

Bessie's parents were not church-going people, and the nine Jones children seldom attended Sunday school. She felt the convicting power of the Holy Spirit moving on her heart in the Henderson Methodist Church during a revival meeting. But the conviction became so heavy at school during an arithmetic class that she burst into tears. She determined that she would go to the altar, just like the big folks, that night if she were allowed to go to church. She followed through on her decision and was gloriously saved that night. She stood, shouted, and praised God for deliverance from sin. Later her mother warned her about her shouting and praising God in church with a threat that if she didn't stop, she would be forbidden to go to church. She was obedient to her parents' desire but lost her joy and love. She began to wander off with her worldly friends.

Bessie had tasted the good things of the Lord, and even though she was drifting along with a worldly crowd, she was never satisfied and longed for the joy and love she had experienced as a child of nine years of age. At the age of seventeen she had her mother's consent to attend the fourth annual camp meeting of Denton Camp in Denton, Maryland. Bessie enjoyed the preaching, and on July 27, 1901, she again sought the Lord and prayed until she had prayed through. She believed at the time she was sanctified.

Before she returned home, she knew God wanted her to say grace (return thanks) before each meal at home and to establish a family altar time even though her family was unsaved. When she asked permission, her mother granted her that privilege. One day her parents purchased a Bible for her. Years later, her mother could confess that the Bible was bought for her because her father believed she would "tear the family Bible up" since she was always reading and studying the large family Bible. It was the only Bible in the home, and she hungered to know more about what was in it. The Bible was her favorite book, and she spent much time in reading it and praying.

Bessie began attending the Holiness Mission in the town of Henderson. Here she heard the holiness message preached and saw it lived out in the lives of these people. A month after her experience at Denton Camp, while scrubbing clothes on an old-fashioned washboard, she felt convicted to receive the blessing of sanctification. She immediately went to her bedroom and consecrated herself to God. He cleansed her heart and sanctified her. The Holy Spirit now reigned supremely in her life. Her eyes fell upon the passage of Ps. 32:8—"I will instruct thee and teach thee in the way which thou shalt go: I will guide thee with mine eye" (KJV). At once she felt called to preach. God used that verse to make her aware that He would instruct her on how to preach and where to go to preach, and He would take care of her while she traveled to these places. She wrote, "I was no longer my own; I belonged to the One who died for me."

The people at the mission saw God's call was upon her, and they often asked her to take charge of the services. Since she had no theological or Bible school training, she depended entirely upon God to instruct her. He gave her the messages to preach.

Doors began to open for Bessie to preach locally in the mission and in tent meetings. Her first revival was held in Weatherly, Pennsylvania, in a Holiness Christian church. She traveled there by train and spent six months in Pennsylvania holding meetings in several different places. The holiness message was not popular, and preaching that message brought persecution and reproach.

After she returned home, calls came to hold meetings along the east side of the Chesapeake Bay (Virginia, Maryland, and Delaware). She conducted revivals in most of the Pilgrim Holiness churches in that region. Many of these churches did not have church buildings. Some of her contemporary women preachers/workers in the area at that time were Etta Gibson (Hoffman), Bertha Haymond (Pitcher), Mary Brown (Olsen), Ethel Brown (Roser) and Cora Downes (Boyer). During her evangelistic days she was instrumental in starting several churches. She held meetings at Tilghman's Island, Wachapreague, Virginia; Georgetown and Harrington, Delaware; Salisbury and Denton, Maryland; and Bridgeville, Delaware. The tent meeting at Bridgeville resulted in the planting of the Epworth Methodist Church. She traveled for six years in evangelistic work.

Bessie Jones was born April 15, 1884, near Henderson, Maryland. She was the second of nine children born into the Jones home. She became the mother of three children: Etta, Roland, and Russell. Each of them was dedicated to the Lord by George B. Kulp, and all three became ministers of the gospel. Each of her eight grandchildren have been active in their local churches. Three granddaughters married ministers.

One granddaughter is the wife of one of the general superintendents of The Wesleyan Church. One great-grandson prepared for missionary service, and another great-grandson is preparing for the ministry.

Bessie married Willard Mitchell January 9, 1907. Willard was one of the early holiness leaders of the district. He was for years the president of the Denton Holiness Association, which later became the Eastern District Pilgrim Holiness Camp.

She was ordained July 26, 1919. Signatures on her ordination parchment were those of George B. Kulp, Charles Cowman, G. E. Helsly, and Oswald Chambers.

Bessie and Willard became a ministerial team. They pastored together at the Hillsboro, Maryland, church for nine years. Each Sunday afternoon they traveled to Harrington, Delaware, for church services. They pastored this church also for the same nine years.

Some people were meeting in a rented hall on the third floor, over a feed store in Dover, Delaware. This group asked the Mitchells to come for a revival. They conducted the revival, and that meeting was the beginning of the Pilgrim Holiness Church in the capital city of Delaware. After the meeting they went back to Dover each Thursday and Sunday evenings for services. Their schedule now called for a morning service at Hillsboro, an afternoon service at Harrington, and an evening service at Dover. They drove the "Model T" Ford about 100 miles each Sunday to meet this schedule. After one year of this routine the Mitchells moved to Dover (1916). The church changed locations several times, but the church was organized with nine charter members while they were pastors. They pastored there for seven years before Bessie's ill health forced them to resign. Over forty full-time Christian workers had come from this church by 1960.

Willard died in 1933. Bessie's health was better by that time, and she assisted her daughter, Etta, in pastorates at Gridletree, Maryland, and Cape Charles, Virginia. Again her health forced her to cease active church work.

Since she had had such a wonderful, convicting, and saving experience as a child at age nine, she felt compelled to take the message of salvation to children. She conducted children's services at the Denton Camp for many years and wrote letters of encouragement to all those who accepted Christ as their Savior in those meetings.

Bessie Mitchell came to love Denton Camp. It was here she was saved, received light on holiness, and was ordained. Here she conducted children's meetings, and several outstanding future ministers and leaders sought and found the Lord under her ministry. She attended every camp from age seventeen until her death, July 12, 1960, except four, and these she missed only because of illness.[159]

Nora L. Andrews

R. L. and Nora Andrews were received into the North Carolina Conference of the Wesleyan Methodist Church in 1911. At one point R. L. left the conference for another church home, but Nora stayed on as a faithful member of the conference. R. L. later returned to the conference to serve with his wife as a ministerial team again.[160]

The Liberty Wesleyan Church of Summerfield, North Carolina, was organized in 1911. Nora was the pastor of this young church in 1911 and 1912. She traveled alone by horse and buggy from Greensboro to Summerfield about fifteen or twenty miles. She had to travel by dirt road and ford both Reedy Fork and Haw River to reach Liberty Church.

Bales Memorial Wesleyan Church was also organized in 1911. Nora was appointed pastor of this church in 1912. At the 1913 conference she was again appointed pastor of the Liberty Church; she was joined that year by her husband, R. L. Andrews.

Both of them were assigned to the High Point, Hickory Chapel, and Providence churches in 1915–16. She was the pastor of Eden First Church in 1919.[161]

The Conference *Minutes* listed Nora as an ordained minister on the retired list in 1936. She was also listed as an evangelist that year. But in 1938 she was listed as retired and was so listed until 1946. Nora died in 1947.[162]

Jennie Reid Clawson

While teaching at Central Holiness University, in Oskaloosa, Iowa, Joseph B. (J. B.) and Jennie Reid Clawson, along with three other families, became enthusiastic about buying land in northern Wisconsin at Stone Lake to do pioneer church work.[163] They agreed to start a Wesleyan Methodist church there. The first Sunday they conducted services in the pine grove on their land. Their first convert was a woman who had kept a saloon for many years. In 1911 J. B. and Jennie were appointed pastors of the newly organized Stone Lake Church. As they began to branch out, J. B. Clawson preached in seven different places, mostly in the surrounding schoolhouses, while Jennie taught in the Stone Lake School and preached in the churches. They walked to all their places of worship. There she realized the joys, sorrows, and sacrifices of a pioneer pastor. Jennie was ordained by the Wisconsin Conference of the Wesleyan Methodist Church in 1915. In 1916 a church of seventeen members was organized at Stanberry and was added to the Stone Lake circuit.

J. B. was elected president of the Wisconsin Conference in 1917 and held this office until 1945. While he carried out his responsibilities as conference president, Jennie cared for the home and their two adopted children, Andrew and Norma, as well as pastoring eight churches during this time. She served with her husband at Stone Lake and Stanberry 1911–18. She pastored Burr-Valley 1920–24. During this pastorate a church building was built, in 1922. The Beulah church was organized August 26, 1924, as a result of a tent meeting. She was the first pastor. The first service was held in a home. There were twenty-four members, and at least half of them were women. Jennie served the Valton church two times, 1926–29 and again in 1935–38. She pastored Baraboo 1929–35, Hayward 1938–40, Rice Lake 1940–49, and Spooner 1949–53.[164]

Jennie was a teacher of rare and unusual ability, a student of the Word, and a scholar of life. She was a counselor, a friend, and an intercessor and knew the power of prayer. She was a loving mother and a homebuilder. She was a spiritual leader to a vast number of people whom she contacted in her broad fields of activity.

Her interests were many and varied. From the time of its organization in 1919 until 1945, she was president of the Woman's Home and Foreign Missionary Society of the Wisconsin Conference.

Jennie played a great part in organizing the Wisconsin Conference Camp Meeting Association. Much of her time was also given in assisting and encouraging ministers of the conference on the course of study. For many years she taught in the Ministers' Institute.

Jennie Clawson was born in Jewell, Ohio, July 29, 1877. The family moved to Kansas during her childhood. After graduating from the University of Kansas (with honors), she taught in the Wesleyan Methodist School at Eskridge, Kansas. While teaching here, she found God dealing with her heart, and she began realizing her need of a personal experience of salvation. She was converted under the ministry of Rev. Ira Bradley. Later, while still teaching at Eskridge, she was sanctified under the preaching of Beverly Carradine.

From Eskridge she went to teach English at Houghton College, in Houghton, New York. While teaching there, she met and married Joseph B. Clawson, one of her students, on June 13, 1906.

Leaving Houghton, the couple moved to Oskaloosa, Iowa, where she became one of the members of the teaching staff at Central Holiness University. While there, she was mightily used of God as an instrument in the ushering in of a gracious revival that will always be remembered in the history of the school.

Throughout these years of teaching, God was preparing Jennie for the pioneer work and pastoring in Wisconsin. She had the ability to work effectively with all ages. The young and old were captivated by her storytelling.

Although her health was failing, she carried on a ministry with the youth of the church. She weekly conducted a good-size class of high school students who chose to attend the released-time Bible class. She taught her last class just four days before she went to be with the Lord, January 17, 1953.

A few hours before her death she asked her husband to read John 14 to her. After the reading

she said with such adoration, "Isn't it wonderful!" Soon she entered into His presence and the place prepared for her.

Mrs. Gertrude David

Gertrude Davis served in Indiana under the International Apostolic Holiness Church from 1911 to 1919 and under the International Holiness Church from 1920 to 1922. When that body merged with the Pilgrim Church and the merged body took the name of Pilgrim Holiness Church, she served under the Pilgrim Holiness Church in Indiana from 1923 to 1935. She and her husband, Earl E., were missionaries to Natal, South Africa. She lived a useful life. Gertrude was known for her faithfulness and sacrifices. She died in 1935.[165]

Mrs. Hattie Dunkleburger Dilk

Hattie Dunkleburger Dilk was born March 26, 1888 and was converted at age seventeen. She attended God's Bible School in Cincinnati, and for a number of years she and her sister Katherine (Inman) traveled in evangelistic work. They both preached and sang. Hattie was ordained in 1913 by the Indiana Conference of the Holiness Christian Church.

She pastored the New Carlisle, Medora, and Oaktown churches in Indiana. She was a delegate to the General Assembly of the Pilgrim Holiness Church in 1924.

Hattie died September 9, 1963, at her home in North Vernon, Indiana.[166]

Ella E. Shaw Ewers

Ella E. Shaw was born in Bunkerhill, Michigan, November 9, 1872. She lived there until she was eighteen years old. On October 2, 1889, she married a minister, E. F. Ewers. They became the parents of three children.

Ella and E. F. served under the direction of the International Holiness Church Michigan District, Indiana Conference of the Holiness Christian

Church, Michigan District Pilgrim Holiness Church, and East Michigan District Pilgrim Holiness Church. Both were ordained ministers.

E. F. Ewers was for many years associated with Bible Holiness Seminary of Owosso, Michigan, which later became Owosso College (later merged into what became Indiana Wesleyan University, Marion, Indiana). During this time they became the first pastors of what later became the Pilgrim Holiness Church in Owosso. The church was started in 1911, and they pastored there until 1917.

The couple pastored together for forty-eight years. Some of the churches they served were Phelps, Ellsworth, Owosso, First and Second Churches in Detroit, Jeddo, Jackson, Durand, Pontiac and Pigeon, all in Michigan. They also served churches in Indiana and New York.

E. F. Ewers died November 3, 1950. They had observed their sixty-first wedding anniversary the previous month, October.

One year Ella's report to conference revealed that she had conducted twenty prayer meetings, preached forty times, made 262 calls, had eight seekers at her altars, and seen eight healings that year in her work. That year she was on the unstationed list!

Ella served for many years on the memorial committee. She was faithful in all her duties and strongly adhered to the old-fashioned way. She died in 1957.[167]

Oneida Jane McMillen Gleason

Oneida Jane McMillen was born December 5, 1888. Her father, John, was a country doctor, and her mother, Mary, was an accomplished musician. Mary was a second cousin of United States President James Buchanan. Mary died in 1894, leaving Donald, age twelve, and Oneida, age six. In time Dr. McMillen married a widow who also had two living children. Together they had three more children: Sim, Lois, and Albert. Soon after Oneida completed normal school and received a certificate to teach, she felt a call to the ministry. Her doctor father was adamantly opposed to her answering this call. He not only

refused to take her and her heavy luggage to the train to go to New York, but he stood on the porch as she left, shouting, "And if you die up there, tell them not to bother to send your body home." As Sim, Oneida's younger half-brother, watched her departure, he determined to find the God his sister knew and served. He became Dr. S. I. McMillen, who served under the Wesleyan Methodist Church in Sierra Leone and in later years became the Houghton College doctor and a noted author.

After Oneida's arrival in New York state, she was asked to keep house for and nurse Rev. Sarah E. Shultz, who was then pastor of Lynndon Park Wesleyan Methodist Church in Falconer, New York. In September 1911, when a change of climate became necessary owing to the physical breakdown of Sarah Shultz, Oneida was appointed supply pastor for the remaining months of the conference year. In the spring of 1912 she was given a unanimous call to become the regular pastor and for fourteen consecutive years served in that capacity. February 3, 1924, during her ministry there a new sanctuary on the other side of town was dedicated. Oneida continued to serve as pastor of this group. From this group Misses Grace and Stella Wood were sent to India, and ten ministers and five ministers' wives went into full-time service. At the time of the dedication of the new church, three young people were training for Christian service: Hazel Jones, one of Oneida's converts, who would soon go to India, was training as a nurse in Geneva, New York; Sigrid Stein was at Houghton College preparing for work in Africa; and Sim I. McMillen was studying medicine in the University of Pennsylvania preparatory to entering medical missionary work in Sierra Leone, West Africa.

Oneida McMillen met Rufus Gleason when he came to hold evangelistic meetings for the Falconer church. They were married May 6, 1925. They traveled the country ministering in churches and tent meetings—and one night when she was preaching, her father gave his heart and life to the Lord. In February 1926 their daughter, Helen, was born. Thereafter Oneida served pastorates, one of which was the Second Church in Central, South Carolina.

Before her marriage she had pastored the Lynndon Park Church in Falconer, New York, from 1911 to 1925. During this time she also served the Ashville church from 1917 to 1920. After her marriage, she and her husband went to the Cateechee, (Central Second Church), South Carolina. This church later became Trinity Church in Central, South Carolina. They spent one year here, and then she went into evangelistic work. From 1929 to 1936, they pastored Canton First. Oneida was the founding pastor of Pittsburgh First, 1944–45. Her next pastorate was Akron, Ohio, Grace Church, from 1948 to 1958. The Oneida Gleason Memorial Church in Salem, Ohio, was her next pastorate, 1958–67.

By the time Helen was three years old, Rufus had a prolapsed stomach due to carrying heavy book-laden suitcases on and off trains while en route to and from evangelistic meetings. He was also suffering from severe stomach ulcers. In 1929 he and Oneida accepted a call to be joint pastors of the First Wesleyan Methodist Church in Canton, Ohio. They served in that capacity for seven years, although Rufus spent months at a time convalescing at the ten-acre farm near Chatauqua Lake, which he and Oneida owned. During this period they bought a big tent and held camp meeting on their property every summer. Oneida cleaned, painted, papered, and refinished countless pieces of secondhand furniture to prepare accommodations in their old farmhouse for evangelists and workers.

When Helen was five, Rufus took over the pastoral duties two months while Oneida and Helen visited conference churches in deputation work (home ministries) with Dr. and Mrs. S. I. McMillen, returned missionaries serving Sierra Leone, West Africa. Oneida was conference president of the Woman's Home and Foreign Missionary Society (WH&FMS) at that time. Throughout her life Oneida lived and breathed missions and youth ministry. She gave thirteen years of capable and excellent leadership as president of the WH&FMS of the Allegheny Conference of the Wesleyan Methodist Church. She was missionary delegate to General Conference in 1931. In an article entitled "Fifty Years in Panorama" Oneida writes,

Tender memories are aroused when we recall that January 1, 1906, less than three months after beginning her second term on the African field, the brilliant life of our own Marie Stephens was snuffed out by blackwater fever. Can it be that this incident was the "corn of wheat" which fell into an African grave to bring into being our conference society, which was organized later that year?

The report continues with details of the launching of missionary work in India in 1910 and in Japan in 1918 and concludes with this paragraph:

This consuming passion for souls stands out as a mighty, impelling force coloring the entire picture of our progress. It is the answer to more than thirty-five of our sons and daughters having given service in Africa, India, Japan, China, South America, Haiti, and Puerto Rico. These with the large number in home fields help to make up the panorama of our fifty years of progress.

While the Gleasons were still co-pastors of Canton First Wesleyan Methodist Church, Oneida served as superintendent of Bethshan Home, a home for unwed mothers. She would put Helen in the car with her and travel, usually late at night, to neighborhoods that were sometimes fraught with danger, to pick up unwed mothers. She counseled both women and staff and directed all activities of the home. She served on the Board of Mangers of Bethshan for twenty years.

In 1936 Rufus and Oneida resigned as co-pastors of Canton First Wesleyan Methodist Church. Rufus's health had deteriorated so badly that he was forced to retire to their ten-acre property near Chatauqua Lake, and Oneida went into evangelism.

Oneida was the first president of the Allegheny Wesleyan Methodist Youth. She served from 1932 to 1947. She also was superintendent of the young people at Stoneboro Camp from 1934 to 1960. As superintendent, she preached each morning of camp, led story hour each afternoon on the playground with the children, led a daily 6:00 P.M. young people's prayer group, led the Saturday evening ring meeting, and originated and remained in charge of the Hallelujah March. The Hallelujah March occurred on the last night of Stoneboro Camp, starting after the last seeker had gotten victory at the altar. Campers lined up around the wall of the tabernacle and shook hands with other campers as they filed past. It was a time for remembering and thanking God for friends and spiritual victories. Oneida Gleason became a confidant and friend to hundreds of youth and their parents. When she walked across the campgrounds, she was stopped every few feet and asked for counsel. She was youth evangelist at Stoneboro Camp (Allegheny), West Chazy (Champlain), and Victory Camp (Ohio). Each year she had a main theme for her series of camp meeting messages. She held revival meetings for Houghton College during the school year. Because she was so well known, her evangelistic slate was always full.

Oneida served as pioneer secretary for the Allegheny Conference of the Wesleyan Methodist Church from 1940 to 1946. The job entailed selecting places to start and establish new churches and supervising the pastors who were sent as permanent workers. Marjean Bennett Dayton traveled with her for a time as song leader. The church congregations were extremely poor financially. She often stayed with the people in their homes until she could get a nucleus for a church and a pastor. She lived in a one-room apartment in 1944–45 while she planted and established the Wesleyan Methodist Church in Pittsburgh. She also built and pastored Akron Grace Wesleyan Methodist Church (1948–58). In 1958 she moved to Salem, Ohio, the location of Allegheny Wesleyan Methodist College. Here she founded, built, and pastored a new church. This group of people honored her by naming the new church Oneida Gleason Memorial. She left Salem in 1967 and moved to New York state, where she realized a lifelong dream of acting as housemother for her twin grandsons while they were at Houghton College. "No greater love" could be used to describe Oneida's love for her daughter, Helen, and her grandchildren.

Oneida Gleason gave almost sixty-three years of service to the Lord. Most of those years were served in the Allegheny Conference. She was ordained at Canton, Ohio, on March 19, 1922. Seven years were spent in the Lockport Conference. She served on many conference committees and boards.

She had a miraculous healing from cancer. The doctor gave her less than six months to live. But God wonderfully healed her, and she lived over thirty-five years longer. During the last fifteen months of her life she was instrumental in giving comfort to a family whose house burned to the ground, and just one week before her death she led an unchurched woman to the Lord. After almost eighty-six full years, Oneida Gleason departed to be with her Lord on October 19, 1974. The epitaph on her tombstone summarizes her life of devotion. It simply says, "God's chosen vessel."[168]

Katherine Edith Dunkleburger Inman

Katherine "Katie" Edith Dunkelburger was born in Three Oaks, Michigan. She was converted in early life. She and her sister, Hattie Dunkleburger (Dilk) entered evangelistic work. They traveled, sang and preached. Katie married Richard D. Inman in 1923. She pastored the Michigan City, Indiana, church for two years; Sandford for one year, and Seeleyville for four years. She again entered into evangelistic work. Katie died June 13, 1950.

Katie was ordained in 1913 by the Indiana Conference of the Holiness Christian Church. She served under their direction from 1911 to 1919. When that group merged with the International Apostolic Holiness Church to form the International Holiness Church, she worked for them from 1920 to 1922. After their merger with the Pilgrim Church to form the Pilgrim Holiness Church, she served with the Indiana District of the Pilgrim Holiness Church.[169]

Ora Turner

Ora Turner and her husband, E. E. Turner, were the pastors of the Amboy, Indiana, Wesleyan Methodist Church in 1911. She was ordained in 1912. In 1914 and 1915 she was involved in college work at Olivet in Illinois. She was granted a letter of standing in 1916.[170]

Deborah Wharton

Deborah Wharton was listed in the 1911–15 *Minutes of the Indiana Annual Conference Holiness Christian Church.* In 1923–24, according to the *Minutes of the Annual Assembly of the Illinois and Missouri District Pilgrim Holiness Church,* she served in that district. She returned to Indiana in 1925. She was listed in the *Minutes of the Annual Assembly of the Pilgrim Holiness Church Indiana Conference* from 1925 to 1934 and 1949 to 1950. She moved to the Michigan District, according to the *Minutes of the Annual Assembly of the Michigan District Pilgrim Holiness* Church, and served there from 1934 to 1948. Her 1936 report of her evangelistic work revealed she had made seven hundred pastoral calls, prayed in three hundred homes, and had twenty-eight seekers that year. When the Indiana District was divided in 1951, she was listed in the *Minutes of the Annual Conference of the Northern Indiana District Pilgrim Holiness Church* until 1967. At that time she was listed as retired.

Vura Morris

Vura (sometimes spelled "Vera") was under the direction of the Indiana Conference of the Wesleyan Methodist Church in 1912. She and her husband, Walter, were the pastors of the Mt. Olive church from 1912 to 1913. In 1914 they pastored the Elwood church.

Vura graduated in 1914 from Fairmount Bible School, Fairmount, Indiana (later merged into what became Indiana Wesleyan University, Marion, Indiana). She was deeply conscious of God's leadings and a very serious student of the Word. She was sincerely devoted to the Lord[171] and was ordained in 1914.

The Morrises were the pastors of the South Bend church for two years and were assigned to general evangelism for another two years. During the pastorate at South Bend, Vura was appointed pastor of the Seybert Mission for one year. The Morrises served as missionaries to India from 1919 to 1924.

For the next four years they served as pastors of the Liberty church, which was on the Boxley charge, Elkhart, and the Blue River charge. During the 1927 conference year the conference granted both Vura and Walter letters of standing.[172]

Vura died March 24, 1965. She had served in India as a Wesleyan missionary for five years and nine years as a co-pastor with her husband. She was the mother of five children.[173]

Miriam Coulter Jennings Watson

Miriam Coulter was born in Huntington County, Indiana. She married Walter S. Jennings on August 16, 1911. During the following two years they were the pastors at Roseburg, Indiana. Both Walter and Miriam were students at Fairmount Bible School, Fairmount, Indiana (later merged into what became Indiana Wesleyan University, Marion, Indiana). She was an excellent student, deeply devoted and thoroughly consecrated to the Lord. She graduated from Bible school in 1915[174] and was ordained August 19, 1916, by the Indiana Conference of the Wesleyan Methodist Church.[175]

Miriam and Walter moved to the Houghton, New York, area in order to attend Houghton College. During this time they pastored the Olean, New York, Wesleyan Methodist Church. They were prospective African missionaries in 1917, but they accepted the Mt. Etna circuit (Lancaster, Indiana) that year and resigned in June 1918 to go to Sierra Leone, West Africa. They served one term at Kabinkola, 1918–21. They were home one year on furlough and returned to Sierra Leone, 1921–23, but Walter became seriously ill, and they were forced to return home. He died in December 1923.[176]

Miriam, now the mother of a small child, Lowell, returned to college. She graduated in 1931 with a degree in education from Marion College, Marion, Indiana (now Indiana Wesleyan University). Her son, Lowell Jennings, and his wife, Mary Faith, would become missionaries to India and Sierra Leone. She was elected as the superintendent of the Indiana Conference Young Missionary Workers Band (now Wesleyan Kids for Missions) in 1924 and served in that office until 1951. In order to support herself and her son, she taught school in the Huntington area.

She was a faithful and excellent Sunday school teacher in the local church and served as class leader for many years. She married Charles Ode Watson, a farmer, July 19, 1940. After her marriage to Mr. Watson, they lived in Florida for a time, and she taught a Sunday school class there. He died in 1959. In 1965 Miriam moved to Gastonia, North Carolina, to be near her son. She continued to teach a Sunday school class for another ten years. She remained a member of the Mt. Etna church for sixty years. She died May 21, 1985.

Stella Crosby Corum

Stella Crosby was one of seven children, She was born September 10, 1882, in South Dakota into a homesteader family. Her mother died when she was very young, and her older sister, Hattie Crosby (Manyon), cared for her. In 1904 the entire family moved to Houghton, New York, where the children could attend a Christian school. Stella graduated from the academy and Houghton College. After graduation from Houghton, she worked in several missions. In 1912 she was the superintendent of the Olean, New York, Mission. Under her consecrated efforts, the work prospered. Two ladies, Mable Morris and Gladis Gates, assisted her with their excellent help.[177]

In 1913 Stella requested to be released from her duties as superintendent of the Olean mission and served as the pastor of the Wesleyan Methodist Church in Avon, South Dakota, from 1913 to 1915.[178]

Stella was a member of the Wesleyan Methodist Church from childhood. She was ordained by the Wesleyan Methodist Church. At some point her name became Corum. She preached for a time for the Church of the Nazarene. She died July 12, 1965, in San Diego, California.[179]

Mary Lottie Anderson Bradshaw Cameron

Mary Lottie Anderson was a woman acquainted with sorrow and grief. She was born December 21, 1878, in Ohio. Her father abandoned her at age one. At age ten she began working for her living.

She was converted at age sixteen as she walked to the church altar. In 1906 Rev. G. C. Bevington came to visit in her mother's home, and she and her mother were led into holiness. They were persecuted by the local church people because of their testimony to being sanctified.

Mary united with Levi Bradshaw in marriage April 12, 1896. They were blessed with the birth of three daughters before Levi died June 20, 1903. Their entire family had contracted small-pox. He was buried before daylight without a funeral. Mary was left with three little girls aged two, four, and six.

On October 25, 1904, she married Charles Cameron. They became the parents of seven children; two of them died early in life. Charles apparently was not a Christian at the time of their marriage, but she led him and all her children to the Lord. Some of the children did not remain true to the Lord.

In 1913 she joined the International Apostolic Holiness Church (later became the Pilgrim Holiness Church). Mary Lottie Cameron's godly life had influenced her daughter Celia, and she was saved at age ten and called to preach at age eleven. Mary was a prayer warrior and a great personal worker. God had also given her the gift of healing. She walked hundreds of miles to homes in order to pray for the sick and neglected people.

After rearing ten children, Mary began preaching and doing home missionary work. She opened missions and churches. She took the ministerial course of study, and though she only had a fourth-grade education, she made "fine grades" and was a student all her life.

Sorrows continued following Mary her entire lifetime. Her husband, Charles, was killed May 13, 1932. Her daughter Addie died of a stroke in June 1946. One year later, Mary was carried out for dead from the Pilgrim Holiness Church in Wellston,

Ohio, of which she was the pastor. But God granted her recovery and enabled her to continue to pastor until her death October 21, 1949.[180]

Anna Matilda Hamilton

Anna Matilda Hamilton was born March 28, 1885, at Macksburg, Iowa, and departed this life December 9, 1989. She was converted at age nineteen and sanctified a few months later. When Anna was converted she also received a call to the mission field. She sailed for China in 1913 and served there until ill health forced her to return to the United States.

Following her return from China, Anna ministered in city mission work on the West Coast. She also served in pastorates in California and Kansas. This work was done under the Church of the Nazarene. She was ordained in 1920.

In 1936 Anna was married to J. S. Hamilton of Argonia, Kansas, and joined the Pilgrim Holiness Church in Argonia. She was listed as an ordained minister in the Western Kansas District of the Pilgrim Holiness Church from 1937 to 1947. From 1948 to 1950 her name was listed by the California-Arizona District. She returned to the Kansas District in 1951. From 1951 to 1968 she served under that district and retired from the active ministry in 1962. At the time of her death she was listed as a retired ordained minister in the Kansas District.[181]

Ronald R. Brannon, former general secretary of The Wesleyan Church, was Anna's district superintendent when she was ninety-four years old. She was vitally interested in every church in the district and was concerned that some pastors and churches had not reported a single conversion to Christ the year prior to his visit. She asked, but not critically, "If those pastors and churches are not getting people saved, what are they doing?" She was unable to attend district conference or functions, but the pastoral appointments list and the district superintendent's itinerary were kept in her Bible as a part of her daily prayer list. Just a few days before Christmas and only a few weeks before her 105th birthday, she laid aside her Bible and prayer list to enter into the very presence of her Lord.[182]

Lydia B. Alphanalp Harrington

The first record on Lydia B. Alphanalp was found in the *Minutes of the Annual Session of the Indiana Conference of the Holiness Christian Church,* 1913–15. She was ordained in 1913 and the next two years she was listed as a missionary to Japan.

The Pilgrim Holiness Advocate, August 22, 1929, on page 13 recorded that she married George Harrington in 1916. She was born May 5, 1859, in Massachusetts and was converted in May 1907. Her death occurred July 8, 1929.

Katherine "Katie" Pitts Nemyer

Katie Pitts was born December 17, 1868, in Germany. She emigrated to the United States in 1884 and located in Coshocton, Ohio. The next year she moved to Wabash, Indiana. She married John Nemyer August 4, 1887, and became the mother of five children. Katie was a good mother and wife.

She entered the Indiana Conference of the Holiness Christian Church in 1913 as an evangelist. She died January 12, 1918.[183]

Bessie Ice Petry

Bessie Petry was a good student at Fairmount Bible School in Fairmount, Indiana (later merged into what became Indiana Wesleyan University, Marion, Indiana). She graduated in 1913.[184] She was the pastor of the Anderson, Indiana, Wesleyan Methodist Church from 1919 to 1920. She was appointed with her husband, Lee, to the Mt. Zion, Howard County church for one year in 1922. Bessie was ordained by the Indiana Conference in 1923. That year the Petrys moved to the Huntington charge and remained in that pastorate for four years. Their next place of service was the Lewis Creek charge, followed by pastoring the Summitville church.

Lee Petry died in 1931. After his death, Bessie was listed as a conference evangelist for many years. In 1964 she was listed as a retired minister.[185]

---⧜⧜---

Lillian Roberts

Lillian Roberts was ordained as a minister by the Indiana Conference of the Holiness Christian Church in 1913. She served that group until it became part of the International Holiness Church by merger. The last time she was listed was in 1922.[186]

---⧜⧜---

Minnie Gay Shelor Billers

The Minutes of the Annual Conference of the Carolina District International Apostolic Holiness Church, 1914, listed Mrs. W. H. Billers as pastor of the Beulah, Virginia church.

From 1916 through 1918 Minnie was the pastor at the Samos, Virginia, church under the Southern District of the International Apostolic Holiness Church.[187]

The Minutes of the Annual Assembly of the Virginia District of the Pilgrim Holiness Church 1922 records her and her husband as the pastors of the Coates' Store Pilgrim Holiness Church. The International Apostolic Holiness Church through two mergers had become the Pilgrim Holiness Church. Minnie Biller was an ordained minister.

Minnie Gay Shelor Biller was born April 8, 1881, and died July 6, 1923. She married W. H. Biller October 29, 1906. She was the mother of two sons and five daughters. During her last three years she worked in the mountains of Virginia in an area where there was no school or church. The people knew nothing of salvation or holiness. God enabled her to build a church building on a lot debt free. According to the report in the *Pilgrim Holiness Advocate* of October 4, 1923, she was reported to be one of the best workers in the Virginia district.

---⧜⧜---

Mary Cruse

Often districts were realigned and their names were changed. The Carolina and Southern Districts of the International Apostolic Holiness Church, and the Southern District of the Pilgrim Holiness Church, provide an example. Mary Cruse ministered as a pastor of Bethlehem and St. Paul in these districts. Her husband, W. C. Cruse, died around 1960. She continued on the roll in the North Carolina District of the Pilgrim Holiness Church until merger with the Wesleyan Methodist Church in 1968.[188]

---⧜⧜---

Carrie Yoder Ferguson

Carrie Yoder was born in 1881. She expressed a desire to be a minister at age eight. She was converted when she was sixteen and was sanctified at age twenty-two. She began immediately to preach in tent and camp meetings and to organize churches. She was elected secretary at the first meeting of the Apostolic Holiness Church of Pennsylvania and served in that office for many years. The object of the Apostolic Holiness Church was the salvation of souls, the sanctification of believers, and the advancement of the neglected doctrines of divine healing and the Lord's return. In order to accomplish these goals, they held conventions, tent and camp meetings, and revivals. Many churches were planted as a result of their tent meetings. They were especially concerned about the care of new converts, and to prevent them from attending cold and formal churches, they organized an auxiliary, which would be called the International Apostolic Holiness Church of Pennsylvania. This group was organized in 1914. Carrie was not only the first secretary of this group, but she was also on the first examining board. She was one of three persons elected as directors of *The Bethel Herald,* a paper published by the Apostolic Holiness Church. She was elected the associate editor also. Carrie also served on the missionary board as well as the camp meeting committee.[189]

The purpose of the tent meetings was to establish a group that could be organized as a church. Carrie organized a church at Augustaville, Pennsylvania, January 10, 1915. Another church was organized that year with twenty-two members at Summit Hill by Brother

Sutton and Carrie Yoder. She was the first pastor of the church at Augustaville. She also was the pastor at Sunberry, Pennsylvania

Carrie Yoder married Thomas E. Ferguson in 1920. He was a pastor in the district. They were co-pastors of churches located in Stroudsburg, Millersburg, Camden, Lock Haven, and Milroy, Pennsylvania. They served the latter church for twelve years.[190]

Through Carrie's efforts, the Milton camp meeting and several churches were established in what is now the Pennsylvania and New Jersey District. She worked with Seth C. Rees and George B. Kulp to help establish the work of the district. She was ordained by the Pennsylvania and New Jersey District[191] and was elected a delegate to the General Assembly two times.

For fifty years she worked for the salvation of souls and the establishment of churches. It was said of her that "she gave her all in glad service for the Master." Carrie A. Yoder Ferguson completed her earthly work December 21, 1951. She was, at the time of her death, co-pastor of the Milroy Church.

Lizzie James Indy

According to the *Minutes of the Annual Session of the Indiana Conference of the Holiness Christian Church* 1914–15, Lizzie James was ordained a minister in 1914. The next year she was married to Mr. Indy (first name unknown). No further records were found for her.

Maggie Kirkman

The Minutes of the Annual Conference Carolina District International Apostolic Holiness Church recorded Maggie Kirkman and her husband, W. C., the pastors of the Mt. Olive Church in Greensboro, North Carolina, in 1914.

The Minutes of the Annual Conference Southern District International Apostolic Holiness Church listed them as pastors in 1916, and in 1918 as pastors at West Durham and Hillsboro. Mrs. Kirkman died at the beginning of the annual change of pastors in 1918.

Lulu Bowman

Lulu Bowman apparently served as a pastor at New London, Indiana, under the Indiana Conference of the Holiness Christian Church in 1915. She was ordained in 1917. The records of the Indiana District of the International Holiness Church and the Indiana District of the Pilgrim Holiness Church listed her as an evangelist. In 1922 she was received into the Indiana Conference of the Wesleyan Methodist Church as an ordained minister from the Pilgrim Holiness Church. She was listed as a general evangelist She was in the Wesleyan Methodist Church for only three years and then returned to the Pilgrim Holiness Church.[192]

Ethel Sager Wilson Carroll

The publishing of salvation literature was a priority with the Pentecostal Rescue Mission. Ethel Sager had worked in a printing office  in Cortland, New York, before she was saved. She came to the Pentecostal Rescue Mission in Binghamton, New York, and worked for three and a half years in the printing department for the mission.[193]

Ethel married David E. Wilson, an outstanding evangelist, in 1913. Two children came to bless their home, Emerson and Augusta (Brecheisen).

Ethel pastored the Schenectady Mission 1915–18. She often was employed as a pastor while her husband was traveling from place to place in revival meetings. She also was a very good businesswoman and was able to help finance the home base while her husband was away in meetings. She served also as an evangelist for a number of years.

Ethel was ordained by the New York District of the Pilgrim Holiness Church in 1941. She retired from the active ministry in 1967.[194] Sometime after this (her previous husband had died), she married Mr. Carroll. Her earthly race ended June 4, 1977.

Etta B. Nichols

Etta Nichols was the pastor of Eden, North Carolina, First Church 1915–18 and 1920–23. During the 1923 conference year, J. L. Armstrong was her assistant.[195]

Etta B. Nichols conducted a mission work in Stuart, Virginia. On October 3, 1919, a church was organized. A lot had been purchased earlier. Mrs. Minnie Shockley had been given a tract of land by her father and believed the Lord spoke to her and told her that she would build a church where holiness could be preached. She gave the timber from her land. The church was erected in 1912 and was first called Shockley Mission but in 1917 was called Minnie's Chapel. Etta B. Nichols was the pastor.[196]

Etta was called to preach and became a member of the North Carolina Conference of the Wesleyan Methodist Church. She had pastoral and evangelistic appointments in that district. She was married to J. B. Nichols, and they were the parents of two sons. She died June 7, 1936, in Spray, North Carolina.[197]

Sarah E. Redding

Sarah E. Redding was born in Perry County, Pennsylvania, July 25, 1875. She died in Cedar Falls, Iowa, December 7, 1950.

Sarah was converted early in life and later sought sanctification. She was called to preach and then attended Cleveland Bible College. She graduated in 1915. Sarah was a Bible preacher and expected the Word to produce results when presented under the anointing of the Spirit. People gladly listened to her preaching.

She helped to organize the Second Wesleyan Methodist Church in Canton, Ohio.[198]

Gertrude Gertie Smith

Gertie Smith is first mentioned in *The Minutes of the Annual Session of the Kansas Conference of the Wesleyan Methodist Connection* in 1915. That year she gave an exhortation following the preaching of a Sister Folter.

Much of her ministry was given to the Concordia Mission in Concordia, Kansas, to which she was appointed in 1919, the year the mission started. It was begun because the people of the community wanted the mission. At first prayer meetings were held in the homes, but the many children in the area wanted a Sunday school. The missionary board secured a schoolhouse, and a Sunday school was organized. Some time later an empty house was converted into a mission with rooms for worship and a residence for workers. The attendance was good. Many persons were saved. Children from the neighborhood flocked to the Sunday school. Men would stop at the mission and were saved. Gertrude was the superintendent of the mission 1919–25. Ill health brought her resignation in 1925—but the following year she was again appointed to the work there.[199]

Lydia Organ Swick

Another woman minister, Lydia Organ Swick, came into the Pilgrim Holiness Church from the Brethren in Christ/Pentecostal Brethren in Christ Church. She was born May 14, 1867, in North Lewisburg, Ohio. She gave her heart and life to Christ early in life. In 1905 she moved to Sugar Grove Hill, Ohio. There were many children in the area and they were without a Sunday school. Lydia became instrumental in starting a Sunday school and a midweek prayer meeting. She sold her home and placed most of the proceeds from the sale in purchasing a section of land that became the campground. In 1907 she helped to get a tent meeting started, which lasted for six weeks and resulted in many people being saved. Some years later a tabernacle was built and a camp meeting was started, which held annual meetings.

Lydia was always helping young people get established. She had the God-given ability to recognize talent and ability in others and was always ready to take a back seat in order for others to go forward.[200]

She served under the Brethren in Christ Church until a group from that Church organized the Pentecostal Brethren in Christ Church. She was often one of the speakers at the ministerial meeting at conference time for the Brethren in Christ. In 1915 Lydia was given a mission worker's license. She was in charge of the Bainbridge Mission in Springfield, Ohio from 1915 for a number of years. Her duties included serving as a class leader (Bible study leader) and having charge of the Sunday evening service. Many people were converted under her ministry. In 1917 she conducted a revival meeting at Dill's Schoolhouse and became the pastor of the flock there.

She helped in many revivals, made missionary calls, worked in missions, and led prayer meetings. In 1919 she was ordained by the Brethren in Christ Church at conference time. She held a tent meeting in Marysville, Ohio, a revival at West Side Mission (she received $16.40 for this meeting), and the records revealed that she usually preached 85 times a year. In 1922 she requested her ministerial credentials be transferred to her then-current name, (Mrs. J. W.) Swick. She continued to serve under the Pentecostal Brethren in Christ Church until that group merged with the Pilgrim Holiness Church in Ohio.[201]

There were several years that her name did not appear on the list of ordained ministers, but in 1927–54 she was listed in the *Minutes of the Annual Assembly of the Ohio District Pilgrim Holiness Church*. In 1948 she was living in Springfield, Ohio. She died July 15, 1956.

Velma Berkgren

Often a name of an ordained woman minister would show up in the minutes with no previous record of her ministry. Such was the case of Velma (Mrs. C. F.) Berkgren.

The minutes state, "On May 15, 1916, the Western Kansas/Eastern Colorado District was organized at a meeting held in Humboldt, Kansas. Reverend Mrs. Velma Berkgren was elected secretary. She held this office continuously until the fall of 1926." She was ordained in

1923. The *Minutes* show she was the pastor of the Oakley Church for a number of years. She may have died during the 1954–55 conference year.[202]

Sadie Betz Kercheval Fields

Sadie Betz received her local preacher's license in 1916. She was under conference direction from 1916 to 1922. She completed her training at Fairmount Bible School, Fairmount, Indiana, and when it was merged into the new Marion College, Marion, Indiana (now Indiana Wesleyan University), she was in the first graduation class of Marion College's Theological Department in 1921.[203]

Her first solo pastorate was the Kirklin and Greenwood churches, from 1922 to 1925. She was ordained by the Indiana Conference of the Wesleyan Methodist Church in 1924. She spent four years in evangelistic work. In 1931 she was assigned the pastorate at Muncie, Indiana, and was there for three years. The next three years she was an evangelist. She was the assistant pastor at Bryant in 1937, but she resigned that position to marry Rev. Harry W. Kercheval. She co-pastored with him for thirteen and a half years at Marion George Street, Shelbyville, Atlanta, Kirklin, and Matthews. During the pastorate at Matthews, Harry died, but she continued on until the end of the conference year 1951.

In 1952 she married Rev. C. C. Fields, and they co-pastored the Grant City and Carthage churches. C. C. Fields died in 1978.[204]

Sadie Kercheval Fields served the Wesleyan Methodist Church for twenty-nine years. She died February 8, 1980.[205]

Ora Belle Sanderson
Irvine Dooley

Ora Sanderson was born February 10, 1889. She spent her early childhood in Laketon, Indiana. Her parents owned a grocery store and she helped in the store. She was the first one in her family to be converted in the Wesleyan Methodist church there.

She felt the call to preach at a young age. A lady in the church told her she believed God was calling her to preach, and that helped to confirm her call. She preached her first sermon in the Laketon Church at the age of sixteen. She attended Fairmount Bible School, Fairmount, Indiana (later merged into what became Indiana Wesleyan University, Marion, Indiana) for one year, but she was financially unable to continue. She completed her studies by use of the correspondence study course. She was ordained by the Indiana Conference of the Wesleyan Methodist Church in 1950.

Ora's parents moved to Leesburg, Indiana. She married Walter Irvine and lived in Leesburg in a house her husband built. She was the mother of six children, two of which died in infancy. The other children were Harold, Rev. Eunice Hansen, Esther Clark, and Miriam Bruce. Miriam has attended the Warsaw Wesleyan Church all her life.

Ora rode the streetcar from Leesburg to Warsaw. It stopped at the courthouse, and then Ora and Miriam would walk from there to the church. Levi Hill was the pastor of the Warsaw church, and he was the superintendent of schools at Silver Lake. She would stay in town and help with calling on the people of the church. Ora pastored the Warsaw Wesleyan Methodist Church for three years (1934–37). During her pastorate she raised funds to buy ground on the corner of Market and Pine Streets. She used a poster and sold bricks on the poster for ten cents each. When all the funds were in and they were ready to purchase the lot and move the small church building to the purchased land, Levi Hill was appointed pastor to make sure it was completed.

Ora continued to attend the Warsaw Church, and Flora Addington became the pastor. Attendance declined. E. J. Pitts, the conference president, came to close the Warsaw church. He paced back and forth reciting all the reasons the church should be closed. Ora Irvine was declaring all the reasons the church should remain open. Finally she asked E. J. to keep the church open for one more year, and he agreed. The Warsaw church is now a thriving church with several hundred in attendance.

Ora often filled the pulpits of pastors who were ill and at other places whenever she was needed. Russell Klinger was the pastor of the Larwill church, and much of the time he was too ill to preach. She filled the pulpit at Larwill during this time.

Ora's husband, Walter, was injured in an automobile accident in 1944 and was paralyzed from the neck down. He died September 7, 1947. In November 1976, Ora married Rev. Dennis Dooley, whom she had known from Bible school days. She died approximately eight months later, on July 6, 1977.[206]

Mary F. Greene Seekins

Mary Greene was given the name of Mayme Frances when she was born January 9, 1877, in Bartholomew County, Indiana. Her immediate family called her Mayme, but she eventually became known throughout the world as Mary. She spent her early life in Shelby County, Indiana.

W. J. Seekins was the pastor at the Lewis Creek Wesleyan Methodist Church and invited Jacob Hester to be the evangelist for a revival meeting at his church. Among those saved in the meeting were Hiram and Ella Drake and Mary Greene, then a young lady of fifteen or sixteen. Mary gave her heart and life to Christ in that revival. Mary's family opposed her newfound faith and made life miserable for her. Ella Drake prayed for Mary, and often she would "be led by the Holy Spirit" to hitch up the horses and go to the Greenes' home. She would bring Mary home with her for the entire day Sunday. The Drakes and the pastor encouraged and nurtured Mary spiritually. Gipsie M. Miller in her book *History of the Woman's Missionary Society Wesleyan Methodist Church* reported that Mary was called to India as a missionary while she was hanging up a dishtowel in the pantry. That may sound foolish, but that's the way life was with Mary. She was gifted with an unusual wit, and God used that wit daily in her life for good.

She believed she should prepare for her life's work, and in 1910 she enrolled at Fairmount Bible School, Fairmount, Indiana (later merged into what became Indiana Wesleyan University, Marion, Indiana). Her parents did not help her financially. She did domestic work in a home in Fairmount, where the owners treated her like a slave. But Mary was determined to stay in school. Marcille Bostic's mother and her aunt were also in school there. Their parents, members of the Lewis Creek church, would butcher hogs each year, and their father would bring meat and homemade bread to the girls. One day they were frying ham, and the delicious smell of the ham entered the cottage where Mary lived. She was hungry and had prayed that God would send her something to eat. Marcille's aunt took a ham sandwich to Mary. Many years later when Mary was home on furlough, she told how God had answered her prayer that day with a ham sandwich.[207]

Mary graduated from Fairmount Bible School in 1916. She was described as an energetic woman who dared to speak her mind. She knew God personally, and she prayed her way through Bible school.[208] She did not have money to buy paper to write her assignments on, so she used discarded wrapping paper and paper sacks. Funds came from unexpected places to help her. The day of commencement, J. D. Baker, president of the Bible school, asked Mary what she was going to do now. She had vowed that she would not tell anyone she was going to India until someone said he or she knew she was to be a missionary to India. Mary's lips were locked. J. D. Baker looked at her and said, "I know you are going to India."

Mary was ordained August 19, 1916, by the Indiana Conference of the Wesleyan Methodist Church. She served two terms in India (1917–25 and 1928–32). She developed a heart problem and was not able to return to India after that.[209] Mrs. Kenneth Knapp and many others said, "She came out of India, but she never got India out of her."

Many of Mary's dresses were made by Marcille Bostic's mother. Mary was a tall woman with a large frame, and it was difficult for her to find dresses that fit. She did not like the color pink. She loved to wear the Indian sari.

The following story reveals Mary's courage even in times of danger. Hazel Jones and Mary were together in the mission house. During the night they heard someone throwing pebbles on the roof of the house. This was done by the thieves to discover if there was anyone in the house. Mary and Hazel were in an upstairs room. Mary used the Gujeraiti language and called out, "I'm going to get the gun and unlatch the door." She put on her heavy shoes and tramped down the stairs all the time talking and saying "I'm going to shoot." And shoot she did! Four or five men ran from the compound.

Mary would go anywhere and do everything. She taught and preached wherever she was needed. She taught in the Bible school for three years, worked in the orphanage, and did village evangelistic work while in India.

Alton E. Liddick, missionary to India who would become executive secretary of world missions, recalled that Mary was comfortable using Gujeraiti, the native language, and while in India spoke only in that language. Mary loved the poor people of India, and she was always available to help them. When she went into the villages to teach and preach, she would pitch her tent near the village and get to work. There are Christian leaders in India today because of her influence, godly life, and work.

When business meetings of the missionaries in India would become "tight," Mary would say something witty, and the tension would break. Charles Carter recalled that when he was a student at Dakota Wesleyan University, he read where Mary Greene was to speak at a new Wesleyan Methodist church. He went to the meeting out of curiosity. He was financially very poor at the time. During the offertory Mary began to wail and shake her tambourine. She walked the aisle and stopped by his side. She wailed and shook the tambourine until she had collected all the money he had in his pocket. Marcille Bostic recalled that she did the same thing at a church picnic at Lewis Creek Church. She stopped in front of a man who was known to keep every penny he had, but her wailing and shaking the tambourine resulted in his leaving the picnic broke and Mary being exhausted!

When Mary returned home because of ill health, she spent her time and strength in traveling over the United States raising money for missions and encouraging young people to answer the call to go to India. Every young woman was a potential missionary candidate for India. Men were slow to answer the call. Mary declared from the pulpit, "If you men are afraid to go to India, get a young woman and hide behind her skirt and go with her." She was an "enlightening and forceful speaker." Her missionary messages were filled with wit and persuasion. Her deputation work (home ministries) was done during "hard times," when money was not easy to come by. But whenever Mary spoke of her beloved India, the offering plates would overflow with money for India. Once when she spoke with inspiration and unction in the Ohio Conference, the offering received was $1,300. Her messages always made the sin-burdened life of the Indian people real and demanded action from her hearers.

She married W. J. Seekins, her first pastor, September 4, 1918. He was many years her senior, but their home was blessed with God's presence. For a time they lived on the Seekins farm near Sheridan, Indiana, but later they moved to Fairmount, Indiana. This author became personally acquainted with Mary at this time. She always prayed for and encouraged the young people of the Fairmount Wesleyan Methodist Church. W. J. Seekins died in 1944. She deeded her home in Fairmount to the Department of World Missions in 1945. Her desire was that it be used as a home for missionaries on furlough.

Mary served as vice president of the general Woman's Home and Foreign Missionary Society for seven years, 1939–46, and as the area chairperson of the East Central Area from 1943 to 1947. In one quadrennial report she had spoken 591 times and traveled 47,221 miles.

She preached her last sermon at the Lewis Creek church near Flat Rock, Indiana, July 8, 1956. She was physically feeble but had unusual strength under the anointing of the Holy Spirit. Her final days of her earthly life were spent in a nursing home in Edinburg, Indiana. She entered her heavenly rest August 3, 1957. One of the final acts of worship (and so like Mary Greene Seekins) related to her ministry was an offering for missions taken at her funeral.[210]

Florence E. Heath Salisbury

Florence Heath formed habits of studiousness and thoroughness in her childhood. These habits followed her all through life. She was gifted with a singing voice of rare beauty and sweetness. She was converted at age thirteen but drifted away from the Lord. She was beautifully reclaimed and restored when she was twenty. Florence began working as a song evangelist and assisting her father in revival meetings. Her mother joined them, and for three years they traveled as an evangelistic team. During this time Florence began to feel the call to preach. She and her mother became a team, and for fifteen years they worked together in five states and ten denominations. God blessed their efforts with great success.

Shortly before her mother's death, Florence joined the Wesleyan Methodist Church in the Allegheny Conference. She was a successful evangelist for eight years and served as a pastor for twelve more years. She was the pastor of Wesleyan Methodist churches at Indiana, Harbor, Middlefield, Templeton, and East Springfield. All these churches were in the Allegheny Conference in Ohio and Pennsylvania.

Florence was born June 22, 1872, in Pennsylvania. She married Rev. A. E. Salisbury February 24, 1932. During her active ministerial days she was the pianist at the Stoneboro Camp Meeting for several years. She also served as the secretary of the conference Woman's Home and Foreign Missionary Society. She was a devoted and active member of the Women's Christian Temperance Union. Her life was exemplary, and she was characterized by her ability to look beyond the faults of even the most unlovely and speak only of their virtues. She died in her home in Waterford, New York, January 3, 1940.[211]

Clara Buntain Webb

Clara Buntain began her ministerial preparation in 1916 in the Indiana Conference of the Wesleyan Methodist Church. She graduated in

1918 from Fairmount Bible School, Fairmount, Indiana (later merged into what became Indiana Wesleyan University, Marion, Indiana). She was gifted with musical abilities and sang alto in a quartet while in Bible school. She attended Bible school by faith, and God provided for her.[212]

No service records were found for her from 1918 for a number of years. There was a Clara Buntain, an ordained minister, in the Indiana District of the Pilgrim Holiness Church from 1929 to 1933.[213] Her name also appeared in 1933 in the *Minutes of the Annual Assembly of the Ohio District Pilgrim Holiness Church.* In 1936 she assisted in a literature demonstration before the conference of the Ohio Wesleyan Methodist Church.[214]

Clara taught school for many years in North Carolina and Kentucky. She worked in home missionary work in the mountains of Kentucky. While working at Zion's Hill Mission there, she met D. C. Webb. He and his wife, Lula Giard, were workers there also. Lulu died, and many years later, in 1940, D. C. Webb and Clara Buntain were married. Together they established Wheelrim Mission in the Kentucky mountains. They started a Sunday school and ministered to one hundred families in a ten-mile radius there. Clara moved her conference membership to the Kentucky Conference in 1943.[215] Ill health forced them to resign at Wheelrim, and they moved to the South Carolina Conference and worked at the Blue Ridge Mission—but they returned to Wheelrim in 1950. D. C. Webb died at the Wheelrim Mission in 1951.[216] Clara remained there until she transferred back home to the Indiana Conference in 1953. She retired in Larwill in the house where she had been born December 1, 1886.[217]

Pearl Dean

Mrs. Pearl Dean was born May 29, 1885, at Cyle, Indiana. She was a charter member of the Apostolic Holiness Union (later the Pilgrim Holiness Church) and was present in the house of Rev. M. W. Knapp at the time of its organization. She acted as the secretary for that organizational meeting. She preached her first sermon in 1903 at

Moores Hill, Indiana, and was ordained July 1905 at Hutchinson, Kansas, by Rev. Seth C. Rees.

Pearl married William S. Dean April 29, 1905. She assisted William in evangelistic work for four years and in pastorates at Orleans, Cory, Bicknell, and Anderson, Indiana; Battle Creek, Michigan; Rossburg, Spencerville, and Cambridge, Ohio.

She served as pastor for some thirty years at Middletown, Providence, Scott City, Shelburn, Linton, and Merom. She was successful in erecting new church buildings in Merom and Scott City and was the pastor at Middletown (now Prairie Creek) from 1924 to 1930. The church had several youth who were gifted with musical abilities. She enjoyed the music of the young people and encouraged and used them in the services. Her husband was an evangelist and was not home much of the time. In those days ministers came only every other Sunday to minister at the Middletown church. They conducted services each Sunday morning but only every other Sunday night. She did not live in Middletown. Pearl was a delegate to the General Assembly of the Pilgrim Holiness Church in 1924.

While Pearl's ministry started around 1905, there were no records found before 1917 for her. She died December 16, 1958.[218]

Ruth Billheimer Drake

Ruth Billheimer Drake was appointed with her husband, W. H. Drake, by the Indiana Conference of the Wesleyan Methodist Church to pastor the Anderson Ninth Street and Middletown Wesleyan Methodist Churches in 1917. She began her studies on the course of study at this time. They had this assignment for two years. The next three years they were the pastors of the Mt. Zion, Howard County, and Mt. Olive churches. They next pastored the Laketon Church.[219]

Both Herbert and Ruth were ordained in 1923. This year they began to pastor the Lancaster Church. The church was heavily in debt on the parsonage. They began a campaign to pay off the parsonage debt. They placed a "do-without box" in the back of the church. The women were encouraged to give the money they received when they sold the eggs that were laid on Sunday. This money was to apply on the principal of the debt. The men gave ten cents per week to apply on the interest.[220]

The couple co-pastored Miami, Santa Fe, Pleasant Grove circuit, Peru East Washington Street, and Amboy churches. Herbert died in 1953 while they were pastoring Amboy. She continued on through the conference year of 1954.

A new church at Sweetser, Indiana, was organized June 21, 1954. Ruth was appointed the pastor of this newly organized group. She was an excellent church planter, and the work prospered. A beautiful new church building was erected and dedicated in 1960. Ruth directed the building program and assisted in the construction. She became ill and was forced to resign November 20, 1962.

Ruth was the mother of six children, and she and her husband cared for eight orphans. Ruth had filled her father's pulpit when she was eighteen. She served the Lord and the Wesleyan Methodist Church for forty-six years. She was welcomed home in heaven April 11, 1963.[221]

Verna Jackson

Verna Jackson was received to pursue the course of study in 1917 in the Indiana Conference of the Wesleyan Methodist Church. She taught English at Fairmount Bible School in 1919–20. Verna was in the first graduating class of the Marion College (now Indiana Wesleyan University) Theological Department in 1921.[222]

She and her husband, Amos, were co-pastors of the Miami, Fowlerton, and Larwill churches from 1921 to 1927. She was ordained by the Indiana Conference of the Wesleyan Methodist Church in 1923. For about five years she was inactive because of her health. One daughter, Lois, was born during this time also.

She returned to the active ministry in 1933 and again was co-pastor with her husband at Plymouth, Marion Nelson Street, Marion Home Corner (now Brookhaven), and Back Creek churches.[223] They took turns preaching each Sunday. It was rumored that whenever it was announced that she would be preaching, a large crowd would come out. To remedy this situation, they began not to announce who was preaching in the services.

Amos M. Jackson was the Indiana Conference president for six years. Verna was an excellent encourager of all the pastors' wives. She was my first conference president's wife, and she taught me many things about being a pastor's wife and a co-pastor. Her wisdom and advice were welcomed.

Verna was also very interested in mission work. In fact, she and her husband had prepared themselves to be missionaries, but the door to mission work never opened for them. Instead, God opened the doors for them to become pastors. Verna served as the Indiana Conference president of the Woman's Home and Foreign Missionary Society from 1939 to 1950.

Verna retired in 1957 from the active ministry. Her husband, Amos, died October 6, 1973.

Zelia B. Miner Johnson

Zelia B. Miner was born in 1884. She was converted at an early age and called to the ministry as a youth. She entered Houghton Seminary, Houghton, New York (later Houghton College) in 1905 and received her theological training there.[224]

There were no records of her service until 1917. She apparently had been the assistant pastor of the Seneca Falls, New York, church in 1916. She had become very ill and was hospitalized, and the churches had taken a freewill offering of $45.37 to help cover her medical expenses. She gratefully received the offering. She had resigned her position at Seneca Falls. However, that year, 1917, she was appointed pastor of the Groton and Mainesburgh, Pennsylvania, churches. She was assigned the Wallace church in 1918.[225] She apparently was ordained by the Rochester Conference of the Wesleyan Methodist Church (Central New York) and was so listed in 1927. She married Rev. Ezra H. Johnson in 1926 and served as his assistant at the Westfield and Jasper, New York, churches. They resigned as pastors at Jasper in 1930 and were granted letters of transfer to the Lockport Conference (Western New York).

The couple co-pastored the Emporium and Rich Valley churches in the Lockport Conference and were engaged in evangelistic work for two years. When the pastor of Rich Valley died unexpectedly in 1935, the church requested to have their "old pastors back"—Ezra and Zelia Johnson. Some of the records are missing from 1937 to 1941. In 1942 they were the pastors at Allegany and in 1944 at Cadwells, New York. Both of them were listed as retired in 1948. She was given a transfer to the Rochester Conference in 1960. Ezra had died in 1956.[226]

Zelia was appointed the assistant pastor to Bernard A. Draper at Sandy Creek in 1960. She remained there until the close of conference in 1963. She served as an evangelist for three years and retired in 1967.

Chloie Neeley Meeks

Chloie Neeley was the second of seven children in the Neeley family. Her mother had dark hair, a keen personality, and a sense of humor. Her father was a businessman and owned a grocery store. He traveled all over the countryside selling things from a wagon.

Chloie was converted at age seven in her parents' home as she knelt at her mother's knees. Two years later she was sanctified in a "pretend" meeting. She asked Jesus to take the bad feeling from her heart and make her heart pure and clean. The evangelist had observed this pretend meeting and sensed that God was working in her heart. He asked the children what had happened, and Chloie gave her testimony.[227]

Chloie was a blond, blue-eyed, very feminine lady. Her eyes sparkled with life. She was gifted musically and played the piano and guitar and sang. After she graduated from high school, she traveled that summer with Amelia Bueker, a missionary from India, and her sister, Fern. She sang and led the singing in meetings in Ohio, Kentucky, and West Virginia. During that summer she began to hear God calling her to India.

Chloie and Fern Neeley sang in Holiness Christian Churches in Illinois, Indiana, and in St. Louis. A group from Oblong, Illinois, had been conducting prayer meetings and became acquainted with the girls and Ellis A. Meeks, a student in Beulah Bible School in St. Louis. The group was impressed with the spirit of these young people and their devotion to God. Under the direction of the district superintendent, this group was organized in 1921 as a church in the International Holiness Church (later Pilgrim Holiness Church). Among the charter members were the E. L. Neeleys and all seven of their children.[228]

Chloie heard God calling her to be a minister as she worked in the garden. She began to argue with God by saying to Him (she had five brothers), "Why don't you call one of *them* to preach?" On Easter Sunday she became convinced that God was calling *her* to preach, and she promised God she would be one of His ministers.

Chloie entered Beulah Bible School in St. Louis. Here she met Ellis A. Meeks, who had just arrived after serving in the army. She often accompanied him on the piano when he sang tenor solos. They soon discovered they had many similar interests, including a call to India as missionaries. They were married in 1922 in Chloie's home in the spring, and just before Christmas they were in New York ready to sail for India.

The couple learned the Hindu language in a school high up in the mountains. God enabled them to learn it in a few months. They visited people and prayed for a miracle in order for them to be able to reach the people with the gospel. God granted them another miracle. A man had tried to kill a dog with a knife. The Hindu people do not kill any kind of animal, so a Hindu man brought the dog to the Meeks. Ellis had been a doctor's helper in the army. He bandaged the dog and used what medicine he had, and the dog got well. People heard about the care the dog had received, and they began to come for medical help for themselves. But before they received medicine, they were taught about God and His love for them. People began to get saved, and the church began to grow. Chloie and Ellis also had a training school for preachers in India.

Four children were born into their home: Virginia (Wright), Ruth (Carpenter), Paul, and

Mary Jane (Duckworth). The Meeks served seven years in India, but Ellis's health became poor and they returned to the United States. They traveled for two years in deputation work but were not able to return to India. God opened the door for them to pastor churches, including some church plants. Chloie was ordained in 1917.

Chloie and Ellis were a pastoral team. He was an evangelistic preacher and moved about while preaching. She was not a "mover"; she stayed behind the pulpit. They worked together and planned their preaching. They took turns preaching, one in the morning and the other at night. They preached series of messages together. He would preach on a theme in the morning, and she would continue the same theme at night. They also worked as a team in calling on church members and the unsaved of the community. Chloie did much counseling, especially with young women, and often gave marriage counseling to couples and even conducted the marriage ceremony.

Jesse Tewell, a former district superintendent in Illinois, credits Chloie for his salvation, because she visited in his home week after week and kept him in church. She prayed him through to victory time and time again. When Don and Vera Close were pastors at Lawrenceville, Illinois, Vera was ill and struggled spiritually during this time of illness. Chloie visited and counseled her week after week until she was much better.

Chloie was deeply concerned about the education of her children. Virginia and Ruth attended Bible Holiness Seminary in Owosso, Michigan (later Owosso College, eventually merged into what is now Indiana Wesleyan University, Marion, Indiana). Chloie did laundry to pay the school bills. They were in Owosso two years, and then Virginia, Ruth, and Paul attended Frankfort Pilgrim College in Frankfort, Indiana (later merged into United Wesleyan College, Allentown, Pennsylvania). Chloie ironed hundreds of shirts to pay school expenses in order that her children could graduate.

Ellis and Chloie were the pastors of churches in Oblong, Robinson, Charleston, Bridgeport, Olney, and Martinsville, Illinois. She was the president of the district missionary society for many years. In the later 1960s Chloie served in the Philippines as a volunteer missionary for two years. The Filipinos loved her. Her life and service were marked by a strong devotion to Christ, an intense missionary zeal, faithfulness to her local church, and a consistent walk with Christ. She was active in the district and local church work until her death March 16, 1982. She was "relentless in her desire to build the Kingdom of God."[229]

Ella M. Slipp

Only a few records were found for the Alliance of the Reformed Baptist Church of Canada. The first record found was from 1917. Ella Slipp was a licentiate at that time, but she was ordained in 1920. She was from the Ft. Fairfield, Maine, church, of which she was pastor for a number of years. She took a great interest in a young minister, Frazier Dunlop, who would become a leader in the Reformed Baptist Church. Ella's name does not appear after 1956 in the *Minutes,* and she died either in 1955 or 1956.[230]

Vera G. Macy Willis

Vera Macy of Chapman Creek in the Kansas Conference of the Wesleyan Methodist Church gave eleven years as a missionary to Sierra Leone, West Africa. Her first term was shortened because she became very ill and needed to return home on the "first boat available." That term was 1919–21. However, she was reappointed and was able to return in 1924–28 and again in 1929–32. She was one of several persons who pioneered the Bendembu station. She played a key role in the life of Bai Bangura, who became the superintendent of the West Africa District.[231]

Vera was born in 1890. She began her ministerial labors in 1917, according to the Kansas Conference *Minutes.* She was listed as an ordained minister in 1922. After she returned home from Africa in 1932, she worked as an evangelist for one year. The following year she was appointed the pastor of the Cedar church and remained there until the end of the conference year in 1936.[232] During 1937 she married Rev. J. M. Willis, a pastor from the Oregon Conference. She was granted a letter of transfer on July 21, 1937, to the Oregon Conference. J. M. and Vera were the pastors of the St. John church in Portland, Oregon, for three years. From 1941 to 1943 they pastored the Aumsville church. The next year J. M. retired, but Vera was employed as a general evangelist for the next two years. In 1946 she and Kathleen Kelsven were supply pastors for a few months after the pastor left to become the pastor of the Miltonvale, Kansas, church. She served as an evangelist for five years after that. She retired in 1952. Her husband, J. M. Willis, died in June 1958, and Vera died October 18, 1970.[233]

Vera was active in both the Kansas and Oregon Conferences. She served as conference president of the Woman's Home and Foreign Missionary Society in both conferences for a number of years. Her interest in missions resulted in her being on the conference mission boards and other mission-related committees. She was the Southern District organizer for eighteen years and also served as the conference superintendent of the Young Missionary Workers Band (now Wesleyan Kids for Missions).

Vera ended her earthly ministry October 18, 1970, in Salem, Oregon.

Grace Wood, Stella Wood, and Katrina Ruse

The Wood family lived on a farm near Cato, New York. There had been seven children born into the family, including three sets of twins. Clarence was the oldest child, followed by Grace and George, the first set of twins; Jean (whose twin died in infancy); and last of all Stella, whose twin also died in infancy.

The parents were godly, thrifty, and wise. Each child was given tasks to do and developed a good sense of responsibility for the assigned task. They were instructed in the way of the Lord. Each Sunday was reserved for Sunday school and church attendance.

A tragic train accident took the life of their mother when the children were quite young. At first the three girls carried on the household duties. The school was about a mile from their home, and Grace and Jean took turns staying at home to prepare the noon meal for the men who worked in the fields. The father finally decided to get a teacher for the children, and they were home-schooled. Miss Helen Root became their teacher, and she not only taught from the textbooks but also instilled in their minds Christian principles for living a godly life. She took the job with Mr. Wood's understanding that she was waiting to go to India. It may have been her burden for the lost ones of India that resulted in the call of both Grace and Stella to India as well. Miss Root did go as a missionary to India under the Free Methodist Church later.

Grace was about twenty years old when she came into the full light and definite experience of salvation. After Mr. Wood married again, the girls were released from home duties. Both Grace and Stella felt the call of God to go into Christian service. They enrolled at God's Bible School in Cincinnati, Ohio. An urgent call came for workers to come to the mountains of Kentucky. Grace worked with this group for a time. She returned to Cincinnati and worked a year in the office of God's Bible School.

Grace felt led to accept and pioneer (plant) a mission church in Cleveland, Ohio. She was the pastor for three years. Her next assignment was the job of matron of the Bethshan Rescue Home in Canton, Ohio, a home for unwed pregnant girls. It was a trying position, but she admirably filled the task. She next accepted the challenge of pioneer evangelism with D. B. Hampes in Portland, Oregon. While working with Rev. Hampes, Grace received a definite call to India.[234]

Grace spent three terms (about six and a half years each) in India in the Gujarat District under the Wesleyan Methodist Church. She was a wonderful missionary, serving in the orphanage, schools, evangelistic fields, and medical work from 1917 to 1946. Grace knew how to adapt herself to various races and to all kinds of Christian groups, regardless of denomination. She had a large number of prayer partners who supported her in prayer daily. She loved youth and saw things from their viewpoint. She was in great demand as a missionary speaker while home on furlough (home ministries).

Grace entered into whatever she was doing with all her heart. She was deeply devoted to Christ and was always quick to speak and act—but when her ideas were rejected, she quickly turned to other thoughts. She never pouted or held a grudge.

When it came time for Grace to return from India and retire from her missionary activities, she became so burdened for the work in Australia that she went there to help in the work. She arrived in that country in December 1946. Her saintly presence and moral and spiritual encouragement during those early days were instruments used of God to help establish the work there. She labored in Australia until 1949.[235]

Grace returned home and lived with Stella in Marion, Indiana, for a time. Later they moved to Georgia and finally settled in Wesleyan Village in Brooksville, Florida. Grace died July 14, 1982, at the age of one hundred.[236]

It is difficult to separate Grace and Stella in their ministries. Therefore, we will insert Stella's service here with that of Grace. Stella received her call to be a missionary to India in 1907. She wanted to go out under the Wesleyan Methodist mission board, but they did not have an established work in India. In 1908 she went to Cleveland to assist Grace in the pioneer church there. During this time Stella became acquainted with Grace Chadwick, the pastor of the Barberton, Ohio, Wesleyan Methodist Church. Miss Chadwick was also burdened for the people of India and encouraged Stella to be patient. Miss Chadwick spoke of the need to get the gospel to India at the Stoneboro Camp of the Allegheny Conference. She was instrumental in awakening the denomination to India's need.[237]

Rev. and Mrs. A. E. Ashton had spent several years in India as missionaries under the Vanguard organization of St. Louis. Their work in India was basically orphanage work for the starving boys and girls from the great famine in that country. The Ashtons came to the United States in 1910 to seek out a holiness denomination to take over their work in India. They made a proposition to Rev. Eber Teter, the missionary secretary, offering the title of a mission compound of five acres at Pardi,

India for six hundred dollars. The proposition was accepted. The Ashtons joined the Wesleyan Methodist Church in Fairmount in 1910. That year the Ashtons and their children were accompanied by Stella Wood to India. They arrived in India in December 1910.[238]

Stella soon learned even while studying Gujeraiti, the native language, that a missionary must do many different kinds of work. She carried heavy responsibilities and burdens. The mission was in a crisis time. The workers were disgruntled because the Wesleyan Methodist Church "had taken over the mission." Stella had to deal with a moral problem that would have been "difficult for a man to straighten out." There was a heavy financial burden, and Stella did all the bookkeeping records. She realized the need for a Bible school and started one during the monsoon season, which lasted three months. She did all the teaching in the school in addition to her other administrative work and responsibilities.[239]

The mission board felt it necessary for Stella to return home after a five-year term to do deputation (home ministries) in the interest of the work in India.[240] She returned to India in 1917 with her sister Grace and Mary F. Greene of Indiana. This was during World War I, and the women waited several weeks on the West Coast before they could get passage on a boat for India. These women did very capable work. They acquired the language of the people and cheerfully bore the sacrifices involved in their missionary work.

Stella returned home and began to pastor churches. In 1927 she was elected to be ordained at a time she chose. She was serving under the Iowa Conference at the Wyanet, Illinois, Wesleyan Methodist Church (the Iowa Conference included Illinois beginning in 1927). Her pastoral record revealed that she was joined at the Wyanet Church by Katrina Ruse.

Katrina Ruse was born March 15, 1894 in Anderson, Iowa. She was converted at age nine at the family altar. She felt called to the ministry and attended God's Bible School in Cincinnati, Ohio. In October 1927 she went to Wyanet, Illinois, to be the coworker of Stella Wood. This was the beginning of eighteen years of pastoral work together.

Stella chose to be ordained in 1930. That year, she and Katrina transferred their conference membership to the Wisconsin Conference. They were the pastors of the Beulah Wesleyan Methodist Church near Richland, Wisconsin, from 1931 to 1933. They pastored the Mill Creek church in Wisconsin from 1933 to 1935.[241]

In 1935 they returned to the Iowa Conference to pioneer the Albert Lea, Minnesota, Wesleyan Methodist Church. They first worshiped in a tent and then met in homes. The church was organized on June 7, 1936. They served this congregation for eight years. Katrina Ruse was ordained in 1936. This pioneering church became a thriving church under their leadership. Also during the 1936 conference year a parsonage was purchased for the church at Albert Lea.

They served the LaPorte City, Iowa, church from 1943 to 1945. The parsonage was purchased in the spring of 1945 while they served there.[242]

During the pastorate of Albert Lea, Stella was elected the editor of *The Wesleyan Missionary*. She possessed a missionary passion, a bent toward literature, deep spirituality, and a loyalty to holiness and the ideals of the Church. She was elected in 1936 and assumed the office in 1937 and continued until her retirement in 1951.[243] She completed her pastoral service in 1945. The office was then established at the Missionary Center in Marion, Indiana.[244]

Katrina Ruse was elected the corresponding secretary of the general Woman's Missionary Society in 1947. She did highly commendable work in developing the missionary study enlargement program. Katrina died April 26, 1949, at the Missionary Center in Marion, Indiana.

After Grace and Stella moved to Georgia, Stella served the North Georgia Conference in various offices. She was the secretary of evangelism, president of the conference Woman's Missionary Society, and editor of the conference paper, *Invigoration*.[245]

When they moved to the Florida Conference, she served as the conference Woman's Missionary Society Prayer Partner Secretary from 1957 to 1959. Stella and Grace were the first residents in the missionary section of Wesleyan Village at Brooksville. Stella conducted a worldwide correspondence during this time. These letters were

gems of counsel, exhortation, and inspiration. Many persons were led to the Lord through this ministry. Stella had a long illness but gave a radiant witness to everyone of the sufficiency of God's grace for every need. She died March 22, 1973.[246]

Bertha Fortner Bolender

Bertha Fortner was born October 13, 1898, in Kentucky. Her mother died when she was seven years old. She spent 1907 attending grade school at God's Bible School in Cincinnati, Ohio. She was soundly converted there at age eight.

"In the year 1914 at God's Bible School camp meeting under the ministry of John T. Hatfield, I sought sanctification. This marked a new and special epoch in my spiritual life." This was her account of her heart-cleansing experience.

Bertha's education continued at home in Butler County, Kentucky's one-room schoolhouse until age sixteen. She returned to God's Bible School, and it was there that she met fellow student Harry Hill Bolender from Felicity, Ohio. They were married on commencement day, June 1, 1918. Two children were born to them, Warren Hill and Vera Juanita Gibbs.

The Bolenders began their life's work of sixty-five years of ministry at the small church in Union City, Indiana. They were the pastors of Pilgrim Holiness and Wesleyan churches in Kentucky, Arizona, Nebraska, Colorado, Kansas, Missouri, and Tennessee. They also did missionary service in the West Indies on the islands of Barbados and Antigua, from 1944 to 1958.

Bertha was ordained to the ministry in 1927 by General Superintendent Seth Cook Rees of the Pilgrim Holiness Church at Colorado Springs.

Bertha was also active in the districts in which they served. She was the district Sunday school promotional secretary and missionary society treasurer on the Kentucky District. She served as the Tennessee District missionary society president also.[247]

Harry H. and Bertha Bolender celebrated their seventieth wedding anniversary June 1, 1988. Bertha completed her earthly walk January 26, 1993.[248]

Charlotte "Lottie" Bardiah Buttermore

Charlotte Buttermore was called "Lottie" in the Conference *Minutes*. She was born December 7, 1876, in Minnesota. She was converted as a child, was baptized, and joined the Wesleyan Methodist Church at age ten. Lottie graduated in 1913 from the theological department of Miltonvale Wesleyan College, Miltonvale, Kansas (later merged into what is now Oklahoma Wesleyan University, Bartlesville, Oklahoma). She was ordained by the Iowa Conference in 1920.[249]

Lottie gave twenty-six years of service to the Lord in pioneering works in the north central area of Minnesota. Her first assignment was in 1918 as a home missionary in northern Minnesota under the direction of the mission board. She received twenty-five dollars for the year's work. In 1920 she was stationed at Williams, Minnesota, at another mission work. She was not limited to the work at Williams, for in 1922 she gave her annual report, which included her work at Trommold, Manganese, and Williams, Minnesota. She also served at the mission at Bain, but she was released from the work there and was appointed pastor at Bethel until a pastor could be secured. On June 1, 1923, she returned to Bain. Other appointments included mission work at Rockford and Hammond.

In 1935 she moved to Miltonvale, Kansas, and assisted the pastor of Cedar, Kansas.

She served the Iowa Conference for a number of years as a member of the committee on itineracy and orders (now district board of ministerial development). Lottie was faithful to God's call and ended her earthly work July 29, 1962.[250]

Alice Cochonur

The Minutes of the Annual Session of the Eastern Kansas and Oklahoma District Pilgrim Holiness Church listed Alice Cochonur as an ordained minister in 1918. She was a pastor in 1924–25. No other record was found of her work.

Mrs. Bessie F. Hatcher

Bessie Hatcher was a unique woman who was gifted with an unusual sense of humor. Harold Crosser said she had been a vaudeville comedian before her conversion. David Tonnessen recalled she had been a Broadway actress and singer in her early life before coming to the Lord. David related that she never left her talents for the stage or musicals, as she wrote such favorite gospel songs as, "Let Me Burn Out for Thee," "Keep on the Firing Line," "He Will Not Fail Me Now," "I Would Not Want to Miss It," and others.[251]

Bessie Hatcher was born March 29, 1882. This warrior of the Cross died in June 1960. She was ordained by the Pennsylvania and New Jersey District of the Pilgrim Holiness Church in 1930. She began her ministry service in 1918, according to the *Minutes of the Annual Convention of the Apostolic Holiness Church of Pennsylvania Inc.* She was the pastor of the Trenton, New Jersey, International Holiness Church from 1920 to 1922. She served as the supply pastor of the Wesleyan Methodist church at Carney's Point, New Jersey, and had a very good relationship with the Middle Atlantic States Mission Conference of the Wesleyan Methodist Church. She was asked to conduct devotions in their conference meetings. She was also requested to act in an advisory relationship to their missionary board with regard to the camp meeting work.[252]

Most of Bessie Hatcher's ministry was spent in evangelism. She was elected the district evangelist. This work called for the conducting of many tent meetings over the conference each year as well as revival meetings in storefront buildings and other places. The intent of these meetings was the planting of new churches. The work demanded long hours and much physical labor as well as the preparing and preaching of the gospel. Bessie was gifted of God for this type of ministry. She served for many years on the foreign mission board of the district. She was gifted musically and played the piano. In 1930 she was elected a ministerial delegate to the

General Assembly of the Pilgrim Holiness Church.[253]

David Tonnessen gave the following two interesting vignettes that reveal her strength of character, her sense of dignity, who she was, and her mission.

Wesley Grove Camp had been a Methodist camp started in 1910 and closed about 1920. Bessie Hatcher walked the nearly one mile from her home in Yardville, New Jersey, to the old tabernacle site at the camp and prayed every day for at least one hour that a church group would come and take possession of the property. An amusement park group was attempting to get the rights to buy the property and set up various amusement facilities. Her efforts paid off, for in 1931 the Middle Atlantic States Conference of the Wesleyan Methodist Church was able to get the property and operated the camp there until 1971.

Bessie was a self-assured, resolute, and rather opinionated person. She insisted on getting rides to the evening service at camp and demanding that she be let out immediately next to the tabernacle door, although cars were not supposed to drive that close. She would get out of the car with her cane and oversized straw hat. During the first hymn she would walk the entire length from the rear of the tabernacle all the way down to the second row. As she walked down the aisle she would nod rather obsequiously to various ministers and other people. Just about the time the first hymn was over, she would be at her seat. She would turn around, gaze across the entire auditorium, nod to whoever was at the podium and then be seated. At rather appropriate times, she would take off her straw hat and send it like a spheroid around the room. Sometimes it would either get lodged in the wooden rafters or narrowly miss the speaker at the podium. Needless to say, this provided great mirth to all the teenagers, children, and a great number of adults.

Taking all of the above in perspective, she was a mighty voice in the community for prayer and testimony. Many evangelists also remember her ability to bake pies, because she brought pies to them during camp.

In her later years, Bessie earned part of her living by writing poetry for greeting cards. Her gospel songs were written portraying her Christian life at the time.

> He stills the storms and
> He calms my fears
> He forgive my sins and
> He dries my tears
> He is the same through endless years
> He will not fail me now.

Flora A. Pitts Goodwin Addington Becker

Flora A. Pitts was a student at Fairmount Bible School, Fairmount, Indiana (later merged into what is now Indiana Wesleyan University, Marion, Indiana) and graduated from the three-year course in 1919 and the four-year course in 1920. She was a good student and sought to help and advise the younger students. She was active in the literary programs of the school.[254]

Flora was appointed to go to India in 1920 but was not able to get there until 1921. She served until 1925. In 1925 she was ordained. She spent some time in the Kentucky Conference of the Wesleyan Methodist Church. Flora Pitts and Vera Lippold were the pastors of the Frankfort Height Wesleyan Methodist church in Illinois. This church was under the Kentucky Conference. She resigned that church November 17, 1932, and the following year was granted a letter of transfer back to the Indiana Conference. She was active on the conference level in Kentucky, serving on several committees and was conference secretary in 1930 as well as conference treasurer of the Woman's Home and Foreign Missionary Society.[255]

In 1935 she married Mr. Goodwin (first name unknown), and during that conference year she was appointed the pastor of the Amboy mission, Amboy, Indiana. Mr. Goodwin soon died, and on September 3, 1936, she married Asa R. Addington. She was the pastor of the Warsaw church for a short time but resigned to be assigned to conference evangelism. She retired from the active ministry in 1948. Mr. Addington died, and July 5, 1961 she married John Becker. Flora was still on the superannuated list in 1968.[256]

Emla Margaret Black

Emla Black took seriously the words of Jesus to give a cup of water to the thirsty, feed the hungry, visit the sick and imprisoned, and care for the strangers. She was born in Greenville, Pennsylvania, June 30, 1889. She became a registered nurse and then moved to Los Angeles to work in private nursing. While there, she took the civil service exam and became a public health nurse with the Mexicans.

In California she met Charles and Lettie Cowman, founders of the Oriental Missionary Society (now OMS International). They lived and breathed the gospel work in the Orient. God used them to awaken a call to Korea. In 1919 she sailed for Korea and worked among the Koreans for twenty years. She ministered in country evangelism and taught in the Bible seminary. She was an ordained minister and a member of the Rees Memorial Tabernacle in Pasadena, California (a part of the Pilgrim Church, which later merged with the International Holiness Church to form the Pilgrim Holiness Church).

Emla was in an accident in 1941, which prevented her from returning to Korea. But her heart's desire was still to help the Koreans. She worshiped with the Koreans in Los Angeles and sent relief packages to Korea. She sought out other people whom she felt would become interested in the Koreans, who were suffering much because of World War II.

Emla worked for her Lord for thirty-eight years under the Oriental Missionary Society in Korea and other places. She was remembered as a warrior of the Cross who was always cheerful, willing, and faithful to her duties. She had a radiant personality, was a blessing to many, and was much loved by those who knew her. Emla died May 7, 1957.[257]

Gladys H. Wellman Coates Coleson

Gladys Wellman was the daughter of B. F. Wellman, an elder (ordained minister) in the North Michigan Conference of the Wesleyan Methodist Church. She married Clarence V. Coates, and they were the pastors of the Lakeview church from 1914 to 1915. Their next pastorate was at White River, for three years. In 1919 she was recommended to study at Fairmount Bible School, Fairmount, Indiana (later merged into what is now Indiana Wesleyan University, Marion, Indiana), and that year they pastored the Roseburg Wesleyan Methodist Church in Indiana. Clarence died in 1920.[258]

Gladys returned to the North Michigan Conference and became the pastor of the Hart Wesleyan Methodist Church. She was ordained in 1920. She also was the pastor of the Walkerville church. She married Ralph Coleson, who began to study for the ministry in 1928. They co-pastored the Walkerville, Hart, Walkerton, Dice, Dighton, Pisgah Heights charge, and Weidman churches. She apparently was the leader of the team at least in the early years of their marriage. They were married around 1922, and Ralph was not ordained until 1932.

Gladys spent some years in evangelism also. She was active in the conference Woman's Home and Foreign Missionary Society and held several offices in that group. She was also active in the conference and served on many committees of the conference.[259]

Rev. Robert Cooper, former pastor and conference president of the North Michigan Conference, wrote,

> When I went to the Hart Wesleyan Methodist Church in 1957, Ralph and Gladys were members there. They had retired and lived at Mears, Michigan. I was present with Ralph and Gladys at the time of her death in 1959. Just before she died, she raised up with an exalted look on her face, and her lips moved, but there was no sound.[260]

Eva M. Dauel

Eva M. Dauel was born March 28, 1881, at Mount Vernon, Illinois. She had been baptized and joined the Christian Church as a child. In 1907 she was converted and gave her heart and life to God. She was later sanctified under the ministry of Rev. Carl H. Dauel, the evangelist.

That year she married Rev. Dauel, and for over fifty years she assisted him in pastorates, in the Rescue Home for girls in Denver, as superintendent of the Fifth Street Mission in Los Angeles, California, and for a number of years as the superintendent of the combined California, Arizona, and Oregon District.

Eva was ordained by the California District of the Pilgrim Holiness Church in 1931. Together, she and Carl were the pastors of the Rocky Ford, Colorado, church, and the Whittier and Olinda, California, churches. Carl died in 1946. Eva went to work with her sister, Katherine Hollowell, pastor of the Adams Memorial Pilgrim Holiness Church in Eastmont, California, as her assistant. She served in that capacity for over ten years, and when Eva became too ill to continue, they both resigned from the pastorate. Eva died December 7, 1957. She is remembered for her cheery spirit and warm smile. Her obituary was found in the *Pilgrim Holiness Advocate,* January 11, 1958, and in the *California District Journal and Minutes of the Annual Conference,* 1958.

Ida O. Fausch Franklin

Ida Fausch was born January 24, 1881, at Germanie, Wisconsin. She was converted in her early life. Her goal in life was to become a schoolteacher, and that goal was reached. After teaching for a number of years, she became aware God was calling her into another area. In 1906 she became affiliated with the Christian Crusaders and did evangelistic work for them for a number of years. When the Crusaders disbanded, she united with the Wesleyan Methodist Church. She took all the prescribed courses for ordination but was not ordained by them. She assisted in the pastoral work at the Hobert and Copmish, Wisconsin, churches.

November 24, 1909, she married James F. Franklin of Otterbein, Indiana. He was not a minister, but he was a constant and great helper in the Church. They became acquainted with the Indiana Conference of the Holiness Christian Church and joined that group in 1919 as it merged with the International Apostolic Holiness Church to form the International Holiness Church. In

1922 that group merged with the Pilgrim Church, and the name chosen was the Pilgrim Holiness Church. The Pilgrim Holiness Church ordained Ida in 1928. She served most of her ministerial life in missionary work in Wisconsin.

On Sunday, July 13, 1958, Ida attended Sunday school and the two worship services, as was her custom. In the early hours of July 24, she died.[261]

Monna M. Rogers

In 1919 the Ohio Conference of the Wesleyan Methodist Church offered words of thanks for the work Monna Rogers had done in the district and bid her Godspeed in her new work at Miltonvale College, in Miltonvale, Kansas (later merged into what is now Oklahoma Wesleyan University, Bartlesville, Oklahoma). While Monna worked outside the Ohio Conference, she maintained her conference membership in Ohio.

Monna taught and worked at Miltonvale College. In 1927 she began teaching at Marion College, Marion, Indiana (now Indiana Wesleyan University). She was ordained by the Ohio Conference in 1930 and spent two years as pastor of the Curtis Ridge and Senecaville churches. She was engaged in missionary, Women's Christian Temperance Union, and general evangelistic work for a number of years. She served as the Delaware County Women's Christian Temperance Union president also. She was active in the conference Woman's Missionary Society (WMS) and held several offices in that organization. She served on many conference committees also.

Monna M. Rogers died November 19, 1977.[262]

Florence M. Sell Timberman Fretz

Florence M. Sell was the pastor of Bird Lake Church in the Michigan Conference of the Wesleyan Methodist Church for a time. She was a member of the Ohio United Brethren Conference at the time but gave a good and satisfactory report. She pastored one other Wesleyan Methodist church, in Coldwater, Michigan. In 1920 she was ordained by the Michigan Conference of the Wesleyan Methodist Church. She was the pastor of the Prattsville Congregational Church in Michigan for a time also.

Florence Sell was born in Ohio in 1882. She was a graduate of Huntington College, Huntington, Indiana, attended Taylor University, in Upland, Indiana, and graduated from Chicago Evangelistic Institute (which later became Vennard College).

Florence married William A. Timberman in 1924; he died in 1946. They were the parents of three daughters. She married Clarence Fretz in 1970, and he died the same year. She had five stepdaughters. Florence died May 23, 1984.[263]

Sadie D. Shoemaker Shafer

Joy Smith wrote her mother's story in these words:

Sadie D. Shafer was born September 22, 1891 in Pennsylvania. She was saved at eleven years of age during a revival at the Windham Center Baptist Church.

When Sadie was thirteen, she and her parents were introduced to the holiness message. They gladly received this message.

In July 1915, she assisted her father in conducting cottage meetings at Oak Hill, N. Y., a nine-mile drive from Binghamton in a horse-drawn wagon over unpaved roads. There would be as many as five people in the wagon. At times they would need to lighten the load to continue their journey, which meant that some would have to walk part of the way. Many times it stormed, but that did not stop them. Sadie even went alone by horse and buggy to call in the homes of both saved and unsaved families. There was an ardor and intensity about their ministry that was contagious.

At first only a few attended the cottage meeting, but as time went on, people started coming even from the city until the house would be packed with 100 or more. By winter they were having three services each Sunday. Sadie wrote, "Such singing, shouting and praying through! Many found the Lord and were delivered from their evil habits, sensuality, and pride. We preached against all forms of sin and worldliness. We stressed not only the saving of the soul but also entire sanctification, the cleansing of the heart from the carnal nature. There were several preachers called from this group."

During this time she met the Shafer family. One of her converts was Carl D. Shafer, whom she married on August 6, 1918. Others of the Shafer family were also saved during the three years she ministered at Oak Hill. This congregation later organized and built a church at Finch Hollow, N. Y.

In 1918 Sadie and her husband went to pastor the church at Cortland, N. Y. Then in 1920 they moved to South Colton, N. Y., and continued their pastoral ministry. They were called to pastor the Reformed Methodist Church of Johnson City, New York, in 1917.

In time the Pentecostal Rescue Mission in Binghamton became the Pilgrim Holiness Church of New York state. Through this Conference the Shafers were assigned pastorates in Brookdale, Pennsylvania, and Madrid and Russell, New York. In 1946 they became a part of the Pennsylvania and New Jersey District of the Pilgrim Holiness Church, and Carl served a while as custodian at Allentown Bible Institute. In 1948 they were assigned to what turned out to be their last pastorate, at Ashland, Pa. Although Carl occasionally filled the pulpit, Sadie carried the preaching load in all the places they served. Carl worked faithfully to support the family during all those years. They served faithfully wherever they went and loved their people. They prayed earnestly for them and saw lives changed. Prayer was one of Sadie's greatest ministries.

Sadie was ordained by the New York District of the Pilgrim Holiness Church on April 19, 1941, and Carl on April 25, 1942.

Sadie's active ministry spanned a period of 40 years, beginning in 1915. At her death she was a member of the Falconer, N. Y., Wesleyan Church.

On September 22, 1991 family members and friends gathered to celebrate Sadie's 100th birthday. In a strong voice she spoke for twenty-five minutes responding to questions about her life and ministry. From experience and faith she said, "The love of God never changes. The goodness of God never changes. It pays to walk in all the light that God gives us."

Mary Olsen Conklin read a tribute to Sadie at her funeral. She noted that to know Sadie Shafer was to learn that God was the focus of her life. Pleasing Him was what truly mattered; human applause, earthly honors, whether bestowed or withheld, did not determine her course. Others watched with admiration her steadily exemplary, sacrificial life; her faithful, uncomplaining ministry; the concerned care afforded the sheep of her assigned flock. Her orthodoxy could not be challenged; her grasp of Scripture was impressive; her counsel embodied solid, practical wisdom. Her vigorous support of heart holiness remained a life-long hallmark, as did her role of earnest intercessor.

She had a remarkable letter-writing ministry. When failing eyesight brought new difficulties, the letters continued to go even after blindness had become total, when other hands set down on paper the messages she framed. Those letters manifested a lively interest in what was going on in the Church as well as in people's lives.

Martha Stuart wrote that Sadie was a gentle, unassuming lady, unapologetic, however, and firmly orthodox. She never breached confidentiality or prudence. She was outstanding in her compassionate outreach. She would move after a service around the church stopping to talk with one after another of the "little people," to whom few others had spoken.

Sadie ended her earthly walk January 13, 1992.

Joining Hands, Adding Ministries

Many world events that would affect the religious world occurred during the 1920s. Adolf Hitler began his rise to power within the Nazi party in Germany. Worldwide air travel had its beginning when Charles N. Lindberg flew nonstop from New York to Paris. In the United States, Prohibition went into effect and women won the right to vote. The Ku Klux Klan cut a ruthless swath across the South and was active even in the North.

Among the churches that would eventually be a part of The Wesleyan Church, it was a time of uniting smaller groups and developing denominational structure. In 1922 the International Holiness Church and the Pilgrim Church (centered in Pasadena, California) united and took the name Pilgrim Holiness Church. The same year the Pentecostal Rescue Mission of New York merged into the Pilgrim Holiness Church. In 1924 the Pentecostal Brethren in Christ merged with the Ohio District of the Pilgrim Holiness Church. In 1925 the People's Mission Church (centered in Colorado) merged with the Kansas District of the Pilgrim Holiness Church. It was now a body that spanned the continent and enjoyed strengthened leadership and membership. Its mission fields touched many areas of the world, and the church began to develop a denominational structure.

For the Wesleyan Methodists, this decade brought success at last in making the nonuse of tobacco a test of membership. In 1923 its missions department was divided into two, one for foreign missions and one for home missions. The development of youth work was authorized on the local and conference (district) levels.

The event that may have had the greatest impact upon the church in the following decades occurred in the 1920s: the stock market crash of 1929. This marked the beginning of the Great Depression that would last until 1940. Church budgets were slashed. Giving became more sacrificial, and some programs were cut from the Church's activities. Yet there was still an urgency to get the gospel to every person at home and abroad. Women continued to hear the call of God to preach, and they responded in obedience. Here are some stories of women who began their ministries during this period.

Hazel Rogers Banker

Hazel Rogers was born on the upper peninsula of Michigan in North Laird, August 22, 1894. Her parents moved to Odessa, Michigan, when she was six. She graduated with honors and was valedictorian of her high school class. She passed the teachers' examination and taught for six years in a school near her home. She was converted at the age of ten and joined the Wesleyan Methodist Church at East Odessa. From that time on, she was very active in church work. Hazel was the church organist for many years in her local church. When the Young Missionary Workers Band (now Wesleyan Kids for Missions) was organized, she became very active in that work. It was while she was teaching school that she felt definitely called to the mission field, and she went to Houghton Seminary, Houghton, New York (later Houghton College) to prepare for missionary work in India.

At Houghton she was described as "a plain, common girl, but one whose every act spelled character." While at Houghton this girl won the esteem of all with whom she came in contact. Her sincerity, faithfulness, and ability were soon evident. At various times she was president of the student body, cheerleader, and editor of the school paper, but her chief interest was always in the spiritual life of people. She spent three years at Houghton. She was ordained by the Michigan Conference of the Wesleyan Methodist Church in Hastings, Michigan, on August 13, 1922. She set sail for India in September of that year.

Hazel met Floyd Earl Banker at Houghton. They learned to care for and love one another. In the spring of 1924 the missionary board sent this young man to India. The day after his arrival, on March 18, 1924, Hazel and Floyd were married. To this union three children were born: Alice Florine, Genevieve, who died when she was eighteen months old, and Helen Ione.[1]

Hazel's life was dedicated to Christ and the carrying of the gospel to the people of India. She spent a total of thirty-seven years of faithful service for the Lord to the people of India. Hazel was so devoted to the work in India that on May 13, 1944, she transferred her district ministerial membership to the India Conference. On October 2, 1949, she moved that membership back to the Michigan Conference.

Hazel very ably led devotional periods at conference session when they were home on furlough (home ministries). Before she left for India, during 1920–21 she held several offices on the conference level. She was an interesting and anointed speaker and often spoke with her husband when they were on furlough. Floyd and Hazel returned home to the United States in 1948. They were the pastors of the Allendale, Michigan, church for two years. She served as assistant pastor. They then returned to India for another term of service.[2]

Hazel died July 18, 1959. A great warrior in Israel had fallen after several months of suffering. "She was most influential in her contacts with the students who attended the Bible School, and today she lives on in the lives of a great many Christian workers whom she influenced through the years." On Wednesday night of the Michigan Conference in 1959, Ethel Zuber gave a fitting tribute to Hazel Banker. A scholarship fund for the students in Yeotmal, India, was established in the name of Hazel Rogers Banker.[3]

Hazel coauthored the most complete history of the work in India with her husband, Floyd. The book, *From Famine to Fruitage,* was published by Wesley Press in 1960.

Mrs. Mae Bumgarner

Mae Bumgarner was born July 16, 1899. She was a person who was unknown to many, but to those who knew her, she was a lady of integrity and commitment to the Lord. She had helped in the organization of the Wilmont Wesleyan Methodist Church in Whittier, North Carolina, and served as its pastor for many years. She died September 17, 1993.[4]

W. E. Clark

Mrs. W. E. Clark and her husband were both ordained ministers in the Indiana District of the Pilgrim Holiness Church. They served for a number of years as evangelists. In 1929 he became field secretary for Frankfort College, Frankfort, Indiana (later merged into United Wesleyan College, Allentown, Pennsylvania). She was an excellent preacher and soul winner.[5]

Mrs. Clara A. Cook

Clara A. Cook was an ordained minister in the South Ohio Conference of the Wesleyan Methodist

Church. She served as conference secretary for thirty years and was a minister of the gospel for over forty years in the Wesleyan Methodist Church. She served as an evangelist part of the time and was active in the First Wesleyan Methodist Church at Dayton, Ohio. She was the mother of one son, Howard.[6]

Lettie B. Cowman

Lettie led her husband to the Lord after being saved only one month. She knew little about soul-winning, but they knelt at a chair in their home, and he received the Lord into his life. Charles died in 1924.[7]

Lettie and Charles came to God's Bible School, Cincinnati, Ohio, in September 1900. They had been accepted to go to Japan under the Methodist board of missions. Their short stay of six weeks resulted in the beginning of the Oriental Missionary Society. Lettie and Charles were the cofounders of this faith missionary society. They broke with the Methodist board of missions and decided to go "by faith" to Japan.[8] They were both ordained in Chicago in January 1901 by Seth C. Rees, Martin Wells Knapp, and Charles Stalker.

Lettie Cowman was a gifted missionary and writer; she was a zealous and able speaker. Even though they organized another missionary group, the Oriental Missionary Society, she kept her local church membership in the Rees Memorial Pilgrim Holiness Church in Pasadena until a few years before her death. Her ministerial membership was in the California District of the Pilgrim Holiness Church.

Lettie saw the work in the Orient spread from Japan to China, Korea, India, and South America. When Charles died in 1924, she was elected to serve as president of the Oriental Missionary Society until 1950. Lettie died at age ninety April 17, 1960.[9] She is remembered as the compiler of the well-known devotional book *Streams in the Desert*.

Anna Evans

Anna Evans was ordained by the Kentucky District of the Pilgrim Holiness Church. Her husband, Arthur L. Evans, was also a minister but was not listed by the Kentucky District. Anna manifested a sweet spirit and had a good personality. She was busy with weekend revivals, children's rallies, and conventions. She taught for two years in a holiness school and spent some time in Mexico. She was an evangelist among the Cubans in the South as well. Anna was an experienced chapel worker in prisons and spent a total of eighteen years in youth and children's work. She served as an evangelist 1954–66, and from 1962 to 1967 she served at Central Florida Bible Institute, in Intercession City, Florida. By 1966 she was superintendent of this Bible school. Arthur L. Evans died May 22, 1966.[10]

Mary P. Garrett

The *Maryland State News (Delaware State News and Daily Eagle)* Sunday, January 23, 1977, edition had this headline: "She Broke Sex Barrier Long Ago." The subtitle read, "To 'Miss Mary' Lady Preachers Are Nothing New." The article was about Mary Garrett of Dover, Delaware.

It seemed funny to her after all these years people were still arguing about women ministers. Mary Garrett crossed the sex barrier to become an ordained minister in 1926. She had been preaching for several years before her ordination. Mary would stand in the middle of a big cornfield all by herself. Her small frame would cast a long shadow across the stubbly field in the late afternoon. When the wind blew just right, her parents, who were finishing the farm chores, could hear her voice, and her father would say, "Listen—Mary's preachin' again." Mary knew at age eleven what she wanted to do and what God was calling her to do. She would be a pastor no matter what!

Despite admonitions from those who tried to discourage her, telling her that the ministry was not for women, she carefully planned her course. She graduated from school and took a job as a teacher in a one-room schoolhouse. When the weather was bad and she couldn't drive the team of horses, she would walk to the schoolhouse.

On Sundays the determined young woman went to church on the third floor of Hinckle's

Feed and Grain Store in Dover. Her mother supported her decision to go into the ministry. Mary dreamed of the day when she would be able to attend God's Bible School in Cincinnati. She saved her money and bought a calf. When it was time to sell the cow, she received enough money to get her into school. She went by train to Cincinnati. She returned to Dover in 1922 and served the Delmarva Peninsula area until she retired in 1968 at the age of seventy.

She moved to Crisfield, Maryland, where she began preaching regularly. When it was time to leave, the townspeople asked her to stay. She told them she would stay only five more weeks—but she remained for five years and reopened a church there. Not everyone wanted her to stay. Some felt she should be run out of town because she was a woman preacher, but Miss Mary "paid them no never mind."

Mary would often be called when people were ill, and she would go, usually walking, taking with her whatever medicine she managed to buy with her meager savings. She conducted funerals for those who died. She received much of her salary in vegetables in the summer, which were canned for use in the winter.

She moved to Cape Charles, Virginia, and pastored there for seventeen years. Even here she met with opposition from those who scorned women who dared to preach. Sometimes under this pressure she wondered if she had made the right choice. One night before a tent service where she was preaching she prayed, *Lord if I'm just puttin' this on and doin' somethin' I shouldn't be, I don't want Your help—I want to be a failure Friday night when I preach. But if You have called me, give me a sign. Let somebody come to the altar and pray until You save them.* Friday night she looked for her sign, and there was a young man kneeling at the altar.

Miss Mary was the pastor of churches in Crisfield and Goldsboro, Maryland, Cape Charles, Quimsby, and Exomore, Virginia; and Cedar Grove, Delaware.[11] When she retired in 1968, she left behind a string of revitalized rural churches. She planted the church in Crisfield and reopened the Cedar Grove church. Mary Garrett completed her earthly journey October 10, 1978.

She had spent her entire ministry in the Eastern District of the Pilgrim Holiness Church.

Laura L. Shepard Grossman

Laura L. Shepard was born September 4, 1891, near Warsaw, Ohio. She was converted in January 1904. She attended God's Bible School in Cincinnati, Ohio, and worked as the assistant registrar and advisor for a number of years at the school.

She was ordained by the Pilgrim Holiness Church in 1927.

Laura married Elmer W. Grossman July 19, 1935. For a brief period they worked together in the ministry, but she became ill and was bedfast for a number of years. She died at age fifty-three on November 25, 1944.[12]

Gertrude Hugley Harris

Gertrude Hugley was born April 23, 1902, in Opelika, Alabama. There were several siblings in her family. She lived to be eighty-seven years of age. The last sixty were spent in Dayton, Ohio. She prepared for the ministry and graduated from Wilberforce University, in Wilberforce, Ohio.

During the last twenty some years of her life, Gertrude was confined to her home because of an illness that caused her much internal suffering and outward affliction of open sores on the skin and face. This was attributed to poisoning from garden sprays. During all this she was a stalwart woman of prayer and never lost interest in the work of the South Ohio District, where she held her ministerial membership.

She was married to James B. Harris in 1923. He preceded her in death in 1981.

Her work in the South Ohio Conference of the Wesleyan Methodist Church was varied, but she was diligent in every place she served. She served as pastor of the Cutler, Ohio, Wesleyan Methodist Church. This was a small rural church that required her to travel by public transportation at least 125 miles one way.

Gertrude served in several district offices and on district boards. She influenced many youth when she was district youth president. As district conference evangelist, it was her responsibility to visit various churches during the year, preach, and serve communion. This required many miles of travel and also gave her the opportunity to proclaim the gospel and preach the holiness message. She also served as district Sunday school secretary for a time.

Perhaps her greatest contributions to The Wesleyan Church were her sacrificial labors for little remuneration, adorning the doctrine of holiness and the beacon of light she shed for those who followed after her.

For a time she did some missionary work among the Native Americans. She quoted them as saying, "White man's religion too tough."

When Eugene Ramsey was the president of the South Ohio Conference, he was able to turn to her as a valuable confidant on district interests even during her illness.[13] Gertrude Harris's funeral was June 24, 1989.

Beulah Knight Landrey

Beulah Knight was the second child of Richard and Hattie Knight. Richard had been called of God to preach, but he became a wandering farmer, traveling from farm to farm in Canada. They eventually settled near Winchester, Ontario. During a revival meeting in a little church, Beulah looked at her father during the invitation and said, "Papa, may I go?" and without waiting for an answer, she took him by the hand and led him to the altar. Both father and child received the pardoning grace of God that night. Both father and daughter were sanctified later in the meeting. Richard became one of the respected and loved ministers in the Canada Conference of the Wesleyan Methodist Church.

Richard died, and Beulah, only fifteen, was granted a permit to teach school. The stress of the schoolroom caused a drain on her spiritual life, and she drifted away from God. But God's love and her mother's prayers followed her, and she found peace in the barn where she had gone to pray. She determined that no obstacle would keep her from taking the gospel to India's millions of hungry people.

She presented herself to the missionary board after she had completed a three-year course at Chicago Evangelistic Institute (which later became Vennard College, University Park, Iowa). They told her she was too young to go. She felt led to take up nursing and graduated from the Civic Hospital in Ottawa, Ontario. Still she was not sent to India. She and her sister, Aileen, formed an evangelistic team called the "Knight Sisters." They gave five years to this ministry in the 1920s. Still she was not sent to India. She received a call to serve as matron and nurse at the Bethshan Home for unmarried mothers in Canton, Ohio. This service ended in 1932 when she married John Landrey, whom she had met three years before at a camp meeting in Michigan. John also had a call to minister in India. Still, no India.[14]

Beulah and John planted and co-pastored Wesleyan Methodist churches in Pennsylvania in the early 1930s. They were the pastors at Rochester, Beaver Falls, and New Castle, Pennsylvania, in the Allegheny Conference. In 1937 the call came: "Get ready to sail for India." Beulah and John were both ordained on August 24, 1937, and they went to India in 1938. They served under the department of foreign missions for sixteen years in India. While in India she served with her husband as an evangelist and church planter and in leadership development. Her nursing skills enabled her to minister to the sick and hurting, providing opportunities to share the gospel of Christ.

They returned to the United States in 1953. Beulah co-pastored at the Camden, New Jersey, Wesleyan Methodist Church and the Ponca City, Oklahoma church. She also served as director of nursing at the Fairhaven Home, a ministry to unwed mothers in Sacramento, California. After John retired, they moved to southern California, where Beulah was very active in the life and ministry of the Arrow Highway Wesleyan Church as long as her health permitted. John died August 31, 1985.

Beulah was the mother of four sons; Richard died in 1937. Of the other three, John Mark is a Christian educator and writer, James Paul is president of the Latin America Mission, and Jerald Burton is a minister.[15]

Elsie Myrtle Chapman McGaughey

Elsie Chapman was born December 21, 1886, in Denver. She grew up in a homesteader family. She left home in 1905 to make her own way. She was lonely, and one day after her day's work was completed, she went to her upstairs room, knelt, and prayed. She found Jesus as her Savior and experienced forgiveness, peace, and joy.

On October 8, 1905, she married Charles McGaughey. They became the parents of three boys and one girl.

The Lord had been preparing Elsie to preach for a number of years. On Thanksgiving Day 1920 she preached for the first time, and from that day on she preached! She was a great soul winner. Hundreds of people were saved under her ministry as she served in the Pilgrim Holiness Church and helped to open new places of worship. Her husband died February 11, 1921. She died December 8, 1954.[16]

Alice Jean Hampe McMillen

Alice Hampe was born to Daniel and Anie Hampe, church planters in western Pennsylvania and Ohio. Their church planting work took them to Washington and Oregon when she was a child. Alice was a wiry girl, possessed with a spirit of adventure. She had a great love for books, art, and nature. She surrendered her talents, time, voice, self, and life to God. When the needs of Japan were presented, she felt God calling her to Japan as a missionary. Alice studied at Seattle College (now Seattle Pacific University). In 1920 they moved to Houghton, New York. Alice entered Houghton College to continue her training to become a missionary. Her faith in God to supply her material needs at college was rewarded, and she graduated from Houghton College in 1925.

Alice applied to the missionary board to serve in Japan. Two doctors declared her physically unfit for foreign service. When people suggested she try other mission boards, she flatly refused, saying she was a Wesleyan Methodist and that she would go under their board. She simply laid the problem at the feet of Jesus and waited for Him to open the door. She completed more work at Houghton and served as dean of women. Alice was active in the Young Missionary Workers Band (now Wesleyan Kids for Missions) and often spoke in their services and did extensive writing for them. She walked through each door God opened. She became a close friend of Oneida McMillen (Gleason) and often visited in that Pennsylvania home. There she met Sim I. McMillen, Oneida's brother. They were both interested in missions, but their calls were to two different fields: Japan and Africa. However, God led them to serve together in Africa.[17] After their marriage they went to Sierra Leone in 1929 and served four terms there, ending in 1941. S. I. McMillen gave his time and energy to spread the gospel through meeting the physical needs of the people. Alice, an ordained minister, was in charge of the Mount Loma Bible School, a training school for Christian workers. Her work was highly valued in the development of the native ministry.[18]

Alice was an excellent speaker. When she spoke, there was usually a response of youth deciding to answer God's call to service or a fairly large sum of money received for missions. In 1949 she became professor of freshman Bible at Houghton College while Dr. McMillen became the village doctor. She taught for a number of years. She was vitally interested in the Woman's Missionary Society and served as general vice president of the society from 1947 to 1963. Alice J. McMillen was "queenly in bearing, and beautiful of spirit." She died January 24, 1986.[19]

Elsie Moyer

Elsie Moyer was born at Colebrook, Ashtabula County, Ohio, and spent her entire life of seventy-three years in that vicinity. She departed this life June 20, 1949. She was the mother of three daughters and one son. Her husband, John, died in 1921. Elsie retired from the active ministry in 1941.

Even in retirement she was a faithful witness to the Christ she loved and served. She preached whenever she was called and labored in prayer for the salvation of the lost.

Elsie was the pastor of the following Wesleyan Methodist churches: East Conneaut and Clarks Corners, Ohio; East Springfield and North Springfield, Pennsylvania. She served the North Springfield church as pastor for fifteen years. Elsie not only cared for her flock spiritually but also helped them in illness by nursing them, praying for them, and staying up many nights with the ill.[20]

Anna May Orkney

The Minutes of the Annual Convention of the International Holiness Church of Pennsylvania and New Jersey, 1920–22, and *The Minutes of the Annual Assembly of the Pilgrim Holiness Church of Pennsylvania and New Jersey,* 1923–25, listed Anna May (Mrs. John) Orkney as an ordained minister serving as a missionary in Seoul, Korea.

Lenora M. Rolfe

Lenora M. Rolfe, also listed as L. M. Rolfe, was first mentioned in the *Minutes of the North Michigan Conference* of the Wesleyan Methodist Church in 1920. She was appointed the pastor of the Cob-moo-sa circuit and remained there until she resigned April 3, 1922. That conference year she served as an evangelist. In 1923 she was on the retired list of ordained ministers.

Lenora served on many conference committees during her lifetime. She also served on several conference committees of the Woman's Home and Foreign Missionary Society.

Robert Cooper, a former president of the North Michigan Conference, wrote that she was highly honored and respected in the conference. Lenora departed this life in 1947 in Cadillac, Michigan.[21]

Viola C. Shinn

Viola Shinn was born in Kentucky in 1888. She was converted early in life and sanctified shortly after. She was employed in regular work near her home and assisted in revival meetings as opportunity afforded. She was a member of the Holiness Christian Church and was the pastor of the Owensboro and Tell City, Kentucky, churches.

She married Charles E. Shinn September 8, 1923. They had one child, who died a few days after birth. Viola and Charles did missionary work for the Pilgrim Holiness Church in Louisville, Kentucky, and in the Los Angeles area.

Together they were the pastors of the Oak View, Murrietta, and Templeton, California, churches. They were called August 15, 1933, to pastor the Murrietta church and left in 1937. They apparently went back to Kentucky and then returned July 27, 1937, to assume the duties of the pastorate at Murrietta until 1940.

In 1931 Viola was elected assistant superintendent of the Los Angeles Mission. She was the pastor of the Riverside church from June 19, 1938, to August 15, 1939.[22]

The Shinns retired and moved to Buena Park, California. Viola died there January 8, 1964.[23]

Mrs. H. P. Thomas

Mrs. H. P. Thomas was listed as an ordained minister in minutes of the *State Assembly International Holiness Church of Kentucky* in 1920–21 and in the *Minutes of the Annual Conference of the Kentucky District Pilgrim Holiness Church* in 1922. No record was found of her appointments.

Edith Trotske Reed

There were reports of evangelist Edith Trotske (sometimes spelled "Trotzke") in *The Pilgrim Holiness Advocate* in the 1920s. Meetings were held in Fairbanks, Kempton, and Merom, Indiana. One reported that she had been a full-time pastor for many years and was an anointed evangelist. God gave her souls wherever she went.

Edith Trotske was born March 18, 1889 and was converted in 1908. She spent twenty-one years in evangelism. She was the pastor of the Jackson Hollow, Sanford, New Goshen, and

Seelyville, Indiana churches. In 1955 she was listed as Mrs. Edith Trotske Reed. Apparently she was married during the previous conference year.[24]

Edith Trotsky Reed died in December 1963.

Miriam Auxier

Miriam Auxier served under the Indiana District of the International Holiness Church as pastor of the Walkerton, Indiana, church. Minnie Snyder served as her assistant pastor.

Miriam was ordained by the International Holiness Church in 1922. After this group merged with the Pilgrim Church to form the Pilgrim Holiness Church later that year, Miriam served under the Indiana District of the Pilgrim Holiness Church.[25] During 1924–26, she was the pastor at the Carlinville, Illinois, church, and again Minnie Snyder was her assistant.[26]

Rev. Ernest Batman, a former secretary of the Northern Indiana District, reported that "Sister Auxier was often a delegate to conference when I was District Secretary. When I had a difficulty pronouncing her name, she would say, 'It is Ox-ear.' She was a very pleasant lady. She was from one of our churches in the northern part of the state."

Miriam Auxier served as an evangelist for many years. She was a gospel singer, pianist, and guitarist.

Mary E. Beitzel

The Minutes of the Annual Assembly of the Indiana District of the International Holiness Church of 1921–22 listed Mary E. Beitzel as an ordained minister in the district. *The Minutes of the Annual Assembly of the Pilgrim Holiness Church Indiana Conference* from 1923 to 1939 listed her as a missionary to Africa.

Elsie Bradley

Elsie Bradley was born in Wisconsin in 1890. She married William Bradley in 1911. They were the parents of two daughters and one son.

Their first appointment was the pastorate at the Effingham, Illinois, church. This pastorate was followed by several years of evangelistic work in Illinois, Indiana, Michigan, and Wisconsin until his health begin to fail. They moved to Sheboygan, Wisconsin, in 1927. He died in 1941.

Elsie was ordained by the International Holiness Church in 1920. The couple served most of their ministerial lives under the Indiana District of the Pilgrim Holiness Church.[27]

Mary K. Elrod

In 1921 Mary K. Elrod assisted in revival meetings during the summer months. Her service was very satisfactory. No further mention was made of her in the *Minutes* of the South Carolina Conference of the Wesleyan Methodist Church until 1945. At that time she had been appointed the pastor of Buck Creek on August 22, 1944. She served that church for three years.

Mary was born in a Methodist home. She attended a camp meeting held at Piedmont, South Carolina, by the Wesleyan Methodist Church. She attended Asbury College, in Wilmore, Kentucky.

Her life was cut short by cancer, and she died in 1948.[28]

Mary Friend

Mary Friend's record began with the 1921–22 year in the *Minutes of the Annual Conference of the International Holiness Church of Indiana*. She was the pastor of the Orleans and Medora church in 1923 and the Linton church in 1924. Mary was a delegate to the General Assembly in 1924 of the Pilgrim Holiness Church. Her ministry was under the Pilgrim Holiness Church. No further records were found for her until 1934 and none thereafter.[29]

Florence Harris

In the *Wesleyan Methodist Church: A Brief History of the Steps Leading to the Organization of the Middle Atlantic States Mission Conference and the Minutes of the First Session* in 1921, Mrs. Florence Harris, an ordained minister, served on the standing committee for presidency. She was actively engaged in the organizational meeting held April 14, 1921 and was appointed a general evangelist and was listed as a general evangelist as long as she was in the Church.

Mrs. Harris served on the Itinerancy and Elders Orders Committee (now District Board of Ministerial Development) from the beginning until 1925, when she resigned and requested that her name be dropped from the roll. Her request was granted.[30]

Hattie Hickman

Hattie Hickman was converted in a Methodist camp meeting in Staunton, Virginia, and was called to preach at the same time in 1915. She worked in a mission while she prepared to preach, and she did revival work for another two years.

She then went to West Virginia and began serving under the International Holiness Church (later Pilgrim Holiness Church). She was ordained by Rev. George B. Kulp and worked under Seth C. Rees, Dr. Godbey and L. W. Sturk.

Hattie Hickman spent most of her ministerial years in evangelism, organizing and pastoring churches in West Virginia. After her health and eyesight failed, she spent her time in a ministry of prayer.

She was the pastor of Bramwell, Cooper's, Clarksburg, Logan, and Fayetteville churches, all in West Virginia.

In her evangelistic work, she often helped in the organizing of new churches in West Virginia. One year her report told of three tent meetings. An infant church at Three Mile was helped, but the "tobacco devil" and many other devils were stirred, and they fought some battles. People said they would "hang us to a limb," and they did shoot at the back of the tent.

A tent meeting held at Dunbar, West Virginia, lasted for three weeks. People laid in the straw like dead folk. They threw away their tobacco, and the tent was full every night. "Most of the crowd" was on the outside. Here the converts were encouraged

to go to the Charleston Church, which was only five miles away and easy for the folk to go to on the streetcar.

The next tent meeting was at Dana, West Virginia. Here a church was organized. She also organized a church at Mt. Hope. Some of the meetings were held in halls. If a church was not organized, she often organized a mission. This was the case at Pax. She held a meeting at the struggling mission at Mullens, and the prospects were not good for this group. A church of twenty-two members was organized at Accoville. Fairmont, where half of the population was Catholic, was a hard place to have a meeting but she was able to organize a mission there. At Mannington she started a Pilgrim Holiness prayer meeting. She seldom received a salary or an offering for these meetings. These accounts were her efforts as a district evangelist for two years.[31]

Hattie Hickman died at age ninety on May 27, 1981.

Ruth Algenia Leverich Luttrull

Ruth Algenia Leverich was born in Lone Tree, Iowa, May 23, 1904. She received her A.B. degree from the University of Evansville and her M.S. degree from Indiana University. Wherever she and A. L. Luttrull lived, Ruth attended college. Her education was extensive. She attended the University of Iowa, Oakland City College, Florida Southern College, the University of Florida, Indiana State University, the University of Southern California, California State (Orange State) University, Chapman College, and the University of California-Irvine.

Her oldest child, Katherine (Palmiro) Baresic, relates her ministerial records:

Mother began filling preaching appointments for Dad when he was in evangelistic work and still in college. She and Dad were married December 23, 1921, and I was born December 18, 1923, so Mother was very young to start out with a baby and take a traction car to Grandview and other Southern Indiana towns to preach.

In July 1925, Dad and Mother were ordained by Dr. Dearing at Oakland City College before they left to serve as missionaries in Agana, Guam.

Mother did a lot of visitation, and I remember her taking a leprous woman to church on Sundays. She helped with programs in the church and taught classes. Dad always said that the native people in Guam did not know how to sing in quartets until Mother taught them at the church. Mother became ill with severe allergies, and they returned home in 1929.

The family moved into the parsonage at Garvinwood General Baptist Church in 1930, and the next year Mother became a part of a radio program on WGBF belonging to James Price and his wife. Later Dad and Mother took over the program. Mother read and answered the mail and planned the program and music. Many times she had stories for the children.

In a few years, they started a Holiness Church (the Tabernacle), opened a Bible School (Mother taught Greek), and had a dairy farm to provide work for the students. She churned butter, and we sold milk daily (except for Sunday) and housed students. She visited the sick, played the piano and organ on the radio and at church, sang in quartets for the radio programs, and went with Dad on radio "rallies." These rallies were an outreach for the radio and our church.

In 1951 Dad and Mother transferred from the International Tabernacle Association to the Southern Indiana Conference of the Pilgrim Holiness Church.[32] They moved to Intercession City, Florida, in 1953, where Dad was the pastor of the Morrison Memorial Church and later president of Central Florida Bible Institute. Mother taught special education classes in Florida besides helping with the pastorate.

They returned to Evansville, Indiana, in 1957 to take the East Side Pilgrim Holiness Church for a couple of years. Mother started some prayer groups in the church and also in towns nearby: Rockport, Grandview, and Owensboro. They returned to Florida for two years, and Mother again taught school.

When Dad went into full-time evangelistic work, they lived in Chandler, Indiana, and Mother taught special education classes in Evansville public schools. Her evenings and weekends were spent in visitation, work with prayer groups, and publishing *The Messenger,* which kept interest alive in contributing to and praying for missions.

Mother died November 25, 1979. She was a busy woman who loved the service of God. I often wondered how Mother was able to cope with all her duties, but she always had time to be a wonderful mother to all of us children.

Ethel M. McCash

The Minutes of the Annual Session of the Michigan Conference of the Wesleyan Methodist Connection, or Church, of America, 1921–27, listed Ethel M. McCash as an ordained minister. She was never given an appointment, and in 1927 she joined another church.

Helena M. Saneholtz

Helena M. Saneholtz served as an evangelist in the "Pioneer Evangelistic Campaign." She describes the job description for this kind of evangelist as a scrubwoman, janitor, provider of food, chauffeur, song leader, musician, altar worker, caller, preacher—everything. This is how she described one of her meetings. A small group of people wanted to have a revival meeting. They asked Helena to come. They had rented an old theater building. There was much opposition in getting the building ready for the meeting. Some town loafers were asked to carry water to the building and help in the clean-up. People were amazed to see her and her two workers with mops and brooms cleaning a theater. Another man had wanted to rent the building also. To cause confusion in the town, he rented a room just two doors down from her building. He started a revival the same night she did. The group that had invited her to come attended their own prayer meeting and didn't come to the revival. She decided to come and live in the community and get to know the people and thereby gain their confidence. She rented a room and moved in. She began calling on all the people in the town, and people became interested. Many did not have cars, so she established a route and began to pick up people to come to the meetings. She went back and forth picking up people for the meeting. When the weather became cold, she purchased oil burners to heat the building. One evening she started the burners and then left to pick up the people. She heard the town's fire alarm go off. The Pilgrim Holiness theater was on fire! Crowds began to flock to the meetings, and several persons were saved. Money came in to meet all the needs of that two-and-a-half-week meeting.[33]

Helena pastored several churches for the International Apostolic Holiness Church in Ohio and the Pilgrim Holiness Church. She often had an assistant or a co-pastor. Ruby A. Wyan (Mrs. Lucian Brown) assisted her on the pastorates at Bradford, Pennsylvania, and Greenville, Ohio, in the 1940s. Helena Saneholtz pastored Murray, Wellston, Defiance, Chillicothe, and Athens, Ohio churches, and the Powassau Church in Canada.[34] She often held revival meetings with Celia Bradshaw. Reports in the *Pilgrim Holiness Advocate*, March 31, 1927, revealed that in one of their meetings there were 152 seekers in the meeting and they preached to overflow crowds.

Helena was ordained by the Pilgrim Holiness Church in the Indiana North District. She worked as an employee for the general church headquarters in Indianapolis for several years. She was the secretary of General Superintendent L. W. Sturk. She also worked in the editorial department, Ministerial Study Course Agency, the Sunday School Department, and the publishing house.

Helena was born in Napoleon, Ohio, November 13, 1898, and departed this life on April 15, 1965. She was a graduate of Bowling Green Teachers College and God's Bible School.[35]

Mrs. Minnie Snyder

Minnie Snyder worked with Miriam Auxier at the Walkerton, Indiana International Holiness Church in 1921. She located in Carlinville, Illinois, in 1924 and served for some years in the Indiana District of the Pilgrim Holiness Church. She was ordained in 1926. Her name appeared for the last time in 1934.[36]

Crystal Sylvia Beecher

Crystal Beecher completed sixty-five years of ministry for the Lord and the Church. She was the mother of two children, Howard and Ima Ruth.

Howard J. Beecher was the pastor of the Brown's Chapel Church near Greenfield, Indiana,

in 1921. Crystal joined him in 1922. Brown's Chapel was a part of the International Holiness Church of Indiana at that time. Crystal was ordained by the Pilgrim Holiness Church in 1937.

She filled the positions of pastor, pastor's wife, and district superintendent's wife during her ministerial life. Howard Beecher was a district superintendent in the Eastern Kansas-Oklahoma, Kansas, Illinois, and Oklahoma Districts. Among the Illinois churches where she pastored with her husband were Brown's Chapel, Bloomington, Decatur First, Charleston, and Pleasant Hill, a church near Lexington, Illinois.[37]

C. B. Colaw, a retired district superintendent from the Tri-State District, recalled that Crystal Beecher had made a great impression on him and had influenced him as a teenager. He said,

> Mrs. Beecher had an immense impact on my life when as our pastors while in my middle teens, they lost a little son about four years of age. The great spirit which was manifested impacted me greatly. The church had voted them out, and before they could move the little boy died. They had the funeral at the church they were leaving and took the casket in their car to the new place for burial.[38]

Crystal died in 1987.

Lona Harriett Dillon Decker

Harriett Dillon was born February 27, 1898, in Warren, Indiana. She was the second of eight children born into the home. She gave her heart and life to Christ while still young at the Plummer's Chapel Wesleyan Methodist Church and soon felt called into missionary work. She attended Fairmount Bible School, in Fairmount, Indiana, and its successor, Marion College, in Marion, Indiana (now Indiana Wesleyan University). Here she met a young man, Carmen Clyde Decker. They were married and became the parents of two children, James and Jane. Both Harriett and C. C. were ordained in the Wesleyan Methodist Church. She was ordained in 1929. Their first pastorate was the Blue River charge in Indiana. In 1921 they accepted the call to go to

Sierra Leone, West Africa. They ministered there for three terms (1921–24, 1925–27, and 1938–41).

During their terms in Sierra Leone they helped to establish work among the people of several villages. When they were home on furlough and after returning from Sierra Leone, they co-pastored several churches in Indiana. Those pastorates were Laketon, Silver Lake, Mt. Etna, Monument City, Plymouth and College Church in Marion, Indiana.

C. C. Decker was a chaplain in the military during World War II. They served a short time as missionaries in Hawaii. Harriett was a school-teacher and taught at Jackson College and Sterling College as well as in the public school systems in Indiana and Florida. They retired and lived in Wesleyan Village in Brooksville, Florida, for almost thirty years. C. C. Decker died December 23, 1977, and Harriett died March 13, 1997, at ninety-nine years of age.[39]

Annie Gerberich

Annie Gerberich was granted her first license to preach in 1922. She and her husband, Lyman Gerberich, were appointed pastors of the Fowler (Ind.) Wesleyan Methodist Church that year. They pastored there until conference time in 1925. At that time they were appointed to the Kirklin, Indiana, church. She was ordained in 1927. They co-pastored the Fountain City charge, Edgerton, Portland, Waveland, Logansport (two times), and the Santa Fe and Pleasant Grove charge. She retired in 1944. Her husband, Lyman, died in 1956.

Mrs. W. C. Kirkman

The *Minutes of the Annual Assembly of the Virginia District of the Pilgrim Holiness Church,* 1922–30, listed Mrs. W. C. Kirkman as the pastor with her husband at Brandywine, Christo, Hemlock, Warren Springs (two times), and Bent Mountain, Virginia. The *Minutes* of 1930 showed that she had died during the past conference year. She had been an active minister in the Virginia

District for ten years. She previously had been a member of the North Carolina District. She was an excellent helper to her husband and often filled the pulpit where they were pastors.

Ida Morgan Kierstead

Ida Morgan Kierstead began to write her life story at age seventy-three but did not complete it. Her grandson, Glendon F. D, Kierstead, provided the materials for some of those early days of his grandparents. She was sixteen when she became a born-again believer. This occurred under the ministry of Rev. G. B. Trafton and a young licentiate, Ella Kinney (Sanders). She was baptized in icy Canadian waters in January after her conversion. She had always had an interest in missions, but after her conversion the burden intensified. Ida was keenly interested in the Bible, and Ella Kinney Sanders helped her in her diligent study of the Word. She worked for eight years as a clerk in a store, but the restlessness of an unsettled heart called her on to something more. Finally she went to Boston and to Fall River Hospital, where she was accepted as a student nurse. She completed the three-year course in two years with very high grades. She graduated in 1901.

After graduation she worked in Boston and completed some nursing specialization. Soon after this Ida became very ill, and her mother cared for her and "never took her dress off" for two and a half weeks. During this time Ida surrendered everything to God and His will. In exchange, God blessed her with "heart purity," sanctification, and a peace that was unshakable during the years to come.

She had become engaged to I. F. Kierstead. He also had a missionary call to Africa. The campground of the Alliance of the Reformed Baptist Church of Canada, Beulah, was at Brown's Flats, New Brunswick, on the St. John River. Ida did not arrive at the camp until after the first Sunday of the camp meeting in the summer of 1905. A large group of people were at the wharf awaiting her arrival. They were in a hilarious mood. I. F. Kierstead had been ordained and accepted as a missionary, but he could not go until he was married. The crowd of friends had hoped that the couple would get married

Rev. Ida Morgan Kierstead and Family

immediately! She spent the night in prayer and concluded that marriage would be the best for both I. F. and her now. She was soon outfitted for the wedding, with a suit, lingerie and even the bridal bouquet. The first marriage in the Beulah Tabernacle was performed in June 1905. The bridal couple was I. F. and Ida Morgan Kierstead.

They set sail on October 4, 1905, for Africa. The trip took six and a half weeks to cross the ocean. They then boarded a train and stopped in Vryheid. This was followed by post cart, a two-wheel cart pulled by ten donkeys, for fifty miles. The trip was completed by horseback. Ida had never ridden a horse before, and for the next few days she sat on cushions!

The Kiersteads worked with Ella and Herbert C. Sanders. Ida studied the Zulu language and was able to speak with the nationals. Her first words in Zulu were "Ask and you will be given." Ida gave willingly of her own dresses to the Zulu women when they were converted. They wanted to get rid of their heathen skirts and dress like a Christian. When they were given a dress, they would hug it up to themselves and dance for joy.

One Sunday morning as Ida led the service, she felt led to have an altar service. Everyone gathered around the altar and prayed. Surges of power swept over the crowd, and a great transformation took place in the people. After that day, in spite of famine, poverty, and sickness, God's grace was evident in these people.

Ida Morgan Kierstead was ordained October 26, 1925. She and her husband, Isaac Freeman Kierstead, were the pastors of a number of churches including Royalton, Fredericton, Saint John, and Knoxville, New Brunswick. These churches were all a part of the Reformed Baptist work in Canada. Her grandson, Glendon Kierstead, said, "I understand she not only helped in the pastoral duties, but she did half of the work."[40]

Irene Kleinschmidt

The Minutes of the Annual Assembly of the California District of the Pilgrim Holiness Church, 1922–26, listed Mrs. Irene Kleinschmidt as the pastor of the Pilgrim Holiness Church in San Diego from 1922 to 1924.

Katie D. Lacey

Katie D. Lacey was listed as an ordained minister in the *Minutes of the Annual Assembly Indiana District of the International Holiness Church,* 1922. No other record of her service was found.

Grace Lamb

Grace Lamb was born in Michigan August 7, 1877. She was saved, sanctified, and called to preach the Word of God in her early years. In 1912 she accepted the responsibility of matron of the Bible Holiness Seminary, in Owosso, Michigan (later Owosso College, eventually merged into what became Indiana Wesleyan University, Marion, Indiana). She served there for fourteen years. She also served in Kingswood Holiness College, Kingswood, Kentucky, for two years. For five years she was the matron of Frankfort Pilgrim College in Frankfort, Indiana (later merged into United Wesleyan College, Allentown, Pennsylvania). For the last eighteen years of her life she was the associate pastor of Fort Wayne Tabernacle, Fort Wayne, Indiana.

A report at assembly time in 1936 revealed that Grace had assisted in 25 services, conducted 260 prayer meetings and services, made 1,040 calls, and prayed in 1,000 homes. Grace became totally blind, but she never complained. Her testimony was that she had a few thorns but a great many roses. During her last illness she hovered between life and death for eight weeks, but during all her conscious moments she prayed for the lost and the advancement of the Kingdom.

Grace Lamb was a good preacher, matron, and teacher. She was firm but kind. Her earthly life ended October 24, 1950.[41]

Lulu Griffin Roberts

Lulu Griffin married Lewis Reibard Roberts in 1914. Together they were actively involved in pastoring churches in Ohio for over fifty years. L. R. Roberts died in 1968. Their pastorates included East Canaan, Athens, Oak Grove, Jackson, Dayton Westside, Bradford, Springfield First, Washington Court House, New Carlisle and Piqua. Her husband also served as superintendent of the Ohio District of the Pilgrim Holiness Church for fourteen years.[42]

Helena Terwilliger Shafer

Helena Terwilliger began her ministerial service under the Pentecostal Rescue Mission of New York. She was listed as an evangelist in 1922 and married Arthur L. Shafer the same year. Helena was the pastor of the Monticello (N.Y.) Pilgrim Holiness church 1924–43. Shortly before she became the pastor, the church became a part of the New York District of the Pilgrim Holiness Church.

Helena was ordained in 1941. She and her husband pastored together for twenty-eight years. She always actively shared the preaching duties. For a time (two to three years) they pastored the Finch Hollow church (later known as Oakdale). She was stationed at Massena, New York, from 1948 to 1956. They retired in 1963, and Arthur died in 1964.[43]

Edith Stearns

Edith Stearns was ordained in 1922 by the Indiana District of the International Holiness Church. That same year that group merged with the Pilgrim Church to form the Pilgrim Holiness Church. *The Minutes of the Annual Assembly of the Pilgrim Holiness Church Indiana Conference,* 1923–34, recorded Edith as a missionary in India. The last entry for her was made in 1934.

Kennie Dawn Adams

The Tennessee District of the Pilgrim Holiness Church owed its existence to pioneer women preachers who were led of God to start churches in the mountains of Tennessee.

Mrs. Kennie Dawn lived in Carthage, Kentucky. God began to speak to her about the lost people in the mountains of eastern Tennessee, and He called her to be a missionary preacher there. In 1923 she and her family moved to Annadel, Tennessee, and she began traveling over the east Tennessee mountains preaching the gospel. Her husband became ill and died, so she moved back to Kentucky. But the call of God kept burning on her heart, and within six months she had returned to Tennessee. She settled first in Friendsville, where she could enroll her daughter in the Quaker boarding school.

One day while praying, she was impressed to go to Clinton and plant a church there. She had never heard of the place, but she purchased two train tickets, one for herself and one for her daughter, to Clinton. She was directed to the boarding house of Fanny Radford. Mrs. Radford later introduced her to Joe and Molly Webster. Prayer meetings were begun in the Websters' home. In 1924 Kennie rented a two-room house. She lived in one room and used the other one for Sunday and Wednesday night services. A small parcel of land was auctioned off in 1926. Kennie Dawn and Fanny Radford purchased the lot by faith for the small congregation, and the first Pilgrim Holiness church of Tennessee was built. Kennie Dawn was a member of the Kentucky District of the Pilgrim Holiness Church, and this church was affiliated with the Kentucky District. The church was organized with seven members.[44] The church at Clinton was dedicated on May 27, 1928. They struggled to be debt free but were "blessed with a zealous pastor, Sister Kennie Dawn." She and her local preachers were busy going into nearby towns and communities establishing Sunday schools and conducting revival meetings. They conducted a revival in an abandoned Methodist church about nine miles from Clinton. The church was not located in a town or village, but the community was stirred, and over 100 persons attended the meeting, some coming as far as six miles over mountain roads.[45]

Kennie Dawn was ordained in 1932. She married Rev. Irvin J. Adams in 1932. She pastored the mission in Sevierville, which she started June 1, 1934. She and Irvin then moved to the pastorate and served the Coal Creek church from 1934 to 1939. This church changed its name in 1939 to Lake City and is no longer in existence. It was one of the original churches in the Tennessee District. The Adamses also pastored the Jamestown church for two years and returned to Lake City and pastored there for another thirteen years until Irvin's death January 16, 1956.[46]

Grace S. Thomas Armfield

Grace S. Thomas was born June 24, 1879. She was converted and joined the Friends Church in 1899. She enrolled in Cleveland Bible Institute in 1905 to prepare for the ministry. She served as pastor of the Alabama Mission for six months. On June 14, 1911, she married Joseph W. Armfield, and to this union one daughter, Mary Esther (McAninch), and two sons were born.

In August 1923 she was received from the Friends Church, on probation, into the Wesleyan Methodist Church in Indiana. She joined the Wesleyan Methodist Church at Mt. Zion, Howard County, Indiana. That year she was appointed pastor of the Waveland-Antioch charge, and she served there for two years. In August 1924 she became an ordained minister of the Wesleyan Methodist Church.

She apparently moved her membership to the Church of God, for in 1930 she was again received as an ordained minister on probation, this time from the Church of God. After this she served as class leader and Sunday school teacher and preached on different occasions. She donated the ground and building of the present Mt. Zion,

Howard County, Wesleyan Church. Grace S. Armfield died August 11, 1933.[47]

N. Grace Davis Birch

N. Grace Davis was born in Truro, Iowa, August 2, 1885. From childhood, Grace had an excellent memory. Her first-grade teacher had a lasting influence on her mind regarding "bad words and wrong deeds." Her parents moved to Jewel County near Burr Oak, Kansas, and she entered the Northbranch Friends Academy in January 1912. She was converted there, and later in 1913 she was sanctified.[48]

Hattie Crosby (Manyon) gave a missionary address at the Northbranch Academy, and from that time on Grace became interested in missions. She graduated from high school in 1916 and immediately began teaching school. She was a very successful teacher. During her fourth year of teaching God revealed His plan for her to go to Africa. She began preparation for this task by enrolling in the theological department at Miltonvale Wesleyan College, in Miltonvale, Kansas (later merged into what became Oklahoma Wesleyan University, Bartlesville, Oklahoma). She completed her work there in 1922. She returned to teaching until the door opened for her to go to Africa.

Grace was elected superintendent of the Kansas Conference Young Missionary Workers Band (now Wesleyan Kids for Missions) at the time of its organization in 1923. She was ordained by the Kansas Conference of the Wesleyan Methodist Church in 1925. She was very active in evangelistic meetings until she left for Africa. At various times she and Vera Macy (Willis) worked together in revival meetings. Both were preachers of the gospel, and both became missionaries. In November 1925 she sailed for Africa.

During her first term in Sierra Leone she was principal of the Boys Boarding School at Binkola and superintendent of all the educational work for the mission in Sierra Leone. Grace spent five terms on the field (1925–28; 1930–32; 1935–39; 1941–44; and 1947–50), working at the Girls School both at Masumbo and Kamabai. She was a choice handmaiden of God.

While home on furlough, Grace spent a year (1934) as a worker in the Zion's Hill Mission in Kentucky and as pastor of the Willis Church in Kansas in 1935. In 1941 she was appointed the pastor of the Mankato pastorate. She worked also for a time in the office of the missions department.

After retiring from missionary service, she married Frank R. Birch, a fellow missionary from Sierra Leone, and foreign missionary secretary 1943–59. On December 5, 1955, she transferred her membership from the Kansas Conference to the Michigan Conference. The Birches eventually moved to Wesleyan Village in Brooksville, Florida. Frank R. Birch died March 26, 1966, and Grace died June 30, 1973.[49]

Mrs. Cora Bromaghin

Cora Bromaghin was received into the Iowa Conference of the Wesleyan Methodist Church in April 1922 from the Willamette Conference. That year she was stationed at the Trommold Mission as pastor. She served that pastorate either as pastor or assistant pastor until October 19, 1925. At that time the mission was organized as a Wesleyan Methodist church, and she was appointed the pastor. She continued to pastor there for the next three years. In 1931 she became the pastor of the Little Pine, Minnesota, church and the next year the Bain church was added to her responsibility. In 1933 she was appointed the pastor at Bain and remained there for another four years. She was on the superannuated (retired) list from 1938 to 1940.[50]

Celia Bradshaw Winkle

Celia Bradshaw was born in Ironton, Ohio, in 1901. Her father was a miner. From age twelve on she was on her own and worked in homes for room and board plus $1.50 a week to help pay for her education.

She began preaching in her mid-teens (age sixteen) while working as a lathe operator in a factory in Springfield, Ohio. Although she was fearful that she would be fired, she felt an irresistible urge to preach. She recalled that one day she "waited until lunch break. I just quoted from the Bible and began to preach, and I guess I talked for about a half-hour with not the least bit of fear. However, when I stopped talking, the doubts returned, and I was sure I had made a fool of myself and was going to get fired." Instead of being fired, she was pictured in the company's newspaper with a story that said, "She preached like Billy Sunday, only she did not require a wheelbarrow full of money when she finished." That was a turning point in her life. She began preaching at churches and planning to make the church her life work. She said there were women preachers around but she did not know them. "So I just followed the path that God wanted me to go."

Celia worked her way through God's Bible College in Cincinnati, Ohio. She then attended the University of Cincinnati and "struggled with the question of marriage for a long time." At one point, she set the date for her wedding but then changed her mind. "I decided that the responsibility of being a wife and mother would demand too much of the time I had promised to give to God's work. I knew I must wait until later in life."[51]

Celia pastored several churches. Among them were Murray City and Dayton First, Ohio. She co-pastored at Defiance and Chillicothe for a number of years in each place. She was ordained in 1923.[52]

Celia married Harold Winkle in 1946. She and Harold moved to Florida in 1948, where she became known as the "pioneer of the Pilgrim Holiness Church in Florida." She was credited with much of the Pilgrim Holiness Church's early growth in Florida. She had spent much of her ministerial career up to this time in pastoring and evangelism, but after 1948 she became a church planter. She was supported in the work of church planting by Marie Waters, an accountant for the city of St. Petersburg and a longtime friend, and her husband, who was a civilian employee at MacDill Air Force Base.

Celia planted and organized the Pilgrim Tabernacle in St. Petersburg in 1949, just one year after they moved from Cincinnati to St. Petersburg. It started as an interdenominational church, but on August 27, 1950, the congregation voted unanimously to join the Pilgrim Holiness Church. She served as the pastor until 1952.

Her second church plant in Florida was the Pilgrim Holiness Church in Bradenton. She continued as the pastor at Bradenton until the early 1960s. At that time she planted her third church, Clearview Pilgrim Holiness Church in St. Petersburg.

Celia was not comfortable with the merger of the Pilgrim Holiness Church with the Wesleyan Methodist Church in 1968, and she moved her membership to the Bible Methodist Church. Under this denomination, she planted her fourth church.

In 1972 she said, "I have had a tremendously rewarding life. The disappointments can never overshadow the satisfaction I have gotten by doing what I believed was expected of me. At times it has been a battle, but a battle which I believe I have won." Harold died in 1978. Celia Bradshaw Winkle died in 1990 at age eighty-nine.[53]

Mary Connelly

The Minutes of the Annual Assembly of the Illinois and Missouri District Pilgrim Holiness Church of 1923–28 and the *Minutes of the Annual Conference of the Pilgrim Holiness Church California District* of 1929–67 recorded Mrs. Mary Connelly as an ordained minister. She was born April 21, 1880 in Lehigh, Kansas, and died January 2, 1967. Her husband, C. E. Connley, preceded her in death. She spent many years as a missionary in India. She lived frugally to support missionary work.

Laura Cook

Two entries were found for Laura Cook. *The Minutes of the Annual Assembly of the Pilgrim Holiness Church Indiana Conference* of 1923 and 1934 listed her as an ordained minister.

Vada A. Deardorf and Mary E. Dice

Vada A. Deardorf and Mary E. Dice were a ministerial team who served the Lord and the Church for thirty-four years together. They were both ordained in 1923. They served as co-pastors in several churches. Among those churches were Robinston, Martinsville, Paris Mission, and Jerseyville, Illinois; Dogwood and Avon, Missouri. They also were engaged in revival and tent meetings together. Both of them were ministerial delegates to the General Assembly of the Pilgrim Holiness Church in 1926 and 1930.

Former district superintendent Jesse Tewell Sr. recalled that Vada Deardorf was a faithful servant of God and the Church. He said in later life she brought the elderly ladies of the local church to camp meeting in her little Chevy and never missed a service. She retired from active service in 1963.

Mary E. Dice was born February 11, 1889, and departed this life June 9, 1953. Early in life she entered nurse's training and became very efficient in that field.

She was converted at the age of twenty-six in the Radical United Brethren Church and later was sanctified and joined the Pilgrim Holiness Church. She definitely felt led to give her life to God's work, and she entered Bible school and took special training to prepare for the ministry. During the thirty-five years of active ministry she served as a faithful pastor, evangelist, and home missionary. Her life was an example of complete dedication and sacrificial service to God and humanity.[54]

Bertha C. Evans

Bertha C. Evans was a licensed minister of the West Virginia District of the Pilgrim Holiness Church in 1923. She was the assistant pastor of the Wayne church for two years and spent some time in evangelistic work. Bertha was ordained in 1928. That year she was the pastor of the Williamson church. She was under appointment by the West Virginia District until 1941.[55]

Kate Glispy

Kate (Mrs. Joe) Glispy pastored the Pilgrim Holiness Church in Seymour, Indiana, in 1923 and the Edinburgh church in 1924. She was under appointment of the Indiana District of the Pilgrim Holiness Church until her death in 1940. In 1929 and 1930 she was listed as an honorary ordained minister.[56]

―❧―

Welhilmina Haines

Welhilmina Haines was the assistant pastor at the Orleans and Medora, Indiana, Pilgrim Holiness churches in 1923. She was ordained in 1924. She was listed as an ordained minister in the Indiana District until 1929. That year she transferred to the Ohio District and served under that district until 1951.[57]

―❧―

Norah Heslop

Mrs. William (Norah) Heslop was a missionary to Japan in 1920, 1922–23. She served in Korea in 1921, according to the *Minutes of the Annual Convention of the International Holiness Church of Ohio,* 1920–23. The *Minutes of the Annual Assembly of the Pilgrim Holiness Church of Pennsylvania and New Jersey District* of 1923–25 listed her as a member in that district. Norah was elected a delegate to the General Assembly in 1924.

―❧―

Jennie Hodgin

According to the *Proceedings of the Annual California District Assembly of the Pilgrim Holiness Church* 1923–32, Mrs. Jennie Hodgin was an evangelist in that district.

―❧―

Ina Louise Joy

Ina Louise Joy was a faithful worker both in the homeland and on foreign soil. She was born in Wayne County, Ohio, September 13, 1876. She was converted in early womanhood and soon after joined the Pilgrim Holiness Church.

She graduated in the first class of Owosso Bible Seminary, Owosso, Michigan (later Owosso College, eventually merged into what became Indiana Wesleyan University, Marion, Indiana). She was ordained in the ministry by George B. Kulp, P. F. Elliott, and W. O. Nease. Her early ministry was spent in the Upper Peninsula of Michigan. She felt the call of God to work in South Africa and began her work there in January 1913. The next year she was united in marriage to Rev. Elmer D. Joy in Swaziland, South Africa. Two children were born to them, a son who died in infancy, and a daughter, Bertha Lucille, who became a missionary to South Africa also. Ina Louise Joy was a devoted coworker with her husband in Swaziland and Mt. Frere, South Africa.[58]

The Joys returned to the United States in 1919 and had planned to return to South Africa, but God's direction led another way. They pastored together churches in Madrid, Nebraska; Bramwell, Parkersburg, and Barboursville, West Virginia; Beulah, Staunton, Richmond, and Lynchburg, Virginia; Binghamton, New York; Belle Ridge and New Castle, Pennsylvania. Her husband was the district superintendent in Virginia from 1934 to 1939. During that time she served as a solo pastor and evangelist.[59]

Ina became known for her saintliness of character and intense passion for souls. She was deeply devoted to God, the Church, and her family. She lived sacrificially during her years of service. She was a patient sufferer and an example of the enabling grace of God during her extended illness of several months before her homegoing July 21, 1952.[60]

―❧―

Laura Wallace Lane

J. Preston Lane and his wife, Laura, had become burdened for the community of East Pasadena, California. In March 1924 they began a house-to-house visitation program with the intent of planting a church. They held an open-air Sunday school in June, with an attendance of nine the first Sunday. Another man, his wife, and teenage children also began a tent meeting at the same time. All the persons involved in the open-air church joined his group.

But the burden had not left the Lanes, and in July they pitched the district tent on their own lot. They had raised enough funds ($383) to erect a wooden tabernacle, and the building was completed on Thanksgiving Day. The church was organized November 9, 1924, with eleven members.[61]

The *Pilgrim Holiness Advocate* dated July 12, 1927, records Laura's obituary on page 12. She was the founder and pastor of East Pasadena (Crown City). She was described as a woman with a penetrating mind, scholastic attainment, forceful personality, and deep spirituality. She was fervently devoted to the truth. Her last exhortation to the Church was "Be true." Her valiant spirit led the Church during a long illness in which she suffered greatly. Her earthly race was completed July 6, 1927.

Clara Orrell McLeister

Clara Orrell was born in Newport, Kentucky, August 8, 1882. In her early childhood, the family moved to Canton, Ohio. Her father was a factory worker at the Deuber Watch Factory, and his wages were low. He did extra work by growing vegetables in large gardens in vacant lots. Her mother was an excellent seamstress and spent much of her time sewing for her seven children and for other people who paid her for homemade garments. Clara learned the joy of working and meeting the financial needs. She developed a practical sense of the value of money that continued throughout her lifetime.

Clara was converted in a revival meeting, held in a rented hall, in the Methodist Episcopal Church. She joined the church and began faithfully serving the Lord by singing in the choir; later she became one of the class leaders.

Education was important to Clara. She diligently studied, and after high school graduation she obtained credentials that enabled her to become a schoolteacher. She taught school for five terms. Later she enrolled as a student in Mount Union College.

She began to attend the Wesleyan Methodist church in Canton where Rev. and Mrs. D. B. Hampe were the pastors. His preaching of holiness convinced her that holy living was the standard for all Christians. She often helped in the street meetings they conducted and went with the women workers to the slum area of Canton to pass out tracts and talk with unsaved persons in the hope of winning them to Christ. When the Hampes left the pastorate at Canton, they were followed by W. H. and Clara Tear Williams. Clara Williams had been an evangelist in her early life and had become a Spirit-filled soul winner. The two women became lifelong friends. Clara Orrell was now in her last term of school and was expecting to become engaged in full-time service for the Lord. She joined the Wesleyan Methodist Church and soon became involved in the work of the Church.

Clara sought and found the experience of holiness of heart at the Stoneboro camp meeting in August 1903. She was also healed of a serious lung condition during that meeting. She taught another year, but in the early summer D. B. Hampe was in Barberton, Ohio, planning to hold a tent meeting and eventually plant a new church. He contacted Clara and asked her to assist in the meeting. Another worker was to be Hattie Crosby (Manyon). The two women made house calls and did personal work among the people. Clara led the singing and played the piano. At the close of the meeting, the Barberton Wesleyan Methodist Church was organized. At the next session of the conference, in March 1905, Clara was appointed the pastor of the Barberton church. They rented a building and used the first floor as a sanctuary and the second as her living area. Her ministry through the years included many kinds of church work, but pastoral work always held first place in her heart. Her preaching was mainly expository with an evangelistic purpose. She was a diligent student of the Bible and developed her voice so she was enabled to speak in all kinds of churches.

Clara and I. F. McLeister were married March 19, 1906. One daughter, Mary Elizabeth, was born to them. She was a gifted child but died January 9, 1932, of tuberculosis.[62]

Their first pastorate was the Akron, Ohio, Wesleyan Methodist Church. It was a pioneer church, and they made house visitations, held street meetings, and conducted revivals. They prayed, studied, held children's meetings, and saw the church grow.

Clara's health was not very good, and they decided to move to Colorado. Clara attempted to plant a church here but was not successful. They moved in 1911 to Pennsylvania. They engaged in tent and revival meetings and organized a church at Wilgus. Indiana in Pennsylvania and Akron, Ohio First were their next pastorates.

I. F. McLeister was elected to the office of general Sunday school secretary in 1919, and they moved to Syracuse, New York. The next year, the president of the Rochester conference invited Clara to accept an appointment as the pastor of the Canandaigua Wesleyan Church. After much prayer, she accepted the appointment and remained as pastor for nine years. I. F. commuted the seventy miles to Syracuse by train. At the end of nine years the church had become one of the most desirable appointments in the conference. While pastoring the Canandaigua church, Clara became burdened with a vision for a church in the Rochester, New York, area. She conducted prayer meetings and formed a group that later united with the Sunday School Union. Later this group became the Gates Wesleyan Methodist Church in Rochester. Her influence continued on when the Gates church pioneered two other churches in the Rochester suburbs. In 1931 the "Mission on Court Street" in Syracuse was turned over to Dr. and Mrs. McLeister. This mission later became the Lyncourt Wesleyan Methodist Church. Dr. McLeister became editor of *The Wesleyan Methodist* and served in that capacity until 1943. So he continued to be busy with denominational work, and he assisted in the preaching at Lyncourt, but the pastoral work was done by Clara for nineteen years.[63] Clara retired in 1950, but the next year she again was doing pioneering work in Skaneateles, New York.

Clara served as the evangelist of the Chambers camp meeting in the early days of the conference. She served for thirty years in faithful ministry there especially as an altar worker.

In 1923 she was elected general president of the Woman's Home and Foreign Missionary Society and held this office for twenty years. She traveled across the entire nation and Canada in the interest of missions. The opening of mission fields in India and South America for the Wesleyan Methodist Church was largely the result of her vision to take the gospel to the entire world. Her leadership ability was used in her travels for the Woman's Home and Foreign Missionary Society and its firm establishment as an auxiliary and the society's growth.

Clara McLeister was the author of three books. She spent many years researching and writing *Men and Women of Deep Piety*. Her first book to be published was a book of poems entitled *The White Slave and Other Poems*. Her last book was *With Christ in the School of Prayer*.

Clara Orrell McLeister, pastor, pioneer in church planting, devoted to conference and denominational interests, entered the ministry in 1904. She was ordained in June 1909. She laid down her earthly tent January 2, 1958, to occupy her heavenly home.[64]

Iva Martin Norman

Iva (Mrs. David) Martin was received from Florida by the Indiana Conference of the Wesleyan Methodist Church. She was ordained in 1923 at conference time and was appointed to pastor the Sheridan, Indiana, church. For the next twenty-one years she served as pastor of the Sheridan, Mt. Zion (Henry County), Kirklin and Mt. Olive, Monument City, Atlanta, Fountain City, Edgerton, and Sims churches in the Indiana Conference. In 1945 she joined another denomination.[65]

Jean Pound

Jean Pound was ordained by the Indiana District of the Pilgrim Holiness Church in 1923. She was a missionary to China and Korea for a number of years. In 1926 she moved her membership to the California District and was under appointment from that district until 1932.[66]

Inez L. Roper

Inez (Mrs. J. Paul) Roper was under appointment with the Pilgrim Holiness Church in California in 1923–24 as an evangelist.[67] *The Minutes of the Annual Session of the Eastern Kansas and Oklahoma District of the Pilgrim Holiness Church,* 1925–26, listed her as a pastor. Those *Minutes* stated she had been ordained in 1916. She spent one year under appointment in the Western Kansas District of the Pilgrim Holiness Church.[68]

The Proceedings of the Annual Assembly California District of the Pilgrim Holiness Church, 1919–42, records her as under appointment with them at that time.

Nettie Winans Soltero

Francisco and Nettie Soltero began their missionary work in a mining town in New Mexico. They had been successful in reaching the people of this community for Christ, but they struggled with a continual pull to go to Mexico.

Rev. Seth C. Rees, pastor of Pasadena Tabernacle, sent a letter to them asking them to consider going to Mexico and beginning a work under the Pilgrim Church of California. After praying, they answered in the affirmative. A farewell service was held for the Solteros in January 1920, and they were presented with their first commission. The church pledged its support of these two members and ordained ministers of their church. The Solteros were to "found and conduct a Pilgrim mission, Bible school, and printing plant in Mexico." After much prayer and study, the Solteros were led of the Spirit to start in a large city, and that city would be San Luis Potosi.

January 27, 1920, they arrived in San Luis Potosi, Mexico. They had traveled by train, and all the passengers had been ill. Francisco became ill with the flu, the dreaded Spanish influenza that had taken the lives of many in the United States in 1918.

They rented a small house, which they used as a parsonage and place of worship. They went door to door inviting people to come to their mission. It was hard work and very discouraging, but eventually people came, and some were saved.[69]

Nettie became concerned about teaching converts to become pastors, so the first Bible school was held in San Luis Potosi. Nettie would teach all morning, take time out for lunch and do the dishes, and return to teaching in the afternoon. The boys lived in their home, and they provided them with food to eat. She served thirty-seven years as a Bible teacher at various locations for the Bible school. Some fifty years later she was still being quoted as an authority on biblical principles, doctrine, and practice. She was deeply loved by believers and nonbelievers in Valles, where she taught for many years.

She became ill on June 3 and died June 5, 1956. Many Catholics who had never entered a Protestant church came to her funeral. The owner of the city bus lines sent two buses to take people to the cemetery and did not charge a fee. A taxicab owner sent six taxis, his own car, and his own truck to take flowers to the cemetery at no charge. Many walked behind the funeral coach. Four national workers asked for the privilege to carry the casket on their shoulders from the mission home to the church out of love and respect for their beloved teacher.[70]

Belle Thomas Swanson

Belle Thomas was ordained in 1923. She married Mr. Swanson (first name unknown) in 1935. Her name appeared on the ordained ministers' list in *Minutes of the Annual Assembly of the Pilgrim Holiness Church Indiana Conference* from 1923 to 1937.

Ethel and Nella J. True

Much can be written about single ladies who dared to trust God and take the gospel to dangerous tribes around the world. Ethel and Nella were sisters, and both of them answered the call to go to Mexico.

Nella was born December 8, 1882, and was converted as a child. At age twenty-nine she surrendered her life entirely to God. She knew God was calling her to minister to the people of Mexico. She gave herself to that task of missions by sacrifice, intercession, and soul-winning.

Both Nella and Ethel were members of Seth C. Rees's church in Pasadena, California. Under his ministry, some fifty persons were called and sent to the foreign fields to win people to the Lord. Nella was thirty-nine when they finally were allowed to enter Mexico. Their work there was a short four years. But they were four very successful years for the advancement of the work in Mexico.

Francisco and Nettie Soltero were the first Pilgrim Holiness missionaries to Mexico, arriving in San Luis Potosi in 1920. Soon they were going into villages outside the city. They received an invitation to take the gospel to Potrerillos. Soltero believed it was too far away to attempt to conduct meetings there, but eventually he made the three-day trip by horseback. The people were hungry. Fifty persons signed a pledge promising to help care for a missionary if one should be sent to them.

An attempt to kill Soltero was made during his three-day stay there. Nella and Ethel were the first missionaries at Potrerillos. The work was with the Otomi Indians. It was a hard place to work; persecution was severe. The home in which they conducted their meetings was burned to the ground. Attempts were made on the lives of the True sisters. Their labors were not in vain, however, for they saw many souls won to the Lord.

News of the arrival of the True sisters was accompanied with reports that they were secret agents of the United States government, which, the reports said, was about to take over Mexico. The people were warned to protect themselves at any cost against these "old cats," the missionaries, and that they should be stoned and run out of town. They were stoned whenever they left their house. The Christian Indians would not allow them to go anywhere without their protection.[71]

Francisco Soltero made the following statements about Nella and Ethel's work in Mexico.

Their time in Mexico was short, but they left indelible memories upon those whom they knew and to whom they ministered. They did not look for the easy places in which to work, but on the contrary they were aggressive, they challenged danger and persecution by remaining in their places as good soldiers of the Cross. Upon one occasion their lives were endangered, but it was a real sacrifice for them to leave their work. More than nineteen years ago they left Mexico, but there remains in the hearts of all who knew them a vivid memory, and sincere gratitude for the work which they did while here among us.[72]

They came home and assisted in deputation work (home ministries). Nella worked even though she had been stricken with cancer. Nella's final words were, "In my Father's house. In my Father's house." She died March 19, 1928.[73]

Nella's service record is recorded in the *Proceedings of the Annual California District Assembly of the Pilgrim Holiness Church,* 1923–27. Ethel continued on under appointment of the California District until 1950.

Cora White

According to the *Minutes of the Annual Assembly of the Pilgrim Holiness Church Indiana Conference,* 1923–36, Cora White was an ordained minister in 1923. She was under appointment by the conference until 1936, when her name was dropped from the roll.

Mrs. Emma Brown

Emma Brown was an ordained minister in the Pilgrim Holiness Church. Records of the International Holiness Churches of Michigan reveal that she was under their appointment 1922–24. That group merged with the Pilgrim Church, and they took the name of the Pilgrim Holiness Church. She preached the "old fashioned" gospel for twenty years for the Michigan District. She also served as matron of Rest Cottage Rescue Home for "unfortunate" (unmarried pregnant) girls and women for twenty years in Grand Rapids. She saw hundreds of ladies redeemed. God abundantly blessed the home by answering prayers for all its needs. The home was supported by free will offerings. It may have been called Prestron Rescue Home. Emma Brown was the mother of two daughters. She was born July 22, 1854, and died June 28, 1938.[74]

Saydee Coulter

Saydee (also spelled "Sadie") Coulter was co-pastor of the Hillsboro, Texas, Pilgrim

Holiness Church in 1924.[75] In 1931 she was stationed at Shawnee, Oklahoma. There were no records of her continuing service, but in 1938–40 she worked in Oklahoma City for a time. Her name was on the roll of the Oklahoma District from 1941 to 1943.[76]

Mrs. Elizabeth Lizzie Craner

Lizzie Craner was a mission worker for the Brethren in Christ. The first record of her work was in 1909. She reported that she was working at the Light House Mission in Dayton, Ohio. Souls were saved and sanctified, and all the needs of the mission had been met. She kept the mission open each night except Monday night until they held a tent meeting, and after the meeting the people requested her to conduct cottage prayer meetings on Monday evening. That was the end of the night of rest. She reported that the poor had been fed, clothed, and looked after in general.

Lizzie made over five hundred calls on sick and needy persons and also went house to house to visit people as she passed out tracts and papers. She often was asked to speak at different places on the "white slave traffic." This was the "business" of men who forced women into commercial prostitution.

Lizzie was ordained in 1917. She held revivals, conducted class meetings, and preached in ministerial meetings, using every opportunity to advance the Kingdom.[77]

The last recorded reference to her was found in the *Minutes of the Annual Convention of the International Apostolic Holiness Church of Ohio, 1924.* She was at Amelia, Ohio, at that time.

Mary Grace Frisk

Mary Grace Frisk served under the California District of the Pilgrim Holiness Church and was a missionary to China for many years. In 1926 she was listed as an ordained minister. She was the pastor of the Rialto, California, church in 1934–36. From 1956 to 1959 the *Minutes* recorded

her as an ordained deaconess, but in 1960–67 she was again listed as an ordained minister.[78]

Elizabeth G. Hardie

Elizabeth Hardie transferred from the Illinois Conference to the Kansas Conference of the Wesleyan Methodist Church in 1924. She was an ordained minister. She was appointed general evangelist from 1924 to 1927. Her husband, Robert, died during the 1926–27 conference year, and she was given a letter of standing on June 8, 1927.[79]

Fern Neeley Henschen

Fern Neeley was the third of seven children, born August 20, 1899. She was very feminine with black hair and snapping dark eyes. She was always full of mischief and enjoyed making people laugh.

Fern was converted at age nine. One summer during her youth, she traveled with her sister, Chloie Neeley (Meeks), and Amelia Baker, a missionary from India. The young ladies were in charge of the music. Their travels that summer took them to Ohio, Kentucky, and West Virginia.

Fern attended Beulah Bible School in St. Louis. There she met Walter G. Henschen, who would later become her husband. He had spent a year as a missionary to Central America and had returned to the United States to teach at the school.[80] They were married July 15, 1920, and became the parents of six children. Two daughters and one son became ministers of the gospel.

Fern was ordained in 1929. She and her husband shared equally the pulpit ministry on their pastorates in the Pilgrim Holiness Church in Illinois, Indiana, and Ohio. He was a student of the Word and a typical professor even in his preaching. Fern was emotional, demonstrative, and a powerful preacher. She loved children and youth, and when they pastored, the children and youth were usually her responsibility.

They eventually moved to Chicago, and Walter became the dean of Chicago Evangelical Institute (which later became Vennard College, in

University Park, Iowa). In 1936 they moved to Cincinnati and both taught at God's Bible School. She taught piano, music, and Bible classes. When she was ill and could not get to the classroom, she taught these classes in her home. At the time of her death, February 18, 1960, she was a Bible instructor at the Bible school.[81]

Fannie Higgs

Fannie (Mrs. A. R.) Higgs was a missionary who served under the Illinois/Missouri District of the Pilgrim Holiness Church. She was ordained in 1928. There were no further entries in her ministerial record after 1939.[82]

Frances Maddox

Frances Maddox began her ministerial work in 1924 with the International Apostolic Holiness Church of Ohio. She pastored several churches in the Western Ohio District of the Pilgrim Holiness Church with her husband, E. M. Maddox. They were the church planters of the church in Troy, Ohio. Frances died August 19, 1971.[83]

Ruby Parr

Ruby Parr served the Indiana District of the Pilgrim Holiness Church from 1924 to 1948.[84] In 1950–56 she worked for the California District. The *Minutes of the Annual Conference of the Arizona District of the Pilgrim Holiness Church* listed her as an ordained minister in 1956–59. But in 1960 she was listed as a deaconess. She continued to serve on the Arizona/New Mexico District until 1965.

Lucy Quillan

Lucy Quillan was licensed by the Illinois and Missouri District of the Pilgrim Holiness Church in 1924. She pastored the church at Ava, Missouri, for a time and served as an evangelist.

She retired from the active ministry in 1963 and died in 1967.[85]

Ruby Levans Reisdorph

Ruby Levans Reisdorph became one of the most powerful and influential leaders of the Wesleyan Methodist Church. God gave her an outstanding singing voice that was used by the Holy Spirit in unusual ways and places to move people toward God. Her Spirit-led singing during a funeral, at the gravesite, on the platform during business sessions of conference, in evan-gelistic meetings, or at mission rallies were examples of her obedience to God's leadings. Her theme song in evangelism was Lucy J. Rider's "Ho, Everyone Who Is Thirsty in Spirit." Her preaching and exhortations were always so spontaneous that it appeared she had never studied or prepared to speak. It was not unusual for her powerful, anointed preaching to result in people coming to the altar in waves, sometimes three or four waves in one service. Her preaching was filled with illustrations of little things that she observed in everyday life, like a withered flower or a beautiful sunset. Her close relationship with the Heavenly Father resulted in a persistent prayer life that gave her the assurance of answered prayer and victory. God honored her prayers with miraculous answers for salvation of sinners, healings, and deliverance from demons and evil spirits.

Ruby was born the third child of six children March 20, 1903, in a log cabin near Pell City, Alabama. She early learned the necessity of helping with household chores. Singing was a natural way of expression for her as a child. Her mother told her, "Your talent is God-given, and you will have to give an account to Him for the way you use it." She learned to play the organ in a very unorthodox way. There was no money for lessons, but she longed to play. During a thirteen-week tent meeting, the children were asked to sit on the floor in the front of the church to make room for the grownups. Ruby and her sister would sit as close to the little folding organ as they could. Ruby would watch the organist position her fingers on the keys as the congregation sang. After the service she would go home and practice those positions, with "one finger" on their organ.

She was converted in 1918. Her wise pastor organized the young people into a Bible study and witnessing group. He led them in textual exhortations as a part of the training. Here was the foundation for her sound biblical preaching. She sought and found heart purity during those high school days.

After graduating from high school, she and the experienced minister, Hattie Avery, were stationed in a mission at Bessemer, Alabama. While working there, she was engaged in a tent meeting with evangelists Nathan Beskin and his wife. On Friday night the evangelist "lifted an offering" to "help Miss Ruby go to Marion College" (now Indiana Wesleyan University). She had work to do at the mission and did not feel she should leave, but after praying she accepted the offer to go. She worked her way through college by singing for funerals, revivals, and weekend meetings; tutoring students; and working at a store in Marion, Indiana.

Ruby became acquainted with Rufus D. Reisdorph at college, and they were married October 25, 1927. Two very gifted persons were then joined in marriage and ministry. Their gifted ministries were not identical, but they were compatible and used mightily by God. His ministry was always given the priority, and Ruby always found a way to use her gifts and skills to complement his work. Ruby was ordained in 1930.

The couple traveled in evangelism. Then Rufus was elected Dakota Conference president in 1929 and served until 1940. He served as general Sunday school secretary and editor, a United States chaplain in World War II, president of Miltonvale Wesleyan College, and general superintendent of the Wesleyan Methodist Church. Ruby was elected general president of the Woman's Missionary Society in 1943 and served

in that office until 1959, when she declined reelection. Her leadership produced many new programs and advancements for the society. She, more than any other president, became a traveling president and visited all the conferences with her missionary message and spirit.

In 1952–53 the Reisdorphs made a tour "in behalf of missionary evangelism" around the world. The tour was successful in every way. The home church became more aware of missionary going and giving. Many persons were saved in their meetings overseas. In 1957 they visited several Caribbean islands and South America. The success of this trip was a repeat of the earlier tour. They served as volunteer missionaries to the Philippines from 1964 to 1976. Rufus died in 1976.

In her early days at Marion College, Ruby was troubled because she did not know exactly what God wanted her to do. She voiced her confusion to evangelist Joseph H. Smith. With great discernment he told her, "Daughter, just keep doing the chores around Father's house. He will show you the next chore and the next." In her retirement years while residing at Wesleyan Village in Brooksville, Florida, she wrote a book about their ministries. She titled it *Chores Around Father's House.*

Ruby was the mother of one daughter, Martha Levene (Marti) Lewis. Marti requested at her mother's death, January 8, 2000, that anyone desiring to memorialize her life could give to the Ruby Reisdorph Memorial Fund, Wesleyan Women International.[86]

Maude Robart

Maude Robart was active in the North Michigan Conference of the Wesleyan Methodist Church. She served as president of the Woman's Home and Foreign Missionary Society and as organizer of the society and of the Young Missionary Workers Band (now Wesleyan Kids for Missions). She was a conference preacher who also served as a deaconess and evangelist in 1924. She was given permission to hold revivals outside the North Michigan Conference. She was a member of the conference Sunday school board and traveled across the entire conference. Each circuit was to take an offering for her whenever she came to represent the conference Sunday schools. She was ordained in 1928. On August 2, 1929, she was granted a letter of standing.[87]

Lydia Harrington Sewell

Lydia Harrington was under appointment in 1924 with the Indiana District of the Pilgrim Holiness Church. Around 1950–51 she was married to Mr. Sewell (first name unknown). When the district was divided, she served with the Southern Indiana District and was so listed under appointment at the time of the merger with the Wesleyan Methodist Church.[88]

Nora Allen Wisemantle

Nora (sometimes spelled "Norah") Allen was ordained by the Indiana Assembly of the Pilgrim Holiness Church. She was from Alexandria, Indiana, and was under conference appointment in Indiana from 1924 to 1935. On March 15, 1928, she married Joseph P. Wisemantle. In 1935 her name was dropped from the roll. She and her husband moved to El Paso, Texas. He had been a successful businessman and banker for many years previously.[89]

Goldie Mildred Williams

Goldie Mildred was born May 24, 1904, in Brown County, Ohio. She graduated from God's Bible School in Cincinnati, Ohio, in 1924. That year she was joined in marriage to L. A. Williams. She was ordained in 1933 under presiding general superintendent Seth C. Rees.

She and her husband began their ministerial service on the Kentucky District of the Pilgrim Holiness Church. They were the pastors of the Ashland, Latonia, and Soldier Pilgrim Holiness churches in that state. She recalled one scary event during their pastorate at Soldier. A man who had just been released from prison came to their church on a

Sunday evening. Her husband was in the pulpit. The man had a gun and sat for a while in the service and then got up and went outside the church. He broke three windows, and referring to her husband, he shouted, "I will kill him!" He came back into the church and shot three times over her husband's head. The congregation was understandably upset and stood to their feet, but L. A. Williams commanded them, "Sit down. He is not going to tear up our worship service." In disgust the man said, "That preacher wouldn't be afraid of the devil!"

The couple co-pastored two churches in Indiana: South Bend and Lebanon. Then they moved to Portsmouth, Ohio, and became the pastors of the Pilgrim Holiness church there. They became the pastors of the Argo, Marshall, and Joliet, Illinois, churches next. While they were pastoring the Joliet church, L. A. Williams died, and Goldie continued on as the solo pastor. After the merger with the Wesleyan Methodist Church, Goldie returned to Portsmouth, Ohio, and was the pastor there from 1971 to 1985.[90]

Erma S. Brannon

Her birth name was Mary Ermena Snyder, but after her marriage to Walter C. Brannon she always signed her name Erma S. Brannon and was known thereafter as Erma. She was born in West Virginia. Her story is told by one of her sons, Ronald R. Brannon, former general secretary of The Wesleyan Church:

She planned a career as a schoolteacher and had begun serving in that profession after training at a West Virginia teacher's training school and at Houghton College. A marriage proposal from a young Methodist preacher-to-be changed all that. Believing it to be of paramount importance to be properly prepared if she were to be a preacher's wife, she enrolled in God's Bible School and graduated in 1925.

The morning after a June 15, 1925, wedding, they boarded a train to go from Spencer, West Virginia, to Aberdeen, South Dakota, where the Dakota Conference was in session. The conference appointed them to plant a new church at Pollock, South Dakota. They were offered no salary, no nucleus of believers, and no building in which to worship.

Mother's call to ministry was to be as a pastor's wife, and ordination was perceived by her as the epitome of preparation. In a poised, almost queenly manner, she preferred to stay in the background. Conversely, she never shrank from any assignment that would support Dad's ministry and advance the Kingdom. When Dad was away preaching camp meetings, revival meetings, or rendering other services, Mother took the pulpit and delivered the sermons. Primarily, though, her role was teacher of Bible studies and Sunday school classes and counselor to many.

Dad was the primary church planter while Mother served in a support role. Four years after being appointed to Pollock, they worshiped in a lovely frame building and had assembled a congregation of new believers. Mother led one of their first converts to faith in Christ at her kitchen chair. The conference asked Dad to move to Aberdeen because of a serious doctrinal problem in the church. They were there nine years, and the church became the largest in the conference even though Dad pioneered several new churches in outlying areas (Ipswich and Loyalton and others). They next went to Billings, Montana, and in the eight years there the church reached membership and attendance comparable to or greater than Aberdeen. During that time, Dad planted other churches, most notably the Joliet, Montana, church. In each of these endeavors, Mother accompanied Dad in visitation ministries and occasionally to the Sunday afternoon services. Often she remained at the primary appointment location to care for calling and counseling interest while Dad carried the preaching load at the pioneer church. Normally, her involvement in home visitation was partnered with Dad. However, when he was away, she did not hesitate to back the car from the garage and go to home or hospital to care for the needy members of the flock. She often served as Bible study or prayer meeting leader. During her prime years, I don't recall a time she was not busy as a Sunday school teacher. Among those whom she taught in her Sunday school classes are Robert W. McIntyre, C. Eugene Cockrell, and Michael Fullingim. Three of her four sons, Dr. Ronald R.,

Elmer E., and Gerald entered the ministry, and the other son, Walter C. Jr., became a leading layman in the Free Methodist Church. He was a schoolteacher.

Mother and Dad were married for sixty-two years. They both were nearly thirty years of age on their wedding date. Often when Dad would return from a camp meeting or revival meeting, members of the congregation would tease him by saying it was all right with them if he went into full-time evangelistic ministry, but they were keeping the assistant pastor.

Her preaching style was didactic and sprinkled with quiet humor. Her wisdom in counseling along with the absence of any evidence of criticism were of immeasurable significance in their ministries. Never was she known to betray a confidence. She had a good scriptural grasp and a clear, balanced application of truth.

Erma S. Brannon completed her earthly tasks February 3, 1987.[91]

Adelene E. Behrent Bubb

In 1924 Adelene Bubb was among the first graduating class of the Beulah Park Bible School, in Allentown, Pennsylvania (later Eastern Pilgrim College, then United Wesleyan College). She married Walter F. Bubb prior to the graduation ceremonies. They were married in the tabernacle by George B. Kulp. She became an effective co-pastor and preacher.

Adelene was ordained and served in the Pennsylvania and New Jersey District of the Pilgrim Holiness Church for more than fifty years. Together with her husband, they pastored churches in Augustaville, Stonington, Rebuck, and Reading, Pennsylvania; and Glassboro, New Jersey. She preached periodically throughout her entire life and occasionally filled engagements within a few months of her death, which occurred September 29, 1980. She retired from active service in 1965.

She was the mother of one daughter and two sons.[92]

Etta Mae Clough

Etta Mae Clough was known affectionately as Miss Clough. She was God's instrument in planting two churches and a mission in the Baltimore area.

She launched First Church in Baltimore in 1924 and served this Pilgrim Holiness church for many years. First Church opened a mission on Christian Street, which was in the slums. It was started during the World War II time, and people could not buy gas for their cars, which they would normally have used to pick up children and bring them to First Church. Etta Mitchell, who became a co-pastor with Etta Clough, pastored the mission for a time, and then the mission was assigned to Rev. and Mrs. Schwartz. Mrs. Schwartz was converted under Etta Clough's ministry. Their daughter, Jenny, became a missionary in China and Taiwan. The Schwartzes served the mission for many years.

Several persons were coming from the Brooklyn and Glen Burnie area, and they desired to have a church closer to them. Etta Clough started prayer meetings near Patapsco Avenue. Soon after this, the Atwood Berry family rented a building on Crain Highway. Meetings were conducted here until the congregation bought property off Oakwood Station Road in Glen Burnie and built a church there. Etta Clough and Etta J. Mitchell were co-laborers at this church for many years.

During those World War II days, many soldiers were stationed at Ft. Meade and attended this church. Etta Clough often took them back to camp after the evening services. Among those men were Braden Shrieves, who became a pastor for several years in the district, Hugh Ammons, whose daughter became a missionary to the Navaho Indians, and Joe Parman, whose son became a missionary in Mexico.

While pastoring in Baltimore, Etta opened her home to several young girls, who then made their home with Etta Clough and Etta Mitchell. This was during World War II. One young lady became the wife of Jesse Crowder. They became very generous donors to Denton Wesleyan Camp and other Wesleyan institutions. Dorothy Ammons, Roselee Emerson Coppock, and many others were assisted by these two young, single lady ministers. Only God knows how many were influenced by them. Some became teachers of God's Word all over the country. Some ended up in the ministry as ordained ministers. Others became full-time missionaries in foreign countries.[93]

Etta Clough was a very humble person and declared she had not done much for the Lord or His kingdom. However, she did not have to take a back seat to anyone. She was a strong, capable, and completely committed person to God and His work. She was an excellent preacher, an exceptional children and youth worker, one given to hospitality, an encourager, and a good musician. She played the piano, accordion, and guitar. She was a disciplinarian. It was not unusual to see her holding a young child in one arm, hand of discipline firmly planted on the head of another child, and directing another child up front reciting a part in the special day program. She was a firm believer that all the members of her church should know the Word by memory and live it daily in life. She made her own visual aids and taught memorization of the Word to perfection. She drilled every child and adult. All her work was preceded and followed by her prayers. She was a woman of patience, understanding and enthusiasm and was a diligent worker who conducted Sunday school, two services on Sunday, and midweek prayer meeting. She scrubbed the floors of the old theater building, now a church, built the fire in the stove two hours prior to the meetings, laid newspaper on the floor to absorb the water from the leaking roof on rainy days, and provided transportation for those in need of a ride to the services. She then played the piano and led the singing from the piano bench, and finally she delivered the Word to the congregation. She even took time to sew a graduation dress for a needy girl in her church. She was always "there" for her people.[94]

Etta was a poet, and many of her poems were published in the *Pilgrim Holiness Advocate*. Recently (within the last three years) she was able

Rev. Etta Mae Clough (r.) and Rev. Etta Mitchell

140

to get her *Bible Stories in Song* published. This is a selection of Bible stories written for children and set to the music of familiar gospel song tunes. The stories were composed by Etta to fit the tunes.[95]

Betty Lou Washburn, an ordained minister in the Chesapeake District, recalled the events of starting a church in the Washington, D.C., area. Etta conducted prayer meetings and started a church here. When the Wesleyan Methodist people came to Washington to plant a church, Etta encouraged her people to attend and help in that endeavor.

Etta Clough and Etta Mitchell were the pastors of the Greenwood, Maryland, church. Etta was a bi-vocational pastor. She worked in an office of a local feed store. During her pastorate there, a church and a parsonage were built. Each was built and paid for within a three-year span.[96]

Dorothy Ammons wrote a letter dated September 27, 1998, with information that Etta Clough within the last few years has been in failing health. She suffered a massive stroke in November 1998 and is living in the Corisica Hills Center Nursing Home in Centerville, Maryland.

Julia Klous Cooke

Julia Cooke served for a number of years as a single lady pastor. Among those churches she served as single or married were Gibbs Chapel, Rain Hills, Rose Hill, Bethel, Wilmington, Roxboro, Mt. Hebron, Old Fort Beulah Heights, all in the North Carolina Conference of the Wesleyan Methodist Church, and Minnie's Chapel and Radford, Virginia. After she retired in 1957, she served as supply pastor at Palestine, North Carolina.[97]

Julia married Charles Cooke. For a time they worked with the Salvation Army in the Mooresville, North Carolina, area. That church wrote a fitting and descriptive tribute to Julia and Charles Cooke. They said the work was done following the depression and the Mooresville cotton mill strike. The Cookes performed outstanding work among the village people and their children. They bought shoes, clothing, and food and distributed them among the people. They furnished recreation for the children and youth and even a fresh air camp at one time. But

they never forgot the spiritual needs of the people. They provided a Sunday school and morning worship service. They preached in a store building, tents and finally rented a building in the middle of the town.

Like many of the women ministers, Julia Cooke had to put up with a lot from the "bystanders" who chanted, "Women should not preach or serve in this capacity. They should be seen but not heard."

After they left the Salvation Army, they joined the Mooresville Wesleyan Methodist church. Charles was a conference preacher, but Julia was an ordained minister. She held meetings, filled pulpits for ministers, did home visitation, and promoted prayer and fasting among the people. She was referred to lovingly as "Cookie." She was a humble, unpretending woman with a great sense of humor. Many of her expressions were considered "funny." She was always happy, even in sorrow. She was gifted with the gift of "helps" and could see a need and then would do something about it. She dressed in typical Wesleyan Methodist garb of that day, clean, well groomed at all times, and sufficiently covered—modest!

Charles, her husband, died March 18, 1958.[98] Julia retired in 1958 because of ill health. She completed her race on earth December 15, 1972, at the age of eighty-one.[99]

Mabel Dukes

Mabel Dukes was born in Ohio in 1902. She graduated from God's Bible School in 1924. She attended Taylor University in Upland, Indiana, and Eastern Nazarene College, near Boston. She was ordained in 1938 by Rev. Paul W. Thomas. She was an avid Bible scholar and an excellent teacher. She married H. D. Dukes in 1924. Together, they were the pastors of Brommes Island, Crisfield, Tilghman, Greensboro, and Ridgely, Maryland churches, and the Dover, Delaware church. She was the mother of two daughters. Her husband served as superintendent of the Delmarva District of the Pilgrim Holiness Church for fourteen years. He died March 25, 1984. Mabel died February 3, 1985.[100]

Louise J. Gifford Henderson

Louise J. Gifford was appointed pastor of the Olean, New York, charge May 1, 1925. Four persons were saved during that conference year. In 1926 she became an ordained minister in the Lockport Conference of the Wesleyan Methodist Church. She was the pastor of the Olean church from 1925 to 1932. In 1932 she married Mr. Henderson (first name unknown) and transferred to the Oregon Conference. She pastored the church at Central, Oregon, in 1932. She was listed by the Oregon Conference as an ordained minister on the retired list from 1937 to 1943.[101]

Margaret Bell Edwards Hankins

Margaret Bell Edwards was born October 29, 1897, in Rio Grande, New Jersey. When she was two years old her birth mother died. The other children of the family went to live with relatives, but she stayed with her father. Her father later married again. She was saved and sanctified at age fifteen and preached her first sermon on holiness. Her stepmother was disgusted with her religious experience and claimed that Margaret was making a mockery of religion. This caused her to seek out a secret prayer chamber in the attic.

Margaret married Raymond Hankins February 23, 1918, at Millville, New Jersey. They became the parents of one son, William Ray. Raymond was a carpenter by trade, but when Margaret attended God's Bible School, in Cincinnati, Ohio, and graduated from the theological course in 1924, Raymond also attended the school with her. Though he assisted her on her many pastorates and served with her on the Jamaican mission field by erecting churches and other buildings at the Caribbean Pilgrim College, he was never ordained.

They served in Jamaica a total of five years. Pastoral work included the Glassboro, New Jersey, church and the Remlik, Boissevain

and Newport News, Virginia, churches. She was licensed to preach in 1923 and was ordained by the Pilgrim Holiness Church in 1925. She also spent some time in evangelistic work.

Margaret was an extraordinary evangelist at home and around the world. The missions department employed her to raise funds for missions everywhere. Sometimes she was gladly received by the pastors and comfortably cared for. Other times pastors objected to her "taking money to convert the heathen" because she would just open more "needy heathen fields." Her reply was "If you or your family were on one of those fields, would you want me to come with the good news of Jesus to you?" This usually broke their hard hearts.

She was always gladly welcomed on the mission fields. Her altars were almost always filled with seekers. Such results were experienced in the Philippines, Peru, Guyana, Suriname, Africa, West Indies, Jamaica, Grand Cayman, and Trinidad. No place was too difficult or inaccessible for her.[102] She traveled by train, bus, car, boat, or horseback.

Her first evangelistic missionary trip to Jamaica and Grand Cayman was paid for from the offering she received at a meeting she conducted in South Bend, Indiana. The worker the church had scheduled did not come, and she filled in at that revival. She took Clara Chizum (now Mrs. William James) with her on that first trip. She saved all the money given to her by the missionary department for her missionary trips. Her husband supplemented this by doing extra work or simply "doing without something" to make up for what was lacking. One time they conducted a revival meeting in a Methodist church in New Jersey. The entire offering was enough for a trip to take her to South America.

After her husband retired and she couldn't do much because of failing eyesight, a couple asked her to go with them to South America and Africa. Her fare and all her expenses were paid.

Raymond Hankins died at age eighty-two on July 8, 1976. Margaret Hankins lived a full and useful life for her Lord and the Church.[103]

Alice Pearl Hoover Lutz Heckart

Alice Pearl Hoover Lutz Heckart was born and raised in Centre County, Pennsylvania. She was converted at age fifteen and two years later felt called to full-time ministry. She attended Allentown Bible Institute, Allentown, Pennsylvania (which became Eastern Pilgrim College/United Wesleyan College).

While serving on her first pastorate in Glen Iron, Pennsylvania, she married Rev. Russell W. Lutz. Together they pastored Pilgrim Holiness churches at Pocono Lake, Delaware Run, Bush Hollow and Loganton, Pennsylvania; and Danville and Bosivane, Virginia. They were also involved in home missions work in Oklahoma for a time. Russell Lutz died during their pastorate at the Loganton church. She continued on as the pastor there until she married Rev. Robert Heckart.

Alice and Robert spent several years as traveling evangelists and also pastored the Big Bow, Kansas, church. They toured Israel several times and ministered in Guyana and Grand Cayman. Robert died while they were living in Colorado Springs. Alice then moved back to Pennsylvania.[104]

She was the mother of two sons, Carl and Leon Lutz. Alice died July 24, 1999, in Allentown, Pennsylvania. She was ninety-one years old.

Martha Hensley Keaton

Martha Hensley was born May 17, 1879. She married John Keaton February 7, 1900, and they were the parents of one son. She was saved and sanctified in 1912 in Ashland, Kentucky. She had been a member of the Church of the Nazarene since 1915 but joined the Pilgrim Holiness Church in 1925. She was ordained September 8, 1931, and served as the pastor of the Fairview, Norman, Olive Hill, and Hitchins, Kentucky, churches. She retired from active service in 1961.

Martha was a very successful minister and was known and respected as a godly woman. She was instrumental in the salvation of her brother,

who became a minister also. She was the mother of one son. She entered heaven September 9, 1962, in Ashland, Kentucky. Her husband died many years ago.[105]

Dorothy Dike Johnson Lehman

Dorothy Dike Johnson was born at Hebron, Illinois, on February 27, 1906. She was saved at age nine and sanctified when she was eighteen. Just one year later she went to Africa as a single lady missionary. She had been called of God to be a missionary at age twelve. She completed a correspondence course in Bible and was ordained in 1933.

Orai Ivan Lehman and Dorothy were married in Kransfontein, Orange Free State, South Africa, December 29, 1942. Dorothy had served as assistant pastor, evangelist, children's worker, teacher in Bantu schools, and superintendent of the Transvaal mission schools.

The Lehmans joined the Pilgrim Holiness Church in 1962 when the Africa Evangelistic Mission with which they had worked for many years merged with the Pilgrims. They worked in the Johannesburg area with the gold miners and also developed a station at Casteel, Transvaal. The Lehmans had three children: Sarah Alice, Orai Dike, and Minnie Jane. All were born in South Africa. Orai Dike and his wife, Linda, are serving in South Africa as missionaries.[106]

Alice Wyatt, Dorothy and O.I.'s oldest daughter, wrote about her mother and their family. She said her mother was a very caring person who always met the

Dorothy Johnson (center) in Africa, 1932

needs of her family and also had time to serve others. She was always concerned about the "people," and even as her health failed, she would wonder if the "people" were being cared for.

Alice continued with the following account of her mother's activities. Dorothy was challenged as a young girl by the missionaries they entertained in her family's home. She left her home in Zion, Illinois, and went to South Africa, where she served for fifty-two years. She was stationed for several years in the African country surrounded by the Republic of South Africa known as Basutoland. It took two days on horseback to get there. She received mail once a month when they would go out to the trading post to get some supplies and the mail.

Later she moved to the Johannesburg area, where the mission had her oversee the schools in the African townships. On weekends and evenings she held services and would teach the adults. She rode the trains in the areas where it was not very safe to travel, but God gave her protection.

She was married at the age of thirty-two and served alongside her husband at Casteel Mission. She enjoyed those years of ministry among the families where she was involved in working with women and teaching them cleanliness, health, sewing, and about God and the Bible. Their three children were born while they served here. All three children and the grandchildren are involved in some sort of Christian ministry.

After a furlough in the States, the family returned to South Africa in 1950 and lived in Boksburg, in the Johannesburg area, so the children could all attend school. Their mother taught the men who were working in the gold mine near their home how to read. She also held services for them in the church next door. She and the children would go with their father on mission trips when they could. Those trips were like a holiday as well as a mission trip to them. They always enjoyed the trips and being around the mission work. The children counted it a privilege to be on the mission field due to their parents' attitude of making their influence in God's work a part of their lives.

Dorothy Lehman was a very good missionary and an excellent mother and wife. She ended her earthly journey June 2, 1983, at age seventy-seven.

Mary Brown Olsen

Mary Brown, a schoolteacher, and her sister, Ethel, lived in Centreville, Maryland. The fruits of their labors included a church in Centreville and a canvas-tent campground in Chestertown, Maryland. "The influence of their ardent labors still continues through the years." These words were written by Etta M. Clough, an ordained minister in the Eastern District of the Pilgrim Holiness Church.

Mary became the wife of Rev. H. J. Olsen, a district superintendent, Bible teacher, general administrator and the editor of the *Pilgrim Holiness Advocate*.

Mrs. Seth C. Rees wrote this tribute about her: "She was a noble woman with a well-ordered household. She had a contagious smile with a silvery laugh. She was lovely in countenance and rich in divine grace."

Mary was known for giving to the needy. She was a tower of strength to her husband and a wise counselor.[107]

Pearl Farr Roush

Pearl Farr was born August 5, 1884, in Indiana. She married Otis L. Roush on May 28, 1907. Four children were born to them.

Pearl was licensed to preach in 1923. Another lady minister, Mary Dice, went to Palestine, Illinois, in 1925 and conducted a tent meeting. A church was started, and Pearl Roush became the first pastor. Pearl was ordained in 1927 by the Pilgrim Holiness Church.

Pearl was the pastor of three churches, all in Illinois: Robinson, Palestine, and St. Marie. On November 4, 1943, the St. Marie Pilgrim Holiness Church was organized, and Pearl became the first pastor of that church. She was a member of the Illinois District until her death. She was elected the alternate ministerial delegate to the General Assembly of the Pilgrim Holiness Church one time.

Pearl preached until her husband retired, and they moved to Montpelier, Indiana. She was devoted to the cause of Christ. Her death occurred September 29, 1954.[108]

Myra Shaffer

The *Minutes of the Annual Assembly of the Illinois and Missouri District Pilgrim Holiness Church* 1925–30 recorded Myra (Mrs. A. M.) Shaffer as a licensed minister in 1925. She was stationed at Malli, Illinois, in 1927. Myra was ordained in 1928. There was no further record of her service after 1930.

Florence E. Baxter Shippee

Florence E. Baxter was born in Ellenburg, New York. She was converted at age ten and called into the ministry. In 1922 she was given a license to be a deaconess, but in 1928 she was received for ordination as an ordained minister in the Wesleyan Methodist Church in the Champlain Conference (now Eastern New York-New England District). She served that district for forty-one years; thirty-seven years were in active service.[109]

She was assigned her first pastorate at Hague and Valley View. During her six years there she assisted a faithful group of people at Ticonderoga, New York. "On April 7, 1926, a group gathered at the home of Miss Ellen Lee in Ticonderoga, New York, to organize a prayer circle. Interdenominational prayer meetings were held with the Reverend Florence Baxter, the first Wesleyan Methodist pastor taking part." This group later became a Wesleyan Methodist Church.

She served the Corinth church for ten years. The work showed good growth under her ministry, and several key families joined the church.[110]

In 1940 she was appointed the pastor of Hadley. During her time there, she married Fred Shippee. He was licensed to preach but was not ordained. He served as her Sunday school superintendent and youth leader. While pastoring there, she conducted a revival at Macomb and many people were saved.

The Shippees moved to Colton, New York. This church had been organized in April 1943 in a home. The church was located on the site of a blacksmith shop and garage and was dedicated on June 11, 1944. Florence was the first pastor and Fred served as her assistant. They remained here for three years.

They were the pastors of the Bakers Mills and Mill Creek churches for five years. They ministered to the Chittendon, Vermont, church for three years and Fort Miller church for one year. During this pastorate they liquidated the debt on the church. In 1958 Florence retired.

Doris Melvin wrote the following about Florence Baxter Shippee:

> Characteristics seen through the eyes of a ten-year old child, I saw a woman who always had a smile and a hug for me. Her laughter was contagious. Others soon, both young and old, joined in response to her joy.
>
> Those of us who knew her saw a loving smile, a tender heart, a person touching many lives for God, someone reaching out to both the young and old, someone willing to work for the cause of saving all, someone preaching aggressively to win everyone to Christ.
>
> Although busy with her own responsibilities, she was always available to assist other churches in need. . . . Because of Mrs. Shippee's ministry in Hadley and Corinth during Charles Dayton's teenage years, he had answered God's call to enter the ministry. . . . Paul Dayton remembered as a young boy going to the altar on a Sunday night when Florence was his pastor. He felt a heavy load was lifted from his shoulders. . . . The crowds were there on Sunday night, and she didn't fool around.

Florence preached for results and did not hesitate to preach on hell and eternal punishment.

Florence Baxter Shippee ended her earthly labors May 11, 1968.

Ila Stewart

The *Minutes of the Annual Assembly of the Pilgrim Holiness Church Indiana Conference,* 1923–27 and 1934 listed Ila Stewart as an ordained minister in 1923. She was the pastor at Mt. Zion that year.

Amy Slaughter

The *Minutes of the Eastern District of the Pilgrim Holiness Church* recorded Amy Slaughter as a minister in the district from 1925 to 1945. She died September 7, 1945. She pastored only one church, the Centreville, Maryland, church. She worked here for several years. When she became physically unable to be actively engaged, she bore her sufferings with Christian fortitude.

Margaret Lohr shared her memories of Amy Slaughter's ministry at Centreville:

Amy's husband, Harry, was a very capable person that shared her faith and zeal but was not a minister. He worked in the background. Without his support she could not have been the minister that she was. Foremost in my memory was one Sunday morning, Amy had fasted and prayed for the services. After she preached she gave an invitation to those who wanted to come forward and give their hearts to God. Some children came forth. One was her daughter, Thelma, another my sister, Etta Clough and myself. That was a lasting, life-changing time for all three of us.

Amy's daughter, Mrs. Earnest Priuth, recalled some precious memories of her childhood and her mother:

My mother was a very caring and loving woman. The Centreville church was a little humble church when she took it. I can't remember her sermons, but I do remember the intensity of her preaching and the prayers around the altar after she preached. The church held cottage prayer meetings in various homes. I remember them loading hymn books and Bibles in the back seat with me before we went out into the country to hold these services. Many people attended. There would be singing, testimonies, and sometimes a short sermon. There were some conversions in these meetings also.

Mama was a good cook; she baked delicious rolls and breads. I recall there were always many visitors in our home. An aunt and cousin always spent the entire summer with us in order to escape the heat of the city and then left before the goldenrod bloomed.

Mama lived like all the other housewives. There was always work to do, washing, ironing, cleaning, raising children, and caring for a garden that provided us with fresh vegetables and canning. I never saw her act frustrated or upset over all the chores. To sum it all up, Mama lived her religion. I never saw her manifest an ill temper or ugly disposition. Unkind words would hurt her, but she didn't answer back. She loved people, and people loved her.

Etta Spring

Etta Spring was given a license to preach in 1925. She served for a time as an evangelist. She was ordained in 1927 by the Ohio Conference of the Wesleyan Methodist Church. That night before her ordination she preached the evening message. She was active in the conference Woman's Home and Foreign Missionary Society.

Her husband, Worthy A. Spring, was granted a letter of standing from the conference September 1927. He became president of Cleveland Bible College (now Malone College) and later the president of Kletzing College in Oskaloosa, Iowa.

Etta retained her ministerial membership in the Ohio Conference until June 3, 1954. At that time she was granted a letter of transfer to the Friends Church.[111]

Esther White and Katie Locke

Esther White and Katie Locke were an evangelistic team for a number of years. They were in much demand across the Midwest. Their evangelistic work included not only preaching the gospel, but Katie also played the trap drums, the cornet, and other musical instruments. They also sang together. They were very "enthusiastic in their ministry." Many Pilgrim Holiness churches were organized as a result of these revival meetings.

According to her obituary found in the *Pilgrim Holiness Advocate* August 3, 1963, on page 14, Katie Locke was born May 10, 1895. She was saved and sanctified in a tent meeting in 1923. At that time she heard God's call to the ministry. Two years later (1925) she and Esther White became coworkers and traveled in home missionary work and revivals for several years.

Both ladies were ordained by the Pilgrim Holiness Church. Their service record may be found in the *Minutes of the Annual Assembly of the Pilgrim Holiness Church Indiana Conference 1939–62* for Katie Locke and 1939–63 for Esther White. They served as the pastors of the Milan, Indiana, Pilgrim Holiness Church for eighteen years. They lived for others, helped many persons who were in distress, and preached without "fear or favor." In her later years, Katie Locke had impaired eyesight because of an illness, but Esther White would read the Bible to her daily, and Katie preached, not being able to see well enough to read.

Katie Locke entered her eternal rest June 11, 1963. Esther White continued on in the ministry and was listed as a conference evangelist at the time of merger in 1968.

Marion Ruth Whitney

Marion Ruth Whitney was born in 1892. She was converted under the ministry of Beverly Carradine. She attended Houghton College, Houghton, New York about 1910. Marion's parents were gospel preachers and singers who established churches in Canada and pastored in the United States. She accompanied them in the work.

She went with her uncle and his family (Adam Shea) to New Jersey in 1930 and became a

Rev. Marion R. Whitney (l.) and her mother, Rev. Mary C. Whitney

member of the Middle Atlantic States Mission Conference of the Wesleyan Methodist Church. She was active in the conference and held many conference offices, including conference Sunday school secretary. Her report in 1930 revealed the Sunday school work was "fair." She stated there was a great need for Spirit-filled teachers "who have the vision and training for the work and a praying church to cooperate with teachers in bringing boys and girls into the church." Marion loved children and was an excellent children's worker.

June 2, 1930, the president of the conference engaged Marion to do some evangelistic work at the North Willow Grove Church. June 23 she was appointed pastor there. The next year she was joined by her mother, Mary, and they pastored the church together. She and Mother Whitney pioneered a church near Philadelphia, directed a church building program, and saw the planting and founding of the Willow Grove Wesleyan Methodist Church. They were the pastors at Willow Grove from 1932 to 1943. On February 10, 1943, she resigned the church effective at the close of the conference year.

Marion was ordained on Sunday afternoon, May 5, 1935, at conference time. She served from 1943 to 1967 as an evangelist and an evangelistic singer. She was confined to a wheelchair from 1950 until her death October 24, 1981. She continued singing, painting, leading neighborhood Bible studies or leading classes for the elderly in painting and singing.[112]

Lillie Andrews

The Proceedings of the Annual Assembly California District of the Pilgrim Holiness Church from 1926 to 1932 listed Lillie Andrews as an ordained minister under their appointment.

Mrs. Earl Baldwin

Mrs. Earl Baldwin served as an ordained minister under appointment in the Michigan District of the Pilgrim Holiness Church in 1924 and

1926. However, she was also listed as an ordained minister under appointment in the Ohio District of the Pilgrim Holiness Church in 1926 and 1927.[113]

Mildred Mae George Barris

Mildred Mae George was born in New Castle, Pennsylvania, May 31, 1903. She was converted in 1920 during a thirteen-week revival campaign held by Mary H. Ellis in the Primitive Methodist Church in New Castle.

In 1924 she felt led of the Lord to enter Taylor University to study music. In the summer of 1925 she and a friend, Sadie Lewis (Jones), represented the university in meetings. The next year she completed her course, and for six years she and Sadie had a fruitful ministry in the field of evangelistic singing.

September 4, 1931, she married E. Ranson Barris. They made their home in West Middlesex, Pennysylvani. There they sponsored two revivals; one was held by the young people of the New Castle Holiness Association and the other by Rev. John Landrey. As a result of these meetings, the West Middlesex Wesleyan Methodist Church was organized in November 1938. Mildred Mae assisted her husband as the pastor of the church. In 1941 she went with her husband to pastor the Allida Smith Memorial Wesleyan Methodist Church.

She received her conference preacher's license in 1944 and was ordained as a minister by the Allegheny Conference in 1947. She served as co-pastor with her husband at Tarentum, Canal, and North Springfield Wesleyan Methodist churches.

She was greatly loved by the people whom they served. She was the mother of two children. During her illness of eighteen years, two of them she was bedfast, she wrote several poems that appeared in *The Wesleyan Methodist*. She also wrote some songs. Two of her songs were published, and the rest were published later. She departed this life January 1, 1953.[114]

Mrs. C. A. Brockman

Mrs. C. A. Brockman was ordained in 1926. She served under the Pilgrim Holiness Church in the Eastern Kansas and Oklahoma District in 1926 and under the Western Kansas District 1927–29, 1931–34.[115]

Madora Thatcher Brown

Madora Thatcher was born May 26, 1874, in Richmond, Virginia. She departed this life December 16, 1955. She was converted early in life. She felt called to the ministry and was engaged in gospel work.

She served as matron at the Star mission in Charleston, South Carolina. For eight years she was a member of the Salvation Army Service Department. She was ordained in 1919 and married Rev. C. M. Brown, July 18, 1922. Together they pastored the First Pilgrim Holiness Church in Marion, Ohio, 1922–31.

Madora was remembered as a woman of deep piety. She was a lover and staunch defender of Bible truths.[116]

Pearl Boggs Butner Allred

Pearl Boggs was born in Yadkin County, North Carolina, September 7, 1890. She was converted at age fifteen and sanctified a year later. In 1913 she was ordained as a minister. She received her education for the ministry at Greensboro Bible Institute in Greensboro, North Carolina.

She married Rev. Gene Herman Butner in 1906. Pearl first served under the International Apostolic Holiness Church of North Carolina as the pastor of the Troy church in Asheboro, North Carolina. In 1916 she was the pastor at Greensboro and was serving under the Southern District of the International Apostolic Holiness Church. She served as an assistant to her husband in 1918 at the South Side Winston-Salem church.[117] Together they also pastored Hillsboro and Burlington, North Carolina, churches and the Pilgrim Holiness churches in Roanoke and Staunton, Virginia. She pastored Bent Mountain and Christiansburg (a mission) in Virginia.

While Pearl was living in Christiansburg in 1945, J. H. Fralin gave Pearl a twenty-five-dollar donation to have a tent meeting in Christiansburg.

Nine people were saved during that meeting. The next year another tent meeting was conducted, and seventeen people were converted. She then organized the first Sunday school. It met in her home, and then a church was started. It was called the Pilgrim Holiness Mission. After G. H. Butner died, Pearl married William S. Allred in 1946. In 1947 a house was built on the old garden spot, and it became the first church building. The name of the church was now called the Pilgrim Mission. A lot was purchased in July 1, 1949, and a new facility was completed in 1950. Pearl Allred was the pastor at Christiansburg from 1947 to 1958. William S. Allred died in 1960, and Pearl Allred retired in 1962.[118]

Marie G. Downer Clement

Marie G. Downer had been ordained by the North Carolina Conference of the Wesleyan Methodist Church in 1926. She transferred to the South Carolina Conference that year and taught at Central College, in Central, South Carolina (now Southern Wesleyan University). She was the pastor of Tuckaseigee, Glenville, and Rock Ridge (all mountain churches in South Carolina). In 1931 she was given a letter of transfer to the North Carolina Conference.

On June 21, 1941, she presented a letter of standing from the North Carolina Conference dated 1931. After seeking legal advice, she was received as an ordained minister in the South Carolina Conference.

Marie did some pastoring for the Christian and Missionary Alliance Church and for about six years worked with an independent church as pastor.

In 1946 she married John A. Clement, becoming his third wife. Both of his previous wives had been preachers. On August 15, 1951, she was granted a letter of transfer to the Kentucky Conference.

Marie worked with the mountain people under very difficult conditions. When she transferred to the Kentucky Conference she was appointed the pastor of the Jamestown work. Apparently there was no salary, for each church was instructed to give a Christmas offering to her for the work at Jamestown. The work there was disbanded March 15, 1953.

She was appointed to the Washington work in 1954. She resigned from that church January 21, 1955, and was appointed to evangelism. However, on April 10, 1955, she was appointed to the Shively pioneer work. The Mission Board gave her ten dollars a week and ten dollars a week for mobile home rent.

March 24, 1956, the conference sent her again to the Jamestown work. She resigned November 21, 1957, and retired from active service.[119]

Myrtle Coleman

The Minutes of the Annual Assembly of the Pilgrim Holiness Church Indiana Conference, 1926–52, revealed that Myrtle Coleman was under appointment in that district for that period of time. *The Journal of Proceedings of the Annual Session of the Southern Indiana Conference of the Pilgrim Holiness Church* recorded she worked in that district from 1951 to 1953. She was the pastor at Coalmont, Indiana, for a time.

Anna Minerva Cork

Anna Minerva and her devoted husband, J. J. Cork, were adequate and model pioneer ministers of the gospel in the International Apostolic Holiness Union and Churches, a forerunner of the Pilgrim Holiness Church in Kansas. Despite the hardships of pioneer life and travel, she remained steadfast in taking the message of salvation to hungry people to schoolhouse revivals, tent meetings, and other preaching points.

A young farmer and his wife, J. J. and Anna Minerva Cork, attended a revival meeting near their farm in Winona, Kansas in January 1906. The young couple were convicted of their sins and were converted. They joined the International Apostolic Holiness Union.

Feeling the tug of God on their hearts to preach the gospel, they left the farm in 1908 and moved to Cincinnati, Ohio, to attend God's Bible School. J. J. graduated in the spring of 1913, and in August, accompanied by Rev. E. G. Marsh, the Cork family set out for Keystone, Kansas.

Keystone was about forty miles from their old farm. Their intent was to hold a meeting and establish a church in that location.

The family traveled by wagon and took a cow for their milk supply, and three tents, two to sleep in and one for cooking and eating. Their other earthly possessions were a stove, cooking utensils, a table, chairs, and beds. The Corks had four children, and they were also packed into the wagon. They found a schoolhouse in Keystone and conducted a revival. A church was organized the next year, 1914, as a result of that meeting.

J. J. and Anna Minerva sponsored a ten-day camp meeting in a tent at Winona in 1914. George B. Kulp was the evangelist. A church was organized in 1915, and a building was constructed. From that time on a camp meeting was held there every year up to and including 1926.

The Corks and J. E. DeCamp went about sixty miles north of Winona for another meeting in a school near Bird City in 1915. Another church was organized after that meeting. About this time the Corks purchased a Model T Ford. This enabled them to pastor both the Keystone and Bird City churches. Some thirty years later they would return to Bird City and pastor another five years there, and under their leadership, the church and parsonage would be moved into town (1948).

J. J. was elected superintendent of the Western Kansas-Eastern Colorado District when it was organized in 1916. Anna Minerva was elected treasurer. They held these offices until the fall of 1926.

Anna was ordained in 1919. She preached the gospel without fear or favor and with great power. Because of her unyielding faith and devotion, eleven churches were planted in Kansas by her and her husband.

Her last years were spent in suffering, but her courage, testimony, and firm grip on God encouraged all those who came to see her in her illness. Anna Minerva Cork died August 19, 1957.[120]

Esther Berg Depew

Esther Berg married Arthur E. Depew in 1926. They were both ordained by the Wesleyan Methodist Church. No record was found of her work until 1931, in the *Minutes of the Annual Session of the Rochester Conference of the Wesleyan Methodist Connection, or Church, of America*. The records showed that she and her husband were transfers from the California Conference in 1931, and they were the pastors at the Haskinsville and Wales Hollow, New York, Wesleyan Methodist churches.

The *Minutes of the California Conference of the Wesleyan Methodist Connection or Church, of America,* 1942–67, revealed they had returned to California and were pastors of the Colton, Bostonia, Lakeside, Sunland, and El Serreno (Los Angeles) California churches. In 1960 Esther was the representative of the Los Angeles County Women's Christian Temperance Union (WCTU), and her conference assignment for the next eight years was as WCTU lecturer and children's worker.

Esther was actively involved in conference work. She served on the itineracy and elders orders committee (now district board of ministerial development), missionary board, commission on child evangelism, and was president of the Woman's Missionary Society.

Sophia Doehring

Sophia Doehring was listed as an ordained minister in the *Minutes of the Annual Assembly of the Michigan District Pilgrim Holiness Church,* 1926–40. She was on the unstationed (without appointment) list in 1936. Her report to conference that year shows she had conducted thirty-six services, preached thirty-six times, conducted seventeen prayer meetings, and held one revival.

Alberta Dunkum

Two entries were found for Alberta (Mrs. W. B.) Dunkum. She was an ordained minister in the Kentucky Conference of the Wesleyan Methodist Church and was listed as a general evangelist in 1926. In 1930 she was involved as a conference evangelist. She was active in the conference Woman's Home and Foreign Missionary Society and the Young Missionary Workers Band (now Wesleyan Kids for Missions).[121]

She died February 15, 1932.[121]

Anna L. Filmore

Anna L. Filmore served the Lord and His Church in many capacities. She was introduced to the Ohio Conference of the Wesleyan Methodist Church in 1926. She preached the afternoon sermon on Thursday of conference. The next year she was ordained (1927). She pastored several churches: Lapeer, Michigan; Greer and Shadley Valley, Fargo, Marengo, and Westview, Ohio; and Black Creek, New York.

Anna was the dean of women at Houghton College, in Houghton, New York, for a few years. She was noted also for her work with children. For three years her conference assignment was as children's worker and Bible teacher. She taught at Houghton College for a number of years. In 1944 she became the dean of women at Cleveland College and served there for three years.

In 1947 she became the national secretary of the National Holiness Association (now Christian Holiness Partnership). The following year she spoke at the Ohio Conference about joining the National Holiness Association, and they did.

Anna Filmore was active in two conferences, the Ohio and Lockport Conferences of the Wesleyan Methodist Church. She served on many of the major conference committees: pastoral relations, duties of conference president, nominations, credentials, Sunday school, and president's advisory boards. She also served as conference secretary of the Ohio Conference and educational secretary of the Lockport Conference.

Anna L. Filmore completed her earthly tasks in 1960.

Mrs. J. B. Fulp

Mrs. J. B. Fulp and her husband were a ministerial team. She was first mentioned in the *Minutes of the Annual Assembly of the Pilgrim Holiness Church Southern District* in 1926. She and her husband were the pastors of the West Durham, North Carolina, church. They served together at Bethlehem, Pleasant Grove, Asheboro, and Biscue. She was also listed as an evangelist from time to time.[122]

Ida Goss Garner

Ida Goss married Rev. Harry Garner in 1921. He died February 3, 1957. She began her ministerial work in 1926 as dean of the women's dorm at Pilgrim Holiness College in Pasadena, California. She was on the active list of ministers until 1960. She died in 1962.[123]

Lorreen Ruth Sears Griffin

Lorreen (sometimes spelled Lorene) Ruth Sears was born March 20, 1898, in Livonia, Missouri. She began preaching at age fourteen. She married Bert J. Griffin September 6, 1923, and they were the parents of two sons and one daughter. After being married, she was involved in evangelistic work, serving with her husband in ministry in the Wesleyan Methodist Church. She ended her earthly tasks September 6, 1967.[124]

Bertha Emma Kienbaum

Bertha Kienbaum gave thirty-four years of service to the Bible Holiness Seminary. in Owosso, Michigan (which later became Owosso College, eventually merged into what became Indiana Wesleyan University, Marion, Indiana) as professor of Greek, theology, biblical literature, and Latin. She taught two generations of students and influenced hundreds of young people for Christ and the Church. Her students loved her and respected her wisdom and counsel. She chided, laughed at and with them, cared for, and prayed for them. Her students often referred to her as "the dean of all." She often told her women ministerial students that they would need to be twice as good at preaching the Word in order to make it in the male-dominated church world.

At age sixty-one, in 1954, she went to Transvaal, South Africa, to set up a Bible school at Brakpan.

Bertha was also a pastor for nine years in Ohio. She and Marcella Dean were co-pastors during that time.

Bertha Kienbaum was born to German Lutheran parents March 20, 1893, near Sandusky, Michigan. She was reared on a farm with four brothers and one sister. When she gave her heart to the Lord, she was put out of her home because of her newfound faith. However she was able later to introduce her mother and father to Jesus.[125]

She made a lifelong commitment to God at camp meeting in Yale, Michigan, on August 24, 1918. The following year she went to Owosso to attend Bible Holiness Seminary. She attended Kingswood Holiness College in Kingswood, Kentucky, and earned a bachelor's degree; two years later she received a bachelor of divinity degree from the same college. She received her master's degree from Taylor University, Upland, Indiana and soon afterward she earned a college life certificate from the state of Michigan. She was an ordained minister.

Bertha taught her last class when she was eighty years old. She often remarked after that that she wasn't doing anything for the Lord. However, the Kienbaum Scholarship at Indiana Wesleyan University, established in her honor, continues to help young people prepare for the ministry. Bertha entered her heavenly rest June 23, 1992, at age ninety-nine.[126]

───── ⚬⚬⚬ ─────

Vera Lauretta Morrell Lacy

Vera Morrell began her ministry as a teenager. She was converted at the age of four. Her parents were devout Baptist people who when they heard the message of heart holiness gladly accepted and lived it. They joined the Pilgrim Holiness Church and became lifelong members. It was in this fertile environment that Vera's faith and Christian life blossomed.

Her family was recognized and respected in the community as godly and spiritual people. Therefore, it was not surprising that a Mexican family, who could not afford the services of their priest to bury their child, came to the Morrell home seeking help. Dad and Mother Morrell said, "I think our daughter Vera can help." So at the age of eighteen, Vera conducted her first funeral service. This was the beginning of a ministry that Vera would have with her Mexican neighbors.

Vera's relationship with the Church began with the International Holiness Church. She attended Colorado Springs Bible School and Christian Academy (later merged into what became Oklahoma Wesleyan University, Bartlesville, Oklahoma). She was gifted with many talents. She could preach, sing, and play the piano. Often she was asked to provide the music for revivals and special services that were held in schoolhouses and churches on the prairie east of Colorado Springs.

Following one of those prairie revivals, Vera received her first pastoral appointment. Several people were converted during a revival at Haswell, Colorado, where Vera had served as the song evangelist. Following the revival a church was organized with the evangelist as the pastor. It soon became evident that he did not have the necessary skills to nurture and build the congregation. After several people left, he decided to return to evangelism, and Vera was appointed as the pastor.

It was during this pastorate that she and a young man, Delbert W. Lacy, developed a relationship. He was a layman at that time. He drove thirty-five miles each Sunday morning to be under her ministry and, of course, to continue their courtship.

God called Vera Lacy to the ministry, and she was faithful to that calling throughout her lifetime. The "preaching" aspect of her ministry was somewhat curtailed following her marriage to D. W. Lacy, December 24, 1932, but she did continue to preach on occasions. She filled the pulpit while her husband was away in meetings or for other reasons and occasionally took other speaking engagements. She always maintained that her husband was the better preacher, and she was content to let him do the preaching. Her contribution to their pastoral ministry, which took them to Virginia, Nebraska, Colorado, and Indiana, was in the area of youth ministry, planning the special days for the church, teaching in the Sunday school, having Bible studies, and, of course, music.

When Vera's husband was appointed to serve as president of Colorado Springs Bible College, her influence was felt in the student life on campus. When he was elected to serve as superintendent of the Rocky Mountain District, and later the Northern Indiana/Central Indiana Districts, her influence was felt as the gracious "First Lady" of the district.

During those years of district and general church ministries, Vera did more than support her husband's ministry. She had a ministry of her own. Because of her training and skills as a bookkeeper, her expertise was often sought by the college bookkeeper while they were at Colorado Springs Bible College. While D. W. Lacy served as the superintendent of the Indiana Central District, she organized the district Women's Missionary Society and served as its first district director. Her concern for the "women in the parsonage" caused her to plan annual retreats for the district ministers' wives. She gave leadership to those retreats as long as her husband was district superintendent.

Few women have sacrificed so selflessly and so completely as did Vera Lacy. To serve the churches in their area often meant living in substandard parsonages. When they took their first organized church at Bladen, Nebraska, they had no food in the house, not even milk for their baby. When the only man in the church came to inquire about their needs, Brother Lacy did not tell him of their lack of food. He would trust the Lord. Vera thought God wouldn't mind if he had let the man know. In a short time the member came back with a wheelbarrow load of food he had gleaned from the Works Progress Administration. He said God would not let him rest until he had brought them food. She clothed her family from the used clothing stores and even made her clothing from the material she could salvage from her husband's worn-out suits.

The reasons why they had sacrificed in these ways (with their pastoral abilities they could have graced the largest churches in the denomination) were three in number. They began pastoring during the Depression, and there was little or no money to be had. The churches in the Rocky Mountain District, where they served, were small and could not afford to support their pastors well. The salary as president of Colorado Springs Bible College was only $100 a month. The last reason probably should have been listed first. They committed themselves to the ministry and sought outside employment only when it did not interfere with their ministry.

Vera's daughter Verla summed up her mother's ministry when she wrote,

She devoted herself to others. Her selflessness was total, and her concern for others reflected her conviction that those who did not know her Christ would not share in the joy of eternity. Her caring was undaunted by tidal waves of apathy or avalanches of resistances. Her commitment was total.

The Northern Indiana District ordained Vera L. Lacy to the ministry in 1967. It was a goal that she had reached for during her entire ministry but was kept beyond her grasp by changing requirements for ordination that were made while she served others. Like her husband, who always put the Church ahead of his personal needs, she, too, would sacrifice her ordination goals rather than neglect her family or her church.

Her influence can be seen in the lives of her three children, who are all educators. Her son, David Lacy, is a retired public school principal from the Tipton, Indiana school system; Verla (Lacy) Powers, Ph.D., serves as a professor at Mid-America Nazarene University in Olathe, Kansas; and Ilene (Lacy) Carter teaches home economics in Illinois.

Vera Laurette (Morrell) Lacy was born August 28, 1908. She went to be with her Lord April 27, 1991.

"It was Sister Lacy's intention to pour out her life in service to her Lord and His Church. That is what she wanted to do—give it entirely to Jesus. Her life always set the highest example of Christian living and service."[127]

Harriet E. Miller

Harriet Miller began her ministerial studies in 1926. The records are not clear as to when she began serving the Church. One source recorded her as the assistant pastor to her husband, J. W. Miller, at Spartanburg, South Carolina, in 1930. Another stated she began in 1932. All her pastoral work was done at Spartanburg and Lyman Wesleyan Methodist churches. Her husband died January 25, 1940. Their last accomplishment together was the building of a new structure at Harveytown, near Lyman Mill. This church had been formerly known as the Lyman Church, but after his death the name was changed to Miller Memorial. Harriet stayed on as the pastor for another three years after his death. During her pastorate, in 1941 the church experienced a gracious revival; they paid their conference assessments in full and reduced the church debt to $227. The following year the mortgage was paid off, gas heating was installed, and the building was repainted. Her son, John James Miller, had been called to preach, and he assisted his mother from 1940 to 1943.

Harriet Miller served as a general evangelist for four years. A write-up about her evangelistic work in the *Wesleyan Methodist,* September 8, 1943, stated she had been a successful pastor, was spiritual, carried a burden for the lost, and knew the problems of a pastor.

She was appointed the district tithing secretary in 1944 and held that position until 1947. In this position, she visited the district churches and preached on tithing as well as conducted revivals.

Harriet was born September 5, 1889, and departed this earthly life December 23, 1963.[128]

Anna Pike

The first record found on Anna Pike was in the *Minutes of the Annual Session of the Kentucky Conference of the Wesleyan Methodist Connection, or Church, of America* in 1926. She was an ordained minister at that time. Anna and her husband, A. F. Pike, were the pastors of the Louisville, Kentucky, Atwood Street Wesleyan Methodist Church that year. She was elected the alternate ministerial delegate to General Conference in 1926.

In 1928 she was received as an ordained minister by the Indiana Conference of the Wesleyan Methodist Church and was appointed

as a general evangelist. She was listed as an evangelist until 1932.

Anna was granted a letter of transfer to the Kentucky Conference in 1937. However, before the year ended, she was again received by transfer from the Kentucky Conference back into the Indiana Conference. She served as an evangelist for another two years. Her name was dropped from the roll of ordained ministers in 1939.[129]

Mary L. Pratt

According to the *Minutes of the Annual Session of the Kentucky Conference of the Wesleyan Methodist Connection, or Church, of America* in 1926–33, Mary L. Pratt was ordained at the conference session in 1926. She and her husband, Lewis, were the pastors of the Holton, Kentucky, Church that year. She served on the conference statistical committee and was vice president of the conference Woman's Home and Foreign Missionary Society that year also. She had no other appointments.

Martha D. Pridgen

Martha Pridgen was born in Kansas in 1889. She became a school teacher and established the first high school in Staton County, Kansas.

She began her ministerial work under the International Holiness Church in 1926 and was ordained in 1929. She served under the Ohio District of the Pilgrim Holiness Church from 1929 to 1953. During this time she was the wife of Charles P. Pridgen, who was the Ohio District superintendent for seven years.[130]

Martha served under the Pilgrim Holiness Church in the Lousiana and Alabama District from 1954 to 1956 and in the Florida District from 1956 to 1967. Part of this time she was listed as an evangelist.[131]

In 1975 she transferred her district membership to the South Carolina District. She died December 9, 1983. She was the mother of one son.[132]

Mattie B. Rice

Mattie Rice served under the Pilgrim Holiness Church. The *Minutes of the Annual Assembly of the Illinois and Missouri District Pilgrim Holiness Church,* 1926–28, listed her as stationed at Onargo, Illinois. The *Minutes of the Annual Assembly of the Kentucky District Pilgrim Holiness Church* listed her at Flat Rock, Kentucky, in 1928 and at Ashland in 1929. She was elected as an alternate ministerial delegate to the General Assembly at one time.

Mary A. Robinson

Mary Robinson was the wife of Rev. C. H. Robinson. She was an English woman and spoke with a British brogue. She transferred from the Rochester Conference to the Champlain Conference of the Wesleyan Methodist Church in 1926. She and her husband were the pastors of the Corinth and East Corinth churches in 1927. Mary served under the Champlain Conference until 1942. In 1939 she worked with the Fairhaven Rescue Home in Sacramento, California. She was under appointment with the Oregon Conference from 1942 until her death about 1965. She never served a church in Oregon as pastor but served as evangelist and city missionary. In 1957 she retired. Her work in Oregon and Seattle was largely with street people, the homeless, and in slums. She was a woman of strong character, great influence, and good example.[133]

Ina Spaugh

Ina Spaugh died February 4, 1974. She was an ordained minister in the Pilgrim Holiness Church. She and her husband, O. J., spent most of their lives as missionaries in Latin America (Guatemala) and among the people in southern Texas in and around Lyford and McAllen. She lived a cheerful, godly, and devoted life. She was the mother of a son and daughter.[134]

Jennie Vestal Cox Ware

Jennie Vestal Cox Ware served forty years in churches on the North Carolina District of the Pilgrim Holiness Church. It was said that "she graced churches with her presence, watered the churches with her tears, undergirded churches in her prayers, and lifted them heavenward in her preaching."

She was married first to Henry Cox, who died in 1911. Jennie and Henry had three children. In 1918 she married Rev. W. P. Ware of Reidsville, North Carolina. When he received light on holiness, he sought out a holiness church. The Pilgrim Holiness Church was organized in Reidsville, and he became a charter member and the pastor until his death July 7, 1928. He married and buried more people in that town than any other preacher. After his death, Jennie, who had served as his assistant since her marriage, became the solo pastor at Reidsville and was the pastor until her death November 3, 1942.

In the formative years of the North Carolina District, Jennie served as a pioneer pastor and evangelist. She was generous with her finances and gave substantially of her means to support the Church and to assist ministerial students in obtaining an education. She paid part of William S. Deal's way through Bible school as well as many others.[135]

Anna B. Willson

Gerald A. Wolter, editor of *The Iowa Conference Centennial 1853–1953,* recorded Mrs. Anna B. Willson as pastor of the Fayette, Iowa, Wesleyan Methodist Church. Miss Sylvia Sampson had conducted a Sunday school here for a number of years. The church was organized July 29, 1926. Anna and her congregation first worshiped in a church formerly used by another denomination. Later they purchased a lot and moved in a church building in 1928.

Anna B. Willson was ordained August 20, 1933. Ruby Kogel served as an assistant to Anna at Fayette in 1935.

Anna was the pastor of the Laporte City, Iowa, church for one year, 1936–37. This church had been organized in 1935. She retired from active ministry in 1937. Her funeral was conducted June 20, 1962.[136]

Rev. Paul Davis, a former president of the Iowa Conference, writes the following information about Anna Willson. She had been the pastor of the Fayette Church when he was a high school student. She encouraged him to go into the ministry. She was an older lady at that time. He writes, "She was a perfect lady with great dignity and poise."

Edna N. Wood

Edna Wood began her ministerial preparation in 1926. She was already married to Asa H. Wood at that time. They began to pastor jointly at the Blanchard church in the North Michigan Conference of the Wesleyan Methodist Church. The following year Trinity was added to their responsibility but in October 1927 they resigned from both churches, and she became the pastor of the Sparta church. In 1929 Asa and Edna accepted the Sparta church together. They remained at Sparta until 1934, when they were appointed the pastors of the Ferry church. She was accepted for ordination in 1936. From 1937 to 1941 they were the pastors of the Golden Wesleyan Church (now known as West Golden). Both their daughters married young men from that church.

Asa and Edna were granted letters of transfers to another church. Apparently that church was the Pilgrim Holiness Church. The next report from them was made from Imperial, Nebraska. In 1945 they were received by letter of transfer from the Pilgrim Holiness Church into the Nebraska Conference of the Wesleyan Methodist Church. They were the pastors of the Atkinson, Nebraska, church from 1945 to 1951 and served in conference evangelism for the next two years. On July 17, 1954, they transferred to the North Michigan Conference.[137]

Asa Wood died in 1955. Edna was appointed to the staff of Brainerd Indian School, near Hot Springs, South Dakota, that year and served in that capacity until the close of the l960 conference

year. She retired from the active ministry in 1961 and moved back to Michigan. Later her daughters placed her in the extended care facility at Hart, Michigan, where she died in 1977.

Besides assisting in the pastoral work, Edna was active in the women's missionary endeavors. She served on various district women's missionary committees and as president of the North Michigan Conference Woman's Home and Foreign Missionary Society for three years. She was also active in the Nebraska Conference Woman's Home and Foreign Missionary Society during their years of service in that conference.[138]

Ruth Mildred Bowman

Ruth Bowman jokingly called herself "the Pennsylvania dutchess." She was born in Bowmanstown, Pennsylvania, December 24, 1904. She was converted at age fifteen and four years later was sanctified. She also received her call to preach that year. She was licensed to preach in 1921 and was ordained in 1927 by George Kulp of the Pilgrim Holiness Church.

She was in the first graduating class of the Beulah Park Bible School, Allentown, Pennsylvania (later Eastern Pilgrim College/United Wesleyan College) in 1924. She also attended God's Bible School, Eastern Pilgrim College, and Frankfort Pilgrim College, in Frankfort, Indiana (later merged into United Wesleyan College). She served as the dean of women on both the Frankfort and Owosso campuses. Ernest Batman, former district superintendent of the Indiana Central District, wrote about his association with her as dean of women at Frankfort:

Although she highly approved of Ada [his wife-to-be] and my dating, she always made it difficult for this bashful boy to get permission for a date with Ada. However, once I had gotten up enough courage to get her permission, she often would find a way to give us a little more dating freedom. She was a great lady, and real friend of young people. I had her for a weekend meeting in my first pastorate. She was a "barn stormer" and preached with enthusiasm.

While on the staff at Owosso Bible College, Owosso, Michigan (later merged into what became Indiana Wesleyan University, Marion, Indiana) she gave the following annual report at conference: she had preached fifty times, led twenty prayer meetings, prayed for eighteen healings, had twenty-five conversions, seen twenty seek sanctification, and held two revivals.

In the United States she pastored the Summit Hill and Muney, Pennsylvania, churches. She spent several years in evangelistic work also. She served on the faculty of Eastern Pilgrim College, Owosso College, and Frankfort Pilgrim College.

In June 1949 Ruth Bowman began her ministerial work on the island of Grand Cayman, in the West Indies. She was appointed the pastor of the West Bay church, and the Northside church was under her direction also. Because of a physical problem, she returned to the United States in 1953. August 1957 she returned to Grand Cayman. She adopted Grand Cayman as her home and retired there. Ruth Bowman died January 15, 1991, and was buried in Grand Cayman.

Ruth had a unique personality and an anointed ministry that endeared her to thousands across the United States and in the West Indies.[139]

Helen Cooper

The Minutes of the California District Pilgrim Holiness Church listed Helen Cooper under appointment from 1927 to 1934. She was ordained in 1928. Helen served as the pastor of the Fresno Pilgrim Holiness Church in 1930.

Mrs. A. F. Duncan

Mrs. A. F. Duncan was ordained in 1926. She served under the Pilgrim Holiness Church on the Western Kansas District from 1927 to 1942 and under the Kansas District from 1943 to 1951.[140]

Emma Erby

Emma Erby had been ordained by the Gospel Workers of America when she was received by the Indiana Conference of the Wesleyan Methodist

Connection as an ordained minister in 1927 and was appointed to be a general evangelist. Her death occurred the next year, 1928.[141]

Mrs. Charles Harvey

The Minutes of the Annual Assembly of the Ohio District of the Pilgrim Holiness Church, 1927–34, listed Mrs. Charles Harvey as an ordained minister in 1927. She worked under that district until 1934.

Vera Anna Hunter Hiles

Vera Anna Hunter was born March 26, 1891, in New Jersey and was called to preach at age seventeen. She taught school for eight years. November 16, 1918, she married Lewis C. Hiles in Coeur d' Alene, Idaho. He had just returned from Japan, where he had served as a missionary. The following year, 1919, she was ordained.

L. C. Hiles and Vera Anna together pastored the following churches: Athol, Idaho; Goodland, Kansas; Mineral Springs, Virginia; Camden, New Jersey; Napoleon, Ohio; Morrison and Dacoma, Oklahoma. They served ten years as missionaries to British Guiana (Guyana) and four years as missionaries in the Virgin Islands.

She served under the Kentucky, Pennsylvania and New Jersey, Ohio, Oklahoma/Texas, and Central Districts of the Pilgrim Holiness Church. At various times she was involved in home ministries and evangelism as well as serving as a pastor. The last fifteen years of her life were spent in Hopeton, Oklahoma. She was the mother of two daughters. Vera died September 19, 1967.[142]

Mary E. Huntsman

The Minutes of the Annual Session of the Champlain Conference of the Wesleyan Methodist Connection, or Church, of America, 1927–29, revealed that Mary (Mrs. Cecil) Huntsman was received for ordination in 1927 and she was to choose her own field of labor until 1929, when she transferred to the Rochester Conference.

While they served in the Rochester Conference, Cecil and Mary were the pastors of the Haskinville, Canandaigua, Halifax, and Carsonville, New York, churches. Mary was active in the conference serving on several committees and as superintendent of the Young Missionary Workers Band (now Wesleyan Kids for Missions) from 1930 to 1935.

In 1937 the couple transferred to the Allegheny Conference and served as pastors at Greenville, North Salem, Pittsfield, Wolf Summit, Walgus, Tarentum, Nu Mine, Punxsutawney, Massillon, Brownsville, and Carrollton, all in Pennsylvania.[143]

Bertha V. Richards Ketch

Bertha Richards joined the Rochester Conference (now Central New York District) of the Wesleyan Methodist Church in 1925. She became the assistant pastor to Rev. Frank S. Lee in 1925 at Rome, New York. After his death, she served the church as the pastor until she received a call to pastor the Wallace Church. She was ordained at conference time in 1927.

Bertha's ministry at the Wallace Church (1927–39) saw a gradual and constant growth. It became the largest church in the zone. Bertha was an excellent speaker and a fine pastor. The church purchased their present parsonage during her tenure. Growth meant the need for more Sunday school rooms, so several rooms were added to the church.[144] In 1933 Bertha married William Ketch.

After a year or so of working in evangelism, the president of the conference took Bertha to an independent church in Avon, New York, and in 1941 she was appointed pastor of this work. In 1944 the Church was officially organized as a Wesleyan Methodist church. The next year she had the first daily vacation Bible school. She collected donated books and started a church library in 1948. A Young Missionary Workers Band (now Wesleyan Kids for Missions) was organized in June 1949. She served this church from 1941 to 1949.[145]

Bertha Ketch was actively involved on many conference committees. She served for nine years as assistant conference secretary and served as a member of the itineracy and elders' orders committee for eleven years. She was a teacher for the conference study course. Bertha retired from the active ministry in 1950.[146]

Ethel Lenore Leach Poff

Ethel Lenore Leach was born May 30, 1890, in Omaha, Nebraska. Her parents were homesteaders in Oklahoma, and she lived in Oklahoma until her marriage to Albert F. Poff in 1910 in Oklahoma. She was the mother of eight children. Two of them died in infancy.

Ethel was converted at age eleven and sanctified sometime later. For a number of years she served as a deaconess and was later ordained. In her early ministry she was involved in mission work at Guthrie, Oklahoma. Many years later she became the assistant pastor to her husband. They served Pilgrim Holiness churches in Oklahoma, Colorado, and Nebraska. She spent thirty-eight years in the ministry. God's work was the most important thing in her life. She gave herself to the work of the Kingdom and the Church. She died April 20, 1957.[147]

Grace A. Schneider

Miss Grace A. Schneider began her ministerial work under the International Apostolic Holiness Church as an evangelist in 1921. She was a teacher at Kingswood School for a time. In 1923 she organized the church at Youngsville, Pennsylvania.[148] In 1927 she transferred to the Virginia District and was assigned the pastorate of the Biller's Crest church.[149] No further record of her work was found until 1942. *The Proceedings of the Western Kansas District Assembly of the Pilgrim Holiness Church,* 1942, stated that she had been ordained in 1940 and was under their direction through 1942. She transferred to the Michigan District in 1945.[150]

Diana Ferns Wyman Miller

Diana Ferns was born in Hemmingford, Quebec, February 3, 1982. She was the oldest of five children. The earliest records found for her reveal that she was a deaconess and served as the assistant pastor at the Wesleyan Methodist church in Mooers, New York, in 1927. She continued to serve there until 1930, when she became the assistant pastor at Chillenden, Vermont. In 1932 she was ordained. Diana Ferns married Rev. Orion Gould Wyman of Wells, Maine, on August 25, 1930.[151]

Diana and O. G. Wyman transferred to the Lockport, New York, Conference in 1933. They were the pastors at Forestville (1933–36) and Ashwood, near Lyndonville, New York, (1936–40).[152] They transferred back to the Champlain Conference in 1941 and became the pastors of the Chazy church. O. G. Wyman died November 11, 1942, and Diana stayed on as the pastor through 1943. On January 11, 1944, she married Rev. S. Harry Miller. Together they pastored the Bakers Mills and Mill Creek circuit and the Colton church. Diana was assigned to evangelism from 1950 to 1956. She retired in 1957. Her husband, S. Harry Miller, died in 1963, but she was still listed as a retired minister at the time of the 1968 merger.

Diana was active in the work on the conference level and served on many committees. She served as conference treasurer of the Woman's Home and Foreign Missionary Society for a number of years. She received her ministerial training at Houghton College, in Houghton, New York. She also did nursing, but there was no record of her education in this area. Her sister-in-law described her as a very nice person, gentle, caring, and helpful. Her preaching was always interesting and helpful and was presented in a most pleasing delivery.[153]

Mary Augsburg

Proceedings of the Annual Assembly California District of the Pilgrim Holiness Church, 1928–31, listed Mrs. Mary Augsburg as an ordained minister, and she served during that time under their direction.

Mrs. Belle Bleakley

Belle Lee Bleakley was an ordained minister in the Pilgrim Holiness Church. Records show that she pastored only one church: Newkirk, Oklahoma. She served under several different districts only because the name of the district changed from time to time. She preached the gospel for over seventy years. She died January 18, 1949.[154]

Mrs. Sophia Bicker

The Minutes of the California District Pilgrim Holiness Church from 1928 to 1934 listed Sophia Bicker as an ordained minister serving under their direction.

Bertha Ward Chapman

Bertha Ward Chapman graduated in 1913 from Fairmount Bible School, in Fairmount, Indiana (merged into what became Indiana Wesleyan University, Marion, Indiana). She was described as cheerful, optimistic, and a good student. She was active in gospel work during her time at the Bible school.[155] She served as pastor of the Otterbein, Indiana, church for a time but resigned during the year in order to pastor Lafayette Second church. She was ordained August 1933. Most of her ministerial work was in conference evangelism. She served under three conferences in the Wesleyan Methodist Church: Indiana, Ohio, and Florida.[156]

Ethel Corya

One reference was found for Ethel Corya, an ordained minister, in the 1928 *Minutes of the Annual Assembly of the Ohio District Pilgrim Holiness Church.*

Bertha Fowler

Bertha Fowler was received from the Methodist Episcopal Church by the Kentucky District of the Pilgrim Holiness Church in 1927. She was ordained in 1928 and was the pastor of the Vanceburg, Kentucky, church that year. The next year she was working in Mexico and had moved her district membership to the California District Pilgrim Holiness Church.[157]

Mrs. Rachel McCune

The *Minutes of the Annual Conference of the Kentucky District Pilgrim Holiness Church* in 1929 recorded Rachel McCune as being ordained in 1929, and she was stationed at Kingswood, Kentucky. No mention was made of the type of work she did.

Maude Norman

Maude Norman was a conference preacher in the Indiana Conference of the Wesleyan Methodist Church in 1928. She was assigned the pastorate at the Fowlerton, Indiana, church that year and continued as the pastor until the close of the conference year in 1933. During this time she was also appointed pastor of a new church that had been started in Gaston, Indiana, and remained the pastor until conference in 1932. Maude Norman was ordained in 1931. She served as conference educational secretary from 1934 to 1936. During the conference year of 1936–37 she turned in her credentials and joined another denomination. Eugene L. Kierstead, former president of the Indiana Conference and denominational publisher, was greatly influenced by her ministry during her pastorate at the Fowlerton church.[158]

Hazel Rose

Hazel Rose began her preparations for the ministry in 1928. She was appointed a conference evangelist in 1931. Hazel Rose helped in getting a new Wesleyan Methodist church started in Converse, Indiana. That church was organized in 1931, and she served as the associate pastor with George Pence. There were some outstanding conversions in the Converse community. One man who was saved gave up tobacco and his membership in a secret order. He testified to his unsaved friends about the joy of serving the Lord. Five or six children were saved in the first meeting, and they brought their parents and other relatives to the Lord and the Church.[159]

Hazel Rose organized the Sims, Indiana, Church. This church was received into the conference during the 1932–33 year. She was assisted by Robert Kendall. She was appointed the pastor at Sims and served there until 1936. She was assigned to the area of conference evangelist for a number of years. During this time, in 1937 her work in East Marion (mission) was recognized by the president of the Indiana Conference, E. J. Pitts.[160]

Sylvia Rowand

Sylvia Rowand was ordained in 1928 by the Ohio District Pilgrim Holiness Church. She was active in that district from 1928 to 1963. She apparently retired from the active ministry in 1963 and was so listed until merger time. She lived in the Cincinnati area all this time.[161]

Gussie Simpson

Gussie (Mrs. Raymond) Simpson was ordained by the Kentucky District of the Pilgrim Holiness Church in 1928. She was the pastor of the Soldier and Olive Hill churches and was responsible for building the church building at Olive Hill.[162]

In 1931–33 she was the assistant pastor of the Bramwell, West Virginia, Pilgrim Holiness Church, according to the *Minutes of the Annual Session of the West Virginia Assembly of the Pilgrim Holiness Church.* The next year she was not assigned to a work. She served under the Eastern District of the Pilgrim Holiness Church from 1935 to 1937.[163] In 1939 she was received by the Pennsylvania and New Jersey District and was under that district from 1939 to 1946.[164] The next record was found in the *Minutes of the Annual Assembly of the Ohio District Pilgrim Holiness Church,* 1947–54. She was listed as living in Nelsonville, Ohio, during those years. Apparently she remained in Ohio, for she was living in London, Ohio, 1959–61 and in Springfield from 1961 to 1966. She became inactive in church work in 1963. She lived in New Carlisle, Ohio, at the time of the 1968 merger.[165]

Florence White

Florence White was a very gifted preacher and an excellent schoolteacher. She taught school during 1921–23 and 1945–56. She was matron and teacher at the Pilgrim Holiness Bible School at Proton Station, Ontario, and during the summer months she led groups of the Bible school students in summer tent evangelism. She was also a gifted evangelist. Even after she retired from active ministry, she continued to be militant in leading people to Christ. Florence ended her journey on this earth August 2, 1975.[166]

The chapel at the Bible school at Proton served as the meeting place of the Proton Pilgrim Holiness Church from 1924 to 1941. Florence, a student at the time, served as the assistant pastor from 1928 to 1930. She was the pastor during the conference year 1934–35 and served again as the assistant pastor 1936–39.

In 1930 she conducted evangelistic services in Sault Ste. Marie, Ontario, in a mission. In the early 1930s a tent meeting was held, and a mission was opened at Wiarton. That mission continued until 1946. Florence and Gladys White were in charge of the mission for a time. A work had been opened at Oshawa, and Florence White and Florence Hobbs were the second workers here. During her ministry, Florence White was assisted by several other women, including Gladys White, Florence Hobbs, Lily Johnson, Lily Baker, and Florence Allen. Florence White was listed as an ordained minister in 1934.

Florence was the pastor of the following Pilgrim Holiness churches in Canada: Proton, Oshawa,

Massey, and Bruce Mines. She served one year at the Massey church with little or no salary and at great sacrifice in order to keep the holiness message in that community. From 1956 to 1963, Florence and Gladys White were the pastors of the Bruce Mines Pilgrim Holiness Church. They began their pastorate there living in their mobile home for a few weeks but later took rooms with Mrs. Eli Taylor, a member of the church. In 1957 these women built a parsonage on the property of the church. The first five years of their ministry there the church board pledged $50 a month toward the pastoral salary. In 1963 they raised their pledge to $75 a month.[167]

Mrs. Cathrine Hazewinkle Wing

The *Minutes of the Annual Assembly of the Michigan District Pilgrim Holiness Church,* 1928, revealed that Cathrine Hazewinkle served under that district in 1928. She transferred to the North Michigan District of the Wesleyan Methodist Church and served as the pastor of the Lounty Line and Turner churches from 1934 to 1936. She resigned from that pastorate May 4, 1936. She had been elected to be ordained that year. On July 30, 1937, she transferred to the Pilgrim Holiness Church, and no other records were found of her service.[168]

Lillian Beard

Lillian Beard served as the pastor of the First Pentecostal-Pilgrim Church in Pasadena, California. This church became known as the Pasadena Rees Memorial Tabernacle. Lillian served in the California District of the Pilgrim Holiness Church from 1929 to 1941.[169]

Emeline Hamel Berg

Emeline Hamel was born November 16, 1914, in Haverhill, Massachusetts. She attended a Nazarene Sunday school, and at age ten she gave her heart and life to Christ. When she was fifteen she felt definitely called into the ministry. She began teaching Sunday school classes and speaking at youth meetings.

She had no financial resources but was determined to attend college. Emeline did housekeeping work for residents around the college while she attended Eastern Nazarene College in Wallaston, Massachusetts. During her college days she joined the Pilgrim Holiness Church.

At age twenty-six (1940) she was asked to become the pioneer pastor of a new church started by the Pilgrim Holiness Church in Boston. She pastored that church for two years. Again, in 1942, the Church asked her to pastor another new church in the Cape Cod area. She pastored this church for two years also. She was ordained by the Pilgrim Holiness Church September 9, 1945 in Haverhill, Massachusetts. During this time a thirty-seven year old bachelor preacher, Clifton Fletcher Berg, asked her to marry him. She consented, and they were married at Johnson City, New York, August 27, 1945. Clifton was scheduled to leave for the jungles of Guyana, South America, and they left for missionary service March 25, 1946.[170]

Clifton always felt the call to "go beyond," and during their sixteen years of missionary service, he went farther into the interior and made several exploratory trips and established contacts with the primitive Indians in new areas. While in Guyana, Emeline acted as schoolteacher, nurse, and mother to their four children.[171]

The Bergs returned to the United States and lived in Haverhill for one year. Clifton took the pastorate at Ravena, New York. While he pastored the Ravena church, Emeline was asked to supply pastor the Albany Wesleyan Church on Sunday mornings. Clifton and Emeline than swapped pulpits on Sunday evenings—she preached at Ravena, and Clifton preached at Albany. They worked like this for a year until a full-time pastor was found for the Albany church. Clifton served as superintendent of the New York District for a year. They moved to Johnson City, New York, to pastor the Oakdale Wesleyan Church in 1969. Clifton retired in 1975.[172]

Early in the 1970s the American Indian Movement was very active at the Onondaga Reservation in New York state. The Wesleyan Methodists were invited to begin a work on the reservation in 1958 by the tribal chief. A church building had been constructed, and both Native American and white men and women came. The first missionaries learned the Indian language. In the 1970s, when the Movement became very active, all whites were evicted, and only full-blooded Native Americans were allowed on the reservation. The church was broken into and set on fire. The altar and all the records were destroyed. Three women began repairing the church, scraping the charred walls, stripping the floor, and repairing the altar.

In 1975 Clifton and Emeline came to build a bridge between the church and the reservation. Clifton went door to door and visited everyone. He made hospital calls and tried to establish good relationships. In 1981 he became ill and couldn't continue as the pastor. Emeline stepped in and took over the pastorate until another pastor could come. After Clifton's death, March 1984, Emeline again returned to the Onondaga Wesleyan Church in July 1984 and continued as the pastor until 1988. She was accepted by the Native Americans and was able to make the gospel real to them. For a time she was assisted by her daughter, Kathleen Spencer.[173]

Emeline retired from the active pastoral ministry at age seventy-two, but she continued to be available for pulpit supply. On May 10, 1998, the New Hope Wesleyan Church honored her by naming her the "mother of the year."

Mrs. Edwin Brown

The *Minutes of the Annual Assembly of the Ohio District Pilgrim Holiness Church* showed Mrs. Edwin Brown as an ordained minister in 1929. She was on the active list until 1949. At that time she was living in Toledo, Ohio. She was listed as a minister through 1965.[174]

Mrs. J. A. Butler

Mrs. J. A. Butler was ordained by the Kentucky District of the Pilgrim Holiness

Church in 1929. She was listed at Kingswood that year. She remained on the list of ordained ministers through 1933, according to the *Minutes of the Annual Assembly of the Pilgrim Holiness Church Kentucky District, 1930–33.*

Catherine Channel

Catherine Channel was listed as an ordained minister from 1929 to 1934 in the *Proceedings of the Annual Assembly California District of the Pilgrim Holiness Church.*

Alice Coulter Coone

Alice Coulter was born in 1885 on the island of St. Croix, American Virgin Islands. She came under the influence of pioneer missionaries to that island in her early life. She was saved and sanctified under their ministry and became a volunteer as a teen in helping them to spread the gospel throughout the West Indies. She worked until 1918 among her own people with Irene Blyden (Taylor, who became the mother of Drs. Ira and Wingrove Taylor) and with Rev. James W. Coone, who became Alice's husband. James W. Coone died in 1918, and Alice came to the mainland. In 1922 she was ordained in the New York District of the Pilgrim Holiness Church. She served as pastor, evangelist and in whatever other capacity in which her talents could be used. *Minutes of the Annual Session of the Rochester Conference of the Wesleyan Methodist Connection, or Church, of America* recorded that the Taylor charge was without a pastor in 1929. Alice Coone of the Pilgrim Holiness Church took the work and continued through the years.

In 1936 she returned to her people in the West Indies, in Barbados, and the last three years were spent in Trinidad. She was an effective deputation (home ministries) worker. Her selfless service to souls, of devotion to God and zeal for the cause of Christ ended with her death February 9, 1948.[175]

Mrs. Mae Eckert

The *Minutes of the Annual Assembly of the Pilgrim Holiness Church of Pennsylvania and New Jersey, 1929–31,* listed Mae Eckert as an ordained minister in 1929, and she was listed in that manner for the next two years.

Irene Falor

Harold and Irene Falor were received January 1929 as conference preachers into the Ohio Conference of the Wesleyan Methodist Church. They were appointed pastors of the Belmont Church. At conference time, they became the pastors at Dayton and were under the mission board. They served this church until 1931. Irene Falor was ordained by the Ohio Conference in 1930. She served as the conference superintendent of the Young Missionary Workers Band (now Wesleyan Kids for Missions) from 1929 to 1931.[176]

Mattie Estella Frazee Hanna

Mattie Hanna was an ordained minister of the Illinois-Missouri District of the Pilgrim Holiness Church at the time of her death May 21, 1936. She was born December 9, 1875. During her childhood she expressed the desire to either become a missionary or a teacher. She lived to see both of these desires fulfilled. Her missionary labors were confined to the states of Illinois, Indiana, Ohio, and Kentucky. She was a gifted teacher and spent ten years teaching in the country schools of Iroquois County, Illinois. She was a graduate of Onarga Seminary and Marion Normal College, in Marion, Indiana (later merged into what became Indiana Wesleyan University). After her marriage to Elmor Hanna, they both attended God's Bible School in Cincinnati.

Mattie was converted June 29, 1901, in one of those country schoolhouses where she had taught. This cultured and educated schoolteacher was astounded and shocked by the improper use of the English language by the evangelist who was preaching there, but her hunger for God was greater.

Another convert in that schoolhouse meeting was Elmor Hanna. Mattie and Elmor were united in marriage in Chicago on September 13, 1906. They became the parents of two daughters and four sons.

The Hannas served the following Illinois appointments as pastors: Onarga, Dow and Jerseyville, Carlinville, Ottawa, and Oblong. They also pastored churches in Ohio and Indiana. They spent many months in evangelistic and home missionary work. For a time Elmor Hanna served as the superintendent of the church's orphanage at Kingswood, Kentucky. Mattie Hanna was a faithful, efficient helpmeet and co-laborer of her husband in this varied ministry. Two outstanding characteristics of Mattie Hanna's life were her loyalty to the highest standards of holy living and her willingness to sacrifice her personal interests and comfort for the cause of Christ.[177]

Carrie M. Hazzard and Lois E. Richardson

The work of God's kingdom was blessed with the Spirit-filled and powerful team of Carrie M. Hazzard and Lois E. Richardson. Both ladies were Canadians. Lois was born in Kingston, Ontario. Carrie began her career in the banking business, but sometime later she became a friend of Lois E. Richardson. Both felt called to the full-time ministry. In the later 1920s they became associated with the Middle Atlantic States Mission Conference of the Wesleyan Methodist Church. They were both listed as deaconesses in 1929.

Rev. Carrie M. Hazzard (r.) and Rev. Lois E. Richardson

During this time the Wesleyan Methodists were attempting to establish new churches in the large metropolitan areas. One such project was the Camden, New Jersey church. Ira Ford McLeister in his book *History of the Wesleyan Methodist Church of America* (Syracuse, N.Y., 1934, 269), describes this new work:

Another most interesting and encouraging church project in this conference [Middle Atlantic Mission] is located in the city of Camden, where the church has been developed and brought into the denomination largely through the labors of Rev. Miss Lois E. Richardson and Rev. Miss Carrie M. Hazzard, who were formerly connected with the full salvation church work in Canada.

Both of them were listed as ordained ministers in the 1930 *Minutes*.

These women were the pastors of this church for twenty-five years. The report in 1929 stated the church had been "legally incorporated and the title to the church building had been transferred" and the deed properly recorded. They had experienced several good revivals, and a number of new members had been added to the church roll. Extensive improvements had been made on the church building. The Camden church became the largest church in the Middle Atlantic Conference, with more than 250 members, including many business people. A healthy church will produce persons called into the active ministry. During their tenure at Camden, some twenty-five ministers and other full-time workers were called out for service. Among them were many men like George Bross, Stephen Pillsbury, James Mills, and many others. Several persons were also called into full-time missionary service.

Another sign of a healthy church is the planting of new churches. While Carrie Hazzard and Lois Richardson were pastors at the Camden church they conducted Friday night cottage meetings at Florence, New Jersey. There an increasing interest and a definite revival in the community became evident, and the people chose to become an organized church. The heavy duties at Camden had not hindered these women from a burden for the people in Florence. September 28, 1940, the cornerstone service was held for the new church at Camden. On November 7, 1943, the mortgage was burned on the beautiful new Camden church. On May 26,

1944, the Florence church was organized. Both women were assigned to the Camden and Florence churches as the pastors for two years after Florence was organized. Through their diligent and untiring labors, these women also organized a new church at Riverside, New Jersey, May 10, 1946. This work was later disbanded.

November 28, 1951, Lois E. Richardson and Carrie M. Hazzard resigned as the pastors at Camden. They entered evangelistic work as Hazzard and Richardson Evangelists. Revivals and camp meetings were held in the United States and Canada. Everywhere they preached the altars were lined with seekers. The revival they conducted in Belleville, Ontario, resulted in the need to build a larger building. Sometimes the woman preaching would get no further than a short exhortation when the altar would begin to fill up, and extra chairs would be set out to make room for the seekers.

Carrie M. Hazzard was described as a very elegant, articulate, and educated woman. Lois E. Richardson was an elegant speaker also. Her exhortations on the importance of camp meetings and youth camps brought results. She was lovingly referred to as "Mother Richardson" when she was introduced to the conference. She served as vice president of the Wesley Grove Camp. Both ladies served on important district committees.

During the years of 1960–62, these women became the pastors of the Philadelphia church. They converted a garage facility into inviting Sunday school classrooms and installed pews to make an attractive sanctuary.

Both ladies played an important role in the establishment of the Wesley Grove Camp, located about six miles from Trenton, New Jersey. The Middle Atlantic Conference acquired the property at Wesley Grove and took over the management of the camp January 11, 1935. The first camp meeting was held there that year. Both of the ladies gave helpful remarks about the work and organization of the camp. Lois requested that the pastors and wives consider purchasing camp meeting equipment.[178] Lois made a project of keeping the grounds and

cottage areas beautified with rock gardens and other improvements.

Lois E. Richardson died July 27, 1982. Besides her pastoral and evangelistic work, she also served under the Oriental Missionary Society. Both of them did missionary work in thirty-one countries, assisted in founding a hospital and supporting and promoting orphanages in South America and Korea. Lois also sponsored many young people entering college. Her funeral was conducted in the Florence church.[179]

Carrie M. Hazzard died June 17, 1997. Her funeral was also conducted in the Florence church. It was reported that these women ministered worldwide to missionaries and had significant influence in the lives of outstanding Wesleyan pastors and denominational leaders. Even when confined to a nursing home, Carrie carried her witness for the Lord with dignity in her declining health. A memorial fund was established to honor her to assist in missionary work in Haiti.[180]

Elizabeth Currie

The first recorded service record on Elizabeth Currie was found in the *Minutes* of the Kansas Conference of the Wesleyan Methodist Church in 1924. She was ordained at conference time that year. She served as the assistant to her husband, L. S. Currie, at Bethel, Excelsior, Clay Center, Hollis Langley, and Topeka North churches. She served as the solo pastor at Langley for two years and also served as an evangelist for a number of years. She was put on the retirement list in 1955.[181]

Iona Hall

Iona (sometimes spelled "Ione") and Everette W. Hall transferred from the Missionary Bands of the World to the Indiana District of the Pilgrim Holiness Church in 1929. They served under that district 1929–35. Then they transferred to the

California District, where they were listed from 1936 to 1938. They transferred back to the Indiana District in 1938 and were under appointment there until 1946.

In 1947 they transferred from the Pilgrim Holiness Church to the Wisconsin Conference of the Wesleyan Methodist Church. There Iona and Everette served as supply pastors of the Appleton, Wisconsin, church.

In 1949 they resigned and transferred to the California-Arizona District of the Pilgrim Holiness Church, where Iona was listed 1949–60. From 1961 to 1965 Iona was listed by the Idaho-Washington District, although there is no record of her ministerial duties during that time. From 1966 to 1967, Iona was listed by the Michigan District with her assignment in the field of education. At the time of the 1968 merger, she was listed as a pastor by the East Michigan District of the Pilgrim Holiness Church.[182]

Mrs. Katherine Hollowell

Katherine Hollowell was born in 1887 and died April 7, 1976. She was saved at age thirteen. Her ministry began in a small mission in Denver. Her father was converted under her ministry there. She served in California as pastor at Sierra Madre, Long Beach, San Diego, and Adams Memorial, in Los Angeles. These churches were in the California District of the Pilgrim Holiness Church.

Her ministry at Sierra Madre ended on November 1, 1932. There had been no deaths and no marriages. She had done a good work of grace among the children. Jennie Whitaker had held a revival for her. Jennie preached powerful messages.[183]

Her work at Long Beach, California, was summed up in a newspaper clipping from the *Long Beach Press-Telegram*.

Women of the Pilgrim Holiness church believe that if you wish a thing done well, do it yourself. Tired of conducting services in rented quarters . . . the nineteen members decided to build a sanctuary of their own on a lot owned by the church . . . and on December 1, 1937, men and women of the congregation started to do the building themselves. The church was headed by a woman pastor, Reverend Katherine Hollowell. Donning old clothes, Mrs. Hollowell and members of her congregation, including the women, were seen daily with saw and hammer putting up the new church. The first unit was opened on February 16, 1938, with a revival meeting with Miss Ruth Grizzelle, preacher and musician. Rev. Hollowell declared that "We are building on the pay-as-you-go plan, and when completed the Pilgrim Tabernacle will be free of debt."[184]

After she retired, she served as minister of music at Buena Park Wesleyan Church and at the time of her death was the associate pastor there.

Edith Downs Wernz Houston

Edith Downs Wernz was widowed at a very young age, having lost her first husband (Wernz) in a work-related accident. In 1926, at age twenty-five, she met Laurence Stanley Houston at God's Bible School, in Cincinnati, Ohio. In 1929 they were married, and both were ordained by the Ohio District of the Pilgrim Holiness Church.[185]

A tent meeting had been held in Elizabethtown, Kentucky, and a group of people had shown an interest in organizing a Pilgrim Holiness Church. The Houstons were chosen for this assignment and opened a mission there in 1930. Over the next five and one-half years, over 2,500 transients passing through the town in those Depression days were fed and many of them housed overnight. The Houstons also ministered to the needy people of Hardin County, Kentucky, particularly in feeding and clothing school children. County funds were actually allocated to L. S. Houston to help in this part of their ministry.

In 1935 the Houstons moved on to serve Kentucky pastorates in Carrollton, Ashland, Frankfort, and Cloverport. L. S. Houston also served for fifteen years as superintendent of the Kentucky District. In 1961, ill health forced L. S. Houston to retire, and the couple settled once again in Elizabethtown. After his death, Edith Houston remained in Elizabethtown. At the time of the 1968 merger, she was listed as a retired ordained minister. She died February 6, 1971.[186]

Mary Stone and Jennie Van Name Hughes

The *Pilgrim Holiness Advocate,* March 25, 1926, reported that Mary Stone, a widely known Chinese preacher, physician, and surgeon, spoke at the regular monthly missionary meeting of the Pilgrim Tabernacle in Pasadena, California. Jennie V. Hughes, an associate with Mary, was with her. The tabernacle was filled to capacity. A march was made, and the people laid their monthly offering on the altar for their work in China. The offering was six hundred dollars. Dr. Stone told of the work accomplished in Shanghai in the building of the hospital, school, and church. Miss Hughes fired hearts in her appeal to send the gospel to China.

Shih Mai-yu was born in 1872 at Kuikiang, China. Her father was the first convert in the Yangtze Valley and became a Methodist preacher. Her mother was the principal of a mission school. Shih Mai-yu was educated in the Methodist mission schools. She earned her medical degree from the University of Michigan in 1906 and did post-graduate work at Johns Hopkins. She was one of the first two Chinese women to receive the M.D. degree in the United States. She became known worldwide as Dr. Mary Stone.

She returned to China and founded the Elizabeth Denton Sanforth Methodist Hospital. She was the head of this institution for twenty-five years and personally trained more than five hundred Chinese women as nurses.[187]

Jennie Van Name Hughes was born in America. She followed God's call to China and became well known in the educational field. Her mission work began with the Methodists in 1905 at Kuikiang. Jennie was a woman with outstanding ability, a tireless worker for the Kingdom, a forceful speaker and writer, as well as an able administrator. She personally gave foster care to thirty-seven Chinese children in her home while she worked in the orphanages. Many of them became strong Christian leaders.[188]

Their sponsoring church (Methodist) in America became corrupted with doubts about creation. These "scholars" doubted the truthfulness of the Bible. Biblical stories were myths. God was love, and therefore He would not punish humans for sin. They only needed to be better educated, wear better clothing, and live in a good environment to be better persons. Their church sent missionaries to China who preached this "gospel."

Mary knew her people needed the Savior who would save them from their sins and make them "new creatures" from the inside out. She took her concern to the General Conference of the Methodist Episcopal Church in America. She pled with the leaders. Many were moved to tears; others violently opposed her, demanding compliance to modernism. Mary spent three nights in prayer and then resigned.

Jennie also came under their fire. The leaders of the church issued an ultimatum to Jennie: her school curriculum must be changed to conform to the modernistic teachings. Jennie promptly resigned.

Mary and Jennie were cut off from their work in China. They had no support, supplies, or equipment, and they had broken their relationship with their church for "the truth's sake." They would simply trust God for their future work in China.

Mary selected $600 of surgical instruments at a store and asked them to hold these. She promised to be back "tomorrow or the next day" to pay for them. The next morning a lady gave her a check for $600. She received a check for $5,000 in a letter with a statement that she would receive this amount annually until the donor died. Without any appeal, money just rolled in, sometimes as much as five and ten thousand dollars at a time. Someone gave $20,000 to start a hospital.

These women co-founded Bethel Mission of China in 1921. They purchased eight acres in Shanghai. The compound consisted of "lawns, trees, gardens, cement driveways, walks, and playgrounds." A hospital, high school, chapel, dormitories, and several residences were on these grounds also. The compound would eventually consist of two hospitals, two city missions, three orphanages, one Bible seminary (the only one in Free China), and one high school. In 1938 they were God-directed to establish a trade school in Hong Kong.

Delbert Thornton, a missionary with the Hephzibah Faith Missionary Association, and Paget Wilkes held holiness meetings in Shanghai in August 1925. Both women from that time on gave a definite testimony of sanctification.

Seth Rees on his travels to China was profoundly impressed by the excellent missionary work that he saw being done by the Bethel Mission under the direction of Mary Stone and Jennie Hughes. Seth Rees's membership roll in Pasadena had as high as twenty-two foreign missionaries at a time. Among them were Mary Stone and Jennie V. Hughes.[189]

Doctors, nurses (2,500 at the time of Dr. Stone's death), and Bible teachers the world over found a relationship with God and received their training from these dedicated women.

Both ladies were ordained ministers in the Pilgrim Holiness Church. Jennie completed her earthly journey December 2, 1951.[190] Her funeral was conducted in the Rees Memorial Pilgrim Holiness Church in Pasadena, California. Lundy Hill and Rev. Mrs. Seth C. (Frida) Rees were the officiating ministers. Mary Stone ended her earthly journey December 12, 1954.[191]

Edna Scott Kenyon

Edna (Scott) Kenyon was born October 15, 1891 in Iowa. She completed her earthly race April 1, 1961, in Asheboro, North Carolina. She married Rev. John T. Kenyon in 1929. She was a loving mother to eight stepchildren, four daughters, and four sons.

Even as a child she was obedient to God. She was healed of tuberculosis when she was a teenager. She attended God's Bible School in Cincinnati, Ohio, and was ordained by the Pilgrim Holiness Church in 1931.

Edna worked side by side with her husband in the ministry, home, or wherever there was a need. Her motto and practice was "A task worth doing at all is worth doing well." A few days before her death she admonished some of the young people to "get established; get your feet on the Solid Rock."

Just before she died she told her loved ones, "It is not 'Good night'; it is 'Good morning.'"[192]

Viola Christina Brannon Leyh

Viola Brannon was born in West Virginia in 1893. In her early twenties she broke her relationship with a young banker and left her position in the business world as well as her comfortable surroundings to respond to God's call upon her life. She furthered her education by attending God's Bible School in Cincinnati, Ohio.

She met William Jennings (W. J.) Leyh at Bible school, and following their graduation in 1925 they were married. Viola joined W. J. in pioneering the Wesleyan Methodist Church in South Dakota. She was ordained by the Dakota Conference in 1929. W. J. and Viola faithfully served that conference for fifty years. She served as a co-pastor with her husband. Their pastorates included Mobridge, Richland, Aberdeen, Huron, Redfield, Ipswich, Tolstoy and Loyalton. Their longest pastorate was at Richland (Mina, South Dakota) for seventeen years. While pastoring the Ipswich church, they pastored a group meeting in a schoolhouse that became the Loyalton church. They were the first pastors of the McIntosh church. These were pioneer days, and the comforts of life were few.

Viola was very supportive in each local church that she co-pastored with her husband. She served as a Sunday school teacher, president of the Woman's Home and Foreign Missionary Society, hostess, preacher, visitation pastor, and full-time supporter of her husband. However, her work was not limited to the local church.

Viola served on the local, district, and general level of the Woman's Home and Foreign Missionary Society. In 1940 she was elected president of the Dakota Conference Woman's Home and Foreign Missionary Society. She held this office until she was elected West Central Area chair of the society in 1952.

Upon the formation of the Beckman (Board) Foundation in 1948, Viola Leyh faithfully served on this board for many years. This board carried out the wishes of the estate of Willie E. Beckman in sharing his assets with world missions, Native American ministries, Wesleyan colleges, Philippine missions, and the Dakota Conference.

The Philippine mission work was left in the hands of the Dakota Conference, and on July 21, 1961, the work was incorporated as a United States board. Viola Leyh was elected to serve on this board. The members were responsible for raising funds for the Philippine missions as well as giving guidance to the missionary policy.

Viola was a faithful supporter of the Native American ministries in South Dakota. She influenced many young people and encouraged them as they fulfilled God's call upon their lives.

Viola was the mother of two daughters, Oleta Freeze, a faculty member of Southern Wesleyan University, in Central, South Carolina (formerly Central Wesleyan College), and Erma Jean Johnson, retired minister's wife.

When Viola was approaching her ninetieth birthday, her daughter Erma Jean asked what she felt her ministry for Christ was at this time in her life. Without hesitation, she replied "I now have plenty of time to pray." Viola's times of prayer ended August 10, 1986.[193]

Elsie Ross Newton

In 1929 Elsie Ross Newton was listed as an ordained minister according to the *Minutes of the Annual Assembly of the Pilgrim Holiness Church Indiana Conference, 1923–50*. She served under that conference until 1951, when the conference was divided, and she continued her ministry under the Northern Indiana District from 1951 to 1967. She retired from the active ministry in 1967.[194]

Laura Raymer

Laura Raymer began her earthly journey in 1880. In May 1900, at age 20, she married Henry Raymer.[195]

Laura's ministry began in 1929. She was the pastor of the Bradley, South Dakota, Wesleyan Methodist Church from 1929 to 1941. She was the pastor; her husband was a farmer.[196] She was ordained in 1936.

She then resigned from the Bradley church and became a supply pastor in a holiness mission.[197] This mission may have been located in Hawarden, Iowa. She was the pastor of two other churches, Bushnell and Garden City, South Dakota. She was the second pastor of the Garden City church. The church had purchased an old granary east of the business district and remodeled it into an attractive chapel with a high steeple. They placed a bell over a new entry.[198]

She was the mother of three daughters: Alline Wall, Gertrude Kepthart, and Loretta Wilson; four sons, Robert, John, Howard, and Arthur. After her husband died in 1951, she moved to Hartford City, Indiana, to be with a daughter. She retired from active ministry in 1956. She ended her earthly journey January 13, 1970.

Frieda Rich King

The *Minutes of the Annual Assembly of the Pilgrim Holiness Church Indiana Conference, 1929–30, 1934*, listed Frieda Rich as an ordained minister in 1929. She apparently served three years or so in that district and then married a minister and became Frieda King. They continued to pastor in the Indiana District/Northern Indiana District until 1967, when they retired, according to the *Minutes in the Conference Journal Pilgrim Holiness Church Indiana North Conference 1951–67*.

Ruth Newton Rogers

Ruth Newton was born June 18, 1904, at Clemson, South Carolina. She graduated from Central Wesleyan College, in Central, South Carolina (now Southern Wesleyan University), in 1929.

Her first ministerial assignment was pastor of the Springdale, Alabama, Wesleyan Methodist Church, which she served from 1929 until 1934. One of her first tasks there was to arrange for a funeral and burial. This included building a casket and getting plow lines to lower the casket into the grave.

In 1934 Ruth went to Brunswick, Georgia, to pastor a mission church and continued there through 1945. She had a strong ministry with children and a radio ministry that helped in the building of the church. Her children's ministry reached into other areas, including the Hortense Camp Meeting and the Little Rock Camp Meeting. She was appointed the pastor of the Ashburn, Georgia, charge December 21, 1946.

About this time Ruth was involved in a serious auto accident that broke her back and had to resign this pastorate. The doctors did not think she would walk again, but God healed her and she went on to engage in very heavy and strenuous work at a mission near Tampa, Florida. She was appointed December 16, 1947, to this mission as pastor, with W. Bert Rogers and Grace Bryant as assistants. She transferred to the Florida Conference in 1950, and sometime between 1947 and 1950 she married W. Bert Rogers. They co-pastored, she the pastor and he the assistant at Tampa until 1963. She was ordained in 1950. They accepted the pastorate at Ida and were there at the time of the 1968 merger. Bert Rogers died in 1973, but Grace continued to pastor until 1976. Poor health forced her to retire, and she moved to Sea Breeze Manor in Hobe Sound, Florida. She died May 28, 1997.[199]

Mrs. M. H. Russell

Mrs. Russell's name was found on the rolls of the Kentucky, Louisiana/Mississippi, Southern and North Carolina Districts of the Pilgrim Holiness Church. She apparently was stationed at Kingswood, Kentucky, for a time. In the Southern District she was listed at Bryson City and at Durham, North Carolina. Her husband died in the early 1960s, and her name continued on the roll.[200]

Phoebe Stone

Dr. Phoebe Stone was the second daughter (first daughter was Mary Stone) of a sanctified Chinese couple living in Kuikiang, China. Her father was the first convert in the Yangtze Valley, and he became a Methodist preacher. Her mother was the principal of a mission school.

Phoebe gave her heart to God as a child. She was called to the ministry of healing through medical missionary work. She was a graduate of Johns Hopkins University and worked with her sister, Mary Stone, in Shanghai, China.

Phoebe served God with success in capable and sacrificial service to the spiritual and physical needs of the sick and the poor of China. She was a model of God's grace. She was a brilliant student, and a devoted and Spirit-filled servant.

Near the end of her earthly life, in 1929, she became a member of the Rees Memorial Tabernacle in Pasadena, California. Shortly after this, she returned to her native land, China, and was ordained by Rev. G. Arnold Hodgin, assistant general superintendent of the Pilgrim Holiness Church. She entered her heavenly rest May 29, 1930.[201]

Mildred P. Stratton

Mildred P. Stratton was born in 1901. After graduating from high school in 1919, she taught school for four years. Revs. Clinton and Effie (Campbell) Bard arranged for Robert Stratton and Mildred to meet at the Stoneboro Camp in 1921. Seven years later, June 6, 1928, they were married at Ashville, New York, with Rev. Effie Bard officiating.

Mildred was given a local preacher's license in September 1927. She and Robert were ordained together on Wednesday evening, August 7, 1929, by the Ohio Conference of the Wesleyan Methodist Church at Victory Camp at conference time. Together, they co-pastored Greer and Shadley Valley, Findley, Jelloway, Findley (two times), Oakland Park in Columbus, and Sunbury, all in Ohio. The conference president, L. D Wilcox, was ill, and Robert took over many of his appointments before 1948. Mildred pastored the Jelloway church by herself for three years. Their annual salary during those early years of their ministry ranged from $245 to $742.

Robert Stratton was elected president of the Ohio Conference of the Wesleyan Methodist Church in 1948 and held that office until 1953. Mildred always assisted him in whatever task the

Lord called him to do. They were caretakers of the Victory Camp grounds for a number of years.

Mildred was active in the conference and served as Woman's Missionary Society (WMS) president, Young Missionary Workers Band (now Wesleyan Kids for Missions) treasurer, WMS vice president, statistician, and conference treasurer.

Mildred is the mother of six children: John R., Wayne, Samuel, Helen Rhoten, Ruth Anna Elder, and Martha Alt.

Mildred is a faithful servant who loves the Lord and loves people. At a special service commemorating the seventieth anniversary of Victory Camp in 1996, Mildred gave this word from her wheelchair: "I've still got the fire!" Mildred celebrated her one-hundredth birthday September 4, 2001, in a healthcare facility in Columbus, Ohio. She created a charitable gift annuity with The Wesleyan Church at age ninety, naming Wesleyan World Missions as the ministry from the annuity.[202]

Ida Tate

Ida Tate served under the California District of the Pilgrim Holiness Church from 1929 to 1962.[203]

Grace Elizabeth Sanders Tilestad

Grace Sanders, the youngest daughter of Dr. and Mrs. H. C. Sanders, was born September 19, 1908, while they were home on furlough. She was four years old when they returned to South Africa. Grace was reared in South Africa, where her parents served as pioneer missionaries under the Alliance of the Reformed Baptist Church of Canada. She returned to Canada in 1929. In South Africa, English and Dutch governesses were hired to teach the children. But they were required to be examined by inspectors in order to pass each grade. This required a trip by donkey wagon to Paulpietersburg. It took several days to make the wearisome round trip of about twenty miles.

Grace was converted at a very early age and was baptized at age six. Her parents taught her

sewing, cooking, music, physical training, nature studies, swimming, how to fish and use a gun (self-protection from snakes), and to ride donkey and horseback. Her father also taught her how to do office work as a bookkeeper and stenographer. She also learned how to care for the sick, administering first aid and assisting with the medical work. When she was seventeen, her older sister, Faith, took a correspondence theological course from Eastern Nazarene College. Faith would get all the younger children up at six o'clock each morning to study with her.

Grace's sanctification experience changed her life. She was sixteen at the time. From then on she had an increasing concern for the unsaved about her and a great desire to take the message to the heathen. When the possibility of reaching children became apparent to her, she organized a Sunday school. When she rang the church bell, children would come running down the hillsides to attend. She was enabled by God to win all thirty-two children to Him during the nine months before she returned to Canada in 1929. By this time she was actively engaged in the mission work and was partially supported by the Salem, New Brunswick, church. When she left for Canada, she told the weeping people her heart was remaining with them and she would return.

It came as a shock to her when God asked if she would be willing *not* to return to Africa. It was a great struggle. But during the eight years at home, the unsaved of her own people in Canada burned her heart. She found active Christian work at Wood's Harbour, Nova Scotia. She was the pastor there for almost four years. Her salary was the freewill offerings, and the most she received in a year was sixty dollars. She lived with a family whose income was cut off. They ate toddle (pork scraps potato soup), or bread and butter or toast dipped in hot water with a little butter, but they never went hungry.

Three months after arriving in Wood's Harbour, Grace organized a Reformed Baptist Church. They met in the community hall but were forced out of it. Then they met in homes. They were in the midst of a revival and fierce persecution. But God enabled them to purchase a vacant house and a strip of land. The house was renovated;

God provided an organ and pews, and they soon had a beautiful church. In her monthly missionary meetings, which drew many people, God began to increase the burden for the heathen of Africa. The missionaries in South Africa had sent an appeal for workers. At Beulah that year (1936) it was decided that her brother, Charles, and she would be sent back to Africa.

Charles and Grace were both ordained at Amherst in the Baptist Church. Exactly eight years to the day from the time they had left Africa, they were back at the Hartland Mission Station. The work at the dispensary grew, but the high infant and maternal death rates were alarming to Grace. She went to Swaziland and took an obstetric course and another one in the Ante-Natal Clinic and Child Welfare Department. She returned to Hartland and opened an Ante-Natal Clinic.

She made mattresses and pillows from banana leaves and horsehair. She used goatskins for rubber sheets. She had no telephone, so when a difficult case came in, she would send one of the native men, using her lady's bicycle, to get the district surgeon some three-and-a-half to four hours away. Even after he had used all his human skills, he would shake his head in despair for the young mothers. Grace often spent hours in praying for her young mothers' recovery. Thank God He brought them through.

Government rulings caused many changes in the work at Hartland. She was sent to Boksburg to study in order to qualify for registration as a midwife. When she returned, the government had demoted the hospital into a dispensary, and no patients who required hospitalization were allowed to stay.

Besides the medical work, Grace carried on a Sunday school and did evangelistic work, walking or riding horseback to spend time with the natives in their homes. The medical work had meant so much to these people that they now opened their homes and hearts to preachers of the gospel.

Grace was scheduled for a furlough in 1948, but her brother, George, was in an accident that broke his leg and nose as well as some teeth. Mrs. Kierstead, missionary wife at Altoona, became very ill and was moved to Vryheid. Grace was asked to minister at the Altoona station. She served alone there for eight months out of the next two years. She walked as far as five miles to visit the sick and minister to the natives physically and spiritually. Some were instantly healed of physical ailments.

The Altoona station had a thriving school of over a hundred children enrolled. Because of the lack of help, Grace taught thirty-eight girls, ranging in ages from about eight to sixteen, to sew.

Grace went home in 1950. She returned to South Africa in 1956 and served for a time at Louwsburg. She loved people. She was an excellent nurse and a person in whom people often confided. She married David Tilestad, and they made their home in Vryheid. She died there July 28, 1980, and was buried there.[204]

Surviving
and Much More

The Great Depression resulting from the stock market crash in 1929 held the nation in its grip and caused great suffering worldwide from 1929 to 1940. Churches felt the crunch financially, but an emphasis on revival and evangelism resulted in growth in the churches. Prohibition had a short life and was repealed; however, the Church's stand against the use of intoxicating beverages stood firm. Some ordained women were given their district assignment as temperance speakers for their districts. Perhaps one of the most significant changes in the nation and eventually the Church came about during this decade when the maximum workweek of forty hours was established. Front porches were added to homes, where the head of the house could relax in the evening with his feet propped on the porch railing. People had more time to do as they wished. Some chose to volunteer for church work; others sought to fill their time with worldly pleasures and pursuits. This decade saw the first commercial television broadcast. This invention would change the church world in many ways in years to come. World War II began in 1939. Although the United States did not enter the war until 1941, it affected the nation in the late 1930s and eventually brought about religious and moral changes that would affect the church world in many ways.

In the Church the youth movement, home missions, and Sunday schools were gaining momentum. The Pilgrim Holiness Church completely restructured itself beginning in 1930. The Wesleyan Methodists adopted the "storehouse tithing plan" in 1935. In spite of the Depression, this plan brought an immediate upturn in financial strength. Women were still listening for and hearing the call of God to take the gospel to the unsaved on this continent and around the world. Here are some of the stories of these heroic women and their activities during this decade.

Cary Adelaide Anthony

Cary Adelaide Anthony was listed as an ordained minister in 1930. She was under district appointment from 1930 to 1966 with the North Carolina District of the Pilgrim Holiness Church.[1]

Bessie Bennett

Bessie Bennett, an ordained minister in 1930, was under appointment in the Indiana District of the Pilgrim Holiness Church from 1930 to 1938 and 1948 to 1950. In 1951 the Indiana District was divided into two districts, Northern and Southern Indiana Districts. She was listed as under appointment from 1951 to 1962 in the Southern Indiana District.[2]

Mary Carlson

The *Minutes of the Annual Assembly of the Ohio District Pilgrim Holiness Church,* 1930–34, records Mary Carlson as an ordained minister in 1930. She was under appointment in that district until 1934. Her husband was Guy Carlson.

Ezma Wilma Morgan Durham

Ezma Morgan was born in Grand Junction, Iowa, on October 18, 1909, and she died October 7, 1990.

Ezma married B. F. Durham in 1936. Together they were the pastors of Pilgrim Holiness churches in Falmouth, Kentucky; and in West Virginia, Texas, Kansas, Louisiana, and Indiana. She was commissioned by the Kansas District and was appointed to supply the church at Lucas, Kansas, for six years.

Part of their ministry was in evangelism. She and their son, John, assisted in the music. B. F. and Ezma Durham never retired. They were always looking for opportunities to serve. They supplied several churches on the Indiana Central District of The Wesleyan Church while the church searched for a resident pastor.

Ezma is remembered as a dedicated person with a beautiful serving spirit. She was kind with her words and witty with her remarks and wisdom.[3]

Gertrude Farmer

Some of the most grueling ministerial work was done by women in the Blue Ridge Mountains work. Among those faithful workers was Gertrude Farmer. She began her mountain missionary work in 1931 and was the pastor at Buck Creek. While she was the "senior" pastor at Glenville, North Carolina, Bertha Stamey was her assistant. This work was located in the North Carolina Conference of the Wesleyan Methodist Church but was under the South Carolina Conference. Her pastorates included Buck Creek, Glenville, Tuckaseigee, Rock Ridge, and Clyde,

North Carolina.[4] She served the Buck Creek work for eight years. The conference journal reported in 1939 that under the wise supervision of the pastor, Gertrude Farmer, and her co-laborers, an addition was made on the building to double the seating capacity. They were in a continual spiritual revival at the church there at Tuckaseigee. While she was pastoring Buck Creek in 1952, the church sold a lot known as the Buck Creek School lot, and the proceeds were to be used to improve the parsonage. Gertrude spent several years as an evangelist also.

Gertrude was often the speaker for the Woman's Home and Foreign Missionary Society public meetings. She was elected the alternate Young Missionary Workers Band (now Wesleyan Kids for Missions) delegate to General Conference in 1934.[5]

Stella Gassaway

Stella Gassaway was born November 23, 1875, in Casey, Illinois. She married Leroy Gassaway in 1893. They had been married forty-four years at the time of her death June 24, 1937.

She was ordained by the Indiana District of the Pilgrim Holiness Church in 1930. She served as the pastor of the Rosemont Church in Terre Haute for many years and preached fearless messages. She was the mother of two daughters.[6]

Carrie S. Gick Goebel

Carrie S. Gick was a maiden lady who served the Indiana and Northern Indiana Districts of the Pilgrim Holiness Church for some thirty years. She was ordained in 1930. Rev. Ernest Batman, former superintendent of the Indiana Central District of The Wesleyan Church, wrote,

She was the secretary of the Educational Board for a number of years. She used to scare me to death when I had to meet that board as a young preacher. When I accepted a pastorate in Indianapolis, she was a member of the congregation. She took this young preacher boy under her wings and helped him overcome his fears of General Officials.

Carrie moved to Intercession City, Florida, to teach in a Christian school, and in 1958 she married a banker from New York. She retired from the active ministry in 1962. She was still on the list of ordained ministers at the time of the 1968 merger.[7]

⸺⸰⸺

Marie Goodman

Minutes of the Annual Session of the Indiana Conference of the Wesleyan Methodist Connection, or Church, of America, 1930–31, recorded that Marie Goodman had been received as an ordained minister from the Church of the Nazarene. She was the supply pastor at Deming during the conference year 1930. The following year she was involved in evangelism and was granted a letter of standing that year.

⸺⸰⸺

Mary E. Powers Harvey

Mary Powers was a native of Spartanburg, South Carolina. She married Lorenzo A. Harvey in 1923 and assisted her husband in pastoring churches in North Carolina and Kansas. She served as matron at Central College, in Central, South Carolina (now Southern Wesleyan University) for a few years. Her husband was a professor at Central for fifteen years and two years at Miltonvale Wesleyan College, in Miltonvale, Kansas (later merged into what eventually became Oklahoma Wesleyan University, Bartlesville, Oklahoma). Part of the time while he taught at Central in the music department, Mary served as the dietitian there.

The *Minutes* recorded Mary as an ordained minister in 1948. She may have been ordained before that time. Some of the churches they pastored in North Carolina included Old Zion, Rose Hill, Roxboro, Hendersonville, Bethel, Greensboro, and Broadview (Emmanuel). They pastored the Lawrence (Ks.) Wesleyan Methodist Church. Mary was also active in the Woman's Home and Foreign Missionary Society and served as the conference secretary of that organization for a number of years.

In 1962 she was given a citation for twenty-five years of service to the conference. Even in

retirement, this ministerial couple spent many years in ministering in hospitals and nursing homes. Mary Harvey died November 2, 1989. Her husband preceded her in death on May 1, 1985.[8]

⸺⸰⸺

Olive Lucinda Hodge

Olive Lucinda was born the sixth of ten children into the home of Francis and Clementine Berkebile in Anderson, Indiana, on June 4, 1904. Olive was saved at age fourteen and received her call to the ministry a short time later. She pursued this call over the objections of her parents. On October 26, 1926, she married a young widower, Paul H. Hodge, who was a Wesleyan Methodist pastor. Paul had a four-year-old son, Marville, at the time of their marriage. God blessed their home with two daughters, Norma and Kathryn, and three sons, Paul, James, and Cecil.

From the beginning of their marriage, Olive and Paul were a ministerial team and worked effectively in building God's kingdom. She was ordained in 1935. They were the pastors of Wesleyan Methodist churches in Anderson, Indiana; Enid and Ponca City, Oklahoma; Houston, Texas; and Los Angeles, Pasadena, and Sunland, California. During their time of pastoring the Enid, Oklahoma, church, Paul served as conference president, and Olive took on the full responsibility of pastoring the church while he traveled for the conference. He began his president's report by saying, "Being assisted by my wife in the pastorate at Enid, I have been able to serve the conference in the following ways." When they were assigned a church, they shared the pulpit, taking turns preaching.

In August 1938 Paul drove to Ponca City, Oklahoma, to see about planting a church there. He rented a hall, and in September a meeting was conducted with Harold Baker and H. H. Harris as evangelists. The meeting was successful, and a church was organized with twenty-eight members. Paul and Olive became the pastors there in 1940.

Olive was a leader in the conference also. She served on the conference Sunday school board, pastoral relations committee, and midyear convention committee. She was president of the

Woman's Home and Foreign Missionary Society for four years and was elected as a delegate to the society's general conference.

When she retired from the active ministry, Olive worked for a time as a salesperson. After Paul's death, she moved to Pasadena to be near her family. Her life was one of service to the Lord and her family. When she was no longer physically able to serve in public ministry, she spent much time in prayer. Olive Hodge went home to be with her Lord on March 6, 1994. She had fought a good fight; she had kept the faith.[9]

Rachel Naomi Brown McCune Howell

Rachel Naomi was born October 20, 1902, to Rev. and Mrs. C. C. Brown. She graduated from Kingswood (Kentucky) Bible College in 1924. Rachel married Rev. Orth McCune July 28, 1925, and he died August 1927. One daughter, Mary Elizabeth Conner, blessed their home. On June 18, 1930, Rachel married Rev. Ewart O. Howell. They became the parents of Esther L. Felsburg, Ruth Overmeyer, and sons William and James.

Rachel's father was a noted evangelist and leader in the Pilgrim Holiness Church and the holiness movement. She traveled with her father and sang in evangelistic meetings with her brother and sisters. She was ordained in the Pilgrim Holiness Church. As a pastor's wife, she worked extensively with children, youth, and music in the local church.

Rachel and E. O. Howell held pastorates in Chattanooga and Jamestown, Tennessee; Pineville, Louisiana; Frankfort, and Lebanon, Indiana; Fort Lauderdale, Florida, and Urbana, Illinois. He also taught at Frankfort Pilgrim Bible College, in Frankfort, Indiana (later merged into United Wesleyan College, Allentown, Pennsylvania) while pastoring in Indiana. He served as the superintendent of the Louisiana-Mississippi District for a number of years. Rachel always found a place of service during all these years. She "exemplified the fruit of the Spirit in her loving, giving, showing kindness to all, and in being thankful."

She was a loving mother who never got upset over various incidents that happened. She always took time to play games and was available to her grandchildren. One grandson wrote, "I will always think of Grandma most as being Christlike. Her Christianity was never legalistic or judgmental. . . . [It was always] natural, peaceful, easy to be around and very attractive without being in any way ambiguous."[10]

Esther E. Hunter

Esther Hunter received her license as a conference preacher (licensed minister) in 1930. She and her husband were appointed to conference missionary evangelism. Esther was active in the conference work and served as conference secretary for at least six years. She was a member of the itineracy and elders orders committee (now district board of ministerial development). She served as president and society organizer of the Kentucky Conference Woman's Home and Foreign Missionary Society.

While her husband, Jacob E. Hunter, served as president of the Kentucky Conference of the Wesleyan Methodist Church, Esther was involved as a general evangelist. She served as assistant pastor to her husband at Brooksburg and Milan churches in the Kentucky Conference; the Brunswick church in the South Georgia Conference; and the Lebanon church in the Indiana Conference. The Lebanon church was their last pastorate. Esther died in 1958.[11]

Mrs. Carrie Koehler

Little could be found on Carrie Koehler. According to the records found in the *Minutes of the Pilgrim Holiness Church Western Kansas District,* 1939–62, she was serving under that district. She became inactive in 1962 and was deceased in 1963. She had been ordained in 1930. She may have been Carrie Faidley. Carrie Faidley, according to the Western Kansas District *Minutes,* was ordained in 1930 and was under the Western Kansas district appointment until 1938.

Amy Bingham West Lee

Amy Bingham was born December 2, 1894, in Jackson, Ohio. She died March 27, 1958, in Nelsonville, Ohio. She married Charles West February 19, 1913. After his death she married William Lee in July 1951.

Amy was converted and sanctified as a young girl. She was called to preach and was true to that call. She was a strong believer in entire sanctification and lived a consistent life. She was a loyal and dependable Pilgrim.

Amy Lee was ordained by the Pilgrim Holiness Church. She served several churches in southeastern Ohio and was in charge of a mission in Columbus, Ohio, for several years. She started a work in New Lexington, Ohio, but that work was closed due to her failing health and strength. Her last pastorate was the Murray City, Ohio, Pilgrim Holiness church.[12]

Florence Genevieve Lee

Florence Lee was born in 1859 and died March 17, 1958, in Vancouver, Washington, at the age of ninety-eight. She was ordained by the California District of the Pilgrim Holiness Church.

After the conversion of her husband, William H. Lee, they sold everything to follow Jesus. They were the founders of the People's Mission Church in Colorado, which merged with the Pilgrim Holiness Church to form the Rocky Mountain District.

Florence Lee was a gifted and versatile woman whom God used in many ways.[13]

Rita E. H. Lee

White persons involved in the work of the Underground Railroad network during the slavery era endangered their lives. African Americans doubly exposed themselves and their families to death if caught. Rita Lee's parents were involved in the Underground Railroad and assisted fugitives by hiding them. They assisted in many marvelous escapes.

Rita Lee (Mrs. Jesse) was a person with great influence among the South Ohio Wesleyan Methodist Church people for many years. She had been greatly influenced by Rev. Eber Teter, the church's missionary secretary.[14]

She spent many years in evangelism and was the pastor of two Ohio churches: Hillsboro and Dayton First. She was an accomplished musician and singer. She was active in the missionary, young people's, and Sunday school departments of the local church. For many years she served as the co-compiler of the South Ohio Conference minutes.

Rita Lee not only served well in her local churches and conference, but she also had a great influence on the communities of those churches. She was the founder and director of the DeSota E. Bass Memorial Center in Dayton. This center was established for community service on June 25, 1933, and was operated under the South Ohio Conference. Many children were helped by the center, which was a work of charity for the entire community. Ill health caused her to give up this leadership.

She also served her community by being the matron and counselor at the Women's Christian Association. While pastoring the Hillsboro church, she was a member of the Hospital Twig and president of the National Association for the Advancement of Colored People.

Her last pastorate was the First Wesleyan Church in Dayton, Ohio. She completed her earthly tasks October 29, 1980.[15]

Jennie Louise Nichols Lynn

Jennie Louise Nichols was born in Huntington, West Virginia. She loved sports and she played on the West Virginia girls' state champion basketball team in 1922. She planned to major in physical education in college. However, during her senior year in high school, she was converted, and God called her into the ministry.

She received ministerial training at Kingswood Bible College, in Kingswood, Kentucky, and completed her work in 1930 at Frankfort Pilgrim College, in Frankfort, Indiana (later merged into United Wesleyan College, Allentown, Pennsylvania). She majored in speech and expression. She taught seven years at the college. While in Bible college she pastored a mission in Frankfort.

Louise was ordained in 1945. She spent more than fifty years in the field of evangelism, specializing in children's ministries. However, she did fill the pulpit on occasion in her local church. She was an excellent vacation Bible school director. She demanded discipline, earned attention, and made stories come alive for all the children.

Late in life (1953) she married Walter Lynn.

She was characterized by a pleasant disposition and very jovial. She was a hard worker and knew how and where to fit into a needy situation. She was always ready to lift burdens other people carried. She entered her eternal rest November 23, 1992.[16]

Mrs. Mary E. Lyons

Mary Ecroyd Lyons (sometimes spelled "Lyon") graduated from the Friends School in Chester, Colorado, in 1898. She taught for a number of years in the Friends day school in Pennsdale.

After her marriage she became a minister in the Wesleyan Methodist Church. Her first and only assignment was in 1930, to the South Bradford church in the Rochester Conference (now Central New York District). The name of the church was changed to Armenia Mountain in 1931. She was the pastor of that church for about thirty-five years. She had a license to preach and was studying on the course of study for ordination. She was an excellent student and received grades of ninety-five percent and ninety-eight percent on all the books she passed. However, she never qualified for ordination. The Rochester Conference made her an honorary elder (ordained minister) at the time of her retirement from active service in 1962. She completed her earthly walk with the Lord October 18, 1967.[17]

Mrs. O. M. Maris

Mrs. O. M. Maris was ordained by 1930. She was the pastor of the Gove, Kansas, Pilgrim Holiness Church in 1943. The *Minutes of the Annual Assembly of the Kansas District,* 1931–43, recorded this information, and no other entries were found.

Mrs. D. I. McCracken

The first entry found for Mrs. D, I. McCracken was in the Pennsylvania and New Jersey *Minutes* of 1930. She was a godly woman who graced the parsonages wherever they were pastoring. She was the assistant pastor to her husband on their pastorates. She was a good preacher "in her own rights" and often ministered to God's people from the pulpit. She labored incessantly for the salvation of souls and the advancement of God's cause. She was an ordained minister and the mother of one daughter, Agailia. The McCrackens were the pastors of the Muncy, Pennsylvania, Pilgrim Holiness Church at the time of her death June 25, 1950.[18]

Ethel Oden

The first recorded ministry for Ethel (Mrs. Charles L.) Oden was found in the *Minutes of the Annual Assembly of the Ohio District of the Pilgrim Holiness Church,* 1929–37. She served on the pastorates of Morehead, Soldier, Elizabethtown, and Maysville, on the Kentucky District, from 1937 to 1953.[19] *Minutes of the Annual Assembly of the Pilgrim Holiness Church Illinois District,* 1954–64, recorded her on the pastorates of Charleston and Decatur, Illinois. In 1965 she transferred to the Southern Indiana District and was there at the time of the 1968 merger.[20]

Isabel Myler Reiff

Isabel Myler was born January 27, 1882 in Pittsburgh. She was converted in early life. She attended Cleveland Bible Institute in Cleveland, Ohio (now Malone College).

She spent most of her early years in the ministry in evangelistic singing and preaching. She pastored one church, Oil City, Pennsylvania. She married C. Jay Reiff in 1929 when she was forty-seven. Together they pastored Pilgrim Holiness churches in Pennsylvania and Indiana and did evangelistic work. Often she alternated preaching the Word with her husband in revival meetings.

In 1958 they retired from active pastoral work and made their home in Fostoria, Ohio. Isabel Reiff died March 28, 1967.[21]

⁓⊷⊶⊷⁓

Grace Sherman Russell

Grace Russell was ninety-five years old when she wrote several letters to me in 1998. She had been a resident of the Bradford County Manor for several years. She was still carrying on an active prayer ministry for the Central New York District pastors. She also was involved in ministry at the manor. She moved about in a wheelchair and called on other residents. Her eyesight was almost completely gone, but she still carried on an active correspondence with many people.

Grace Russell began her ministerial work in 1930. She was enrolled in the Wesleyan Methodist course of study (a study course conducted by teachers and students by mail), but she also had attended Houghton College, Houghton, New York for a time. When she married Cecil Russell, he was the pastor of the Wesleyan Methodist church at Batchely, New York. They remained there for another year after their marriage. According to her letter, they served for a time on the Onondaga Indian Reservation near Syracuse, New York. The Onondaga tribe accepted them and gave them Indian names.

They also pastored together at the Bath church. She must have been the leader of the ministerial team, for her name always appeared first, followed by his name. She was ordained while they were pastoring at West Jasper. The *Minutes* recorded that she was the pastor at West Jasper and became ill with pleurisy and that her husband, Cecil, and a young man from Houghton College supplied the pulpit during her illness. She was ordained in 1935.

She spent many years in youth and child evangelism work. She became ill with multiple sclerosis and was unable to continue in the active pastoral work. She was the mother of three children. They moved to Houghton, New York, after she became ill, and as her strength began to return, she was able to care for "student roomers," which helped to pay for the education of her children. She taught a

Sunday school class and preached whenever the opportunity arose and she was able to do so. Since she could no longer be in the active preaching ministry, she began to write. She became the author of two books, *Jesus, Teach Us to Pray* and *You Want to Have a Happy Marriage.*[22]

⁓⊷⊶⊷⁓

Ethel Goldie Skinner

Ethel Goldie Skinner was born in 1913. She was converted July 13, 1930, at age seventeen in an "old fashioned" camp meeting. In August of that year, God called her into His ministry. "By faith" she attended Bible Holiness Seminary in Owosso, Michigan (later Owosso College, eventually merged into what became Indiana Wesleyan University, Marion, Indiana). She sang in a ladies' quartet, and each weekend they traveled with H. T. Mills, president of Bible Holiness Seminary, to help pay for her tuition, which was ninety-nine dollars a year. To cover her expenses at school, she worked ironing boys' shirts—"fully starched."

After she finished at the seminary, she traveled in evangelism with Mary Kraft from Grand Rapids and later with Helen Fair from Ohio.

She and Gaylord V. Skinner were married September 17, 1937, in New Ringold, Pennsylvania, during a revival meeting. G. V. Skinner had a definite call to the ministry and fulfilled that call for fifty-nine years in evangelism and pastoral duties until he died October 25, 1996. Ethel worked by his side during all this time. She conducted Bible studies, prayer meetings, and daily vacation Bible schools. They preached in camp meeting tents for seven years. She also served as her husband's secretary. She made calls in hospitals, homes, and especially on widows, and conducted funerals, served communion, and helped in the music by playing the piano or organ.

Ethel's personal ministry also included counseling and preaching. She was an evangelistic preacher and was ordained in 1940. She was the instrument God used to show His healing power in several incidents. In a camp meeting in Halifax, Pennsylvania, she prayed for a very sick baby. She asked the parents to set the child up and give him some food, but they were afraid to do that since he had been sick for so long. Finally, after much persuasion, the child did eat and lived. That was over sixty-eight years ago.

She and her husband worked with Cecil and Alice Clifton at the Wesleyan Methodist church and in their radio work. A lady from that radio audience came to them for help. She was demon possessed. The demon(s) would throw her to the floor and cause her body to jerk. After prayer, God delivered her from the power of the demon(s).

In 1998 Ethel Goldie Skinner was still active with the music and piano for each service at Evergreen Valley Wesleyan Church in Burton, Michigan.[23]

Mary Taylor

Mary Taylor served in the Indiana District of the Pilgrim Holiness Church from 1930 to 1938.[24]

Anna Hazel Nichols Upshaw Turner

Anna Hazel Nichols was born October 15, 1892, in Dayton, Ohio. She was converted early in life. She played the organ and was a member of the choir in her early days. She married Thomas Upshaw, and one daughter was born to this union. Thomas died (year unknown), and then she married William Turner. He died in 1935.

Mrs. Turner organized a choir. She worked for and paid for a pipe organ to be installed in the church.

She attended school at Payne Theological Seminary in Wilberforce, Ohio. She was ordained by the Wesleyan Methodist Church and was the pastor of the Richmond, Indiana, and Hillsboro, Ohio, churches.[25]

Olive Marie Whited West

Olive Marie and Charles A. West were a ministerial team in life, and they both ended their work just a few days apart. Charles died

January 12, 1961, and Olive followed in death just twelve days later, on January 24, 1961. For thirty years they worked side by side in several churches assigned to them by the Allegheny Conference of the Wesleyan Methodist Church. Their first appointment was in 1930 at Templeton, followed by Wilgus, East Conneaut, Wolf Summit, Cecil, White Memorial, North Springfield, Sagamore, and the final pastorate at Pine Grove, from which they both entered heaven. They had also spent some time in evangelistic work.

Olive began her ministerial preparation in 1937. She was first appointed as co-pastor with her husband at Wolf Summit, West Virginia. She pursued the course of study faithfully until 1953, when she was received for ordination.

She was a devoted wife and mother of three children. Her motherly sympathies led her to reach out to all who were in need.[26]

Nona Wilson

Nona Wilson was licensed to preach at the annual assembly of the Illinois and Missouri District of the Pilgrim Holiness Church in 1930.[27] There was no record of her service again until 1943. She was listed as under appointment with the Illinois District from 1943 to 1968. She was ordained in 1951. From 1955 to 1968 she was listed as inactive.[28]

Ella V. Simon Zuch

Ella V. Simon was born September 11, 1892, in Long Eddy, New York. She completed her earthly journey April 17, 1999, at the age of 106. In 1927 she went to God's Bible School, Cincinnati, Ohio, for the two-year Christian workers' course. She met James C. Zuch of Red Key, Indiana, while attending school, and they were married July 24, 1929.

Ella and James began their ministerial work in the Kentucky Conference of the Wesleyan Methodist Church in 1930. They were the pastors of the Brooksburg church. Sometime between

1930 and 1933, Ella was ordained. James became the president of the Kentucky Conference 1932–34. During part of this time, Ella was listed as a general evangelist.

In 1937 there was a note in the *Minutes of the Kentucky Conference* thanking the Zucks "for being the founders and organizers of the Milan, Indiana, church this last year."[29]

They were appointed as pastors of the Vine Street Wesleyan Methodist Church in Cincinnati December 19, 1937. They had an outstanding ministry at the church for six or more years. They also spent many years in successful evangelistic work.[30]

They moved to West Palm Beach, Florida, in 1943. James had suffered from asthma for a number of years, and it was hoped this move would help him physically. Here they began work on the Riviera Beach church. They literally built the church building with their own hands and with their own financial means.[31]

In Florida they became associated with Rev. H. Robb and Geraldine French and Francis French. Robb had felt for some time the need of a spiritual oasis for people spending their winters in Florida. Together they found in the tiny village of Hobe Sound fourteen primitive acres along the Intracoastal Waterway. They developed these acres into a camp meeting and housing area for Christian people spending their winters in Florida. All of them were diligently and sacrificially giving and serving in this project. They spent many hours in the hot sun fighting sand fleas, mosquitoes, and snakes while clearing the property. The first camp meeting was conducted there in 1947. In the early days of the camp, the Zuchs could be found cleaning, cooking, caring for guests, and praying.

James C. Zuch died in 1958. Ella retired from active service in the ministry in 1956. She made her home at the Sea Breeze Manor, Hobe Sound, Florida, until her death.[32]

Ella was always involved in the conference work in each of the conferences in which they served. She was elected to preach the opening sermon of the 1934 conference in Kentucky. In that conference she served on the itineracy and elders orders committee (now district board of ministerial development) and was secretary for the conference Woman's Home and Foreign Missionary Society. In the Ohio Conference she served as the conference superintendent of the Young Missionary Workers Band (now Wesleyan Kids for Missions), the committee on morals, and the pastoral relations committee.

Anna Briggs

Minutes of the Annual Conference of the Pilgrim Holiness Church California District from 1931 to 1948 listed Anna Briggs as under appointment for that time.

Dorothea Calhoon

The Minutes of the Annual Assembly of the Idaho-Washington District Pilgrim Holiness Church, 1931–35, recorded Dorothea (Mrs. C. C.) Calhoon as stationed at McGuire, Port Falls, and Weippe, Idaho. The Oregon District was started in 1940, and she appears on the stationed list in *The Minutes of the Annual Assembly of the Oregon District Pilgrim Holiness Church,* 1940–48. In the *Minutes of the Annual Conference of the Northwest District of the Pilgrim Holiness Church,* 1949–66, she was listed without an appointment.

Edna Mae Carter

Edna Mae Carter was born July 11, 1908, in Indianapolis, and she died in the same neighborhood February 2, 1991. She came to know the Lord as her Savior at the age of eight at the Wheeler Rescue Mission in Indianapolis. At that early age of eight, in fact within twenty-four hours, God began to call her to minister to children. She felt called to start a Sunday school. Twelve children came, and she won her little girl friend to the Lord. The attendance increased, and her father asked the leader of the mission to permit a Sunday school to be organized. Edna Mae became aware of the needs of children in overseas places as a child, and she eagerly filled mite boxes to help support Chinese orphans. By the time she was eleven, she knew God had called her to the work of missions.

During high school years she worked at Wheeler Mission part-time and served others with love and compassion. She graduated from Indiana Bible College and then was employed as a social worker. She became known as the "sunshine girl" to the elderly shut-ins and the underprivileged.

She came under the holiness influence by the Missionary Bands of the World and joined their St. Clair Street church in Indianapolis in 1923. The Missionary Bands recognized her call and gave her a ministerial license to preach. She was ordained in 1931. The group sent her to minister in Paraguay, and she worked there until 1936. She returned home to care for her aged parents until their deaths in 1943 and 1944. During this time she worked at the Wheeler Mission and at the Missionary Bands headquarters.

In 1949 she returned to full-time missionary work and was sent to Jamaica. She labored there until her retirement in 1977. She was involved in children's work, directing vacation Bible schools and conducting evangelistic campaigns. She also served as youth director and organized the first Wesleyan Youth Conference in Jamaica. The Missionary Bands of the World and the Wesleyan Methodist Church merged in 1958, and she became an associate missionary under the Wesleyan Methodist Church in Jamaica. She retired and moved to Wesleyan Village in Brooksville, Florida, until she was forced by ill health to return to Indianapolis.

Wayne Wright was the general secretary of Wesleyan World Missions at the time of her death. Here is his tribute to her and her work:

It is marvelous to see that God can take simple instruments and make them into something useful, provided the instrument is yielded and willing. Edna Mae was not extraordinarily talented from the world's standpoint. Her full surrender to Christ, her willingness to follow His call, and her devotion to doing what she could have combined to make her life something worthwhile in the Kingdom of God.[33]

Nellie Hamilton

Nellie Hamilton served two years as pastor of a Friends church. In 1931 she was ordained by the Ohio Conference of the Wesleyan Methodist Church. Almost all her ministerial work was done in the area of evangelism. She was known as a traveling evangelist. She wore a dark-colored cape and was "quite a firebrand" of a preacher. She retired from the active ministry in 1963 but was still listed as retired at the time of merger with the Pilgrim Holiness Church in 1968.

In 1953 the Ohio Conference decided to disband the Wooster, Ohio, church. But Nellie Hamilton desired to do what she could to revive the work. She was given the opportunity, but the work was closed December 1, 1953, and the property was sold. She received twenty dollars a week for her work while pastoring this church.

Nellie was active in conference work also. She preached the conference sermon in 1952. She served on several conference committees, including pastoral relations, courtesy, and the young people's society's executive committee, and as reporter.[34]

Pauline Patterson Ludwig

Pauline Patterson began ministerial work and study for the ministry in 1931 in the Kansas Conference of the Wesleyan Methodist Church. She was ordained in 1946. Her ministerial work was primarily that of a children's worker. In 1949 she married Harold Ludwig and was granted a letter of transfer to the California Conference.[35]

She assisted her husband in pastoring the El Sereno church in 1949 and was assigned to conference evangelism for a time. She was on the unstationed (without appointment) list for a number of years, and in 1961 she withdrew from the conference.[36]

Olga Marie Norman

Olga Marie Norman and her husband, G. I., came into the Lockport Conference of the

Wesleyan Methodist Church in 1931. They were from Chicago and were received from the Church of the Nazarene as local preachers. She was ordained at the conference session in 1932.[37]

In 1932 G. I. and Olga were appointed pastors at the Olean, New York, church. During their tenure there (1932–39) a "heaven-sent" revival occurred. They conducted a radio program and had summer tent meetings and other evangelistic meetings. As a result of their labors, the church began to grow. Many were added to the church, and a Sunday school record of two hundred was reached.[38]

The conference records were missing for 1937–41, but the Normans were appointed pastors at McRae Brook Mission, located near Eldred, Pennsylvania, in 1942. The mission had been in existence since 1938, but during their pastorate, in June 1942, the church was organized.

Olga Marie Norman was a woman of faith in her great God. They lived a distance from the McRae Brook Church. But by faith, she would get her five children, George, Daniel, Fred, Della, and Olga Marie dressed and ready for church. They would walk to the end of the land and wait for a ride to the church, where she would preach. Always God answered her prayers, and they would arrive on time. One day a man came to the door of their home and handed her the keys to a car for her to use to get back and forth to the church. In Olean, a businessman gave them a house to live in. Olga related this personal information about her mother's prayer life. She stated also that her father was the upfront person and sometimes boisterous. But her mother was the calm, quiet, behind-the-scenes worker. She added "class" to their work and ministry.

Olga transferred her ministerial standing to the Ohio Conference May 26, 1943. She and G. I. were appointed pastors of the Dayton Northridge Church in 1943. They pastored that church until 1950, when they were appointed pastors of the Calhoun and Mt. Olive (Six Mile) churches in

South Carolina.[39] She also served as her husband's assistant at the Clemson, South Carolina, church. She was known as a meticulous housekeeper, but during all the years they pastored she always had time for people, and to her everyone was special. She was a real "people person."

They returned to the Ohio Conference in July 1954 to become the pastors of the Middletown, Ohio, Wesleyan Methodist Church. They organized that church on April 9, 1955, with thirty-two charter members. Four years later, 1959, they resigned and became the pastors of an independent work in Greensboro, North Carolina for a short time.[40] In 1960 they transferred to the Allegheny Conference.

After moving into the Allegheny Conference, they pastored churches in Tuscaloosa and Montgomery, Alabama, and did extensive evangelistic work. Many of their calls in evangelistic work came from the Bible Methodist Church. G. I. Norman died November 9, 1974. After his death, Olga did not travel much in evangelistic work. She did pastor a church in Alabama, and the church was dedicated during her ministry there.[41] Olga Marie Norman entered her heavenly home July 29, 1997.

Dorotha Irene Dobbie Robbins

Dorotha Dobbie was born in 1910. She was ordained by the Ohio District of the Pilgrim Holiness Church in 1931. She was a gifted musician and spent twelve years in general evangelism before she married Rev. Marshall H. Robbins.

Together they pastored in western Ohio. She was serving as the associate pastor with her husband at the time of her death at Troy, Ohio. She died May 1, 1976.[42]

Helen Frances Davidson Stark

Helen Frances Davidson was born in 1904 at Bakers Mills, New York. She was endowed with a sweet disposition and an unselfish nature. These traits characterized her entire life. Her early childhood was spent in the Adirondack Mountains. Her father was a pastor, and she accompanied him each Sunday to a distant church when they moved to Horican, New York. She became

actively interested in spiritual things at this time. And when her oldest sister and her husband sailed for Africa, she expressed her desire to become a missionary. She was seven years old and never swerved from that desire. At this time she organized a Young Missionary Workers Band (now Wesleyan Kids for Missions) and acted as its superintendent even when she was seven. During the summer months of her high school and college days, she worked on the farm in the hay fields.

She entered Houghton College, Houghton, New York, in the fall of 1920 and served as a stenographer to earn a large share of her college expenses. This heavy load of work and studies did not prevent her from spending an hour each morning in devotions with God. She was sanctified during her college days. She was active in the student missionary group on campus. In 1925 she graduated with an A.B. degree and completed the advance course in theology.

Helen taught one year at Cadyville, New York, after graduation but felt led to return to Houghton the next year as the dean of women. On June 30, 1928, she married Price P. Stark. She remained at Houghton on the teaching staff at the college and seminary and preached whenever the opportunities came.

Helen and Price sailed for Sierra Leone in 1931.[43] They served three terms in that country. While home on furlough in 1936, Helen served as the assistant pastor at Driftwood in the Lockport Conference (now Western New York District). In 1942 they transferred their conference membership to the Champlain Conference (now Eastern New York-New England District) and in 1943 Price was elected president of the conference.[44] Helen had been assisting him on the pastorate at

Mooers, and when he was elected president, Marjean Bennett (Chapman Dayton) came to assist Helen in the pastorate. In 1946 they returned to Sierra Leone for another term. This term completed their ministry in Africa.

Helen assisted her husband in pastoring the Castle Garden and Bradford, Pennsylvania, churches and the East Aurora, New York, church in the Lockport Conference after they returned from Africa.

Helen served as the general president of the Woman's Missionary Society from 1959 to 1966. Her administration was a time of advancement for the society. When she completed this ministry, Helen and Price made their way to Jamaica, and they both taught in the Bible school there for two years. In 1968 they retired in Brooksville, Florida, and were actively engaged in local church work.[45] Price died in 1984, and Helen completed her earthly work November 22, 1994. She was the mother of two daughters.

Bessie Ruth Aslin

Bessie Ruth Aslin was born December 24, 1905, in Peabody, Kansas. She graduated from Pacific Bible College in 1930 and was employed as a schoolteacher for several years. She was ordained in 1948. She married Thomas Elbert Aslin on August 3, 1930. They were the parents of one daughter. The Aslins spent the early part of their ministerial work in pastoring churches in Kansas, North Carolina, Nebraska, Colorado, Missouri, Texas, and Tennessee.[46]

In 1948 the Aslins became missionary pastors of the White Park Pilgrim Holiness Church in Bridgetown, Barbados, serving that church until May 1953. They returned in December 1959 and were the pastors at White Park for another two years. They served a total of seven years in Barbados.[47]

The Aslins served under appointment in several districts of the Pilgrim Holiness Church: Rocky Mountain, Kansas, Tennessee, North Central, and Texas.[48]

Ruth loved the Lord and gave faithful and devoted service to Him. She died April 24, 1967.

Mary E. Bennett

Mary E. Bennett was received to pursue the course of study for ordination in 1932. She was ordained before 1942.

In 1942 she began serving as the executive secretary of the Buffalo Bible Institute. She served in that capacity for five years. She was appointed the pastor at the Forrestville, New York, Wesleyan Methodist Church July 2, 1945, and continued to serve through 1951.

Mary was active in the conference work. She served as the assistant conference secretary in 1946 and was elected conference secretary in 1947. She served through 1956. Her skills in secretarial tasks enabled her to serve as co-editor of the conference paper, "The Circuit Rider," later called the "Itinerator," from 1946 through 1956. She served as the editor of a booklet published by the Lockport Conference (now Western New York District) for their centennial celebration, called "Our Heritage Lockport Conference Centennial 1861–1961."

 Her interest and gifts in child evangelism enabled her to serve with distinction on the conference level of the Sunday school board for eight years, on the committee for child evangelism, and conference Sunday school secretary for four years.

These skills brought her to the attention of the general Church, and she served as the promotional secretary and child evangelism director of the Sunday school department 1951–55. In 1955 she was elected the general superintendent of the Young Missionary Workers Band (now Wesleyan Kids for Missions) for one quadrennium.

Her interest and involvement in the temperance movement resulted in her election for a period of time as president of the Women's Christian Temperance Union (WCTU) of East Aurora, New York.

In 1959 she became the pastor of the Cuba, New York, Wesleyan Methodist Church in the Lockport Conference for four years. During this time the Cuba church became aware of its place and responsibility in the local community.

Mary was employed at Houghton College, Houghton, New York, in 1963 in a secretarial position in the development, public relations, and alumni offices. She was Robert Luckey's secretary for seven years. But she never lost interest in the district work and served as the district director of the Young Missionary Workers Band.[49]

Mary Bennett was an excellent speaker and traveled over North America in the interest of the general Sunday school department and the Young Missionary Workers Band. She spoke at Christian education banquets, Sunday school rallies, and other special events, often using the "diagrammatical wheel" and flannel graph board to illustrate her messages.

Gipsie M. Miller described Mary E. Bennett from the biblical injunction "Never lag in zeal . . . be aglow and burning with the Spirit, serving the Lord." All there was of this radiant woman was thrown into service for God.[50]

Mary Bennett died June 1, 1970. Her Christian concerns, thoroughness, neatness, efficiency, promptness, and unfailing good cheer were her hallmarks.[51]

Lois Crouse Bingham

Lois Bingham was an ordained minister in the Pilgrim Holiness Church. The first record of her service was found in the Southern District. She was serving as a missionary in Jamaica from 1932 to 1935. In 1938 she was located in Wilmore, Kentucky, and was under the appointment of the Illinois District from 1938 to 1940.[52]

From 1941 to 1943 she served under the California District, and in 1945–47 she was listed under appointment in the North Carolina District. She and her husband, Buelle E., were the pastors at Fayettville in 1947.[53]

Esther Close

Esther Close was born into a rugged and fiercely independent family. Her father, Henry Close, had been a "gunslinging militia" cowboy in a furious range war in Wyoming. He moved to Kansas and bought a team of horses, farm machinery, and a furnished house. He was now ready to start farming and find a wife. He saved his wages of five years being a cowboy, but he had also acquired a tremendous thirst for liquor that stayed with him all his life. Esther's mother, Lula Mae Duensing, was a divorced mother of two sons, Ed and Will, and an infant daughter. She joined a caravan moving west to settle homesteads in Kansas, Oklahoma, and Nebraska. She rented an entire railway car to transport her personal goods, which included her livestock. She located in Overland, Kansas, and bought a herd of cattle. She took on the work of a cowhand and spent long hours in the open range watching the cattle. An itinerant Methodist preacher and his wife lived not far from her ranch. When her herds moved close to their cottage, she would spend time with the pastor and his wife. They talked to her about the Savior. One January afternoon, crushed with conviction, she made her way to their home during a terrific snowstorm. She could not wait another day; she must be saved. But with no encouragement at home, her faith faltered. She married Henry Close, and they set up housekeeping in a sod house on his recently acquired homestead.

Rev. Esther Close riding in an oxcart used in her midwifery ministry in India

Esther was the sixth of ten children. Dewey "Dick" and Ray became Pilgrim Holiness ministers. Virgil, Nick, and Paul became navy career men. Edna became a teacher, and when Lula Mae's health failed, she was a surrogate mother to Ruth, Margaruite, Hallie, and Esther.

Lula Mae was reclaimed, and she earnestly sought to bring up her children in the Lord. At family altar time there was always an empty chair, for Henry was never present. With the help of some of her neighbors, Lula Mae started a Sunday school, and for ten years she served that school. A number of the children were saved. Eventually a church was established.

Esther attended school in a one-room sod building that was later replaced with a wood frame structure. A revival came to Winona, Kansas, in 1917 when Esther was thirteen, and she was converted. She had dropped out of school after the eighth grade because she was not a good student and her mother was afraid for her to go to Colby or board in town to attend school. However, after her conversion she read the Bible each day, because she had been told that it was "what a good Christian did." She began to sense God's call, and He seemed to be pointing to God's Bible School in Cincinnati, Ohio. She worked and earned enough money for one semester and entered the school in 1926. Since she did not have a high school education, she was required to take those classes. She worked from 7:30 A.M. until 12:30 P.M. She attended Bible classes in the afternoon and high school classes at night, from 7:30 to 10:30 P.M.

Each weekend the students were involved in practical ministry; therefore, she went house to house in visitation to the elderly and sick. Esther's closest friend at God's Bible School was Roberta Macmillan, who became Mrs. Clarence G. Keith. The Keiths became missionaries to Africa.

Esther graduated from God's Bible School in 1932. The nation was in the Great Depression. People were without work and food. She filled Ray Close's pulpit in Center, Colorado, during that first summer after graduation so he could work and earn money to support his family. In the fall she returned to Cincinnati and came in contact with R. W. Wolfe of the Pilgrim Holiness

Church in eastern Kentucky. He offered her a pastorate at Willard, Kentucky, but he also suggested that she get someone to go with her. Elma Talbot, a God's Bible School graduate, went with her. She led the singing and worked with the children. Their people were desperately poor. There was no parsonage, but the church was able to get a house (which was part of an estate) for them to live in rent-free. Their salary was sixty-two dollars a year for the two of them. Food, milk, canned goods, produce from their gardens, cornmeal, and flour were given to them. These women did not think of themselves as being impoverished. Their church interior looked like a barn, for it had never been plastered. The front wall about eight to ten feet above the pulpit had a scattering of bullet holes where "errant missiles" entered the building. Willard had its share of feuds, killings, and random violence.

The Sunday morning attendance was between forty and sixty, but since the church service was "the only show in town" on Sunday night, over two hundred people would then crowd into the old church to hear Esther, the "green" preacher. Elma married a local preacher before the year ended, and Frances St. Claire came to help Esther. Esther was ordained by the Kentucky District of the Pilgrim Holiness Church in 1934.

After eighteen months, the district superintendent moved Esther from Willard to Jamestown, Tennessee. Again there was no parsonage, and she made her home with the local families. One home was that of Sergeant Alvin York, the most decorated soldier of World War I. In less than a year God began to call her to missionary work in India.

While she pastored Willard, Billie Holstein, a missionary to India, went under the Pilgrim Holiness Church but later established an independent work that she called "baby-fold." It was a kind of orphanage for abandoned infants. Esther learned from Billie the spiritual needs of the people of India. During this time she began to realize that "when you follow the Lord, you do not need to know the end. . . . Faith is just taking one step at a time."

The Pilgrim Holiness Church accepted Esther as a missionary but gave her no support.

She resigned her pastorate and went to Kansas to tell her family good-bye. Her trip from Kansas to New York involved enough speaking engagements to get her fare to India, and she had thirty-five dollars left over! She said God stretched her money like rubber. She learned to live a life of faith—no salary, no support. She prayed, and funds came from sources she didn't even know.

She worked for several months on the Nepal border, but it became evident that she must learn the language. While in language school she again met Billie Holstein. Billie offered her a job helping with her work. That involved the care of twenty to thirty babies; almost all of them were unwanted baby girls. While working there, Esther became very ill. Billie prayed and laid hands on her, and she was healed.

In November 1940, Esther developed nephritis. A friend in the United States prayed for her, and Billie called a Canadian missionary doctor. He declared that she had kidney failure and hepatitis and admitted her to the hospital. She begged the doctor to let her go home, for she had run out of funds. He simply said, "I don't charge those who work for Christ."

She was convinced that she should leave the "baby-fold" in 1941. Her brothers, Ray and Dick, told her about the Oriental Missionary Society (OMS) and its close ties with the Pilgrim Holiness Church. She applied and was interviewed. They asked her one question, "How is your health?" She had to tell them about her kidney and liver condition. They firmly stated she would never pass the physical examination. However, when the report was written out, it stated "nothing at all out of order with the kidneys and liver." She began working for OMS in the fall of 1942.

During her furlough she took more training in child evangelism at Cleveland Evangelistic Institute (now Malone College). Back in India she worked in the Bible school and did office work and visitation in the hospital. When there were conventions, she was in charge of the kitchen and had nationals working for her. During the end of this term of service, she had become involved in midwifery. She was advised to get more training under the British medical system since even a registered nurse's credential from America was not recognized. She remained eighteen months longer in India to complete the midwifery course. Now she had been exposed to the sick and suffering of India. Here she learned also to give to those who refused to pay and slipped away even without saying thanks. Esther had never been a good student, but God enabled her not only to pass the course but also to get the highest grades in the entire province.

While on furlough this time, she discovered that a new policy of OMS required each missionary to raise his or her own money to return to India as well as all their expenses in traveling. God provided a car and even a driver's license!

The next term, Esther was sent to central India to open a clinic and to practice midwifery. She saw an average of fifty to sixty patients each day. She delivered over five hundred babies, and by the grace and mercy of God and the faithful prayers of His people, not one baby died. She traveled to see her patients on her bicycle, or sometimes a patient would send an ox cart to take her to them. She sometimes received fifty cents for her work or more often nothing. She was enabled by God to lead many dying women to God.

During her third term she opened a clinic and assisted in a little church clinic next to the government school. There was a government hospital close by, but many came to her clinic, because the women felt much more comfortable with Esther. The hardest thing for her was not physical privation or snakes but the dehumanizing influence of Hinduism on the women.

In 1968 she felt God was saying to her that her time in India was over. Haiti was the next stop on her journey. Retirement was just five years away. She went to Haiti and was in charge of the obstetrics department. The women came to her, usually twenty a day. From 1969 to 1973 she delivered hundred of babies, including six sets of twins and seven babies by breach births. She enjoyed the attitude of the Haitians. They were cheerful, affectionate, and childlike and greeted each birth of a boy or girl with joy and delight.

Esther Close lives in retirement in Greenwood, Indiana, and at the time of this writing is nearing her one-hundredth birthday.[54]

Hazel L. Goss

Hazel L. Goss was listed in the *Minutes of the Annual Assembly of the Idaho/Washington District Pilgrim Holiness Church,* 1932–60. In 1960 she was on the inactive list.

Cora Hathaway Hart

Cora Hathaway was listed as an ordained minister in the *Minutes of the Annual Assembly of the Ohio District Pilgrim Holiness Church* in 1932. She was listed in the *Minutes* until 1955. She apparently was married in 1947 to Mr. Hart (first name unknown). No other information was found except that she lived in Howe, Indiana, for three years (1948–50) and in Leipsic and Napoleon, Ohio.

Ruby Kagle

Some women ministers were pastors and worked with another woman minister in local churches. Ruby Kagle seemed to be the leader when she and another woman were assigned a pastorate. Ruby began her ministerial service in 1932, when she began to work on the course of study for ordination in the Iowa Conference of the Wesleyan Methodist Church. She was appointed with Vera Brainerd to pastor the Rockford, Iowa, church. On May 3, 1935, she was appointed to supply the LaPorte City church.

The *Wesleyan Advocate,* February 3, 1975, page 18, reported that she was ordained by the Iowa Conference in 1934. She was the pastor at Rockford again in 1936. She served as a home missionary in Montana from 1937 to 1941. The next year she began her missionary/teacher ministry at Zion's Hill, Kentucky. She worked at the Zion's Hill Mission from 1942 to 1946.[55]

In 1947 the Iowa Conference granted her a letter of transfer to the Middle Atlantic States Conference. She was appointed with Faith Burkett as pastor of the Wattstownship,

Pennsylvania, Wesleyan Methodist Church and served that church through 1955. Ruby was active in the Middle Atlantic States Conference in the Woman's Missionary Society. She served as the mission study secretary and reading course secretary from 1955 to 1967. Ruby also spent several years in evangelism work.[56]

Ruby Kagle had taught school for two years in Montana before she entered the ministry. She attended Miltonvale College, Miltonvale, Kansas (later merged into what became Oklahoma Wesleyan University, Bartlesville, Oklahoma). Her ministry included work in Montana, Kentucky, Iowa, and Pennsylvania. She was actively engaged in the Paulsboro, New Jersey, church before her retirement, and her membership at the time of her death was in the Pennsylvania and New Jersey District.[57]

Lillian R. Lash

Lillian R. Lash was a retired ordained minister of the Pilgrim Holiness Church at the time of her death. She was a member of the Berkley Hills Pilgrim Holiness Church in Grand Rapids, Michigan. She married Orval Lash December 25, 1902.

She pastored the Leesburg and McLuney, Ohio, churches and Ashley, Michigan, church. She had also taught school for many years and she ran a nursing home in Grand Rapids.[58]

May Markee

May L. Markee was already an ordained minister when she transferred from the Wisconsin Conference to the Iowa Conference in 1932. However, no records were found for her before 1932. She and her husband, Wesley W., were appointed the pastors of the Wyanet, Illinois, Wesleyan Methodist Church in 1932 and served there through 1934. On July 11, 1935, they asked for and were granted letters of transfer, which they held until 1937. At that time they transferred to the Free Methodist Conference in Wisconsin.[59]

Corda A. May

Corda A. May was ordained in 1932 by the Kentucky District of the Pilgrim Holiness Church. She served as the pastor of the Coal Creek Mission in Tennessee for two years.[60]

She began her ministry in the West Virginia District of the Pilgrim Holiness Church in 1934. She served the West Union, Three Mile (two times), Spring Ford, and Ravenswood churches in that district. In 1944 she resigned her pastorate at Three Mile and was involved in evangelistic work. She died in Waterloo, Ohio, in 1965 or 1966.[61]

Margaret Taylor Holgate Miner

Margaret Taylor was ordained as an elder (ordained minister) in the Wesleyan Methodist Church in 1932. She and her husband, Raymond, were appointed pastors of the Smyrna, Delaware Wesleyan Methodist church. The church grew from six in Sunday school to over one hundred in three years.

The Taylors planted a new church at Paulsboro, New Jersey, following their pastorate at Smyrna. When the attendance reached seventy in number, they built a church building. The Taylors also planted churches in Baltimore, Maryland and Richmond, Virginia.[62]

While Margaret was an ordained minister and did her share of pastoral work and preaching, she was also a full-time schoolteacher. She taught school "to pay expense." She used her car to haul in loads of children for Sunday school and vacation Bible school. She was a woman with great energy. She would spend hours calling in the homes of children and adults, lead the singing, teach a Sunday school class, and preach. She was in charge of the special programs given at Easter and Christmas as well as on other special occasions. Margaret was also a chalk artist and often drew pictures during the services for the children. She had a happy cheerful spirit and taught the children

189

with enthusiasm. Many of these children gave their hearts to the Lord.

Because she loved children and enjoyed working with them, an opportunity was given to the Taylors to become house parents at Hephzibah Children's Home in Macon, Georgia. They accepted that invitation and served there for two years.

They were then contacted by the superintendent of the Florida District of the Pilgrim Holiness Church. He wanted them to do pioneer work (plant churches) in Florida. They accepted the challenge and became the pastors of the Clearwater church for three and a half years. Around 1983 some men were attempting to move the church sign, but they were having a difficult time trying to break the sign loose from its foundation. Margaret was watching them and finally said, "Brothers, I mixed that concrete, and I mixed it well." It hadn't crumbled in over thirty years.[63]

The "History of Largo Wesleyan Church" contained the following information on the planting of that Wesleyan Methodist church by Margaret and Raymond Taylor in Largo, Florida. The church was started in the spring of 1954, and the services were held in the home of Revs. Raymond and Margaret Taylor. The church was organized on April 15, 1954, with ten members. They purchased a site and planned to build the church in three phases so they would have a place to worship immediately. The first service was held in the building on January 2, 1955. Three families totaling fifteen persons and several others began coming, and it was necessary to construct the rest of the building. Much of the work was done by volunteers, but Clarence Martin and the conference president, Foster Piatt, supervised and did a great deal of the work. The completed church was dedicated February 5, 1956.

The seventh annual session of the Florida Conference of the Wesleyan Methodist Church was conducted in the Largo Church. Very soon after this, Raymond Taylor had a stroke and died on July 11, 1956. Margaret Taylor was asked to continue pastoring and did so for about five years. The children and youth work prospered under her leadership.

She married Mr. Holgate (first name unknown) and after his death married Floyd Miner, a retired sales consultant for Borden Dairies, in 1977. Both of them were active members of the Clearwater Wesleyan church in 1985. He served as the church treasurer. She was listed as the pastor of visitation. A typical week for her would be ten or fifteen visits and prayers with folk who were ill or confined to their home, four to eight hours in various funeral homes in the area, a nursing home service with personal greetings to about forty lonesome elderly people, teaching a Sunday school lesson on Sunday, and conducting the missionary service on Wednesday night. In 1998 at the age of ninety-two she was residing in a nursing home.[64]

Cora Reynolds

Cora Reynolds was ordained by the Ohio District of the Pilgrim Holiness Church in 1939. She had served as a missionary nurse in South Africa for a number of years. She met Alfred Reynolds, and they were married in South Africa in 1924. Alfred died in Africa in 1937.

Cora and her two children, George and Alice, returned to the United States, and she served as the school nurse at God's Bible School, in Cincinnati, Ohio, from 1938 to 1950. During part of that time she was the pastor of the North Bend Pilgrim Holiness Church (1943–48) also. She was employed as a nurse at Dunham Hospital in Cincinnati from 1950 to 1962. She died February 12, 1981.[65]

Elsie Taylor

Elsie Taylor began her ministerial work in 1932. She also was enrolled in the course of study for ordination that year. She served as the assistant pastor to her husband, Frank, at the Hague and Valley View churches from 1932 to 1936 and at the Macomb church from 1937 to 1941. Part of that time they also served the Heuvelton church. These churches were in the Champlain Conference of the Wesleyan Methodist Church.[66]

She and her husband also served pastorates in the Rochester (now Central New York District) and Lockport (now Western New York District)

Conferences of the Wesleyan Methodist Church. The Champlain Conference (now Eastern New York-New England District) ordained her in 1954.

She was the mother of one daughter, who wrote, "She was a merciful person, and in her there were law and love, the two mightiest forces in the universe. She was one who cared." She died December 12, 1975.[67]

Agnes M. Baily

Agnes Baily grew up in the Jersey City, New Jersey, Wesleyan Methodist church under the ministry of Frank Butterfield and A. J. Shea. After graduating from college, Agnes went to the West Coast to assist on home mission church planting projects. Agnes tells her story:

My ministerial life began in the Portland, Oregon, area. I was first called out there to assist in planting a new church. This was in the mid-thirties. I worked in the northeast section of Portland and helped to start the Russelville church, which became a fairly strong church. In those early days my travel in the northwest was mostly by train, or I was transported by members who drove me to places of service by car. While in Oregon, I was ordained to the Christian ministry. I played the piano for their camp meetings.

I returned home to New Jersey because of the illness of my mother. While at home, through various circumstances, I became reacquainted with a friend from God's Bible School in Cincinnati, Ohio. This resulted in my marriage to Percy Baily of Roanoke, Virginia.

We spent four years in Marion, Indiana, after our marriage, while Percy finished up his college work. Our first pastorate was in Shippensburg, Pennsylvania. We pastored there for six years, 1950–56, and saw good growth. Occasionally I would take a service, although I never became really comfortable in the pulpit. While in Shippensburg, a Nazarene brother visited our church occasionally, and someone told me that he said, "Every time I go there, that woman is 'yapping' in the pulpit." That was not very flattering, and didn't make me feel any more comfortable in the pulpit!

Our older children were born in Marion, Indiana, and our third child was born in Shippensburg, Pennsylvania. Philip, our oldest,

is a successful pastor in the South Carolina District.

Our next move was to Richmond, Virginia. We pastored there for nine years. By this time it became apparent that my forte was in the teaching ministry. Most of my teaching has been in the books of the Bible. I taught a large adult class for seventeen years while we were in Roanoke First Church. My style of preaching was more on the instructional nature, discipline rather than evangelistic. My dress for the pulpit was usually a suit or at least a very tailored navy dress with a small lace collar.

My teaching ministry has covered about fifty years. Since there is no Wesleyan church in the area where I now live, I am teaching at a Nazarene church in White Stone, Virginia.

All the time I was married, Percy and I worked together harmoniously, although I did not share the pulpit on a regular basis.

Agnes was extremely active in all district functions including the Woman's Missionary Society and Wesley Grove Camp. She served as Woman's Missionary Society conference secretary from 1956 to 1965 and president of the Woman's Missionary Society for two years. The *Minutes of the Middle Atlantic States Mission Conference* recorded Percy and Agnes as the pastors of the Sussex, New Jersey, church from 1956 to 1967.[68]

Lillian James Bailie

Lillian James and Thomas Bailie were married November 26, 1924. Thomas was the pastor of a rural congregation that did not have a church building from 1930 to 1935. The church was located in Watford City, North Dakota, in the Dakota Conference of the Wesleyan Methodist Church. Lillian began her ministerial ministry in 1933. She was granted a license to preach that year. Apparently Watford City was on a circuit with Riverside and Johnson Corners. In 1934 Lillian was ordained and she assisted her husband in pastoring the Almont Wesleyan Methodist Church from 1934 to 1941. Besides assisting her husband, she was elected the conference secretary of the Woman's Home and Foreign Missionary Society. She served in this office through 1941.[69]

Lillian assisted her husband in pastoring the Artesian, Avon, Houghton, and Belle Fourche,

South Dakota, churches. They also pastored the Forsythe, Montana, Wesleyan Methodist Church. In 1957 they transferred to the Wisconsin Conference.

On September 1, 1956, they became the pastors of the Baraboo Wesleyan Church, and remained there until 1958. At that time they moved to the Beulah church and pastored that church through 1961. In 1962 they were placed on the retired list of ministers and moved their ministerial credentials to the Illinois Conference.[70]

The Illinois Conference needed pastors, and Lillian and Thomas were the supply pastors at Roseland, Illinois from 1962 to 1965. From that time on they were listed as retired. However, she directed the day care center of Hope Wesleyan Church for a number of years during her retirement. Forrest Gearhart, former district superintendent of the Illinois conference, remarked that Lillian was retired when he knew her but that she was an effective minister and always tried to make her husband the more visible of the two of them. She was a very gifted woman whom God used to advance His kingdom. Both of her sons became ministers/pastors, and Meredith Bailie is now serving as a pastor to our missionaries.

Lillian was born March 25, 1901, in Kentucky. She served the Wesleyan Methodist and Wesleyan Churches for forty-four years. She died November 17, 1991.[71]

─────

Coral W. Goodman Butcher

Coral Goodman married Charles Henry Butcher August 30, 1916. They were the parents of Orval, Alice Mae (Heavilin), Claton, William, and Leon. Leon preceded her in death. They took their first pastorate in Valton, Wisconsin, with the Wesleyan Methodist Church. A few years after that, they held a tent meeting in Dunnville, Wisconsin, and some twenty-five to thirty quarry workers were saved. The Butchers moved there and planted a church.

They were invited to Eau Claire, Wisconsin, by some Christians and planted a Wesleyan church there. Coral and Charles served here for nearly twenty years. Coral was a woman God had gifted

in many ways. She was an excellent helpmate and an adventurous pioneer in helping to plant churches in the Wisconsin Conference. She served that conference in pioneering for thirty-six years.

Coral was ordained in 1940. While they pastored the Eau Claire church, twenty-seven Christian leaders/workers were called from the church. They resigned from that church in 1943 and for two years served as conference evangelists. At age forty-nine Coral returned to teaching so they could plant more churches. They accepted the work at Stevens Point, and from this place they worked to plant other churches nearby for the next six years. Stevens Point was organized March 22, 1951.

Coral was involved in conference work also. She served as the conference superintendent of the Young Missionary Workers Band (now Wesleyan Kids for Missions) from 1939 to 1953. She was a member of the itineracy and elders orders committee (now district board of ministerial development) for ten years.[72]

Their son, Orval, planted the Skyline Wesleyan Methodist Church in California. Claton, another son, was also pastoring in California. In 1953 they transferred their ministerial membership to the California Conference and served as pastors of the Bostonia work for about two years. In 1955 Charles was elected president of the conference, and they resigned to give full-time service to the conference work. He served for one year. In 1956 Coral and Charles became the pastors at San Gabriel until her death November 4, 1961.[73]

─────

Zelda Clevenger

The *Minutes of the Annual Assembly of the Pilgrim Holiness Church Indiana Conference,* 1933–36, listed Zelda (Mrs. Samuel) Clevenger as an ordained minister in 1933. In 1936 she was dropped from the roll of ordained ministers.

─────

Verna A. Clinefelter

The *Minutes* of the Allegheny Conference recorded Verna A. Clinefelter as assigned to "choose her own field" of service in 1933 and as a missionary in 1934. She was listed as retired from 1948 to 1966. No other service records could be found for her.[74]

Dorothy Dunbar Cretsinger

Dorothy Dunbar was born September 3, 1909, near Concordia, Kansas. She was the oldest of three children born into a Wesleyan Methodist parsonage family. Her mother died when Dorothy was ten years old. She attended high school and college at Miltonvale Wesleyan Academy and College, Miltonvale, Kansas (later merged into what became Oklahoma Wesleyan University, Bartlesville, Oklahoma). She worked as a dental assistant in Concordia, Kansas, and during this time felt God's call into the ministry. During the summers she did evangelistic work, both singing and preaching. Dorothy was ordained in 1937 by the Kansas Conference of the Wesleyan Methodist Church.

Dorothy married Rev. A. L. Crestsinger June 19, 1938, and they set up their first home in Guthrie Center, Iowa, where he was the pastor. Three children, Mary Esther Ashby, Lois Jean, and Jonathan, were born into their family. The children were coached to memorize Scripture verses, and a scripture was found to provide guidance for nearly every situation in life.[75]

After Dorothy was married, she moved her ministerial membership to the Iowa Conference. She assisted her husband in pastoring churches at Guthrie Center, Firth, Albaton, and Bennezette in that conference. In 1952 they transferred to the Dakota Conference.[76]

In the Dakota Conference Dorothy assisted her husband at the Loyalton, Rawlins, Terry, Johnson Corners, and Bushnell churches. Besides assisting her husband in these pastorates, she was often assigned the task of missionary evangelist.[77] She was elected as president of the conference Woman's Missionary Society in 1953 and served in that office for many years. She was also involved in the general Woman's Missionary Society and held the office of recording secretary from 1959 to 1966. From 1948 to 1959 she directed the prayer partner work through a monthly page in the *Wesleyan*

Missionary.[78] One of her former district superintendents reported that Dorothy had two emphases as a preacher: "Prayer—Missions, Prayer or Missions." Whenever she spoke she revealed her heart and love for world missions.

Nellie Cummins

The *Official Record of the Annual Assembly of the Virginia District of the Pilgrim Holiness Church* recorded Nellie Cummins as ordained in 1933. She served for a time in a mission at Pocahontas, Shacklefords, Virginia. From 1937 to 1944 she was listed as an evangelist.

Ione Driscal

Ione Driscal began her earthly walk April 20, 1906, in Grand Rapids, Michigan. Her mother, a devoted Christian, died just eighteen days after her birth. Through the influence of a stepmother, she attended a Wesleyan Methodist Sunday school. Even as a small child she was inclined to religious subjects and was impressed with missionary speakers when attending the Hastings, Michigan, camp meeting. She and her father were baptized on Easter Sunday, when she was thirteen, and they both became members of the Wesleyan Methodist Church that Sunday. When she was fifteen her interest in missions became centered on Africa.

Ione graduated from high school at age seventeen, and she chose Houghton College, Houghton, New York, for preparations for her educational and religious career. She was a good athlete, president of the college (youth level) Young Missionary Workers Band, and a regular attendant of both the prayer services and services at the local church. She graduated from Houghton at age twenty-one with a diploma in theology and an A. B. degree with history and religious education as her majors.

She taught in high schools in New York after her graduation with the understanding that she was to be released when the mission board was ready to send her to Africa. She filled her "hope chest" with articles suited for her coming work in Africa. She sailed for Africa in 1933.[79] She served as an educational missionary for a span of thirty-two years. Her valuable contribution to the educational development in Sierra Leone was recognized by Queen Elizabeth in 1957 when Dr. Driscal was honored by Queen Elizabeth as a member of the British Empire. She was one of two Wesleyan lady missionaries so honored for their service in Sierra Leone.

Ione taught and trained the future mothers of Africa to sew, cook, care for their families, and most of all to love Christ and study the Word of God. While she was employed to teach and although she would become the director of all the African educational work and be the principal of the only girls school in northern Sierra Leone, her deep interest in evangelizing the lost of Africa took her on extended treks through northeastern Sierra Leone. She visited, preached, and evangelized in towns and villages where no white woman had ever been.

She possessed a pleasing and sympathetic personality and was a favorite speaker of young people when she was home on furlough. During her furloughs she also tried to better equip herself for her life's calling. She earned a master's degree from Winona Lake School of Theology and did graduate work at the University of Michigan. She also taught at Houghton College during furloughs, was dean of women at Taylor University, Upland, Indiana and also dean of women at Houghton College.

Ione was ordained in 1937. From 1963 to 1965 she served as a missionary in Puerto Rico.[80] She was faithful to the work that God had called her to do and to which she had committed herself. Her earthly walk ended June 11, 1998.[81]

Wilhemina Endicott

Wilhemina Endicott was from Camden, New Jersey, and she was credited with her Bible school studies from Allentown, Pennsylvania in 1933 by the Middle Atlantic States Mission Conference of the Wesleyan Methodist Church. She became a licensed preacher in 1934 and a candidate for missionary work. In 1939 she began to work with the India Homeland Mission Society. She served in that capacity through 1943.

She was ordained in 1947 and was the supply pastor at Dover, Pennsylvania. Most of her ministerial work was in evangelism. She was on the reserve list of elders (ordained ministers) from 1964 to 1967.[82]

Lois Fairchild

Lois Fairchild was listed as ordained in 1933 and was on the roll of ordained ministers in the Kansas District of the Pilgrim Holiness Church from 1933 to 1937.[83]

Constance Fitch

Constance Fitch transferred to the Virginia District of the Pilgrim Holiness Church in 1933. She was on their roll in 1934.[84] The *Minutes of the Annual Assembly of the Pilgrim Holiness Church of the Pennsylvania and New Jersey District* listed her on their roll from 1935 to 1948. *The Conference Journal of the Pennsylvania and New Jersey District of the Pilgrim Holiness Church* listed her on their roll from 1949 to 1963. She was released to work outside the denomination in 1962. Her husband, Willard R. Fitch, had pastored churches in the Pennsylvania and New Jersey District and had served under the Oriental Missionary Society. No record was found of her activities.

Georgia Tomey Goodman

Georgia Tomey Goodman (often listed as Mrs. R. L. Goodman) was listed on the records of the Kentucky District of the Pilgrim Holiness Church, 1943–62, as an ordained minister. She served the Bowling Green church 1944–46, Ashland 1946–47, and Paris 1947–49. She then was listed by the Florida District in 1964 and by the East Michigan District (as a pastor) 1965–66.

Georgia and Rupert Goodman celebrated their fiftieth wedding anniversary August 1, 1993. They were the parents of six children. Together they pastored churches in Kentucky,

Florida, Michigan, and Indiana. Mrs. Goodman tells her ministerial story:

My roots are in the Methodist Episcopal Church. In our small town, Elnora, Indiana, people freely visited other churches, especially during revival meetings. In the spring of 1935, a woman evangelist, Cora White, held a six-week revival meeting at the Pilgrim Holiness Church. In the fifth week of that revival I was converted at the age of twelve. From that day, I have tried to walk with God. It was in August of 1941, at Frankfort camp meeting, that I quietly but consciously received the baptism of the Holy Spirit.

At age fifteen I joined the Pilgrim Holiness Church. The Reverends E. I. and Verna Faidley were the pastors. The Elnora and Epsom churches were on the same charge. Mrs. Faidley conducted and preached on alternate Sundays at these churches.

As was the custom in small churches, they immediately put me to work and conferred on me a local preacher's license, stating that the church sensed God had called me to preach. I served as evangelist in a number of churches in southern Indiana. Then I traveled for a year with an evangelist couple, leading the singing, singing duets, and conducting children's meetings. Those thirty-minute children's services were a regular part of most revivals in the 30's and 40's. I would preach at least once during the revival hour during those meetings.

I entered Frankfort Pilgrim College in 1940 and took the courses leading to ordination. I spent my weekends and vacations working in revivals and camp meetings.

On August 1, 1943, Rupert L. Goodman, a fellow graduate from Frankfort Bible College, and I were ordained to the ministry by Dr. R. G. Flexon in the morning. We were united in marriage in the afternoon by the Reverend L. S. Houston at the Maysville, Kentucky, camp. After our wedding, we sat through an extremely long missionary service.

After we were married I took my place as a helpmate doing whatever—teaching Sunday school classes, directing daily vacation Bible school, missionary president, playing the piano, conducting Wednesday night Bible studies, preaching when my husband was away in revivals or ill, calling, all the standard duties of pastor's wife, helping to raise six children, entertaining guests such as special workers for two to three weeks revivals two to three times a year. In between and during all these activities, I earned a B.S. and Master's degrees in education. I was always busy.

We pioneered [planted] a church in Paris, Kentucky, starting in an abandoned building across

from the railroad tracks. Those were eight good soul-winning years. Later we planted the Villas Church in Fort Myers. Donna Freed Tesh, an extremely gifted minister's wife in North Carolina, was the first convert.

Did we have a certain style of dress? We certainly did. Sleeves were down to the wrists, skirt was nine inches from the floor, a modest neckline, a double panel petticoat, no jewelry or makeup.

Most of my sermons were evangelistic when I was a girl evangelist. After I became a pastor's wife, my sermons were usually "practical/devotional."

Most of our means of transportation in the early years was by Greyhound bus and occasionally by train. On our first pastorate we had no car, so for two years we did our moving about by walking until we purchased our first car, a relic of pre-World War II. Later we had nice cars. Our living quarters ranged from two rooms partitioned off a storefront mission to lovely modern homes. We learned that the type and kind of dwelling had little to do with our happiness but had a lot to do with our conveniences.

Retired [this was written in April 1998], I still teach a Sunday school class, and for eleven years I have headed up L.I.F.T., our local church's women's ministry. I am grateful for any part we had in those who found salvation and growth during our ministry. And I am exceedingly thankful that all our children are Christians and are involved in their local churches.

Mrs. H. S. Harrold

Mrs. H. S. Harrold was ordained in 1933. She served under the Ohio District of the Pilgrim Holiness Church from 1933 to 1946.[85]

Della J. Turner Hotle

Della J. Turner was born October 7, 1873, at College Springs, Iowa. At the age of seventeen, while studying to be a schoolteacher, she was converted. She was sanctified in 1893 and preached her first sermon the same year at Mt. Pleasant, Iowa. She was ordained to the ministry July 25, 1895.[86] She was married September 5, 1895, to Frank C. Hotle. The ceremony was performed by Rev. Thomas H. Nelson, superintendent of the Missionary Bands of the World.

Six children were born into their family. One son, Elvin, became a minister.

A great-grandson, Dr. Marlin Hotle, superintendent of the Tennessee District of The Wesleyan Church, wrote the following tribute to Della Hotle in a letter to the author, dated January 24, 1999.

My great-grandmother was also a lady preacher. In fact, my great-grandfather, Frank C. Hotle, was sanctified under her ministry. They are listed in the book *Conscience and Commitment* as the cofounders of our work in India. Frank was raised in the Methodist Episcopal Church and was attending the Methodist College at Mt. Pleasant, Iowa. While there, a group of young women from the Pentecost Bands came to Mt. Pleasant and conducted a series of meetings in a great hall on the square. This was in the fall of 1892. My great-grandfather, thinking the women were from the Salvation Army, attended out of curiosity. He was convicted by both their spirit and ministry and sought holiness of heart during the meeting. Soon he started traveling in evangelism with two of these young women. One of them, Della J. Turner,

was the one preaching when he was sanctified and would later become his wife and partner in ministry for nearly 50 years. They were married while he was pastoring the Pentecost Bands headquarters church, Salem Park in Indianapolis, and almost immediately left for India. My grandfather was born during the eight years they served there. I have heard it said that while Frank was a gifted speaker, in many ways Della could do a better job moving an audience than he.

Della and Frank Hotle went to India in the fall of 1897. In a few years they had orphanages caring for three hundred children, four mission stations, a brick chapel and schools, all free from debt, and many converts.[87] They had not planned to do orphanage work, but the great famine hit India in 1897. Hundreds of starving children needed food and shelter. Della spent seven years in preaching the gospel and working among the people of the land. She was especially active in caring for the famine-stricken children. Frank was instrumental in raising thousands of dollars for famine relief work in India by making pictures of the starving and dying, which were sent to other parts of the world.[88] While they were home on furlough, Della spent a year in giving lectures and raising money for relief work also. They returned to India but were forced to come home because of Frank's health. They had spent eight years in India.

After they returned home, Frank established a missionary training home in Terre Haute, Indiana, and also edited a missionary paper there. They united with the Pilgrim Holiness Church in 1933 and served for some time as pastors at Sheridan and in Indianapolis, Prospect Street Church.

From the time of Della's conversion, she was actively engaged in the work of the Lord as long as her strength permitted. On the Sunday before her death she realized that her earthly journey was about completed, and she made her own funeral arrangements. Afterward she rejoiced and praised God almost continually until she lapsed into a coma. She died July 2, 1953.

Leah Lucille Parker Isgrigg

Leah Parker was born May 10, 1908, on a farm south of Decatur, Indiana. At the age of two and a half, neighbors found her and her father hanging with ropes around their necks in the barn and apparently dead. They were able to revive Leah but not her father. When she was about fourteen, her mother remarried. Soon after this, Leah gave her heart to the Lord in a little country Quaker Church. A couple in the church, Frank and Mary Martz, who had no children, took her into their home, clothed and cared for her, and provided for her training at God's Bible School in Cincinnati, Ohio. While she was in Bible school, God called her to preach His Word. Ernest Batman, former superintendent of the Indiana Central District of The Wesleyan Church, remarked that Leah had a passion for preaching and was an excellent communicator of the Word. Her daughter, Ruth Smith, said her eleven years in evangelism (mostly while pastoring also) was given to preaching. Herein lay her strength and talent in God's work.

Also while at God's Bible School she became acquainted with Paul N. Isgrigg. They were not permitted to date but began corresponding by mail on June 17, 1931. They were engaged on October 19, 1932. They were married on September 2, 1933. Leah began her ministerial work by pastoring a Methodist Church near Paris, Kentucky, after her graduation from God's Bible School on May 19, 1928. After her marriage to Paul Isgrigg, she co-pastored with him. Paul had begun his ministerial work as a song evangelist and children's worker in the Kansas District of the Pilgrim Holiness Church. They were the pastors of Fowler, Hutchinson, Osawatomie, Fredonia, and Goodland in that district until 1945. At that time they transferred to the Indiana District and pastored the Fairmount, Huntington, Brown's Chapel, Walkerton, Crawfordsville, Frankfort, Indianapolis, and La Porte churches in that district. They served twelve years in Kansas and thirty-two years in Indiana. Leah was ordained, according to the Kansas *Minutes,* in 1935.

During their ministry some seventy-eight persons were called into full-time Christian work under their influence. Their daughter, Ruth, said it was impossible to know which one had influenced these persons to follow the Lord's leadings since they worked very closely as a team. They both did visitation every day in homes, hospitals, and businesses. Paul was gifted with singing and worked with children in the evening services on Sunday. He believed that as soon as a child was converted, Leah and he should plant the seed of doing God's will in their lives then and in the future.

Paul insisted that Leah preach half of the time when they were pastoring. However, since Paul had some major illnesses, including tuberculosis, skin cancer, and throat cancer, Leah actually preached much more than Paul. Leah was also a woman of great faith in the Great Physician. Paul was healed of each of these diseases, in part at least, by Leah's faith and believing for his complete healing each time.

Leah and Paul became the parents of four daughters, Irene Lucille, born just over a year after their marriage, followed by Helen Bernice and Ruth Evangeline, each a year and a half apart. Six years after Ruth's birth, Rachel Pauline

arrived. Often when Paul and Leah were pastoring different churches, Paul would take two of the girls with him, and Leah would take the other two. No matter which parent they were with, the girls always had to sit on the front pew, where they could be carefully controlled.

Leah played the piano only if there was no other pianist present. She taught Sunday school classes when teachers were absent. She enjoyed playing a part in jovial skits that taught a moral lesson, especially at ministerial retreats. One skit she pulled off quite unintentionally during a revival in the Fairmount, Indiana, Pilgrim Holiness Church. Ruth was eight years old at the time. She saw her mother had an apron dangling below her dress. So during prayer, Ruth sent a note to her mother. Leah was praying out loud but didn't miss a word praying while she read the note. She didn't stop praying until she had pulled the apron from under her dress and tucked it inside the podium. Leah was great at making up songs as she worked around the house. The girls loved her rhyming choruses and learned to do the same themselves.

Ruth asked her sisters, Irene and Rachel, what they remembered most about their mother. They both stated they remembered her joy and appreciation of life and that she was one hundred percent dedicated to the work of God. Ruth then asked if they ever felt neglected because of Leah's joy and dedication to God's work. Their reply was, "Oh, no. We felt like we were in God's work with her and Dad, who loved the Lord so much." Rachel, the youngest, said "In Mother I saw Christ in word and example. She lived a life of complete dedication to God, His work, and her family with much sacrifice and self-denial, love, forgiveness, and a faith that was strong and that endured." As Rachel later declared,

Mother taught us that we did not have problems, only challenges. Happiness is not in what we have or can do but in a relationship with the giver of life and true happiness: Jesus Christ. He leads us into all truth and allows us to be His hands and feet as we journey with Him. And lastly, we are to love everyone and not be satisfied until everyone knows His love.

Leah Isgrigg completed her earthly life's work April 13, 1979.[89]

Grace Goodwin Kauffman

Grace Goodwin left her home in the Dakotas to teach school in Hillsboro, Wisconsin. Here she met and married Jess Kauffman, who shared ownership in a local hardware store. The Kauffmans lived in Hillsboro for many years.

A tent meeting was held in Hillsboro in the summer of 1933, and several interested families met in the Kauffman home for Sunday school and preaching services. Later that same summer a group of sixteen members organized a Wesleyan Methodist church. Grace Kauffman was appointed the pastor by the conference president, Rev. J. B. Clawson. A building was purchased, and the church became known as the Wesleyan Methodist Chapel. These were the days of the Great Depression, and everyone was touched by lack of material needs. Yet the church was rewarded with rich blessings from the Lord.

During her pastorate the church made exceptional progress and contributed to the spiritual life of the community. Grace was also a leader in the Wisconsin Conference as well as a civic leader in the Hillsboro community.

On March 16, 1947, Grace wrote a letter of resignation in favor of calling a full-time paid pastor. She had served the church from its beginning, for fourteen years, and had received no salary.

The Kauffmans moved to Nevada shortly after her retirement and later moved to Montana. Mrs. Kauffman was now in her nineties, but she continued conducting Bible studies. She died in a nursing home at the age of one hundred two. She made a great spiritual impact on many wherever she lived.[90]

Grace was active in the Wisconsin Conference. She served on the committee on itineracy and elders orders (now district board of ministerial development) for ten years. She also served on the Sunday school board, judiciary, camp meeting board, pension board, and pastoral relations committee. She was vice president of the Woman's Home and Foreign Missionary Society for seven years. After she resigned from the Hillsboro church, she worked as a missionary under the mission board for five years. She was granted a

letter of transfer to the Dakota Conference in 1955. She was assigned to missionary work in this conference for a number of years and was the pastor of the Missoula work in Montana for several years.

Grace Kauffman was ordained in 1937.[91]

Louise M. Stroh Kerr

Louise M. Stroh was born May 5, 1897, in Wales, New York. She grew up in New York state and attended a Catholic church during childhood, although she was never confirmed. After her mother's death, she made her own way as a live-in cook and housekeeper. After her conversion she joined the Wesleyan Methodist Church.

She married Neil Clark Kerr December 23, 1916, in Holland, New York. Neil was a layperson who after his conversion became a spirited gospel singer and entered song evangelism work. He died October 10, 1953. The *Minutes* of the North Georgia Conference recorded at the time of his death that he was a good man, full of the Holy Spirit and faith. He was a loyal soldier of Christ.

Louise Kerr began her ministerial work in the Lockport Conference of the Wesleyan Methodist Church in 1933. She was a faithful missions worker at Wales Center, New York. This work may also have been called Wales Hollow. She ministered there until January 14, 1944. She was ordained in 1943. She was granted a letter of transfer to the North Georgia Conference in 1945.[92]

She began her work in the North Georgia Conference by pastoring the Welcome church near Elberton, Georgia. During her three years at Welcome, she directed the building of the parsonage there. She became the pastor of the Wesley Chapel Wesleyan Methodist Church in 1947. She followed Ella Roof Graham, who had been the pastor at Wesley Chapel for forty-three years. Louise Kerr was the pastor for seven years and was followed there by Ella Cawthon and her husband, who also pastored that church for another seven years. Louise also directed the building of a parsonage at Wesley Chapel.

She served as chaplain and matron at Hephzibah Children's Home for one year. In

March 1955 she was appointed as the pastor of the Macon, Georgia, Wesleyan Methodist Church. Other pastorates in Georgia included Greensboro and Union Point. She eventually retired and moved to Springfield, Georgia.

Louise was active in the conference work and served on the committee on itineracy and orders (now district board of ministerial development) for nine years, committees on vacancies, credentials, finance, Sunday school board, pension plan, missionary board, and was secretary of child evangelism.[93]

She was an able speaker and preached true holiness, guiding and pleading for all to live a holy life. She was a very devoted Bible scholar. She conducted several vacation Bible schools, which were very successful in reaching many children for the Lord. She had a very generous and giving spirit.

She was the mother of one daughter, Rose Mary Albrecht. Louise Kerr died September 22, 1996.[94]

Minnie Knecht

Minnie Knecht was ordained in 1930. However, no records were found on her or her work until 1933. Her entire life was devoted to the work of missions. She spent many years working among the mountain people of Kentucky. The *Minutes* did not always state where she was serving in mission work, but the record shows she worked in mountain missions in Kentucky from 1935 to 1942 and in 1951.

She was the pastor at Missions, South Dakota, 1943–46 and worked at Brainerd Indian School for a number of years also. She was listed as retired in 1964 and was so listed at the time of the 1968 merger.[95]

Georgia M. Markey

Georgia M. Markey served the Wesleyan Methodist Church in the Allegheny Conference, in Pennsylvania. She was stationed with her husband, Joseph B. Markey, at the Pine Grove charge in 1933. She served with him at Pittsfield, Erie; the Sandy Lake, Oak Grove, and Zion charge; Zion, East Conneaut, and Alida Smith Memorial.[96]

Etta J. Mitchell

Etta Jones Mitchell began her journey on earth December 23, 1907. Her earthly journey ended June 11, 1994. She was the daughter of Willard and Bessie Jones Mitchell. She, like her mother, was converted as a child and felt God's call to be a minister of the gospel. She was active in her home church in Dover, Delaware (one her mother and father had planted). According to the *Minutes* she was ordained in 1944, but other records indicate the date as 1937.

She began her ministerial work with Rev. Etta Mae Clough in 1933. First Church in Baltimore started a mission in the slum area. Miss Clough had been pastoring First Church. She continued as the pastor there but also served as pastor of the mission. Etta Mitchell assisted her in the work there.

When several persons were traveling from their homes in the Brooklyn and Glen Burnie area, they began to ask for a church closer to their homes. Etta Clough and Etta Mitchell were the planters of another church. Miss Clough started prayer meetings, and the group met in three or four different locations until they were able to purchase property in Glen Burnie. Etta Clough and Etta Mitchell were co-pastors at this church for many years.[97]

Rev. Etta J. Mitchell (l.) with her mother, Bessie Mitchell

Together these women pastored in Wachaprague, Cape Charles and Exmore, Virginia, and the mission in Baltimore. Etta Mitchell also co-pastored with her mother at the Girdletree, Maryland, and Cape Charles, Virginia, churches.

When failing health caused her retirement from the ministry, she continued to work as a licensed practical nurse. Failing eyesight curtailed her activities and eventually led to blindness. She continued her love for and interest in the activities of the Church on the local, district and general levels. Her closing days were lived in Centreville, Maryland.[98]

Ronald Kelley, general secretary of The Wesleyan Church, reported that he did not remember much about Etta Mitchell except that she was a woman of prayer. "When she was having one of her prayer meetings at camp, in her cottage, I either out of fear or respect would walk out of my way so as not to create any disturbance."

Florence Clark Northrup

Florence Clark was saved as a child and felt called to Christian service. She was licensed to preach in 1933 by the Rochester Conference (now Central New York District) of the Wesleyan Methodist Church. In 1933 she served as the assistant pastor of the Boylston Church and later became the pastor. She was ordained in 1935. When the president of the conference, John D. Wilcox, gave his report in 1934, he stated, "We wish to acknowledge and appreciate the splendid work of Miss Florence Clark in the building up of the Boylston church."

After her ordination, she served for nine years on the committee on itineracy and elders orders (now district board of ministerial development). She taught classes on the course of studies, which included the classes on perfect love, homiletics, ethics, "A Plain Account of Christian Perfection," and "How to Conduct a Sunday School."

She was the pastor of West Varick and Shady Grove churches in the Rochester Conference. In June 1946 she was granted a letter of transfer to the Champlain Conference (now Eastern New York-New England District) and accepted the work on the Hoganbugh Indian Reservation, where she ministered to the St. Regis Indians. She worked with the Indians for two years.[99]

Arthur O. Northrup Sr. accepted the pastorate of his home church in Morley, New York, in

1932. After the death of his first wife, he married Florence Clark, and they pastored the Morley and later the Cobleskill church. They were pastors at Cobleskill for six years. Florence and Arthur also pastored two community churches for a few years. Arthur died in 1968.[100]

Florence taught English and Bible literature in the Middlesburgh Central School for nineteen years. She died March 5, 1978.[101]

Sadie Parker

No conference journal minutes were found for Sadie Parker. However, when the North Carolina West District of The Wesleyan Church celebrated its centennial, she was listed as the pastor of the McAdenville Church in 1929–33, Hickory and Sandy Ridge from 1933 to 1935, and Victory Chapel from 1936 to 1938.[102]

Mrs. Sallie Parker

Sallie Parker was an ordained minister serving as an evangelist in 1936 in the North Carolina Conference of the Wesleyan Methodist Church. In 1939 she withdrew and surrendered her ministerial credentials because she was no longer a member of a local Wesleyan Methodist Church.

On July 22, 1941, Sallie Parker was given a local preacher's license and was appointed the pastor of the Harriman Church in the Tennessee Conference of the Wesleyan Methodist Church. The next year (1942) "her ministerial credentials were accepted and she was restored to the proper place and standing." In 1944 she was again appointed the pastor at Harriman. In 1946 she was granted a letter of transfer to the North Carolina Conference, but no service record was found for her at that time.[103]

Edna Z. Patterson

Edna Z. Patterson assisted her husband, C. D., in pastoring the Greenville, Barberton, Brownsville, and Newcastle churches in the

Allegheny Conference of the Wesleyan Methodist Church. Her husband died while they were pastoring the Newcastle church, and she continued on for another year or two at the church. She was then the pastor of the West Middlesex church. She also spent some years as an evangelist in the conference. She was listed as retired in 1955–66.[104]

Mrs. Effie Ross

Effie Ross was in the second year of her ministerial study course work in 1933. She was engaged in evangelistic work in the Oklahoma Conference of the Wesleyan Methodist Church. Her first church in pastoring was the Carevile church in 1935. She pastored the New Hope, Etna, and the Carevile church (second time). She spent many years as an evangelist. On August 20, 1948, she was appointed the supply pastor of the Methodist Church in Erie, Kansas. She was ordained in 1952. From 1962 to 1968 she was without an appointment.[105]

Myrtle M. Ammons Sension

Myrtle Sension was first received to begin her ministerial studies in 1933 in the Middle Atlantic States Mission Conference of the Wesleyan Methodist Church. However, she withdrew from the conference the next year.[106]

The records are missing for a number of years. She was married to Mr. Ammons (first name unknown), and they were the parents of four children: Lester, Frank, Birdie, and Josephine. During the "lost years" she was married to Harry J. Sension and was ordained. They were involved in home missionary and orphanage work in the mountains of Kentucky. They were the mission workers at Wheelrim, Kentucky for a number of years. She was also a pastor on Cayman Island for a time. Myrtle taught school under the Missionary Bands and the Household of Faith at Intercession City, Florida.[107]

The *Minutes of the California Conference of the Wesleyan Methodist Church* recorded the Sensions' transfer from another denomination to that conference in 1950, and Myrtle was appointed to conference evangelism. In 1953 they transferred to the Kentucky Conference. They were stationed at Wheelrim from 1954 to 1958. She was on the list of retired ordained ministers in that conference in 1961. Harry J. died December 3, 1966. Myrtle was still on the retired list at the time of the 1968 merger.[108]

Ina Spark

Ina Spark began her ministerial work in the Kansas Conference of the Wesleyan Methodist Church in 1933. In 1934 she began her theological course at Miltonvale College, Miltonvale, Kansas (later merged into what became Oklahoma Wesleyan University, Bartlesville, Oklahoma), and continued her work at Marion College, Marion, Indiana (later Indiana Wesleyan University). She became the dean of women at Marion College in September 1937 and worked there through 1941. She was ordained in 1939.

She worked at the YMCA in Anderson, Indiana, as a secretary for two years. In 1946–47 she was employed as a secretary at the Holiness Association office in Chicago. From 1948 to 1949 she worked at the Topeka, Kansas, YMCA office as a secretary.

In 1952 she withdrew from the church.[109]

Pansy May Ralston Stalcup

Pansy May Ralston was married on May 11, 1910, to R. C. Stalcup. They were the parents of twin boys and a daughter.[110]

Pansy May Stalcup was ordained in 1930. She served under the Kansas District of the Pilgrim Holiness Church from 1933 to 1947. She was the pastor of the Lincoln church in that district from 1943 to 1945. She lived in Colorado Springs from 1945 to 1947.[111] The next records for her were found in the California District of the Pilgrim Holiness Church from 1960 to 1967.

Esther Steelhead

The *Minutes* of the Pilgrim Holiness Church in the California District recorded that Esther Steelhead was assigned work in that district from 1933 to 1968.[112]

Florence Stewart

Often a woman minister would have been serving the Lord and pastoring churches and no record could be found of her labors. Such was the case of Florence Stewart. In her obituary found in *The Wesleyan Advocate,* December 2, 1968, she was reported to have helped to organize the Brandon, Nebraska, Community Church in 1923. She was married to James A. Stewart, and they were the parents of eight children, six of whom were girls.

James Stewart died in 1944, and following his death Florence pastored the Rocky Ford and Kiowa, Colorado, Pilgrim Holiness churches; the Lewellen and Tecumseh, Nebraska, churches; and the Fall River church in Kansas.

That record does not reveal the influence she has made on the world. Orai and Linda Lehman wrote about her influence on the Cheney family while she was the pastor at Lewellen. Sister Stewart, as she was called by her people, came to pastor that church in 1948. She came to the Cheney home, a farmhouse outside Lewellen, and invited the family to church. The Cheneys had no transportation. Mrs. Stewart came and got them in her car until other transport was obtained. She had room for just a few, and there were eight children in the Cheney family. When the Cheneys were able to purchase a truck, the entire family could attend church. The children rode in the back of the truck. Mrs. Stewart's eagerness to get the children in church was the beginning of their family's church attendance. After they got the truck, the family hardly ever missed a Sunday, and one by one the children were converted. At least three of the children, Wilma Wissbroecker, Linda Lehman, and Robert Cheney, became missionaries and have taken the gospel to foreign lands. When Florence died, she asked that her books be given to Robert Cheney for his library.[113]

Florence Stewart was ordained in 1950. She retired from pastoral work in 1967 and died August 31, 1968.

Ella Grace Cowles Story

Grace Cowles was born on May 27, 1912, while her parents were missionaries in China. In the fall of 1923 she discovered America when her parents returned to the United States. She spent three years in Bible school and graduated in 1933 from the Training School for Christian Workers, a school that is now known as Azusa Pacific University, Azusa, California.

Grace tells her own story, with a few editorial changes.

I graduated from Training School the first part of June, and on June 15, Vernon Gordon Story and I were united in marriage. June 15 of this year [1998] we will celebrate sixty-five years of marriage, and we are still lovers!

June 21, 1933, we filled every cranny of our small '29 Ford roadster with all our earthly possessions and headed for North Carolina. We were on the way to rescue the "perishing" for Jesus, but we knew so little about how to do that big job. The third Sunday of our marriage, Vernon was preaching in Winston-Salem, and I was holding the fort in Elkin.

Elkin was a pioneer work. Our first service was held in a lady's backyard. We served there only during the summer months, but when we left they were worshiping in a store building. Now they have a beautiful church. We are listed in the Elkin's church history as the first pastors.

From 1934 to 1938 we pastored in Erlanger, now known as Lexington, in the North Carolina District. Erlanger was a mill village, and the good people there filled the small stone building to worship the Lord. One tent meeting was held during this time. We moved our people to worship next to a store building and before we left into a real church building.

During those early years in our ministry I often shared the pulpit with Vernon. After the children began to come, I drew back a bit and did more "preaching" at home and working in other areas in the church. In the fall of 1934 when our firstborn, Aletha, was but a few weeks old, Vernon and I were ordained by Dr. Walter Surbrook. Aletha did not attend the ordination service; she had the whooping cough.

I worked to support myself to get through Bible School. That stress with getting married, starting on our "missionary" journey, plus working so hard to accomplish this great task with so little knowledge of knowing how to do the work contributed to a break in my physical and emotional state. This led us to feel we should take a leave of absence. We stayed with Vernon's folk in central California until our second daughter, Becky, was born in February 1939.

By the time Becky arrived, we were refreshed and ready to pastor the small Pilgrim Holiness Church in San Diego, California. We lived in a tiny one-bedroom apartment in the rear of the church. San Diego was an important military establishment. Our home was a home away from home for many young men. Then came Pearl Harbor, and wives and family members came to visit their "boys." I don't know how we found places for them, but they came and went and we did our best to minister to them during this time. Much later, while pastoring in Colorado Springs, we met a mother who told us that Vernon was her son's last pastor; our home was his last home on earth. Our family grew by the addition of two boys during this time.

During this pastorate a lady came to visit me one day. I watched as she carefully placed a pie on the table. It had one piece missing. I kept repeating to myself that I must not forget to thank her for the pie when she leaves. When she was getting ready to leave I thanked her for the pie. She told me she was not leaving the pie for me. It was going to another place!

We were the pastors of an interdenominational church in El Monte, California, after we left San Diego. We moved into an unfinished parsonage. Vernon and I slept in a draped-off part of the living room while the children and Father Story had the two bedrooms. Father Story came to live with us after Mother Story's death. Vernon was able to finish the rooms, and we had a good, busy time for the few years we were there before we accepted the call to the Salem, Oregon, Pilgrim Holiness Church in the Northwest. We knew before we went there that the church was split into bits and pieces, but we felt we would do what we could to build something out of the troubled church for the Kingdom.

Our fifth child, Carolyn, was five weeks old when we headed for Oregon. Father Story was with us also. He lent us money to buy a house, for there was no church or parsonage. We worshiped for a while with the few who had "stayed by the stuff" in a small store building with a very small apartment in the rear until we could find a place to move into. The living quarters were inconvenient. Father Story had to turn the radio up very loud so he could hear! Cooking on a wood stove in the tiny kitchen in the summer was another story! But we were rewarded many times over by God and His people.

One dear friend said she was unchurched until we came to her home and asked her to attend Sunday school. She became a pastor's wife. Vernon and the men of the church built a nice church building. We lived in our own "dream home" for nearly twelve years. That home even had a guest bedroom where we entertained church officials.

I almost always taught a Sunday school class even if it meant keeping a baby in a high chair by my side during that time. Church nurseries had not come into vogue. Our last child, Dorothy, was born while we were in Salem. I often set her in a cardboard carton with things to play with to keep her quiet in the back of the church, while I listened and watched the other children sitting up front.

After twelve years in Salem, it was time to move on to Vancouver, Washington. It was a difficult move to make. We left a large house to housing facilities in the back of an unfinished church. It was a one-bedroom apartment. Three of our children were gone from home, but three were with us, making a total of five persons to fit into that apartment. Our son, Ken, slept in a classroom, and the girls had bunk beds on the back porch. Vernon and I had the one bedroom.

Vernon and I enjoyed singing together while he played his guitar. I often led the singing. During one evening service in Vancouver I asked the people to call out a favorite song and we would sing that song. Two songs came up at the same time. One was from a woman, the other from a man. I chose the lady's first and intended to sing the man's next. The man was greatly displeased and upset. He rose and stalked out of the chapel. After the service I called his home and found I had created a very serious situation. I explained and made apologies, but his wife informed me that he probably would not allow her to give their tithe to church anymore. Well, this preacher's wife did some serious praying that night. The next morning, the man and his wife appeared at the parsonage. He was humbled by my reactions and apologies. He wanted what I had in my heart.

Vernon was able to finish the inside of the sanctuary at Vancouver, and then we felt the call of God to the Pilgrim Holiness Church in Portland, Oregon. We had pastored there for four years, and then a bombshell exploded. We were voted out! It shocked many people and the community. When the smoke cleared and the people discovered the rumors about us were untrue, the church wanted to vote again. We felt we could not accept the call unless the vote was unanimous for us. That vote resulted in one negative vote. That was our answer, and we moved to the Rocky Mountain District. Years later, the person who voted against us wrote and asked us to forgive her.

We pastored the Colorado Springs Knob Hill church in the Rocky Mountain District for fifteen years. The church began to grow, and the building was inadequate for the growing attendance. Vernon and the men remodeled and enlarged the church. Here we again ministered to many military persons. Many of them had been made to feel they were not wanted by some congregations since they were of the "transient population." We accepted them in our church and home whether they were black or white, and some even made their home with us.

For ten years I served as the director of our district missionary societies. That was a wonderful experience and a great responsibility. I was privileged to go on a tour with missionary ladies to Jamaica and Grand Cayman. Many memories of God's work among these island peoples are imprinted in my book of memories. I was also asked to serve on a merging committee to arrange for the merging of the Pilgrim Holiness and the Wesleyan Methodist missionary societies.

For a period of time I wrote a number of stories mostly of true incidents. Some were published. In 1973 Wesley Press printed an edition of a book I wrote titled *Footprints on the Sands of China*. For years I had worked in domestic house cleaning so I would have money to support missionary projects. Since the writing of the book, I have given the money from the selling of the book to missions.

When I was in my 50's the Lord healed me of a thyroid goiter. He lengthened my life so I could mother our six children. Aletha Story Sheets and husband, James, are retired pastors and were in evangelism for many years crisscrossing the country preaching and singing for the Lord. Becky Story

Lewis became a pastor's wife and also works for Sara Lee. Vernon Luther became the pastor of a church in San Pedro, California. Ken is a family counselor. Both sons have masters and doctorate degrees. Carolyn Story Fowler (Mrs. David) has been a pastor's wife and is gifted in working with children, as is Dorothy (Mrs. Randy) Dayton.

Vernon and I retired from active pastoring in 1977 and moved to a little town south of Colorado Springs. We had hoped to go to heaven from there, but our children soon believed we should move nearer to some of them—three out West and three in the East. In 1989 we moved to North Carolina. Vernon and I take turns teaching a Sunday school class. My mind races ahead of my body now since I move with the aid of a cane.

Later Vernon and Grace moved to a one-bedroom apartment at Wesleyan Arms in High Point, North Carolina. Vernon died September 27, 1999.[114]

Mary Tombs

The *Minutes of the Annual Assembly of the Pilgrim Holiness Church Indiana Conference* from 1933 to 1945 listed Mary Tombs as an ordained minister.

Elizabeth Traver

Elizabeth Traver's home church was Belle Fourche, South Dakota. She was licensed to preach in 1933 by the Wesleyan Methodist Church. Elizabeth served as an assistant pastor to her husband, Frank J. Traver, at Brentford, Northville, and Bushnell churches. She was ordained in 1941. She served one year, 1941, as the solo pastor at Bushnell. She also pastored the Sturgis, South Dakota, church. She apparently lived in Vale and pastored that church at the same time. Elizabeth was assigned to missionary work for a number of years also. She was on the retired list of ordained ministers from 1959 to the merger in 1968.[115]

Beulah Arnett

Beulah Arnett served as an ordained minister in the Indiana District of the Pilgrim Holiness

Church from 1934 to 1953.[116] She and her husband, J. L., transferred to the Northwest District of the Pilgrim Holiness Church in 1954 and were the pastors of the Tacoma, Washington, Pilgrim Holiness Church until 1960.[117]

Wilma Bakke Parker

Wilma Bakke was first licensed to preach in 1934. She was from the Rice Lake, Wisconsin, area.

Norma L. Stuve, daughter of the president of the Wisconsin Conference of the Wesleyan Methodist Church, J. B. Clawson, wrote the following facts about Wilma.

> During the time when the Reverend Estelle Lienard was pastoring the Rice Lake Wesleyan Church, four members of the Bakke family joined the church. As they became involved in the work of the church, Wilma and her brother, Charles, became a musical team. Their gifts were a great blessing and added much to the services. They joined the Lienards in holding Sunday afternoon services in Spooner until 1936. At that time the Spooner church was organized.

> In 1938 this brother-sister team went to fill in at the Mt. Pisgah and Oak Ridge churches. Plans had been made for Wilma to be ordained, but while staying in the home of one of her parishioners, she came down with the mumps and was not able to go to the church. Even so, plans were carried out, and she was ordained in 1942 by the conference president, J. B. Clawson.

> Charles returned to his work in Rice Lake after several months, but Wilma continued as the pastor for four more years. She was assigned to the category of missionary evangelism work for the next nine years. In 1956 she was given a letter of standing.

> Wilma had a winsome personality and a wonderful sense of humor. She was loved by all. She returned to Rice Lake and was active in her home church for a number of years. Later she married Norman Parker from Rice Lake and they moved to Colorado and later to California. Wilma died in 1996.[118]

Mary A. Bowman

Mary A. Bowman was a conference preacher in the Wesleyan Methodist Church, Indiana Conference, from 1932 to 1934. She began pastoring in 1934 at the Deming, Indiana, church. She was the pastor there through 1937. She was assigned to conference evangelism from 1938 to 1943 and was ordained in 1940. In 1941 she was granted permission to pastor a church in another denomination. In 1945 she joined another denomination and was dropped from the conference roll of ordained ministers.[119]

May Cornfield

Many women preachers were under appointment in the Ontario District of the Pilgrim Holiness Church. Few were ordained. Often these women were assigned to one or more preaching points. That meant they traveled from one preaching point to another to perform their duties. May Cornfield and Bertha Short were assigned as pastors at Lion's Head in 1934. Bertha also served at Farwich during this time. May Cornfield assisted Brother A. Jackson in 1935.[120]

May served with R. Gordon at Lion's Head in 1939. Myrtle Watson and May were the pastors at Lion's Head from 1940 to 1945. May Cornfield was ordained in 1940. In 1944 Dyer's Bay was added to their assignment but was removed the next year. May was under district appointment until 1952. She later became a deaconess.[121]

Nina V. Baggs
Edwards Downing

Nina V. Baggs was born April 4, 1895, and died April 27, 1990. She married Jefferson Eli Edwards in 1913. To this union were born Herbert Edwards, Gertrude (Norman N.) Bonner, Madge S. (Daniel R.) Bursch, and Kathryn Martin. Jefferson Edwards died in 1924. In 1936 Nina married Harrison Downing in Mitchell,

South Dakota. She became the stepmother of Elsie (Herman) Nettleton.

Nina was ordained by the Hephzibah Faith Missionary Association in 1936. She ministered under the Pilgrim Holiness Church and later The Wesleyan Church for many years. She pastored churches in Colorado, Nebraska, Iowa, Oklahoma, and Texas before she retired. She was an able minister of the gospel and a woman of prayer. Harrison Downing died in 1981.[122]

Nina was called to preach and she conducted revival meetings in South Dakota, Iowa, and Nebraska. While the children were young, around 1925, and after the death of Jefferson Edwards, Myrtle Downing came to live with them and cared for the children while Nina was gone in meetings.

After Nina's marriage to Harrison Downing, they moved to Glenwood, Iowa, to pastor the church there until 1940. At that time they moved to Gavilan, New Mexico. They served in the Oklahoma/Texas District of the Pilgrim Holiness Church from 1950 to 1952 and in the North Central District from 1952 to 1958. Together they also pastored in the Texas District from 1959 to 1967.[123]

Emma M. Garman

On the flyleaf of Emma Garman's Bible were found these words:

Born the first time November 10, 1880
Converted January 2, 1895
Sanctified August 12, 1906
Divinely healed September 14, 1908
Baptized September 26, 1908
Received my call by God to Christian work July 1908.

She apparently worked under the Pentecostal Rescue Mission in New York as a slum worker in her early days of ministry. She was under appointment according to the *Minutes of the Annual Assembly of the Pilgrim Holiness Church of Pennsylvania and New Jersey* in that district from 1934 to 1937. During the 1937 year she was received by and worked in the Kentucky District of the Pilgrim Holiness Church from 1937 to 1946. During those years she worked in the Pikesville Mission and the Tyrone Mission.[124] She

also worked with Rev. Johnson's mission, and for a period of time she operated a mission under her own supervision.

The first mention of her ordination was in 1934, and she was apparently ordained by the Pennsylvania and New Jersey District of the Pilgrim Holiness Church. She was an ardent and tireless worker. She was gifted with the ministry of helpfulness. Emma often filled pulpits for other ministers, and she supplied the pulpit in her home church. She was given to the task of home visitation. Her funeral was conducted October 6, 1959.[125]

Mary Good

The first recorded entry of Mary Good's ministry was found in 1934. She was listed as an ordained minister at that time. She continued in the Indiana District of the Pilgrim Holiness Church through 1950. At that time the conference was divided, and she became a member of the Northern Indiana District. She retired in 1962 and was still listed as an ordained minister at the time of the 1968 merger. She taught home economics and health in the high school at Frankfort Pilgrim College for a number of years.[126]

Erna E. Kenschaft

Erna E. and Irma O. Kenschaft (Weaver) were sisters who worked together in ministry. They also were assisted in ministry by Ruth (Betty) North for a number of years.

Erna was a conference preacher (licensed minister) from the Middle Atlantic States Mission Conference of the Wesleyan Methodist Church in 1934. That year the Kenschaft sisters conducted a young people's meeting before the regular service at conference, and Irma was introduced to the conference. Erna gave the devotions before conference. These women were involved in evangelistic work for a number of years. On March 21, 1938, Erna was granted a letter of transfer to the Rochester Conference (now Central New York District). She remained with that conference from 1938 to 1940 when she returned to the Middle Atlantic States Conference.

In 1941, Erna and Ruth (Betty) North were assigned as the pastors of the Shippensburg, Pennsylvania, Wesleyan Methodist church. In 1941 "a rising vote of appreciation was tendered to Shippensburg pastors for the faithful and sacrificial service they were rendering." In 1944 "by motion the assembly arose to its feet in appreciation of the untiring and faithful efforts of the pastors at Shippensburg." These women received the evening offering for their salary, which amounted to anywhere from fifty cents to six dollars a week. They used orange crates for chairs and an ironing board for a table. One man, a defrocked Nazarene preacher, tried to have the women thrown out of town. Banks refused to loan them money, and another person tried legally to put their storefront building up for sheriff's auction sale. The women found employment, which was extremely difficult to do in those days. One paycheck went to pay the church's bills, and they lived on the other. These jobs brought in twenty-five cents an hour and twelve dollars a week. But the church grew numerically and spiritually. One year the *Conference Journal* reported an old-fashioned revival and expressed appreciation for the "faithful and competent labors of Erna Kenschaft and Betty North."

Erna and Ruth (Betty) began pastoring at the Georgetown, Delaware, church in 1949 and continued as the pastors until 1959. This church situation was worse than at Shippensburg. The denominational officials had removed the former pastor because of a string of personal debts. It took them four or five years to establish a good relationship in the business world for themselves and the church. Again they had to obtain secular work outside the church in order to meet living conditions. Half of the people in this church did not believe or practice the holiness message. But they were able to bring into the church twenty-nine believers who did believe in holiness. The work they did with the children was successful. Many memorized the Word of God. They resigned at Georgetown and soon had a call to return to Shippensburg.

In 1960 Erna and Ruth (Betty) found themselves again as the pastors of the Shippensburg church, and they stayed until their resignation in 1966. This time around, the church paid them an adequate salary. In 1962 the Shippensburg church had a dedication service for a new church entrance and foyer, pews, carpeting, and piano.

Erna was ordained in 1961. She was employed as a Christian worker in the Friendly Acres Children's Home for a few months.[127]

The conference president, Rev. Bradley, asked these women to take another church. This one had been closed for six months because no one wanted to go there. Again these women heard the remark, "It will be only until we can get a man to take the church." That was said at Shippensburg, Georgetown, and now at Watts Township. After much prayer, they accepted the call. As Erna sat on the platform and saw the filth and cobwebs, she doubted that she could do it again. The words from Psalm 90:17 came to mind: "And let the beauty of the LORD our God be upon us: and establish thou the work of our hands upon us; yea, the work of our hands establish thou it" (KJV). That settled it. They would take on yet this, another difficult assignment.

Fifteen pickup truckloads of debris were hauled from the property. They again sought and found secular work to meet their financial needs. This work brought them fifty cents an hour. The year was 1967. They eventually became state employees. The old church was cleaned up, as well as the parsonage. Some of the men and women from the Shippensburg church came and helped with the cleaning and remodeling. They employed an exterminator to come out once a month to keep the livestock under control—snakes, four-legged critters of all sorts, and bugs. Eight years had passed, and then they became aware of more serious problems. They had seen an increase in interest and attendance. About thirty-five children were being ministered to in the Sunday school. But a bus from a charismatic group about ten miles away was coming each Sunday and getting their children, along with the children from the Methodist church, Church of the Brethren, and United Brethren. Ruth (Betty) developed a bleeding ulcer and had to resign her secular work. Erna also resigned hers. They stayed on at the church for a few more years trying to recover from the "sheep stealers."

Erna retired and resided in Brooksville, Florida. After her move to Florida, she did some interim pastoring at Lynn Haven, Florida. Erna was a gifted speaker and a great prayer warrior. After seven months of suffering physically, she declared, "Though He slay me, yet will I trust Him." Surely she must have heard her Lord say, "Well done, my child, come up higher," and on December 3, 1982, He took her home.[128]

Velma Knox

Velma Knox was a conference preacher (licensed minister) in 1934 under the Wesleyan Methodist Church. She was assigned to evangelism and remained in that category through 1939. She was ordained by the Kansas Conference in 1939.

She became the pastor of the Cedar church in 1940–41. At various times in her ministerial work she was assisted by Mildred Nantz. They were the pastors at the Eskridge and Arkansas City churches. She retired in 1966 and moved to Topeka, Kansas. She died January 1, 1984.[129]

Irene Tanier Lang

Irene Tanier Lang recorded her story. She was converted at the age of twelve. Soon after that, she began playing the piano for congregational singing at the newly organized Pilgrim Holiness church in her hometown, Liberty Center, Ohio. When she was sixteen, around 1930, she went to North Carolina to sing and play the piano in tent meetings with Eunice Fulp. Eunice's father was the evangelist.

She went to Detroit in 1934 and worked for a year in a relief mission. This was during the Depression. Rev. and Mrs. Beard had charge of the preaching services, and their son, Kenneth, and Irene were in charge of the music. After each evening service each person attending was given a loaf of bread and sometimes vegetables. Irene called in the homes of the people. She was moved by their poverty and longed to help them, but she also was very poor and had no money.

During the summer of 1935 she worked and saved a few dollars to help to get in Bible school.

That fall she enrolled at the Bible Holiness Seminary in Owosso, Michigan (later Owosso College, eventually merged into what became Indiana Wesleyan University, Marion, Indiana). She worked for her room and board. A lady paid for her piano lessons, and she took as many subjects as possible with her limited finances. Her mother did ironing for a lady, which took all day. She was paid one dollar. Her father paid the ten cents tithe so her mother could send her the entire dollar. This dollar paid for her school supplies and stamps. Irene graduated in 1937. She took more subjects by correspondence, and in 1944 she was ordained.

In the summer of 1937, Anna Sherman (later Kilwy) and Irene went to West Virginia to sing in tent meetings. One Sunday the evangelist and Anna and Irene were invited out for the noon meal. After they visited in the home for a long time the evangelist said they would have to get back to the church for the afternoon service. The women were really hungry. After the afternoon service, the daughter of the family brought them a *full* meal. The father was drunk and didn't tell his wife he had invited them to dinner. After he sobered up, he remembered.

Often their sleeping accommodations were not good. In one of those meetings, Anna was unable to sleep at night. The bedbugs were eating her up. The lady with whom they were staying sprayed them. Irene's mother unpacked her clothes in the woodshed when she came home from that meeting!

That fall, Irene's home church called them to be their pastors. Anna was to do the preaching, and Irene was to be in charge of the music. They lived with Irene's parents. The following year Anna married Rev. Willard Kilwy, and Irene was asked to become the preaching pastor. She struggled with that call, for she said it wasn't any easier for a woman to pastor in 1938 than it is today. But she yielded to God's will and began to pastor the Liberty Center church.

There were people coming from Grand Rapids, Ohio, to her church in Liberty Center. They asked her to hold prayer meetings in their home. These meetings grew, and in the summer of 1939 she conducted a tent meeting on the schoolhouse lawn in Grand Rapids with Melroy Ward as the evangelist and Daniel Woodward as the song evangelist. The Grand Rapids Pilgrim Holiness church was organized in the last meeting. They worshiped in the town hall for a while, but it wasn't heated well; so when cold weather came, they went back to worshiping in a home. Irene felt she needed help since she now was pastoring the Liberty Center and Grand Rapids churches. Clara (Sherman) Mayo helped her for one year.

Ray Richards, a member of the Liberty Center church, felt called to preach and held a successful revival in Liberty Center. He consented to help her with the churches. One Sunday he would be at Grand Rapids and she would preach at Liberty Center. The next Sunday they would exchange places. Ray was a carpenter by trade, and he and some of the men and women from the Grand Rapids church built a small cement block church in 1940. Richards and Irene worked together for five years. Then the district superintendent decided the churches should have separate pastors. Irene continued at Liberty Center another three years and Richards at Grand Rapids for five more years.

Roy Beltz, of the general home missionary department, sent Irene in 1948 to Massey, Ontario. Darlean (Zimmerman) Allgire, a convert of the tent meeting in Grand Rapids and a graduate of Owosso, became her assistant pastor. They also conducted Sunday afternoon services on the Ojibway Indian Reservation in a little log cabin. There were no seats for the Native Americans to sit on. Ray Richards came to hold a revival at Massey. Irene's father came with him. During the day, these men made seats for the Native Americans, and they put siding on the parsonage. Ray Richards preached each night.

Irene worked with the children, and Darlean worked with the youth. They didn't conduct services on the reservation in the winter because it was impossible to travel on the roads. She served the Massey church for two years.

The next two years she and Darlean pastored in the Durham, Ontario, church. They lived in an upstairs apartment over the cement block church. One time when they had company, Irene had no meat for the meal. They visited a family and their three children, and Darlean shot two pigeons. The mother cleaned the pigeons and told Irene how to cook them. They had the meat for their guest.

In 1952 she returned to pastor the Grand Rapids, Ohio, church. Eventually, the church grew to the point where the little building couldn't hold all the people. They had to build a church, but Irene felt she was not the person to do this. She resigned after pastoring the church a second time for another eleven years. That church currently has property worth $750,000.

The district sent her to Leipsic, Ohio. The church was growing, but in her fourth year (1969) Irene became very ill. She was in the hospital for three months, but after being on sick leave for six months, she returned to finish the year. She could not longer pastor but was not prepared to do anything but work in the ministry.

At Christmas time the previous year, Roy Lang called to see if she was having a service on Christmas Eve. His wife had died. They had been members of one of her churches, and he had served for many years as Sunday school superintendent. They began keeping company and they were married July 9, 1968. She was fifty-four. He was a wonderful husband, and they shared fifteen years together before he died with leukemia. She filled in as pastor one summer at Douglas Road Wesleyan church in Toledo, Ohio after her marriage. One summer she was a fill-in pastor in Defiance, Ohio, and for four months at Grand Rapids between pastors. At the age of eighty-four she was still teaching a Sunday school class of senior citizens and filling the pulpit when the pastor was on vacation. She walked with a walker and sat in a wheelchair while she taught and preached. Irene Lang died January 3, 1999.

Her influence continues on in the ministry of many of the children and youth whom she pastored. Among them would be listed Lois (Mrs. Paul) Downey, missionary to Brazil for many years; Mary Ann Goldsmith, pastor's wife; Larry Bittenger, missionary and pastor; Bernard Christy, pastor; Darlean Line and Joanne (Mrs. Ogle) Yates, both pastors' wives.

[God] "acts on behalf of those who wait for him. You come to the help of those who gladly do right, who remember your ways" (Isa. 64:4–5). Those words were proven true of Irene Lang's life. The most money she ever got was $35 a week from a church. The district gave her $50 a week when she pastored at Leipsic. At Grand Rapids she received $2.50 each week. But after her marriage to Roy Lang, she had a nice home and Social Security check to get along on. God does take care of His children.

Helen Minkler

The *Minutes of the Annual Session of the Ohio Conference of the Wesleyan Methodist Connection, or Church, of America* recorded that Helen Minkler had been received into the conference as an ordained minister in 1934. She was listed as an evangelist for three years. In 1939 she requested to be dropped from the roll of ministers.

Mildred Nantz

Mildred Nantz had completed the theological course by 1934 at Miltonvale College, Miltonvale, Kansas (later merged into what became Oklahoma Wesleyan University, Bartlesville, Oklahoma). She was listed by the Kansas Conference of the Wesleyan Methodist Church as a conference preacher (licensed minister). August 26, 1936, she was appointed as the pastor of the Fairview charge. She was ordained in 1938 by the Kansas Conference. She resigned from the Fairview charge March 27, 1941, in order to be appointed to pastor with Ada Shutts at North Topeka, Kansas. The rest of her ministerial appointments were assignments with other women as assistants. From 1942 through 1943 Velma Knox and Mildred pastored the Willis church. They labored together as the pastors of the Eskridge church from 1944 to 1947. They became the pastors of the Arkansas City church from 1948 to 1951. Mildred also spent a few years in evangelistic work. She died November 15, 2001, at the age of ninety-seven in Topeka, Kansas.[130]

Nora Hitesman Powell

Nora and her husband, Richard T. Powell, were ordained in 1934. According to the *Minutes of the Annual Assembly of the Ohio District Pilgrim Holiness Church,* they were under appointment in the district until 1939. At that time they were on the list of ordained ministers in the Pennsylvania and New Jersey District. They were in that district until the end of 1943.[131]

No records were found for her again until the *Minutes of the Annual Assembly of the Ohio District Pilgrim Holiness Church* in 1954 and 1955. From 1956 to 1962 she lived in West Carrollton, Ohio, but there was no record of her ministerial activities.[132]

The *Minutes of the Annual Conference Texas District of the Pilgrim Holiness Church* recorded her as under appointment from 1963 to 1968.

Elizabeth E. Savage

On September 10, 1933, the president of the Middle Atlantic States Mission Conference of the Wesleyan Methodist Church formed a temporary organization of the Trainer, Pennsylvania, church with fifteen members. On October 1, 1933, the president completed a permanent organization of the church with seventeen members, including Elizabeth E. Savage and her husband, Harley J. Savage. Elizabeth Savage was the pastor. The church showed signs of growth and a "good degree of spiritual life and vigor." In 1934 this new church, under the guidance of its pastor, hosted the annual conference.

Elizabeth Savage was ordained May 5, 1935. She preached the evening message, and there was a "goodly" number of seekers. Elizabeth was active in the conference work and served on many conference committees and boards, including pastoral relations, missionary board, judiciary, and statistical. She served as the president of the conference Woman's Home and Foreign Missionary Society for four years.

Elizabeth was appointed to general evangelism in 1936. She and her husband became involved in a church-planting project in Wilmington, Delaware, and were appointed as the pastors. From 1936 through 1944 they pastored the Wilmington church. On January 20, 1944 they were appointed to supervise the Smyrna, Delaware, work until conference time. Harley J. Savage was ordained in 1941.

Elizabeth and her husband served for two years as general evangelists. In 1947 they were under appointment with the Oriental Missionary Society. On April 4, 1950, they were granted letters of standing and joined another denomination. However, on August 23, 1950, the Savages joined the Trainer, Pennsylvania, church and their names were placed on the conference ministerial roll again.

In 1951 and 1952 Elizabeth E. Savage was appointed as a conference evangelist. On October 30, 1952, she was upgraded to a general evangelist, and this appointment continued until 1961. In 1953 she gave a "stirring and anointed" report that she had sensed problems in the Philadelphia and Sussex churches and had spoken to the Lord on their behalf. In 1955 she reported on a revival at Middletown, Delaware, March 6–13, 1955. On October 22, 1957, Harley J. Savage died.

Elizabeth apparently had some exposure to Jamaica during this time, as she reported in 1960 on Jamaican home life in the conference's public Woman's Missionary Society service. She led devotions in the 1961 conference session. From 1961 to 1962, Irma O. Weaver and Elizabeth E. Savage pastored the Trenton, New Jersey, church.[133] Elizabeth flew to Jamaica in October 1961 to teach a term in the Bible school.[134] She reported to the conference on Jamaica in 1962. From 1962 to 1963, Elizabeth Savage was listed as a missionary in Jamaica. Since her name does not appear on official denominational lists of missionaries, it is possible that her service in Jamaica was outside the Wesleyan Methodist Church. In 1963 she was appointed as a conference evangelist. In 1964 she married a man by the name of Williams. From 1964 to 1967 she was on reserve, and in 1967 she was listed as "superannuated" (retired).

Mrs. Jeanette Sebree

The only record found for Jeanette Sebree was in the *Minutes of the Annual Assembly of the Pilgrim Holiness Church of the Pennsylvania and New Jersey District* from 1934 to 1936. She was listed as an ordained minister in 1935. She was the pastor of the Bealsville church in 1936.

Mattie Shelton

Mattie Shelton was under appointment according to the *Minutes of Annual Assembly of the Pilgrim Holiness Church Indiana Conference*, 1934–50. She was listed as ordained in 1934.

Eunice May Huff Shirbroun

Larry Johnson, a former district superintendent, remembered and described Eunice Shirbroun as a chapel speaker at Miltonvale College while he was a student there.

She often spoke in chapel. She was a powerful proclaimer of the Word of God. Her hearers received the impression they must pay close attention because "this is the Word of God." She had a low deep tone voice. She would take her Bible, open it, and within three minutes she was preaching with a "head of steam" like a steam engine. She was a soul-stirring, spirit-filled, preaching machine. She was a "Deborah" when she spoke, firm, committed, and undaunted. But she always made her listeners believe there is HOPE for any circumstance.

Eunice was born May 10, 1914. Her call to the ministry came while she was a junior in high school at Miltonvale. She was first enrolled on the conference roll in 1934 while she was a student at Miltonvale College, Miltonvale, Kansas (later merged into what became Oklahoma Wesleyan University, Bartlesville, Oklahoma). She was ordained in 1938 in the Iowa Conference. Eunice began her ministerial work as the pastor of the Tuttle Grove Wesleyan Methodist church in 1936. This was a rural church, and she did all her visitation by walking for a year or two until she could purchase a secondhand car. That church may now be called Orange Center Church, near Coon Rapids, Iowa. Her future husband, George Edward Shirbroun, was a member of her first congregation. They were married January 19, 1938, and became the parents of Mary Ann Hillen, George Franklin, and John Wesley.

Eunice pastored Bethel, Waverly Chapel, and Rockford churches in the Iowa Conference and the Heber church in Kansas. The Rockford church worshiped in an American Legion hall. She presented a new Sunday school to the conference at Waverly in 1943. Soon after this, she became the first pastor of that group. Her husband, George, was a great prayer warrior, and he served as a Sunday school superintendent for over twenty years. He died January 31, 1952.

Eunice was dean of women at Miltonvale Wesleyan College from 1954 to 1957. She served with the Navigators and was on staff at St. Paul Bible (Crown) College, in St. Bonifacius, Minnesota. She also served as an evangelist and in her retirement served as the minister of visitation at the E. R. Dodd Memorial Wesleyan Church in Emily, Minnesota. She believed her strong point in the ministry was calling and visitation. She loved people. She was also a supply pastor for several churches in the Emily area during her retirement.[135]

Mrs. Ina Mitchell Shreve

Ina Mitchell Shreve began her ministerial work in the Kansas Conference of the Wesleyan Methodist Church in 1932 as a conference preacher (licensed minister). She apparently was married in 1934 and was ordained at conference that year. She spent several years as a missionary to Peiping, China, beginning in 1935. No other records were found on her until 1946, when she was introduced to the Kansas Conference and she was again appointed as a missionary to China until 1950. In 1951 she was the supply pastor at Twin Falls, Idaho. The next six years she served as a missionary to Cuba. On May 10, 1958, she was granted a letter of transfer to the Allegheny Conference.[136]

Ada Shutts

The *Minutes of the Annual Session of the West Virginia District Assembly of the Pilgrim Holiness Church* listed Ada Shutts as the pastor of the Vienna Pilgrim Holiness church in 1934. She was the pastor of the Berkeley Springs church from 1935 to 1938. Ada was on the Indiana District of the Pilgrim Holiness Church list in 1939.

There was no record of her ordination, but in 1940 she was received as an ordained minister from the Pilgrim Holiness Church by the Kansas Conference of the Wesleyan Methodist Church. She served as the supply pastor of the Topeka North church until she resigned July 4, 1942. She began teaching at Intercession City Bible College in Florida immediately after her resignation.[137]

Flora Belle Slater

Flora Belle Slater was born January 31, 1906, in Monroe, Washington. She was the oldest of eight children born to Charles L. and Maude Slater, pioneer missionaries for the Pilgrim Holiness Church. She was saved as a very young child and by age nine knew that God definitely had called her to be a missionary. She followed in the steps of her parents by making a lifelong commitment to the cause of world missions.

Flora Belle attended God's Bible School, in Cincinnati, Ohio, and Kingswood Holiness College, in Kingswood, Kentucky. She took courses in business and in practical nursing in  addition to her Bible college work. Before her first foreign missionary assignment she worked in Peniel Mission in San Francisco.

Her first missionary assignment was to Mexico in 1934, where she worked for several years with Francisco and Nettie Soltero in both evangelistic and Bible school ministries. While working with these outstanding pioneer missionaries, her strong missiological convictions were established. During an extended four-year furlough and deputation work, she was assigned the task of initiating the missionary society work for the Pilgrim Holiness Church by Rev. Paul W. Thomas, then secretary of foreign missions.

As the years passed, other fields of service opened up for Flora Belle. She served a term in Puerto Rico. In March 1947 she arrived in Peru to be in charge of the Bible school at Chiclayo. During a time of convalescence from an illness that shortened her work in Peru, God spoke to her about the need for a Bible school on the island of Mindanao in the Philippines. With God-given restored health, she was on her way to the Philippines in 1951. After a short tour of the work on Luzon, Flora Belle proceeded to Mindanao, where she worked to establish a self-supporting Bible school. Her crowning ministry was her more than twenty years of service in the Philippines. She joined Rev. Paul William and Frances Thomas in 1952 and together they pioneered a great work that has maintained a spirit of revival and dynamic church growth until the present era. She poured her life into the training of pastors and Christian workers, most of whom became active in the leadership of the Church in the Philippines. Among those leaders was Saturnino Garcia, former general superintendent of the Philippine General Conference. He was converted and mentored under her leadership. Flora Belle became known affectionately as "Mother Slater" among those to whom she gave herself so lovingly and completely for so many years. She was the president of the Bible colleges on Mindanao and Luzon and spent a year helping to establish the mountain Bible school among the people of northern Luzon.

After retirement in 1972, the needy world still beckoned her. In 1972 she went to Indonesia as an associate missionary, where she continued her much-loved work of ministerial training with two of her "children" from the Philippines, Rev. and Mrs. Daniel Pantangan. The Pantangans had pioneered the work in Indonesia.

With advancing years and illness, she waited for the Lord's angels to come and take her home from a nursing home in Florida. Her release came April 10, 1996. The Flora Belle Slater Memorial Scholarship Fund was established by Wesleyan World Missions for the Bible colleges in the Philippines so that needy students could be assisted in their preparation for the ministry.[138]

Laura Storkman

Laura Storkman was ordained in 1934 and served through 1935 with the Kansas District of the Pilgrim Holiness Church.[139]

Jessie Lee Bingham Surbrook

Jessie, her sister, Olive, and brother, Buell Bingham, provided the special music for the evangelistic team headed by Walter L. and George Surbrook. From the efforts of this group many came to know the Lord, and two churches were established at Kannapolis and Siler City, North Carolina.

Jessie was born July 3, 1903, in Randolph County, North Carolina. Her education included Greensboro Literary and Bible School in North Carolina; Olivet Nazarene College, in Kankakee, Illinois; and further training at Hayes State Teachers College in Kansas. She taught English and music (voice and choir) at Pilgrim Bible College, in Kernersville, North Carolina (later merged into United Wesleyan College, in Allentown, Pennsylvania) and Owosso Bible College, in Owosso, Michigan (later merged into what became Indiana Wesleyan University, in Marion, Indiana).

She was married to Walter L. Surbrook April 8, 1932, and they became the parents of two daughters, Ruth (Mrs. James) Smith and Esther. Following their marriage, they established their home in the Detroit area. They jointly served in the fields of evangelism, education, administration, and the pastorate. They had a rich ministry among many people. She kept house and tried to keep life as normal as possible with her husband gone so much of the time as general superintendent of the Pilgrim Holiness Church (1933–46). She taught in elementary school for a few years. Her daughters remember her as a loving mother who gave to them the gift of a love of music and reading. She taught the girls to sing in parts in the car as they traveled to summer conferences and camps. She was a gentle, gracious lady who was not easily upset. She was a good balance for Dr. Surbrook, who always wanted things done "yesterday." Jessie Surbrook died November 16, 1992.[140]

Mrs. H. C. Walker

The *Minutes of the Annual Assembly of the Ohio District Pilgrim Holiness Church,* 1934–55, recorded Mrs. H. C. Walker as an ordained minister in 1934 and as active in the ministry through 1947. No service record was found for her after that date, and all that was recorded was that she was living in Cincinnati, Ohio, from 1948 to 1967.[141]

Irma Kenschaft Weaver

David Tonnesson wrote about his memory of the Kenschaft sisters:

[Irma] was best known for the many years being the director of services and activities for the children and youth through the age of thirteen at conference and camp time in the Middle Atlantic States Conference. Irma, Elizabeth Ruth North, and Erna Kenschaft acted as a trio in operating the services. Erna played the piano, Ruth was the energetic and dramatic song leader, and Irma took care of the rest of the program.

Irma Kenschaft was born in Philadelphia July 15, 1905. She entered the ministry as a licensed preacher from Trainer Wesleyan Methodist Church, where Elizabeth E. Savage was the pastor. She was active in the evangelistic field until 1950. She was elected the conference child evangelism secretary and served in that office until 1961. That year Irma and Elizabeth E. Savage were appointed as pastors of the Trenton, New Jersey, church. In

1962 Irma was the solo pastor at Trenton and was still pastoring there at the time of the 1968 merger.

Irma was active in church work on the conference level. She served on the conference Sunday school board 1939–58, as conference Sunday school secretary 1939–55, on the committee on child evangelism 1950–61, as superintendent of the conference Young Missionary Workers Band (now Wesleyan Kids for Missions) 1939–42, as Woman's Missionary Society vice president 1959–65, and on the mission board 1951–58, as well as other committees.

While she was the conference Sunday school secretary, she visited each Sunday school in the conference. One year the conference president reported sincere appreciation was due the Sunday school secretary for her emphasis on the extension work of the conference through the Sunday school.[142]

Irma was ordained in 1958. She was the mother of two children, Charles "Bud" and Dorothy Pepper. She and her husband Edgar F. Weaver moved to Brooksville, Florida, when they retired. He died February 20, 1990. Irma was a "second mother," a role model and a mentor to a host of people. She completed her earthly walk August 26, 1997.[143]

Cleona Wright

Cleona Wright was a pastor in the Ohio District of the Pilgrim Holiness Church. Among the churches she pastored were the Morgan Center and Mt. Olivet churches. She was under the Ohio District from 1934 to 1946. Her husband, Emmett, was a composer of gospel songs and faithfully worked with his wife in evangelism. He died February 7, 1940.[144]

The next service record that was found for her was in the *Journal of Proceedings of the Annual Session of the Southern Indiana Conference of the Pilgrim Holiness Church.* She was listed as an evangelist from 1951 to 1953.

Flo Andrews

The records reveal that Flo Andrews' ministerial work was all done under the Pilgrim Holiness

Church in Indiana. She was ordained by the Indiana District in 1935 and served under that district until 1950.[145] When the district was divided in 1951, she was under appointment with the Southern Indiana District from 1951 to 1967.[146]

Kathryn Beaver

Kathryn Beaver will long be remembered for her passion for missions and the missionary work of The Wesleyan Church. Her wit and humor made her a favorite person among all the children and youth on the Fairmount, Indiana, campgrounds.

Kathryn served as the Indiana Conference treasurer of the Woman's Missionary Society from 1956 to 1963. In 1963 she was elected the conference president of the society. She gave a total of thirty-five years of service to conference missionary work.

Kathryn began her conference service in the Indiana Conference of the Wesleyan Methodist Church in 1935 when she was assigned as assistant pastor to her husband at the Jonesboro, Indiana, Wesleyan Methodist church. In 1940 they left the Jonesboro church to become the pastors at the Plymouth, Indiana, church. She was ordained at conference time in 1943. She co-pastored with her husband in Marion, Indiana, at Nelson Street Church, at Lafayette Schuyler Avenue Church, and a second time at the Jonesboro church.[147]

When her husband, Garl, became involved in general church activities, Kathryn worked at the Marion College library and in the district Woman's Missionary Society work. They accepted a call to pastor the Dayton, Ohio, Northridge church. Her husband's sudden death by a heart attack brought Kathryn back to Marion, Indiana.

Kathryn was a gifted teacher and always had a large Sunday school class in the churches where they pastored. The Lord also used her musical skills in His work on the local level. She was the mother of one son, David.

Thelma Cloer Brown

Thelma Cloer was called by the strong inner voice of God at the age of eleven to be a minister.

Thelma was born May 7, 1922. She was married to D. Wayne Brown June 9, 1943. She was a supply pastor for a church in the North Carolina District of the Pilgrim Holiness Church and was active in evangelism for eight years before her marriage. She was ordained in June 1946 by the California District of the Pilgrim Holiness Church.

She and her husband were the pastors of five churches over a period of twenty-two years. Two churches were in California: Long Beach and East Los Angeles. Three were in Michigan: Croswell, Ann Arbor, and Flint. In 1966 her husband was elected by the Pilgrim Holiness Church to be the general secretary/treasurer. At the merging General Conference in 1968 he was elected to the same post until 1972, when the office was divided and he became general secretary. He served in the office until he retired in 1982. D. Wayne Brown died January 24, 1994.

Thelma was the mother of two children, Judi and Donald. Donald died in 1991. Thelma was a faithful worker, mother, and wife. She always sought to fill in wherever she was needed in the ministerial work with her husband.[148]

Catharine Delores Carr Carlson

Catharine Delores Carr, nicknamed "Peggy" by her family, was born in Meadville, Pennsylvania, in October 1904. After high school she attended and in 1927 graduated from Asbury College, Wilmore, Kentucky.

Catharine and her college friend Frances Beard went to work with Mrs. McConnell at her Kentucky Mountain Bible School and Mission after graduating from Asbury. She taught in the school and participated in the religious services of the mission.

After two years at Kentucky Mountain Bible School and Mission, Catharine enrolled in Chicago Evangelistic Institute (later Vennard College, University Park, Iowa) and graduated with a master's degree in religion in 1931.

She took a train from Chicago to return to her home in Erie, Pennsylvania. Catharine was observed reading her Bible by a Wesleyan

Methodist minister, who was seated across the aisle. They began to converse. He was going to Erie to attend the Allegheny Annual Conference of the Wesleyan Methodist Church. He suggested that it would be good for her to attend. She did, and as a result of that "chance" meeting she joined the Wesleyan Methodist Church and began her ministerial work with them.

Catharine pastored the Ashville, New York, church from 1935 to 1936. In 1937 she was ordained. She also pastored the East Clarksburg and Bethel charge in West Virginia and Grace Wesleyan Methodist Church in Akron, Ohio.

While pastoring Grace in Akron she became acquainted with Arthur G. Carlson, a widower and devout Christian layman. He was a conference trustee, treasurer, and a leader in Akron First Church. He had long been active in the local church ministries and had a deep desire to be involved in full-time work for the Lord. They were married March 26, 1942. Mr. Carlson had four children: a married son, two daughters who were attending Houghton College, and a fourteen-year-old son. Catharine's warmth, wisdom, cheerfulness, and loving ways filled the void in this family.

Catharine continued to pastor the Akron Grace Church. Mr. Carlson stepped out in faith and began the course of study for ordination. The last year she pastored Grace Church he was her assistant.

In 1946, Catharine accepted the pastorate of the Carrollton Tabernacle with Arthur as her assistant. They were appointed to the Pittsfield, Pennsylvania, church, and while there, Arthur G. Carlson was ordained in 1953. A pastorate of the Mentele and Spruce Grove charge (Heilwood, Pennsylvania) of five hard strenuous years resulted in ill health forcing him to lighten his workload. At conference time they were assigned to the Warren, Pennsylvania church. During the second year of their ministry there, Arthur died suddenly in October 1961. Catharine continued to pastor the church until the close of the 1964 conference year.

She became the assistant principal and a teacher of the Christian Day School at Stoneboro, Pennsylvania. This school was sponsored by the Allegheny Conference. Later she moved to Canton, Ohio, and there she taught in a Christian school for a time. In Canton she attended a Nazarene church with her children. When she was asked to teach a Bible studies group she enthusiastically accepted. Catharine always put her heart and soul into everything she did. She manifested a strong purpose in her walk with the Lord. She was a cheerful and rejoicing person. In all her ministry she aggressively followed her calling in preaching, though in the church world it was not easy to be a "woman preacher."

During her retirement she was diagnosed with abdominal cancer and had surgery. The surgeon said she had two weeks to two months to live. But when he went into her room a few days after the surgery, she was sitting on the edge of the bed with a joyous and happy look on her face and a strong upbeat note in her voice. She knew she was in God's hands. The surgeon decided at that moment that since she had a desire and purpose for living, he should try radiation. There followed weeks of suffering from the radiation treatments, but God intervened and she got better.

She made two extended trips to Haiti to help in the work there where her stepdaughter, Elizabeth, and her husband, Henry Ortlip, had been working for many years with the Wesleyan Methodist Church. Her presence and help were a blessing to the Ortlip family and many others as well.

She went home to be with her Lord in February 1975 from complications with diabetes.[149]

Reba Hooker Coleman

Reba Hooker Coleman began her ministerial studies in the Indiana Conference of the Wesleyan Methodist Church in 1935. She pastored the Mechanicsburg, Indiana, church and was engaged as an evangelist until 1941. She was ordained in 1940.

Reba spent many years working at the Zion's Hill Mission in the mountains of Kentucky. She again entered the evangelistic field of work. Later in life she married Rev. Oscar Coleman.[150]

Eunice Hunsinger Davidson

Eunice Hunsinger was a conference preacher (licensed minister) in 1935 in the Kansas Conference of the Wesleyan Methodist Church. She was the pastor at Wesley Center and later assisted her husband, A. G. Hunsinger, there. In 1941 they became the pastors of the Idana church and remained there until 1951. Eunice was ordained in 1944. A. G. Hunsinger died in 1951 or 1952.

In 1952 Eunice became the pastor of Wesley Chapel until 1956. After that she pastored the Morgan Chapel, Clay Center, and Leavenworth churches. On July 23, 1966, she married Paul Davidson. She and Paul pastored the Leavenworth church for another year and then became involved in the Wesleyan Indian Mission work.

Eunice was engaged in several committees and boards on the conference level and served from 1958 to 1960 as the editor of the paper titled *Wesleyan Visitor*.[151]

Myrna Allen Deal

Myrna Deal wrote some facts about her life and work:

I feel honored that God called me at an early age to preach, although I am unworthy of such a high calling.

As a young person I enjoyed trying to help people and visiting the aged and sick. I did some work as an assistant before I was married. I also pastored two churches after marriage while my husband did evangelistic work.

My husband was very supportive and was a great encouragement to me. His help was tremendous. We worked together in pastoring and in evangelism in the United States and overseas. We did missionary evangelism in many countries.

While he was district superintendent (North Carolina, 1942–49; Pacific Northwest, 1950–58; and California, 1963–64), I did some pulpit supply work and teaching in a Christian day school. We always enjoyed working with young people.

Our years in God's service were happy, and we got to celebrate our 60th wedding anniversary before he went to heaven.

I was ordained by the Pilgrim Holiness Church October 10, 1934. My preaching style was evangelistic and teaching. I still teach a Sunday school class, do visitation, and speak on different occasions. I also promote the sale of my husband's books. He was the author of over forty books.

Mrs. Deal wrote the preceding memo April 15, 1998.

Dr. William S. Deal died January 25, 1992. The Deals were the parents of one daughter, Evangeline Deal Shelton (married to Dr. Larry Shelton). Myrna Deal also wrote articles that were published in the *Pilgrim Holiness Advocate*. She was elected and served as president of the Northwest District missionary society of the Pilgrim Holiness Church.[152]

Elizabeth Choate

The *Minutes of the Annual Session of the Rochester Conference of the Wesleyan Methodist Connection, or Church, of America 1935–1941* stated Elizabeth Choate had completed all requirements for ordination and was elected to be ordained in 1935. In 1940 she was listed as a missionary at the Emmaus Rest Home, Kobe, Japan. The following year the record stated she was "transferred."

Vera Pearle Carter Close

Vera Carter was born June 12, 1914, in Longton, Kansas. She worked as a young girl at the Kresge's "dime store" in Wichita, Kansas. She often heard the Salvation Army band as they played and sang on the street corner downtown. "Whosoever will . . . 'tis the loving Father calls the wanderer home. . . whosoever will may come." Vera's heart longed to come home. On December 31, 1930, at age sixteen, she made her way down the aisle of the sawdust floor of the Friends church and was marvelously saved by the blood of the Lamb.[153]

Vera graduated from high school and knew God was leading her into the ministry. She had an outstanding singing voice, and her music teacher was upset when Vera told her God was leading her to attend Bible school in Colorado Springs. Her voice teacher tried to persuade her to seek a career in music, but Vera wouldn't budge. In exasperation the teacher declared she would never be known outside her county.

Her father had a terrible temper and was a heavy drinker. He made all kinds of threats and proclaimed he would kill her if he found out she had slipped off to school. She certainly would not get a dime from him to pay her tuition. Vera later would be described as having a strong will and determination, which she had given entirely to God. These traits were manifested in her determination to go to Bible school. She worked at a store to earn money for her first semester, and her mother cleaned houses and did "washings" for the rich people in Wichita to help her. Another strong character trait she developed early in her Christian life was the effectual prayer of faith. She had the money for school but no transportation. She prayed, and within two days she received a phone call from her pastor. He and his wife were going to Colorado Springs. Would she like to go with them?[154]

Vera packed her belongings in boxes and left for school. Her father came home and found she had left. In a rage, he turned all the pictures of Vera toward the wall. He tried to strangle her

Rev. Vera Close leading singing at regional youth convention, 1948

mother, but God intervened and prevented him from doing her physical harm.

While attending Colorado Springs Bible College (later merged into what became Oklahoma Wesleyan University, Bartlesville, Oklahoma) she formed a friendship and evangelistic team with Vera Howerton. They became known as the "Two Veras." They worked together for four years. They sang in prairie schoolhouses and in established churches in the cities and villages all over the United States. Their voices blended so perfectly that it was impossible to distinguish who was singing what part. Their ministry resulted in many converts from among children, youth and mature adults.

Vera's singing voice was an instrument used by God to convict and draw people to God. When she sang people longed to know the Person about whom she was singing. Even after she retired, she would often be asked to sing at church. Vera would call her good friend Joy McDonald on the phone. Joy would place the phone by the piano and begin playing the song Vera would sing the next morning. Vera in her home some distance away would practice for the service the next day. Vera never had to warm up before singing. She would simply clear her throat and begin singing.

At first Vera ministered only by music, playing the piano and singing, but it soon became evident that churches could not support both singers and preaching evangelists. In a telephone conversation to me, she said she was pushed into preaching because of the financial crunch during the Depression. That might have been the "push" but God had given Vera the gift of evangelistic preaching also. Many persons of all walks of life were led to Christ during those four years of preaching and singing. Names like Gordon, Gilbert, Colaw, Beecher, persons who would become district superintendents, and other leaders in the Pilgrim Holiness Church and The Wesleyan Church, pastors in the Church of the Nazarene and Free Methodist Church and a bishop in the United Methodist Church filled her pages of memories of persons saved or helped in her meetings.

In one of those meetings, the evangelist was the new district superintendent from Oklahoma. The pastor's wife was ill, and Vera, seeing a need, took over the domestic chores of cooking and cleaning. The evangelist watched her at work both in the home and in the Church. He observed how passionate she was about the Lord's work. They fell in love, and three months later, December 22, 1937, Dewey Richard (Dick) Close and Vera Carter were married.

The marriage did not hinder this "God-called" woman from service for her Lord. Dick Close was the pioneer district superintendent for the Pilgrim Holiness Church in Oklahoma and Texas for sixteen years. The call and passion of Dick and Vera Close was to plant churches. During this time they were involved in planting some fourteen churches during a fifteen-year period, besides co-pastoring churches in Tulsa, Enid, Blackwell, Bethany, and Hopeton, Oklahoma. Vera's category/listing in the district journal was usually "pastor with D. R. Close" *and* "evangelist." Sometimes she would be the solo pastor at a church. For example, in 1940 she served as the pastor at the church at Newkirk. That year there was an added note stating she had held fifty-six meetings, had thirty-three seekers, and thirty-one persons finding sanctification.

During D. R. and Vera Close's lifetime of service to the Church, they planted a total of seventeen churches. Often Dick was credited for this great feat, but he emphatically declared he could not have done any of this without Vera. John A. Dunn, former general director of the Wesleyan Investment Foundation, recalled that Vera had also served for one month as district superintendent!

Whenever they were conducting revival meetings or laying the plans for planting a new church, Vera would suggest that they "go visit the schoolhouses." There were small rural schools all over the countryside. Vera would put on a program for the children, telling Bible stories, playing the piano, and singing. The children would tell their parents about "this woman" who came to school and spoke and sang. People came from all over the countryside to the meetings.

Vera's preaching was compelling and persuasive. Those who heard her preach recall how she could bring fear into everyone's heart when she talked about "there was a certain rich man" from

Luke 16:19–31. She was also gifted in giving the evangelistic invitation and with discernment in inviting persons to the altar on a one-on-one invitation.

Her ministry with children was outstanding. She made each Bible story come alive, and the children felt the emotions and joys of those who were touched by the hand of Jesus.

She was a great counselor and always gave a listening ear to those who needed her help. She had the ability to draw people out and get them to reveal what was troubling them.

Vera was also a woman of confidence. During the Korean War, a young man from the church where they were pastoring wanted to get married while he was home on leave. Dick was out of town. Vera decided she would perform the wedding. She played the prelude, sang the songs, performed the ceremony, played the postlude, and organized the reception. The *Oklahoma City Times* was so impressed with this event that they came out, took pictures, and placed the story with a picture of Vera and the couple on the front page of the paper.

Vera was a giant in many ways, but she was also human and felt the emotional, mental, and physical pain in the difficult places. She suffered grief when she, Shirley, and Beverly were involved in an automobile accident that took the life of Beverly. Though she was grieving over the loss of her daughter, she taught Jo Anne, another daughter, to come face-to-face with death and grief and still believe in God and His mercy. God's grace kept her singing.

Vera was also a public servant. She was a leader in the Women's Christian Temperance Union, which worked against the legalizing of alcoholic beverages. She organized the largest parade in the history of Oklahoma City for the "dry" politicians. And they won.

Vera was a family person. She loved her husband, daughters, and grandchildren. On the flyleaf of her Bible she wrote these words:

> Have tried hard to raise Jo Anne and Shirley to live Christian lives first, and to prepare them for life with education, second. Many tears and prayers have ascended to the throne for guidance in their lives. Not one tear was wasted—God bottled them all and poured them out in later life. I do not regret having worked hard in secular as well as the ministerial world to aid them in their education.

She never allowed her mind to be idle, and she sought to better herself in order to serve Christ better by studying at various places where they pastored—Phillips University, Bethany Nazarene College, and Northwestern State University—and even in retirement she took classes at the University of Colorado and at the Community College of Colorado Springs.

Vera served as a minister for several different churches, Tulsa, Enid, Blackwell, Bethany, and Hopeton, Oklahoma; Lawrenceville, Illinois; Lima and Dayton, Ohio. She was licensed in 1935 by the Kansas District of the Pilgrim Holiness Church and was ordained by that district in 1938.

Vera was the mother of three daughters, Jo Anne, director of World Hope International; Shirley, associate professor of voice and opera at Houghton College, Houghton, New York; and Beverly. Jo Anne received from her mother musical talents of piano and voice but also those gifts of counseling, compassionate ministries, and preaching. Shirley has been blessed with the skillful talent of piano and a gifted voice to sing not only hymns and gospel songs but also opera, for which she has won fame. As earlier stated, Beverly died as a result of the automobile accident. The year was 1956.

Vera had wanted Shirley to sing a certain song at her funeral. It was an Elvis Presley gospel song. Shirley had not sung that style and type of song for years and did not have the time to learn it. One summer when Shirley came home Vera told her, "You don't need to learn that song, Shirley. I've already taped it. And I'll tell you this much—if you want anything done in life, you have to do it yourself. And so I'll sing at my own funeral!" She had taped the song at the age of eighty-one, and there was not an error in pitch, tone, or performance. That tape of the song "His Hand in Mine" was played at her funeral. Vera Carter Close completed her work and walk on this earth Sunday, March 22, 1998.[155]

Viola Dillon

According to the records found, Viola Dillon began her ministerial work in 1935 in Colorado Springs. She was listed by the Southern District of the Pilgrim Holiness Church 1935–36 and in 1940.[156]

Her records were found from 1940 to 1944 in the Indiana District of the Pilgrim Holiness Church. From 1946 to the 1968 merger she was listed by the North Carolina District.[157]

Ethel Entry

Ethel (Mrs. H. E.) Entry came into the Allegheny Conference of the Wesleyan Methodist Church in 1935. She had been recommended by Templeton First Church. She was appointed to serve with her husband at the Templeton church that year. She was ordained in June 1936. The next year she was appointed as a general evangelist. She and her husband moved to Houghton, New York, and Houghton became their home base for their evangelistic work. In 1955 Ethel took a position teaching school in a Christian day school in Colorado Springs and remained in that area until her husband died in May 1957. Though her residence and work had been largely outside the Allegheny Conference, she retained her conference membership there. She died April 6, 1958.[158]

Nellie Holden Ewell

Two sisters, Luella (sometimes spelled "Louella") and Nellie Holden, were involved in evangelistic tent meetings in their early days on the Eastern Shore. *The Pilgrim Holiness Advocate* of January 8, 1942, reported that it had been over ten years since these women began evangelistic work together. They had been continuously in church revivals, camps, and tent meetings. A tent meeting held in Viola, Delaware, had lasted for several weeks. Often it was raining, but there were always good altar services. They had conducted tent meetings at Crisfield and Salisbury, Maryland; Deltaville Camp, in the German's Tabernacle in Gloucester County, and Five Points, Virginia; Tunnesville, New Jersey; Milroy, Pennsylvania; and New Liberty, Maryland.

They also pastored churches at Crisfield and Broomes Island, Maryland, and Quimby, Virginia. When Nellie was pastoring the Cape Charles church, she asked Ronald Kelly's father about him.

His father explained that Ron was in college preparing for the ministry. That pleased her, and she said, "That's good." She further stated, "I told my people that they were going to have to raise their salary if they wanted a pastor after I was gone. A young man can't take care of his family on the salary you're paying. And furthermore, he'll not have to live on the salary I'm getting. They'll either pay more or close this church." (Dr. Ronald Kelly's home district was the Eastern District. He currently is the general secretary of The Wesleyan Church.)[159]

Nellie Holden was under appointment by the Eastern District of the Pilgrim Holiness Church from 1935 to 1967. In 1956 she married Oscar Ewell, and together they served as pastors of the Cape Charles church. She believed her gift of singing was an added asset to her ministry.[160] Louella Holden was also under appointment by the Eastern District of the Pilgrim Holiness Church from 1935 to 1967.

Mrs. Frank W. Henry

Mrs. Frank W. Henry was never listed by a given name in the conference journals. She is first mentioned in the *Minutes of the Annual Assembly of the Pilgrim Holiness Church Southern District* in 1935. She was listed as the pastor at Winston-Salem, North Carolina. The next entry found for her was in the North Carolina District in 1947. She served as pastor at Silor, Pleasant Grove, Burlington, and Spray. She was still in the district at the time of merger in 1968.[161]

Martha Ingram

Martha (Mrs. Thomas C.) Ingram was listed in the *Minutes of the Annual Assembly of the Oklahoma/Texas District Pilgrim Holiness Church,* 1935–37. Her name appeared on the roll in the *Minutes of the Annual Assembly of the Oklahoma/Texas/Louisiana District Pilgrim Holiness Church,* 1938–40, and 1944–46. In 1941 she was listed as the assistant pastor at the Plainview, Texas, church in the *Minutes of the Annual Assembly of the Pilgrim Holiness Church Texas District.* All the other years she was listed without appointment.

Cleo Jones

The *Minutes of the Annual Assembly of the Pilgrim Holiness Church Indiana Conference,* 1935–39, recorded Cleo Jones as an ordained minister in 1935, and she served in that district through 1939.

Pauline Kernan

The *Minutes of the Annual Assembly of the Ohio District Pilgrim Holiness Church* listed Pauline Kernan as ordained in 1935, and she served through 1937 in that district.

Ruth Klopfenstein

Ruth Klopfenstein was on the roll of ordained ministers in the Indiana District of the Pilgrim Holiness Church in 1935–36. Her name did not appear again until 1941–53.[162]

Marie Wilson Phinney

Marie Wilson was born January 29, 1913, in southeastern North Carolina. She was a tiny baby weighing two and one-half pounds. Her parents had wanted a baby boy who would become a preacher like his grandfather. They knew God had used women in the past, and perhaps He would use their daughter. Marie gave her heart to the Lord at age ten and was baptized in the river. She was interested in spiritual things as a child and made friends easily.

At age sixteen she graduated as valedictorian of her class. She completed the secretarial and accounting courses at Edwards Business College in High Point, North Carolina. This training enabled her to work her way through all her college education. During this time she met J. A. Huffman, dean of the school of theology at Marion College, Marion, Indiana (now Indiana Wesleyan University). He encouraged and helped her to enter Marion College in September 1930. She was now seventeen. The congregations of the

Hickory Chapel and Hayworth Memorial Wesleyan churches in High Point were a great influence on her. In 1931 she declared herself as a missionary candidate. She graduated from Marion College with a bachelor's degree in theology in 1934. She took post-graduate classes at Winona Lake School of Theology and the Homer Rodeheaver Music School. She also took courses on a master's degree at Marion College. While in college, she made a complete surrender to God and was sanctified.

On March 20, 1935, Marie married E. Sterl Phinney, a Marion College graduate. She began living in a parsonage (a total of five) on March 27, 1935, in Bryan, Texas. During this pastorate her first son, Edward Sterl Jr., was born.

In 1937 the Wesleyan Methodist mission board invited them to become missionaries to Japan. They left Texas by train carrying all they owned in two suitcases, one for the baby boy and the other for the two of them. They were on the way to Japan. Those years in Japan were difficult days. World War II began. The mission board instructed them to sell all the mission property because all foreign owned properties in Japan were being taken over by the military regime. In a miraculous way the properties were sold within two days. Sterl had to take the money by ship to Singapore to the international exchange center to cash it into U.S. checks. He did it with great risk of being robbed and meeting with physical harm. Their second son was born in Japan. The next letter from the mission board instructed them to return to the United States. Sterl believed that God would send them to South America and they would be so instructed by the next letter.

The letter did not come. They returned to the United States, and after a time they were given the use of a mountain cabin in the Big Horn Mountains. Still there was no letter. Two long months passed, and then the letter arrived in Buffalo, Wyoming, all tattered and torn. It had been sent to Japan and arrived after their departure. It was returned to the Wesleyan Methodist headquarters and finally forwarded to them in Buffalo. It stated that some of the board felt they should be the first missionaries to Medellin, Colombia—the land Marie had felt called to for many years.

Marie and Sterl spent one term in Colombia. Their third son was born there. Oh, what about that money from the sale of the properties in Japan? Well it went to Colombia. The Phinneys had packed their luggage and were waiting for their visas to enter again, but they were not permitted to return because of Marie's health. Everything they owned was in Colombia.

The Indiana Conference was in session at this time, and Marie and Sterl were appointed as the pastors of the Bluffton, Indiana, Wesleyan Methodist church.

Sterl suffered a heart attack and died in 1973, and the oldest son died in 1996. Since Sterl's death Marie has had short terms as a volunteer worker in Bolivia, Puerto Rico, Jamaica, and Mexico and was on a Wesleyana Cruise that visited Wesleyan churches on five Caribbean islands.

Marie worked for fourteen years as a civil servant, two years in forestry in Oregon, and twelve years for Social Security in Indiana. For fifteen years she served as a nanny for professors' children in the Earlham College Community at Richmond, Indiana.

On May 2, 1994, she retired at Wesleyan Village in Brooksville, Florida. Here she keeps busy singing in the choir, helping in nursing homes, serving others who hurt, and trying to keep up with acquaintances around the world by correspondence and phone.[163]

Helen Schmidt

Helen (Mrs. C. M.) Schmidt began her ministerial work in the California District of the Pilgrim Holiness Church in 1935. She remained on the conference roll through 1968. She served as pastor of the Dixon Pilgrim Holiness church 1961–62 and again in 1965–68.[164]

Annie Short

Annie Short was ordained in 1935. She and her husband, S. D. Short, were the pastors of the Powasson Pilgrim Holiness Church in the Ontario District from 1935 to 1937. From 1938 to 1940 they were the pastors at Massey. Her name remained on the roll of ordained ministers until 1956.[165]

———⟨∞⟩———

Elsie Spain Mason

Elsie Spain was from the Independence, Iowa, Wesleyan Methodist church. She was appointed by the Iowa Conference during the 1935 conference year to be the assistant pastor at Waterloo. In 1936–38 she (age twenty-three) and Vera Brainerd (age fifty-three) served as the pastors at Bennezette. Here the church provided them with a cow. Since Elsie had grown up on a summer resort/farm in northern Minnesota, she knew just how to care for the cow. Elsie liked to pray at the church altar when she could not sleep. But there was no lock on the door, and she soon found how dangerous it was for a single lady to be pastoring by herself. A married man began stopping by, and she began to pray elsewhere.

From 1938 to 1940 Elsie attended Miltonvale Wesleyan College, Miltonvale, Kansas (later merged into what became Oklahoma Wesleyan University, Bartlesville, Oklahoma). She earned part of her tuition by getting up at 4:30 A.M. to stoke the furnace at Hillcrest Cottage. This was the beginning of a lifelong habit of early morning devotions as she watched the furnace and prayed.

In 1940 Elsie was listed as a conference preacher (licensed minister) doing missionary work. She was ordained in 1941 and was assigned to Bentley. She had to walk everywhere. Most of her people lived three or four miles away, so she learned short cuts—via or across railroad tracks and pastures. One family lived twelve miles away, so a pastoral call took all day for that one. The teacher/principal of the high school was dating a fifteen-year-old girl who attended the services with her parents and gained undue influence over the whole family. He attended services regularly but sat and wrote through the entire service, "rewriting the Bible as it should be."

From 1942 to 1943 Esther Nauman and Elsie were the pastors at Dundee, Iowa. Offerings averaged about $2.50 per week. Esther worked part of the time at the small hospital/chiropractic building in Manchester. Before she started work, the two ladies seldom had meat on their menu. One day coming home from the country, they spotted and killed an opossum. Sunday they could hardly wait for dinner—'possum, potatoes, carrots, rutabaga, and onion simmering on their wood heater. She thought it was good, but she said that it was her first and last 'possum.

A minister friend gave her name and address to Rev. Charles Esley Mason, and he began visiting her at Dundee. She accepted her friend's recommendation, and they were married within the year. From 1943 to 1945, the Masons pastored at Firth, Nebraska. In 1944, Nebraska was organized as a separate conference. Esley (as she called him) and Elsie shared preaching and Wednesday night services. Elsie taught Sunday school and conducted mission services. Elsie's abilities were recognized by the Nebraska Conference. In 1944 she was chosen to be on the local board of trustees of Miltonvale Wesleyan College. In 1944, 1945, and 1946 she was elected to the Nebraska Committee on itinerancy and elders orders (now district board of ministerial development). The team was not well matched, since at least two of their pastorates asked that she be the pastor and Esley find other employment to supplement the salary.

From 1945 to 1946 the Masons pastored at Neligh, Nebraska. From 1946 to 1947 they were the supply pastors at the E. R. Dodd Memorial Wesleyan Methodist Church in Emily, Minnesota. In 1947 they were to choose their own field, and in 1948 they were granted letters to the Dakota Conference. Apparently they pastored at Garden City, South Dakota, during this time. In 1949 the Masons were back on the Nebraska roll and were listed as "supernumerary" (on reserve). In 1950 Esley joined another denomination (possibly Methodist, as they once pastored a Methodist church). Elsie continued as part of the Nebraska Conference until 1961, but without any specific appointment. In 1961 she transferred back to the Iowa Conference and from 1962 to 1966 was listed as a conference evangelist.

From 1950 to 1969, Esley, Elsie, and their three children lived in North St. Paul, Minnesota. Esley worked at Swift and Company. Elsie became a layperson in practice, first in a Nazarene church and then as a charter member of the Oakdale Wesleyan Methodist Church. She worked at St. John's Hospital and took courses from the University of Minnesota to earn her B. S. degree.

Esley was severely injured in an auto accident in 1966. Elsie went to Angle Inlet, Minnesota, to teach in 1969 as she now had to support her family. Esley died in 1971. And in 1972, with all bills paid and the children grown and employed, Elsie went to teach in Brainerd Indian School in South Dakota. She retired from there in November 1982 due to ill health.[166]

Helen Vincent

Helen Vincent served in the Eastern District of the Pilgrim Holiness Church from 1935 to 1940, according to the *Minutes of the Eastern District Pilgrim Holiness Church.*

Gladys J. White

Gladys and Florence White were sisters and schoolteachers who also spread the gospel of Jesus Christ in Canada under the Pilgrim Holiness Church. Gladys was converted as a child. She began early in life to prepare for the ministry and the call of God for her life. She graduated from McMaster University; Toronto Bible College; Frankfort Pilgrim College, Frankfort, Indiana (later merged into United Wesleyan College, Allentown, Pennsylvania); and the College of Education of Toronto.

Gladys was ordained in 1935. She worked as an assistant pastor to her sister, Florence, at the Wiarton church. She was the solo pastor at Thessalon and Patton churches in 1938 and 1939. The next year she was the pastor at Wiarton and Proton. Her helpers were H. H. Shaw, L. Baker, and Florence White. She returned to pastor the Wiarton church in 1945 and 1946, and this time George Jackson assisted her. She also was the pastor at Bruce Mines and Durham. She and her sister, Florence, were the church planters at Bruce Mines. They pastored there for seven years.

Gladys's work also included working with the Upper Canadian Bible Society and teaching at the Pilgrim Bible College in Proton, Ontario. She served as principal of the high school department of the Bible school from 1948 until it closed in 1950. She was also involved in evangelistic tent meeting work and in missionary work in northern Ontario.[167]

Alma Acton

Alma Acton was listed as an ordained minister in 1936 in the Illinois and Missouri District of the Pilgrim Holiness Church. She served under district appointment from 1937 to 1945 in the Iowa/Missouri/Arkansas District and under the Illinois District until 1967.[168]

Florence M. Carlson

Florence was a minister in the Ohio District of the Pilgrim Holiness Church from 1936 to 1937. According to the *Minutes of the Annual Assembly of the Pilgrim Holiness Church Indiana Conference 1938–50,* she joined that district in 1938. When the district was divided in 1951, she served under the Northern Indiana District until 1967.

She was an ordained minister. *The Pilgrim Holiness Advocate* reported November 2, 1933, page 4, that she had accepted the call to the staff of the *Pilgrim Holiness Advocate.* She was the office editor of that paper for twelve years. The office was located in Indianapolis.

In 1946 she went to Cincinnati, Ohio, to work in the office of *God's Revivalist.* She became the editor of that publication in 1951 and served there for many years.

Florence M. Carlson died May 13, 1974.[169]

Mary Carnahan Crandall

Mary Carnahan was converted at age eight. She graduated from Houghton College, Houghton, New York, in 1935 with a degree in Christian education. She was not sure what God really wanted her to do with her life. She had won public speaking contests as well as one in Bible reading at commencement. Professor Frank

Wright of Houghton College told her this was the evidence for which she had been looking. She must be called to preach.[170]

After graduating from the ministerial course at Houghton College, she went to Barrington, Vermont, to assist the pastor there. She assumed it would be mainly music and evangelism, but the pastor became ill, and she had to do many of the regular pastoral duties, including some preaching. Perhaps that was when she realized she could preach and possibly should. As her job description had not been what she intended and felt led to do, she did not stay there long.[171]

In 1936 she was assigned the pastorate at Boylston Wesleyan Methodist church. Here she worked closely with one of the leading families, the William Presleys. Presley was a descendant of a circuit-riding preacher who helped to start many Wesleyan Methodist churches in the New York area.

For a time, Mary did housecleaning and other work for Sears Oil Company in Rome, New York. Then she went to pastor the Wesleyan Methodist church, a tiny work in Groton, New York. She lived in a room up over the entryway, and there was not enough salary to support her. During this time her father helped her financially. She was a very determined and faithful woman to the work until God released her from that pastorate. Mary Carnahan was ordained by the Rochester Conference (now Central New York District) of the Wesleyan Methodist Church in 1937.

From 1938 to 1941 she was involved in general evangelistic work as a gospel singer. An article in *The Wesleyan Methodist* described her as an experienced pastor and evangelist, singer, and young people's and children's worker. She prepared well for the services and was talented in vocal and instrumental music. She was a wise and earnest altar worker.[172]

Mary served as an associate pastor with Laura Ames at the Pine Meadows and Redfield charge during the 1942 conference year. These women also served as Sunday school teachers. One student walked six miles from home to church in order to be taught about Christ by these women. During the 1940s many meetings were held in the home of Nellie Olin because the church woodstove was not safe.[173] In 1943 Mary became the second full-time pastor of the Redfield church. For a time, she walked several miles to an old schoolhouse for a second preaching and teaching service each Sunday. Her pastorate at the Redfield church lasted ten years. She married John W. Crandall in 1952 and mothered his three sons. He became the official pastor and continued there until his death in 1975.

For thirty years much of Mary's livelihood came from being the postmaster at Redfield, in the foothills of the Adirondacks. She was noted for her excellent ministry to the children of that community. Mary and John worked well together to see that the small village and township had a multifaceted church ministry to all ages. Part of the time the church ministered to a black family whom they transported to church events. After her husband's death, Mary returned a second time to pastor the church.

When their son, Edward Crandall, was unable financially to return to seminary, he was asked to supply a church in Camden. When he returned to Asbury, his parents conducted afternoon services in the same building (1962–65).

Mary Crandall moved to Houghton, New York for the last four years prior to her homegoing August 27, 1981.[174]

Marcella Dean

Marcella Dean was saved in a holiness tent meeting. After the meeting was over, she walked five miles to the Madisonville Pilgrim Holiness Church. She overheard some people talking about the tent meeting. "What was the tent meeting like?" someone asked. Another person responded, "Not much—just one girl!" Marcella Dean decided at that moment she would give back to the Pilgrim Holiness Church more than they paid for that tent meeting! And she did. She repaid the Pilgrim Holiness denomination in her tithes, offerings, and service much more than the financial cost of the tent meeting.

Her parents were very upset when she told them she had gotten saved. They had not wanted her to get involved with "those holiness people."

Their medical doctor had been talking with them about her. He told them Marcella had a good brain. Her parents wanted her to go to college, and the doctor planned to pay for her education at Oxford College in Ohio. They reminded her that she had only two more years of high school and that she was going to go to Oxford. They believed she had destroyed the plans for her bright future.

Marcella would later spend some time (1954–56) in Transvaal, South Africa, as a missionary, but her missionary activities began immediately. She prayed for the conversion of her parents. Her father was the first to be saved, and he was delivered from the addiction of tobacco. She prayed her brothers would become ministers, and God honored her prayers by calling three of the four. Marcella became an ordained minister in the Pilgrim Holiness Church in 1936.

Early in her ministry Marcella and Bertha Kienbaum were co-pastors of a church in Ohio. Her ministry was varied from preaching, teaching, writing, public social work, missionary, and children's ministry.

She will be remembered for her work in the missionary work with the children. There was no organization for the children. She said, "In the Pilgrim Holiness Church we always pled poverty, and we didn't put out very nice (printed) materials." Marcella had just received her graduate degree in education. She wanted things to be attractive and beautiful. But she was always cautioned to not spend much money. During the time she was in this office (at the headquarters in Indianapolis) she wrote teaching materials for children's and adult ministries. Her papers were always filled with object lessons, patterns, missionary games, and choruses.

After her retirement from social work for the Owosso, Michigan, public schools, she held camps, workshops, and vacation Bible schools. She spoke and held workshops for the International Sunday School Convention in Cobo Hall, Detroit, for twelve years.

She was an instructor at Owosso College, Owosso, Michigan (later merged into what became Indiana Wesleyan University, Marion, Indiana) for a number of years as well as in the public school system. Her love for children and youth kept her mind alert to ways of teaching and holding their attention.

She served as the junior church director at Flint, Michigan, Brown Street Wesleyan church. In 1980 she became director of Christian education at the Owosso Wesleyan Church, where she held children's church as late as January 1994. She retired from active service May 31, 1994. Her friends and many of her former students set up a scholarship fund at Indiana Wesleyan University to honor her and her work.[175]

Elma Honeycutt

Elma Honeycutt grew up knowing what it meant to move all across the western United States. Her father was a frontiersman, and her mother came west from Missouri on a covered wagon. She was born in a sod house. She related that most of the time they went to church in a buggy. Her mother taught her children to pray by saying a few words and having them repeat them after her.

After her father "lived his claim out," he sold it. He bought one of the first Fords that came off the line. Then he packed the family and their belongings in the car and headed west to the state of Washington. The rainy weather did not suit them, and they moved back across the mountains to Idaho. That area was too cold, and they became homesick, so they moved back to Oklahoma. Next they moved just across the border into Texas, where they lived in an underground dugout house. She grew up on this Texas farm. She learned to work on the farm. She and her sister would milk nine cows (by hand) before they walked to school each morning. In the evening their task was to gather the eggs.

Elma and her older sister attended God's Bible School in Cincinnati, Ohio. They both met their future husbands there and were married in a double wedding.

In 1933 she and her husband, W. E. Honeycutt, began their ministerial work in Covington, Kentucky, with the Pilgrim Holiness Church. Their ministry covered forty-five years. Her husband suffered a heart attack while they were serving a church in Pennsylvania, so they moved to Virginia to be near one of their daughters. When his health improved, they began pastoring together again. This time it was the Severn Presbyterian Church at Naxera. But his health eventually deteriorated again and forced them to enter the Ware Convalescent Center. At the time of his death they had been married fifty-seven years and ten months.

Elma then resided in the Walter Reed Convalescent Center. She was asked to be the chaplain of the center. She now makes her daily calls on the residents by holding on to the back of a wheelchair. She conducts devotions at the center, plays the piano, and reads her poetry to the residents. She has played the piano in public for seventy-three years. She began writing poetry at age thirteen and has had three books of poems published.[176]

Elma's husband served as a home mission district superintendent for a time. They served churches in seven different districts. She pastored or assisted in pastoring the Lawrenceville and Janesville, Illinois, churches as well as the Julian Brookside church in the Pennsylvania and New Jersey District and the Baton Rouge, Louisiana church.[177]

Fern Amanda Haines Mahin

Fern Haines's faith in God meant more than life to her. She was born July 31, 1893, in Bladen, Nebraska, and was saved as a child. While teaching school, she met Ross L. Mahin. They married and lived twenty-one years on a farm near Cedar, Kansas.

Fern was the mother of four children. She was faithful in training them in the precepts of God. She served as pianist, Sunday school teacher, and the local Woman's Home and Foreign Missionary Society president.

Fern began her studies for ordination in 1936, and she and her husband entered their ministerial work in 1938. They were the pastors of the Wesley Center Church in the Kansas Conference of the Wesleyan Methodist Church.

They pastored together the churches at Victor, Chapman Creek, Chanute, and Manketo. They were both ordained August 6, 1944, and served the Wesleyan Methodist Church for twenty-five years in pastoral work.

Fern was also active on the conference level and served on several committees and boards. She took part in the ordination service in 1952.

Her death occurred December 17, 1962.[178]

Mannie Moffatt

Mannie Moffatt served the Virginia District of the Pilgrim Holiness Church from 1936 to 1964. She was the pastor of the Deltavilla, Virginia, church for a number of years. She died during the 1964 conference year.[179]

Gipsie M. Miller

Gipsie M. Miller wrote her ministerial story:

My "call" was unusual in that the local boards of two of my husband's churches recognized it before I did, and they offered to grant me local preacher's license. I thanked them and explained that I was not called. I had a dim view of women preachers!

One day in the quietness of my regular prayer time, I heard a voice saying, "I have . . . ordained you." (John 15:16, KJV). I was startled. Was God really calling me to the ministry of preaching? I was not sure how my preacher-husband would feel about this since we had never discussed such a thing. So I prayed, "Lord, if You are indeed calling me to preach, then You tell Dewey."

Dewey was my late husband, the Reverend Dewey O. Miller, at that time pastor of First Wesleyan Methodist Church, Roanoke, Virginia. I do not now remember how much time passed after my unexpected call until one day my husband said to me, "Have you ever thought about ordination?" I then shared with him what had gone on between the Lord and me. Dewey encouraged me in every way possible and was my esteemed mentor.

I had no ministerial training. My aspiration had been a business career. I had gone to business college, and at the time of our marriage, I held a responsible job in a bank.

I received local appointment in 1947 and commenced the Ministerial Study Course offered through the Conference. It was completed in 1951, but I waited for another confirmation before taking the vows of ordination—converts at the altar under my preaching. It was given, and I was ordained by the North Carolina Wesleyan Methodist Church Conference at Colfax, North Carolina, August 7, 1952.

The nature of my ministry was missionary evangelism. I was already officially connected with the district Woman's Missionary Society, and after the Lord laid His hand on me for ministry, I experienced a new burden for it and a new confidence about the work I was doing. My ministry through WMS had the outlets of preaching, writing, and extended ministry.

My preaching missionary sermons were based on Scripture texts and delivered by faith in the power of the "unchanging commission." Another door that opened for me was writing. I wrote for the WMS Prayer Calendar and the *Wesleyan Missionary* for a total of ten years. I wrote the programs for the WMS in the *Guide* for seven years. I originated the *Community Missions,* a promotional and inspirational quarterly to advance the program. I authored the books *History Woman's Missionary Society Wesleyan Methodist Church; Community Missions Manual;* and *Effective Community Missions.*

I contributed one chapter to *Of Noble Character,* edited by Joy Bray. I also wrote numerous skits, dramas, installation services, and the Ceremony of Merger for the Pilgrim Holiness and Wesleyan Methodist Women's Missionary Societies held October 29, 1968, at Louisville, Kentucky.

I was never an assistant pastor to my husband; neither of us desired this appointment for me. I did take services while he was away in revivals. In the local church I was simply the pastor's wife. I did those things a pastor's wife usually does. I visited with him, and I also carried on a visitation ministry alone. I taught Sunday school classes, conducted prayer meetings at church and in the homes, directed VBS, and was active in the music program, sometimes as pianist, sometimes as choir director. My extended ministry in missionary evangelism led to preaching as the doors opened to me.

I became active in the local WMS while still a teen. I became a district officer at age twenty-four. For thirty-nine and a half years I was a district officer, thirty-two of which were as president. For five years I was a general WMS officer as Community Missions Director.

My appointment now (1998) with the North Carolina West District is "Retired Ordained Minister, Director Emerita WW [Wesleyan Women]."

Mrs. Miller celebrated her ninetieth birthday November 12, 1998.

Vivian Taylor Saunders

Vivian Taylor Saunders served with her husband for fifty years as a pastor and missionary. The *Minutes of the Annual Assembly of the Pilgrim Holiness Church Southern District* listed them as pastors at Gold Hill and Albemarle in North Carolina, from 1936 to 1941.

They also were the pastors of Erlanger, Burlington, and Salisbury churches in the Pilgrim Holiness Church in the North Carolina District. They served as missionaries to Barbados and Guyana from 1954 to 1960.[180]

Vivian Saunders served on the committee for the merging conference of the general Women's Missionary Society. At the time of the 1968 merger, she was elected vice president of the Southern Area WMS. She also served for a number of years on the general WMS executive committee and as the district WMS president for nine years.

Vivian Taylor Saunders was born June 30, 1914, at Hagerstown, Indiana, and was saved and sanctified in 1930. She graduated from the theological course at God's Bible School, Cincinnati, Ohio, in 1933. While there she met Dallas Roy Saunders, and they were united in marriage May 24, 1934. They were the parents of four children.

Vivian was a born leader. She used her musical skills and talents of singing and musician, children's and youth worker both in the local churches where they pastored and on the mission field. Both Vivian and Dallas were ordained in the North Carolina District of the Pilgrim Holiness Church. Vivian died January 29, 1985.[181]

Bertha Ellen Stamey

It is impossible to put into a few words the dedication and commitment of Bertha Stamey to the mountain people in South Carolina and to her Lord. Rev. James Wiggins, superintendent of the South Coastal District of The Wesleyan Church, wrote a tribute of her life that was read at her funeral. The following facts that reveal her character and devotion to the mountain people were taken from his tribute.

James Wiggins and his siblings grew up under two lady preachers, Bertha E. Stamey and Gertrude Farmer. These godly ladies were missionaries to the mountain people who owe a great debt of gratitude to them for their devoted, loving, and untiring efforts to share the love of Christ and nurture everyone in the faith.

Bertha Stamey was a woman with a call. Her preaching and exhorting were anointed with the power of the Holy Spirit. To live and labor among the mountain people demanded more than a normal commitment.

She was a woman with compassion. Like her Master, she reached out to these people in tangible ways to meet the physical and spiritual needs of people. James Wiggins related that after chopping wood for her, she would give him a box of used clothing or other items that his family desperately needed.

Bertha had a compelling urge to reach the lost. She was not content merely to pastor and meet the spiritual needs of the community and the Glenville Church, but she tried to start Sunday schools and Bible studies in other communities as well. Pine Creek community was an example. This village was located eight to ten miles across the mountains, but she went to these people each Sunday afternoon with the gospel.

She lived a consistent Christian life. One of Jim's eight sisters remarked that Bertha Stamey was as near to a perfect example of living the Christian life without spot or blemish that she ever knew.

Bertha was a woman with a conservative, frugal lifestyle. She sought to put Christ and His kingdom first in her life. She lived without luxuries, pinched pennies, and paid the district assessments.

Her consecration was total. Her all was on the altar for Christ. She lived in the Spirit and walked in the Spirit. She modeled Jesus in her capacity to love the lowly and unlovable. She reached out in love to those who had little education, who lived in poverty and unfavorable circumstances in this life. She made them feel important. They may have been nobodies in the world's eyes, but she made them feel like somebodies in Christ. She took the youth to camp meeting and always involved all the children in the special programs at the church.

Bertha was born December 11, 1902, and she answered the call to "come home" May 7, 1998. Her father was a Wesleyan Methodist minister. Bertha began preparing for the ministry in 1936. She often had other lady ministers working with her on her assignments. Her first assignment was with Gertrude Farmer at Glenville in 1940. For a period of twenty years she pastored the following churches in the South Carolina Conference of the Wesleyan Methodist Church: Buck Creek, Glenville, Tuckasegee, Greenville Woodside Avenue, Eden, Glendale Converse, and Easley Alice. She was ordained in 1954. Nellie Linder also served as her assistant while she was pastor at Glenville.

The Glenville and Buck Creek work was known as the Blue Ridge Mountain Mission work in the early days. Bertha was a prayer warrior, and many things were accomplished in her churches because she touched heaven with her prayers. In 1945 the Glenville church was remodeled, and Sunday school classrooms were added to the building. The interior was finished with sheet rock and Celotex. That year a parsonage was purchased. In 1949 she became the pastor of the Greenville Woodside Avenue Church and the church was painted that year. In 1951 all the indebtedness was paid off, and in 1953 a new parsonage was purchased and construction of the basement unit of a new church was begun. In 1954 the basement church was completed. Her sacrificial and efficient labors added to the church in many ways.[182]

Elsie L. Schael Thomas

Elsie (Mrs. C. A.) Schael was born in Twinsburg, Ohio, June 11, 1903. She was converted as a child and was sanctified as a teenager. She attended Cleveland Bible Institute (later Malone College) for one year and then transferred to Marion College, in Marion, Indiana (now Indiana Wesleyan University). Here she met Walter Lewis Thomas, whom she later married.

Elsie entered into her ministerial preparation in 1936 and began that year to be an assistant to her husband on his pastorates. Among those pastorates were Byron and Fishersburg churches. She was ordained in 1943. They spent several years on the pastorates until his health failed. Elsie taught in the public school systems for twenty-two years.[183]

Ida B. Thompson

Ida B. (Mrs. C. A.) Thompson was received as an ordained minister from the Church of the Nazarene in the Middle Atlantic States Mission Conference of the Wesleyan Methodist Church in 1936 and was appointed a general evangelist that year. She served for one year as pastor of the Smyrna, Delaware, church. In 1938 she gave devotions at conference and was appointed to evangelistic work. No other reference was found on her.[184]

Geneva L. Jones Tysinger

Geneva L. Jones began her preparations for the ministry in 1936. She retired from the active ministry in 1958.

Rev. Melvin L. Gentry, a minister in the North Carolina West District of The Wesleyan Church, wrote the following tribute to Geneva L. Jones Tysinger June 3, 1998:

> Geneva L. Jones was a person endowed with leadership qualities, which God directed into the ministry. In early life she embraced the doctrine of heart holiness and often testified to her personal experience of sanctifying grace. She was not ashamed of the gospel of Christ.

She was ordained by the North Carolina Conference of the Wesleyan Methodist Church in 1943. She was also in demand as a licensed practical nurse. She combined both of these certifications as a strong witness for Christ. Her life of faith, prayer, and hard work was a great influence on many lives and especially on her own family. Her children and grandchildren are actively involved in The Wesleyan Church in the High Point and Thomasville, North Carolina, area.

Her voice could be heard from the prayer rooms at the Shady Grove Campground in Colfax, North Carolina. She was an intercessor for the evangelists and workers and was faithful at the altar encouraging and exhorting seekers who responded to the invitation in the camp services.

Her early years of ministry were invested in pioneering (planting) a church in Lexington, North Carolina. Later she was appointed the assistant pastor of Memorial Park Wesleyan Church and First Wesleyan (now Central) Church in Thomasville, North Carolina. She served both of these two churches for ten years each.

Geneva was married to Thomas Cicero Jones in 1904, and they became the parents of three sons: Otho, J. C., and Howard; and two daughters, Bessie Hilliard and Sadie Potts. After many years of widowhood, she married J. E. Tysinger in 1956.

Geneva's life of Christian service came to an end July 22, 1981.

Alice L. Bushnell Waldron

Alice Bushnell became the wife of Edward E. Waldron, and they were both faithful ministers in the Pilgrim Holiness Church. Before her health failed and her physical suffering began, she entered willingly and faithfully in ministry in several pastorates with her husband. They jointly pastored in Lansing, Michigan; Lamal, Colorado; Clymer, Pennsylvania; and Medora, Madison, and Grand View, Indiana.[185]

Ophie Pearl Walker

Pearl Walker was an educated woman. She was a graduate of Frankfort Pilgrim College, Frankfort, Indiana (later merged into United Wesleyan College, Allentown, Pennsylvania);

Kingswood Bible School, Kingswood, Kentucky; and God's Bible School, Cincinnati, Ohio.

Pearl Walker was born September 24, 1901, and died January 12, 1963, while pastoring the College Corner Pilgrim Holiness church. She was converted at age ten. After she was sanctified, her goal and aim were to be employed in the Lord's work. She began preaching at an early age, delivering messages described as "heaven sent and Holy Ghost anointed."[186]

The first reference found of her work was in 1936. She was an ordained minister at that time and served in the Indiana District of the Pilgrim Holiness Church through 1950. At that time the district was divided, and she became a ministerial member of the Southern Indiana District. She was the pastor of nine churches. Part of the time she was an assistant to her husband, Elza. She pastored the College Corner church for twelve years.[187]

She was described as a Spirit-filled Christian who faithfully followed the Lord. Her life was an inspiration to those she served. She was the mother of two children.

Mrs. Jennie Whitaker

Jennie Whitaker may have begun her ministerial service under the Pilgrim Holiness Church in California. Her name was on the roll of the California District from 1936 to 1941. She was the pastor of the Pilgrim Holiness Church in San Diego in 1938.[188]

The Wesleyan Methodist, July 30, 1941, page 12, reported in the column "Church News and Reports" that Jennie Whitaker, an ordained minister, had joined the Tennessee Conference of the Wesleyan Methodist Church as a conference evangelist. The *Minutes* revealed she was placed on the conference roll after she had passed the course on the *Discipline.* She became the associate pastor of Knoxville, Tennessee, Second Church with O. C. Rushing in 1942. Most of the time that she was under the direction of the Tennessee Conference, she was listed as a general evangelist. In 1948 her name was dropped from the roll of ordained ministers, but

she was reinstated in 1950. Her problem seemed to center around the fact she was not a member of a local Wesleyan church. In 1959 she requested her name be dropped from the roll, and the record stated that there was nothing against her character.[189]

Augusta Wilson Brecheisen

Augusta Wilson Brecheisen was born into the home of traveling evangelist David E. Wilson and his wife, Ethel Sager Wilson, on March 7, 1916. Augusta's famous father was a gifted communicator and Bible expositor with a phenomenal memory, probably a photographic memory. He preached four hundred times a year in eighty-five denominations around the world for forty-five  years. While he was holding revivals, his wife, Ethel, kept the home fires burning, caring for their two children and pastoring small churches. Her tiny pastoral income, along with a gift for real estate investment, allowed David E. Wilson freedom to preach in churches of all sizes regardless of the amount of the offerings he received. Every two to three weeks Ethel would bundle up the children and take her husband to the railroad station. He would board the train for another trip to a church for another meeting.

Religious work was Augusta's heritage. While her father was winning scores of people to the Lord, her mother was busy ministering to the spiritual needs of her little flocks. Her mother was the prayer partner of her father, who may have been hundreds of miles away. She witnessed and experienced the sacrificial support her mother gave to her father's work.

It is not strange that Augusta met her future husband at the Ludlow Falls, Ohio, camp meeting. Her father was the camp evangelist. Loren and Dale Brecheisen were the camp musicians.

Loren was born on a small farm near Petoskey, Michigan. His father died when he was four years old. His mother raised eight children on a very meager income. Loren was gifted in musical abilities. He and his brother, Dale, formed a vaudeville-like duo and performed in northern Michigan resorts. Loren played the piano and sang.

Augusta was licensed to preach in 1937 and was listed as an evangelist. Her district ministerial membership was in the New York District of the Pilgrim Holiness Church. She became an educator and taught at Bible Holiness Seminary, Owosso, Michigan (later Owosso College, eventually merged into what became Indiana Wesleyan University, Marion, Indiana). Loren was a student at the Bible Holiness Seminary, where she taught. They fell in love and were married June 1, 1940. Both Loren and Augusta were ordained in 1943.

Neither Augusta nor Loren ever pastored a church. They served the Lord and the Church for forty-five years as evangelistic singers throughout the United States, Canada, and Hawaii. When asked what was the most discouraging aspect of their ministry, Augusta quickly answered: the breakdowns with cars and trailers and weather problems. They traveled by car and trailer. Augusta taught their two children, Jerry and Ethel, in the trailer—it was their home and school. She related that God always provided for them though many times they didn't live under the best arrangements. They lived life on the road. Every two or three weeks they would be tearing down and setting up the musical equipment. Perhaps the one burden they lived with was trying to meet all the financial needs and never knowing if the offerings would be enough to make the payments on the accordion or other pressing needs. But God never failed them.

Augusta and Loren celebrated fifty years of marriage in 1990. When asked what had been the most rewarding and fulfilling part of her ministry, she replied, to see souls won for Christ and the making of many lasting Christian friendships.[190]

Susie Britton

Susie Britton was given an offering of twenty-six dollars for her sacrificial work at the Williamstown, Kentucky, church. She had labored at the church during the 1936 year, and the conference gave her the offering in 1937. She was also ordained at conference time in 1937. Her sacrificial labors continued at the Williamstown church for three years.

Susie was a pastor in the Kentucky Conference of the Wesleyan Methodist Church from 1936 to 1957. She pastored the Milton, Mt. Zion, and Sylvania churches. She was a conference evangelist for a number of years and retired from the active ministry in 1957.

Susie was also active on the conference level and served on the committee on finances and what is now called the district board of ministerial development. She died February 28, 1958.[191]

Laura Cheneworth

The records were not clear about Laura Cheneworth's ordination. She was under appointment with the Indiana District of the Pilgrim Holiness Church from 1937 to 1942. Her death occurred probably during the 1942–43 district year.[192]

Mrs. J. D. Craik

Mrs. J. D. Craik was ordained in 1936 by the Kansas District of the Pilgrim Holiness Church. Her entire ministerial work was done in Kansas. She became inactive in 1958 and retired in 1966.[193]

Beatrice Dodge

Beatrice Dodge was a Pilgrim Holiness missionary. Her missionary career began in 1937 and took her to Barbados, in the Caribbean, and to Guyana, in South America. She was ordained in 1942. She was still serving as a missionary in 1963.[194]

Christine Fowler

Christine Fowler was a conference preacher (licensed minister) and young people's evangelist in 1937. She was a successful youth worker for several years.

In 1947 she was ordained. The next year she began teaching at Sanford Biblical College. During that year she also held fourteen meetings. She served from 1949 to 1952 as the secretary of the Kentucky Conference of the Wesleyan Methodist Church. On January 3, 1950, she was appointed by the president of the conference to the pioneer work at Lewisport, Kentucky, and Catherine Harrington was her assistant. Catherine also held revival meetings during this time. The work at Lewisport was not successful. She also pastored the Newburgh church in Kentucky and was a general evangelist for many years. She was listed on the inactive list at the time of the 1968 merger.[195]

For a time, Christine was a student in college and during this time was assigned as the associate pastor of Knoxville, Tennessee, First Church.[196]

Hallie Giltner

Hallie Giltner pastored the Holton church in the Kentucky Conference of the Wesleyan Methodist Church from 1937 to 1943. She then spent two years in evangelistic work but returned to the Holton church for another year in 1947. She was ordained that year.

Hallie taught at Sanford Biblical College for a time but returned to the pastorate in 1954. From 1954 to 1957 she was assigned to Milan and in 1958 returned to pastor the Holton church for another six years. She was engaged in evangelistic work at the time of the 1968 merger.[197]

Mrs. Harley Hoffman

Mrs. Harley Hoffman served as an assistant pastor in the Pennsylvania and New Jersey District of the Pilgrim Holiness Church. She was ordained

in 1937. Most of the years she was listed as inactive. In 1965 she retired and was so listed in 1967.[198]

Eunice Irvine Hansen

Eunice Irvine served the Wesleyan Methodist Church for twenty years as a single woman minister. She related the following facts about her ministry before and after her marriage.

Eunice was born September 9, 1916. She lived in the small town of Leesburg, Indiana. After her graduation from high school, she worked for a lady in Lake Tippecanoe in the summer and in Alexandria, Indiana, in the fall. She then decided to help a lady who was ill and lived in Peru, Indiana. While working in Peru, she attended a revival meeting at the East Washington Street Wesleyan Methodist Church. She had been converted in a children's meeting during the Fairmount, Indiana, Wesleyan Methodist camp meeting at the age of eleven, but during high school days she had drifted away from the Lord. During the revival meeting she was convicted of her sins and prayed through in her room. From then on her life was changed.

She obtained work in a basket factory in Peru but felt a call to preach and knew she needed to attend college. She quit her job and made plans to go to college. Before starting to college, she held her first revival meeting in Hoopston, Illinois. Some people were saved in that meeting.

She attended Marion College (now Indiana Wesleyan University), Marion, Indiana, from 1939 to 1940. She left college and became the assistant pastor at the Warsaw Wesleyan Church. The next year she became the pastor. At the end of the conference year 1942 she returned to Marion College and graduated with a bachelor of religion degree in 1943.

In 1945 she organized a Wesleyan Young People's Society at the Warsaw church with sixteen members. She also began leading young people's Bible studies. Eunice was also a leader in the conference Wesleyan Young People's Society. She served as the conference youth secretary for two years. During all this time she was active in holding evangelistic meetings and "Kids' Krusades." Eunice was ordained in 1944.

Her father was injured in an automobile accident in 1944 that left him paralyzed from his neck down. She spent most of her time at home helping to care for him until September 1946.

In 1949 she went back to Marion College and received her A.B. degree.

Eunice spent a few years working in the missionary office of the Free Methodist Church at Winona Lake. One of her duties was preparing the missionary news page for their monthly magazine. She left that office when she married Wendell Hansen November 2, 1957. Dr. Hansen became president of Great Commission Schools in Anderson, Indiana, and she taught in the kindergarten at the school.

Eunice returned to Marion College for a semester after they left Great Commission Schools. She taught at Westfield-Washington Elementary School for eighteen years. During this time she earned a master's degree in education at Ball State University, in Muncie, Indiana.

On weekends Eunice, her husband, and their small son presented programs in churches. They used trained birds to speak and perform in presenting the gospel message of salvation. Through this ministry many hundreds were won to the Lord. Their video of the performing birds has now been seen on national television in Japan, England, and Russia. There have been many write-ups about their ministry in newspapers and magazines. They were still presenting this unique ministry in 1999.

The Hansens have a daughter, Sylvia, and a son, Dean.[199]

V. Dorothy Johnson

V. Dorothy Johnson served as a missionary to Sierra Leone, West Africa, from 1933 to 1936. She was a member of the Oregon Conference of the Wesleyan Methodist Church and was ordained. She was listed in the *Oregon Minutes* from 1937 to 1942, but no other service records were found of her work. She died in Portland, Oregon, April 13, 1962.[200]

Vivian Stanley Bardsley Johnson

Vivian Stanley Bardsley Johnson writes her own story:

During camp meeting in the summer of 1936 I experienced a very definite call to full-time Christian service. My call was further confirmed when Rev. E. J. Pitts, conference president of the Indiana Conference, told me that the conference board had voted to give me a scholarship at Marion College (now Indiana Wesleyan University). The scholarship was renewed each year until I graduated in 1940.

In the fall of 1937 three young ladies, Jane Plew, Mary Chapman and Kathleen Kelsven, joined with me in forming a girls' gospel team. I did the preaching, and the girls sang. The gospel  team was well accepted throughout the Marion, Indiana, area, and we were involved nearly every Sunday during the three years following its formation.

Following my graduation in 1940 the conference board gave me credit for my involvement with the gospel team in preaching and ordained me. I was granted a general evangelist appointment. The eight years from 1940 to 1948 I was working full time as a general evangelist. According to my records, I held 130 meetings in eight years in eight states. (Revival meetings in those days lasted from two to three weeks.)

On August 29, 1948, I was married to Rev. Orval Bardsley. Orval's first wife had passed away, leaving him with four young children ranging from four to twelve years of age. In addition to these four children, Harold, Annabelle, Paul, and Betty, God gave us another daughter, Linda. All our children are Christians and members of The Wesleyan Church. Harold was a pastor for a number of years and is now serving as district superintendent of the Indiana North District of The Wesleyan Church. His son, Mark, is a pastor. Linda's husband, Joe Kelly, is also a pastor. Annabelle has a son who is a pastor.

After my marriage to Orval, I held revivals from 1948 to 1980 in most of the churches we pastored. I also preached on Sundays from time to time. Orval and I were co-pastors at Dowagiac, Michigan; South Bend, Mt. Zion, Henry County, Westfield, Indianapolis First, Jonesboro, and Sweester, Indiana, churches. We retired from the pastorate in 1980 because of Orval's health problems. He died in 1986.

In 1989 I married Rev. Howard Johnson, a retired Wesleyan pastor from the Iowa/Minnesota Conference. Because of a stroke and other health problems, I have not preached often during the past few years. We have spent our winters in Brooksville, Florida, at Wesleyan Village, where we take part in the prayer chain that gives prayer support to missionaries all over the world and to local needs as well.

Vivian preached repentance, regeneration, and holiness. Her preaching was always with a tender and weeping heart. Tears were her trademark. She was honored in 1964 for twenty-five years of service, and she co-pastored for another sixteen years.

Vivian was born in Madison County, Indiana, in 1911. She entered her heavenly home October 13, 1999.[201]

Caroline Bescon McQuigg

Caroline Bescon McQuigg was converted in a revival meeting in the Fargo, Ohio, Wesleyan Methodist church in 1926. Her supreme desire was to help people come to know God.

She began her ministerial studies for the ministry in 1937. She and her husband, Harry, were appointed to the pastorate at Sunbury, Ohio, and were both ordained in 1943 by the Ohio Conference. They also were the pastors of the Chippewa Lake church for three years. In 1948 they opened a new work at Jelloway and insisted that it would be a Wesleyan Methodist church.

Caroline died as a result of an auto accident November 1, 1949.[202]

Mabel Metzger Rathbun

Mabel Metzger Rathbun was born in Lincoln, Kansas, in 1903. She married Lee Rathbun, who was a farmer and schoolteacher. During the time he was finishing his college work in preparation for full-time teaching, Mabel was converted through holiness preaching at a country church. Her transformed life was influential in bringing her husband to the Lord.

When Lee Rathbun completed his college work, they moved to Colorado Springs, where he taught high school mathematics. During this time they both felt called to the ministry, and from 1937 to 1939 they pastored a church in Kansas. Mabel was ordained in 1937.

Mabel Rathbun was considered by the Pilgrim Holiness Church to be a "choice minister." For more than twenty-five years she and her husband were instrumental in either starting or establishing churches in Simms, Oakdale, and Pineville, Louisiana.

Mrs. Rathbun had diabetes and as a result was blind for many years. Nevertheless, she continued to prepare her messages with the help of her husband and continued to preach with blessing and effectiveness. Until restricted by her last serious illness, she helped her husband with the general pastoral duties at the Oakdale church.

Mabel Rathbun died June 18, 1965. She was the mother of Elsie Marie Hooter and Warren Lee Rathbun.[203]

Florein Strohl

Florein Strohl was converted as a young girl. She had never heard about sanctification or living a holy life, but she longed for something more. That deep craving of her heart was met, and years later when she heard the holiness message of full surrender to God and death to self, she knew she already had that experience. She was a member of a Methodist church and the teacher of the ladies' Bible class, but she felt led to join the Pilgrim Holiness Church about 1920.

Florein was born August 26, 1878, near Napoleon, Ohio. She married Arthur Strohl in 1897. Arthur died in 1932.[204]

After Arthur's death, Florein moved to Liberty Center, Ohio, and helped to establish the Pilgrim Holiness Church there. She was ordained in 1936.

She lived for a time in Lansing, Michigan, but later moved to Colesville, Pennsylvania, to live with her daughter and son-in-law, Rev. and Mrs. J. Franklin Lint. She worked zealously in several local churches where her son-in-law pastored and served the Lord faithfully.

Florein Strohl was the pastor of the Highland and Linden Hall, Pennsylvania, churches in the Pennsylvania and New Jersey District of the Pilgrim Holiness Church. She died March 21, 1964.[205]

Agnes Tellefsen

Agnes Tellefsen was licensed to preach in 1937 by the Middle Atlantic States Conference of the Wesleyan Methodist Church. She had attended God's Bible School in Cincinnati, Ohio. She was listed as an evangelist in that conference until she transferred to the Oregon Conference May 24, 1939.

Agnes was active in the conference. She served as the Sunday school secretary and secretary of evangelism. Her duty in the latter office was to report to *The Wesleyan Methodist* the revival schedules of the conference. She often led in the devotional periods of conference and frequently led the singing.

She moved back to the Middle Atlantic States Conference in 1943 and served as a general evangelist until 1945. No other reference was made to her work after 1945.[206]

She was ordained by the Oregon Conference and was the pastor of the Russelville Wesleyan Methodist Church. She served in that conference from 1939 to June 3, 1943. She was active also on the conference level there and served on several committees and boards as well as being the vice president of the conference Woman's Home and Foreign Missionary Society.[207]

Jeanette Zufall

Jeanette and Harry A. Zufall served in several districts of the Pilgrim Holiness Church. She was first mentioned as the pastor of the Stonington church in the Pennsylvania and New Jersey District.[208] The next record of her work was found in the West Virginia District from 1942 to 1948. The 1942 record showed that she had transferred from the Pittsburgh District. She was the assistant pastor at Terra Alta, West Virginia, in 1943 and was listed as the pastor of O'Toola, West Virginia, in 1944–45. They remained in that district through 1947.

Jeanette was listed as a co-pastor in the Illinois District from 1948 to 1950. This may have been the Marshall Pilgrim Holiness church. She served as an evangelist in 1951.[209] They returned to the West Virginia District in 1952 and remained there until they moved to the Eastern Ohio District in 1965.[210]

Ruth Alexander

Ruth Alexander, nurse, preacher, evangelistic singer, and skillful church planter, was ordained August 1941 during the annual conference of the Michigan District of the Pilgrim Holiness Church in Owosso, Michigan. God called her to preach, and the inward compulsion would never leave her. She felt that it was the greatest honor that could be bestowed upon her. Ruth did not know how to "take it easy." Every task she performed was done with all her heart, mind, and strength. W. N. Miller, a former superintendent of the Michigan District of the Pilgrim Holiness Church declared,

As a public speaker, Rev. Ruth Alexander had the ability to have her listeners weeping or laughing with her. With this ability she sincerely honored her Lord and led many souls to Him. Her training and ability as a registered nurse could have assured her of a more prosperous, secure life, but the call of the Master was so strong that she left all and followed Him.

Ruth was the oldest of six children. The family was very poor, and she early learned the necessity of economizing. This enabled her to survive on her meager salary as a minister. She was an avid reader as a child and read virtually everything in the local public library. Her younger brothers and sisters begged her to tell them stories, and her extensive reading filled her mind with many good stories. She became an experienced storyteller while a child herself and used that gift in her preaching ministry.

When she was eleven years old, Rev. L. W. Sturk, his brother, J. D., and Rev. B. E. Manker pitched a tent and conducted a tent meeting in her hometown. Nearly one hundred people were saved, and Ruth and her mother were among them. A Pilgrim Holiness church was organized, and Ruth became a charter member at age twelve. She began teaching Sunday school classes at that time. When she was fourteen she was elected or appointed to the church board. Ruth said it was not because she was so smart, but she could read and write, and many of the people in the church could only sign their names.

Ruth graduated from high school at age seventeen. In September of that year, she entered Butterworth Hospital School of Nursing in Grand Rapids, Michigan. She loved her patients and gave them excellent care. Here the nurse's uniform gave her a sense of worth, for everyone was on the same level in that wardrobe! She completed the course in three years.

After graduation, Ruth was employed by Butterworth Hospital and was in charge of the maternity nursery for five years. Then one day her mother's doctor phoned her to tell her that her mother had suffered a heart attack and that she should come home immediately. She cared for her mother for one and one-half years after that. She promised her mother that she would care for the younger children after her mother's death. Her brother Henry was a student at Marion College, Marion, Indiana (now Indiana Wesleyan University). The rest of the children were at home, the youngest aged eleven. She planned to return to the nursing field as soon as she completed her responsibilities at home.

However, God had other plans for her. Ruth began to feel the call of God to preach. She struggled for several months before she surrendered. She wondered how God could open the doors for her, a woman, to minister.

Since there was no Pilgrim Holiness church in the town where she was living, she attended a Wesleyan Methodist church. She led the singing and taught a Sunday school class. One Sunday the pastor was making the announcements and told the church he had not asked Sister Ruth but felt impressed to announce that she would be preaching the next Sunday night. That was March 1938. She preached, and she said, "I told them everything I knew in twenty-five minutes." Eight persons responded to the altar call that night. She preached on Sunday evening for the next two weeks, and more people were saved. She felt this was God's confirmation of her call to preach the gospel.

Henry told her there was an opening for a school nurse at Marion College. She applied and was accepted. Before she left for Marion, she had her third marriage proposal, but she pushed aside the desire to be a wife and mother because God had called her to be a minister. She entered Marion College in September 1938.

Ruth and her brother Henry formed an evangelistic team and spent a year and a half holding revival meetings. The salary for many of these meetings was change wrapped in a handkerchief! She learned to pray for her financial needs. She was in need of dresses for these meetings, and God provided by giving her five or six used but very expensive and clean dresses from a lady who had been severely burned on her arms as a child. All the dresses had long or three-quarter length sleeves, a requirement that Ruth followed whenever she was in the pulpit. Henry eventually married a Christian girl, and the team broke up. Ruth continued in the evangelistic field for another year, lugging her accordion and luggage on and off buses and trains. One wealthy widower came to the altar in one of her meetings and claimed to get saved. He would meet her bus or train whenever she was holding a meeting nearby. She finally convinced him that she was not interested in marriage and stopped meeting her at the bus or train depot. She was then back to carrying her luggage and no longer rode in his limousine!

In 1942, Ruth planted a Pilgrim Holiness church in Cheboygan, Michigan. The district rented a dirty old store building for three months. The building had two small dingy rooms in the back, which became the living quarters for Ruth and Marie Hildenbrand. Ruth did not know how to plant a church, but after praying she decided the first thing was to clean the building. She scrubbed, cleaned, and prayed for two weeks until Marie came. The empty building needed seats. After much prayer, she bought ninety-one chairs by faith. When the dirty chairs were delivered, she had the needed one hundred dollars and a place to store the extra chairs (since her building could hold only forty chairs. Ruth and Marie worked all day getting the building ready for the services, practicing and praying. Each evening they would walk the streets of the town, greeting people and inviting them to the meeting that would soon be held. They had ten persons present at the first meeting. People were converted. The little group had to move three times in two years in order to accommodate the crowd. They finally purchased a house, and they moved into it for their services. At the end of six years of labor, scrubbing, scouring, digging ditches, painting, carrying cement, lumber, and stones, besides making house calls on foot (she had no car), Ruth had planted a church—but she had wrecked her health. She was forced to spend the next year resting and recuperating. It became a common saying in the district that no man wanted to follow Ruth Alexander as a pastor. She was a hard act to follow. She just worked too hard.

After all the men ministers on the district list had been exhausted, the Dearborn church contacted her to become their pastor. Ruth remarked, "A woman preacher must have the courage of a lion, the hide of a rhinoceros, and it helps if you don't have feelings." There was no parsonage at Dearborn so Ruth lived in her own home in the city mobile home park. This church had a bad reputation in the community, and growth was extremely slow. During her seven years as pastor, they were able to purchase a parsonage. The records showed the church had grown from twenty-seven to seventy-two.

The district council (now district board of administration) asked Ruth to again enter home missionary work. They wanted her to start a church in Bay City, Michigan, but this didn't materialize, and she went to Mt. Clemens to plant a church. On the first Sunday there were forty persons present. Ruth stayed nine months.

In May 1957 she received a call to pastor the Greeley Avenue Church in Detroit. The church was financially broke, had an ugly exterior, water stains on the ceiling, and a basement half full of water. Again Ruth began the process of cleaning, painting, and redecorating the sanctuary, and eventually they covered the exterior with bricks and landscaped the yard.

At Greeley, Ruth took on the "terrible boys" class. They were eight ten-year-old boys. Ruth won the boys, and they became her helpers. That class doubled in size and raised $365 for the church. By now the church had outgrown the building. The parking space was limited, and there was no way to expand. They purchased a nice brick ranch house and a large adjoining lot. The old church was sold, and they were forced to use the house—Ruth's parsonage—as a church. She played the accordion in the kitchen, the song leader led from the living room, while the church was seated in the dining and living rooms. Ruth lived in one bedroom and walked through "the church" to the kitchen to prepare her meals. They began construction on the new church, and it was ready for occupancy on Easter Sunday.

In January 1967 Ruth, who had known for several months that her health was deteriorating, gave up and entered the hospital. She had five major medical problems, and one required surgery. It took six months to get back a degree of health. The church faithfully carried on with the aid of ministers on Sunday, but she finally was forced to resign because of her poor health.

Her doctors told her she could never go back into home missionary work, but she could return to nursing two days a week. She continued to work as a nurse for ten years until she was forced to retire at age sixty-five. She witnessed to patients and counseled them in spiritual matters. Those years of working at the hospital enabled her to become eligible for Social Security. After her retirement she enjoyed five years of fairly good health. She filled pulpits for pastors and served as an interim pastor at Lansing Trinity Church, when Rev. William Doe died. During her retirement years she also wrote her life's story, *The Parson Was a Lady*. Ruth suffered from kidney failure for a number of years but continued her "arm chair" ministry and won her neighbor to Christ just a few days before her death, January 30, 1991.

Ruth summarized her life and work like this:

There have been heartaches, misunderstandings, tears, troubles, anxious hours, and sleepless nights. But there have been victories, rewards, fun, pleasure, joy, satisfaction, and spiritual blessings immeasurable. The Lord has given me hundreds of spiritual children. I have laughed . . . I have cried . . . I have loved . . . I have lived.[211]

Faye Baker

Faye Baker was a conference preacher (licensed minister) in the Oklahoma Conference of the Wesleyan Methodist Church in 1938. The conference urged her to complete the course of study for ordination. She was married to Rev. Harold Baker July 3, 1936, and they spent the next nineteen or twenty years in general evangelistic work. She was ordained in 1940.

Faye Baker will be remembered for playing her accordion and singing with her evangelist husband in revivals and camp meetings across the nation. In August 1954 Harold and Faye accepted the pastorate of the Muncie, Indiana, Wesleyan Methodist church. He died November 11, 1957, while serving that church.

Faye served under the direction of the Oklahoma Conference from 1938 to 1963, although she was not active in the ministry after her husband's death. In 1963 the *Minutes* showed she had withdrawn from the conference because she failed and refused to report to the annual conference for more than two years.[212]

Blanche Burres

Blanche Burres and her sister, Florence (who later became Mrs. Florence Dyer), were a ministerial team for a number of years. Blanche was born in Floyd County, Indiana, in 1887. She was converted at age eighteen. She graduated from Cleveland Bible College in 1938. Her first recorded assignment was at the Elizabeth church in the Kentucky Conference of the Wesleyan Methodist Church. Florence was her assistant at Elizabeth, Brooksburg, Louisville Ninth Street, and Winchester, Kentucky, churches.[213]

Blanche organized the Clear Fork Wesleyan Methodist church in southern Indiana in 1938. She was responsible for the completion of the building program of the Louisville Ninth Street church and the builder of the parsonage in Winchester, Kentucky. She also reopened a church in southern Indiana.[214]

Blanche was ordained in 1945 by the Kentucky Conference. With Florence as her assistant, she pastored the North Charleston Church during the 1947–48 conference year in the South Carolina Conference. That church later became know as the Plantation Wesleyan Methodist Church.[215]

Blanche was active on the conference level and served in various offices and on many committees—pioneer evangelism, vacancies, Sunday school board, tithing secretary, secretary of child evangelism, and the camp meeting association directors board. She was a good soul-winner and an able minister of the gospel.

She was an effective evangelist and served several years in the field of evangelism. Her last pastorate was at Elizabeth, Kentucky, with Florence as her assistant. Blanche completed her earthly work September 2, 1983.

Ruth Campbell

The only records found for Ruth Campbell were in the minutes of the *Kansas District Pilgrim Holiness Church Annual Conference* of 1960–68. That record showed she had been ordained in 1938. From 1960 to 1968 she was the pastor of the Humboldt, Kansas, Pilgrim Holiness church.

Naomi Clevenger

Naomi Clevenger was ordained by the Pilgrim Holiness Church in 1938.[216] Rev. Ernest Batman, former superintendent of the Indiana Central

District of The Wesleyan Church, recalled that she was from the Kokomo, Indiana, Trinity church. She traveled in evangelism for a number of years before marrying. He remembered that when he was a lad she held a tent meeting near English in southern Indiana and stayed with his grandparents. She was an excellent preacher. After marrying, she joined the Church of the Nazarene and pastored churches in southern Indiana.

The Minutes of the Annual Assembly of the Pilgrim Holiness Church Texas District recorded her as the pastor of the Hillsboro, Texas, church for one year, 1941.

Mrs. Florence Burres Dyer

Florence Burres Dyer and her sister, Blanche Burres, were a ministerial team. Her first recorded ministerial assignment was at Elizabeth, Kentucky. She served as the assistant to her sister at Elizabeth, Brooksburg, Louisville Ninth Street, and Winchester, Kentucky. She was ordained in 1945 by the Kentucky Conference of the Wesleyan Methodist Church.[217]

Florence served as the superintendent of the Zion's Hill Mission in Kentucky from 1947 to April 12, 1948. She was appointed as the pastor of the Paoli church August 23, 1948, and became the assistant to Blanche at the Winchester church in 1949.

She was married in 1957. She spent several years in evangelistic work also. Her last recorded pastorate was with Blanche at the Elizabeth Church in 1962.

Florence was active on the conference level church work also. She served as the president and organizer of the Kentucky Conference Woman's Missionary Society 1948–51, and as vice president 1957–58. She served on the conference Sunday school board, missions committee, child evangelism committee and the ways and means committee. She and her sister, Blanche, often sang together at conference time during the devotional periods.[218]

She also assisted her sister, Blanche, in pastoring the Charleston church in the South Carolina Conference. This church became known later as the Plantation Church.[219]

Helen Francis

Helen Francis was ordained in 1938 and served from 1938 to 1942 in the Ohio District of the Pilgrim Holiness Church.[220]

Christina Hobbs

Christina Hobbs's record began in 1938 in the Ontario District of the Pilgrim Holiness Church in Canada. She was stationed in Proton in 1939. Christina was ordained in 1942 and remained on the assembly roll through 1950. She was later listed in 1954. No other records were found.[221]

Ruth Elizabeth North

Ruth Elizabeth "Betty" North, during the summer of 1998, recorded on tape the highlights of her life and work for the Lord. The following details were taken from that tape.

She was born March 5, 1917, in Scranton, Pennsylvania, and was named Ruth Elizabeth, but she was known as Betty. She was a third-generation Salvationist. She had one brother, James, who was eight years older than she. She spent her childhood attending Salvation Army meetings and preparing to serve the Lord in the Salvation Army.

At age six Betty was aware of her need to be saved, and God did save her, but she did not become established in the Lord. Her family attended three services on Sunday in different surrounding communities. They moved often, and changing schools was a nightmare for Betty. She gave her heart "repeatedly" to the Lord, and He was faithful in guiding and keeping her heart tender. As a young teen, Betty had a uniform and a bonnet and went through the beer gardens with her tambourine and the *War Cry* magazine soliciting money and giving away the magazines as she had been taught.

Her parents were assigned to the Salvation Army Fresh Air Camp near Philadelphia, which served two hundred underprivileged children during the summer months. The group of campers changed every ten to fifteen days. Here

Betty learned to swim, play tennis, and volley-ball. By the time she was seventeen, she had her first job. She was the lifeguard at the large pool at the camp and earned ten dollars a week.

The winter months at the camp were lonely. But she and her schoolmates enjoyed sledding parties there. She became captain of the basket-ball team in high school but was forced to give it up because of a heart problem. She also completed the Salvation Army corps cadet classes and was ready for officership courses at the training school in New York. She was involved in the local Salvation Army programs with the juniors and youth as well as the open-air street meetings. She played in the Salvation Army band even though she couldn't read music.

Betty helped her brother, who was stationed outside Philadelphia, after his wife gave birth to their first child. She did bookkeeping and other office duties and gave out food each morning to the needy. These were the days of the Great Depression, and there were many needy persons. She enjoyed the work but became disillusioned with the circumstances there and returned home. However, even at home she was disappointed with some of the behavior at the local corps and became even more disillusioned. She turned her back on the Lord and decided that even though she knew God had called her to Christian work, she would never work for the Salvation Army or any other church organization.

Her parents were heartbroken with her deci-sion. She lived in outward sin and rebellion for one year. Her mother was invited to an all-day meeting at the Trainer, Pennsylvania, Wesleyan Methodist church. She attended that meeting, and it was announced that the Kenschaft sisters had something special to offer the young people. That something special was a ten-day camp meeting in Ora, New Jersey, for two hundred young people, and it was free. Her mother talked with the Kenschaft sisters and registered Betty for the camp. Betty was angry but finally agreed to attend.

The workers at the camp were "the Duck sisters," Lois Richardson and Carrie Hazzard; Brother Ortlip, the artist; and Marion Whitney. Betty did not surrender to God during that camp, but she longed for "the real thing" these people

had. The Kenschaft sisters were conference preachers (licensed ministers) in the Middle Atlantic States Conference of the Wesleyan Methodist Church, and they kept a constant check on her. When Rev. Harold Baker, an evan-gelist, held a revival meeting at their church, they encouraged her to attend. Betty resisted the call to repentance, but when Rev. Baker came down and stood before her and prayed, *O God, we call on heaven and earth to record the decision of this girl,* she could resist no longer and was gloriously saved. That night Betty also broke off a relation-ship with her gentleman friend.

In December 1935 the Kenschaft sisters took Betty with them to many churches where they had scheduled revival meetings. Betty became the energetic song leader for the team. In 1938 Erna Kenschaft and Betty were asked to pastor the Shippensburg, Pennsylvania, church, a storefront church that had been a pool hall and previously was called the "Bucket of Blood." It was located in the slum area of the city. A group of people had wanted a holiness church but they weren't sure if it should be a Nazarene, Free Methodist, or Wesleyan Methodist church. They asked the conference president, John Wilcox, to have Betty North, Erna and Irma Kenschaft (Weaver) pastor their group "until they found a man pastor." Erna and Betty said they would stay, but Irma Kenschaft Weaver left the team for other places of work. These women stayed for six or seven years. They used orange crates for chairs, an ironing board for a table, and canvas cots for beds. A pot-bellied stove provided them with heat.

They were plagued with all kinds of prob-lems. A sixty-five-year-old unfrocked minister decided to run them out of town by getting signa-tures on a petition. The conference president called a trial meeting and asked that all the sign-ers be present. Only two of the signers showed up. The conference president then kindly exposed the man publicly with papers and data on the behavior of this former minister. The women were to receive the Sunday evening offerings as their salary. Sometimes it was six dollars; other times it was fifty cents. Those who opposed the women quickly informed them that they would no longer lavishly support them.

It was conference time, and Betty and Erna gave their report. It looked as if the church would have to close. But a lady gave the conference president one thousand dollars to be used if they cared to stay and build a church. They returned to Shippensburg and began to look for a lot. They found two lots; each would cost five hundred dollars. They were purchased, and the women looked for employment to keep body and soul together and began the task that lay ahead of them.

After Betty, Erna, and the conference president had been promised a loan to build their new building, the bank president refused to give them the loan. They had just completed the building, and it had been dedicated. Forty years later they found that a member of the bank board was the president of the local lumber company whose bid had been much higher than the bid from another lumber company in a neighboring town. The president of the local lumber company was seeking revenge, so they were denied the loan. The pressures of bill collectors were almost more than the women could take. Then one day a Christian lawyer came and told them he had come to place a sign on the church that declared the entire property was up for a sheriff's sale. He did not want to do this but was forced to do so by the law. The sign had to be placed on the front and back of the property. Then he stated, "There is no penalty if you remove them."

The women quickly removed the sign as soon as they heard his car leave. They sat weeping on the basement steps. Betty and Erna sought employment. This was not easy, because since they were women, no one wanted to employ them. They finally found work in an Arrow Shirt factory and made twenty-five cents an hour. After three years, Betty found work in a local newspaper office as a linotype operator and made thirty cents an hour. The United States was involved in World War II. Erna accepted a federal government job, and then Betty became a policewoman and receptionist at a military base. They used one paycheck to live on, and the other they applied to the church debts. They spent their evenings and Saturdays visiting the people in the neighborhood, witnessing, and inviting them to church. At first people came out of curiosity, but God was also working on their hearts.

After six months, the women decided to tackle the town czar. He owned most of the Shippensburg's businesses. His office was directly back of the church. They prayed, and the conference president and the women walked over to talk with this man. The conference president laid all the facts before the man and ended by saying the church property was up for sheriff's sale. He pointed out that the church could be changed into an apartment building if it didn't "go as a church." There was already a six-room apartment on the lot in back of the church. Surely all this would appeal to a businessman.

After a few minutes he asked if they had been to the local bank where he was president. They assured him they had and the bank had refused to give them the loan. He reached for the phone and called his bank. He informed them two women and a man would be there shortly and they were to be given all the money they wanted. They thanked him profusely, and then he said, "If you need me again, come. If you don't, then don't bother me." And as a parting statement he said, "I'll shoot the first bidder if that church has to go on the auction block."

The community people were coming to church and soon began to tithe their income. They began to grow spiritually and increased their support in other ways. Slowly the creditors were paid off. The church was getting closer to becoming an organized church. Betty was ordained at Wesley Grove in New Jersey in 1945.

They had spent two years in the old pool hall and six years in the new church. The entire debt was liquidated. The mortgage was burnt. Betty and Erna resigned, because now there was a man with a family who would come and pastor the church. A salary was also set for the new pastor. The annual conference of 1946 "arose in appreciation of the splendid and unselfish service of Betty North and Erna Kenschaft at Shippensburg."

In a few months they accepted a call to pastor the Georgetown, Delaware, Wesleyan Methodist Church (1950). Here again they faced unbelievable challenges that were worse than at Shippensburg. Here the former male pastor had left a string of personal debts amounting to thousands of dollars.

The denominational officials had asked him to separate himself from the entire church. The women sought and found secular work in order to survive. The church was paying them a total of twenty dollars a week for the two of them. They ministered at the church for four or five years before they were accepted with any degree of credibility financially in the community. Betty finally found a good job that enabled them to maintain a better standard of living and still have time for church visitation and work. Here the holiness message was accepted by half of the congregation. The children's work flourished. But after about eight years, they were able to add only twenty-nine more members, so they decided they would resign.

Soon after their resignation, the Shippensburg church wanted them to return and be their pastors (1960). This time they would receive an adequate salary. They accepted the call and served there for another seven or eight years. Betty had a beautiful choir of young people who honored God with their voices and godly lives. Some of these youth became pastors, pastors' wives, schoolteachers, and a chemist.

During this second term, these women were able to do some renovation of the building. The church was rewired and updated electrically. New pews were put in the church, and a new heating system was installed. The apartments that belonged to the church were also renovated. Many new people, young couples with children, were being added to the church. And, of course, another man and his family were available to take their place when it was time to leave.

The conference president now asked them to take another church until they could find a man to fill the pulpit. The church was a mountain church near Harrisburg, Pennsylvania, and it was called Watts Township Church. The church had been closed for six months because no man would go there. After much prayer, Betty and Erna agreed to become the pastors. Neither had ever lived in the country, much less the mountains. Their first service was held in September 1967. Erna sat on the platform and looked the place over during the song service. What she saw was dirt, filth, and cobwebs, which hung from the light bulbs. She couldn't believe God

had sent them to another tough assignment. This church gave them twenty-five dollars a week plus the expenses of the utilities of the parsonage and the church.

Their first task was to find employment. They first accepted employment as house cleaning maids at a motel. It was hard and dirty work. All the rooms opened from the outside, and they trudged through snow and rain from building to building with buckets and mops. They received fifty cents an hour for this work. But the church and the parsonage also needed a good general cleaning. They removed fifteen pickup truck loads of debris from around the parsonage and church. They papered and painted every room as well as doing other repairs on the church. And they installed an electric outdoor light to scatter the darkness of the mountain nights. The church at Shippensburg came to help them with the cleaning on Saturdays. Before the work was completed, wall-to-wall floor coverings were installed, pews and walls were painted, and a new pulpit and communion table were purchased. The parsonage was cleaned up, a new stove for cooking was purchased, and three and one-fourth acres of grass around the parsonage had been mowed and trimmed. Once a month they had to have an exterminator come to care for the livestock—all kinds of four legged critters, snakes and bugs—that inhabited their area.

An even more serious problem became evident after eight years of working at Watts Township. A new church about ten miles over the mountain began to come each Sunday morning and gather the sheep and lambs from the Wesleyan Methodist, Methodist, Church of the Brethren, and United Brethren churches into their bus. All kinds of goodies were given to the children to bribe them to get on the bus. Erna and Betty had good government jobs, so the financial burden was lifted. But this "sheep stealing" thing caused Betty to develop bleeding stomach ulcers, and she had to resign her job. Betty was at peace only when Erna was reading to her from the Bible. Even during all this trouble the Lord gave them wonderful victories in their church.

In 1978 they moved to Florida. They pastored the Lynn Haven Church in the Florida Panhandle.

They went house to house inviting people to come to know Christ as their Lord. Then Betty was stricken with colon cancer, and they were forced to move to Brooksville, Florida. Surgery, rest and healing came slowly. Erna was stricken the next year with lupus and died in 1982.

Betty sought and found employment at the Salvation Army as a probation officer. This enabled her to pay her hospital bills and maintain her mobile home. Betty was still residing at the Wesleyan Village in Brooksville, Florida, in 2002.[222]

Alma G. Hollenback

Alma G. Hollenback was received during the 1937 conference year into the Indiana Conference of the Wesleyan Methodist Church. She was received from the Church of the Nazarene and was appointed as a conference evangelist. Like all other ordained ministers coming from another denomination, Alma was to serve on probation. Before the end of the conference year, she and her husband transferred to the North Michigan Conference. Alma and her husband, U. T. Hollenback, were appointed pastors of the Brockway Church in Michigan from 1939 to October 15, 1940. August 18, 1942, they transferred to the Indiana Conference and both served as evangelists. In 1943 they were granted letters of standing. Alma was the mother of three children.[223]

Esther Margaret Johnson

Esther Margaret Johnson was born August 10, 1898, in Eau Claire, Wisconsin. Her family moved to Webb Lake, where Esther attended elementary school. She graduated from high school in Superior and then earned a teacher's certificate at Eau Claire. She then started her teaching career. She and her parents moved to Rice Lake and became charter members of the Rice Lake Wesleyan Methodist Church.

During the ministry of Rev. Estella Lienard, a group from the Rice Lake Wesleyan Methodist Church held Sunday afternoon services in Spooner, about twenty-five miles from Rice Lake. Esther was called to become the first pastor of the newly organized church in Spooner. She served that church from 1936 to 1939 and also returned to teaching.

In 1940 she was ordained and served for one year at the Rice Lake Wesleyan Methodist Church. However, Esther's hearing became worse, and she was forced to give up teaching. Her assignment by the conference was missionary evangelism under the conference mission board from 1941 to 1952.

Esther was active in the conference work and served on the Sunday school board for some time, twelve years as a member of what is now the district board of ministerial development, and eight years as the conference Woman's Home and Foreign Missionary Society treasurer.

Norma L. Stuve recalls a young lady saying to her, "If I ever become a Christian, I want to be one like Esther Johnson." After Esther's retirement, she moved back to Rice Lake and passed away in a nursing home there May 15, 1995.[224]

Mary Price Joiner

Mary Price Joiner was born in Trappe, Maryland, in 1901, the daughter of Rev. and Mrs. A. A. Price. She was converted at the age of five and was sanctified while attending Greensboro Bible School in North Carolina. She also attended Beulah Park Bible School, Allentown, Pennsylvania (later Eastern Pilgrim College/United Wesleyan College).

Mary assisted Rev. Alfred Clark in planting a Pilgrim Holiness church in Greensboro, Maryland. She was the pastor of the Centerville Pilgrim Holiness church for six years. She and her husband, Walter, planted and organized the Ridgely Pilgrim Holiness church and were pastoring that church at the time of her death.

About two months before her death, Mary stated, "It would be wonderful to be called home from the pulpit working for our Savior." On Thursday evening she was preaching at the Denton church. She preached a great message of faith and soul-stirring confidence in God. She sank into a pulpit chair and went to heaven a few hours later March 2, 1951.

Mary Price Joiner served in the Eastern District of the Pilgrim Holiness Church from 1938 to 1951. She was ordained by that district. She was the mother of one son.[225]

Edna Loh

Edna Loh served in the California District of the Pilgrim Holiness Church from 1938 to 1956.[226]

Ethel Gilkerson Lucus

Ethel Gilkerson was one of the young ladies from the Eastern District of the Pilgrim Holiness Church who actively preached the gospel mainly on the Eastern Shore of Maryland. In her early evangelistic work she traveled by train or bus to meet her scheduled meetings. Ethel was an evangelistic type preacher, "a real firebrand for God." She played a guitar and sang as well as preached. In many of her meetings she served both as the singer and preacher. Apparently her ministry began around 1938, and she was single during all this time.

She married Rev. B. H. Lucas around 1947, and together they did some evangelistic work, taking turns preaching, and they also pastored the Pilgrim Holiness Church in Cambridge, Maryland. Their taking turns preaching was known at that time as preaching "turnabout."

In 1952 they planted an independent work in Garden City, Michigan, and she served as co-pastor with her husband until his death in 1983. They had been married for thirty-six years and shared as a team in the ministry the entire time. After his death, Ethel continued to pastor until July 1992—a total of forty years in pastoring. While her husband was living, they worked as a team. They did everything together. They made house calls (visitation) and did everything that could benefit the church and community in which they served.

Ethel was known for preaching "whatever the Lord laid on her heart." She ministered in various places—tent meetings, storefronts, armories, living rooms, and camp meetings. The Lord gave her success in gathering in the harvest, and she had many converts.

Ethel moved her district membership to the Tennessee District of the Pilgrim Holiness Church in 1961. A convert, Barbara Claus, provided the preceding facts about her ministry in April 1998. At that time Ethel was a member of the Clinton, Tennessee, First Wesleyan Church.[227]

Ethel L. MacFadgen and Virginia M. Miller

Ethel L. MacFadgen and Virginia M. Miller were single lady ministers who were originally from the Pentecostal Rescue Mission of New York. Mission records show that Ethel and Virginia were pastoring the Haverhill, Massachusetts, church or mission December 27, 1935. The salary for the two of them at that time was five dollars a week. They spent four dollars and fifty cents for their rent, and they gave fifty cents tithe to the church.

Virginia Miller was ordained in 1941, and Ethel MacFadgen was ordained in 1942 by the New York District of the Pilgrim Holiness Church. These women continued to pastor the Haverhill church until the close of 1958. From 1959 to 1963 they were listed as evangelists.[228]

Minnie L. Morgan

Minnie L. Morgan apparently served in the California District of the Pilgrim Holiness Church from 1938 to 1945. The California *Minutes* recorded her in that district until 1968.[229] However, the *Minutes of the Annual Assembly of the Oregon District Pilgrim Holiness Church* recorded her as a transferee from the California District in 1945–48, and the *Minutes of the Annual Conference of the Northwest District Pilgrim Holiness Church* listed her as a member of that district in 1949.

Constance Ngo

Proceedings of the Annual Assembly California District of the Pilgrim Holiness Church, 1938–52, recorded Constance Ngo as a member of and under appointment in that district.

Wilma F. Jones Reiff

Wilma F. Reiff was born in Kansas in 1904. She graduated from Colorado Springs Bible College (later merged into what became Oklahoma Wesleyan University, Bartlesville, Oklahoma) with both A.B. and master's degrees. She received her doctor of theology from Pikes Peak Seminary and taught in the public schools for twenty-eight years and in Bible colleges for six years.

Wilma married Edward L. Reiff in 1933. She was an ordained minister and was listed in the records of the California District of the Pilgrim Holiness Church (spelled "Reifer") 1938–39, Louisiana and Alabama 1954 and 1955, Arizona 1959 and 1960, and Arizona-New Mexico 1962 through 1965, the last two years as retired. She died March 30, 1987.[230]

Flora Kean Ressler

Flora Kean was born March 11, 1901, in Ohio. She was converted as a child at age eleven and sanctified at age sixteen. She graduated from Marion College, in Marion, Indiana (now Indiana Wesleyan University). She became a member of Harrison Chapel, a Wesleyan Methodist church near Pataskala, Ohio. She married Menno D. Ressler June 29, 1934. To this union one daughter was born, who died in infancy.[231]

Flora heard God's call and answered that call by working at God's Holiness Mission in Columbus, Ohio for many years. She was the pastor of the Cooks Corners (and in charge of the work at Burke) and Bakers Mills churches in the Champlain Conference of the Wesleyan Methodist Church (now Eastern New York-New England District).[232]

Flora was ordained by the Champlain Conference in 1948. She completed her earthly tasks March 17, 1950.

Gertrude Hooth Shaw

Gertrude Hooth Shaw wrote her life's story, *Echoes of the Past*, in 1993.[233] She was born January 18, 1912, the oldest of eight children. The family lived on a farm along the shores of the Georgian Bay in Bruce County in Ontario. Her father was a farmer, stonemason, and auctioneer. They had no modern conveniences, and Gertrude grew up with coal oil lamps, washtubs, scrubbing boards for doing the laundry, and no rugs on the floor.

Gertrude learned to play the pump organ. She was converted at age twelve in a home church service. After her conversion she often spoke in the cottage prayer meetings. All the services were conducted in the homes of the people in the community, and she was frequently the preacher. They usually walked to these meetings. A Methodist church was built in their community, but the preacher did not believe in Jesus' cleansing blood. Eventually most people quit going to the church. Gertrude's family began to attend the Pilgrim Holiness church in Lion's Head. These meetings were also held in the homes of interested people. Later a Pilgrim Holiness church was built at Ferndale, about eleven miles from their home. During the winter they traveled to church in a horse-drawn sleigh.

Gertrude attended the Bible School at Proton Station. Those who graduated from the Bible school pastored Pilgrim Holiness churches. Their training included four years of work at the Bible school, and then they were required to complete the denominational ministerial course.

Gertrude and her college roommate, Mary Cuthbertson, started a church in the village of Sauble Falls in Bruce County. They worshiped in the local schoolhouse. The girls carried their Aladdin lamp from their home, and that provided light for the service. The school was about a quarter of a mile from their home. They had no transportation, so they walked—to church, to visit their church families, and everywhere else they needed to go. They had no furniture, so they slept on the bed springs on the floor. They had no salary, so they plucked and cleaned chickens to sell to tourists, delivered milk, picked berries, fished, and cleaned houses to earn money.

At the end of the summer, following the planting of the church at Sauble Falls, the Ontario District of the Pilgrim Holiness Church asked Gertrude to plant a congregation at Tobermory. A tent meeting had been held earlier, and this prepared the way for her to start this church. A family who desired to have a Sunday school and a church provided her with room and board in their home. She conducted Sunday school on Sunday afternoons and an evening worship service. A prayer service was held on Wednesday nights. She visited in homes, read the Scriptures, and prayed. She walked everywhere she went. There was no snow removal, and the snowdrifts were high. The temperature was often around twenty degrees below zero. One day she received a threatening letter from a person who declared she would be killed if she continued to preach. Gertrude preached from the pulpit located in front of a large open window. She "exercised her faith" in God and His protection and continued on as the pastor until the district sent a man to replace her. Early in the 1930s the district asked her to pastor the Dyers Bay mission church. There was a log house parsonage and a little frame church building. Her youngest sister stayed with her. They stuffed moss scraped from rocks between the logs to keep the cold wind out of the house. There was no well, but they carried water from a nearby spring. Often there was no wood to heat the house or cook, so the girls burned weeds for fuel. Bread was cheap, and that was their staple food at mealtime.

On November 3, 1937, Gertrude married James Edmund Shaw. Jim was a devoted Christian and supported Gertrude in her church work. They continued to live in the parsonage. The house was so cold that everything froze at night but usually would thaw out before breakfast. Jim had no work, and the offerings from the church were very small. In the spring Jim was able to obtain a job and received two dollars a day for his work. Gertrude continued to pastor at Dyers Bay until the fall of 1940. She served the 1944–45 district year again at Dyers Bay.

Six children blessed their home. Gertrude did not pastor for a number of years while serving her family as a full-time homemaker and mother. One son, Dale, became a Wesleyan pastor.

In 1964 district superintendent L. B. Reese asked Gertrude to pastor the chuch of Bruce Mines. They had experienced a series of hardships on their farm, including the burning of their feed mill, in which they lost everything. There was no reason for them to remain on the farm, so on Thanksgiving Day, November 10, 1965, Gertrude began pastoring the Bruce Mines church. There were twenty-two persons present at the first service. They lived in the parsonage for two years, but in 1967 they purchased a house with all modern facilities. She continued to pastor the church for nine years. Her salary was twenty-five dollars a week. Jim supplemented her salary by working as a handyman. During this time the church had grown, and they needed Sunday school rooms, so Jim gave of his time and labor to add four Sunday school rooms on the west side of the church.

In retirement at age eighty-six at the time of the writing of her book, Gertrude attended Sunday school regularly and hosted home Bible studies in her home.

Ann Shaw, her daughter-in-law and publisher, made the following statement about Gertrude:

> In the twenty-seven years that I have been privileged to know her, I have not heard her "defend" her call to serve God through the work of the church. I have only heard her confidently confirm it. She didn't talk much about it. She just did it. She invested her life in helping people discover Jesus Christ as Lord and Savior. Her mission field began at home.[234]

————

Maggie Jean Carlin Spear

Maggie Jean Carlin (Mrs. R. A.) Spear was listed by the Alabama Conference of the Wesleyan Methodist Church in 1938 as an elder (ordained minister), serving the following year in evangelistic work. She pastored Ways Creek 1939–40, Wolf Creek 1940–42, and Golden Grove 1942–43, 1955–61 and 1963–64. In other years up until her retirement in 1967, she served as an

---

evangelist or in conference missionary work or was free to choose her own field of labor.[235]

Loretta Raymer Wilson

Loretta Raymer was born October 12, 1917. She was the youngest child of Laura Raymer, an ordained minister in the Dakota Conference of the Wesleyan Methodist Church. She remembers as a seven-year-old her mother propping up her study course books on the ironing board and the kitchen cabinets as she went about her housework. By 1938 Loretta was a conference preacher (now a licensed minister) in the Dakota Conference, serving as a song evangelist and children's worker.

On May 29, 1939, Loretta was married to Charles R. Wilson, by Charles's father, O. G. Wilson, later a general officer in the Wesleyan Methodist Church.[236] Loretta and Charles transferred to the Kansas Conference that year and were ordained there together. From 1941 to 1943 they served in the Oklahoma Conference at Cedar Grove. They also held a revival at Wichita Falls, Texas, in May 1942, which led to the organization of a church there. From 1943 to 1958 they served again in Kansas. While Charles served pastorates in these years, Loretta was sometimes listed as an evangelist, more frequently as a song evangelist and children's worker. In 1958 they transferred to the Lockport Conference (now Western New York District). Charles eventually became a college professor, first at Houghton College, Houghton, New York, and then at Taylor University, Upland, Indiana. Loretta describes her own ministry:

I never questioned my own call to ministry and thank God for the opportunities I have been given. Over the years I have worked with my husband, Charles, in evangelistic meetings (mostly singing for my part), D.V.B.S., and in later years, women's ministries, retreats, and such. Shortly after retirement and a move to Ft. Wayne [Indiana], I became chaplain to two groups: Ladies Auxiliary of the Ft. Wayne Rescue Mission and the Christian Women's Prayer Breakfast of Ft. Wayne. For each of these groups, I gave monthly devotions and also had the privilege of leading the prayer for government leaders at the prayer breakfast for seven years.[237]

M. Catherine Millis Bloom and Martha Bloom Raper

Two sisters-in-law carried on a long and effective evangelistic and pastoral ministry as a team known as "the Bloom sisters." Martha Bloom was born April 1, 1922. She grew up in the New Castle, Indiana, Wesleyan Methodist church. As a child, she sang in the choir. By the time she was seventeen, she had settled the issue of total obedience to the Lord in her life.

When Martha was ten years old, her brother Richard, eleven years older than she, married Miriam Catherine Millis, December 24, 1932. Catherine was born March 21, 1910, at Greensboro, Indiana, not far from New Castle. She was called to preach as a child. Both Martha and Catherine could sing, and as Martha reached adulthood, it seemed natural that they should launch into the Lord's work as a team.

They served under the Indiana Conference of the Wesleyan Methodist Church from 1940 to 1960. Catherine was ordained in 1944, and Martha was granted standing as a lay special worker. Their first meeting was a revival in July 1940. They sang this time without accompaniment, practiced hard, and achieved real harmony. Catherine did the preaching. In the years that followed, their schedule of meetings was always full, often five years in advance, and churches were frequently packed out. For the first two years, Richard was not a part of the team. He worked at a steel mill but would drive them to their meetings and then pick them up at the end. After that, he traveled with them full-time. They would eventually travel a million and a quarter miles without an accident.

In 1953 they traveled to the West Coast, where Catherine served for nine months as supply pastor of the Pasadena, California, Wesleyan Methodist Church. They had an old six-cylinder Pontiac that could barely pull their heavy house trailer up and over the mountains—plenty of thrills trying to pass trucks even slower than the Pontiac!

In 1960 they transferred to the South Carolina Conference and continued their evangelism. In 1963 Catherine became pastor of the Carlisle, South Carolina, Wesleyan Methodist church. She served there for five years, and Martha served as her assistant. They gathered seventy-five boys and girls from preschool to sixteen years of age and worked with them each week. The principal of the high school said he could tell which children were from the church.

In 1968 they returned to evangelism. But at the South Carolina campground in July, Richard died. The two ladies then traveled alone. For a time they served an independent church, Morning Springs, near Carlisle. Catherine began to fail by the winter of 1988 and died in 1995. Martha married Edward Raper, and they eventually retired in Brooksville, Florida.

The Bloom sisters had faithfully served the Lord and the Church for forty-nine years, fourteen years pastoring, the rest in itinerant evangelism.[238]

Anna Mae Yarnell Bowman

Anna Yarnell was born May 8, 1907. She grew up in Barry Township, Schuylkill County, Pennsylvania. She prepared for the ministry at Beulah Park Bible School (later Eastern Pilgrim/United Wesleyan College) in Allentown, Pennsylvania, and at Nyack College, Nyack, New York. She was ordained by the Pittsburgh District of the Pilgrim Holiness Church in 1940. She co-pastored with another woman minister at Belle Ridge prior to her marriage.

She married Mark Bowman and they co-pastored at Elizabeth, Pittsburgh, Washington and Cherryville in Pennsylvania, and at Cambridge and Denton, Maryland. Mark became superintendent of the Eastern District of the Pilgrim Holiness Church and served until his death in 1965. After her husband's passing, Anna Bowman pastored at Oxford, Maryland. Then she returned to Pennsylvania and pastored at Penns Creek. She also taught at a Christian school at Penns Creek. After fifteen years, she retired and moved to Mt. Carmel, where she continued to preach as supply pastor from time to time in a number of churches in the area. She also ministered in child evangelism and at a Mt. Carmel nursing home. She had two sons, Luke and John. She died November 29, 1999, at the age of ninety-two.[239]

Ila M. Bruce

The records of the Michigan District of the Pilgrim Holiness Church indicate that Ila M. Bruce was ordained in 1939. She pastored at Traverse City 1940–42. Her name appears on the list through 1952, one year as an evangelist and three years in education.[240]

Winifred Eastman

Winifred Eastman was born at Valley, Wisconsin, in 1912. She graduated from Vernon County Normal School and taught at two rural schools. She attended Miltonvale Wesleyan College, Miltonvale, Kansas (later merged into what became Oklahoma Wesleyan University, Bartlesville, Oklahoma). She was apparently recommended by the Topeka First Wesleyan Methodist Church for status as a conference preacher (now licensed minister), and she was so credentialed by the Kansas Conference in 1939. She began the course of study and served as the assistant to Rev. Vivian Haun in the pastorate at Hardy, Nebraska 1940–42, 1943–48. She was ordained in 1943. The planting of a church in Denver, Colorado was underway. In 1948 she went there, got a part-time job to support herself, and gave the rest of her time to helping with the church. She was listed 1949–53 as assistant pastor at Colorado Springs. Some years she was listed as a conference evangelist. From 1955 to 1965 she was "unstationed" (without appointment). Apparently beginning in 1955, she served in a team ministry with Rev. Norma Henderson in pastoring the Valton Friends Church near Wonewoc, Wisconsin. Her conference appointment in 1966 and 1967 reflected this ministry. She retired from there after twenty-one years in 1976. She died January 31, 1988, at the age of seventy-six.[241]

Verna Harris Faidley

Verna Harris was born in Burns City, Indiana, September 28, 1901. She prepared herself for the

Lord's work, graduating from the Missionary Training School in St. Louis and God's Bible School, Cincinnati, Ohio. She was ordained by the Indiana District of the Pilgrim Holiness Church in 1939. She married E. I. Faidley. They had one son and three daughters. She served under the Indiana District, 1939–50, and, after the division of Indiana into two districts, under the Southern Indiana District, from 1951 until her death on September 13, 1965. She and her husband did both pastoral and evangelistic work. Churches they served included Elnora, Bicknell, Shoals, Mitchell, Westport, Madison, Bedford, Oaktown, and Medora.[242]

Ruth Finnefrock

Ruth Finnefrock was born June 24, 1909. While in high school, she was called to preach. She married William Finnefrock, who apparently was also a minister. They had one son. She was ordained in 1939 and was instrumental in planting the Lancaster, Ohio, Pilgrim Holiness Church and became its pastor, serving there for twelve years. She also pastored the Kenton, Ohio, church for two years or more. She died January 18, 1947.[243]

Eva Grace Frye

Eva Frye was born February 12, 1888. She was converted in 1898 and sanctified in 1908. She married Rev. William Arthur Frye (known as "Pappy" Frye), but the point in their lives at which this occurred could not be ascertained. His first pastorate was a four-year service beginning in 1913 for the Brethren in Christ. He became part of the Holiness Christian Church, which merged into what became the Pilgrim Holiness Church. He served pastorates in Springfield, Ohio, and in Elwood, Frankfort, Indianapolis, and West Terre Haute in Indiana. She preached her first sermon in Frankfort in 1939 and was ordained by the Indiana District of the Pilgrim Holiness Church that year. She appears on the appointments of the Indiana District 1939–41 and then transferred to the Illinois District 1942–50.

She pastored at least one church in Illinois. She came back to the Southern Indiana District, and her name appears in their records 1951–66. She died May 30, 1967. She was known as a great helpmate to her husband, a friend to all, and a great prayer warrior.[244]

Marie Roth Hahn

Marie Roth was born on a farm near Clay Center, Kansas. Her parents later moved into Clay Center, and she began working at Swenson's Mercantile store in 1917. She remembers being one of the few who escaped the great influenza epidemic. And she remembers a parade when World War I ended with a casket being pulled down the street with the "Kaiser" in it. While working at Swenson's, she met Guy M. Hahn. They both left to attend Miltonvale Wesleyan College, Miltonvale, Kansas (later merged into what became Oklahoma Wesleyan University, Bartlesville, Oklahoma). They were married there August 17, 1920. Both were later ordained.

By 1938 the two were pastoring the Valton Wesleyan Methodist church in Wisconsin. At the 1939 annual conference session, she was continued as co-pastor of Valton and was asked to continue the study course and to return for ordination the next year. She was ordained by the Wisconsin Conference in 1940. Her husband continued to pastor Valton until 1945. In 1941–42, her assignment was evangelism and overseeing the Bethel charge. Then she resumed service with her husband in Valton. In 1945 the Hahns also served Mt. Pisgah and Oak Ridge for six months. From 1945 to 1950 Guy served as Wisconsin Conference president (now district superintendent). She continued as pastor at Valton 1945–48. From 1948 to 1949 she pastored Spooner, and from 1949 to 1950 she served as president of the conference Woman's Missionary Society (she filled this office 1945–50) and in evangelism. She indicated many years later that she sometimes served smaller churches that could not afford a pastor while her husband served in positions that did support them. In 1950 the two joined their labors again to co-pastor Stone Lake 1950–51 and Rice Lake 1951–53.

In 1953 Guy and Marie were granted permission to pastor a Methodist church in Nebraska. Apparently this continued for several years, and beginning in 1956 both were listed as "unstationed" (without appointment). Guy died in 1960 at the age of sixty-five.

Marie Hahn continued to live in Nebraska until about 1980, when she moved back to Clay Center, Kansas. She decided at age ninety-six not to renew her driver's license. She was still living at the age of one hundred one. Asked about changes she had seen in her lifetime, she said, "I've seen change from going places in a horse and buggy to going to the moon."[245]

Estella Hancock

Records on Estella Hancock are rather fragmentary. It appears that she was ordained by the Ohio District of the Pilgrim Holiness Church in 1939 and remained on their list until 1942. Then she transferred to the Illinois District, possibly going through the Pennsylvania and New Jersey District. She was listed by the Illinois District 1942–45. Then she returned to the Ohio District and pastored the Ashley Pilgrim Holiness Church 1946–55. In 1955, after the division of Ohio into two districts, she was listed by the Eastern Ohio District. From 1959 on, she was listed by the Western Ohio District as living in Springfield, Ohio.[246]

Jessie Hathaway

The *Minutes of the California Conference of the Wesleyan Methodist Church of America,* 1958, contain the following record:

Rev. Jessie Hathaway, a pioneer minister of the California Conference, died April 22, 1958. She pioneered the Sunland Church, pastoring from 1930–38. She continued to live near the little church and watched with much prayer and enthusiasm the growth and development of this vine of her planting, and lived to see the near completion of the lovely building which was dedicated seventeen days after her passing. She left a monument to her memory of prayer, cooperation and interest in souls that will live on into eternity.

Vivian Haun

Vivian Haun appears on the records of the Kansas Conference of the Wesleyan Methodist Church in 1939. She was apparently recommended to the conference by Topeka First Church. She was licensed as a conference preacher (now licensed minister) and appointed as an evangelist while pursuing her studies at Miltonvale Wesleyan College, Miltonvale, Kansas (later merged into what became Oklahoma Wesleyan University, Bartlesville, Oklahoma). In 1940 she was shifted to the course of study and appointed to pastor the Hardy Mission in Nebraska, with Winifred Eastman as her assistant. They continued in this assignment 1940–48. In 1948 the Hardy group was organized as a church with twelve members. Eventually they leased a church building with an option to buy when the other denomination was ready to sell. Vivian Haun was ordained in 1943. From 1948 to 1951 she served as a conference evangelist. From 1951 to 1965 her listing was "choose own field" or "unstationed" (without appointment). Beginning in 1965, she pastored Willis. Vivian Haun was elected as a delegate to one of the General Conferences when it was very unusual for a woman to serve in that capacity.[247]

Lela Montgomery Jeffers

Lela Montgomery was born May 15, 1890, in Evansville, Indiana. She was converted in Evansville in 1904 and sanctified in February 1905. She preached her first sermon when she was seventeen at Kinmundy, Illinois, and was the first person licensed to preach by the Southern Illinois Methodist Conference. She spent seventeen years in evangelism and married Angus R. Jeffers June 25, 1923. She was ordained by the Indiana District of the Pilgrim Holiness Church August 21, 1939. She appears on the district conference's records, 1939–49. Lela assisted her husband on his pastorates. They were serving in Muncie, Indiana, when she died, February 28, 1950.[248]

Ethel Jordan

Ethel Jordan was born August 24, 1882, in Vernon County, Wisconsin. She became active in church work even before she was converted, which occurred when she was twenty-three. Believing that the Lord was calling her to some special work, she studied at God's Bible School in Cincinnati, Ohio. She engaged in extensive Sunday school and general church work. She served as matron of an orphanage and also at a rescue home. Some time was also spent in pastoral and city mission work.

In 1928 Ethel Jordan entered missionary service in Africa under the Pilgrim Holiness Church. She spent twenty years there, two terms of ten years each. She served in Cape Province, Natal, and Northern Rhodesia (now Zambia). She served as teacher, preacher, visitor, and friend to the nationals. Her first furlough was from April 1938 to March 1940. It was during that time, in 1939, that she was ordained by the Ohio District of the Pilgrim Holiness Church. She appeared in their listings through 1954 and then was listed by the Western Ohio District from 1955 on. She retired after her return from the field in 1950 or shortly after. She lived in the mission home in Indianapolis for a time and then moved to a retirement home in Hillsboro, Wisconsin. She was still living past her one hundredth birthday, praying for the missionaries and their labors.[249]

Anna Sherman Kilwy

Anna Sherman was born April 2, 1915 in Sharondale, Kentucky, to Nicholas and Parascisia Yansur Sherman. She found the Lord early in life in West Virginia and felt called to the Lord's work. She graduated from Owosso Bible College, Owosso, Michigan (later Owosso College, eventually merged into what became Indiana Wesleyan University, Marion, Indiana). She married W. L. Kilwy in 1938 and had one daughter, Bonnie.

Anna Sherman Kilwy engaged in home mission work in West Virginia with Irene Tanier, laboring in Madison, Welch, and Ravenswood. At the time of her death it was said that "God alone knows the heartache, tears, and sleepless nights she spent at some of these places." Then she served as assistant pastor to Tanier at Liberty Center, Ohio.

In 1939 she and her husband were both ordained by Walter L. Surbrook. She was listed in the records of the Ohio District of the Pilgrim Holiness Church, 1940–53. Her husband pastored churches in Ohio at Berrysville, Port Clinton, Cincinnati, Toledo, and Greenville, and she apparently assisted him. It was at Greenville that she died, November 20, 1953.[250]

Alberta Klatt Kindschi

Alberta Klatt first appears in the records of the Oklahoma Conference of the Wesleyan Methodist Church in 1939. She was received to work and was assigned to evangelism. On March 6, 1940, she married Paul L. Kindschi. O. G. Wilson conducted the ceremony. In 1941 the Kindschis transferred to the Dakota Conference. Here she served as a song evangelist and children's worker and was ordained June 7, 1942.

In 1944 the Kindschis transferred to the Iowa Conference. Her appointment was pastoring with her husband at Waterloo First Church 1944–49. From 1949 to 1951 she was listed as a children's worker. From 1951 to 1954 she served as secretary to the conference president (now district superintendent). From 1954 to 1960 she was listed as a children's worker. From 1960 to 1961 Alberta was employed at the new World Headquarters of the Wesleyan Methodist Church in Marion, Indiana. In 1963 she was listed as a children's worker. Otherwise, from 1961 on, Alberta was listed as "unstationed" (without appointment).[251]

Josephine Alpha Johnson King

Josephine Johnson was born in Wisconsin in 1909. She was called into the ministry while she was young. She graduated from the high school program at Miltonvale Wesleyan College, Miltonvale, Kansas (later merged into what became Oklahoma Wesleyan University, Bartlesville, Oklahoma) and then from the Lutheran Hospital School of Nursing. She then returned to Miltonvale and completed the college's theological program. She married Lloyd King.

In 1938 the Wisconsin Conference of the Wesleyan Methodist Church listed her as co-pastor with her husband of the Gull Lake and Chitasmo charge, and they continued there until 1940. In 1940 she was ordained, so now she was both an ordained minister and a registered nurse. From 1940 to 1943 she co-pastored the Burr charge; from 1941 to 1942 this included Valley, and in 1942–43 she also had responsibility for a pioneer work near Camp McCory. From 1943 to 1952 she was listed as co-pastor at Eau Claire; on June 7, 1951, they celebrated Eau Claire's twenty-fifth anniversary. During these years she served various offices and committees in the Wisconsin Conference, including conference youth president and treasurer and vice president of the Woman's Missionary Society. She often served as camp nurse. From 1952 to 1953 she was listed as co-pastor of the Mt. Pisgah and Oak Ridge charge.

From 1953 to 1961 the Kings retained membership in the Wisconsin Conference but were granted the privilege of serving in the Kansas Conference. From 1953 to 1959 they supplied the Abilene (Ks.) Wesleyan Methodist Church, and from 1959 to 1961 they supplied Immanuel Church in Kansas City. Lloyd King died in 1960 in their last year of service at Immanuel.

From 1961 to 1966 Josephine was given permission to study for occupational missionary work. She became a cytology technologist and worked at the state laboratory in Wichita, Kansas, until shortly before her death. She died September 26, 1978, at the age of sixty-nine.[252]

Elva Lanchaster McCullough

Elva Lanchaster and her husband, Lorin S. McCullough, were saved in the Lawrenceville, Illinois, Pilgrim Holiness church. Both were called into the ministry. They pastored several churches,

including Bridgeport, Palestine, Charenton, Marshall, Decatur, and Ottawa, all in Illinois, and Parkersburg, in West Virginia. She was listed by the Illinois District from 1938 on and was ordained in 1943. Lorin served part of the time as a general evangelist, and she also was listed as evangelist part of the time.

From 1951 to 1962 they served at Bridgeport. They engaged the people to pray and pay tithes and to believe. They started with eight church members and a Sunday school of fifty. On Mother's Day 1956, attendance peaked at 275, with seventy-five mothers present. That year they broke ground for a new church, and it was completed in 1957. Membership had grown to seventy-two.[253]

Lorin died September 23, 1972. Elva remarried, and her name became McCullough. She and Lorin had a daughter named Jean. Elva retired in 1978 after a fall and a broken hip. Rev. Jesse Tewell, former superintendent of the Southern Illinois District of The Wesleyan Church, described her as an outstanding preacher with a sparkling personality. She authored a book on some of their evangelistic experiences.[254]

Sylvia J. Lee

Sylvia J. Lee was born to Leslie and Nellie Lee January 3, 1911. She graduated from high school in Hillsboro, Wisconsin, in 1929. She completed the courses at Keefe Business College in LaCrosse and then worked as bookkeeper for the West Salem Garage until the Depression terminated her job.

In 1934 Sylvia was called to the home of Jess Kauffman to assist them during an influenza epidemic. In June of that year, Rev. Mrs. Kauffman, pastor of the Wesleyan Methodist Church, led Sylvia to salvation through Christ. Feeling a call to the ministry, she went to Miltonvale Wesleyan College, Miltonvale, Kansas (later merged into what became Oklahoma Wesleyan University, Bartlesville, Oklahoma). After graduation, she returned to Hillsboro, serving as a pulpit supply while supporting herself by working at the Hillsboro Hospital.

As early as 1934, the Wisconsin Conference took note of Sylvia, receiving her to study under the direction of the conference; she had already passed one book in the course of study. Then in 1939 she was "received to travel" (recognized as ready for appointment). In 1940 she was appointed to missionary evangelism. In 1941 she was appointed to evangelism and to work under the conference president (now district superintendent). She was to finish the reading course so she would be ready for ordination. In 1942 Sylvia was ordained and served in evangelism until 1946. From 1946 to 1953 she served as pastor of Burr and Valley. During this time the Burr church was completely remodeled. In 1954 she was placed on reserve but was to supply on Sundays at Wisconsin Rapids. From 1954 to 1967 Sylvia was listed as being on reserve and then in 1967 was listed as "unstationed" (without appointment).

Because of her business training, she served the conference for several years on the auditing committee, as educational secretary twice and on the statistical committee twice. She was the assistant secretary in 1945 and the conference secretary 1946–55. In 1955 she was given a rising vote of thanks for her "efficient service as conference secretary."

During the years Sylvia was on reserve, she spent seven years as a telephone operator for the Hillsboro Telephone Company until local operator service was discontinued in 1960. She was then elected city clerk in Hillsboro until 1969 when ill health forced her to resign. Her last days were spent in St. Joseph's Nursing Home in Hillsboro. She died May 9, 1973, at the age of seventy-two.[255]

Imogene Snyder McFarlin

Imogene Snyder McFarlin was ordained by the Indiana District of the Pilgrim Holiness Church in 1939. She was listed in their records from 1940 through 1950. In 1951 and then through 1958 she was listed by the Southern Indiana District. In 1959 she transferred to the Kentucky Conference of the Wesleyan Methodist Church. Rev. Ernest R. Batman, former superintendent of the Indiana Central District of The Wesleyan Church, said Imogene did mostly child evangelism before she married William McFarlin.

After that, they worked in evangelism. He was the preacher, and she worked with the children and assisted with the music. When they transferred to the Kentucky Conference, they pastored New Shiloh 1959–60. William died April 6, 1962, and Imogene in November 1963.[256]

Beulah Moorefield

Beulah Moorefield was first listed by the North Carolina Conference of the Wesleyan Methodist Church (which then included Virginia) in 1939 as a "conference preacher" (now licensed minister). She was listed as an "elder" (ordained minister) by 1945. She served as the associate or assistant pastor with her husband, Arthur, at the following churches: Rock Hill, Christenburg Memorial, Thomasville Second, Midway, Roanoke Second, Winston-Salem, and Thomasville Memorial Park. She was cited for twenty-five years of service in 1959 while serving Winston-Salem. She was on reserve 1961–64 but then renewed her assistant pastoral role beginning in 1964.[257]

Esther May Nauman

Esther May Nauman was first listed by the Iowa Conference of the Wesleyan Methodist Church in 1939, instructing her to "remain in school." In 1940 she was listed as a "conference preacher" (now licensed minister). From 1941 to 1944 she was in evangelistic work. She was listed "in the hands of the conference president" (now district superintendent) in 1944. In 1945 Esther was ordained and appointed as pastor of the Maywood Chapel in Waterloo, Iowa, but resigned before the year was over. In 1946 and 1947 she was authorized to choose her own field of labor.[258]

Elvina Anna Hovland Perkins

Elvina Anna Hovland married Eldred Victor Perkins in 1936 at the Burr, Wisconsin, campground during the camp meeting of the Wisconsin

Conference of the Wesleyan Methodist Church. They began their ministry in 1939 at the Superior, Wisconsin, church; while there, they started the Darrow Road church. In 1943–45 they co-pastored Oak Ridge and Pisgah. Eldred was ordained in 1942. Elvina became a conference preacher (now licensed minister) in 1941, but no record of her ordination was discovered.

In 1945 they transferred to the Iowa Conference, where they pastored a new group which became the Falls Avenue Wesleyan Methodist Church in Waterloo, Iowa (later Sunnyside Temple and still later Cedar Valley Community Church). They continued here until 1953.

In 1953 they transferred to the California Conference. They pastored the Bostonia church in the San Diego area and coordinated church planting in California. Later they started the Sacramento Arcade church. Then they moved to Arizona to lay the groundwork for a new church in Scottsdale. In 1964 they were back in Madison, Wisconsin, to begin a new church. Eight years later they moved to Bolingbrook, outside Chicago, to pastor another new church. And then they moved to Mukwonago, outside Milwaukee, to begin a new church. They returned to California to serve the Christian and Missionary Alliance, starting a new church and helping with church extension work. In 1985 they returned to service in The Wesleyan Church to begin a work in Corona, California. They served there until April 1990, when Eldred had heart surgery.

The Perkinses moved to Florida in March 1991. Elvina was the mother of David, Linda (Mrs. Lyle Williams), Sharon, and Robert (he died in 1948).[259]

Ruth Nichols Sanchez

Ruth Nichols, a graduate of Miltonvale Wesleyan College, Miltonvale, Kansas (later merged into what became Oklahoma Wesleyan University, Bartlesville, Oklahoma), went to work among Mexican immigrants in Carlsbad, California, in 1933. In 1937 she moved to Oceanside, California, where there was a growing

Sunday school, and opened a mission there. A parsonage and a church were built and were dedicated in 1940.

Ruth Nichols was apparently from Enid, Oklahoma. She was introduced to the Oklahoma Conference of the Wesleyan Methodist Church in 1939, was requested to complete the course of study, and was assigned to continue in the Mexican work. She was ordained in 1941. She married Jose Sanchez in 1945. In 1946 the Oklahoma Conference recognized that she was working in the bounds of the California Conference, and in 1947 she was granted a letter of transfer.

From 1947 to 1955 Ruth Nichols Sanchez served most of the time at Oceanside, part of the time at Carlsbad. From 1955 to 1956 she was listed by the California Conference as a missionary evangelist and from 1956 to 1961 as supervisor of the Mexican work. From 1961 to 1963 she was on reserve and then went on the "unstationed list" (without appointment).[260]

Ruth Patterson Saunders

Ruth Patterson was born February 26, 1916, in the hills of Harrison County, Ohio, to Mr. and Mrs. Chester D. Patterson. Her parents were later called to preach and became elders (ordained ministers) in the Allegheny Conference of the Wesleyan Methodist Church. Ruth learned to read at the age of four, was converted at seven, and graduated from high school at sixteen. In high school she won first place on two occasions in a Prince of Peace speaking contest. Shortly after conversion she heard a voice saying, "Will you go for Me as a missionary?" Later the voice made it clear that she was to go to Africa. For a time she suffered a spiritual lapse but was restored at the age of fourteen. While she was quite young, her parents took a four-year course at Cleveland Bible Institute (now Malone College), and when she graduated from high school, she returned to the Institute to prepare for her life's labors. While there she and Norman Saunders, a young man from Poquoson, Virginia, were attracted to each other. They were married August 29, 1938, at her parents' home at Barberton,

Ohio. Ruth Patterson Saunders was ordained by the Allegheny Conference in June 1939.

The Allegheny Conference listed Ruth 1939–40 as an evangelist, in 1940–42 as co-pastor at Niles, Ohio, 1942–46 at Salem, Ohio Greenwood, in 1946–49 as missionary to Africa (Sierra Leone), in 1949–51 as on furlough (now "home ministries"), in 1951–57 as missionary to Africa, in 1957–62 as co-pastor at Greenfield, in 1962–66 as missionary to Africa. At the age of eighty-three, she looked back on their years in Sierra Leone as "years of joy and blessing." She was still active in her local church, teaching a Bible Class, serving as women's president, and providing pulpit supply for absent pastors.[261]

Ethel Schaar

Ethel Scharr was first mentioned in the records of the Kentucky District of the Pilgrim Holiness Church in 1939 as pastor at Tyrone. In 1941 she was ordained. In the *Pilgrim Holiness Advocate*, January 1, 1942, page 12, she was described as a consecrated worker, a splendid preacher, and a well-balanced messenger of truth, and it was stated that God was honoring her work. She was also listed by Kentucky in 1943. In 1947 and 1948 she was listed by the Idaho-Washington District. The August 12, 1948, issue of the *Pilgrim Holiness Advocate*, page 15, described her as an excellent preacher, apparently teamed with Mabel Martin, who played the guitar and mandolin. They were described as "godly," providing evangelistic preaching and singing. Ethel Schaar then was listed in the records of the Eastern District, 1949–53.

Naomi Schumaker

Naomi Schumaker was born in Clay County, Indiana. She was converted at eighteen in a tent meeting and became a member of the Seelyville Pilgrim Holiness church. Her ministerial service began as an evangelistic singer. She entered upon the course of study and preached her first sermon at the Sandford, Indiana, Pilgrim Holiness

church. She was ordained. Her name appears on the records of the Indiana District and the Southern Indiana District of the Pilgrim Holiness Church from 1939 to 1951. She served as assistant pastor or pastor at Seelyville for a total of twelve years. When the roads were icy, she walked four miles to the Seelyville church to fill her place. She pastored at Shelburn four years, Vincennes one year, and Terre Haute Northside five years. She was ill for some time at Northside but kept on with her ministry until she fell unconscious in the service November 11, 1951. She died December 13, 1951.[262]

Sena Spoolstra

Sena Spoolstra was listed by the Michigan Conference of the Wesleyan Methodist Church in 1939 as an elder (ordained minister) under the direction of the conference president (now district superintendent) in evangelistic work. In 1940 the Hudson church was without a pastor, so the president sent Sena and her husband, Andrew, to serve there. In 1941 they were granted letters of standing.[263]

Helen Ruth Strong

Helen Strong received her call to preach at seventeen and met her future husband, Forest Wayne Strong, at eighteen. A year later, in 1934, they were married. In 1935 they began ministerial service in the Pilgrim Holiness Church. They served 1934–40 as circuit preachers in five different areas of Tennessee. From 1940 to 1955 they were apparently in Montgomery, Alabama; at least part of this time Helen was listed as "unstationed" (without appointment). In 1955 they moved to Selma, Alabama, and started a church in a wooden tabernacle. Over time a church building and parsonage were built. Thirty-seven years after they arrived, 1992, they retired from Selma and moved to Florida.

Helen died January 29, 1999, at the age of 83. She was survived by four daughters, seventeen grandchildren, thirty-one great-grandchildren and thirteen great-great-grandchildren.[264]

Lola Lea Vickers

The minutes of the Eastern District of the Pilgrim Holiness Church listed Lola Lea Vickers as a licensed minister in 1939, an ordained minister in 1946, and she continued on the list through 1967, but there were no other indications of the nature of her service.

Madge Howard Wilson

Madge Howard was born in Jackson, Michigan, May 23, 1915. She was converted in Jackson in October 1926 and sanctified December 31, 1934. She worked in the field of evangelism following completion of the three-year theological course at Owosso College, Owosso, Michigan (eventually merged into what became Indiana Wesleyan University, Marion, Indiana). She received some medical experience while employed as ward helper at Ann Arbor State Hospital, Ann Arbor, Michigan.

She married Ermal Leroy Wilson, August 9, 1939, at Jackson, Michigan. She was also ordained by the Pilgrim Holiness Church in August 1939. Madge and Ermal Wilson began missionary service in Africa, February 9, 1940. The first six years were spent in Swaziland, followed by a little over a year in Natal. After a furlough, in 1948 they went to Mt. Frere, Cape Province, for two years. They then transferred to Brakpan, Transvaal, and served for two years. From 1952 to March 1955 they labored again in Mt. Frere.

Returning home, Ermal Wilson served for a time as assistant secretary of foreign missions. From 1958 to 1968 he served as general secretary of foreign/world missions for the Pilgrim Holiness Church. From 1968 to 1972 he served as the first General Secretary of World Missions for the newly merged Wesleyan Church.

At some point, Madge Wilson earned an M.A. degree from Indiana University. After their return from Africa, she taught at Frankfort Pilgrim College. Madge Wilson died January 24, 1967. She and Ermal had three children: Paul, Evangeline, and Victor, all three born in Africa and all three involved in ministry.[265]

Roberta Wylie

Roberta Wylie was the daughter of a Wesleyan Methodist minister and his wife. She was saved at the age of sixteen and a little later was sanctified. She was described as a most consistent person with a great deal of common sound judgment. She was called to foreign mission work, but to fulfill that call she had to climb over an unbelievable number of obstacles.

Her schooling was often interrupted. She worked at the Textile Institute in Spartanburg, South Carolina. For two years she pursued her education by working in the mill one week and going to school the next. She was delayed three more years by illness and family concerns. Her mother died and left a baby to be cared for. Roberta assumed responsibility for the little one. School had already begun two weeks before at Central Wesleyan College, Central, South Carolina (now Southern Wesleyan University). But the Lord opened the way for her and the baby to go to Central. When she was nearly through the junior college at Central, she went to the Booth Memorial Hospital in New York and graduated as a trained assistant. Then she went to the medical center in Jersey City and came out as a nurse.

Even though she now had training, the door was closed to her for missions. As early as 1930, she spoke at the North Carolina Conference of the Wesleyan Methodist Church as a "missionary-elect." But this was during the Great Depression, and there were no funds to send her. So she invested this time in service as superintendent of a rescue home for fallen girls in Greensboro, North Carolina.

Finally, in 1937, she went to Sierra Leone, West Africa. She served at first as a nurse at Kamakwie Hospital. Most of the time she was there by herself, ministering to both physical and spiritual needs of the many who came for help.

In all, she served in Sierra Leone three terms: 1937–42, 1943–46, and 1948–53. She was listed on the North Carolina Conference appointments from 1939 on. While she was home in 1947, she was granted authorization to administer the sacraments. But this did not satisfy the British government in Sierra Leone. So in 1948, while she was in Sierra Leone, the North Carolina Conference ordained her *by proxy* in its session—which was made possible by a ruling by General Conference President R. S. Nicholson.

Roberta Wylie's listing was returned missionary, 1953–62; returned missionary on reserve, 1963; reserve, 1964–65; and unstationed (without appointment), 1966–68. She died November 5, 1971, at the age of sixty-four.[266]

Mrs. M. L. Brown

Mrs. M. L. Brown was quite possibly the Helen Horst listed by the Pittsburgh District of the Pilgrim Holiness Church in 1939. Mrs. Brown was ordained by this district in 1940 and was listed also 1941–44. In 1942, she was assigned to Clinton, Pennsylvania.[267]

From Wartime to Post-War Boom

The first half of this decade brought the Holocaust, with its unbelievable slaughter of the Jews and other peoples in Europe. Pearl Harbor thrust the United States into two-front participation in the Second World War; the blinding atomic blasts at Hiroshima and Nagasaki heralded the end of the long struggle. Millions of young men were sent into battle and many young women filled supporting roles in the military. Millions of women were drawn into factory labor. Because of the family separation caused by war and the exposure of wives to new friendships in the workplace, divorces multiplied and the very family structure was threatened. Women's dress and hairstyles changed radically. Movies became perhaps the leading form of entertainment. Missionaries were cut off from financial support, furloughs, and replacements by the war. Denominational leaders and evangelists traveled only with difficulty. Even pastors found themselves restricted in access to their flocks.

The second half of the decade brought a great wave of optimism. The war effort had broken the hold of the Great Depression, and the end of the conflict introduced a prolonged prosperity such as had never been known. There was an enormous increase in the construction of churches and parsonages. Denominational departments multiplied. World missions made significant and rapid advances. The Wesleyan Methodists drastically restructured to provide their first full-time central leadership. A flood of veterans, forever changed by war experiences, poured into church colleges to prepare for ministry. In 1946 the Holiness Church of California merged with the Pilgrim Holiness Church, and in 1947 some churches and mission fields of the Hephzibah Faith Missionary Association joined the Wesleyan Methodist Church. And still, throughout the decade, a significant number of women responded to God's call. Here are some of their stories.

Roma Lapham Acuna

Roma Lapham was born April 15, 1910, to William and Lacy Lapham. She became a Christian in 1931 and served the Lord for sixty-five years. She graduated from Houghton College, Houghton, New York, in 1934. While at Houghton, she helped in a Sunday school and preaching ministry. She graduated in 1940 from Marion College, Marion, Indiana (now Indiana Wesleyan University) with a master's degree in religion.

In 1940 Roma went to California to join Ruth Nichols in Oceanside, working among the Mexicans. Beginning in 1942, she was listed by the Lockport Conference of the Wesleyan Methodist Church (now Western New York District) as an "annual conference preacher" (now licensed minister), assigned to the Mexican Mission in Oceanside. In 1942 Roma and Delores Lobdell started a mission in Vista, where a Sunday school had been started in 1935. The Lockport Conference ordained Roma in 1943, and until 1949 her listing showed her at the Mexican Mission in Vista.

In 1946, Roma helped name and care for a child she legally adopted two months later. His name was Stephen Roman Morales. She fell in love with and in 1949 married Alberto Acuna, a native of Mexico who had been in the United States since 1916. He had been a charter member at the work in Carlsbad, California, and they lived there for a time. She inherited eight grown stepchildren whom she loved dearly, and she and Alberto raised Stephen to love the Lord. In 1949 she transferred to the California Conference. From 1949 to 1952 she was listed in child evangelism. In 1951 she became a public school teacher and taught kindergarten until she retired in 1975. From 1956 to 1959 she was also pastor of the Vista Wesleyan Methodist Mexican chapel. In 1962, the Acunas bought a house in Vista and continued to be active in the Vista church. Roma Lapham Acuna passed away February 3, 1996.[1]

Gracia L. Fero Banker

Gracia L. Fero was born January 30, 1912, to Rev. Albert D. and Pearl Fero in Sandy Lake, Pennsylvania. She was converted at an early age. In 1933 she graduated from Houghton College, Houghton, New York.

 She volunteered for missionary service for the Wesleyan Methodists in India, but frail health closed that door. So she taught on the high school level at Allentown Bible Institute (later Eastern Pilgrim/United Wesleyan College), Allentown, Pennsylvania, 1936–37, and at Zion's Hill, a Wesleyan Methodist mission school in the mountains of Kentucky, 1937–38.

From 1940 to 1942, the Allegheny Conference of the Wesleyan Methodist Church listed her as assistant pastor at the Akron, Ohio First Church. The conference ordained her in

1942. From 1942 to 1943, she pastored Summit (Rock Run), probably in Ohio; and from 1943 to 1945 Blue Eye Chapel and from 1948 to 1951 Soldier, both missions/pioneer churches in Pennsylvania. In between were two years of witnessing and one in evangelism.

From 1951 to 1963 she served as editor of the *Wesleyan Missionary*, a magazine published by the Woman's Missionary Society. Rev. Gipsie M. Miller, in writing about Gracia Fero Banker, said,

Mrs. Gracia F. Banker's greatest gift to the *Wesleyan Missionary* was Gracia, herself. When she was elected editor in 1951, she brought into the office far more than journalistic ability. Her spiritual acumen, developed across the long years of walking with God with the faith of a little child, enabled her to editorialize with the freshness of the morning dew. A quality was there which could not be explained by the tricks of the trade in professional writing.

Rev. Banker was the author of several booklets: *God's Disciplines, Not of This World, The Way to Security,* and a tract, "The Adequacy of the Calvary Cure."

In 1961 she married Rev. Floyd E. Banker, former missionary to India. From 1963 to 1968, they served during the school years as missionaries to Jamaica, where Gracia taught in the Bible school. They traveled following this in missionary evangelism in India, Australia, Papua New Guinea, and Japan. They retired to Wesleyan Village in Brooksville, Florida, in 1969. Gracia dispensed Wesleyanaphone messages to Village prayer meetings, ministered in duets or the ladies sextet, and sometimes directed the choir. She died December 14, 1991.[2]

Edna Barnes

Mrs. Edna Barnes was listed as under district appointment in the Indiana District of the Pilgrim Holiness Church 1940–51. When the district was divided, she was listed by the Northern Indiana District 1951–52. In 1952 she transferred to the Southern Indiana District and was listed there that year and 1954–57. In 1957, the Northern Indiana records tell of her transferring back into that district from the California District; however, the California District has no records of her there. She apparently served in some capacity with her husband, Omer W. Barnes, on their pastorates. Rev. Ernest R. Batman, former superintendent of the Indiana Central District of The Wesleyan Church, said of Edna Barnes, "She was a very saintly lady, highly respected, and dearly loved by the people they pastored."

Ethel C. Bennett

Ethel (Mrs. Frank) Bennett was born November 21, 1880, in Ross City, Ohio. She attended Ohio Northern University and taught school in her early life. She was converted and became an earnest, active Christian. She believed that she was called to the ministry. She entered the ministry in the Pilgrim Holiness Church and was ordained by the Ohio District in 1940 at the age of sixty. She was listed by the Ohio District 1940–55 and by the Western Ohio District 1955–59. She lived most of these years in Springfield, Ohio. She was described as a faithful wife and a loving mother. She died July 19, 1959.[3]

Alice Boyd

Alice Boyd was a native of Kansas and a graduate of Miltonvale Wesleyan College, Miltonvale, Kansas (later merged into what became Oklahoma Wesleyan University, Bartlesville, Oklahoma). She was from Iowa Union and was listed as a conference preacher (now licensed minister) by the Kansas Conference of the Wesleyan Methodist Church in 1939 and was appointed to serve that year as pastor at Iowa Union. She was continued there the following year, 1940–41. In 1941 she was ordained and served as assistant pastor at Albert Lea, Minnesota, 1941–42. From 1941 to 1943 she was a conference evangelist, and from 1943 to 1949 she was listed as an evangelistic singer and a children's worker.

She was teaching school during this time and felt the call of God to China. On September 18, 1948, she arrived in Hong Kong and spent eight months in language study. With her accordion, she could and did take part in outdoor evangelism, even though she did not as yet have command of the language. The advance of communism in China forced her to spend most of her time in Hong Kong, where she taught Bible in the public schools. Her listing 1949–50 was as a missionary to China.

From 1950 to 1952, she was again listed as an evangelistic singer and children's worker. But in 1951 she was elected general corresponding secretary for the Woman's Missionary Society and served in that office until 1959. From 1959 to 1962 she was told to choose her own field. From 1963 to 1966 she was listed as secretary and parish worker at the Houghton, New York, church. In 1966 and 1967, she was listed as secretary to the Billy Graham Association.[4]

Aldene Headly Bradley

Aldene Headley married William Calvin Bradley in 1939. They pastored for the Pilgrim Holiness Church in Maryland and Pennsylvania before moving to Indianapolis. They sailed for Africa in 1946 and served three terms in Zambia, Swaziland, and South Africa; two years were spent with the European work in Port Shepstone, Natal. They returned to the United States in 1965 and pastored churches in Virginia, Maryland, and Kentucky. They retired in June 1984. Aldene passed away, December 6. 1984.[5]

Marjean Bennett
Chapman Dayton

Margaret Jean Bennett, known throughout her life and by personal choice as Marjean, was born in 1919. She graduated from Houghton College, Houghton, New York, in 1940. The Champlain Conference (now Eastern New York-New England District) of the Wesleyan Methodist Church listed her that year as a conference preacher (now licensed minister) and appointed her to travel under the direction of the conference president (now district superintendent). In the fall of 1940,

Marjean and Anne Ross held special meetings at Heuvelton, New York, and several sought the Lord at the altar of prayer.

From 1941 to 1953, Marjean was appointed to evangelism. In 1943, Rev. Price Stark was elected conference president. In 1944, Rev. Helen Stark and Marjean cared for the pastorate at Mooers, New York. In 1945 Marjean was ordained. In 1952 she married a widower, Rev. Howard H. Chapman, became stepmother to his small children, and assisted him in pastoral duties at West Chazy, New York, 1952–57. From 1957 to 1961, she was to choose her own field of labor. During that period, she served two different interim periods as supply pastor at the Elizabeth Street church in Plattsburgh, New York. From 1961 to 1963, she was on reserve, and in 1963–65 unstationed (without appointment). Then followed two years assisting her husband in the pastorate at Elizabeth Street.

In the years of her appointments other than pastorates, she remembers many forms of service: Working in churches in New York, Pennsylvania, Ohio, Michigan, West Virginia, Florida, and Canada; pastoring a Pilgrim Holiness church in Middlebury, New York; serving as song leader to Rev. Oneida Gleason, pioneer secretary of the Allegheny Conference; working in the same conference with Rev. Gracia Fero (Banker); serving as youth pastor of the Schenectady, New York, church.

In 1975 Howard Chapman passed away. In 1982 Marjean Bennett Chapman married a Christian layman, Chester Dayton. She continued to sing and preach, visit those in need, and carry on all aspects of ministry as opportunity afforded.[6]

Helen Dentler

The record of the Allegheny Conference of the Wesleyan Methodist Church listed Helen (Mrs. J. W.) Dentler on its ministerial roll beginning in 1940. She may have been ordained that year. She co-pastored at Keepville 1941–42, Ashville 1942–45, Carrollton 1945–46, Mount Calvary 1946–47, New Mine 1947–50, Vanport 1950–56, West Middlesex 1956–64, Loyal Oak 1964–66. The conference included churches in eastern Ohio, western Pennsylvania and a few in West Virginia.

Flossie Doll

Flossie Doll was ordained in 1940. Her name appears on the records of various midwestern districts of the Pilgrim Holiness Church. In 1940 she was in the Iowa-Missouri-Arkansas District. In 1942–44 she was in the Western Kansas District. In 1944 she was an assistant pastor, again in the Iowa-Missouri-Arkansas District. Beginning in 1945, she was listed by the Kansas District, serving in 1948–49 at the People's Mission in Wichita. From 1953 on, she was not listed with her husband, J. John Doll.

Louise Traver Goodsell

Louise Traver was born into a home in which two ministers preceded her. Her mother, Elizabeth Traver, was eventually ordained. Her father, Frank Traver, was never ordained and passed away in 1939. Being raised in a pastor's home in the Dakota Conference of the Wesleyan Methodist Church, Louise grew up enjoying the work and the people. She started giving readings and sharing talks early in life. She filled the pulpit for her father in Bushnell, South Dakota, when he was seriously ill and for her mother a year later.

She studied for the ministry at Miltonvale Wesleyan College, Miltonvale, Kansas (later merged into what became Oklahoma Wesleyan University, Bartlesville, Oklahoma). She had to stay home for a year and did some of her work by correspondence. Her mother was still completing the course of study, and they studied some of the books together. Louise graduated from Miltonvale in 1939.

In 1940, she married Gordon Goodsell, and they became pastors of the Watertown, South Dakota, church. In 1941 the Dakota Conference ordained Gordon and Louise Goodsell, and Louise's mother, Elizabeth Traver.

The Goodsells served primarily as planters, establishers, and revivers of churches. From 1940 to 1947, they served as the first resident pastors at the Watertown church, and they built the church building. Louise Goodsell says that her husband was "most supportive" of her ministry, and they served together filling in for each other whenever needed. He was often involved in construction. From 1947 to 1951, they took over First Church in Rapid City, South Dakota, at a time when it was near death and planted it all over again. While there, Gordon helped to build the first Wesleyan Native American chapel in Rapid City. In 1951 the Goodsells transferred to the Nebraska District. From then until 1956, they served at Grand Island, first as occupational missionaries, then as pioneer pastors. Services were held in a tent, which a storm took down three times. In 1954 they presented the newly organized church to the conference. From 1956 to 1957, they were conference evangelists. In 1957 they transferred back to the Kansas Conference. From 1957 to 1964, they pastored the Belle Fourche, South Dakota, church, and from 1964 to 1967 the Aberdeen, South Dakota, church. From 1967 to 1968, they were conference evangelists. Beginning early in 1968, Gordon served as supply pastor at Sundance, Wyoming, and later that year they began service together at Pierre, South Dakota.

Louise Traver Goodsell has been described as a great Bible teacher. She had a special gift in speaking to children and could pull them into a Bible story until they would sigh or shout or yell, "Yea!" But she was also versatile, at home in the children's meeting but equally at home preaching to a tabernacle filled with adults.

In 1998 Bartlesville Wesleyan College (now Oklahoma Wesleyan University), into which Miltonvale Wesleyan College had merged, honored Louise Goodsell as Alumna of the Year. The tribute mentioned that the Goodsells had paid their way for two mission trips to Haiti, assisting Wesleyan missionaries there. And upon retirement they served as the Dakota camp managers. They raised four children and had seven grandsons.[7]

Ruth Bake Hamilton

Ruth Bake Hamilton is listed in the records of the Indiana District of the Pilgrim Holiness Church as being ordained in 1940. She continued to be listed through 1945.

Mrs. Ada Scott Hodson

Ada Scott Hodson was born in Decatur County, Indiana, possibly in the 1870s. It is difficult to draw the recorded details into anything like a clear account. She is said to be the sister of Rev. Myrtle Jane Webster Brown, wife of Rev. C. C. Brown (see chapter 1), yet there is no mention of "Webster" with Ada. She may have been a half-sister with a different father, or she may have married a man named Scott earlier, but she married a Mr. Hodson in 1943 when she was quite elderly. She apparently was converted near the same time as Myrtle, just before the beginning of the 1900s. She is said to have been used mightily by the Lord in home missionary work in the Holiness Christian Church, which merged into what later became the Pilgrim Holiness Church in 1919. The two sisters are given at least partial credit for the existence of the Lawrenceville, Illinois, church. Yet Ada Scott Hodson does not show up on the official records until she is listed in the records of the Indiana District of the Pilgrim Holiness Church, 1940–51, and the records of the Southern Indiana District, 1951–56. She died when she was past eighty years of age.

Marie Hubby

Marie Hubby was born in a parsonage. She appears on the records of the Iowa Conference of the Wesleyan Methodist Church as appointed on October 16, 1939, with her husband to pastor the Atkinson, Nebraska, church. The Atkinson church was apparently organized the same day. The 1940 conference session listed her as a conference preacher (now licensed minister). They continued to serve at Atkinson until 1942. Then followed pastorates at Howardsville, Iowa, 1942–44, and Spencer, Nebraska, 1944–49. In 1944 they participated in the organizing session of the Nebraska Conference. In 1949 the Nebraska Conference ordained Marie Hubby.

In 1949 the Hubbys became the pioneer pastors at the Wayne church, which was organized August 2, 1952. They continued service there until

1954. Then from 1954 to 1955 she was listed as a conference evangelist. Most of the years she served the Nebraska Conference, she was president of the conference Woman's Missionary Society.

On July 30, 1955, the Hubbys transferred back to the Iowa Conference. From October 1954 they had been pastoring the Rudd, Iowa, church and continued there until 1957. For 1955 to 1956 they also pastored Rockford. Then from 1957 to 1966, they pastored the Cedar Rapids church. In 1966 they assumed the pastorate at Marshaltown.

Following retirement, the Hubbys pioneered an interdenominational open air chapel at Cripple Creek Mountain Estates in Colorado. They had two children, Bonnie Bass and Bruce. Rev. G. M. Hubby died November 19, 1987. For several years, Marie Hubby served as chair of the West Central Area of Wesleyan Women of The Wesleyan Church.[8]

Kathleen Kelsven Edwards

Kathleen Kelsven's call to ministry was mainly to work with children and youth. But she also had some pastorates along the way.

Kathleen was listed by the Dakota Conference of the Wesleyan Methodist Church from 1940 to 1943 as a song evangelist and children's worker. The conference ordained her June 7, 1942. That summer she served as the children's worker at a holiness camp meeting in North Dakota and taught a vacation Bible school in South Dakota. In 1943 she transferred to the Oregon Conference.

The Oregon Conference immediately elected Kathleen as its secretary, and she served in that office from 1943 to 1958. In 1943–44 she was listed as "field representative" and in 1944–46 as children's worker and song evangelist. During these years, she lived with her parents in Sheridan, Oregon, and traveled mainly by bus. She taught Sunday school and worked with children's and youth camps, in children's and youth services in camp meetings, and in vacation Bible schools. She also supplied pulpits. Some secular work was necessary.

From 1946 to 1947, Kathleen Kelsven and Vera Willis supplied the pioneer pastorate at Salem, Oregon. From 1947 to 1949, she served in evangelism. From 1949 to 1952, Kathleen was pastor at Holgate, a new work in Portland, Oregon; she was assisted the last year by Marjorie Gjesdal. From 1952 to 1953, she was again in evangelism.

In the summer of 1953 she married Burdette Edwards, and together they were appointed assistant pastors in Seattle. After a few months she became the pastor, and Burdette was her assistant. He had to work, and this led to a successful career in social work. When Kathleen was pregnant, she had one outfit for dress-up wear. A preschooler told her, "You must like that coat; you wear it every Sunday." She readily agreed. Burdette developed throat problems, and she was busy with a growing family; they resigned the pastorate in 1956.

Kathleen had served in many other offices and on many committees by the time she completed her service as conference secretary in 1958. The conference honored her in its 1958 session. Burdette died in January 1997.[9]

Eula Kennedy

Eula Kennedy's name does not appear in the official records of the Pilgrim Holiness Church until 1940. But two itinerant Methodist evangelists from Kentucky came to Clarksburg, Indiana, and held a revival that led to the organization of a church that became a Pilgrim Holiness church. Eula was the first pastor, beginning in 1937. She also established a Pilgrim Holiness camp meeting at Clarksburg.

In 1940 the Indiana District of the Pilgrim Holiness Church ordained Eula. She pastored the Lawrenceburg, church 1940–52, the Seymour, church 1952–60, and the Rising Sun, church beginning in 1960 and continuing past 1967.[10]

Rev. Ernest R. Batman, former superintendent of the Indiana Central District of The Wesleyan Church, speaks of Eula Kennedy as the girlhood pastor of his wife, Ada Batman. He describes her as an outstanding pastor, a very dedicated lady, and an excellent communicator of the Word.

Reland Elam Key

Reland Elam was from Bubb County, Alabama. She was the first person to graduate with a Th. B. degree from Central Wesleyan College (now Southern Wesleyan University), Central, South Carolina. She was appointed by the Kentucky Conference of the Wesleyan Methodist Church in 1940 to serve with Ruby Irwin as pastors of the Jamestown, Kentucky, pioneer work. Reland Elam had been ordained by the Alabama Conference that year. In 1942 she was received by the Kentucky Conference from the Alabama Conference as an elder (ordained minister). She continued at Jamestown at least until 1944. From 1945 to 1947, she pastored New Albany, Indiana (the Kentucky Conference included the southern part of Indiana), being assisted by Ruby Irwin 1946–47. For a short time in 1947, Reland Elam was pastor at Glenville in the South Carolina Conference, with Ruby Irwin as her assistant. From 1947 to 1950, Reland was back at Jamestown. From 1950 to 1952, she was listed as in "pioneer work."

In 1952, Reland married a widower, Rev. Ven Key. From 1952 to 1955, they co-pastored Pekin. From 1955 to 1956, Reland was a conference evangelist. The Keys co-pastored Shively 1956–57 and Pekin again 1957–59. Then in 1959–61, she was a conference evangelist again and was "unstationed" (without appointment) 1961–62.

In 1962 she transferred back to the Alabama Conference and served 1962–63 as assistant pastor at the Ensley Church in Birmingham. She went on the superannuated list (retired) in August 1963 due to ill health. Reland Elam Key died February 15, 1964. Her husband, Ven Key, died May 19, 1969.[11]

Lila Cairns Manker

Lila Cairns was born in 1892 and grew up near Hastings, Michigan. In 1916 she married a Pilgrim Holiness minister, Bernard E. Manker. It appears that Lila Cairns Manker's ministry moved gradually from pastor's wife eventually to her own extensive

pastoral career. She later admitted that she had fought her ministerial call for a long time. Bernard pastored Pilgrim Holiness churches at Elkton, Sault Ste. Marie, Ellsworth, Merrill, and Flint. Lila had acquired a normal school certificate in Barry County (Hastings) and apparently taught school during part of this time.

In 1939 they took the pastorate at Hastings, near her childhood home. By 1940, Bernard was moving into full-time evangelism with meetings  in both the United States and Canada. Lila's battle over her call was settled, and she was ordained in 1940. At first she filled in when her husband was gone, and then she was chosen by the congregation to be the pastor. She served twenty-three or more years as pastor of Hastings. Ill health forced Bernard's retirement in 1950, and he passed away September 19, 1960. He and Lila had one daughter and four sons.

Lila Manker left a tremendous impression on those to whom she ministered. The widow of a Free Methodist minister remembered Lila's children's meetings in a storage garage at camp meeting in Owosso, Michigan, and giving her heart to the Lord following one of those services. Another widow remembered when Lila married her and her husband, insisting that both be Christians before she would do it. One man recalled how wicked he had been as a seventeen-year-old. He was invited by a recently converted uncle to attend Lila's service. He said her preaching was largely teaching but always aimed at decisions. In the second service he attended, he was at the altar repenting of his sins. Because he was in the Marine Corps Reserve and was thus involved there on Thursday nights, Lila called a board meeting and had prayer meeting changed to Wednesday night for the sake of his spiritual growth. One lady recalled riding with her mother and Lila to youth rallies. Lila was notorious for her driving. She prayed audibly all the way,

"Dear Lord, help us find this road. Dear Lord, help us pass this truck. Dear Lord, help us to have enough gas." After praying, she paid little attention to other vehicles—she just passed the truck!

While Lila Manker was still pastoring at Hastings, she led the congregation in erecting a beautiful new brick church building. It was in the 1960s that she declined to serve longer. She had determined that if she ever had six negative votes in the annual pastoral vote, it was time to move on. Afterward, she went to a Free Methodist church at Stony Point that was failing and served there for quite a while. She taught piano in her home until her death.

Lila was known for her success in praying for healing. This was also a battle for her—she could pray for herself, but to preach about healing was another matter, but the Lord won this battle too. One lady had a difficult time giving birth, and the doctor warned that the mother probably wouldn't make it. Lila was called, she visited, went home to pray, and called, saying, "The Lord has told me you're going to be all right." Soon the mother was completely well. The doctors told one man in 1950 to take his wife quickly to see her family in Hastings as she was soon to die. Lila prayed for her. The man lived until 1980, and his wife lived until 1995.

When Lila Manker was in her early nineties, she could not understand why the Lord did not heal her of her arthritis. Finally she felt assured that the Lord would heal her on New Year's Day. It was a complete healing—on January 1, 1986, at the age of ninety-three, she went to be with the Lord, where there is neither pain nor sickness.[12]

Alta May Mendenhall

Alta May Mendenhall was converted in 1891 in Hartsville, Indiana. In 1906 she joined what became the Pilgrim Holiness Church. She preached her first sermon at Columbus, Indiana, in 1928. She received a local preacher's license in 1928 and was licensed by the district in 1930. She appears on the records of the Indiana District of the Pilgrim Holiness Church, and after the division of Indiana into two districts, the Northern Indiana District, 1940–52. She was ordained in

1940 and served six years as assistant pastor of the Jonesboro, Indiana, church. She died February 28, 1953.

Mrs. Alice Zoe Norris

Alice Zoe Norris was born October 23, 1885, in Lake City, Illinois. Her name appears in the 1940 records of the Idaho-Washington District of the Pilgrim Holiness Church as pastor at Hermiston, Oregon, for 1940–41. It appears again in the records of the Oregon District 1945–48. She was the pastor at Maysville, Washington, 1945–47 and was ordained in 1946. Then her name appears on the records of the Northwest District of the Pilgrim Holiness Church 1949–64. She was pastor of the Port Angeles church 1953–57 and supplied there again 1958–59. She died January 26, 1965.

Bertha Ruth Meyer Prichard

Bertha Ruth Meyer was born January 21, 1902. She lost her eyesight at age twenty-five but amazed everyone as to what she could accomplish without seeing.

Bertha Meyer's name appears in the records of the Kansas Conference of the Wesleyan Methodist Church, 1940–67. In 1940 she was listed as a "conference preacher" (now licensed minister), and she was to serve under the direction of the president (now district superintendent). Beginning that year, she was appointed as a singing evangelist and children's worker. At the 1941 conference session, she sang a song in one of the devotional periods. In 1947 she was ordained, and from 1947 to 1949 she and A. Hulet pastored the Wesleyan Hope Mission in Kansas City. From 1949 to 1954, she served as a conference evangelist.

In 1951 Bertha Meyer married James Prichard, who was also blind. They set up a broom-making business in Horton, Kansas, and people were amazed at what two people deprived of sight could do. They lived frugally and invested heavily in all the denominational departments and interests of the conference. James Prichard died in 1958. From 1954 to 1967, Bertha was listed as doing "parish work" or "pioneer work" in Horton. She died January 11, 1967.[13]

Elizabeth Thompson Reed

Elizabeth Thompson was born in 1951. Her parents were not saved in her early years. But in 1926, the Dover, Delaware, Pilgrim Holiness Church bought an old Methodist campground and held services there. Her parents were saved and sanctified in the meetings. Elizabeth was eleven years old, and she, too, wanted to be saved. She hesitated, for she saw no children responding. Her mother told her she was old enough to know what she was doing. The next evening she "sneaked out" and knelt in the straw at the altar. Etta Mitchell (whose story is also told in this book) knelt in front of her and gave her the words to say. Elizabeth repeated them after her. Elizabeth then led her younger sister to the Lord—her first convert!

While Rev. Paul Elliott was her pastor in the early 1930s, he asked her to prepare a paper for a district youth convention entitled, "An Ideal Pastor from a Young People's Viewpoint." After she presented the paper, it was published in the *Pilgrim Holiness Advocate*. In later life she read the paper repeatedly to see if she were living up to her ideals.

She met her husband-to-be, Newell W. Reed, in 1934 at the Dover church. They were married July 24, 1939, in Tennessee, where he was attending the university in Chattanooga. Both were ordained in 1940. They had one daughter, Janet (Mrs. Roger Bradley).

They served the following churches: Hooper's Island, Trappe, Broome's Island, Hurlock, and Greensboro—all in Maryland—and Elizabeth in Pennsylvania. Elizabeth Thompson Reed never allowed herself to be called "assistant pastor" as she thought the people should think of only one person as their pastor. But she served in an enormous range of ministries: Sunday school teacher, vacation Bible school director, children's

club director on local and district levels, missionary president, music and tabernacle speaking in children's camp, conducting children's services at Denton, Maryland camp, church pianist, organist, choir director, arranger of music, conductor of singspiration services, musician and speaker in nursing homes. Her community service included the Garden Club, World Day of Prayer, Women's Christian Temperance Union, playing for funerals at local funeral homes, working in community missions, conducting child evangelism services one day a week after school. She also spoke at youth rallies and conventions and supplied many pulpits. She felt called to provide "helps" and to "fill in the gaps." Elizabeth divided her sermons into four categories: think sermons, joys and hope sermons, gloom and doom sermons, and special sermons (holidays, special occasions).

The Reeds celebrated their sixtieth wedding anniversary, August 3, 1999. In 1998 Newell W. Reed had been supplying a small church in the country, Holden's Chapel, Suddlersville, Maryland for seventeen years. They were planning to celebrate sixty years of ministry in 2000.[14]

Hazel Rees

The records of the Indiana District of the Pilgrim Holiness Church reveal that Hazel Rees was ordained in 1940. She continued to be listed in 1941, 1942, and 1943.

Mrs. W. L. Robinson

The records of the Kentucky District of the Pilgrim Holiness Church reveal that Mrs. W. L. Robinson was ordained in 1940. She continued to be listed 1941–47.

Bessie Mae Carroll Taylor

Bessie Mae Carroll was born in Martin County, Indiana, February 21, 1922. She was saved when she was eighteen, sanctified at twenty-one. She spent seven years in evangelistic work with her father before she was married. She attended Immanuel Missionary College. She married Francis Asbury Taylor in Colorado Springs June 16, 1947. Francis taught at Immanuel Missionary College and served as its president for a time.

The Taylors pastored churches in Colorado, Kentucky, and Indiana. They served on the mission field in Haiti and Africa and joined the Pilgrim Holiness Church in 1962. They served pastorates at the Ash Street church in Tipton, Indiana, and Mt. Hope Chapel in Michigantown, Indiana.

The Taylors had four daughters: Ida, Rebecca McQuiston, Carlo Glass, and Marlina Brandon. The couple celebrated their fiftieth wedding anniversary, June 16, 1997.[15]

Ivah B. VanWormer

Ivah B. VanWormer is listed in the records of the Allegheny Conference of the Wesleyan Methodist Church in 1940 as a conference preacher (now licensed minister) serving as co-pastor with her husband, Rev. H. C. VanWormer, of the Dixonville, Pennsylvania, church. She was so listed 1940–44. She was ordained in 1942. From 1944 to 1945, she was a general evangelist. From 1945 to 1953, she was listed as assistant to the conference president (now district superintendent), who was her husband. From 1953 to 1966, she was listed as president of the conference Woman's Missionary Society and assistant to the president of the conference.[16]

Mrs. Oma Williams

Oma Williams was ordained in 1940 by the Ohio District of the Pilgrim Holiness Church. She pastored the Crown City church, 1940–53. She was in evangelistic work 1954–55. She continued to be listed in the district conference journals until 1962, when she retired.[17]

Ellen Roark Atkinson

Ellen Roark was born January 2, 1914, in Bull's Gap, Tennessee. Her family moved to Indiana, and Ellen attended high school in Delphi. She graduated from Union Bible Seminary in Westfield, Indiana, and continued her education at Owosso Bible College, Owosso, Michigan. She was ordained by the Indiana District of the Pilgrim Holiness Church August 19, 1941.

Ellen's niece, Rachel J. Satterfield, lost her parents when she was six, and she went to live with her grandparents, Ellen's parents. Ellen was her model and encourager, although she was gone from home by that time. Rachel said, "When Aunt Ellen came home, I would have to get on my knees and pray, listen to scripture, and hear stories. Ellen was a prayer, a good speaker and could read the scripture in an eloquent manner." Ellen's father was very proud of her and often showed visitors a picture of her. With pride in his voice, he would say, "She is a preacher." This produced some smiles and some frowns. Some would ask if she were married, and he would say, "Not yet." Ellen was also gifted in music, singing and playing piano, guitar and accordion.

Ellen was listed by the Indiana District 1941–45. On November 10, 1945, she married Rev. Fred Atkinson in Anderson, Indiana. They raised eight foster children prior to the birth of their own son, John, in 1953. From 1947 to 1961, they co-pastored Wesleyan churches in Fairview, Enid, and Henrietta in Oklahoma; Albuquerque, New Mexico; Hillsboro, Texas; and Burlington and Norway in Indiana. She became inactive in 1962. Fred Atkinson died May 25, 1986.

Even in retirement, Ellen continued to share the light and love of Christ through other routes of ministry. She worked as a nursing assistant in two nursing homes, then at Home Hospital in Lafayette, Indiana in the maternity ward. She never ceased to visit with people everywhere, sharing Christ's love with everyone she met. She was always encouraging and lifting the spirits of those about her.

Ellen Roark Atkinson finally retired to Brooksville Florida, where she died on Easter Sunday, April 13, 1998.[18]

Fylena Beard

The Ohio District of the Pilgrim Holiness Church listed Fylena Beard in 1941 as serving at the Third Street Mission in Columbus, Ohio. She lived in Columbus and worked at or headed this mission at least until 1956. She was ordained by the Ohio District in 1944. When Nota Higgins applied to go as a missionary to the Amerindians of Guyana, in South America, the general board of the Pilgrim Holiness Church asked the Third Street Mission to supply her transportation, equipment, and support. Fylena Beard replied that they could not as they were only a few and all were poor. But they did! They raised her support and equipment for her first time out. In 1962, Fylena Beard was released to work outside the Pilgrim Holiness Church.[19]

Helen Brock

Helen Brock was born in 1909. She was listed by the Indiana Conference of the Wesleyan Methodist Church in 1941 and 1942 as pursuing the course of study. From 1943 to 1947, she pastored at Matthews, 1947–48 at Larwill, 1948–50 the Santa Fe and Pleasant Grove Circuit. She was ordained in 1950 and was appointed as a conference evangelist. However, from October 1950 to February 1952, she pastored South Salem. From then until 1956 she was a conference evangelist. From 1956 to 1963 she was back at Matthews and from 1963 to 1964 back at Pleasant Grove. Then followed two years on reserve and in 1966 she went on the unstationed list (without appointment). Helen Brock died October 16, 1968.[20]

Faith F. Burkett

Faith F. Burkett, of the Camden, New Jersey church, was received by the Middle Atlantic States Conference of the Wesleyan Methodist Church in 1943 to pursue the course of study. She was given credit for work done at Bible school. From 1944 to 1947, she taught at Zion's Hill Mission, Rock Lick, Kentucky. The 1944 session of the conference took up an offering, one-half of which was to support her. She was ordained by the conference June 26, 1946.

In 1947 Faith F. Burkett and Ruby Kagle were appointed pastors of the Watts Township church in Pennsylvania. They served there until 1956. David Tonnessen, an attorney who served on the General Board of Administration of The Wesleyan Church for several years, knew these ladies and their ministry. He said that both were trained as schoolteachers, Faith on the Maryland Eastern Shore and South Jersey, and Ruby, he thought, in Kansas. He said Watts Township was a rural/wilderness church. The two ladies literally were missionaries, teaching folks how to read and write and practice the social graces, and above all, ministering to their spiritual needs. He said they labored long hours in hard conditions and almost never asked for anything. He said their love for people first helped to keep several small churches in that area going, and some of them produced outstanding workers who served the Church at large over a number of years.

Faith Burkett served in various offices and on various committees and boards for the conference, especially in the areas of Christian education and missions. She served as conference treasurer of the Woman's Missionary Society 1956–66. She was a conference evangelist 1956–57, unstationed (without appointment) 1957–61, conference evangelist 1961–64, and after that was listed on reserve.[21]

Elizabeth Copeland

Elizabeth (Mrs. William) Copeland was licensed by the Pittsburgh District of the Pilgrim Holiness Church in 1941. She was listed by that district 1941–43 and 1958–63. She was ordained in 1958 but was on the inactive list 1958–63. Elizabeth was listed by the Eastern District, 1963–67.[22]

Mary Crystal Miller Dunbar

Mary Crystal Miller was born October 10, 1896, in St. Francis, Kansas. After her father's death, she moved to Miltonvale, Kansas. While attending Miltonvale Wesleyan College (later merged into what became Oklahoma Wesleyan University, Bartlesville, Oklahoma), she was saved and sanctified. After completing her studies, she taught school for five years.

On June 16, 1920, she married a widower, Rev. E. H. Dunbar. E. H. pastored the Excelsior charge, Hall, Morgan Chapel, Chapman Creek, and Topeka First Church (nine years at this one). Mary worked devotedly and untiringly as a pastor's wife. Eventually she became convinced that she was called to preach. In 1941 the conference asked her to continue the course of study. In 1942 and succeeding years, she was appointed to evangelism. She was ordained in 1944.

Mary had a keen interest in missionary work. In 1937 she was elected president of the conference Woman's Home and Foreign Missionary Society and continued in that office until six months before her death, April 5, 1947, in Topeka. She was the stepmother of Rev. Dorothy Cretsinger and Rev. Claire Dunbar. A memorial service was held at the 1947 conference session.[23]

Dorothy Gallagher

The minutes of the Ohio District of the Pilgrim Holiness Church listed Dorothy Gallagher in 1941, 1942, and 1943. She was ordained in 1941.

Irene Ipe Green

Irene Ipe of the Holiness Tabernacle Association was introduced to the 1940 session of the Indiana Conference of the Wesleyan Methodist Church. She apparently had had experience as an evangelist. From 1941 to 1947, she was a conference preacher (licensed minister) appointed by the Indiana Conference as a conference evangelist. In 1943 she was also assigned to conference missionary work at Hudson Lake. Beginning in 1944 she was also listed as a theological student, apparently at Marion College (now Indiana Wesleyan University), Marion, Indiana. In 1948 she graduated from the college and was ordained by the Indiana Conference.

From 1948 to 1956 she continued as a conference evangelist. From 1956 to 1957 she was a teacher at New Carlisle, and from 1957 to 1958 she served at Brainerd Indian School in South Dakota. From 1958 to 1964 she was either listed as on reserve or "unstationed" (without appointment). She apparently married Mr. Green (first name unknown) in 1963 and on July 2, 1964, requested that her name be removed from the role of elders.[24]

Willa Edna Nelson Harvey

The July 30, 1941, issue of the *Wesleyan Methodist* carried a report of the session of the Tennessee Conference of the Wesleyan Methodist Church. It listed Harrison A. and Willa E. Harvey as pastors of the Beaumont church. At this point this couple would have been fifty-nine and fifty-two years of age respectively. They had had thirteen years of service in the Salvation Army, and possibly earlier service under the Wesleyan Methodists. Willa Edna Nelson Harvey was born in North Carolina. The Harveys were married in 1918.

From 1942 to 1943, the Harveys served as superintendents of the Heritan Street Mission under the supervision of First Church (probably in Nashville). Beginning in 1943 they were again listed as pastors at Beaumont, apparently on Stair Avenue in Knoxville. Willa was ordained by the Tennessee Conference in 1944, and from 1946 to 1948 she was a general evangelist. She was elected as president of the conference Woman's Home and Foreign Missionary Society in 1942, 1944, and 1946.

In 1948 she was granted permission to reside outside the conference, and on July 24, 1948 she was granted a letter of standing to the North Carolina Conference. Apparently the letter was not used. From 1949 to 1952, she was again a general evangelist. From 1952 on she was listed as superannuated (retired).

Harrison served as pastor and evangelist and for a time as vice president (now assistant district superintendent) of the Tennessee Conference. He preached until he was ninety years of age and died December 30, 1973, at the age of ninety-two.

Willa Edna Nelson Harvey was described as a woman of great dignity with a sweet smile, who gave to others the "cup of cold water" and the gospel. The Harveys had one daughter and four sons; two sons and three grandchildren were called into the ministry. Willa was a member of the Oak Ridge, Tennessee, church when she died at the age of ninety-six, December 7, 1984.[25]

Ruth E. Hoien

Ruth E. Hoien appears on the records of the Allegheny Conference of the Wesleyan Methodist Church in 1941, as co-pastor with her husband, Clifford, at Punxsutawney, Pennsylvania. From 1944 to 1945, she co-pastored at Wolf, Summit, and Rock Run. Beginning in 1945, she was always listed as assistant pastor. They served at Templeton (Pennsylvania) Zion from 1945–46, Akron (Ohio) Kenmore 1946–48, Middlefield (Ohio) 1948–58, Mt. Calvary 1958–63, and Oak Grove from 1963 to at least 1967.[26]

Nellie Linder

Nellie Linder was an alumna of Central Wesleyan College (now Southern Wesleyan University), Central, South Carolina. She was listed in the records of the South Carolina Conference of the Wesleyan Methodist Church in 1941 as a conference preacher (licensed minister) and for 1941, 1942, 1943, and 1944 she was appointed as assistant pastor under Bertha Stamey at Glenville in the Blue Ridge Mountain Mission Work. She resigned December 20, 1944.

Nellie Linder later appears as a deaconess in the records of the Arizona District of the Pilgrim Holiness Church 1960 and 1961, and the Arizona-New Mexico District 1962–65. She had moved to Phoenix in about 1957 to assist in starting Calvary church. She conducted a successful children's church for over two years, while she was "up in years." She established a ministerial scholarship at Central Wesleyan College out of her estate.[27]

Clara B. Walters Manker

Clara Walters was born in Michigan in 1900. She married Dayton A. Manker in 1919. After a year of farming, they went to Owosso Bible School in Owosso, Michigan, a Pilgrim Holiness school (later merged into what became Indiana Wesleyan University, Marion, Indiana). Then Dayton served as a pastor at Coldwater, Cadillac, and Beulah churches for the Wesleyan Methodists. Clara served alongside him as the pastor's wife.

Dayton A. Manker became president (now district superintendent) of the North Michigan Conference and served in that office for nineteen years. Clara was president of the conference Woman's Missionary Society for at least the 1948–55 period. The Mankers lived in Cadillac, and there were several churches fairly close to Cadillac. Rev. Manker faced an emergency one Sunday morning with one of the nearby pulpits empty and was scheduled elsewhere. In desperation, he asked Clara to fill that pulpit. Reluctantly she agreed to help out. She was such a "hit" that everyone, including her husband, was surprised. She apparently was never licensed or ordained, but this was the beginning of her "substitute" ministry. She often filled in for vacationing or ill pastors. On April 1, 1943, she was appointed pastor at Pisgah Heights for the rest of the year. Her preaching was not profound, but rather, her daughter, Flossie Manker Peterson, says, "She had a natural ability to communicate. She was blessed with an abundance of common sense and a good sense of humor. She explained truths from the Bible in a manner appreciated and understood." Some even said that she was a better preacher than her husband.

In 1950 Dayton A. Manker stepped out of the presidency in North Michigan to become pastor of College Church in Miltonvale, Kansas. Later, after "retiring," they served the Appleton church in the Wisconsin Conference, and he was conference president in Wisconsin for three years. Clara continued to work alongside him, playing the piano, singing, teaching in and superintending the Sunday school. She became an artist when seventy-five years old. The Mankers had one son and two daughters.

Clara Walters Manker died March 8, 1987, at the age of eighty-six. Dayton A. Manker died January 23, 1994, at the age of ninety-five.[28]

Pauline Billheimer Putney

Pauline Billheimer was born in 1899, the daughter of a Wesleyan Methodist pastor, Rev. C. A. Billheimer, and his wife. She graduated from Marion College (now Indiana Wesleyan University), Marion, Indiana, in 1924. She married Amos Putney in 1925. She was licensed as a conference preacher (licensed minister) in 1941 and served as an assistant pastor alongside her husband. They pastored eleven Wesleyan Methodist churches in the North Michigan, Indiana, and Kentucky Conferences over a thirty-five-year period. She taught Sunday school from the time she was a teenager. She conducted neighborhood Bible classes and child evangelism meetings. The Putneys had several foster children and two of their own, Everett Putney and Aurie Higgenbotham. Pauline Billheimer Putney died February 13, 1981, at the age of eighty-two.[29]

Dorothy Frances Ragsdale

Dorothy Frances Ragsdale (known commonly as Frances) was born November 20, 1917, near Alexandria, Indiana. She completed a two-year Bible course at Union Bible Seminary, Westfield, Indiana. While at Bible school, she met Paul Ragsdale, a native of Washington, Indiana. He was studying to be a missionary and she to be a minister. Her plans did not include marriage and a family, but Paul persisted. After a six-month courtship by mail, they were married September 26, 1937.

Frances was ordained in 1941 by the Indiana District of the Pilgrim Holiness Church. In December of that year the Ragsdales were planning to sail to the Philippines for missionary service, but Pearl Harbor canceled those plans. Then in the spring of 1942, in spite of submarine-infested waters, they and their son John sailed to Grand Cayman Island for five years of service. After a furlough, in 1950 they went to serve in the Union of South Africa. After another furlough, in 1960 they went back to Africa to Jembo Mission in Northern Rhodesia (now Zambia). They spent a total of fifteen years in Zambia.

The Ragsdales had five children: two sons, John Ragsdale, former president of United Wesleyan College in Allentown, Pennsylvania, and James; and three daughters, Rachel, Carol, and Ruth (wife of David Smith).

Frances Ragsdale was credentialed by the Indiana District of the Pilgrim Holiness Church, 1941–51, and by the Northern Indiana District, 1953 until the 1968 merger. She was a member of the Mooresville, Indiana, Wesleyan Church at the time of her death, August 28, 2000, at the age of eighty-three.[30]

Mrs. Myrtle R. Rogers

Myrtle R. Rogers was originally from Jerseyville, Illinois. The records of the Iowa-Missouri-Arkansas District of the Pilgrim Holiness Church show her as a pastor there from 1941 to 1943 and 1944 to 1948. She was listed in the records of the Central District 1949–50. From 1951 to 1962, she was listed in the records of the Illinois District, 1951–52 as evangelist, 1952–53 as pastor, 1961–62 as pastor at Jerseyville, and 1962–63 as pastor at Casey. From 1963 to 1968 she was again listed in the records of the Central District. Myrtle R. Rogers died July 20, 1998.

Grace Rohland

Grace Rohland was listed in the records of the Ohio District of the Pilgrim Holiness Church from 1941 to 1953. She was ordained in 1941. She lived in Cincinnati from 1948 on.

Madalyn Johnson Simpson

Madalyn Johnson is first mentioned in the records of the Oklahoma Conference of the Wesleyan Methodist Church in 1939. On June 23, 1941, she went with the vice president (now assistant district superintendent) of the conference and his wife and Alice Vermillion to Wichita Falls, Texas, to find a place to pitch a tent and get ready for a tent meeting. In 1943 she was recommended to travel (enter ministry), given credit for work at Miltonvale Wesleyan College, Miltonvale, Kansas (later merged into what became Oklahoma Wesleyan University, Bartlesville, Oklahoma), and was listed as a fourth-year student on the course of study. In 1943, she was appointed as a song evangelist. An announcement with accompanying picture appeared in the denominational paper in June 1943, saying that she was entering the evangelistic field and was of sterling character with zeal and ability and a passion for souls. She had a local preacher's license and was a graduate of Miltonvale. She was a song evangelist and children's worker, a good pianist, and led the singing and sang specials.

She was again appointed as a song evangelist in 1944, 1945, and 1946. In 1945 she was ordained. By 1946 she was the wife of Walter E. Simpson, and on April 25, 1947, she was granted a letter of transfer to the Dakota Conference.

In the Dakota Conference, she and Walter pastored Baker and Knobs 1947–49, Belle Fourche 1949–51, and Brookings 1951–53. From 1953 to 1954 she was listed in missionary work and served as secretary of the conference Woman's Missionary Society. In August 1954 they transferred to the Iowa Conference, where they served the South Troy, Minnesota, church 1954 to 1955. By 1955 they were pastoring Aberdeen, South Dakota, and transferred back to the Dakota Conference in 1956, serving at Aberdeen one more year. On May 28, 1957, they transferred out of the Dakota Conference.[31]

Irene Steger Fields

There are only bits and pieces of Irene Steger Fields' life available. When she was converted, her first husband, Steger, left her. She is mentioned in the official records of the Indiana Conference of the Pilgrim Holiness Church in 1941. The minutes of the 1948 session of the Kentucky Conference of the Wesleyan Methodist Church record that Irene Steger of the Pilgrim Holiness Church had been approved to serve as evangelist at the Milton, Kentucky, church. She had ministered for Rev. Pommerehn and Rev. Stanley Kendall that year.

At one point, Irene was pastoring the Westport, Indiana, church. A Mr. Maddock saw two women struggling to raise a tent. He went to help them and was invited to attend the upcoming tent meeting. The two evangelists were Katie Locke and Esther White (see chapter 2). Mr. and Mrs. Maddock were converted during the meeting. The church had been about to close, and Irene Steger had been sent there since it was thought that she could do no harm. One family with ten children as well as other families began to attend, and the attendance went from nothing to 75–100 in seven years. The church had a great ministry among the youth through its music. Some were called into the ministry and as missionaries and song evangelists during her pastorate. She apparently led the church in erecting a church building and acquiring a parsonage.

At some point, Irene Steger also pastored the Riverside church, later known as Eagledale in Indianapolis. She also served for a number of years as president of Letts Camp, an interdenominational camp in southern Indiana.

In later years, following the 1968 merger that produced The Wesleyan Church, Irene Steger was a charter member of the Gateway Wesleyan Church at Plainfield, Indiana, and later attended during the early stages of the church plant at Avon, Indiana.

Irene Steger had a daughter, Mary (Miller). After Irene's first husband died, she married a Mr. Fields (first name unknown)[32]

Ruth Zehner

Ruth Zehner and her husband, Lester W. Zehner, were ordained in 1941.

Gertrude Bonner

The lady who became Mrs. Gertrude Bonner received her call to missionary service as a girl of twelve in a missionary convention in Faith Home Chapel in Mitchell, South Dakota. She married Norman N. Bonner August 27, 1939. For a time, the Bonners pastored a church in Glenwood, Iowa.

In 1942 they were sent by the Hephzibah Faith Missionary Association of Tabor, Iowa, and Mitchell, South Dakota, to Haiti. The trip was via the Bahamas and involved a wild trip with a violent storm that wrecked their ship. In Haiti they helped to open the mission work, evangelize, establish congregations, and teach in the Bible school. In 1947 various parts of the Association merged into the Wesleyan Methodist Church, including the mission work in Haiti.

In 1947 the Bonners were sent to South Africa under the Pilgrim Holiness Church and  served there until 1960. Here they were involved in evangelism, pioneering the work among the "European" people, planting churches and teaching in the Bible school at Brakpan. Gertrude taught piano and organized and directed choirs. Norman was given the African name "Matileza," which referred to one who goes out and levels the ground before the building can go up. Gertrude was given the Africa name "Izinayo" for "feet," because she was always on the go—a busy wife, mother, and helper of others. In South Africa a woman preacher was not accepted. But R. G. Flexon ordained her there November 4, 1956. She enjoyed "sharing" and was able to do that since her husband was superintendent over the work in South Africa, Swaziland, and what is now Zambia. Gertrude had difficulty learning the language in Natal, South Africa. She was having difficulty buying some turkey eggs. But she failed to get the right "click" in her pronunciation and found out she was asking for turkey *heads!*

From 1960 to 1969, Norman N. Bonner served as president of Central Pilgrim College (later Bartlesville Wesleyan College/Oklahoma Wesleyan University, Bartlesville, Oklahoma). After that, he taught at Western Evangelical Seminary in Portland, Oregon (now a part of George Fox University). Through Norman's encouragement, Gertrude earned a master's degree from the seminary while they were there. They also traveled to and ministered in other countries—Guyana, Vietnam, the Philippines, Hong Kong, Korea, Taiwan, and Japan.

The Bonners had two sons, Robert Bonner and Stanley. They celebrated their sixtieth wedding anniversary in 1999. They reside in Brooksville, Florida.[33]

Mrs. M. M. Conrad

Mrs. M. M. Conrad's name appears on the records of the annual conferences of the Western Kansas District of the Pilgrim Holiness Church 1942–52. She was ordained in 1942. From 1944 to 1953, she served the Hutchinson mission. Her husband died July 5, 1952. Her name also appears on the records of the Iowa-Missouri-Arkansas District 1945 and 1946.

Catherine Craig

Catherine Craig pastored the Santa Barbara, California, church in 1942.[34] As far as the official records are concerned, her name appeared on the minutes of the annual conferences of the California District of the Pilgrim Holiness Church, 1946–68.

Lorene Crowder and Edith L. Miers

Lorene Crowder and Edith L. Miers were teamed together for most of their ministerial service.

Lorene Crowder was the daughter of Rev. E. E. Crowder. She was ordained by the Indiana District of the Pilgrim Holiness Church in 1942 and was listed in their annual records until the state was divided into two districts in 1951. Then she served under the Northern Indiana District.

Edith L. Miers was born in 1914. She was converted May 12, 1935, and sanctified July 8, 1938. She was ordained by the Indiana District of the Pilgrim Holiness Church in 1942. She began her ministry as a song evangelist and was listed in the annual records of the Indiana District until the division into two districts in 1951. Then she was under the Southern Indiana District.

Apparently Lorene and Edith joined forces in 1952. A picture of the two of them appeared in the *Pilgrim Holiness Advocate* July 12, 1952. And by 1953 Edith L. Miers had transferred to the Northern Indiana District, and the two of them were both listed by that district from then on. They sang, held vacation Bible schools, and did some preaching. In 1958 both were listed as evangelists. From 1964 on, both were listed as inactive. They were very active in their local church and supported missions and the district's ministries. Edith L. Miers died January 29, 1986, at the age of seventy-one.[35]

Henrietta M. Griffith

Henrietta M. Griffith became a Wesleyan in her middle years, but her ministry began long before that, and she served The Wesleyan Church even then in various ways.

Henrietta was born November 30, 1923, in Stockton, New Jersey. She was saved at the age of fourteen in 1937, at the first revival she ever attended, in a Methodist church with a Nazarene evangelist. Very soon she was teaching a Sunday school class for primary boys. At age fifteen she was in charge of twenty-five "beginners" in a vacation Bible school. She was sent to several lay training classes and became active in the Epworth League. A church-sponsored Bible content contest prize paid her way to a youth institute. Here she took a course in home missions and received a call from the Lord to work in Kentucky.

Henrietta graduated from high school in 1942, and she dates her call to preach from that year. While visiting a Methodist church one summer, Henrietta was given a tract by a lay preacher. He urged her to read the tract and to be filled with the Spirit. She was sanctified in 1943.

Henrietta completed junior college at the College of South Jersey in 1943 and earned an A.B. degree at Asbury College in 1945, a theological diploma from Kentucky Mountain Bible College in 1948, and a master of religious education degree from Asbury Theological Seminary in 1950. She also took graduate studies at the University of Kentucky.

In 1947 Henrietta taught sixty children in eight grades in a one-room school at Beech Grove in McCreary County, Kentucky. Quite a culture shock for a city girl from the East Coast! In 1948 she and Eunice Kirk rode horseback to pastor Jetts Creek and Mill Branch churches. She was ordained by the Kentucky Mountain Holiness Association in 1949, and in 1950 she became a high school teacher at Mt. Carmel High School, in Lawson, Kentucky. A year later she moved a mile up the river to teach at Kentucky Mountain Bible College, where she remained.

For about thirty-five years, in addition to teaching Bible and Christian education classes, Henrietta directed the Christian Service Department of Kentucky Mountain Bible College, sending out some forty students in ministry each week. She also pastored Kentucky Mountain Holiness Association churches at Wrigley, Kentucky, 1964–70, and Consolation, Kentucky, 1976–85. She also preached in revivals, gave Bible studies, and conducted Christian education seminars in several states, including services with Wesleyans and Nazarenes. She was also very active in the Women's Christian Temperance Union on local, state, and national levels, serving as Kentucky WCTU president beginning in 1992 and serving as National Christian Outreach Director 1989–92 and being appointed again to that office in 1998.

Shortly after the 1968 merger that created The Wesleyan Church, Henrietta became a Wesleyan, with her ministerial membership in the Kentucky Conference. She spent six weeks or more on Wesleyan mission fields in both West India and Central India, preaching in a holiness conference at Rajnangoan, a revival at the leprosy hospital and in several churches.

In 1994 Kentucky Mountain Bible College honored Henrietta M Griffith for her service as Christian service director and for helping the school to become accredited. She was commended by the visiting accreditation team and elected to honorary membership in the Delta Epsilon Chi Honor Society of the Accrediting Association of Bible Colleges. In 1999 the Kentucky Conference gave her a retirement plaque commemorating fifty-seven years in the Christian ministry.[36]

Dorotha Shook Hazelwood

Dorotha Shook reported as an annual conference preacher (licensed minister) to the 1942 session of the Tennessee Conference of the Wesleyan Methodist Church. She was a third-year student on the course of study. In 1944 she was continued on the course of study and appointed as a conference evangelist. She was ordained in 1946, and in 1946 and 1947 she was appointed as a conference evangelist and in 1948 as a general evangelist. In November 1948 she was appointed pastor of Byrd's Chapel, followed in 1949 with her appointment to general evangelism and in 1950 to child evangelism. In 1951 she was appointed to pastor Mountain View.

Dorotha served as president of the conference Woman's Home and Foreign Missionary Society in 1947 and 1948 and was on the conference missionary board from 1947 to 1950.

In 1952 she married Mr. Hazelwood (first name unknown) and in 1952, 1953, and 1954 was on the "unstationed" (without appointment) list.[37]

Alice Mae Butcher Heavilin

Alice Mae Butcher was the daughter of Rev. Charles and Rev. Coral W. Butcher (see chapter 4), Wesleyan Methodist ministers who were pastoring in the Valton area of Wisconsin. Alice Mae as a child and youth lived with parents who not only were pastoring but were continually looking for other needy groups or places to plant Wesleyan churches. Alice Mae participated in their ministries to the extent that she could.

She enrolled at Marion College (now Indiana Wesleyan University), Marion, Indiana. In 1942 she was received by the Wisconsin Conference of the Wesleyan Methodist Church to study and travel under the conference's direction. She continued to be listed as pursuing study through 1947.

In 1945 Alice Mae graduated from Marion College with an A.B. in education. By now her parents were planting a church at Stevens Point, Wisconsin. Soon they were reaching out also to  Wisconsin Rapids and they conducted a weekly radio broadcast. Alice Mae secured a job teaching biology and Spanish at the high school and joined her parents in their ministries. In 1946 Alice Mae went back to Marion College to take additional courses. Ronald A. Heavilin, a native of Marion, had come home from World War II. They met, and by 1947 they were married. Ron transferred from Marion College to Stevens Point State College. He completed a B.S. in education in two years and became principal of a grade school in town. He also now was a part of the ministry team.

In 1948 the believers at Wisconsin Rapids were organized into a Wesleyan Methodist church, and Ron and Alice Mae were appointed the pastors. They bought a small house that Ron converted into a small chapel and a parsonage apartment. They served there until 1953 and also did outreach work to Sherwood and perhaps other points.

In 1953 Ron and Alice Mae were called by the Lord to take teaching positions for the United States government with children of military personnel in Puerto Rico. This enabled them also to assist Rev. and Mrs. Robert Crosby in the new Wesleyan Methodist mission in Puerto Rico. They initiated an English-speaking service in the San Juan area, Ron preaching, Alice Mae assisting. They also assisted in a weekly radio broadcast in Spanish.

In 1955, Alice Mae's parents left their pastorate at Bostonia, at the edge of El Cajon, California, since Charles was serving as conference president (now district superintendent). Ron and Alice Mae succeeded them at Bostonia in February 1955. Alice Mae's ministry here was predominantly with the Sunday school, vacation Bible school, women's ministries, visitation, counseling, and choir directing.

In 1957 the Heavilins returned to Puerto Rico. Ron was now superintendent of the mission and pastor of the Spanish-speaking church. By this time the Wesleyan Academy had been established in the basement of the Caparra Wesleyan Methodist Church. Alice Mae substituted for teachers as needed and taught English in the various classes and helped Ron in outreach ministries. There were now five congregations in Puerto Rico, and soon they were organized into a conference, and Ron was named president (now district superintendent), and Alice Mae assisted wherever needed.

In 1963 the Heavilins went to serve in Honduras. Ron was superintendent of the mission and manager of the Christian bookstore. Alice Mae directed the English day school, which had 100 students in six grades, all in one room.

In August 1964 the Heavilins were back in Puerto Rico. In 1966 they were home on furlough, crossing the continent six times and holding over three hundred services. In 1967 they returned to Puerto Rico where Ron directed the Academy. Alice Mae taught second grade bilingually and also taught English to kindergarten and first grade and interpreted for English-speaking preachers. They also aided the outreach churches.

In 1969 they moved back to San Diego. Ron had hypoglycemia and was encouraged to get involved in physical work. He took on the task of building enlargements to the rapidly growing Skyline Wesleyan Church, pastored by his brother-in-law, Orval Butcher. Alice Mae became the leader of the Intercessors, ladies who met every Tuesday morning to pray for needs at home and abroad. In the fall of 1990 they moved to Marion, Indiana, where she frequently led College Wesleyan Church in its monthly adult missions prayer meeting.[38]

Grace S. Miller Hoien

Grace S. Miller transferred as an ordained minister from the Church of the Nazarene into the Dakota Conference of the Wesleyan Methodist Church in 1942. She and her husband, Rev. Julius Miller, had done evangelistic work in the Midwest. From 1942 to 1943 they pastored at Northville and Brentford. He died in 1943. She pastored Brentford from 1943 to 1945. She married John Hoien, retired from active ministry, resided in California, was listed as unstationed (without appointment) from 1945 on. She died during the 1965–66 conference year.[39]

Esther V. Jones

Esther V. Jones was born November 15, 1879, and was converted at the age of twelve. She and her husband, John C. Jones, had ten children. There was no Sunday school, so she invited people to Sunday school at the Walnut Grove schoolhouse, driving her horse and buggy through the corn to meet them there. The Sunday school was organized in 1907 and eventually became the Big Bow, Kansas, Pilgrim Holiness Church. She was called to preach in 1926, took the course of study, and was ordained by the Western Kansas District in 1942. She pastored for a few years at Big Bow. She died November 12, 1966.[40]

Vivian Robinson Griffin Keller

Vivian Robinson was born February 8, 1907, at Deercreek, Oklahoma. On May 1, 1927, she married Floyd N. Griffin. Soon they both felt they were called to the ministry and became ordained ministers in the Pilgrim Holiness Church. They pastored eight churches in the Kansas District.

The official records identify six of those churches. Vivian was apparently ordained in 1942. She co-pastored Toronto 1943–44, Syracuse 1944–48, Scott City 1948–50, Garden City 1951–53, Hutchinson 1953–57 and St. Francis 1957–62. Floyd Griffin passed away in 1962 at St. Francis. They had two sons and a daughter, who passed away in 1975.

Vivian Griffin became inactive after Floyd's death. Then on September 6, 1964, she married an evangelist, J. Orvan Keller. They served in evangelistic ministries until they became pastors of the Winona and Brewster churches. They retired in 1968, living in Hutchinson, Kansas, and serving actively in the church there as long as they could. He passed away in 1980. Vivian was an excellent pianist and used that gift in retirement. She passed away April 15, 1994.[41]

Delores Lobdell

Delores M. Lobdell was born in Detroit in 1913. She was from an unchurched family but met Jesus Christ and committed her life to Him. She attended God's Bible School in Cincinnati, Ohio. She later graduated from Marion College (now Indiana Wesleyan University), Marion, Indiana, receiving a degree in secondary education.

In 1942 she joined Roma Acuna in starting a mission for Mexicans in Vista, California, where a Sunday school had been started in 1935. In 1945 her name appears on the records of the Michigan Conference of the Wesleyan Methodist Church as a conference preacher (licensed minister), a first-year student on the course of study, and under appointment by the home missions department to the work in Vista. She continued under this appointment until 1948.

In 1948 she was ordained by the Michigan Conference and appointed to evangelistic work. In 1949 she was again appointed to evangelism and made conference secretary of child evangelism, an office which she held until 1955. In 1950 she was also appointed pastor of the East Odessa

church at Lake Odessa, Michigan, a pastorate she served until 1963.

Her work as child evangelism secretary was by no means something done when there was nothing else to do. In 1950 the conference asked her to hold five promotional meetings in early January 1951 throughout the conference for child evangelism. In 1952 she reported conducting six vacation Bible schools, three children's revivals, and two weeks of Bible Crusaders Camp; she was reaching 654 children each week, and there had been 125 conversions—all of this while she was also pastoring East Odessa. In 1953 she reported 54 enrolled in child evangelism teacher training, 38 workshops held, a child evangelism banquet with Rev. Mary Bennett (see chapter 4) as the speaker. She had also held promotional child evangelism and home missions meetings in the Illinois Conference.

After her tremendous service in child evangelism ended in 1955, Delores took a position as biology teacher at Northview Schools, Grand Rapids, Michigan, while still pastoring East Odessa. Later she renewed her migrants mission ministry. She apparently began work at "Texas City" in 1959. This was a migrant camp on the Jack Rhoades farm at Morrison Lake, near Clarksville, Michigan. The Rhoades family provided a tabernacle there, dedicated June 28, 1959. The conference recognized the ministry by appointing her to minister there 1960–65. Her pastorate at East Odessa continued to 1963, but from 1963–65 Texas City was her sole assignment. She gave extensive reports of the work in 1960, 1961 and 1962. In 1960 one group of 250 Mexicans had spent a very brief time there, and another group of 75 were there until Labor Day and had been ministered to. In 1961 there were 90 African-Americans and 75 Mexicans there at the same time; that year nearby Wesleyan Methodist churches cooperated in a revival meeting at the camp. In 1962, twelve were converted and some wished to join the church, and they were seeking to provide a simple structure for that.

From 1966 on she was listed as unstationed (without appointment). In 1967 she moved to Houghton, New York, and taught science at nearby Fillmore High School. In the 1970s she moved to Drummond Island, Michigan. She taught at Cedarville High School on the mainland and pastored the Protestant church on Drummond Island. When she retired to Florida in the 1980s, she continued to minister to the people in her mobile home park, teaching Bible classes and conducting services. She died in Lakeland, Florida, October 22, 1997, at the age of eighty-four.[42]

Evelyn Meister

Evelyn Meister was listed in 1942 by the Kansas Conference of the Wesleyan Methodist Church as a conference preacher (licensed minister). She was to travel under the direction of the conference president (now district superintendent) and along with Sarah Billeyss was to pastor Formosa. In 1943 she was continued at Formosa. She was ordained in 1944, and from 1944 to 1948 she pastored Cedar. From 1948 to 1949 she pastored the Quinton Heights church in Topeka. From 1949 to 1954 she was listed as a general evangelist and children's worker, and from 1954 to 1955 as a conference evangelist and children's worker. From 1955 on she was listed as "unstationed" (without appointment).[43]

Victoria Dennert Moulton

Victoria Dennert was born September 6, 1912, near Aberdeen, South Dakota. She attended school in Bath, South Dakota, until she was nine, and then the family moved to Boone, Iowa. After graduating from high school there, she believed she was called to the ministry and enrolled in Boone Bible College. Here she met Wilbur Moulton. They were married in Canton, South Dakota, July 31, 1937.

They entered the ministry together and were ordained in 1942 by the General Baptists. In 1950 they were listed by the Kansas Conference of the Wesleyan Methodist Church. They were apparently received as "conference preachers" (licensed ministers). They pastored together at Artesian 1950–59. In 1957 their ordination by the General Baptists was accepted, and they were received into full standing as ordained ministers. They pastored Mt. Vernon 1959–61, Brentford and Northville 1961–64, served with the Native American Mission 1964–66, and pastored Medicine Rock beginning in 1966.

After the death of her husband, Victoria continued her ministry by entertaining people after the Sunday church services. She had one son, Robert. She died at Minot, North Dakota, March 2, 1997. The Kansas District of The Wesleyan Church dedicated its 1997 conference *Journal* to the memory of "Vickie" Moulton, as she was known.[44]

Estella Royal

Estella Royal was received by letter of transfer as an ordained minister from the Georgia Conference into the North Carolina Conference of the Wesleyan Methodist Church December 11, 1941. In 1942 the North Carolina Conference records indicated that she was appointed to evangelism. In 1943 she appeared on the records of the North Carolina District of the Pilgrim Holiness Church and was listed by them 1943–48. The first two years she apparently served as an evangelist and then became pastor at Bethel.

Ida Sellers

Ida Sellers' ministry apparently began at least five years before she and her husband came under the Wesleyan Methodists. The *Wesleyan Methodist*, July 30, 1941, spoke about the Heriton Street Mission in Knoxville, Tennessee, with its superintendents, Henry and Ida Sellers. In 1942 the Tennessee Conference records indicated that Ida Sellers was a first-year student on the course of study. Ida and Henry Sellers were officially appointed at the mission by the Tennessee Conference beginning in 1946. She was continued as a student until her death, November 2, 1949. At the time of her death it was indicated that they had pastored at the mission for thirteen years, carrying the beginning back to 1936. She was considered an excellent preacher. She excelled in house-to-house visitation, by day and by night as needed—ministering to the sick, praying for the sinful, leading great numbers to Christ. Over 200 people came to the hospital to pray for her, and over one thousand came to her funeral. Her doctor said he had never seen anything like this testimony to her effect on people's lives. Henry Sellers died December 7, 1955. They had one daughter and one son.[45]

Bertie M. Shaw

Bertie M. Shaw transferred from the North Georgia Conference of the Wesleyan Methodist Church to the South Georgia Conference as a conference preacher September 28, 1942. In 1944 she was listed as a third-year student, assistant to her husband, C. E. Shaw, as pastor at Lakeland, Florida. They continued at Lakeland under the South Georgia Conference until 1950. Bertie M. Shaw was ordained in 1947.

In 1950 the Shaws transferred to the new Florida Conference and continued to pastor at Lakeland, with Bertie as the assistant, until 1956. She was placed on the conference missionary board in 1951. She retired in 1956 and died in 1958.[46]

Stella Mae Shaw Hughes

Stella Mae Shaw was recommended by the Tennille, Georgia, Wesleyan Methodist Church to the North Georgia Conference in 1942 to travel under its direction. She was received August 2, 1942, as a conference preacher (licensed minister), and was appointed to serve as an evangelist and children's worker. On September 6, 1942, she was transferred to the South Georgia Conference. The South Georgia Conference appointed her to be a conference evangelist in 1942 and ordained her in 1943. In 1944 she married an evangelist, Fred Hughes. Her appointment in 1944 and 1945 was as a conference evangelist, and in 1946 and 1947 as a general evangelist.

Early in 1948 Stella and her husband transferred to the South Carolina Conference. Until 1949 they served the Walhalla church, Fred as pastor and Stella as assistant pastor. From 1949 to 1951, she was appointed as an evangelistic singer and children's worker. From 1951 to 1952, Fred served as pastor and Stella as assistant pastor at the Providence church. In 1951 Stella brought a good message to the conference on child evangelism.

She was elected conference child evangelism secretary, and the conference president was authorized to set up a schedule for her to visit each church to promote child evangelism. In 1952 and 1953 she was appointed to evangelism.

In January 1954 Stella and Fred Hughes transferred to the Florida Conference. From 1954 to 1955, Stella served as assistant pastor with her husband at Cocoa. From 1955 to 1956, she was assistant pastor with her husband at Merritt Island. Both of these years she served as conference director of child evangelism. In 1956 Stella was appointed as a conference evangelist.

Fred and Stella transferred back into the South Georgia Conference in January 1957 and served the Perry, Georgia, pioneer work until 1958. In 1958 they were appointed to general evangelism. On December 1, 1959, they joined another denomination.[47]

Addie Smith

Addie Smith and her husband, Kenneth, were spoken of as having pastored in New York, Kansas, and Michigan. She appears first in the records of the Champlain Conference (now Eastern New York-New England District) of the Wesleyan Methodist Church in 1942 and 1943. Both years she was appointed associate pastor of Bakers Mills and Mill Creek. In 1943 she was recommended for ordination.

Addie Smith was ordained by the Kansas Conference in 1944 and was appointed to conference evangelism. From 1947 to 1954 she was "unstationed" (without appointment). In 1954 she withdrew. While still listed in the Kansas Conference, she appeared on the records of the Michigan District of the Pilgrim Holiness Church, beginning in 1951. She was listed as in pastoral service 1951–53, 1954–55, 1956 and 1957. Then she was listed by the East Michigan District as in pastoral service 1960–62.

Addie Smith died November 1, 1968. She was described as a dedicated, tireless, and faithful worker with a genuine loving concern for people. The Smiths had three daughters.[48]

Anna E. Smith

Anna E. Smith was an ordained minister who served under the Pennsylvania and New Jersey District of the Pilgrim Holiness Church. She ministered to a Tuesday night youth meeting in the Glassboro, New Jersey, church for many years. Then she served as pastor at Turnersville for twelve years. Her last pastorate was at Millville, New Jersey. It was said at the time of her death that several were then in the ministry who found the Lord under her ministry.

Anna E. Smith was the wife of J. Harry Smith. They had three daughters. Anna died October 28, 1961, at the age of sixty-seven.[49]

Edith Rose Smith

Edith graduated from God's Bible School, Cincinnati, Ohio. She felt called to Africa but was not accepted because she had a heart murmur. A lady friend asked her to join her in evangelistic work and suggested that after a while at that she would know what God wanted her to do. They started in Harrison County, Indiana, with United Brethren churches. Sometimes they had children's services, sometimes they were the singers, sometimes Edith preached. They held meetings at New Albany and Westport in Indiana. They spent the summer in the Kentucky mountains in meetings. In August they were back in Indiana, holding meetings for the United Brethren, Methodist Protestants, Pilgrim Holiness, Nazarenes, and Wesleyan Methodists, in missions, brush arbors and tents. Edith's first co-laborer got married. Others teamed with her at times. The last lady was Pilgrim Holiness. They went to Letts Camp in southern Indiana where Edith had the children's services. Here she met a young Pilgrim Holiness minister, Lester Smith.

Edith and Lester were married in 1940 and spent forty-seven years co-pastoring Pilgrim Holiness/Wesleyan churches. They took turns preaching, but Edith says Lester always took the business side of the work. Edith was ordained in 1942. Their first church was at Alton. From 1942 to 1952 they served a ten-year pastorate at Scottsburg, Indiana. They planted the church, and then World War II delayed construction of the building, and they waited and saw it through. Then came a sixteen-year pastorate at North Vernon, Indiana, where they built a new parsonage, and a nine-year pastorate at French Lick, Indiana, where they remodeled the church. Then they retired, but they were asked to take a small church at Holton, Indiana, fifteen miles from their home. They accepted, young people started to come, and they stayed for ten years. They finally did retire due to ill health in 1989, and Lester died April 22, 1991. Sometime during their busy years of pastoral service they found time for ministry visits to the West Indies, with two revivals in Cayman and services in Jamaica, Haiti, and Puerto Rico. Lester and Edith Smith had two sons, Roy and Benet, and one daughter, Ruth.[50]

Helen Reynolds Smith

Helen Reynolds was first listed by the Lockport Conference (now Western New York District) of the Wesleyan Methodist Church in 1942. She was to continue to travel under the direction of the conference and she and Herman A. Smith were appointed to pastor the Cuba, New York, Tabernacle. Apparently they were married by the time of the 1943 conference session, and they were continued at Cuba. Helen was ordained in 1944, and the Smiths were appointed pastors at Higgins, New York, 1944–48. Then they pastored at Olean, New York, 1948–53. They resigned on September 29, 1953, and on February 19, 1954, were granted letters of transfer to the Canada Conference.

In 1954 and 55, Helen Reynolds Smith's appointments were to serve as assistant pastor at Ottawa. In 1957 she was listed by the Oregon Conference as an ordained minister transferring from the Canada Conference. She was placed on the "unstationed list" (without appointment), and in 1960 she requested that her name be omitted from the roll.[51]

Madelene Knotts Smith Yarbrough

Madelene Smith was appointed by the Indiana Conference of the Wesleyan Methodist Church as co-pastor with her husband, Rev. Layland Smith, of the Huntington Etna Avenue Church in 1942. The following year the Indiana Conference ordained Madelene. The Smiths served in Indiana at Huntington 1942–44 and at Kokomo South 1944–52. They then served at the Eau Claire, Wisconsin, church 1952–55. After this they returned to Indiana to pastor the South Bend church 1955–68. In 1968 Madelene went on the "unstationed" (without appointment) list. During each of the Smiths' pastorates, church buildings were erected or remodeled. Their Sunday schools experienced outstanding growth.

Layland died in 1982. Madelene's only daughter, Judy Huffman, passed away later. Madelene eventually married a Mr. Yarbrough (first name unknown).[52]

Sybil Beckett Yoder

Sybil Beckett was born in 1920 in Salem, Oregon. Her parents enjoyed almost sixty-five years together. Her father died three weeks before their sixty-fifth wedding anniversary.

Church was the center of the family's life. Sybil was converted at age seven in a children's tent meeting on their street. Revival services at the Friends Church kept her spiritually vital in the years that followed. She was called to be a missionary at age thirteen.

High school was followed in 1937 with her enrollment at Portland Bible School. Then the family moved to Colorado Springs. In college she met Arreld E. Yoder, and they were married June 15, 1942. She experienced the infilling of the Holy Spirit in the first year of marriage. They pastored in Hartman, Colorado for two and one-half years. Then they were sent to Guatemala, where they taught school and served as missionaries. Services were held generally in brush arbors, and travel was by train and horseback.

When they returned home for deputation work (home ministries), a group from Pennsylvania called them to plant a church among the Dutch people. They established a church and a school in Gratz, Pennsylvania. Two single ladies were brought from Colorado Springs to teach in the school. An eleven-room house provided the Yoders with five rooms, the school with three, and the two ladies with three. Sybil taught the upper grades.

R. G. Flexon asked the Yoders to serve the Pilgrim Holiness Church in Puerto Rico. Daisy Buby already had a Bible training school in session, and Sybil taught in the school. Services were held in several places on the island. Sybil played a portable organ or accordion in the services and taught Sunday school. It was felt that a central church needed to be built, but the cost of property and real estate appeared to be prohibitive. The work was turned over to the Church of the Nazarene. While in Puerto Rico, in 1954, the Yoders adopted a baby boy, David Allen.

In 1955 they were transferred to Guyana, in South America, where Arreld pastored the large Georgetown Pilgrim Holiness Church. Sybil served as Sunday school superintendent, and they had 1,200 in attendance on rally day. They rode their bicycles to various Saturday and Sunday afternoon Sunday schools, with David in a little chair on Sybil's bicycle. In 1956 they were transferred to Paramakatoi, in the interior of Guyana, where Sybil took over a school of 120 children. The Yoders lived in a "mud and wattle" seven-room house.

The Yoders came home on furlough in 1959. Their home ministries work was interrupted by Arreld's stroke and heart surgery. In the years from 1959 to 1978 the Yoders supported themselves as salespersons. Beginning in 1982, they pastored the Medford, Oregon, church for a year and a half, and then Arreld suffered a second stroke. A third stroke in 1992 took his life. He was buried three days before a planned golden wedding anniversary celebration.

Sybil afterward traveled to the Holy Land in 1992. She accompanied medical teams to Peru in 1993 and 1995 as their interpreter. In 1997 she visited a World Gospel Mission work in Bolivia as part of a ladies' work team. At one Northwest District of The Wesleyan Church ladies retreat, she served as the keynote speaker, and she conducted a seminar on "Building Coping Skills" at the 1998 ladies retreat.[53]

Junia M. Apple

Junia Apple finished a two-year Christian worker's course and a two-year junior college program at John Wesley College in High Point, North Carolina. Then she married Rev. Charles E. Apple in 1943. She joined him in pastoral duties at Franklinton, North Carolina. In 1945 Junia was ordained by the North Carolina District of the Pilgrim Holiness Church. That same fall both Apples entered Owosso College and Seminary in Owosso, Michigan (later merged into what became Indiana Wesleyan University, Marion, Indiana). Three years later, each graduated with a Th. B. degree.

From 1948 to 1985, the Apples pastored the following churches in North Carolina: Gold Hill (built a new parsonage), Lexington, Thomasville Mt. Zion, Burlington, Franklinville (two times), Ramseur-Kildee, Elkin, and Seagrove-Whynot.

In 1985 they retired but continued to provide pulpit supply as needed. In this capacity they ministered in 40 different churches in North Carolina.

Junia described her ministry as that of a supportive pastor's wife, which included being an assistant to the pastor, preaching when her husband was away in revivals, teaching in Sunday school and vacation Bible school, directing the choir, serving in the missionary circle, directing Christmas and special day programs. She conducted prayer meetings and assisted in visitation. She also worked in district youth camps for ten years.[54]

Mary Magdalene Bradford

Mary Magdalene Bradford was born in 1915. A revival conducted by Rev. L. S. Houston in the Ashland Heights, Kentucky, Pilgrim Holiness Church reached several young people. One was Mary, saved in her teens. She was called to preach and prepared for the ministry at Frankfort Pilgrim College, Frankfort, Indiana.

Mary was first listed in the Kentucky District records in 1943. In 1943 she was listed as pastor at Rush, Kentucky. In 1948 she was ordained. The ordination report in the *Pilgrim Holiness Advocate* spoke of her as a good, Spirit-filled gospel preacher, one who preached positively yet tenderly. From 1950 to 1953, she pastored the Willard church. For a year she was an evangelist. From 1954 to 1956 she pastored at Catbelsburg. From 1956 to 1959 she was again in evangelism. In 1960 she was listed in the Eastern District's records and from 1963 to 1967 was listed by the Kentucky District as inactive.

Mary's last years were spent in caring for the sick and elderly and serving faithfully in the Ashland church where she had been converted. She died October 16, 1983.[55]

Grace David

Grace and her husband, Russell David, were originally from Wisconsin. Russell was at one time a bartender or tavern owner, but he found Christ as Savior. Together they followed God's call into the ministry. Grace's name appeared first in the records of the Iowa Conference of the Wesleyan Methodist Church in 1942 as received to study and to travel (serve) under the direction of the conference. Beginning in 1943, she was listed as being in school. Both Grace and Russell enrolled at Marion College, Marion, Indiana (now Indiana Wesleyan University) and later graduated. In 1948 she was listed as a conference preacher (now licensed minister) and in 1949 was appointed to evangelism.

On November 22, 1949, the Davids were granted letters of transfer to the North Michigan Conference. Russell became the pastor and Grace the assistant pastor at the Kaleva church. Grace was ordained in 1951. The Davids served Kaleva 1949–53 and Cadillac 1953–58. From 1958 to 1966 they were listed as co-pastors at Fremont, and in 1966 they began service as co-pastors at Lakefield. Grace served as the conference president of the Woman's Missionary Society for many years beginning in 1956, serving simultaneously on the conference missionary board. She was also elected conference world missions secretary in 1966.

Russell died in 1972 at the age of 65. The Davids had two sons, Eugene and Ramon. Grace later moved to Zeeland, Michigan, to be near Ramon. She passed away in 1996.[56]

―――――

Dollie Gum

Dollie Gum was attending Miltonvale Wesleyan College, Miltonvale, Kansas, when she was received to travel (serve) by the Oklahoma Conference of the Wesleyan Methodist Church in 1943. She was listed as a conference evangelist. In 1944 she was to continue in college and in service to the Kansas Conference. In 1945 she was ordained by the Oklahoma Conference and appointed as a conference evangelist. The ordination story in the *Wesleyan Methodist* spoke of her as an evangelistic singer and preacher. She served as pastor at Alva, Oklahoma, August–November 1946. In 1947 she was listed as a general evangelist and from 1948 to 1950 again as a conference evangelist. She served on the conference Sunday school board 1945–47 and as educational secretary 1946–47, and conducted devotions in the conference in 1946. She requested to be dropped from the roll in 1950.[57]

―――――

Bertha Haas

Bertha Haas was born in 1892. She joined the Pilgrim Holiness Church in Chillicothe, Ohio, in the early 1930s. She was ordained by the Ohio District of the Pilgrim Holiness Church in 1943 and was listed on the records of that district 1943–54 and on the records of the Eastern Ohio District 1955–61. She passed away February 25, 1962. She worked hard and faithfully as long as health permitted, preaching in churches, on street corners, and in homes. She was known as a woman of prayer and faith, a friend and an inspiration to all who knew her.

―――――

Grace Hamilton

Grace Hamilton was ordained in 1943 by the Indiana District of the Pilgrim Holiness Church. She was listed on the records of that district 1943–50 and on the records of the Southern Indiana District from 1951 on. She and her husband, Clarence, had four children who were special workers: Mae and Mildred sang together, Max and his wife Barbara sang together, and Paul sang alone. All of them served as song evangelists in local churches and Max in camp meetings as well.[58]

―――――

Mrs. Nannie E. Hunter

Nannie E. Hunter was born in 1899. She was a commissioned minister in The Wesleyan Church at the time of her death. She had served in the bounds of the Southern Indiana District of the Pilgrim Holiness Church as pastor of the Sycamore Community Church near Rising Sun, Indiana, 1942–64. Her church membership was in the Lawrenceburg, Indiana, Wesleyan Church at the time of her death. She lived across the street from the Lawrenceburg church, faithfully attending every service. She delighted in preaching when the pastor was away and in giving the midweek lesson. She seemed to become inspired as she shared the word of God. When her health failed, she moved to a retirement center. She had a son, Floyd, and two daughters, Betty Nelson and Ruth Schweers. She died June 3, 1993, at the age of ninety-four.[59]

―――――

Marion Koth

Marion Koth was ordained by the Dakota Conference of the Wesleyan Methodist Church in 1943. She was appointed to missionary work 1943–48 and then was "unstationed" (without appointment) for a year. From 1949 to 1953 she was listed as supply pastor of a Methodist church in Washington. In 1954 and 1955 she was listed as serving as a supply pastor outside the denomination. In 1956 she withdrew and joined another denomination.[60]

―――――

Luella Lloyd

Luella Lloyd was first listed by the Kansas Conference of the Wesleyan Methodist Church in

1943 as a singing evangelist and children's worker. She continued with that appointment until 1955. She was ordained in 1946. From 1955 to 1958, she was the assistant pastor at Salina, Kansas. In 1958 she and her husband, Willard, were listed as supply pastors at Lynch, Nebraska.[61] On July 15, 1959, they transferred to the Nebraska Conference and continued service at Lynch. In the 1960–61 conference year they were pastoring at Chanute, Kansas, and by March 11, 1961, they had transferred back to Kansas. They continued service at Chanute until 1963, and from 1963 on they were listed as pastors at Williams Chapel.[62]

Mary S. Logan

Mary S. Logan is listed in the district conference records of the Ohio District of the Pilgrim Holiness Church in 1943 and 1944 as an ordained minister.

Anna Martin and Ada Dishong Chess

Anna Martin and Ada Dishong (later Chess) ministered together in a period of their lives about which the most vivid memories are still available. The official conference (district) records seem to indicate that they spent most of their ministry years in different parts of the country.

Anna Martin left home at the age of seventeen to go to Alma Bible College in Zarephath, New Jersey. This school was connected with a tiny holiness denomination known as the Pillar of Fire. For many years she traveled back and forth across North America in her single-seat 1927 Ford. She held meetings in places where she thought God wanted her to start a church. The college always sent another young lady with her, and some five or six individuals accompanied her at different times.

Anna Martin had apparently teamed up with Ada Dishong when they traveled to the vicinity of Barnsboro, Pennsylvania, apparently in the late 1930s. Both of the ladies were preachers, and they sang duets together, with Anna playing the ukulele. In this area lived two of Ada's sisters, Catherine Martin Dongell and Sophie Martin McCombie and their families.

Anna and Ada started services in a miner's hall and sometime later negotiated with a farmer who owned an abandoned church to rent that building. There were eleven children in the Dongell family. Mrs. Dongell had led most of them to the Lord, although her husband was not yet converted. The services conducted by Anna and Ada, along with revivals led by Rev. J. R. Swauger and others, not only deepened the Dongell children in the faith but led to their father's conversion and the conversion of many in the neighborhood. The church probably never got much larger than the fifties in attendance, but many were called from it into Christian service. These included Arthur and Mabel Fields, Wesleyan Methodist pastors in Brooklyn, New York; one Dongell daughter, Ruby, who married a minister; three Dongell brothers, Ed, Herbert, and Oliver, who went into the ministry; Philip J. Birchall, who went into the ministry; a brother-and-sister team, Mary and Walter Fowler, who served for over forty years as America Rescue workers; and several others. Herbert Dongell has pastored several churches and also taught at both Allentown Bible School, Allentown, Pennsylvania (later Eastern Pilgrim College/United Wesleyan College) and Central Wesleyan College, Central South Carolina (now Southern Wesleyan University). Rev. Philip Birchall has pastored Wesleyan churches throughout his lifetime. Oliver Dongell pastored until his death.

At some point this rural church became the Pleasant Hill Wesleyan Methodist Church, Emeigh, Pennsylvania. The first official notice was in 1943, when the Allegheny Conference listed Anna Martin as pastor at Emeigh. She was continued there in 1944 and was appointed as a general evangelist in 1946. In 1947 she joined another denomination. Ada Dishong first appears on the official records in 1947, also in the Allegheny Conference, being appointed as a general evangelist in 1947 and 1948.

Anna Martin was not officially a part of the Wesleyan Methodist Church, 1947–51. But the Dongells remember that she and Ada Dishong went from Emleigh to start the Johnstown, Pennsylvania, Wesleyan Methodist Church.

Anna Martin came back into the Wesleyan Methodist Church from the Pillar of Fire in 1951, being received by the Kansas Conference. She was received as an elder (ordained minister) on trial on the strength of her credentials from the Allegheny Conference, dated May 5, 1947. She was listed as a conference evangelist 1951–55. She was listed as unstationed (without appointment) from 1955 on. From 1955 to 1958, she served as pastor of the South Dayton Community Church, apparently near Denver.

Ada Dishong continued to be listed by the Allegheny Conference. In 1953 she married Glenn Chess. She was a conference evangelist 1953–55, on reserve 1955–57, conference evangelist again 1957–62, unstationed (without appointment) 1962–66. In 1966 she was listed as superannuated (retired).[63]

Viola Melling

Viola Melling was ordained by the Ohio District of the Pilgrim Holiness Church in 1943. She was listed on their official district conference records 1943–53. She lived in Arcanum, Ohio.

Beulah Moyer Miller

Beulah Moyer was born in 1905 and was converted at age eighteen. She attended Kingswood Bible School in Kingswood, Kentucky, and Frankfort Pilgrim College in Frankfort, Indiana. She was listed on the official records of the Tennessee District of the Pilgrim Holiness Church 1943–60. She was ordained by that district in 1943. She was the founder and pastor of the church at McEwen, Tennessee, and she also ministered in evangelism and home missions.

On August 19, 1960, Beulah married Rev. W. C. Miller. Their first pastorate was at Ravenswood, West Virginia. At the time of her death, they were pastoring Bethel Tabernacle in Fishersville, Virginia. She died July 27, 1965, in Waynesboro, Virginia.[64]

Mrs. Helen Poole

Helen (Mrs. George) Poole appears on the records of the conferences of various districts of the Pilgrim Holiness Church. She was ordained in 1943 by the Ohio District. She appears on their records 1943–54 and on the records of the Eastern Ohio District 1955–59. She lived in Marion, Ohio, 1948–50, Cincinnati 1950–53, Dayton 1953–55, and Greenville 1956–59. She appears on the records of the Kentucky District 1960–62 and on the records of the Pittsburgh District in 1963, serving as co-pastor at West Newton. She was back on the records of the Eastern Ohio District 1965–67.

Mrs. Elizabeth F. Pugh Robertson

Elizabeth F. Pugh served the Allegheny Conference of the Wesleyan Methodist Church. Conference records indicate that she served as pastor at Sagamore 1943–47, Ashville 1947–58, and Riverview 1958–65. In 1965 her name became Robertson, and in 1965 and 1966 she was listed as a conference evangelist.

Ruth Mengel Schaltenbrand

Ruth Mengel was originally from West Virginia and was part of a family trio and a female ministry team. She graduated in 1933 from Owosso Bible College, Owosso, Michigan (later merged into what became Indiana Wesleyan University, Marion, Indiana). On June 8, 1938, she married Walter Schaltenbrand, and they pastored Pilgrim Holiness, and later Wesleyan, churches for many years. Ruth was ordained by the Pennsylvania and New Jersey District in 1943. She transferred to the New York District in 1945, where she and her husband served at Middleburg at least 1948–55. The Schaltenbrands appeared on the Eastern District roll 1957–65 and were back in Pennsylvania and New Jersey 1966 and 1967. They co-pastored at Roxana, Delaware; Delmar, Maryland; and State College, Pennsylvania (listed there 1966 and 1967). Ruth retired in 1974. The Schaltenbrands had three sons, Walter R., Philip, and Wayne. They lived to celebrate their fiftieth wedding anniversary in 1988 and their sixtieth in 1998.[65]

Josephine Sturk

Josephine (Mrs. John D.) Sturk was listed on the official records of the conferences of the Ohio District of the Pilgrim Holiness Church 1943–54 and on the records of the Western Ohio District 1955–67. She was ordained by the Ohio District in 1943. She lived in Cincinnati 1948–50, Columbus 1950–51, Indianapolis 1951–61 and Owosso, Michigan, from 1961 on. Beginning in 1963 she was listed as inactive.

Rose Elizabeth Bickel Surface

Rose Elizabeth Bickel was born October 24, 1894, in a new farmhouse near a little town she called "Spud." Rose was the sixth of seven children, and she was seven years old when her younger brother was born. She described herself as a child as a "little spitfire, stubborn and as quick to fight as any boy." In early childhood she was introduced to the joy of reading, learning to read and write before attending school. Her teen years brought a change as she was now shy and timid. She loved school and especially elocution and Latin.

Rose was not allowed to attend Sunday school and church often. The summer before she was sixteen, she went to a July 4th celebration where she met Earl F. Surface. It was love at first sight, and they were married April 13, 1913. Both were eighteen years of age, and they lived with his parents for two years. That same year they knelt at an altar of prayer and were baptized. Rose became a member of Tabor Evangelical Church. They lived too far to attend regularly, so they began to attend a Wesleyan Methodist church. Later they moved so they could attend both churches. Tabor Evangelical did not preach Christian perfection, but the Surfaces heard it during a revival at the Wesleyan Methodist church, became convinced of the doctrine, and both went to the altar. Rose was not yet satisfied. At home that night Earl called others in to pray. They prayed and talked all night, and Rose gained the victory.

The Surfaces entered the ministry in middle to later life, Earl in 1943, and Rose in 1948, when she was fifty-three years of age. They had three sons and four daughters, the first four of whom had grown and left home by that time. Earl took his first pastorate at the Wesleyan Methodist church in Kirklin, Indiana, apparently in 1943. Rose's name first appears in the records of the Indiana Conference of the Wesleyan Methodist Church in 1948, as a student pursuing the course of study and co-pastor with her husband at Wesley Chapel, near Greensburg, Indiana. Rose was ordained in 1950. Following Wesley Chapel, they co-pastored Cicero (1949–50), Warren (1950–54), Bluffton (1954–56), Martinsville (1956–57) and Edgerton (1957–62). They retired in 1962 but supplied as co-pastors at the Kingsford Heights church beginning in 1964 and again beginning in 1967. Earl died December 20, 1974. Rose passed away May 7, 1981. One son became a minister and one daughter a minister's wife.

Keith Smith, a grandson, recorded the following memories of Rose Surface:

I am convinced that one of Grandma's priceless earthly possessions was her mind. She exercised it daily. Her mental diet consisted of many forms of good and wholesome meals. The bulk of her nutritional needs and desires was drawn from the Word of God. . . .

I cannot help but think of Grandma whenever I come in contact with the game of Scrabble. I am not sure when the two of us played our first game. It would be safer to guess who won that first—and most of the games—since my early beginning. . . .

Some of Grandma's philosophy came to light during those numerous games in a way that I hope lingers for me as many years as I am able to remember. She would often remind me that she "played to win, but never to beat." Our final two games were played a month before she died. I won the first by five. She won the last by over one hundred.[66]

Mrs. Lena Wilson

The *Minutes of the Annual Assembly of the Ohio District of the Pilgrim Holiness Church* reveal that Lena Wilson was ordained in 1943. She continued to be listed among the ministers 1944–46.

Florence Atkinson

Florence Atkinson was received by the Oklahoma Conference of the Wesleyan Methodist Church in 1944 to pursue the course of study. She was listed as a conference evangelist in 1945 and 1946. On January 19, 1947, she was appointed pastor of the Wesleyan Chapel and remained there until 1948. In 1948 she was ordained and appointed again as a conference evangelist. She served the conference in various capacities. She served from 1944 to 1949 as the conference secretary. At the close of her service in that office she was given a rising vote of thanks for her faithful and efficient service. She served 1944–47 on the conference Sunday school board and conducted Sunday school rallies at the conference sessions of 1946, 1947, and 1948. She spoke at the conference memorial services relative to three departed ministers and was in charge of the conference memorial services in 1947 and 1948.[67]

Elizabeth M. Ault

Elizabeth M. Ault was listed by the West Virginia District of the Pilgrim Holiness Church in 1944 and 1945 as an ordained missionary serving in Africa. In 1947 she was listed by the New York District. Her service was with her husband, Donald, in Northern Rhodesia (now Zambia).[68]

Madge Edwards Bursch

Madge Edwards was born in Mitchell, South Dakota, May 7, 1922. Her parents were Jefferson and Nina Edwards. Her father died when Madge

was two years of age. Madge had two sisters, Gertrude (Bonner) and Kathryn (Martin).

Madge's mother felt called to preach, and she conducted revival meetings in South Dakota, Iowa, and Nebraska. Madge was converted in a tent meeting when she was ten years old. Her mother, Nina Edwards, married Harrison Downing in 1935. Nina Edwards Downing was ordained by the Hephzibah Faith Missionary Association in 1936, and the Downings served as pastors, eventually in the Pilgrim Holiness Church.

In 1941 Madge enrolled in the Colorado Springs Bible Training School (later merged into what has become Oklahoma Wesleyan University, Bartlesville, Oklahoma). She earned her theological degree in May 1944. She had met Daniel R. Bursch, her future husband, while her parents were pastoring in Gavilan, New Mexico. He also came to the Bible Training School for one semester before Pearl Harbor. In January 1942 he enlisted and served four years in the military.

When Daniel returned, he and Madge were married in August 1944 in Denver, and they moved back to Colorado Springs. Daniel attended Colorado College, and both taught in the Colorado Springs Bible Training School.

In 1949, Rev. R. G. Flexon asked the Bursches to consider doing missionary work. The Colorado District of the Pilgrim Holiness Church ordained Daniel and Madge, and in July 1950 they took ship for Africa. Their appointment was in Northern Rhodesia (now Zambia). They took charge of the large Jembo Mission station, along with its hospital and boarding school. They were also involved in a teacher training school, plus supervising outstation schools and churches.

Madge taught Bible classes in the boarding school, assisted in domestic science classes, and held monthly or more frequent meetings with the church "band" women. These were commissioned to do visitation, help the sick, and sometimes preach. The Bursches had brought their oldest son, Lowell, with them, aged two and one-half years. He was joined in May 1951 by Charles and in August 1952 by Herbert. Madge home-schooled Lowell. She also helped the nurse at the hospital with deliveries and other regular hospital routine. This opened the door to the village people. Through the boarding schools and outstation schools, the Bursches reached the youth—through chapel services, prayer meetings, regular church services, and revivals.

After five years at Jembo, they were asked to delay furlough and fill in at Mt. Frere Mission in the Cape Province of South Africa. Here they were in charge of two mission stations, a hospital, and a large girls' boarding school.

From June 1956 to July 1957, the Bursches were home for home ministries. When they returned to Africa, Daniel was the field superintendent for all the Pilgrim Holiness work in Zambia, Swaziland, Republic of South Africa, and Southern Rhodesia (now Zimbabwe). They built a missions headquarters at Choma in Zambia. Madge served in many capacities—entertaining guests, meeting with women and others in Bible studies.

The family was home again June–December 1963. When they returned to Zambia, Lowell attended school in Zimbabwe and the other boys at Zambia's capital, Lusaka. The African work was divided, with Daniel as superintendent of Zambia by itself. He was also appointed secretary of education by the education department of Zambia, and he served as chair of the board of Livingstone College, a teacher training school maintained cooperatively by five denominations.

In September 1966, Daniel Bursch was called to be president of Owosso College, Owosso, Michigan (later merged into what is now Indiana Wesleyan University, Marion, Indiana). Madge earned a B. S. in education in 1969 and then teacher certification and a M.S. in elementary education from Eastern Michigan University in 1974. She was also teaching, which she continued to do for fifteen years. She served as president of the local missionary society and spoke in various churches for their missionary programs.

In 1984 Madge retired from teaching. The Bursches began to spend their winters at Wesleyan Village in Brooksville, Florida. In 1986 they wintered instead in Africa, helping in the work, revisiting their previous fields of labor, and renewing contacts with many to whom they had previously ministered.[69]

Ethel Cooley Baldwin

Ethel Cooley is listed in the district conference records of the Indiana and Southern Indiana Districts of the Pilgrim Holiness Church 1944–67. She and her first husband, Lawrence I. Cooley, were from the Brown's Chapel congregation near Greenfield, Indiana. She was ordained by the Indiana District in 1944. She served with Lawrence in home missions and pastoral work. After his death, she served as a volunteer nurse in Haiti with the Wesleyan Gospel Corps. She was married to Earl Baldwin, San Diego, at the time of her death, October 27, 1989.[70]

Clare Elkins

The district conference records of the Michigan District of the Pilgrim Holiness Church indicate that Clare Elkins was ordained by that district in 1944 and that in 1945–46 she was at Colorado Springs Bible School (now merged into what has become Oklahoma Wesleyan University, Bartlesville, Oklahoma).

Mrs. T. M. Fast

The name of Mrs. T. M. Fast appears in the records of several districts of the Pilgrim Holiness Church. She was ordained in 1944 by the Michigan District. She was unstationed (without appointment) in 1944–50 in the same district and in pastoral service there 1950–51, 1953–55. From 1955 to 1960, she was listed by the East Michigan District as a pastor, and in 1961 that district listed her as unstationed. From 1962 to 1965, the Virginia District listed her as pastor at the Radford, Virginia, church, and in 1965 that district listed her as retired. However, she also appears on the records of the Central District, 1964 and 1966. And the Michigan District again lists her in 1967 as transferred from the Central District and as retired.

Mable Dongell Fields

Mable Dongell came out of the community in which the Emleigh, Pennsylvania, Wesleyan Methodist Church had such a very effective ministry. She and her husband, Arthur Fields, became involved with a Wesleyan Methodist church in Brooklyn, New York. The Middle Atlantic States Conference first listed her as a ministerial student from the Brooklyn church in 1944. She continued to be listed that way until in 1950 Arthur and Mable Fields were listed as the pastors of the Brooklyn, New York, Wesleyan Methodist church. Mable completed the course of study in 1951 and was ordained in 1952. She continued as pastor of this same church until 1976—a twenty-six-year pastorate.

Mable Fields was active in her conference. From 1952 to at least 1967, she was the conference superintendent of the Young Missionary Workers Band (now Wesleyan Kids for Missions). From 1955 to 1966, she served on the committee on child evangelism. Her church opened its doors in 1961 to the work of Jewish evangelism under Laura Sells.

Mable Fields retired from her long-term pastorate in 1976 and died November 7, 1978.[71]

Ruby Fletcher

The records of the Kansas District of the Pilgrim Holiness Church reveal that in 1944 Ruby Fletcher was ordained.

Elizabeth Gilmore

Elizabeth Gilmore first served under the New York District of the Pilgrim Holiness Church. She and her husband, George, were missionaries to St. Croix in the American Virgin Islands. She was first listed by the New York District in 1944 as a licensed minister and a missionary. She was ordained by that district in 1950. She continued on the New York District roll until 1958, being listed as a missionary 1953–55. From 1959 to 1967, her name appeared on the roll of the Eastern District. During that period the Gilmores pastored the Seaford, Delaware, Pilgrim Holiness Church. In later years the Gilmores were active in the Methodist Church and circles in Sussex County, Delaware.[72]

Maxine L. Shockey Haines

Maxine Shockey was born in Howard County, Indiana, February 27, 1925. Her father and mother were not yet Christians at that time. She had not heard the name of Jesus except for one or two times before she was ten years old. The Shockeys had moved by that time northeast of Marion, Indiana. A lady minister from Marion opened an abandoned church building in the neighborhood and began evangelistic services. People were getting saved. A little girl invited Maxine to Sunday school. That first time ever in church she heard the gospel for the first time from a lady Sunday school teacher and gave her heart to the Lord. Not long after, her father and mother were also converted.

When Maxine was thirteen, the family moved to Fairmount, Indiana, and Maxine and her parents joined the Wesleyan Methodist church. Maxine's gift of leadership was immediately apparent to the pastor and the church. While still in junior high school, she became what was then called the superintendent of the Young Missionary Workers Band (now Wesleyan Kids for Missions). Among the children she ministered to was a boy three years younger than she, Lee Haines, then known as "Buddy."

As Maxine moved on into high school, she and her friends organized a prayer band that met at the school every Wednesday noon hour. When the prayer band occasionally conducted services in neighboring churches, Maxine preached. When Rev. Will Ott became pastor at the Wesleyan Methodist Church in 1942, he saw that she had gifts for ministry. He said nothing to her but led the church in voting her a local preacher's license. When he presented it to her, she remonstrated, saying that she couldn't do that—no one in her family had gone to college. Rev. Ott replied kindly but firmly, "You can and you will."

Enrolling in 1943 at Marion College (now Indiana Wesleyan University), Marion, Indiana, Maxine worked her way through college, paying every dollar herself. World War II was underway, and she worked in a factory eight hours a night,

five nights a week. The management recognized her leadership ability. They promoted her to supervise several men. In keeping with the prejudice of the time, she as a woman was paid less than the men she was supervising.

Rev. Maxine Haines (l.) speaks in Chiclayo, Peru, 1989, while Angelica Gonzales interprets.

By the end of the fall term of her junior year of college, her health broke from the double load. In December 1945, she moved back home with her parents. By now, Lee M. Haines was a senior in high school. Maxine had been president of the youth group while he was a part of it, and later his Sunday school teacher. (In later years, she delighted in saying, "I taught him everything he knows.") The two had great respect for each other. But now, in a short time, their long-term friendship changed into romance. When Lee graduated from high school, he enrolled at Marion, and Maxine returned to classes. She graduated with a bachelor of religion degree Monday morning, June 7, 1948, and on Tuesday evening, June 8, Maxine and Lee were married.

Maxine had been received by the Indiana Conference of the Wesleyan Methodist Church to study for the ministry in 1944, and she was so listed until 1948. In August 1948 the conference appointed Maxine and Lee to be co-pastors of the Peru, Indiana, Washington Avenue church. Lee still had two years of college to complete. Maxine became the bookstore manager at Marion College, and they drove back and forth between church and college together. Maxine helped with the preaching and calling, taught Sunday school, and filled in at the piano. They served here until 1951, one year after Lee graduated from college.

From 1951 to 1956, the Haineses served as co-pastors at the Blue River Wesleyan Methodist church near Arlington, Indiana. This rural church experienced significant growth. Maxine had a large role in this, starting and teaching a young married couples class that reached a high of fifty in attendance. From 1956 to 1961, Lee and Maxine pastored at the Jonesboro, Indiana, Main Street church. They had been married nine years when their first child, Mark, was born in 1957. Less than sixteen months later, Rhoda joined the family.

From 1961 to 1963, Lee served as the editor of adult Sunday school literature and supervisor of the Sunday school editorial office for the denomination at its new headquarters in Marion, Indiana. This was a difficult time for Maxine. She was not well, and there was no easy handle for her to get hold of for ministry. She concentrated on her children and taught Sunday school. She also wrote some Sunday school curriculum. Lee also missed the human contact of the pastorate.

From 1963 to 1970, Maxine and Lee returned to the pastorate, at the Eastlawn Wesleyan Methodist church in Indianapolis. This was a church plant that was being relocated. They saw the first stage of the church building completed and dedicated and the congregation stabilized. A new parsonage was constructed. Maxine carried a heavy load at Eastlawn in children's, youth, and women's ministries, while caring for the family and working full-time for two extended periods. In 1967–68, when Lee filled the dual role of pastor and also helping full-time in developing the new *Discipline* for the church merger, Maxine picked up some of the administrative role in the Church.

In 1970 the Haines family moved to Marion, Indiana. Lee taught at Marion College (now Indiana Wesleyan University) 1970–80. Maxine became office secretary of the division of religion and philosophy 1971–84. At one point during that period she served eleven or more professors. She became a mom-away-from-home for the religion majors. She suffered from life-threatening physical problems most of the time in these years but carried an enormous load. She held monthly seminars in her home for fiancees and wives of ministerial students, preparing them for their varied roles. Maxine completed a master of arts in ministerial education degree with honors at the college in 1984. Her major research project was subsequently published as *This Ministry We Share*, a manual to aid minister's wives.

In 1984, Maxine retired to begin traveling with her husband. Lee served the denomination as General Secretary of Education and the Ministry 1980–88 and as General Superintendent 1988–2000. Maxine had many opportunities to minister around the world, including counseling and speaking, both with women and with men. She was loved everywhere she went. She was the first woman to address the General Conference of the Immanuel General Mission of Japan, leading them in their devotionals.

In her last years, she began her research for writing this book. She collected files on many hundreds of women who entered the ministry in the various branches of The Wesleyan Church's family tree between 1841 and 1968, especially those who were eventually ordained. She had written at least three-fifths of her book prior to her final hospitalization.

Following Lee's departure from denominational office in July 2000, Maxine and he enjoyed a short period of respite. But in October 2000 Maxine experienced symptoms that led in 2001 to surgery for bladder cancer. There followed chemotherapy, radiation treatments and additional surgeries. Maxine L. Haines passed away, September 16, 2002.[73]

Margaret K. Hankins Hughes

Margaret Hankins was listed in the records of the West Virginia District of the Pilgrim Holiness Church in 1944, 1945 and 1946. After J. S. Hankins's death, Margaret married Robert R. Hughes. They served as missionaries to the West Indies. She was listed by West Virginia 1946 through 1965 as Mrs. Robert R. Hughes. In 1947 and 1963 she was classified as an evangelist. The Kentucky District also listed her in 1961 as an ordained minister.[74]

Grace Kelloway

Grace Kelloway was an American who served on both sides of the United States-Canada border. She appears first on the records of the Ontario District of the Pilgrim Holiness Church in 1945. She was an ordained minister and she served as pastor at Massey, Ontario 1944–47, and then at Proton, Ontario 1947–48. At Massey it was said that she served there with little or no salary and at great sacrifice to keep the holiness message in the community. An attempt had been made at a much earlier time to establish a Pilgrim Holiness Bible school in Proton. The Pittsburgh District listed Grace Kelloway at Transylvania Bible School in Pennsylvania 1950–59 and then as inactive 1959, 1960, and 1961. The Western Ohio District listed her in 1963 as living in Piqua, Ohio, and 1964–67 as living in Pittsburgh.[75]

Mary Beatrice Lelear

Mary Beatrice Lelear was received to study preparatory to travel (service) by the Rochester Conference (now Central New York District) of the Wesleyan Methodist Church in 1944. They granted her a license as a conference preacher. Her husband, Henry, was listed as pastor and Beatrice as assistant pastor at Shady Grove. She continued on the course of study in 1945 and 1946 and was listed as associate pastor at Shady Grove 1945–46. In the mid-1940s, Mrs. Lelear and another lady "drummed up" enthusiasm for indoor plumbing at the Chambers, New York Camp. This resulted in flush toilets and a laundry room being installed in the basement of the "old dorm" in 1948. In 1947 she requested that her name be dropped temporarily. She served as conference vice president of the Woman's Missionary Society 1946–55 and conference director of child evangelism 1954–55. The first children's camp at Chambers was directed by Beatrice Lelear.

In 1955 she transferred her study course credits to the Allegheny Conference. She was ordained by that conference in 1957 and was listed as a general evangelist for children 1957–68. Her husband served as a general evangelist in these and subsequent years. Mrs. Lelear later served as head resident at one of the women's dormitories at Marion College (now Indiana Wesleyan University), Marion, Indiana. Known affectionately then as "Aunt Bea," she had a significant impact on the lives of those under her care.[76]

Wanda Lingo

Wanda Lingo appears on the records of the Eastern District of the Pilgrim Holiness Church 1939–52. She also appears on the records of the Texas District 1943, 1951 and 1952, and on the records of the Oklahoma-Texas District 1944–50. She was listed as co-pastor, with her husband George, in Divine, Texas, in 1943 and as pastor at Divine 1947–49. She was listed by the Rocky Mountain District 1961–63 as co-pastor at McCook, Nebraska, 1963–64 as in evangelism, and beginning in 1965 as a missionary. The Lingos served as missionaries for four years in the West Indies, including Jamaica, Trinidad and Curacao, Netherlands Antilles (pastoring a church in Curacao). They also served in Guyana and Suriname. Besides Divine and McCook, they also pastored Benkelman, Haigler, and Sutherland in Nebraska and Eckley in Colorado. They had one son, Arnold.[77]

Bertha Lapish Nation

Bertha Lapish was converted in a Presbyterian church. She felt a call to full-time Christian service. She attended the People's Bible School in Greensboro, North Carolina. She began preaching in home prayer meetings and revivals and taught the catechism to children from her home, many finishing the First Catechism and some the Second. She always awarded them a testament or Bible when they finished the course.

Bertha served first under the Southern District of the Pilgrim Holiness Church, being listed on its records in 1940 and 1941. After the district was divided in 1942, she served under the North Carolina District. In 1942 and 1943 she was listed as in Bible school. By 1944 she had married Rev. Norman J. Nation. Together they pastored at Bryson City, Whittier, Wilmot and Mebane. They built a campground, and at some point Bertha was ordained. While they were at Mebane, Norman died on a Sunday morning, during or immediately after the service, June 20, 1949 or 1950.

Bertha Lapish Nation continued as pastor at Mebane until 1952. She then pastored Forest City 1952–54 and Beulah 1954–60.

Sometime after the 1968 merger of the Wesleyan Methodist and Pilgrim Holiness Churches, Bertha moved to Mooresville, North Carolina, and joined the First Wesleyan Church. She preached some and helped in a nursing home. She had a special ministry to the poor and unchurched. At one time she had a mission in Mooresville, where she dispensed God's Word as well as what was needed for the body. Through her frugality she managed to buy four or five houses. The rental money funded her care for others, even at times providing temporary housing for a homeless family. In her later years, when she could no longer carry on this ministry, she gave herself to prayer. Bertha Lapish Nation died December 12, 1999.[78]

Ruth Neal

Ruth (Mrs. George W.) Neal served at first in the West Virginia District of the Pilgrim Holiness Church. She was ordained there in 1944, and her name appeared on the roll also in 1945. Beginning in 1946 and continuing to 1951, Ruth served under the Indiana District of the Pilgrim Holiness Church. When the district was divided in 1951, she served from then on in the Southern Indiana District, and after the 1968 denominational merger, in the Indiana South District of The Wesleyan Church. She was listed as pastor at Sandford, Indiana, 1953–56. Ruth Neal passed away January 24, 2002.

Veda Roe Olson

Veda Roe was born August 20, 1911, in Mankato, Kansas, and was saved in 1935. She enrolled in 1941 as a ministerial student at Miltonvale Wesleyan College, Miltonvale, Kansas (later merged into what has become Oklahoma Wesleyan University, Bartlesville, Oklahoma). She married Ivan Olson December 24, 1942.

Veda was received by the Oregon Conference of the Wesleyan Methodist Church to study for the ministry in 1944. She was listed that year as a conference evangelist. In 1947 and 1948 Veda and Ivan were listed as attending school. In 1950 she was returned to her local church where she would have had a local preacher's license. In 1953 she came back on the conference roll as a conference preacher (licensed minister), and she and Ivan pastored at Lebanon 1953–56. In 1956 she once again dropped from the conference roll.

However, Ivan and Veda continued to work as a team, as pastors, as evangelists, in city missions, as teachers of Bible classes. They conducted family crusades for holiness associations and camp meetings. Music was a large part of Veda's life—piano, organ, and stringed instruments. She had a beautiful voice, sang solos and duets, and wrote songs. She memorized more than thirty dramatic readings and wrote over 4,000 poems as well as stories, skits, and plays. She had a special gift in working with children and youth in vacation Bible school and camps and directed children's choirs. She used visual aids including hand puppets, wrote her own skits, learned to be a ventriloquist. Entire families often yielded to the Lord after her presentation to the children or youth.

Veda Roe Olson went to be with the Lord September 7, 1995.[79]

Lena M. Brown Shrieves

Lena Brown was born in Connersville, Indiana, January 29, 1920. When she was ten she was convicted by the preaching of her father and urged to repentance by her mother. While still in her teens she felt God calling her to foreign missionary service. She said that while she was meditating on Matt. 28:18–20, God said, "Lena, Lena, Lena." And she said, "Yes, yes."

After graduating from high school Lena attended Westfield Bible Seminary in Westfield, Indiana, and Frankfort Pilgrim College, Frankfort, Indiana (later merged into United Wesleyan College, Allentown, Pennsylvania). She graduated from Frankfort in 1943 with a Th. B. degree. She went on to Asbury College and received an A. B. degree in 1947. And she earned a practical nursing certificate from the Chicago School of Nursing.

Prior to her appointment to service in Africa, she spent some time as matron in the Beulah Rescue Mission, Terre Haute, Indiana, and as dietitian in the People's Bible School, Greensboro, North Carolina. She also served as an evangelistic singer and children's worker.

Lena Brown was ordained by the Indiana District of the Pilgrim Holiness Church August 22, 1944. She continued to be listed by them, and later, after the district divided, beginning in 1951 by the Northern Indiana District. In 1948 she was appointed as a missionary to South Africa. She spent thirty years laboring in various capacities in such places as the Industrial Institute, Mt. Frere, Cape Province, and at the Wesleyan Bible Institute, Port Shepstone, Natal, South Africa.

After Lena Brown retired, she married a retired pastor, Rev. Braden Shrieves, December 19, 1987. Lena died April 20, 2003, in Spring Hill, Florida.[80]

Lula Smith

The conference records of the Indiana District of the Pilgrim Holiness Church reveal that Lula Smith was ordained in 1944. She was also listed by that district in 1945, 1946, and 1947.

Mina Steele Smith

Mina Steele was born in Charles City, Iowa, December 11, 1912. She attended Miltonvale Wesleyan College, Miltonvale, Kansas (later merged into what became Oklahoma Wesleyan University) and Marion College, Marion, Indiana (now Indiana Wesleyan University) in preparation for the ministry.

Mina was listed at the organizing session of the Nebraska Conference of the Wesleyan Methodist Church in 1944 as the pastor at Atkinson, Nebraska. In 1945 she met and married Lawrence Smith. They made their home on a farm, where their three children were born. They organized a Sunday school, which provided the nucleus for Hillside Chapel, which she served as the founding pastor 1945–56. In 1956 the family moved to Plattsmouth, and she pastored the church there 1956–59. In 1959 they returned to Holt County, where she pastored the Page church until her death.

Mina Steele Smith served in some conference office or some conference committee nearly every year from 1944 to 1964. She was the conference Sunday school secretary 1944 and 1945 and secretary of the conference Woman's Missionary Society 1944, 1945 and 1946. She passed away March 2, 1967, at O'Neill, Nebraska.[81]

Winifred Trimble

Winifred (Mrs. H. A.) Trimble was first mentioned in the records of the Allegheny Conference of the Wesleyan Methodist Church in 1944. From 1945 to 1946, she served as co-pastor at Mt. Calvary. She then served at one or more churches with similar names: Salem 1946–47, Greenwood-Salem 1947–49, North Salem 1949–52. She was co-pastor at Niles 1952–60 and at East Conneaut 1960–67.[82]

Blanche Vampner

Blanche Vampner was born June 24, 1885. She was converted in March 1926 at Coldwater, Michigan, and was sanctified in September 1940. She preached her first sermon in Hartford City, Indiana, in June 1937. The Indiana District of the Pilgrim Holiness Church licensed her as a minister in 1941 and ordained her in 1943. She pastored at Hartford City for two years. She passed away in 1948. She had spent eighteen years in some level of evangelism.[83]

Edna West

Edna West was listed by the New York District of the Pilgrim Holiness Church from 1944 to 1961. She was already an ordained minister in 1944 and was listed as an evangelist. In 1945 and again in 1953–61 she was listed at Port Jarvis.

Erie Wiley

Erie Wiley was listed by the West Virginia District of the Pilgrim Holiness Church 1944–67. She was ordained in 1944. She was serving as an evangelist in 1949 and was unstationed (without appointment) or serving as an evangelist 1953–57 and 1959.

Marcile A. Williams

Marcile (Mrs. Howard) Williams served first in the Eastern District of the Pilgrim Holiness Church, 1944–49. Beginning in 1951, she was serving under the Ohio District. She lived in Langsville, Ohio, in 1951 and in Peebles, Ohio, 1952 and 1953. In 1954 she was serving in evangelistic work. After the Ohio District divided in 1955, she continued to be listed in evangelistic work under the Western Ohio District through 1960. Beginning in 1961, she served in the Illinois District. She was listed as pastor at Bridgeport in 1963 and as an evangelist in 1964. She continued to be listed in Illinois through 1967.[84]

Carrie Barbiein

Carrie Barbiein was received by the Indiana Conference of the Wesleyan Methodist Church as an ordained minister on probation in 1945. She was assigned as a conference evangelist in 1949. However, she withdrew from the denomination in August 1950.[85]

Mrs. Mae Baumgarner

Mae Baumgarner served under the North Carolina District of the Pilgrim Holiness Church in 1945, perhaps at Wilmot. Her name appears on the records of the district again 1955–68. At least part of this time she was pastor at Whittier, and in 1960 Wilmot is mentioned again.

Viola M. Holycross Bondehagen

Viola Holycross (Mrs. Thomas) Bondehagen was received by the Indiana Conference of the Wesleyan Methodist Church in 1945 to study preparatory to travel (service). She was listed as a conference evangelist in 1946, 1947, and 1948. She completed the course of study in 1947. On December 15, 1946, she became pastor of the Lawndale church in the California Conference. She transferred to the California Conference in 1949 and was ordained there that year. She was listed as a conference evangelist 1949 through 1952, then as unstationed (without appointment) through 1959. In 1960 she was listed as withdrawn.[86]

Ruth Brizendine

In a service in Canon City, Colorado, in 1945, Rev. W. F. Drown, superintendent of the Rocky Mountain District of the Pilgrim Holiness Church, was the speaker. After the service, Ruth Brizendine consulted with him and mentioned that she was called to preach. Rev. Drown decided to give her a chance. The next morning Rev. Minnie Barnes asked Ruth to go to Freeport, Kansas, with her and help her in her church there.

Ruth Brizendine filled in at Freeport for a few months after Rev. Barnes left the church. She then returned to Colorado Springs Bible College (later merged into what became Oklahoma Wesleyan University, Bartlesville, Oklahoma), and graduated four years later. She worked at the Pilgrim Holiness headquarters for about a year, hoping to serve as a missionary in South America, which did not work out. She then worked for a time at the Colorado Springs Bible College. Eventually she became the Greek teacher at the new campus in Bartlesville for six years. She also did some graduate work during this time. In 1968 she joined the staff of Brainerd Indian School near Hot Springs, South Dakota. She spent about eight and one-half years there, preaching in the chapel at first; later she served in teaching, secretarial work, and in other capacities. During her years of ministry she also wrote for publication. Ruth left Brainerd to care for her elderly mother.[87]

Ida L. Christenson

Ida Christenson served first as an ordained deaconess in the Pilgrim Holiness Church. Beginning in 1945, she was listed as an ordained minister in the Michigan District and was involved in pastoral service there 1945–1955. When the district was divided, she served in pastoral service in the East Michigan District 1955–68 and after the 1968 merger was a part of the North Michigan District of The Wesleyan Church. At least part of the time, she pastored a church at Honor, Michigan, which met in her home. She was very much involved in her community and in district activities.[88]

Bertha Deal

Bertha Deal's name first appeared on the record of the North Carolina District of the Pilgrim Holiness Church in 1945. She was apparently serving at Walnut Grove at that time. She was ordained by this district. Her name is listed from 1955 on to the merger in 1968. She was instrumental in starting the Taylorsville, North Carolina, church and pastored it this entire period. After the merger, the Taylorsville church was part of the North Carolina West District of The Wesleyan Church. Bertha's health eventually forced her to retire.

Bertha Deal died at Brian Center in Hickory, North Carolina, December 16, 1995, at the age of ninety.[89]

Katherine P. Drown

Katherine P. Drown was ordained June 10, 1945, by the Dakota Conference of the Wesleyan Methodist Church. She and her husband, F. Wilbur Drown, had six children.

Katherine served in the Dakota Conference until 1955, being listed as doing "missionary work." She then transferred to the Nebraska Conference. She was listed as a conference evangelist 1956–57, home missionary 1957–58, and conference evangelist 1958–59. From 1959 to 1964 she was listed as on reserve. In 1964 she retired.

Katherine's obituary described her as an evangelist and supply pastor in the Dakota and Nebraska Districts. She held a number of offices in the Nebraska Conference, particularly in the Woman's Missionary Society. In retirement she served in her local church as missionary society president, church treasurer, and Sunday school teacher. She also served as senior citizens prayer secretary for Wesleyan Indian Missions. Katherine P. Drown died May 24, 1977, at the age of seventy-eight.[90]

Wilma Irene Wondercheck Francis

Wilma Wondercheck was born March 3, 1925, in Atkinson, Nebraska. She was born again in her high school years, under the ministry of Rev. G. M. Hubby, pastor of the newly organized Wesleyan Methodist church in Atkinson.

Wilma graduated from Miltonvale Wesleyan College, Miltonvale, Kansas (later merged into what became Oklahoma Wesleyan University, Bartlesville, Oklahoma) in 1945. She went to stay at the Ralph Ernst farm, near Spencer, Nebraska, to teach vacation Bible school. Here she met George Francis. In the fall of 1945, Wilma was received to travel (serve) under the Nebraska Conference of the Wesleyan Methodist Church. She was appointed assistant pastor of the Lincoln, Nebraska church.

On August 24, 1946, she and George Francis were married in the first of three church buildings at Atkinson. That year they attended God's Bible School in Cincinnati, Ohio. In 1947 the Nebraska Conference appointed them as "pioneer" (church-planting) pastors at Grand Island.

From 1948 to 1953, they served at Page, which had just come into the Wesleyan Methodist Church from the Hephzibah Faith Missionary Association. In their first year at Page, Rev. J. R. Swauger, general secretary of home missions, Rev. Clarence Budensiek, conference president, and Rev. Arnold L. Nabholz were touring the conference and stopped at the Francis home for dinner. The kitchen stove burned white gas and was dangerous and unpredictable. The stove malfunctioned, and the cake fell. Rev. Swauger learned of this, went looking, and had a piece of cake anyway. The Francises' son was born here at Page. In 1950, George supplied at Greeley for a time. In 1951 they were ordained by the conference.

From 1953 to 1956, George and Wilma Francis served at Plattsmouth. New basement units were built for worship and parsonage. Their first daughter was born here. They also supplied an independent church at LaPlatte.

From 1956 to 1958, the Francises were in the "Sand Hills," serving at Tryon. Several "sod houses" were still being lived in at Tryon. Forty miles away, at Arthur, the Pilgrim Holiness church was built out of baled hay. It is preserved today as a museum.

From 1958 to 1960, they served at Naponee; a second daughter was born here. From 1960 to 1964, the Francises pastored Neligh, where in 1944 Rev. J. R. Swauger had organized the Nebraska Conference. This church was quite a challenge—a salary of twenty dollars per week for a family of three children. God provided work that developed George's building skills. From 1964 to 1969 they served Venus, a rural church near Orchard; Wilma also supplied the Page church for a time. Apparently within the five-year period they ended up back at Page (where they had pastored early in their ministry), and someone else pastored Venus.

From 1970 to 1978, they pastored at Wayne and supplied a German congregation in the rural area. From 1978 to 1986, they pastored at

Scottsbluff; George helped to build the church and parsonage at Alliance. From 1986 to 1993, they pastored at Lynch, near where both had been born.

George and Wilma Francis retired in 1993 and moved to Kearney, Nebraska. Here Wilma died May 10, 1999.[91]

Betty Nelle Freeborn

Betty Nelle Freeborn was received by the Kansas Conference of the Wesleyan Methodist Church in 1945 to study preparatory to travel (service). Her 1945 appointment was as college nurse at Marion College, Marion, Indiana (now Indiana Wesleyan University). Betty Nelle was a registered nurse. She served five terms as a missionary to Sierra Leone, West Africa. Her first term was March 1946 to March 1949. During her second term, July 1950 to September 1953, she was elected to ordination by the 1950 Kansas Conference session, but since she was far away in Africa she was later ordained by a committee. The other terms of service were March 1955 to May 1958; November 1959 to November 1962; November 1963 to February 1967.[92]

Bernice Hubby

Bernice (Mrs. William) Hubby was licensed as a conference preacher (now licensed minister) by the Nebraska Conference of the Wesleyan Methodist Church in 1945. She served as pastor at Firth 1945–48. From 1948 to 1949 she was a conference evangelist. She was supply pastor at Paddock and Union 1949–50. Her pastorate at Neligh ran from 1950 to 1960. She was ordained by the conference in 1955. She pastored Napanee 1960–61 and O'Neill 1961–64. She returned to the pastorate at Neligh in 1964.

Bernice Hubby served in many offices and on many committees on the conference level. Most notable was her service on the committee on itineracy and elders orders (now district board of ministerial development) 1957–65.

Bernice Hubby passed away July 10, 1971. At the time of her death, she was remembered as one in whose presence a person could feel the power of God.[93]

Ruth Nicholson Huff

Ruth Nicholson was born July 15, 1914. She completed high school in Mineral, Virginia, May 29, 1933. She earned an A. B. degree through God's Bible School and the University of Cincinnati in June 1941. And years later, July 1970, she earned a B. S. in elementary education from Malone College.

Ruth married Carl W. Huff June 20, 1942. He also became a minister. From 1945 to 1949 they pastored Harrison Chapel for the Ohio Conference of the Wesleyan Methodist Church. In 1949 this conference ordained Ruth. From 1949 to 1950 they pastored the church at Springfield, Ohio, and from 1950 to 1952 they pastored the church at Weirton Heights, West Virginia.

In 1952 they were authorized to choose their own field of labor. They chose the independent Holiness Tabernacle in Lafferty, Ohio. They pastored there for fifteen years, organizing it as a Wesleyan Methodist church in 1957. In 1967 they took another independent church on Robb Avenue in Lima, Ohio. They served there for two years. In 1970, one year after they left, this too was organized as a Wesleyan church.

From 1969 to 1973, the Huffs pastored at the Jelloway-Danville Wesleyan church. Then they retired to become "willing workers" at the Greer, Ohio church, until at least 1996.

Ruth Huff was elected vice president of the conference Woman's Missionary Society in 1961, 1962, and 1964. She was elected to the conference board of education in 1968. She said they pastored two of the hardest churches two years each and gained a young preacher from each— John LeMasters and Kevin Turner.[94]

Bertha Lucille Joy

Bertha Joy was born October 10, 1918 at Lourenco Marques, Portuguese East Africa (now

Mozambique). She was the daughter of two ministers, Elmer D. and Ina Louise Joy, pioneer Pilgrim Holiness missionaries to Africa. Later Joy Mission in Swaziland was named after her parents.

Bertha received a Bachelor of Theology degree from Eastern Pilgrim College, Allentown, Pennsylvania (later United Wesleyan College) in 1943. She later earned an A. B. degree from Westminster College, New Wilmington, Pennsylvania. She also studied at Drayton Business College, Pittsburgh, Pennsylvania and took a practical nursing course from the Chicago School of Nursing.

Bertha had a call to missionary service and was employed by the foreign missions department in 1944. She was first appointed to serve in San Antonio, Texas. On January 10, 1946, she sailed for Africa, where she spent four years at Pilgrim Industrial Institute, Mt. Frere, Cape Province, South Africa. She was in charge of the home economics department there.

Bertha Joy returned home in January 1951. She took further training in home economics, helped her father in his pastoral work, and worked for more than two years as office editor of Sunday school literature in the editorial offices of the Pilgrim Holiness Church in Indianapolis, Indiana.

On June 22, 1957, Bertha Joy returned to Africa. She served at Jembo Mission, Northern Rhodesia (now Zambia), as head teacher of the home economics department until 1964. From 1964 to 1965 she was at the Chabbabboma Mission and in 1965 began service at Choma. Bertha Joy died in Africa in the winter of 1966–67.[95]

Edith Mae Jones McIntyre

Edith Mae Jones was converted as a teen, was sanctified, and was called to the ministry. She joined the Wesleyan Methodist Church at Johnson's Corner, North Dakota. She studied for the ministry at Miltonvale Wesleyan College, Miltonvale, Kansas (later merged into what became Oklahoma Wesleyan University, Bartlesville, Oklahoma).

Edith was married to Robert W. McIntyre September 1, 1944. The Fargo Wesleyan Methodist Church at Marengo, Ohio, had called

Robert to be their pastor on August 15, 1944. On September 11, 1944, the McIntyres transferred from the Dakota Conference to the Ohio Conference and served as pastors at Fargo 1944–47. Edith and Robert were ordained together in 1945.

From 1947 to 1949, the McIntyres pastored the Ashland Park Avenue church in Columbus, Ohio. Part of this time Robert supplied an independent work on Locksbourne Road in Columbus in an unsuccessful attempt to bring it into the Wesleyan Methodist Church. Meanwhile Edith preached on Sunday mornings at the Ashland Park Avenue church.

From 1949 to 1952, the McIntyres pastored the Linden church. On April 1, 1951, they dedicated newly purchased property, housing the church downstairs and the parsonage upstairs. In August 1952, Robert and Edith moved to pastor the Coshocton church. That year Edith was elected to the committee on itineracy and elders orders (now district board of ministerial development) but later resigned.

Four and one-half months later, on January 4, 1953, Edith Jones McIntyre passed away, leaving Robert with two daughters (Judith and Joy) and two sons (John and James). At the 1953 Ohio Conference session, a memorial service was held in which Edith was remembered for her uncomplaining, consecrated service and the lasting influence and inspiration of her saintly life.[96]

Ruth Welcome Miller

Ruth Welcome was born in Haviland, Kansas. She was converted at an early age in a community schoolhouse. She was a graduate of the Friends Bible College and also attended Lindsborg College. She taught in the music department of Haviland Bible College for a number of years.

Ruth married Leon L. Miller in 1924, and they served together in the ministry under the

Pilgrim Holiness Church. They pastored together at Ogallala, Nebraska; Newkirk, Oklahoma; and the First Pilgrim Holiness Church in Colorado Springs. Ruth was ordained in 1945.

The Millers served for eighteen years as missionaries to Barbados in the West Indies. For part of that time Leon was field superintendent of the Caribbean. Then they pastored at Syracuse, Kansas, 1954–57. Leon died during their last year there. At the time of his death, he was president-elect of Colorado Springs Bible College (later merged into what became Oklahoma Wesleyan University, Bartlesville, Oklahoma).

Ruth Welcome Miller transferred from the Kansas District of the Pilgrim Holiness Church to the Pacific Northwest District in 1958, living in Portland, Oregon 1959–62. She retired in 1962 and died May 24, 1982, at the age of eighty-one.[97]

Elsie May Downing Nettleton

Elsie May Downing was born in Parker, South Dakota, May 26, 1915. Her parents, Harrison A. and Nellie May Downing, were farm-ers. Elsie became a Christian as a young girl and early learned to pray. She wanted to sing but was not natu-rally talented for that. There was a rock in the pasture where she sometimes prayed, and there she prom-ised God that if He would enable her to sing, she would sing for His glory. He answered her prayer, and she kept her promise.

While Elsie was in high school, her mother became very ill, and Elsie dropped out of school to take care of her. Elsie and her father prayed much together during this time, and he received a call to preach. After her mother's death, Elsie went back to high school and graduated. Her father married again, this time to a widow, Rev. Nina V. Edwards. He pursued his call to preach, and he and Nina served together in the ministry. The marriage

brought a stepbrother and three stepsisters into Elsie's life: Herbert Edwards, Gertrude (Bonner), Madge (Bursch), and Kathryn (Martin).

Elsie was in her twenties when she graduated from high school. She then enrolled at Colorado Springs Bible School (later merged into what became Oklahoma Wesleyan University, Bartlesville, Oklahoma). There she met Herman D. Nettleton. They were married June 26, 1940. Later they would both graduate in 1951 from Western Bible Institute, El Monte, California (later also merged into what became Oklahoma Wesleyan University), and they did further studies at Northwest Nazarene College in Nampa, Idaho.

The Nettletons co-pastored home missionary churches in the Pilgrim Holiness Church in Nebraska, Idaho, Washington, Oregon, and Texas. Their longest pastorate was at Dalhart, Texas. The Nettletons had four daughters, Esther (Crank, at one time a missionary nurse in Zambia), Louise (McIntyre), Rachel (Eisenbeis) and Lois (Al-Harithy), and one son, Philip, who has pastored and served on several Wesleyan mission fields.

The Nettletons always had a significant ministry with youth and children as well as a prayer ministry with people of all ages. Elsie was known for her gift of hospitality, and for providing food, clothing, and even shelter for many needy people. Elsie Nettleton passed away December 6, 1992.[98]

Louise Nichols

Louise Nichols was ordained by the Indiana District of the Pilgrim Holiness Church in 1945. She continued to be listed by that district through 1949. When the district divided, she was listed in somewhat overlapping fashion by one or both districts (Northern and Southern Indiana) in 1951 through 1953.[99]

Mary Ella O'Connor Penny and Lily Van Slaven Penny

Mary Ella O'Connor married Rev. W. Harold Penny in 1936 in Jonesboro, Arkansas. They had four children, three of whom died. Mary Ella was a licensed minister. She assisted her husband in pastoring in Bladen, Nebraska; Stanley, Missouri; Yakima, Washington; and Coeur d' Alene, Idaho. Mary Ella died in an automobile accident in Sacramento, California, June 18, 1950.[100]

Lily Van Slaven married Rev. Harold Penny in 1953. They had one daughter. Lily had been ordained in 1945. Lily and Harold pastored a Pilgrim Holiness church in Blackwell, Oklahoma. In 1958 they were called to pastor the church in Corpus Christi, Texas. Harold's health was failing. He died December 1, 1958.

Lily Van Slaven Penny continued as the pastor at Corpus Christi until 1960. From 1963 to 1967, she lived in Batavia, Ohio, and pastored the Afton church. In 1967 she was listed by the Western Ohio District as being at Central Pilgrim College, Bartlesville, Oklahoma (now Oklahoma Wesleyan University). In 1968 she appeared on the roll of the Central District of the Pilgrim Holiness Church.[101]

Elizabeth Ann Clark Phillips

Elizabeth Ann Clark was born July 16, 1922, in Denton, Maryland. She was saved in 1937 and sanctified sometime later. She said that as far as she knew, she never had a call to the ministry or even to be a mission-ary except that she told the Lord she was willing to be a missionary if called. She told Him that she did not believe she could be, but she would depend on His grace. Then she fell in love with Dean Howard Phillips, and she knew that he was headed for the mission field and if she married him she would be a missionary.

Both Dean and Elizabeth graduated from Eastern Pilgrim College, Allentown, Pennsylvania (later United Wesleyan College). They were married March 10, 1945, in Harrington, Delaware. They had three children: Joyce Arlene, Doris

Elaine, and John Howard. The Eastern District of the Pilgrim Holiness Church (later Delmarva and then Chesapeake) wished to ordain Elizabeth before the Phillipses departed for the mission field, but she declined for the time being.

In February 1947, the Phillipses were appointed to serve on St. Croix in the American Virgin Islands. Later they were transferred to Antigua in the West Indies. Here Dean was superintendent of the Northern Islands District and pastored the large St. Johns church. At the same time, Elizabeth pastored a small church on the other end of Antigua, preaching there on Sunday mornings.

During their first furlough, the district finally persuaded Elizabeth and she was ordained in the summer of 1954. When the furlough was over, Dean became superintendent of the Trinidad District, and they lived in Port-of-Spain. They brought about the erection of a new church in the capital city. The third term found them back in Jamaica, where Dean was district superintendent 1963–69.

Altogether, the Deans served forty-two years as missionaries in these islands as well as in Guyana. Elizabeth always looked at their ministry as being her husband's with her as his helper. She taught in Bible schools (ethics, Pentateuch, Daniel, general epistles, Acts, Revelation) and adult Sunday school classes. She also used her commercial training in high school as bookkeeper for the various fields. She preached when asked to do so. Although Elizabeth felt "pushed into the ministry," she felt that it had been a blessing to her and others, as a result of her husband and the needs they encountered on the fields.[102]

Ruth Heim Rimmer

Ruth Heim was born March 17, 1916, in Treverton, Pennsylvania. She married John Goodwin Rimmer October 2, 1940, in Tilghmans Island, Maryland. Ruth Rimmer was ordained by the Eastern District of the Pilgrim Holiness Church in August 1945. John and Ruth pastored churches in Maryland, Delaware, and Louisiana.

They had two sons, Paul G. and James R. By 1978 they had moved to Covington, Virginia, to be near family members. John died there that year. While attending the Covington Wesleyan Church, she was asked by the district superintendent to become its pastor, which she did. Ruth Heim died July 21, 1998, in Covington, Virginia, at the age of eighty-two.[103]

Clara P. Sherman

Clara P. Sherman was listed in the records of the Michigan District of the Pilgrim Holiness Church as being ordained in 1945. Her 1945 listing was unstationed (without appointment) and in 1946 it was "education."

Esther Sherwood

Esther (Mrs. Jason H.) Sherwood was ordained in 1945 by the West Virginia District of the Pilgrim Holiness Church. She was listed by this district again in 1946. The Ohio District listed her in 1948 and 1949 as living in Greenville, Ohio; in 1950, 1952 and 1953 in Toledo; in 1951 in Nelsonville, Ohio; and in 1954 in Maysville, Kentucky. The Kentucky District listed her 1954 through 1957. The Eastern Ohio District listed her 1959 through 1962, and again in 1966 as unstationed (without appointment) or retired. The Western Ohio District listed her in 1965 in connection with Washington Court House, Ohio; in 1966 at Union Bible Seminary in Westfield, Indiana; and in 1967 in connection with West Mansfield, Ohio.[104]

Lily Slaven

Lily Slaven was ordained in 1945 by the Kansas District of the Pilgrim Holiness Church. She was also listed in 1946 and 1947 by the Kansas District. The Oklahoma-Texas District listed her in 1945 as pastor at Newkirk. They also included her name in 1948 through 1952. In 1953 she was listed as pastor at Henryetta, Oklahoma.[105]

A. Elizabeth Stephens

A. Elizabeth Stephens was from Thornby, Quebec, which is about halfway between Campbells' Bay and Otter Lake in a northwesterly direction, or fifty miles northwest of Ottawa. She became an ordained minister in the Canada Conference of the Wesleyan Methodist Church and served for many years as the conference secretary.

Elizabeth was first listed by the Canada Conference in 1945. In 1946 she was listed as pastor of Thornby and in 1947 seemed to be serving a larger area that reached perhaps to Campbells' Bay and Otter Lake. In 1948 she was listed as an evangelist. From 1949 to 1954, except for 1951, she was listed as superannuated, which normally meant retired. In 1951 she was listed as "supernumerary" (on reserve). From 1954 through 1967 she was listed as unstationed (without appointment).

Elizabeth's ministry revolved around Thornby. She made her living as a public school teacher. She not only taught the "three R's" but also sought to instill a knowledge of the Scriptures. She used her schoolroom nearly every year for two weeks of revival services. A goodly number of the parents learned about Christ's saving and sanctifying power and were brought to Jesus. She had a church built to bring people to know the Lord. The pastor of the Wesleyan Methodist church at nearby Shawville, Quebec had the oversight of Thornby. Roads were impassable in the winter, so the church would be closed. In the summer, every Sunday afternoon out from the hills came parents, youth, and children. Better working conditions elsewhere eventually attracted people away from the hills. They began keeping the roads open in the winter, and people were attracted to other things outside. The little church was forgotten. And when Rev. A. Elizabeth Stephens retired from teaching, she located in Campbells' Bay. She had no transportation and on July 21, 1960, the little church in the valley at Thornby was sold.[106]

Jenny V. Vincent and Laura Conley Fleming Gibbs

Jenny V. Vincent was born May 16, 1898, in Soldier, Kentucky. She received the assurance of her conversion in 1918 and was sanctified on May 21, 1920. Her reading of the Scriptures and the Holy Spirit led her to the Lord. She was convinced of a call to Christian service from early youth. She graduated from high school in Soldier, Kentucky. She studied for the ministry at God's Bible School, Cincinnati, Ohio, the Pilgrim Holiness college at Kingswood, Kentucky, and through the course of study. She served for eighteen years as secretary of the Kentucky District. She was licensed as a minister in 1945 or 1946 and was ordained by the Kentucky District of the Pilgrim Holiness Church August 5, 1955, at the Maysville campground.

Jennie Vincent served as assistant pastor at Olive Hill, Kentucky, for one year under Rev. Jack Tockett, about six months at Aspen Grove along with "Sister" Walker, one year at her home church in Soldier (1948), over four years at LaFollette, Tennessee (1956–60), and about one and one-half years at Willard, Kentucky (1961–62). She also served as an evangelistic singer, pianist, children's worker, director of many vacation Bible schools. She was under appointment 1955–56 and 1963–67 as an evangelist. She served as district missionary president and district secretary of world missions, and at age sixty-eight she was in charge of the junior youth camp in 1966.[107]

Part of the time Jennie Vincent worked with other ladies, including Hazel Smith and Betty Foster. Her longest-lasting team ministry was with Laura Conley Fleming, a licensed special worker. The team ministry included evangelistic singing and children's ministry as well as the pastorates at LaFollette, Tennessee, and Willard, Kentucky, and covered a total of twelve years, 1949–61. Laura Conley was born September 8, 1922. She married Rev. Kenneth Fleming December 18, 1961. She and her husband pastored the Soldier and Pleasureville, Kentucky, churches. Kenneth Fleming died November 11, 1972. Laura later married Rev. Victor Gibbs August 31, 1991, and

they pastored the Livermore, Kentucky, Wesleyan church. Laura Conley Fleming Gibbs passed away February 19, 1996.[108]

Emma Williams

The Oklahoma District of the Pilgrim Holiness Church in its conference minutes listed Emma (Mrs. R. K.) Williams in 1941 as unstationed (without appointment) and in 1945 as being ordained that year.

Beulah Day Wilson

Beulah Day was a minister in the Pilgrim Holiness Church in Indiana, appearing on the records of the Indiana District 1945–52. An article in the *Pilgrim Holiness Advocate* in 1948 described her as a successful evangelist and a splendid preacher. She married Rev. Albert H. Wilson, February 3, 1953. He was serving at the time as the second assistant general superintendent of the denomination. He passed away August 15, 1956.

Beulah Day Wilson was listed by the New York District 1953–57 as an evangelist. She was described as a good evangelist who had been in pastoral work for many years, with a genuine Christian character and adherence to the truth of God's Word.[109]

Alta M. Adams

Alta M. Adams was an ordained minister and under district appointment 1946–63 in the California District of the Pilgrim Holiness Church. She died during the 1963 district year.

Mrs. V. A. Bacher

The California District of the Pilgrim Holiness Church listed Mrs. V. A. Bacher as an ordained minister under appointment in 1946. The California-Arizona District maintained such a listing for her 1947–55.

Lilia Barton

Lilia Barton was an ordained minister serving the California District in 1946 and the California-Arizona District 1947–49. A Leila Barton (perhaps a spelling irregularity) served as a Pilgrim Holiness missionary to Peru.[110]

Maxine Kettering Bingaman

Maxine Kettering was from the Lawrence, Kansas, Wesleyan Methodist Church. She studied for the ministry at Miltonvale Wesleyan College, Miltonvale, Kansas (later merged into what became Oklahoma Wesleyan University, Bartlesville, Oklahoma). There she met Fred Bingaman, and they were married in 1946. They had three sons, Roger, Harold, and Alan, and one daughter, Darly (Larson).

Maxine Kettering Bingaman was received by the Kansas Conference of the Wesleyan Methodist Church in 1946 to travel (serve) under the conference president. She and Fred served as missionaries at Brainerd Indian School, Hot Springs, South Dakota, 1950–54. In 1952 they were ordained together.

The Bingamans transferred to the Dakota Conference July 29, 1954. They pastored at Sturgis, South Dakota for about six months. From 1955 to 1957 they served as pastors at Houghton, South Dakota. From 1957 to 1960 they served the Avon, South Dakota congregation. From 1960–68 they pastored a rural church in Ridge, Montana. In 1968 they served as assistant pastors to Dallas Wadsooth at Hamilton, Montana. Also in 1968 they moved to Bitterroot Valley. For many years Fred served as president of an interdenominational camp in eastern Montana. He died at Bitterroot Valley, October 27, 1994.

Maxine Kettering Bingaman was known for taking a text and making it come alive with "clarity and charity." Fred did most of the preaching, even though he was quiet, soft-spoken, and public speaking did not come easily to him. It is reported that their congregations listened with a sense of relief whenever Fred announced that Maxine was going to preach. After one of her stirring and anointed sermons, some would say, "I wish she would preach more than she does." She used farm stories about animals, planting and harvesting, working in the fields.

One of her sermons was remembered many years later. She was preaching on Elisha and said he used part of a plow and a yoke of oxen to make a sacrifice to the Lord when Elijah called him to follow the Lord. She said this was more than a sacrifice. He was declaring that he had cut every tie and bond to his life as a plowman of the earth, and now he would labor in God's field for a spiritual harvest.[111]

Mossie Campbell

The records on Mossie Campbell appear to be fragmentary. The Kansas Conference of the Wesleyan Methodist Church received her as an ordained minister from the Pilgrim Holiness Church in 1946 and appointed her and her husband, Russell Lee Campbell, to serve as pastors at Mulberry Chapel mission. They served there until 1948. On June 10, 1948, they were granted letters of transfer. Then Mossie shows up on the records of the Rocky Mountain District of the Pilgrim Holiness Church 1961–67. The three years that her location is given (1961, 1966, 1967) she was in Denver.[112]

Mary Cockran

The Ohio District of the Pilgrim Holiness Church ordained Mary Cockran in 1946 and listed her as pastor at Westboro, Ohio, in 1947 and 1948.

Eunice Conadoll

Eunice Conadoll was first listed by the Allegheny Conference of the Wesleyan Methodist Church in 1946. From 1947 to 1952, she was assisting her husband, Rev. R. W. Conadoll, as "pioneer secretary" (heading up church planting) with seven mission points. From 1952 to 1964, she was her husband's assistant as they pastored Canal, and from 1964 to 1967 she assisted him in pastoring the Indiana, Pennsylvania, church.

Stella Critchfield

Stella Critchfield was ordained by the Indiana District of the Pilgrim Holiness Church in 1946 and continued to be listed by that district through 1950. From 1951 to 1967, she was listed by the Southern Indiana District. From 1951 to 1957, she was listed as pastor at Cannelton, Indiana.

Laura Dudley

Laura Dudley was ordained by the Virginia District of the Pilgrim Holiness Church in 1946. She served with her husband, William R. Dudley, as a missionary to the Philippines. In 1948 she was listed as a returned missionary. And from 1949 through 1952 her name was on the roll of the Eastern District.

Mrs. May S. Heck

The name of May S. Heck appears on the records of the Oregon District of the Pilgrim Holiness Church. She was ordained there in 1946 and was to serve as co-pastor at Bend, Oregon. She continued to be listed by the Oregon District through 1948, then was listed by the Northwest District 1949 through 1951 and by the California District 1952–68.

Mrs. Callie Huddleston

Callie Huddleston was from Owensboro, Kentucky. She moved to California. Her name was listed by the California District of the Pilgrim Holiness Church 1946–51. She was known as a great preacher of "second blessing" holiness. She was said to have done a great work among people of color in Los Angeles. She died July 30, 1951.

Emily V. Hutchinson

The records of the Ohio District of the Pilgrim Holiness Church indicate that Emily Hutchinson was ordained in 1946. She was listed by the Pittsburgh District 1946 through 1948, being appointed as pastor at Jewett, Ohio in 1946 and 1947.

Ruby Irene Berkgren Long

Ruby Berkgren was born near Oakley, Kansas, October 16, 1927. She attended Colorado Springs Bible College and Colorado College. She earned a Th. B. degree. She married Richard Eugene Long August 8, 1947. He was also a graduate of Colorado Springs Bible  College (later merged into what became Oklahoma Wesleyan University, Bartlesville, Oklahoma). Ruby Long was a licensed minister when they were married but was eventually ordained. She taught school for two years and served as dean of women at Colorado Springs Bible College for several years up to 1956.

In July–August 1956, the Longs sailed to Africa for missionary service under the Pilgrim Holiness Church. At first they served at Ebenezer Mission in Swaziland, then at Joy Mission, and in 1960 were transferred to Chabbobboma Mission in Northern Rhodesia (now Zambia). They had three children; two of them died and were buried in Africa. Their second term in Africa began in 1963, again in Zambia. They served a total of thirteen years in Africa.

After the 1968 merger, Richard Long served as superintendent of the Nebraska District of The Wesleyan Church until 1978. He and Ruby pastored Lewellen, Nebraska, for two years and Oshkosh for several years. They served there after 1978. Richard died September 24, 1984, at the age of 56. Ruby continued pastoring for several years and served as Nebraska District secretary.[113]

Velma H. Hertel Manuel

Velma H. Hertel married Rev. Roy Manuel. Her name first appeared in 1947 in the records of the Indiana District of the Pilgrim Holiness Church. She was listed there through 1950. When the district divided into Northern and Southern Indiana Districts in 1951, she went with the Southern District. The Manuels were listed as pastors of the East Enterprise church at Vevay, Indiana 1952 through 1967. She was reputed to be an excellent preacher. She and Roy sang together, and they had a nursing home ministry. She conducted many funerals.[114]

Mayme Parker Mills

Mayme Parker was born in November 1892 at Woolford, Maryland. Later she moved to Cambridge. She was converted as a young woman and identified with the Pilgrim Holiness Church. She was zealous for the Lord's work, had an alto voice, and played the trumpet and the trombone. For over twenty years, she and Mrs. Oscar Ewell (Winifred Mears) were co-laborers, traveling as members of the Vickers Evangelistic Party. They ministered from Boston to North Carolina in "pioneer work," establishing many churches and reopening some that had been abandoned. She spoke of many persecutions, meetings held under adverse circumstances, but the work went forward. Meetings were held in churches, halls, and tents. Crowds sometimes numbered in the thousands, and a great number of seekers found the Lord. She was never happier than when "on the battlefield for the Lord." She married Wilby Mills in 1934.

Mayme Parker Mills was ordained by the Eastern District of the Pilgrim Holiness Church August 5, 1946. She pastored at Bishop's Head, Maryland, for several years. Mayme then returned to Cambridge, served on the local

church advisory board, served as choir leader, and taught the ladies' Bible class. Wilby Mills died in 1956. As Mayme approached the end of her life, she said, "I am ready to go. I have lived all my life for this. I'm covered by the blood." Mayme Parker Mills died October 1, 1957.[115]

Margurite Olson

The name of Margurite Olson was carried on the records of the California District of the Pilgrim Holiness Church 1946–67.

Ruby Powell

Ruby Powell was received to travel (serve) in 1946 by the North Carolina Conference of the Wesleyan Methodist Church. She was apparently serving at Zion's Hill Mission in Breathitt County, Kentucky, at that time. She continued to be listed by this district through 1963. From 1947 to 1950, she was a conference evangelist. She was ordained in 1948. She continued to be appointed as a conference evangelist through 1956, with the additional notation that she was a Bible school and children's worker 1950–54. Beginning in 1957, she was listed as an assistant professor at Central Wesleyan College, Central, South Carolina (now Southern Wesleyan University). This appointment continued through 1961 with the addition in 1960 and 1961 that her area of instruction was "education." For 1962 and 1963 her appointment once again revolved around vacation Bible school and other children's ministries. On January 1, 1964, she was granted a letter for leaving the denomination.[116]

Geneva M. Fiebelkorn Pritchard

Geneva Pritchard was received by the Lockport Conference of the Wesleyan Methodist Church (now Western New York District of The Wesleyan Church) in 1946 to pursue the course of study under the direction of the conference. On June 27, 1946, she was appointed to care for the Leon Wesleyan Mission under the pastoral care of Rev. Howard F. Parks, pastor of the East Leon church.

A small group was meeting in Leon when Geneva and her husband, Clarence, moved there. Sunday morning services were begun. Geneva's appointment there continued for thirty-five years, until she retired in 1981. She also taught educationally handicapped children. The Lockport Conference ordained Geneva in 1950. The meetings were held in a former Baptist church building. In 1951 the congregation was organized with nine charter members and nine associate members. That same year they bought the old Baptist building and extensively renovated it inside and out without incurring any debt. The number of tithers in this church equaled the number of members. Most of the members lived some distance from the church but were faithful in attendance and support.

Geneva Pritchard served on the conference Sunday school board 1947 through 1951 and had other officer and committee assignments from time to time. She and Clarence had one son and three daughters. Clarence died in 1975. Geneva retired from her pastorate in 1981. She passed away January 8, 1987, at the age of eighty-one.[117]

Pearle Ratcliffe

Pearle Ratcliffe was ordained in 1946 by the Oklahoma Conference of the Wesleyan Methodist Church of America. She was appointed as a song evangelist 1946 through 1950. In 1951 the conference granted her a letter of standing.

Kathryn Thomas

Kathryn (Mrs. C. W.) Thomas (also spelled "Catherine" and "Katherine") was listed by the California District of the Pilgrim Holiness Church 1946–58. She then transferred to the Michigan District and was listed there 1959–67. In 1959 the word "education" appeared with her name.

E. Louise Van Matre

E. Louise Van Matre was born January 24, 1906. Her parents were John E. and Lena Starks. Her father had attended Moody Bible Institute and had served in the Spanish-American War. After Havana, Cuba, was taken, Mr. Starks returned to the United States, met Lena, married, and moved to a farm in a sparsely populated area. They started a Sunday school that grew into a Methodist Episcopal church. Louise was the second of four children—one son, three daughters. They had no electricity, so they milked their twelve cows by hand. Family Bible reading and prayer occurred each morning after breakfast. Sunday was observed very strictly—no games. Her father died in 1913 when he fell on a hay fork. The family burned corncobs in the kitchen stove and hauled coal on a sled for the heating stove. Louise attended school in a one-room schoolhouse. She walked one and one-half miles to school. When it was rainy, she drove a horse and buggy to school, and in the winter the horse pulled a sled. The sled was a large box on a board, filled with hay. A fur robe was thrown over the hay, and a bag of hot brick bats was placed near her feet with a robe over them.

By 1935 Louise went to Peru as a missionary under the Holiness Church of California (which merged with the Pilgrim Holiness Church in 1946). She served many years in Peru. She was ordained in 1940. She was listed by the California District of the Pilgrim Holiness Church 1946–62 and by the Arizona-New Mexico District 1963–65. Her service in Peru must have ended about 1967. At that time she went to her critically ill mother in South Dakota and stayed close by until she died in 1974.

In 1974 Louise moved to Beaumont, Texas. But from 1973 to 1984 she was in and out of the United States. She made several trips to Mexico, working with other missions, including a Holiness Gospel Mission. She also returned to the Wesleyan work in Peru, teaching two full years in the Bible school. She also took trips to Cuba and Spain during her busy life. In her later years, she heard from a "spiritual son" in Spain who had been a teenager when she visited there. He was now pastor of four congregations and had been traveling into France and Germany to preach the gospel.[118]

Eva Vernon

Eva Vernon was listed by the Idaho-Washington District of the Pilgrim Holiness Church from 1946 through 1957. In an overlapping fashion, she was listed by the Tennessee District in 1948 as pastor of the Silver Point Mission. And her name appeared in the records of the Texas District from 1954 through 1957.

Jennie R. Wager

Jennie Wager and her husband, William Wager, came to the Middle Atlantic States Conference of the Wesleyan Methodist Church in 1946. Both were ordained ministers who had been part of the Standard Church of Canada. They were introduced to the conference body as members of the Camden, New Jersey, church who were planning to go as missionaries. The Wagers had served in China prior to World War II. Now they were about to return as Wesleyan Methodist missionaries and open a new Wesleyan Methodist mission field.

Based on her credentials with the Standard Church, Jennie was received as an ordained minister. Her 1946 appointment was missionary-elect to China. The Wagers arrived in China October 15, 1946. They established temporary residence on the China Inland Mission compound in Kweiyang, Kweichow. They then chose Tsunyi, the second largest city in the province, as the center for their work. They moved there just before Easter 1947. Here they located a Bible school to train Chinese pastors who would plant indigenous churches. Soon seven points were being evangelized from Tsunyi. However, the political climate was growing ominous as the Nationalist government weakened and the Communists gradually took over. The Wagers held on until July 1949 and then had to leave, turning over the work to the Chinese.

The Wagers with their son Robert were now transferred to Tokyo, where they served until May 1952. They were on furlough 1952–54. From the time they had left China, they had been looking for a way to serve the Chinese people. In March 1954 they found that way, arriving in Taiwan. They worked for a time with the Taiwan Gospel Mission, which was associated with the Voice of China Mission. Then for a time they were on their own. Eventually they went to teach in the Free Methodist Bible school in southern Taiwan. They completed their service there in 1959. They were on furlough 1959 and 1960. Jennie gave a challenging message in the public service of the Middle Atlantic States Woman's Missionary Society in 1959. From 1961 on they were listed as superannuates (retired).[119]

Athelia Bards

Athelia Bards was listed as under appointment by the California-Arizona District of the Pilgrim Holiness Church 1947–56, and by the California District in 1957.

Mrs. Olive Birch

Olive Birch transferred from the Interdenominational Evangelistic Association (California) to the Oregon District of the Pilgrim Holiness Church in 1947. She was also listed by the district in 1948. The district changed its name to the Pacific Northwest District in 1949, and she was listed as unstationed (without appointment) from 1949 through 1954. Beginning in 1955 and continuing through 1967, Olive Birch was listed without a category.

Olive Kindley Coleson

Olive Kindley married Ralph J. Coleson on June 5, 1938. Both of them were fully convinced of a call to missionary service. Olive had at first believed that she must go alone in responding to her missionary call. She prepared at Marion

College, Marion, Indiana (now Indiana Wesleyan University), entering with a five-dollar registration fee and a strong faith in God. She spent four  years in ministerial training, two years in teacher training. She carried a full academic load while paying her own way by doing laundry, cleaning, ironing, clerking at Kresge's or J. C. Penney on weekends and holidays. She was part of a girls' gospel team, responsible for services at a nursing home and children's home. They held a revival at the George Street Wesleyan Methodist Church in Marion. Olive conducted a children's revival at the West Eighth Street Church at 6:00 P.M. Finally, after much searching of heart, she and Ralph decided that since both were called to missions and both had been led of the Lord to the same college, it was all right for them to team up together. It was to be a long life of varied and exciting ministries.

Olive Coleson was received by the Indiana Conference of the Wesleyan Methodist Church in 1947 to study preparatory to travel (service) and was listed from 1947 to 1952 as a missionary to India (what is now the Western India field). Many hours were spent in language study plus "mother responsibilities." And she traveled out regularly with a Bible woman to present the gospel during the week in ninety-nine Sunday schools. During the rainy season she taught Bible to young aspiring preachers.

The Colesons came home on furlough in 1952, and Olive was ordained in 1953. By 1954 their request for visas to return to India had been refused for the third time. So they accepted the pastorate of the Plymouth, Indiana, church where Olive was co-pastor 1954–58. Women were not highly respected here, so Olive kept a low profile, taught youth in Sunday school, conducted vacation Bible school, promoted missions and spoke publicly when invited to do so.

From 1958 to 1959 the Colesons served as missionaries to Sierra Leone, West Africa.

Ralph became ill and had surgery in Africa and two more surgeries after returning home. While he was still recovering from the third surgery, they became co-pastors at the Hartford City, Indiana, church, 1959–61. One man was certain he did not want a woman preacher. But Olive had the pulpit for four weeks while Ralph was recuperating. She prayed and fasted, and the man came to the altar and was saved. From 1961 to 1963, they served as co-pastors at the Kokomo, Indiana, South Wesleyan Methodist church. After a year on reserve, they began a pastorate at Monument Chapel in 1965 that continued for several years.

Olive Coleson was always heavily involved in the Woman's Missionary Society, serving on the local level as president, and the Young Missionary Workers Band (now Wesleyan Kids for Missions), serving as superintendent. She also served as the Indiana Conference Woman's Missionary Society reading course secretary, one year as editor of the prayer page of *The Wesleyan Missionary,* and was elected chair of the East Central Area WMS.

After Monument Chapel came retirement, if it could be called that. The Colesons pastored in Fort Wayne, Indiana, for one year. Then they served as the Wesleyan Seminary Foundation directors at Asbury Theological Seminary, Wilmore, Kentucky, for three years. Then they moved back to Marion, Indiana, where they conducted Sunday morning services at the Wesleyan Health Center for eight years, conducted child evangelism meetings in their home for six years, and volunteered for many other types of ministry.

The Colesons had two children, Dorothy and Richard. Ralph and Olive celebrated their sixtieth wedding anniversary in 1998.[120]

Mrs. Adah L. Fiddler

Adah L. Fiddler was an ordained minister in the Missionary Bands of the World when this small denomination merged with the Wesleyan Methodist Church in 1958. She and Miss Elsie Martin had gone to Jamaica in 1947 and started a workers training endeavor called Westmoreland Training Institute under the Missionary Bands. She was serving as the missionary secretary in the Indianapolis headquarters of the Bands at the time of the merger, and she rendered valuable service in working through details of the merger. Adah Fidler was received as an ordained minister into the Indiana Conference of the Wesleyan Methodist Church in 1958. That year she was appointed as foreign missions office worker. In 1959 she requested not to be continued as an ordained minister.[121]

Mrs. Cora Harris

Cora Harris came to the Kansas Conference of the Wesleyan Methodist Church from the United Brethren Church. Her credentials as an ordained minister were evaluated November 11, 1946, and approved subject to action by the conference itself. But it was not until the conference session of 1951 that she was actually received "on trial" based on her United Brethren credentials. In 1951 she was listed as "supernumerary" (on reserve). In 1952 she was to choose her field of service. From 1953 to 1956 she was once again on reserve, and 1956–58 she was unstationed (without appointment). In 1958 she transferred to the Oklahoma Conference. For 1958–59 she was on reserve, 1959–61 unstationed, and 1961–68 superannuated (retired).[122]

Mrs. Cora B. Kingery

Cora Kingery was received by the 1947 session of the Ohio Conference of the Wesleyan Methodist Church. She still needed to pass the exam on the *Discipline*. In 1948 she was ordained at the campground and was listed as an evangelist 1948–54. On November 12, 1951, she was granted a letter of standing, and on September 27, 1952, the letter of standing was renewed. But apparently she kept returning to the fold. From 1954 on, she was listed as superannuated (retired). Cora Kingery died August 14, 1964.

Opal E. Robinson Royalty

Opal Robinson was born October 15, 1915 in Moville, Iowa. In 1917 the family moved to Billings, Montana, where Opal married Alvin D. Royalty on June 28, 1935. They homesteaded near Cody, Wyoming, living in tents until they built a cabin. The government reclaimed the homestead, and they returned to Billings, where they were employed on a ranch. Both were converted there under the ministry of Rev. W. C. Brannon at the Joliet, Montana, Wesleyan Methodist church.

At the beginning of World War II, Opal and Alvin moved to Seattle, Washington. While there, as laypersons, they helped to organize a new Wesleyan Methodist church. In 1947, their local church recommended Opal to the Oregon Conference of the Wesleyan Methodist Church to study for the ministry. In fact, for a short time they were appointed to pastor the Aumsville, Oregon, church. But they quickly recognized their lack of preparation. They resigned and moved to Miltonvale, Kansas, to study at Miltonvale Wesleyan College (later merged into what became Oklahoma Wesleyan University, Bartlesville, Oklahoma). In 1951, having completed their courses, they transferred as conference preachers (licensed ministers) to the Oklahoma Conference. At the 1951 annual session of the conference they were both ordained.

Opal and Alvin Royalty pastored for the Oklahoma Conference for eighteen years: at the Etna church in Geary, Oklahoma 1951–57; at the Blackwell, Oklahoma church 1957–60; at the New Hope church in Ringwood, Oklahoma 1960–67; and at the Highland church in Harrison, Arkansas 1967–69.

When they retired from the pastorate at Harrison, they served at Brainerd Indian School near Hot Springs, South Dakota. In 1980 they moved into Hot Springs, and Opal became active in the local Wesleyan church there. Alvin died in 1990.

Opal Royalty served as president of the Oklahoma Conference Woman's Missionary Society 1952–60 and vice president 1964–68. She was on the conference missionary board all the years she was president. She served in other official capacities also. She had served as the local WMS president, led the youth ministries and taught Sunday school in each church they pastored, and preached whenever Alvin could not. Opal E. Royalty died March 7, 1997, at the age of 81.[123]

Velma Sarles

Velma Sarles was listed by the Indiana District of the Pilgrim Holiness Church 1947–50 and by the Southern Indiana District 1951–58. She was ordained in 1947. She was listed as pastor at New Albany, Indiana, in 1951.

Lylia Breasure Shrieves

Lylia (also spelled "Lydia" or "Lida") Breasure lived across the street from the Pilgrim Holiness church in Laurel, Delaware. She was a wife and mother in her middle twenties when she was gloriously converted in a revival service at the church. She had one child, a daughter, who died soon after Lylia's conversion. Then her husband, who seemed to want no part of church, divorced her. She held a personal conviction that even though divorced, she could not remarry as long as her ex-husband lived.

During a missionary service at Denton, Maryland camp, Lylia was among many who presented themselves at the altar for whatever God wanted them to do. Later she was privileged to go to South America for a short-term ministry there. She completed her studies and was ordained as a minister.

Lylia took a group of people from the Gumboro, Delaware, Pilgrim Holiness church and planted a church in Millsboro, Delaware. The church started in a Celotex building with a wood shavings floor. After the church grew, she led them through a building program and built a new church in the early 1950s. All of this was accomplished as a bivocational/single pastor. In 1947, Lylia submitted the following annual report: services 3, prayer meetings 30, cottage prayer meetings 3, other services 37, times preached 37, visits 65, dealt with 40 souls personally, support received $105.50, regenerated 15, sanctified 12. It is unclear whether she was pastoring yet, since four years later in 1951 she was still a third-year licentiate.

Lylia also pastored at Goldsboro, Maryland, and late in life in Florida. While at Goldsboro, she invited a little boy to church. He was saved and grew up to be a preacher, Rev. Ken Deusa. After the death of her ex-husband, Lylia married Rev. Braden Shrieves, and they labored together for the Lord.[124]

Mrs. H. L. Solter

Mrs. H. L. Solter was apparently ordained in 1922 by the Kansas District of the Pilgrim Holiness Church. The record of her pastoral service began in 1947. She was co-pastor of Big Bow, Kansas, 1947–52. From 1952 to 1954 she was living in Johnson, Kansas, in 1955 in Portland, Oregon, and in 1957–58 in Johnson, Kansas, again. From 1958 to 1967 she was co-pastor at Johnson, Kansas. From 1967 to 1968 she was co-pastor at Goodland, Kansas. She retired in 1968.

Mabel Sweet

Mabel Sweet was listed by the New York District of the Pilgrim Holiness Church as an ordained minister in 1947 and 1948. For both years she was listed as unstationed (without appointment).

Blanche Ione Tedrow

Blanche Ione Tedrow was born July 9, 1902, in Shoals, Martin County, Indiana. She was converted in March 1927 and sanctified in December 1943. She attended God's Bible School, Cincinnati, Ohio, graduating in 1931. Following graduation, she pastored for three years in Indiana. She also served for a time as office manager of the Midnight Cry Publishing Corporation. At some point she pastored the Wesleyan Hilltop Chapel in Elizabethtown, Kentucky.

The Indiana District of the Pilgrim Holiness Church listed Blanche Tedrow as an ordained missionary in 1947 and continued to list her through 1950. The Southern Indiana District listed her 1951–67. Her first term of service as a missionary began in the autumn of 1947 when she was appointed as a teacher to the Jembo Mission in Northern Rhodesia (now Zambia). Her second term began in 1953. In June 1957 she was transferred to Chabbobboma Mission in the Zambezi River valley area. Her last service in Zambia was in 1962–72. She was in charge of the home economics departments of the schools where she served. But she also did village visitation, preaching and vacation Bible schools. She also taught English, Bible, and Sunday school classes.

Blanche Tedrow declared,

> I am glad that I obeyed the call to Africa. I have found it best to stay in the Lord's will, and from it comes a peace which keeps one encouraged.

> Missionary work is the most gratifying of any that I have done. To see a poor, frightened scantily-clad African girl come into the boarding school, and in a few years go out a beautiful Christian young woman, ready to take her place among mothers and leaders of the coming generation, brings me much satisfaction.

Blanche Tedrow passed away October 15, 1999, at the age of ninety.[125]

Nona Tenney

Nona Tenney is listed in the records of the West Virginia District of the Pilgrim Holiness Church, 1947–62. She was the pastor at Cinco 1947–53 and at Cool Branch Heights 1953–62. It appears that she also pastored at Nitro 1954–55 while pastoring at Cool Branch Heights. Nona Tenney died in 1962 while pastoring at Cool Branch Heights.

Lola Thornburg

Lola Thornburg's name appears on the records of the California District of the Pilgrim Holiness Church 1947–57. She was an ordained minister. She served as a missionary to Bolivia for nine years, even though she was in ill health. She was never able to return to the field but sent necessary items there. She also taught Bible in what became Western Pilgrim College in El Monte, California (later merged into what became Oklahoma Wesleyan University, Bartlesville, Oklahoma). Lola Thornburg died July 5, 1956.

Erma Toma

In 1947 the Ohio Conference of the Wesleyan Methodist Church received Erma Toma. She was to complete her study of the *Discipline* and Wesleyan Methodist Church History. She was ordained in 1948. From 1948 to 1949 and 1950–51 she was listed as an evangelist.

From 1951 to 1957 she pastored the Hyde Park church (later Oakridge) in Dayton, Ohio. She began as a supply pastor October 7, 1951, and became full-time pastor May 11, 1952. There were good increases in attendance, finance and membership. The property on Savanna Avenue was sold for a good price and another property was purchased at the corner of Circle Road and Oakridge Drive. Plans were underway for a new church building. In 1953 Erma Toma conducted devotions at one of the conference sittings—a searching and challenging message. The Holy Spirit's approval accompanied the message of truth. A season of prayer followed. Spontaneous shouts, ringing testimonies and resounding praises swept aside the order of business for a time. The missionary board reported that Erma's church was making remarkable progress in every way, and the church was taken out from under the board's supervision. On May 23, 1954, the new Dayton Oakridge masonry structure was dedicated.

The 1957 conference appointed Erma Toma as a conference evangelist. But on October 1, 1957, she was appointed pastor of Zanesville, Ohio, South Church and on December 10, 1957, pastor of Zanesville North Terrace church. She resigned the North Terrace church June 14, 1958, but continued pastoring the South church until 1965. On June 28, 1963, Zanesville South Church was dedicated with a packed house in attendance. Erma Toma was described as both pastor and builder of this church.

From 1965 to 1966, Erma Toma was a conference evangelist. She then pastored

Senecaville 1966–68. Again she was appointed to evangelism in 1968.[126]

Norah Jane Gevsenbach Witthuhn

Norah Jane Gevsenbach married Ferdinand Witthuhn in 1947. In 1948 they entered service to the Wesleyan Methodist Church as missionaries to Haiti. On August 1, 1951, while on furlough (home ministries), they were both ordained by the Nebraska Conference. They served four terms in Haiti, completing their work there in 1965. They toured the Nebraska Conference for missions in 1956–57. Norah was featured in the conference's public service of the Woman's Missionary Society and spoke in that service in 1963. Subsequent to their service in Haiti, they pastored at Sidney, Nebraska, for five years, retiring in 1971. Ferdinand died July 17, 1987, at the age of eighty-four.[127]

Bernice L. Woodward

Bernice (Mrs. John) Woodward was listed by the Kentucky Conference of the Wesleyan Methodist Church in 1947 as a conference preacher (licensed minister). She was to pursue the course of study and was appointed as assistant pastor of Highland Park. She continued under that appointment until 1949. In 1948 she was ordained. In 1949 she led devotions at one sitting of the conference. From 1949 to 1952, she served as assistant pastor at West Frankfort. On July 30, 1952, the Woodwards transferred to the Ohio Conference.

From 1952 to 1956, John and Bernice were listed as pastors at Marion, Ohio. From 1956 to 1966, they were listed as pastors at the Silver Street church in Marion. In June 1957, the church celebrated their remodeled and enlarged parsonage, the entire church basement remodeled, a new front entrance added, Sunday school rooms built along the entire east side of the church, and new pews. The Woodwards withdrew from the denomination and the conference June 30, 1966.[128]

Gleda Abraham Davis

Gleda Abraham was born January 30, 1910. She and her husband, Paul, served an independent church in Ohio prior to being received into the ministry of the Wesleyan Methodist Church. Gleda was received by the Indiana Conference in 1948 and was listed as studying preparatory to travel 1948–51. From 1951 to 1953 she was co-pastor with her husband at Fowlerton, Indiana. From 1953 to 1956, she was co-pastor at Martinsville. In 1956 she was appointed as a conference evangelist. From 1957 to 1960 she served as co-pastor at Kirklin. In 1960 she was ordained, along with her husband and her oldest son, Richard. From 1960 to 1961 she was to choose her own field of labor, and from 1961 to 1966 she was on reserve. But in 1966 she and Paul returned to Kirklin a second time. She was co-pastor 1966–68 and then was listed as associate pastor. The Abrahams later pastored the Lewis Creek church.

The Abrahams had four sons: Richard, Ronnie, Roderick, and Roger; and two daughters, Rita and Roberta. Roger also became an ordained minister in The Wesleyan Church.

Richard said his mother had three great strengths: simple hope and faith, compassion, and love for her husband and children. Concerning her faith, he told of her husband going ahead to conference one year while she and the six children were to come later to camp meeting. At the proper time, she got everyone in the car, but it would not start. She got everyone out of the car and had them to kneel by the car. She told the Lord that Paul would be expecting them and there was no way to contact him. "Please start this car for your glory," she prayed. They all got back into the car. She turned the key, expecting the car to start—and it did!

Gleda had many health problems, and these problems resulted in ministry and in glory to God. In most of her hospital stays, a roommate or hospital personnel was saved because of her witness. She was instantly healed from cancer and instantly healed after brain surgery. She was confined for twenty-six weeks. God was honored in all of her illnesses.

In Richard's opinion, his father was without doubt the steady, firm leader of the family and the church in spite of the fact that Gleda was more outgoing. Even as co-pastor, she respected her husband as the leader. She was a faithful mother in spite of the busy schedule and the needs of the church people.

Shirley Tharp was a girl in the Kirklin church where the Abrahams served for two periods. She married Roderick, Gleda's son, between the two pastorates. She said this about her mother-in-law:

Gleda was a people person, and her gifts in this area were not confined to any particular age group. With teens she was at her best one on one. For children it was a real treat when she told one of her stories at church. The children were not the only ones entranced as she made the story characters seem real. Gleda planned her work around the needs of the church people. She drove elderly people to doctors' appointments, grocery shopping, and so on.

Since Paul had to work because the churches they pastored could not pay a full salary, Gleda did most of the personal work; however, when there was illness or an emergency, they both were there.

Paul did most of the pulpit ministry. Her turns in the pulpit probably numbered around once a quarter, if that often. The difference in their personalities really came through in the pulpit. He was a reserved and serious type of person, whereas Gleda was outgoing and humorous. Paul would announce two to three weeks ahead of time when Gleda was going to preach. He seemed to enjoy the build-up, and when time came for her sermon, he enjoyed listening just as much as the rest, for she used humor in her delivery.

Paul Abraham passed away April 26, 1978 at the age of sixty-eight. After his death, Gleda later married Charles Davis. She passed away January 8, 1983.[129]

Beulah Andrews

Beulah (Mrs. Clayburn M.) Andrews was listed by the Indiana District of the Pilgrim Holiness Church as an ordained minister in 1946 and 1947 and was pictured with her husband in the 1948 records of that district. She was also listed in the records of the Alabama-West Florida District of the Pilgrim Holiness Church in

1956–59 and in the records of the Alabama-Northwest Florida District in 1960.

Mrs. Howard L. Bland

The records of the Kansas District of the Pilgrim Holiness Church show that Mrs. Howard L. Bland was ordained by that district in 1948. She served as co-pastor at Sharon Springs, Kansas, 1949–50 and co-pastor at Fall River 1950–52. From 1952 to 1962, she was listed by the Oklahoma-Texas District and from 1964 to 1968 by the Central District.

Mary V. Gursky Sims and Louise Hamilton Harrell Close

Mary Gursky was involved in mountain missions in Preston, Kentucky, at least as early as 1947. She was the principal speaker that year in the public Woman's Missionary Society service in the Ohio Conference of the Wesleyan Methodist Church. She was teamed in Preston with Louise Hamilton. Louise had been received by the Indiana Conference in 1942 to pursue the course of study, and beginning in 1945 was listed as serving in Kentucky. Mary was ordained by the Allegheny Conference in 1948 and was listed as serving at Preston. Louise withdrew from the credentialing process in 1948. Mary took a letter of standing from the Allegheny Conference and was listed by the Kentucky District of the Pilgrim Holiness Church in 1949, 1950, and 1951. Then Mary dropped out of the credentialed ministry. The work at Preston had never been brought under the Wesleyan Methodist denomination. The two ladies proceeded to develop a lasting congregation that continued to serve its community long after the ladies departed. In the late 1950s, Louise and Mary sought secular employment in Indianapolis and helped quite significantly, especially in children's work, in the church plant in Lawrence, Indiana, and later when it relocated as the Eastlawn Wesleyan Methodist Church in Indianapolis. Louise eventually married Thaddeus Harrell, and after his death Rev. Ray Close, longtime minister in the Pilgrim Holiness Church. Mary eventually married Frank Sims.[130]

Pearl Keysor

Pearl (Mrs. James) Keysor was ordained by the Champlain Conference of the Wesleyan Methodist Church (now Eastern New York-New England District of The Wesleyan Church) in 1948. She was listed as assistant pastor at the Hadley church in New York 1948–50, and as assistant pastor at the church in Macomb, New York 1950–65. From 1965 to 1968 she was on reserve and then was listed as superannuated (retired).[131]

Mrs. J. Harry Smith

Mrs. J. Harry Smith was listed in the records of the Pennsylvania and New Jersey District of the Pilgrim Holiness Church in 1948 as a licensed minister. From 1948 to 1950 she was pastor at Turnersville, New Jersey, and was also listed as pastor there in 1952. She was ordained in 1943. District records continued to list her from 1948 through 1961.

Edna Marie Wolf Wildey

Edna Marie Wolf was born May 17, 1922, in a rural community about seven and one-half miles southwest of Bluffton, Indiana. The family lived there through the first half of Edna's second grade. The Great Depression was on. Her parents could not pay interest on the farm mortgage, let alone  make full payments. So they lost the farm. The Wolfs moved in with Mrs. Wolf's parents and Edna attended a one-room school the second half of second grade and the first half of third grade. At the end of the year they bought their farm back for half of what they had paid the first time. Edna grew up on the farm, helping with the chores.

Edna was the middle child—four girls, one boy (the youngest). Her parents were Christians. Church was a great part of their lives, along with the daily family altar with its Bible reading and prayer. As far back as she could remember, Edna wanted to be what God wanted her to be. But her spiritual life was up and down until early in 1942, at the age of nineteen and a half, she completely surrendered to the Lord.

While working at General Electric in Fort Wayne, Edna believed that God placed a call on her heart to go to college and study to be a minister. She attended Olivet Nazarene College in Kankakee, Illinois, for two and one-half years. Then she met Thomas Wildey. Tom (as he was usually known) was in the Air Force and received an honorable discharge. God had also called him to the ministry. They were married August 7, 1945. Both then enrolled at Marion College, Marion, Indiana (now Indiana Wesleyan University). While there they lost their only child (a daughter) at birth in September 1946. Both of them earned bachelor of religion and A. B. in religion degrees. And Edna earned teaching requirements for high school.

While still in college, Edna and Tom co-pastored the Wesleyan Methodist church in Sims, Indiana, 1948–50. They were ordained together by the Indiana Conference in 1950. They served as co-pastors of four other churches: Shiloh, near Plymouth, Indiana (1950–55), Lancaster (1955–60), Greentown (1960–64), and Albion (two different times of seven years each for a total of fourteen years—the first time began in 1964). All of their churches grew significantly, and there were several building programs. Thomas Wildey also served for a five-year period as a general evangelist.

Near the end of July 1953, while in a building program at Shiloh, Tom was seriously injured in an automobile accident. He was bedfast and in a body cast for nearly a year and was permanently crippled. It was a miracle year as God and His people made it possible for Tom and Edna to pay all their huge medical bills. And best of all, Tom refused to let the accident cripple his ministry and effectiveness.

Edna filled the pulpit that year, morning and evening. Tom was in demand as an evangelist even while pastoring, and she filled the pulpit in those times as well. The bone surgeon advised Edna to pursue teaching in public schools to make sure they could make it if Tom became permanently incapacitated. So she started teaching in the fall of 1954 in high school—she had a state license for that. But in 1955 they moved to Lancaster, and there were no high school openings nearby. An elementary position was open three miles away. She took it and returned first to Marion College and then to Ball State University to qualify herself for elementary teaching. She did that and more, graduating in 1958 with a master's degree from Ball State. She taught for thirty years along with all the work of being a co-pastor.

After Edna retired, she and Tom went to Florida for seven winters. They asked the Lord to use them there even while they had a good time, and He did. Tom had often said that he hoped he would die preaching or fishing. It turned out to be the latter. On July 21, 1994, he was fishing in the state park about five miles from Albion. He had a massive heart attack and went to be with the Lord. Edna kept busy after his passing, doing visitation in the church and community, calling on the sick, elderly and shut-ins and those in the hospital. Tom had always conducted many funerals, and Edna was surprised after his passing that now she was busy conducting funerals.

Her comment on her life in the ministry was this:

> If I had it to do over, would I want to be a minister in God's work? I would answer with a "resounding YES!" It has been such a joy and so rewarding to be a part of God's work and His will for my life. Thank God for all the times that I've invested time in Kingdom's interest. I even feel more this way as I am nearing my heavenly home, going to be with God the Father, Jesus Christ the Son, and the Holy Spirit, and my loved ones, and the Family of God.[132]

Agatha Adams

Agatha Adams was born February 1, 1916, in Custer City, Pennsylvania. She graduated from Wilmington College and from God's Bible School in Cincinnati, Ohio. She and Arthur T. Adams met at God's Bible School in the 1930s. They were married on August 25, 1940, at a camp meeting in Louisiana where A. T. (as he was commonly known) was serving as evangelist. They had one daughter, Loretta (Lemke).

Agatha was ordained by the Louisiana/ Alabama District of the Pilgrim Holiness Church in 1948. She and her husband served as pastors at the Simons, Louisiana church 1949–50. From 1950 to 1959, Agatha served with her husband in the Pittsburgh District, pastoring the Cherryville, Pittsburgh, Elizabeth, and Washington churches. From 1959 to 1962, she served with her husband in the Western Ohio District, pastoring the Leesburg and Chillicothe churches. From 1962 to 1968 they served together in the Eastern District, pastoring in Delaware at Dover and Millsboro.

Following retirement, Agatha was active in Wesleyan Women at the Leesburg, Ohio, Wesleyan church. Later the Adamses attended the Cypress Wesleyan Church in Columbus, Ohio. The Adamses celebrated their sixtieth wedding anniversary in 2000. Agatha Adams died December 26, 2001.[133]

Elizabeth Ashcroft

Elizabeth Ashcroft was ordained by the Oklahoma-Texas District of the Pilgrim Holiness Church in 1949. According to that district's records, she was under appointment until she died in an accident in Bethany, Oklahoma, June 13, 1956 or 1957.

Mrs. Nina Dean

The records of the South Georgia Conference of the Wesleyan Methodist Church for 1949 indicate that Nina Dean was received as an ordained minister pending receipt of her credentials. She was appointed as a conference evangelist.

Esther Deisker

Esther Deisker (or "Deisher") served under the Illinois District of the Pilgrim Holiness Church. From 1949 to 1960, Sherman and Esther Deisker pastored the Olney, Illinois, church. Prior to 1959, Sherman found a group of people located in what was called Mt. Hope. It had been a Free Methodist church, but it had no pastor and was not holding services. Sherman and members of the group conducted prayer services and other meetings. Sherman Deisker died in 1960. Esther finished out the year as pastor at Olney and was so listed until 1963. She was ordained in 1963. The church at Mt. Hope was organized in 1960. The building was in bad condition. In the spring of 1963 while Esther was apparently pastoring both Olney and Mt. Hope, the Mt. Hope congregation signed a contract with the trustees of the "Methodist Episcopal Society" for the use of Amity Chapel. Mt. Hope Pilgrim Holiness church became known then as Amity Chapel. Esther Deisker was listed by the district as pastor at Amity Chapel, 1963–64. She continued to be listed by the district until 1968, being designated "inactive" in 1964 and 1965.[134]

Judith Hofen

Judith (Mrs. O. R.) Hofen was ordained by the Kansas District of the Pilgrim Holiness Church in 1949. Kansas District records list her from 1948 to 1959. She was listed as co-pastor at Argonia, Kansas, 1949–53 and co-pastor at Osawatomie, Kansas, 1954–59. She then transferred to the Oklahoma District. Oklahoma records show her at Blackwell, Oklahoma, 1960–62, designating her as co-pastor in 1962. The Central District records list her 1963–64, 1966–68, designating her as a pastor in 1963 and as inactive in 1968.

Deborah Hoover Howard

Deborah Hoover was born February 22, 1910 at May's Landing, New Jersey. She found her Lord and Savior in May's Landing. She attended Allentown Bible Institute, Allentown, Pennsylvania (later Eastern Pilgrim College/United Wesleyan College). She served for years as an evangelist and children's worker. It was said that she was never too busy to gather children around her and tell them the story of Jesus in word and song.

Deborah Hoover was ordained by the Pennsylvania and New Jersey District of the Pilgrim Holiness Church in 1949. She pastored the Gloucester City, New Jersey, church (in the Philadelphia metropolitan area), 1948–63. The failing health of her parents caused her to return to Millville, New Jersey, to care for them. But she commuted back and forth between her parents and her pastorate. She married Alonzo Howard November 24, 1962. Deborah Hoover died October 5, 1963, at the age of fifty-three.[135]

Kathryn Savage Johnson

Kathryn Savage was born in 1923 to Rev. and Mrs. L. W. Savage, ordained ministers in the Pilgrim Holiness Church. Kathryn joined the Savage Family ministry team at an early age, singing her first solo when she was eleven. They pastored and did home missionary work, conducting meetings in storefronts and rented halls, and opening several closed churches. In the summers they held revival meetings over much of the Eastern Shore (Maryland, Delaware and the part of Virginia east of the Chesapeake Bay), using the "gospel tent." Two Nazarene churches were established. Kathryn pastored the Seaford Church of the Nazarene for a short time. The tent was cut down on occasions. The family traveled at first by Model T and then Model A.

Kathryn Savage attended Allentown Bible Institute, Allentown, Pennsylvania (later Pilgrim Eastern College/United Wesleyan College), graduating from the academy and completing one year of theological studies. She also earned college credits from the University of Maryland and Salisbury University. She graduated from the School of Practical Nursing with a Maryland license. She was ordained by the Eastern District of the Pilgrim Holiness Church.

Kathryn Savage married Webster Johnson, October 3, 1946, at Blades, Delaware, with the ceremony performed by her father. Kathryn teamed with her sister, Rev. Ruth Savage Morris, as the "Savage Sisters," holding revivals extensively on the East Coast. They used guitars, sang and preached. After Kathryn married, Webster assisted her in singing in local revival meetings and community churches.

Kathryn became employed by the state of Maryland at a psychiatric facility. Her duties included service as director of public information/relations. At first there was no chaplain, so she held weekly church services, conducted group therapy sessions and buried the dead when no one claimed a patient's body. Years later a chaplain was employed and she assisted him as necessary. Once a patient handed her a letter addressed to God. All it contained was "Dear God," a long blank space and the patient's name. She told him that he had not told God anything. The patient replied, "I don't have to—He can read between the lines."

While employed at the hospital, Kathryn pastored two Pilgrim Holiness churches: Centreville, Maryland, and Emmanuel Chapel in Trappe, Maryland. She won a Governor's Award and nationwide recognition through the National League of Nursing for a project she developed known as "Outreach," to aid the seclusive, long-term mental patient.

Kathryn wrote a booklet, *A Sinner Saved by Grace*, the life story of her father. She used the $1,000 she earned from the book's sale to provide two $500 scholarships to young men going into the ministry. One of the young men was Thomas E. Armiger, later General Superintendent of The Wesleyan Church. In 1996, their fiftieth anniversary year, Kathryn and Webster Johnson set up the K. and W. Johnson Scholarship Fund to help those going into the ministry, both male and female.

Kathryn's hobbies included the world's most extensive collection of Christmas seals and membership in the Titanic Historical Society. She served as district historian for sixteen years, retiring in 1997. She had gathered enough materials to establish an archives for what was now the Chesapeake District of The Wesleyan Church. She was still very active in her local church in Cambridge, Maryland, as well as other community churches.[136]

Orpha Mae Case Lehman

Orpha Mae Case was born March 8, 1909, in Dowling, Michigan. She was converted at age

fifteen. She believed God had a special work for her, so after high school she began to save money for Bible school. At God's Bible School, Cincinnati, Ohio, she surrendered all to the Lord and testified that He definitely sanctified her. She was unable to continue at the school and for seven years she worked as a housemaid. A door opened to go to college, and she worked her way through Eastern Nazarene College, graduating in 1941 with an A. B. in biblical literature.

She wondered, "What next, Lord?" She thought maybe she was to be a minister's wife. But no minister came around—except one she was always glad she didn't marry. Instead, there came a call to teach in Bible college. For the next six years she served Colorado Springs Bible College (later merged into what became Oklahoma Wesleyan University, Bartlesville, Oklahoma), and Owosso College, Owosso, Michigan (later merged into what became Indiana Wesleyan University, Marion, Indiana).

Next came a very definite call to the mission field as a teacher. She earned a B. S. in education at George Pepperdine College in Los Angeles in 1948. At some point she also studied at Butler University in Indianapolis.

At the age of forty, Orpha Case boarded the *S.S. Mauritania* in New York City on April 8, 1949, bound for Africa as a Pilgrim Holiness missionary. No one met her in Capetown, nor was there a message as to how to travel the eight hundred miles to the mission station. So for the first four years, she served at Mt. Frere in the Cape Province, at the Pilgrim Bible Institute, teaching in the Christian Homecraft School. About two weeks after her arrival she was told she was to preach the Sunday morning sermon in the native church. She replied that she was a teacher, not a preacher. She was told she was now a missionary and all missionaries took their turn. She preached, and there was a whole altar full of

From Wartime to Post-War Boom

seekers. The single teachers liked to go to the outstation churches, some of which were in a rugged, mountainous area. Orpha would drive the jeep for the group, and she preached the message.

Then she was transferred to what is now Zambia, where she taught Bible and English in the primary school. Then she equipped the new home economics building and taught sewing with an African assistant.

When Orpha Case returned to the States on furlough (home ministries), she was ordained in 1958 at the age of forty-nine, by the Michigan District of the Pilgrim Holiness Church. When she went back to Africa, the Pilgrim Holiness and Brethren in Christ Churches had joined together to build a Christian high school. She taught there until she retired in 1976 at the age of sixty-seven. She was involved in chapels and other services. She traveled as far as fifty and eighty miles once a month to outstations. During school vacations, the teachers would hold vacation Bible schools in the daytime for men, women and children, with revival services at night.

When Orpha retired, she wondered what to do next. She eventually returned to her home church in Battle Creek, Michigan, and for the next six years she worked with her church in a ministry of calling on shut-ins and living with elderly people as a housekeeper.

That door closed, and Orpha Case at age seventy-five said, "What next?" She felt a real tug and almost a homesickness to return to Africa. She told the Lord that she wanted a husband to go with her this time, and if He provided one that would be a miracle. The Lord said, "Expect a miracle!" Shortly afterward, a picture fell into her hand of an old friend, Rev. Orai I. Lehman, with a group of people in Africa. She knew that he had retired, had lost his first wife (see Dorothy Dike Johnson Lehman) and had returned to Africa as a volunteer missionary. She thought he looked lonely, so she wrote him a letter. He replied, and correspondence continued. Both attended the 1984 Festival of Missions in conjunction with the General Conference of The Wesleyan Church in Columbus, Ohio. They greeted each other briefly. The Festival ended, and Orpha stayed for one day of the General

Conference. Passing through the lunchroom, she saw Orai I. Lehman sitting with a friend. She stopped to greet him, the other man disappeared, and Orai hurried to get her a cup of coffee. When she left the lunchroom she had a date for the evening service—her first date in fifty years. Three months later Orai met her plane in Johannesburg. They were married in a church near the mission station.

Orai and Orpha Lehman served six and one-half years as volunteer missionaries. She did the housekeeping. Orai built two church buildings, kept the mission home in repair, preached, and encouraged the Africans. They retired to Bartlesville, Oklahoma, in 1995 when Orpha was eighty-four.

Orpha Lehman went to be with her Lord, January 9, 1999, at the age of eighty-nine.[137]

Betty L. Miller

Betty L. Miller served under three Pilgrim Holiness districts in the northwestern part of the United States. From 1948 through 1954, she was listed in the records of the Oregon District. That district ordained her in 1948. In 1949 she was listed as pastor at Eugene, Oregon, with Evelyn Retenburgh. In 1951 and 1952, Betty was listed as pastor at Eugene. In 1953 she was apparently in El Monte, California. From 1955 through 1959, Betty was listed in the records of the Idaho-Washington District, with no details as to her ministries. From 1960 through 1967 she was listed in the records of the Northwest District as pastor at Raymond, Washington.

Ruth Savage Morris

Ruth Savage was the sister of Kathryn Savage Johnson. The story of Ruth's parentage, early involvement in ministry, and her teaming with Kathryn as the "Savage Sisters" has already largely been covered in Kathryn's story.

Ruth married J. Reed Morris on December 21, 1939. She had already been active in ministry, and by 1949 she was pastoring Pilgrim Holiness

319

churches. Her first two churches were apparently Broome's Island, Maryland, and Bishop Head, Maryland. J. Reed Morris had worked as a waterman. But when Ruth Savage Morris moved to pastor Laurel, Delaware, Reed also became convinced he was called to preach. He drove back and forth to Allentown, Pennsylvania, to get his degree.

The Morrises served two other pastorates, Georgetown, Delaware, and Delmar, Maryland. They served over forty years as registrars of the Denton Camp in Denton, Maryland. In 1971 Ruth Morris donated a kidney to her daughter, Ruth Ann. The Morrises celebrated their fiftieth wedding anniversary in 1989. In 1999 Ruth Morris completed fifty years of active ministry. In their retirement years, the Morrises served as hospital chaplains.[138]

Mrs. Hazel Cline Perry

Hazel Cline Perry's service is recorded in the records of the Champlain Conference (now Eastern New York-New England District) of the Wesleyan Methodist Church. The conference ordained her in 1949 and appointed her as an evangelist 1949–50. She served as pastor at West Sandgate, Vermont, 1950–51. She was appointed as an evangelist 1951–59. She was to choose her own field of labor 1959–61. From 1961 on she was listed as superannuated (retired).

There is also a reference to Hazel Perry as an ordained minister in the records of the New York District of the Pilgrim Holiness Church in 1955.

Emma Mitchell Rundell

Emma Mitchell was born in Carlisle, Kentucky, November 2, 1919. She was converted in 1936 and sanctified in 1939. She prepared for missionary service at Frankfort Pilgrim College, Frankfort, Indiana (later merged into United Wesleyan College, Allentown, Pennsylvania), Asbury College, and Butler University. While at Frankfort, she served as secretary to the president for four years and also served for some time as dean of women.

Emma married Merton Russell Rundell Jr. on June 7, 1948, in Covington, Kentucky. They had two children, Mary Elgra and Merton Russell III. They were ordained together by the Kentucky District of the Pilgrim Holiness Church in August 1949. They began their world missions service in November 1951, with Merton in charge of the Peruvian Training School in Chiclayo, Peru. Emma assisted him in that responsibility.

The Rundells continued to serve in Peru until 1967. In 1967 they were released to work outside the Pilgrim Holiness Church.[139]

Annie Laurie Eubanks Carlson Thompson

Annie Laurie Eubanks was born in Birmingham, Alabama, November 3, 1926. She was saved in June 1940, and soon thereafter joined the Pilgrim Holiness Church. She was sanctified in 1945, and in the same year she believed she had a definite call to missionary work.

Annie prepared for her missionary service by attending Intercession Bible College, Intercession City, Florida; People's Bible College, Greensboro, North Carolina; and received diplomas from Kingswood College, Kingswood, Kentucky; Tate Springs, Tennessee; and the Evangelical Teachers Training Association in Chicago. Her business  training enabled her to work her way through school, serving as typist, stenographer, receptionist, order clerk, and private secretary. She was ordained by the Alabama District of the Pilgrim Holiness Church in 1949.

During her Bible school years, Annie did considerable evangelistic work and conducted vacation Bible schools, often doing a revival and Bible school concurrently. Services were held in churches, a storefront mission, and a rescue mission. Eventually she served in this way in Alabama, Indiana, Illinois, Louisiana, Pennsylvania, Florida, Tennessee, Kentucky, Barbados, St. Vincent, Guyana, Suriname, Trinidad, Zambia, Swaziland, Pondoland, and South Africa. Also while living and teaching in Columbus, Ohio, she served for a number of months as interim pastor at Cypress Wesleyan Church.

In November 1949 Annie Eubanks and Violet Harbert (Manning) were appointed to open Pilgrim Holiness missionary work on the island of St. Vincent in the West Indies. Services were held under trees, under a house built on stilts, and in a rented vacant store building. Churches were organized at Layou and Buccament Bay where a stone building was constructed. Converts were taken by pickup truck for services in outlying villages. There were so many requests for Sunday schools that they had to operate one "Monday school" on Monday after school hours. A number of preaching points were opened during the four years spent on St. Vincent.

The transforming nature of the conversions experienced by the islanders was revealed when they approached a plantation owner about purchasing a piece of his land for a church building in Buccament. He asked what was needed and where. A hillside spot overlooking the bay was chosen. When the paper work was completed and they arrived to make payment, he said, "My workers who attend your church do not steal from me anymore. They are different. They do good work. So I want to thank you by giving you the land for the church. Furthermore, when your people get stones from the river, have them laid aside, and when there is a load, let me know, and I will have them picked up and delivered to your site free of charge."

Native foods brought interesting experiences. Once Annie was presented a pan filled with tiny live guppy-like fish called "tre-tre's." When she asked how to kill and clean them since they were so small, she was told, "You doesn't kill them, ma'am. You just mix 'em up with flour and egg and fry 'em. The hot skillet does kill 'em." All

Annie could think of were those many little eyes looking up at her from the skillet!

Returning home, Annie Eubanks was involved in deputation (home ministries) and convention work. Then in 1954, the general board of the Pilgrim Holiness Church appointed her to serve as general missionary society director. Her responsibilities included promotion of the societies on the national level, preparing program books for both groups, arranging reading courses, overseeing the sorting, preparing and shipping of clothing and supplies to foreign fields, and editing the *Missionary Society News Sheet* and *The Junior Missionary*. She served in this capacity for eight years.

On March 33, 1962, Annie married a layman, Otto E. Carlson, and moved to Kane, Pennsylvania. A struggling little Pilgrim Holiness church in Dubois, Pennsylvania, was looking for a pastor. Although Annie Eubanks Carlson lived two hours away, she was asked to fill in. Ultimately she was voted in as full-time pastor and served there for five years. Otto Carlson was so supportive of her ministry that they moved to Dubois and he commuted eighty miles each way to his job in Bradford, Pennsylvania.

After Otto Carlson passed away, Annie married another layman, Garth C. Thompson. He had been a Sunday school superintendent and teacher. He became a member of the local church board at Brooksville, Florida, and a member of the Wesleyan Bible Conference board of directors. After he passed away, Annie Thompson continued to reside in Wesleyan Village at Brooksville and to teach an adult Sunday school class at the Wesleyan church.[140]

Eunice Rachel Bennett Vreugdenhil

Eunice Bennett was born at Wright, Minnesota, June 11, 1904. She grew up on a farm in South Dakota, the oldest child with five brothers. Her parents did not attend church. She attended Sunday school with some neighbors. She was afraid of thunderstorms, was afraid to die, and had an experience with the Lord that

freed her from the fear of death. But she lost out because she had no instruction and little church contact, and her brothers teased her, causing her to become angry. Later she went forward at a Free Methodist Church. She received the witness of the Spirit that she was saved later in the church yard. One evening, August 9, at age seventeen, she went to the pasture to pray. She opened her New Testament and read, "Go and prepare." The Lord used it to call her to His service. The church people began praying for her but her parents were opposed. She ended up at Wessington Springs High School. She then taught school for a while.

Eventually she enrolled at God's Bible School in Cincinnati, Ohio. She was sanctified there. She then worked in an orphanage in Kentucky. The Lord led her back to God's Bible School, and she did missionary work in Cincinnati. During prayer time in chapel she testified that the Holy Spirit had spoken to her, "Woe is me, if I preach not the gospel." She taught in vacation Bible school that next summer and preached in the evening at a Free Methodist church. The Free Methodist church gave her a local preacher's license. Then she believed the Lord was leading her into mountain missions in Kentucky. She served there 1930–33, walking and riding horseback to visit the people. She lived with them, as it was not safe for her to stay in the parsonage alone. The young men were rowdy and disturbed the church services, but eventually there was a breakthrough, and men were laying their tobacco and guns on the altar and praying, sometimes several nights, until they got the victory. Some preachers reminded her that the Bible said for women to be silent in the church. She responded, "The Lord called me, so what are you going to do about it?"

On March 23, 1934, Eunice married Harmen Vreugdenhil in Mitchell, South Dakota. The Vreugdenhils then went to South Africa under the Hephzibah Faith Missionary Association and served two years there. Their oldest son, Marion, was born there. Later there were three other children added to the family: Ralph, Dorothy (Tollen), and David. After returning to the United States, the Vreugdenhils served pastorates in Nebraska and New Mexico. They eventually left the Hephzibah Faith Missionary Association and joined the Free Methodist Church. Harmen served as a Free Methodist pastor for a time, completing a three-year pastorate at Ortley, South Dakota. He suffered severely from sinus problems and was advised by his physician to leave the lake country for a drier climate. The Free Methodists had no appropriate locations open, so the Vreugdenhils transferred to the Dakota Conference of the Wesleyan Methodist Church.

Eunice Vreugdenhil was received as a licensed minister by the Dakota Conference in 1949. She was appointed with her husband to pastor Medicine Rock and Mills Iron, near Willard, Montana, 1949–50. They were appointed to missionary work 1950–51. From 1951 to 1953 they pastored at Houghton. In 1952 Eunice was received into full standing as an ordained minister. From 1953 to 1956, they pastored at Tolstoy, South Dakota. From 1956 to 1961, they pastored at Brentford, and apparently Eunice pastored at Northville 1958–59 during this time. From 1961 to 1962 they pastored Artesian, and from 1962 to 1964 the ministered at Tolstoy again. All of these were small, rural churches where the Vreugdenhils had to stretch resources to meet family needs. But the children never were aware that they were poor. In 1964 they were listed on reserve, and July 15, 1964, they transferred to the Oregon Conference, where they retired.

In retirement, Eunice Vreugdenhil carried on an extensive correspondence with missionaries around the world and was especially known for her ministry of prayer. Harmen Vreugdenil passed away December 18, 1976, at the age of eighty. Eunice Vreugdenhil passed away October 26, 1997, at the age of ninety-three, at the Hood River Care Centre in Hood River, Oregon.[141]

Dorothy Schnell Williams

Dorothy Schnell was born in Bartholomew County, Indiana, June 23, 1915. She graduated from Trinity Bible College, Evansville, Indiana. She and her sisters sang together before she was married.

Dorothy married Rev. Ray L. Williams August 21, 1943. She was ordained by the Indiana District of the Pilgrim Holiness Church in 1948. Dorothy and Ray served primarily as evangelists, preaching and singing. They pastored at English, Indiana, for a time, and also at Charleston and Bridgeport in Illinois. Ray L. Williams passed away July 1990. Dorothy Williams passed away at Columbus, Indiana, March 30, 1996, at the age of eighty.[142]

Optimism, Tension, and Shrinking Opportunity

World War II had thrust the United States onto the world scene in a more prominent way than ever before. That prominence involved the U.S. in the Cold War with an attending fear of nuclear holocaust. In spite of these developments, the 1950s was a decade of optimism, especially for the Church. It was popular in the culture of that time to belong to and attend a church. The Billy Graham evangelistic campaigns were getting underway, and the media played a large part in highlighting and popularizing mass evangelism.

For those churches that would eventually be united in The Wesleyan Church, the rapid construction of new church buildings, parsonages, and other church-related structures continued. The holiness churches had often been characterized as being "on the wrong side of the tracks." There was now a deliberate move "across the tracks" to more "strategic" locations. There were more aggressive programs of evangelism and church planting, centered in and partially funded by the general churches and the district and annual conference structures. Both the Pilgrim Holiness Church (1958) and the Wesleyan Methodist Church (1959) made the shift to a multiple general superintendency. Interest was developing for church merger on a larger scale than had been previously experienced.

Two small mergers took place in this decade. In 1950 the Trinity Gospel Tabernacle Association of Evansville, Indiana, merged into the Pilgrim Holiness Church. And in 1957 the Missionary Bands of the World merged into the Wesleyan Methodist Church.

One disappointing development in the 1950s was a drastic decline in the number of women entering the ministry in the churches that later united in The Wesleyan Church. The 1930s and 1940s had welcomed the largest numbers, but the 1950s showed a decline of 32 percent from the previous decade. To fully explain this decline would be difficult and is beyond the scope of this study. But the following is an attempt to suggest related factors.

First, there appears to have been a decline in the number of women seeking to enter credentialed ministry. There may be several reasons for that.

World War II had thrust millions of women into the job market, a trend that continued in the 1950s. There were now more and better-paying employment opportunities for women, resulting in fewer women considering the ministry.

There appears to have been a decrease in the number of "clergy couples." That may be partly the result of encouragement by church leaders and educators after World War II for clergy spouses to pursue teaching (and later nursing) degrees so as to supplement inadequate pastoral salaries. Some wives who felt called to service did not pursue preparation for two vocations. They probably served just as zealously and sacrificially as if they had, but they were not credentialed.

The women ministers who had served up through the 1940s had often felt that they were "used." Often, they received difficult appointments that men would not accept and were told at the outset that they would be replaced by a man as soon as the church could support a man and his family. This would not have encouraged potential women candidates in the years following World War II.

A second reason for the decline in the ordination of women in the 1950s may be that there was growing resistance to the ordination of women within the churches. Several factors may have contributed to that.

Many male veterans of World War II had had transforming spiritual experiences on the battlefield and believed they were called into the ministry. They inundated the churches' college campuses, and by the 1950s an enlarged pool of male ministerial talent was available.

Women had often single-handedly planted churches, then brought them into one of the denominations. But by the 1950s, church planting was more structured and more centered on the role of the district or conference. The churches planted by women in the past had often been assigned male pastors soon after coming into one of the denominations. The new church-planting program was thus somewhat conditioned to the selection of male pastors. The interests of the denominations were shifting away from deprived persons and rural or small-town situations to urban and suburban settings. Very few women were recruited for these ventures.

In addition, other avenues of ministry in which women had served in significant numbers had either changed drastically or simply ceased to exist. Ministries to special groups, in which women had provided much of the staffing, virtually disappeared except for that to Native Americans. Ministries to vagrants and addicts were less common. Ministry within "red light districts" and homes for "fallen girls" passed off the scene. That was partly due to the fact that government requirements for such institutions were redefined in ways that the churches found hard to meet. Ministries in the mountains and to the Mexicans in southern California were transferred from denominational responsibility to the districts and conferences, and largely passed out of existence.

Also, both the Wesleyan Methodist and Pilgrim Holiness leaders and ministers joined the broadstream evangelical movement in the newly organized National Association of Evangelicals. This brought them into contact with leaders from other churches that held a male-dominated worldview. Many evangelicals totally opposed the ordination of women, and holiness people began to read their writings and follow them on radio and television. And the accelerated growth the denominations experienced after World War II through church planting and evangelism brought in many new members and ministers who had not previously been conditioned to accept women ministers.

In spite of the changes in church life and the decline in the number of women entering the ministry, there were still those who heard God's call and answered, even in the 1950s.

Alma Aldinger Robertson

Alma Aldinger was born in South Dakota. Her family was not well-to-do, and she was one of twelve children. When Alma was seven, her mother died. A Christian couple, Mr. and Mrs. John Stotz, became like guardians to her and inspired her to church attendance. She was saved at age thirteen and at fifteen felt drawn to missionary service. Her home church was the Mitchell, South Dakota, Wesleyan Methodist Church. She was sanctified as a freshman theological student at Miltonvale College, Miltonvale, Kansas (later merged into what became Oklahoma Wesleyan University, Bartlesville, Oklahoma). She worked her way through college by working at a store, and reading one hour a day to a sightless student who was also preparing for the ministry.

Alma co-pastored for a year in Wyoming. She cared for her father until his death. This experience led her to enroll in nursing school, which she completed in 1949. On June 11, 1950, the Dakota Conference ordained her. Alma Aldinger, minister-nurse, began her service in Sierra Leone, West Africa, in 1950. She was on the mission field 1950–53, 1955–58, 1960–63, and 1964–67, with furloughs (home ministries) in between the foreign services. She then married David Robertson, a Dakota businessman and devout Christian. After his death in 1976, Alma returned to Sierra Leone 1979–81. She carried a heavy and important nursing responsibility, but her first purpose was to evangelize. She was considered to be an able teacher, preacher, and witness of the gospel of Christ, both in the homeland and on the mission field. She supplied the pastorate at Williston, North Dakota for one year.[1]

Hazel Armour

Hazel (Mrs. Marshall F.) Armour was ordained by the Alabama Conference of the Wesleyan Methodist Church in 1950. She served as assistant pastor of the Talledega North Street Church 1950–53. From 1953 to 1954, she was the assistant pastor at Nixon Chapel. From 1956 to 1960, she was the assistant pastor at Anniston First Church. In 1960 she transferred to the Allegheny Conference. From 1960 to 1964, she served as assistant pastor with her husband at Punxsutawney, Pennsylvania. From 1964 to 1967, she served with her husband at Grace church in Akron, Ohio.[2]

Ruth Estella Bixler

Ruth Bixler was born in South Dakota. Her home church was the Wesleyan Methodist church in Mitchell, South Dakota. She attended Wessington Springs College in Wessington Springs, South Dakota, for two years. After teaching for a time, she graduated in 1945 from Marion College, Marion, Indiana (now Indiana Wesleyan University). She served three terms as a missionary teacher in Sierra Leone, West Africa: 1945–48, 1950–53, 1956–59. She was ordained by the Dakota Conference of the Wesleyan Methodist Church June 11, 1950. From 1962 on, she was listed as unstationed (without appointment). She returned to South Dakota and taught school at Aberdeen. In 1965 she received an M.A. degree from Northern State College. She died May 27, 1984.[3]

Mrs. Arnold Bolender

Mrs. Arnold Bolender was listed as an ordained minister, appointed as an evangelist, in the records of the Kentucky District of the Pilgrim Holiness Church, 1950–61.

Leta Bottenberg

Leta (Mrs. W. O.) Bottenberg was listed in the records of the Central District of the Pilgrim Holiness Church in 1950. From 1951 to 1962 she was listed in the records of the North Central District. From 1963 to 1968 her name appeared again on Central District records, with her listing 1965–68 being "retired." Her husband's obituary stated that he pioneered and organized some twenty churches in Kansas, Oklahoma, Missouri, and Arkansas. He served as superintendent of the North Central District for twenty-two years. He pastored at Enid, Oklahoma, until his death October 3, 1973, at the age of seventy-two.[4]

Daisy R. Finnefrock

Daisy R. Finnefrock was listed in the records of the Ohio District of the Pilgrim Holiness Church 1950–51. She lived at Lancaster, Ohio. She was ordained in 1951. She pastored the Bethel church 1951–53. In 1954 she was appointed to evangelism. From 1955 to 1957, her name appeared in the records of the Eastern Ohio District, with her appointment in 1955 being to evangelism.

Esther Grosenback

Esther Grosenback was received to travel (serve) by the Nebraska Conference of the Wesleyan Methodist Church in 1950. Her first service was apparently at the O'Neill church. From 1950 to 1951 she was the supply pastor at Pine Ridge. From 1951 to 1954 she was a missionary to the Native Americans at the Sioux Community Chapel in Rapid City, South

Dakota. The Nebraska Conference ordained her in 1952. From 1954 to 1957, she was listed as a conference evangelist and from 1957 to 1958 as a home missionary. From 1958 to 1965 she was listed as serving in child evangelism. On November 16, 1966, she was again appointed to the Sioux Chapel, and on December 15, 1966, she transferred to the Dakota District. She was listed in 1967 and 1968 as serving at the Sioux Chapel.[5]

Betty Hu

Betty Hu is listed in the records of the California District of the Pilgrim Holiness Church 1950–67.

Hazel Marie Thomas Leatherman

Hazel Thomas spent her childhood and youth in North Carolina. Spiritual growth was fostered by her praying mother and other godly influences from the Pilgrim Holiness church in Kannapolis. Study requirements for ordination were completed at Southern Pilgrim College, Kernersville, North Carolina (later merged into United Wesleyan College, Allentown, Pennsylvania) and at Marion College, Marion, Indiana (now Indiana Wesleyan University).

Hazel taught public school in North Carolina for a short time before going as a Pilgrim Holiness missionary to Africa. She spent a five-year term in Northern Rhodesia (now Zambia) as a missionary teacher. Her special Scripture verses for her missionary service were Psalms 2:8 and 3:6. Returning to the United States, she served as dean of women at the college in Bartlesville, Oklahoma, for one year. The next year she married Rev. Oliver Leatherman. She was ordained by the Kansas District in 1968. She and her husband pastored a small Pilgrim Holiness church in Toronto, Kansas, from the time they were married until the district closed it in 1993.

In retirement the Leathermans continued to reside in Toronto but wintered in Arizona. In

Arizona Oliver conducted worship services each Sunday morning at the mobile home/RV park, and Hazel directed a Bible study once a week.[6]

Ivanelle McCarty

Ivanelle McCarty was listed as a conference preacher in the Illinois Conference of the Wesleyan Methodist Church in 1950. She was assistant pastor to her husband, Clarence C. McCarty, at Hoopston 1950–53. From 1953 to 1959 they served in "pioneer" (church planting) work at Sheffield. From 1960 to 1961 she was appointed to occupational evangelism. From 1961 to 1966, she was assistant pastor to her husband at the Peoria First Church. In 1966 they went off the conference ministerial roll and back to their local church as local preachers.[7]

Jemima Walker Mitchell

The records of the California District of the Pilgrim Holiness Church listed Jemima Walker among the ministers 1950–62. She became Mrs. Mitchell in 1958.

Henrietta News

Henrietta News was listed in the records of the Eastern District of the Pilgrim Holiness Church 1950–67. She was listed as serving at Mt. Carmel High School in Kentucky. She was known in the mountains of Kentucky as a "wonderful holiness preacher" and a great blessing there. She pastored churches for at least fifteen years. In retirement years she was a victim of Alzheimer's disease and resided in the Mt. Carmel retirement home for retired workers.[8]

Laura Weatherholt O'Brien

Oklahoma Conference records show that Laura Weatherholt O'Brien transferred on October 28, 1950, as a conference preacher (licensed minister) from the Allegheny Conference of the Wesleyan Methodist Church to the Oklahoma Conference. In 1951 she was ordained and was appointed as assistant pastor at the Oklahoma City church. She was also pursuing training as a nurse in Oklahoma City. In 1953 she was listed as a missionary evangelist. In 1954, at her request, she was dropped from the roll of ministers, and she gave her credentials to the committee on itineracy and orders (now district board of ministerial standing).

Fern Annabelle Nelson Peterson

Fern Annabelle Nelson was born December 17, 1916, in Omaha, Nebraska. She was saved at the age of twelve and was sanctified in 1935. She attended God's Bible School, Cincinnati, Ohio; Omaha Bible Institute, Omaha, Nebraska; and Van Sant's Business College in Omaha.

Fern married Martin Luther Peterson June 12, 1939, in Omaha. They had one daughter, Linda Louise. They served effectively in evangelistic and pastoral work. Martin was ordained July 1, 1947, and Fern in January 1950. They served many years as pastors and were missionaries in the Caribbean for nearly ten years. They held pastorates in the Central, Rocky Mountain, and Eastern Ohio Districts of the Pilgrim Holiness Church.

The Petersons centered their ministry on Barbados in their first term as missionaries, superintending the district and pastoring a number of churches. Fern became ill, which forced their return to the United States. They spent this time in evangelism and pastoral work. On June 1, 1958, they went to Antigua until the vacancy there was filled. In September 1958 they went to St. Vincent to serve as superintendent and pastor. In June 1960 they went back to Barbados to superintend the district.

Fern Peterson suffered from rheumatoid arthritis for fifteen years and was confined to a wheelchair. Her last few months she was bedfast. She passed away August 26, 1986, at the age of sixty-nine.[9]

Elsie Roberts

Elsie Roberts was listed in the records of the Kentucky District of the Pilgrim Holiness Church, 1950–67. From 1950 to 1953, she served with Dessie Redd as pastors at Tyrone. In 1953 she was listed with Dessie Redd at Preston. Elsie was listed as pastor at Preston 1954 and 1955. She continued to be listed 1956–62 and then from 1963 to 1967 was listed as "inactive."

Mrs. Lala Sports

The records of the South Georgia Conference of the Wesleyan Methodist Church listed Lala Sports in 1950 as being received to pursue the course of study and do evangelistic work under the conference president (now district superintendent). From November 22, 1950, until 1952 she was pastor of the Browning church. In 1951 she became a conference preacher (licensed minister), and in 1952 she was ordained. She was appointed to conference evangelism 1952–53 and served as pastor at Jessup 1953–57. In 1952 she conducted devotions at the conference session. In 1956 she reported improvements to the inside of the Jessup church building and the addition of a concrete porch and steps. In 1957 she was again appointed to conference evangelism and in February 1958 she left the denomination and joined the Church of the Nazarene.

Leora Dora Strope

Leora Dora Strope was received in 1950 to study and travel (serve) by the Nebraska Conference of the Wesleyan Methodist Church. In 1951 she was listed as a conference preacher (licensed minister) and was appointed as youth and children's worker at the Gordon church. In 1952 she was to remain in school. She was listed as a conference evangelist 1954–57 and was ordained in 1956. At some point she also became a registered nurse.

Leora Strope was listed as a home missionary 1957–58. Beginning in 1958, she was listed as a missionary to Haiti. Her support was raised for a number of years by the Nebraska Conference Woman's Missionary Society, beginning in 1957. She served as a missionary to Haiti for two terms: 1958–61 and 1962–63. She was the featured speaker at the WMS public service in the Nebraska Conference session in 1963. She was listed on reserve in 1963 and 1964. She died December 11, 1974.[10]

Emma Whittinghill

Emma (Mrs. Hobart H.) Whittinghill's name appeared on the records of several districts of the Pilgrim Holiness Church. The Kentucky District listed her 1946, 1947, and 1948. The Oklahoma-Texas District listed her in 1950. The Texas District also listed her in 1950 and in 1951 indicated that she had transferred to the Indiana District. The Southern Indiana District listed her 1953–67, indicating that from 1964 on she was pastor at Coalmont.

Mrs. Roy Wilkinson

Mrs. Roy Wilkinson was listed in the records of the Michigan District of the Pilgrim Holiness Church 1950–53 as a missionary, in 1954 as "unstationed" (without appointment), and in 1955 as a missionary. She was listed on the records of the East Michigan District 1956–64 as "inactive."

E. Ruth Willingham

Ruth Willingham felt a pull toward spiritual things as a child. She remembers raising her hand for prayer. Another time she slipped up to the altar when others went to pray with seekers. In her teens she experienced a personal relationship with Christ and received the assurance that her sins were forgiven. She found peace "in saving and sanctifying power."

She attended Northwest Nazarene College in Nampa, Idaho. Since she had worked as a nurse's aid, she started to pursue nursing. Soon she shifted to home economics but still did not feel at ease. In her junior year she switched to religious

subjects. She started going with Ted L. Willingham, who was preparing for the ministry, and after much prayer felt certain that this was the way for her to go. She said that she never "had a specific revelation as to a call to preach" but rather a growing assurance that this was God's will and she experienced satisfaction in the many aspects of God's work.

Ted had attended what is now Azusa Pacific University for his first year of college. Then he and Ruth were married, and he attended Northwest Nazarene for his two middle years. Ruth graduated from Northwest Nazarene in 1950. Then Ted transferred back to Azusa and graduated there. They served their first pastorate at a Pilgrim Holiness church in Yucaipa, California, July 1951–April 1954. From 1954 to 1956 they pastored at Post Falls, Idaho. In 1956 they went to plant a new church at Weeser in northern Idaho, close to the Canadian border. After footers had been dug for the new building, district support was shifted elsewhere. The Willinghams went ahead and planted an independent church in Weeser and pastored it until 1963.

In 1963 Rev. L. B. Reese persuaded them to return to service under the Pilgrim Holiness Church. They moved to Ontario on Bruce Peninsula, which reached out into Lake Ontario, with congregations at Ferndale and Dyer's Bay, near Lion's Head. They served there 1963–68. Ted injured his back in 1965 and spent six weeks in bed plus more time recuperating. Ruth carried on full ministries at both churches, and she and the children drove the twenty miles between through deep snow drifts. From 1968 to 1980, the Willinghams pastored in Toronto at the Amroth church. This was just after the 1968 merger, and this was a former Wesleyan Methodist church. Ruth was recognized and paid as assistant pastor part of the time. At the time of their departure from Toronto, the Amroth congregation helped to plant the Milliken church. From 1980 to December 1981, Ted and Ruth pastored at the Shawville, Quebec, church.

At this point, Ted Willingham began to serve as an institutional chaplain in Palmerston, Ontario. Ruth was also listed in that capacity at least part of the time. She refers to their service as team ministries, with Ted taking the primary role. She never felt that she had to force the door open. There were always plenty of opportunities to serve her Savior.

> There were times of preparing our own teaching materials and special programs; leading Bible study groups; directing Children's Church; doing Cradle Roll ministry with mothers; counseling, assisting in funerals and weddings; serving communion; and preaching from the pulpit. . . . My greatest delight is in the study of God's Word and the opportunities to share it, whether from the pulpit, Sunday school class, Ladies' Bible study group, or on a one to one.

The Willinghams attend the Evangelical Missionary Church of Canada in the community where they live. When a young pastor arrived a while back, Ruth served as his secretary. His denomination did not approve of women in ministry, but when he observed all the ministries she was performing, he bent the rules and called her the assistant pastor.[11]

Blanche Reed Woody

Blanche Reed was a licensed minister in the Illinois District of the Pilgrim Holiness Church in 1950. She and Ruth Tonks pastored the Ottawa, Illinois, church for one and one-half years 1950–51. The Illinois District ordained her in 1952. From 1954 to 1964, she pastored the Moss church in the Tennessee District. In 1965 she married Denzil Woody. In 1966 and 1967 the Tennessee District listed her as being in California.[12]

Mrs. Mamie F. Yaryan

Mamie F. Yaryan was the first convert of the Evanston Avenue Pilgrim Holiness church in

Indianapolis. She was later sanctified and called into the ministry. She was ordained in 1950 by the Indiana District. She was listed in the Northern Indiana District's records 1951–53 as an evangelist. She continued to be listed through 1967, and was listed as an evangelist in 1963. She had three sons and four daughters. One son, Don, served as district statistician for a number of years. Two grandsons, Randy and Wesley Yaryan, became pastors. Mamie F. Yaryan died March 24, 1978.[13]

Irene Frances Hawk

Irene Hawk was born in Butler, Pennsylvania. She was a member of the Christian and Missionary Alliance. She was deeply interested in missions early in life but did not become convinced of a call to missions until after she was relieved of caring for a younger brother and sister. She graduated from Transylvania Bible School in Pennsylvania in 1950 and was ordained in 1964. Her missionary career began in 1951, serving in Cuba 1951–59. She then began service in Peru. It was in 1968 that she became an associate missionary with The Wesleyan Church in Peru.[14]

Mrs. B. S. Jones

Mrs. B. S. Jones was listed among the ministers in the records of the North Carolina District of the Pilgrim Holiness Church 1951–57.

Marjory E. Gjesdal Jones

Marjory Gjesdal was listed in the records of the Oregon Conference of the Wesleyan Methodist Church in 1951 as a conference preacher (licensed minister). From 1951 to 1952, she and a coworker, K. Kelsven, pastored the Holgate church. In 1952 and again in 1953, she and her husband, Donald Jones, were appointed to pastor Holgate. By March of 1953 the Holgate church had been organized and they were needing "to build a superstructure immediately." Marjory was elected to the conference Sunday school board in 1953. The Joneses soon resigned from Holgate and they were appointed to Seattle. In 1954 they were referred back to their local church.

Marjory E. Jones was listed among the ministers of the California Conference of the Wesleyan Methodist Church 1956–65. She was ordained in 1957 and was appointed pastor, with her husband, Donald F. Jones, of a "pioneer project" (church plant) called La Cresta Ivy Chapel. They served there 1957–59. From 1959 to 1961 they pastored the El Sereno church in Los Angeles. From 1961 to 1963 she was on reserve, and from 1963 to 1965 she was unstationed (without appointment). In 1965 Marjory Jones was listed as withdrawn.

Mrs. Bessie L. Kline

Bessie L. Kline was received to study for the ministry by the Nebraska Conference of the Wesleyan Methodist Church in 1951. She was to serve under the missionary board as pastor at Niobrara. On September 17, 1951, her deaconess's credentials were transferred from the Kansas Conference. By 1952 she had completed the course of study and was continued as pioneer (church-planting) pastor at Niobrara. Lots were purchased for a church building, September 12, 1952. Work was begun on the building May 15, 1953. At the 1953 conference session she was ordained and continued as pastor at Niobrara. She resigned May 31, 1954. She became a conference evangelist. In 1955 she was listed as "unstationed" (without appointment). In 1956 and 1957 she was to choose her own field of service. In 1958 she was once again appointed as a conference evangelist. She left to go to the Church of the Nazarene but came back in 1960 and pastored Niobrara again. On March 2, 1961, she was released from her appointment because her health had failed. In 1962, 1963, and 1964 she was listed as "superannuated" (retired).[15]

Ruth Hames Sparks

Ruth Hames married Rev. Carl V. Sparks of Gastonia, North Carolina, on August 31, 1941. She was elected conference secretary of the Woman's Missionary Society in 1942 and again in 1945 and from then on. She was listed by the North Carolina Conference of the Wesleyan Methodist Church as a fourth-year student on the ministerial course of study beginning in 1951. She completed the course of study in 1956 and was ordained in 1958. From 1956 to 1962, she was listed as a song evangelist and children's worker. From 1962 to 1968 she was listed as a children's worker. In 1968 she was listed on reserve.

Ruth Hames Sparks considered her field of service to be ministering to the women of the church and community. At the Sparks' first pastorate in the mountains of North Carolina, a frightened young boy came to their door around midnight, saying his mother was dying and needed prayer. Carl and Ruth followed the boy across streams, over rough territory, up a remote mountain. Carl remembered that this was "bootleg" country, where men had "stills" and were manufacturing what was called "white lightning." They found Ella under old-fashioned conviction. She had been selling the white lightning while her husband served his "year and a day" at the Raleigh state prison. The Sparks prayed for Ella. Early Sunday morning she marched down the church aisle, all smiles—a changed woman.

Carl and Ruth had a regular visitation program in the homes of members and visitors. They called ahead by telephone. They often won burdened persons to the Lord in this way. They also made hospital and nursing home visits.

Both Carl and Ruth earned not only A.B. degrees but also master's degrees in education. Ruth taught for thirty-four years in public schools. In 1980 they went with other Wesleyans on a short-term mission to Haiti and Puerto Rico. In 1993 Ruth received a plaque honoring her for service to Wesleyan Women in North Carolina for forty-three years. Ruth fills in preaching for pastors when needed. She always gives a missionary address and she gives any love offering she receives to missions.[16]

Grace Wolford

The records of the Pittsburgh District of the Pilgrim Holiness Church listed Grace Wolford among the ministers from 1951 through 1961. In 1959, 1960 and 1961 she was designated as "inactive."

Anna Behermeyer

The records of the North Central District of the Pilgrim Holiness Church listed Anna Behermeyer among the ministers from 1952 through 1962. The records of the Central District listed Anna as available for work 1963 through 1965 and as retired 1966 through 1968.

Laura Carson

Laura Carson (or Cason) was listed among the ministers in the records of the California District of the Pilgrim Holiness Church 1952 through 1968.

Virginia Beatrice Cunningham

The records of the West Virginia District of the Pilgrim Holiness Church listed Virginia Beatrice Cunningham among its ministers 1952 through 1961. The records of the New York District listed her as an ordained minister 1962 and 1963, and apparently she was appointed to serve Chittenango in 1963. West Virginia listed her again in 1967 as pastor at Mullens.

Mrs. Mary Evangeline Dunkerley DeHass

The records of the Allegheny Conference of the Wesleyan Methodist Church listed Mary Evangeline Dunkerley as ordained in 1952. She was the pastor at Riverview 1952–54. From 1954 to 1956 her assignment was not listed. Beginning

in 1955 she carried the last name of DeHass. From 1956 to 1958 she was a conference evangelist. From 1958 to 1964 she was pastor at Alliance, Ohio. From 1964 through 1966 she was again a conference evangelist.

Luda Jean Fulmer

On July 31, 1951, Eugene Fulmer was appointed by the president (district superintendent) of the Ohio Conference of the Wesleyan Methodist Church to pastor the North Grand Avenue pioneer church (church plant) in Marion, Ohio. On March 4, 1952, Luda Jean Fulmer transferred from the Allegheny Conference. Her transcript from Transylvania Bible School was evaluated, and she was declared to be a fourth-year student. The Fulmers pastored at North Grand Avenue until May 1, 1952. The Sunday school averaged thirty-six, the afternoon preaching service twenty-nine and the evening service twenty. Attendance dropped by half when the Fulmers left.

On February 25, 1952, two groups at Lafferty and St. Clairsville, Ohio, expressed interest in coming into the Wesleyan Methodist Church. The founders and main supporters of these works were a Mr. Knopf and a Miss Sells. They wanted to unite with the Wesleyan Methodists but wanted the Fulmers to be the pastors. The conference moved the Fulmers with a mobile home to Lafferty to pastor these works. But soon Knopf changed his mind and served notice that the Fulmers would be through July 15! From 1952 to 1953 the Fulmers pastored at Chippewa Lake, and from 1953 to 1956 they pastored at St. Albans. Apparently both were ordained in 1953. From 1956 to 1959 they were listed on reserve. On July 20, 1959, note was taken that they were no longer members of the denomination, and their names were dropped.[17]

Blanche Gilbert

Blanche Gilbert was listed by the North Carolina Conference of the Wesleyan Methodist Church as a ministerial student, beginning in

1952. From 1952 to 1955 she was listed as a first-year student. Beginning in 1955 she was listed as a student at Central Wesleyan College (now Southern Wesleyan University). In 1956 she was also listed as assistant pastor at West Durham, and in 1957 she was listed as assistant dean of women at Central. In 1958 she had completed her work at Central and by 1960 had completed all study requirements. In 1960 she was listed as assistant dean of women at Central and on September 26 of that year she was appointed assistant pastor at Durham. She served in that capacity at Durham 1960–68. She was ordained in 1961. In 1968 she was listed as a district evangelist. In 1976 and 1977 she was appointed as assistant pastor at Roxboro.[18]

Lillie Moore

Lillie Moore was listed on the records of the Southern Indiana District of the Pilgrim Holiness Church 1952–60.

Anna Shaffer

Anna Shaffer was ordained by the Florida Conference of the Wesleyan Methodist Church in 1952. That year she was appointed as a conference evangelist. From 1953 to 1954 she was assistant pastor with her husband of the Greenville circuit, including Pine Island and New Zion. From 1954 to 1955 she was again a conference evangelist. From 1955 to 1960 she was assistant pastor with her husband, Cecil, at Paola. From 1960 to 1961 she was assistant pastor with her husband at Intercession City. From 1961 to 1962 she was assigned work under the conference board of church extension. From 1962 to 1968 she was listed on reserve.

Anna Shaffer served the conference in various offices. She was treasurer of the conference Woman's Missionary Society 1952–61. She was the conference Sunday school secretary (director) 1955–56. And she was elected to the statistical committee 1953, 1954, 1958, 1959 and 1960.[19]

Margaret Smith

Margaret Smith was an ordained minister in the Michigan District of the Pilgrim Holiness Church. In 1956 she was a pastor. She was listed without designation of an assignment 1957–63. In 1966–67 she was released to work outside the church. Following the 1968 merger, she was a member of the North Michigan District of The Wesleyan Church. She lived at Hope, Michigan, in retirement. She was in poor health and passed away in 1978.[20]

Mrs. Mildred Stone Spiker

The records of the Michigan District of the Pilgrim Holiness Church indicate that Mrs. Mildred Stone Spiker was ordained by that district in 1952.

Dorothy Straight

The records of the New York District of the Pilgrim Holiness Church listed Dorothy Straight as an ordained minister 1953–63. Part of the time she was apparently pastoring and part of the time without appointment. She may have pastored the Monticello, New York, church 1952–57.

Hallie Wagoner

The records of the North Carolina District of the Pilgrim Holiness Church listed Hallie Wagoner 1952–68. She was ordained in 1952. She apparently pastored the Atlantic church and the Harkers Island church in the late 1950s and early 1960s, possibly both of them simultaneously for part of that period.

Lois Williams

Lois Williams was listed among the ministers in the records of the North Central District of the Pilgrim Holiness Church 1952–62, and in the records of the Central District 1965–68.

Virginia K. Workman

Virginia K. Workman was listed among the ministers in the records of the West Virginia District of the Pilgrim Holiness Church 1952–67.

Blanche Bond

The records of the Southern Indiana District of the Pilgrim Holiness Church listed Blanche Bond, wife of Brose Bond, among the ministers 1953–67.

Viola Borders

The records of the Southern Indiana District of the Pilgrim Holiness Church listed Viola Borders among the ministers 1953–67.

Eva E. Burchel

Rev. and Mrs. H. C. Burchel of the Standard Church of Canada were introduced to the 1950 session of the Lockport Conference (now Western New York District) of the Wesleyan Methodist Church. H. C. Burchel was received by the conference by letter of standing, July 1, 1950. In 1953 Eva Burchel was received by the Lockport Conference to study preparatory to travel (service). She was continued on the course of study until 1957, when her records were transferred to the Ohio Conference.

In 1957 the Ohio Conference ordained Eva, citing her completion of the course of study under Lockport, and one year of service in Lockport plus one year of service in Ohio. From 1957 to 1958, H. C. and Eva Burchel pastored at Empire. From 1958 to 1960, they pastored at Chillicothe. They served as conference evangelists from 1960 to 1961, and from 1961 to 1963 they pastored Kenton. From 1963 to 1966, both of the Burchels were listed as pastors at St. Albans, West Virginia. But from 1966 to 1967 only Eva was so listed. Both Burchels were listed as pastors at the Mark Street church, Marion, Ohio, 1967 to 1968. Eva was listed as "superannuated" (retired) in 1968.[21]

Martha Duvall

Martha Duvall was listed in the records of the Kentucky District of the Pilgrim Holiness Church 1953–57, serving as an evangelist.

Freda Farmer

Freda Farmer was born August 27, 1923, near Utica, Ohio. She first went to school in the same one-room country schoolhouse where her mother and grandfather had attended. She was 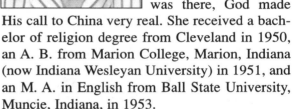 saved at camp meeting at Coshocton, Ohio and later was sanctified.

Freda graduated from high school at Utica. Five years later she began college work at Cleveland Bible College (now Malone College). While she was there, God made His call to China very real. She received a bachelor of religion degree from Cleveland in 1950, an A. B. from Marion College, Marion, Indiana (now Indiana Wesleyan University) in 1951, and an M. A. in English from Ball State University, Muncie, Indiana, in 1953.

In 1953 the Ohio Conference of the Wesleyan Methodist Church received Freda Farmer as a third-year student on the ministerial course of study. On September 2, 1953, Freda was accepted by the Taiwan Gospel Mission, an independent mission board, for missionary service on Taiwan. Changes in the sponsoring board soon required Freda to seek a different sponsoring body. The Ohio Conference assured her of her salary—this word was received by Freda on Christmas Day 1954, a real Christmas present! Roy S. Nicholson, general conference president (now general superintendent) of the Wesleyan Methodist Church, was touring the fields and interviewed Freda on the field. She then was appointed to service by the Wesleyan Methodists and began service in March 1955. She served until June 1958, returned for a second term September 1959—July 1964, a third term September 1965—June 1970, and a further term ending in 1976. The Ohio Conference ordained Freda Farmer, August 2, 1959. Beginning in 1960, the Wesleyan Methodist work at Chiayi, Taiwan, was turned over to the Ohio Yearly Meeting of the Friends. Freda continued service under the Friends board until 1976, but was supported by her own denomination. In 1962 she was transferred to Taipei, the capital of Taiwan. She conducted youth and women's meetings, taught English Bible classes, and assisted in the general work of the Church. From 1967 to 1975, she was a part-time instructor at National Taiwan University and treasurer of the Friends Mission.

From 1977 to 1989, Freda Farmer served The Wesleyan Church as a missionary to Indonesia. At least in the beginning, her work was to attempt to reach the Chinese population of Indonesia. Freda Farmer said that she lived out 2 Corinthians 12:9. In her "weakness of language and many other weaknesses" God's power worked in the hearts of Asians to bring them to Himself.[22]

Alice Lan

Alice Lan was listed among the ministers in the records of the California District of the Pilgrim Holiness Church 1953–67.

Arleen Maudie Likes Wiley Swanson

Arleen Likes was born in Corunna, Indiana, September 2, 1923. A few days before Christmas 1941 she was converted, and she was sanctified four years later. She earned an A. B. degree in religious education and psychology from Asbury College, Wilmore, Kentucky in 1942 and a B. S. in home economics and an M. S. in science and home economics from Purdue University, West Lafayette, Indiana. She also studied at Taylor University, Upland, Indiana, and Ball State University, Muncie, Indiana.

Arleen Likes married Charles A. Wiley Jr. September 2, 1947, at South Milford, Indiana. They had one daughter, Naomi Ruth, and one son, Charles Aden III. The Wileys served for one year as missionaries to Haiti under an independent board. From 1953 to 1959, Arleen taught home economics at Frankfort Pilgrim College, Frankfort, Indiana (later merged into United Wesleyan College, Allentown, Pennsylvania).

On September 9, 1959, the Wileys arrived at Paramaribo, Surinam, to serve as missionaries under the Pilgrim Holiness Church. They soon located inland at Pelgrim Kondre, a jungle mission among the Djukas, or Bush Negroes. Arleen was in charge of the school there. Charles died April 26, 1963, while they were home on furlough (home ministries). Arleen was ordained in 1963. She and her children returned to serve in Surinam for a period of time.

After the 1968 merger, Arleen Wiley was elected general director of the Young Missionary Workers Band (now Wesleyan Kids for Missions). In 1971 she married Rev. Ellsworth C. Swanson, a general evangelist. They moved to North Carolina in 1977 to pastor the Greensboro Calvary church. They also pastored at Ramseur Kildee and Siler City First. Arleen served as district YMWB director for two years, and as district director of Wesleyan Women for seven years. She eventually retired due to ill health. The Swansons moved to Bartlesville, Oklahoma, in October 1995. Arleen is remembered for her dedication and perseverance in the midst of great physical pain. She died February 22, 1997.[23]

Mary Swentzel

The records of the Florida Conference of the Wesleyan Methodist Church listed Mary Swentzel among its ministers 1953–56. She transferred to the Florida Conference as an ordained minister from the Pilgrim Holiness Church in 1953. She served as assistant pastor with her husband at St. Petersburg 1954–57.

Elizabeth Ward

The records of the Michigan District of the Pilgrim Holiness Church indicated that the district ordained Elizabeth Ward in 1953.

Betty Lou Washburn

Betty Lou Washburn grew up in Baltimore, Maryland. When she was converted at age fourteen, she had a lady pastor, Etta M. Clough. Rev. Clough was planting the First Pilgrim Holiness Church in Baltimore, and Betty Lou's mother was a charter member. Betty Lou began to teach a Sunday school class when she was fifteen and to preach when she was eighteen. Rev. Clough knew a couple who wanted a church in the Berkeley Springs area of West Virginia. In cooperation with the district, she secured a building and began sending Betty Lou and Geraldine (Geri) Gangaware down for Sunday services. The young ladies worked in offices in Baltimore during the week and took the train to West Virginia on the weekends. After six months they quit their jobs and moved to their church. Since they had no car, they walked up to six miles in calling on their people.

Betty Lou and Geri took correspondence courses at first. After a year and a half, Geri said that she was going to Allentown Bible Institute, Allentown, Pennsylvania (later Eastern Pilgrim College/United Wesleyan College). Betty Lou went also. There she met Paul Washburn. They were married July 19, 1947.

The Washburns pastored at Quakertown, Pennsylvania, and Lebanon, Pennsylvania. While pastoring at Lebanon, they attended the district conference, where they heard General Superintendent L. W. Sturk make a plea for ministers for the Northwest. The Washburns received what they believed were clear instructions that they were to go. They left in a Ford station wagon shortly after Thanksgiving. They pastored first at Grandview, Washington, where both worked to support themselves. Betty Lou cut asparagus and tried to pick grapes. But the latter left her "sitting

in the volcanic ash and bawling." On July 20, 1953, Paul and Betty Lou Washburn were ordained at the Clarkston-Lewiston campground of the Idaho-Washington District.

Next they pastored at Spirit Lake, in the panhandle of Idaho. One woman had prayed for her husband for seventeen years. He prayed through alone one night while his wife was 200 miles away at camp meeting. The Presbyterian minister said that this man was the most outstanding example of God's grace in that town. Betty Lou applied for a teaching position there. The superintendent asked her what made her think she was qualified. She determined to become so qualified that no would ask that again.

Family illness forced the Washburns to return to the East in 1956. They pastored at Muncy, Pennsylvania, and at Millersburg, Pennsylvania. At some point they also pastored at Wells, New York. They then moved to Shippensburg, Pennsylvania. Here Betty Lou enrolled at Shippensburg University and earned a teaching degree. Then she worked for the school district and earned a master's degree as a reading specialist. They pastored a church ninety miles away and did a lot of supply work and evangelism.

Betty Lou read in the Wesleyan Native American Ministries paper that Brainerd Indian School needed a reading specialist. By now Paul was retired. But they moved to Brainerd, near Hot Springs, South Dakota, where they served 1985–88. Paul installed a septic system, preached, helped Betty Lou with her Bible class, and befriended and counseled the students. Betty Lou developed a remedial reading program for the secondary school. One Native American high school student with a documented learning disability became her special project. She worked with him for three years. The Washburns returned to Brainerd the following year for graduation exercises, when this young man was recognized as the salutatorian of his class.

By 1988, Paul was seriously ill with cancer. They returned to the East once again. Paul died September 3, 1990. As a widow, age seventy-four, Betty Lou was still substitute teaching, preaching occasionally, teaching a senior adult Sunday school class and trying to be an "encourager."[24]

Mrs. Anna Baynum

The records of the Kentucky District of the Pilgrim Holiness Church listed Anna Baynum as an ordained minister 1954–67.

Myrtle C. Bemis

Myrtle C. Bemis was listed in the records of the Southern Indiana District of the Pilgrim Holiness Church as an ordained minister 1954–67. She was listed as the pastor at Coalmont, Indiana in 1954.

Ila M. Bennett

H. S. and Ila M. Bennett transferred as ordained ministers from the Pilgrim Holiness Church to the Wisconsin Conference of the Wesleyan Methodist Church in 1954. They were appointed as pastors of the Wisconsin Rapids church in 1954 and served there until 1965. At that time they became pastors of the Baraboo, Wisconsin, church.

Ila served as the conference secretary of the Woman's Missionary Society 1955–60. She was also active in children's work, and was elected conference secretary of child evangelism in 1962 and 1963. She also served as conference Christian Youth Crusaders director, 1962–64.[25]

Mamie Blankenship

The records of the Allegheny Conference of the Wesleyan Methodist Church listed Mamie Blankenship among the ministers 1954–66. She was ordained in 1954 and served as pastor at English, West Virginia, 1954–61. Beginning in 1961, she was listed as "superannuated" (retired) through 1966.

Margart Grace Brown

The records of the North Carolina Conference of the Wesleyan Methodist Church reveal that Margart Grace Brown was received in 1954 to study. She was given a special illustrative evangelism assignment 1954–57. At that time children's worker was added to her responsibilities. Song evangelism was also added in 1958. In 1959 she transferred out of the conference.

Mary Chapman

Mary Chapman appeared in the records of three different districts of the Pilgrim Holiness Church. The Southern Indiana District listed her in 1954, 1955, and 1956, the first two years as pastor at Fort Branch, Indiana. The Kentucky District listed her 1957–62, pastoring at Livermore 1957–59 and at Augusta 1959–63. The West Virginia District listed her as pastor at St. Marys 1963–68.

Mrs. Irene Creech

Irene Creech was listed in the records of the Gulf States District of the Pilgrim Holiness Church as pastor at Bogalusa in 1954, at Tioga in 1958, and back to Bogalusa in 1959.

Evelyn Dixon

Mrs. Lloyd Dixon was listed among the ministers in the records of the California District of the Pilgrim Holiness Church 1954–59, and Evelyn Dixon was so listed 1960–67.

Mrs. Floyd E. Dunn

Mrs. Floyd E. Dunn was listed by the Illinois District of the Pilgrim Holiness Church among the ministers 1954–61, with the designation of "pastor" in 1954 and 1960. She was listed by the Kentucky District in 1962 and designated as an evangelist in 1963 and 1964.

Erma Hacker

The records of the California District of the Pilgrim Holiness Church listed Erma Hacker among the ministers 1954–67.

Anna Hartley

On September 27, 1954, Anna Hartley was appointed by the Ohio Conference of the Wesleyan Methodist Church as supply pastor of the Southwest Sharon church. The assignment was continued 1955–56. In 1956 her husband, Kenneth J. Hartley, joined her on the supply pastor team at the church, now simply called Sharon. On July 12, 1956, the Sharon church was organized with twelve members. On July 30, 1957, Anna was listed as pastor and Kenneth was listed as supply. This continued until 1960. Anna was ordained in 1958. In 1960, Anna was appointed to reserve status but then was reassigned as pastor at Sharon. From 1961 to 1966, Kenneth and Anna were both appointed pastors at Sharon. From 1966 to at least 1968, they served as pastors at Rittman.[26]

Ruth Frances Berkgren Hogarth

Ruth Frances Berkgren was born in 1925. She graduated from Colorado Springs Bible College and the Friends University of Wichita, Kansas. She also earned a teaching certificate from Wichita State University. She taught at Colorado Springs Bible College and in public school for several years.

Ruth Berkgren married Rev. Virgil Hogarth in 1951. She was ordained in 1954. The Hogarths served first in the Idaho-Washington District of the Pilgrim Holiness Church, 1954–58. They pastored at Spirit Lake, Idaho, and Grandview, Washington. They served in the California District 1960–61, pastoring at Ventura. They transferred to the Kansas District in 1962 and co-pastored at St. Francis, Kansas, 1962–66. They became co-pastors at Wichita First Church in 1966 and then became pastors at Sabetha in 1981. The Hogarths had one son and one daughter. Ruth Berkgren Hogarth died May 17, 1985.[27]

Alma Huppert

Alma Huppert was listed among the ministers in the records of the California District of the Pilgrim Holiness Church 1954–62.

Dorothy Johnson Clark

Dorothy Johnson was saved when she was ten years of age in vacation Bible school in a little Methodist church in Bloom City, Wisconsin. She later "felt the tug of the Holy Spirit" on her mind and heart to go into full-time Christian service. Her pastor encouraged her, and friends guided her. She attended what is now Vennard College, then in Chicago, now in University Park, Iowa. She was first listed on the ministerial roll of the Iowa Conference of the Wesleyan Methodist Church in 1954. She was to continue in school. She graduated from Vennard in 1955 with an A.B. in Bible and Christian education.

After graduation she sent out résumés and had some interviews. But nothing was brought to closure. She went to Wisconsin to stay with her sister and spent a night in prayer. She found confirmation of her call in Romans 10:14–15; her life verse was Isaiah 41:10. She went to the Wesleyan Methodist camp at Burr, Wisconsin. She had hardly gotten out of the car when Rev. Loring Peterson, conference president (district superintendent) approached her about pastoring the church at Hillsboro. As a result, she pastored there 1955–63. In 1955 she was listed by the Iowa Conference as supplying the church in Hillsboro, Wisconsin. By 1956 she had transferred to the Wisconsin Conference and was a conference preacher (licensed minister). She was ordained in 1957. Several were converted at Hillsboro during her ministry, including two older women. A young man from the congregation later went into the ministry.

From 1963 to 1965, Dorothy Johnson was listed as a conference evangelist and children's worker. She teamed up with a lady whose name was Elda Shore. They held vacation Bible schools for Wesleyan Methodists and Free

Methodists, did evangelistic meetings for the Pilgrim Holiness and Salvation Army and children's meetings in the Chicago area. They filled in for a Pilgrim Holiness church after its pastor's death. From 1960 to 1962, Dorothy served as the Wisconsin Conference statistician and from 1962 to 1964 on the conference nominating committee.

Dorothy Johnson and Elda Shore pastored the Free Methodist church at Livingstone, Wisconsin, 1964–65. On May 11, 1965, Dorothy transferred to the Free Methodist Church. She and Elda became pastors at the LaFarge Free Methodist church. One year and seven months later, they were in an auto accident; Elda Shore was killed, and Dorothy was badly hurt. After she recovered, she pastored at LaFarge until 1970. In 1968 she married Vernie Clark. In 1970 she resigned as pastor at LaFarge and became the assistant pastor under a Pastor Dado. Vernie Clark was a widower with two small children. Five years after their marriage, Dorothy gave birth to a little girl.

In 1985 Dorothy Johnson Clark transferred back to what was now The Wesleyan Church, filling in for vacationing pastors, conducting funerals and weddings, and helping wherever needed. She became a part of the congregation at the Mt. Pisgah Wesleyan church in Ontario, Wisconsin. She served as Sunday school superintendent for nine years, taught first and second-graders in Sunday school, served for a time as director of missions, and sometimes filled in for the pastor at a Wednesday Bible study in an apartment complex.[28]

Mary Cloer Jonatis

Mary Cloer (or Clover) was listed in the records of the North Carolina District of the Pilgrim Holiness Church 1954–60. She was ordained by 1954 and apparently served on Formosa (Taiwan) 1954–55. In 1960 she married a Mr. Jonatis.

Marjorie Jones

Marjorie Jones was listed in the records of the Allegheny Conference of the Wesleyan Methodist Church 1954–66. She was ordained in

1954. In 1955 she was appointed as a general evangelist. From 1957 to 1959 she served as pastor with her husband, Donald P. Jones, at Canton, Ohio, Second church. From 1959 to 1966 she was pastoring at Greenwood. In 1966 she was appointed as a conference evangelist.

Carol Kiger

The South Central District of the Pilgrim Holiness Church listed Carol Kiger among its ministers in 1954. In 1956–57 Carol Kiger pastored the South San Gabriel, California, church. She was also listed by the California District in 1963.[29]

Carol A. Lister

Carol Lister was recommended by the Camden, New Jersey, church to the Middle Atlantic States Conference of the Wesleyan Methodist Church in 1954. She was so received but apparently spent at least part of that year serving as assistant pastor to Rev. Arthur Bray at the Austin, Illinois, church. Carol continued to be listed as a student 1955–57. From 1957 to 1959, Carol Lister and her husband, G. Kenneth Lister, pastored the Penn Beach, New Jersey, church. Carol was ordained in 1958. From 1959 on through at least 1967, the Listers served under World Gospel Mission in Kenya, Africa.[30]

Mrs. Emmett Meeks

Mrs. Emmett Meeks was listed among the ministers in the records of the Kentucky District of the Pilgrim Holiness Church 1954–56. She was serving as pastor at Confluence. She was ordained in 1955. From 1957 to 1961 she was listed in the records of the Pittsburgh District as inactive.

Margie F. Morris

The records of the Eastern District of the Pilgrim Holiness Church listed Margie Morris in

1954–55. By 1956 she had transferred to the Pennsylvania and New Jersey District. She was listed there through 1967. For at least the 1962–67 period, perhaps more, she served on the faculty at Eastern Pilgrim College, Allentown, Pennsylvania (later United Wesleyan College). For part of this period she was the librarian. In 1967 she was listed as an educator at Owosso College, Owosso, Michigan (later merged into what became Indiana Wesleyan University, Marion, Indiana).[31]

Olive L. Clark Todd

Olive Clark was born December 7, 1906, in Greene County, Indiana. In 1922 she went to live with John Newton and Elizabeth T. Clark in Terre Haute, Indiana. There she graduated from Hymera High School and from Normal College. She then studied on her own for the ministry. She married Leonard Todd June 30, 1953. She was ordained in 1954 by the Southern Indiana District of the Pilgrim Holiness Church and was listed by the Southern Indiana District 1954 through 1967. She pastored first at Sycamore Park, in Clinton, Indiana, and later at Shelburn. Leonard Todd died January 7, 1994. Olive Clark Todd died October 10, 1994.[32]

Mrs. Robert Ackerman

Mrs. Robert Ackerman was listed as an ordained minister and pastor in the records of the East Michigan District of the Pilgrim Holiness Church. From 1955 to 1958 she was listed as a pastor. From 1959 to 1962 she was listed as unstationed.

Naomi S. Colbert

Naomi married Fred Colbert in 1933. She was received by the Kentucky Conference of the Wesleyan Methodist Church from the Pilgrim Holiness Church as a conference preacher (licensed minister) January 21, 1955. She had engaged in evangelistic ministries for ten years prior to this. The Kentucky Conference (which included the southern third of Indiana) appointed her as pastor of

a church plant known as Vincennes Avenue in Washington, Indiana. She pursued the course of study and pastored this work until 1957. At that time she was returned to her local church to serve as a local preacher. But in 1958 she was again appointed to Vincennes Avenue and continued there after the 1968 merger for a total of more than twenty-five years. In 1964 Naomi S. Colbert was ordained. She was the mother of three daughters and one son. She died May 16, 1987, at the age of seventy-two.[33]

Mrs. Dorothy Darrah

Dorothy Darrah was listed 1955–60 on the records of the Champlain Conference of the Wesleyan Methodist Church (now Eastern New York-New England District). As a conference preacher, she was appointed assistant pastor at Cadyville, New York in 1955. She was ordained in 1958. She continued as assistant pastor at Cadyville until her death May 19, 1960. The church may have been on a circuit, as Dorothy Darrah left a house to be used as a parsonage whenever Cadyville could have its own pastor.

Evelyn Chapman Gisselbeck

Evelyn Chapman Gisselbeck was listed in the records of the Dakota Conference of the Wesleyan Methodist Church 1955–68. In 1955 she was a conference preacher (licensed minister). She and her husband, Eugene Gisselbeck, served as pastors at Medicine Rock and Mill Iron 1955–57. Evelyn was ordained June 16, 1957. That year she was assigned to missionary work. From 1958 to 1961 she and her husband pastored Sand Point, Idaho. From 1961 to 1962 she was assigned missionary work. From 1963 to 1966 she was unstationed (without appointment). In 1966, 1967, and 1968 she was listed as on reserve.

Irene Hanley

The records of the Ohio Conference of the Wesleyan Methodist Church listed Irene

Hanley among the ministers 1955–66. In 1955 she was a conference preacher (licensed minister). From 1955 to 1957 she served as a conference evangelist. In 1957 she was ordained. From 1957 to 1963 she served as a general evangelist. From 1963 to 1966 she was listed as on reserve, doing Jewish evangelism. On July 5, 1966, she withdrew and joined another denomination.

Laura Houch

Laura (Mrs. H. C.) Houch was listed among the ministers in the records of the North Central District of the Pilgrim Holiness Church 1955–62. She was listed in the records of the Central District in 1963 as a pastor and from 1964 to 1968 as retired.

Mary Keck

Mary Keck was listed among the ministers in the records of the Eastern Ohio District of the Pilgrim Holiness Church 1955–57 and 1959–67. She lived in Lancaster, Ohio. Beginning in 1966 she was listed as unstationed (without appointment) or as retired.

Ruth Long

Ruth Long was listed among the ministers in the records of the California District of the Pilgrim Holiness Church 1955–56. She was listed in the records of the Arizona-New Mexico District 1956, 1958–60, and 1963–64. She was ordained. She served for a time as a teacher at the Pilgrim Bible School in Colorado Springs (later merged into what became Oklahoma Wesleyan University, Bartlesville, Oklahoma). Her last years were devoted to vacation Bible schools, child evangelism, and other children's work. She was a member of Phoenix First Church when she died, just before Christmas 1963.

Mrs. Victor Marvin

The records of the Kansas District of the Pilgrim Holiness Church listed Mrs. Victor Marvin among the ministers 1955–67. Her ordination apparently dated from 1918. She and her husband pastored Wichita Trinity Church for fifteen years. In 1965 she was residing in Wichita and in 1966 and 1967 she was listed as retired.

Lillian Montgomery

Lillian Montgomery and her husband, Albert Montgomery, were officers in the Salvation Army and had retired from service. In 1955 they joined the Champlain Conference of the Wesleyan Methodist Church (now Eastern New York-New England District). Lillian was received as a conference preacher (licensed minister). The two served as chaplains at the Franklin County Prison 1955–60. In 1960 Lillian was to choose her own field of service. In 1961 she was returned to her local church to serve as a local preacher. In 1962 she was received to work on the ministerial course of study. In 1963 she was ordained, and from that year until 1968 she was listed as unstationed (without appointment). In 1968 she was listed as superannuated (retired). In retirement the Montgomerys were active in the local church at Malone, New York, and carried on outreach ministry at the Alice Hyde Nursing Home. They had two sons and two daughters. Lillian Montgomery passed away March 8, 1973, at the age of eighty-two.[34]

Thelma Parker

The records of the Pennsylvania and New Jersey District of the Pilgrim Holiness Church listed Thelma Parker among the ministers 1955–67. She was listed as an evangelist 1957–60 and as pastor at Millville, New Jersey, 1964–68.

Lorraine Randall

Lorraine Randall was listed among the ministers in the records of the Champlain Conference of the Wesleyan Methodist Church (now Eastern New York-New England District) 1955–66. She was ordained in 1955. She served as associate pastor at Forest Dale, Vermont, 1955–59. In 1959 a large house was purchased at Gouvernour, and Lorraine and Cliston Randall pastored there 1960–64. In 1964 Lorraine Randall was listed on reserve. From 1965 to 1966 she was assistant pastor at Stony Creek. On May 7, 1966, she gave her credentials to the conference president (district superintendent), and her name was removed from the ministerial roll.

Rose Ellen Swango

Rose Ellen Swango was listed among the ministers in the records of the Southern Indiana District of the Pilgrim Holiness Church 1955–67.

Berdsel Bell

The records of the Pennsylvania and New Jersey District of the Pilgrim Holiness Church listed Birdsel Bell among the ministers 1956–58. She transferred from the Eastern District in 1956.

Mrs. Elmer Braden

Mrs. Elmer Braden was listed in the records of the Tennessee District of the Pilgrim Holiness Church 1956–67. Beginning in 1958, she was listed as an evangelist.

Verneeda Ilene Gewecke Brown

Verneeda Gewecke was born December 21, 1911, at Ingham, Nebraska. She spent her early years in and around Farnam, Nebraska. She married Oliver Jesse Brown on Christmas Day 1933 at her parents' home in Farnam. The Browns had one daughter and one son.

After many years of farming with her husband, Verneeda began a home study course in preparation for the ministry. She was ordained by the Rocky Mountain District of the Pilgrim Holiness Church in 1956. She pastored at Lodge Pole, Sutherland, Arthur (1961–68), and Sidney—all in Nebraska. Verneeda Gewecke Brown passed away December 18, 1999. Her memorial service was held December 21, on what would have been her eighty-eighth birthday.[35]

Mrs. C. A. Bullard

The area of song evangelism and children's work became more prominent during the late 1940s and the 1950s. Mrs. C. A. Bullard served under the North Carolina Conference of the Wesleyan Methodist Church as a song evangelist and children's worker from 1956 to 1960. On August 24, 1960, she was also approved as a child evangelism director. From 1961 to 1962 she continued service in song evangelism and children's work. In 1962 she became the conference director of Christian Youth Crusaders (CYC). By 1968 she had the largest CYC in the denomination.[36]

Elnora Coe

Elnora (Mrs. J. E.) Coe was listed among the ministers in the records of the Texas District of the Pilgrim Holiness Church 1956–58. In 1957 she was identified as co-pastor of the Amarillo, Texas, church.

Mrs. Cora Collins

The records of the Kentucky District of the Pilgrim Holiness Church listed Cora Collins among the ministers 1956–67. She was the pastor at Cynthiana for this entire period. She was ordained in 1965. In 1960 extensive work was done on the parsonage and on the church. New floors were put in the parsonage, three rooms were tiled, one room was plastered, two new windows were installed, three rooms were redecorated, and the foundation was laid for a porch and a bath. The floors of the church were sanded and finished.

Alberta Finnicum

Alberta Finnicum was listed in the records of the Allegheny Conference of the Wesleyan Methodist Church 1956–66. She was ordained by 1956. She served as the pastor of the Harbor Ridge charge this entire period. Her husband, Joseph Finnicum, was listed as her assistant 1957–59 and 1962–63.

Bernice Fredrick

The records of the Pennsylvania and New Jersey District of the Pilgrim Holiness Church listed Bernice Fredrick among the ministers 1956–63. In both 1962 and 1963 she was listed as working outside of the denomination.

Mrs. Albert M. Hood

The records of the Western Ohio District of the Pilgrim Holiness Church listed Mrs. Albert M. Hood among the ministers 1956–67. She was ordained by 1956 and resided most of this period at least in Hartford City, Indiana.

Bernice Huffine

Bernice Huffine was first listed as a licensed minister by the Arizona District of the Pilgrim Holiness Church 1956–58. She was ordained by the Idaho-Washington District in 1962 and was listed by that district through 1965. In 1966 and 1967 she was listed by the Western Ohio District. She pastored with her husband, Albert P. Huffine, at Van Wert and at Lima Community church in Ohio. She retired in 1990, but in 1997 she and Albert began to serve as supply pastors at Lima Community. Bernice loved to write poetry.[37]

Helen Letonek

Helen Letonek was listed in the records of the Allegheny Conference of the Wesleyan Methodist Church among the ministers 1956–66. She was pastor, with her husband, Steve Letonek, of the West Fairfield church for those years. In 1966 she was listed as a worker recognized by the conference.

Zelma Salvador

Zelma (Mrs. Frank) Salvador was listed among the ministers in the records of the North Central District of the Pilgrim Holiness Church 1956–59. She was so listed in the records of the Florida District 1961–67.

Mrs. Margeurite Schwartz

Margeurite Schwartz was listed as a minister by the Eastern District of the Pilgrim Holiness Church 1956–67. She apparently pastored the Baltimore, Maryland Second Church for some time, and is specifically identified in that way in 1960–61 records. She was the supervisor of the girls at the Denton, Maryland camp.[38]

Mildred Smith

Mildred Smith was listed among the ministers in the records of the Northern Indiana District of the Pilgrim Holiness Church 1955–67. She was ordained in 1955. At least as early as 1955, she and her husband, Lewis G. Smith, were pastors of Victory Chapel in Frankfort, Indiana, and they continued service there long after the 1968 merger.

Mrs. Alice Spear

Alice Spear was received by the Nebraska Conference of the Wesleyan Methodist Church in 1956 to study for the ministry and to travel (serve) under the direction of the conference president (district superintendent). By 1959 she was a conference preacher (licensed minister) and was appointed as pastor of the Grand Island church. She was ordained in 1960 and continued her ministry at Grand Island through 1964. She served the conference on the statistical committee in 1962, led devotions in 1962, served on the pension plan board 1963 and 1964 and the committee on vacancies in 1964.[39]

Delpha VanWinkle

Delpha VanWinkle was listed in the records of the Indiana Conference of the Wesleyan Methodist Church 1956–68. She was received as an elder (ordained minister) on probation in 1956. In 1957 she was received into full standing. From 1957 to 1961 she served as registrar at Marion College, Marion, Indiana (now Indiana Wesleyan University). She was listed as on reserve 1961–65. She was unstationed (without appointment) 1965 through 1968.

Viola Wagner

Viola Wagner was listed among the ministers in the records of the Wisconsin District of the Pilgrim Holiness Church in 1956. She was listed in the records of the Illinois District 1956–68. She and her husband, Fred Wagner, pastored the Pleasant Hill church at Lexington, Illinois, for two and one-half years beginning in 1957. A new parsonage was built during their pastorate. Viola Wagner was listed as an evangelist in 1959 and 1963.

Nancy I. White

In 1956 Nancy White served as the assistant secretary of the Lockport Conference of the Wesleyan Methodist Church (now Western New York District). She apparently served some time as assistant to the pastor at Batavia, New York. In 1956 she was appointed supply pastor at Machias, New York. By February 13, 1957 she was granted a license as a conference preacher (licensed

minister). At the 1957 session of the conference she led devotions. She now became the pastor at Machias and served in that capacity until 1959. In 1959 she was ordained and appointed as a children's worker. On July 12, 1960, she was given a letter of transfer to the Canada Conference.

Nancy White had become the pastor's assistant at Belleville, Ontario, on November 1, 1959. Rev. J. S. A. Spearman was not only the pastor at Belleville but also the Canada Conference president (district superintendent). And Nancy was listed by the Canada Conference as the conference president's assistant from 1960 through 1966. She served in this capacity at least until 1968.[40]

Mrs. Helen Winchester

Helen Winchester was born in Wisconsin. Her mother, father, grandfather, and uncle were all ministers. Her father served in home missions, and she traveled over much of the eastern part of the country with him. Her conversion came in October 1933, in Ohio County, in western Kentucky, under Methodist influence. A radio program and Henry Clay Morrison's *Pentecostal Herald* made her hunger after holiness, and she was sanctified wholly. Later came the call to the ministry, which she said that she could never doubt. "I felt I had to answer it, though, or lose my soul." Concerning her call, she declared, "The call has been real, rugged, and rewarding. So many, many places—jails, hospitals and homes—these have been my privilege to enter as well as the pulpit." She was ordained in 1956 by the Kentucky District of the Pilgrim Holiness Church. Her ministerial service was concentrated in the area around the place of her conversion— in western Kentucky.

Much of Helen Winchester's ministry was spent going wherever there were open doors and opportunities. She sometimes helped other ministers in their pastorates or joined in teams for revivals. She labored in Ohio County for several years, particularly in Central City and Cool Springs. She held the first cottage prayer meeting at one of these places in a house on the outskirts of town. Three members of the family living in that house were in the penitentiary at the time. There were descendants of that family in church decades later because of that visit. In Cool Springs an old building was granted for use in services. Every Saturday night it was open, and a fire was going. The first convert was the man who made the place available. In 1958 she was embroidering pillowcases for a church fundraiser. She was alerted by hearing, "You've got to go" several times. She got up and left, not knowing where she was going. She prayed along the way and at the crossroads. She crossed a street to an alley. At the first house she came to, a lady came out crying and saying, "I'm so glad you came!" She had found her neighbor dead. Helen Winchester stepped into the situation, doing even menial tasks to ease the lady's stress.

The Kentucky District listed Helen 1956–67. She was listed as an evangelist in 1959 and as inactive in 1962. Her husband died in June 1962. By 1963 she was pastoring the church at Clay and continued there until 1966. She then moved to Cloverport to assist a Brother Mercer in Glen Dean Mission 1966–67. Then she moved to Owensboro to assist a Brother Todd. Then from 1969 to 1982 she pastored at Livermore. In 1975 Livermore was in great danger because of leaks in the gas lines. Some of the men were dealing with the emergency all night, and it was very cold. Wesleyan ladies provided the men with hot coffee and food. Afterward there was a meeting, and the Wesleyan church was the only church invited. Helen received a ceramic dish in recognition of her part in serving needs at such a time.

Helen Winchester retired in 1982.[41]

Mrs. C. C. Coleman

Most of Mrs. C. C. Coleman's ministerial labors apparently took place before her name appeared on any of the available official district records. The records of the Rocky Mountain District of the Pilgrim Holiness Church listed her from 1961 through 1965. She and her husband, C. C. Coleman, were referred to in the records of the 1966 district conference as faith laborers who had started the Superior and McCook churches,

both in southern Nebraska, near the Nebraska-Kansas state line. When the Grand Junction church was in crisis, they gave their time to get it back on a firm foundation. The C. C. Colemans retired from active service in 1957. Mrs. Coleman died November 23, 1965, at the age of fifty-one. C. C. Coleman died six months later, May 1966 at the age of seventy-two.

Donna Dean

Donna Dean graduated from Owosso Bible College, Owosso, Michigan (later merged into what became Indiana Wesleyan University, Marion, Indiana) and from Spring Arbor College, Spring Arbor, Michigan. She and her husband, Clifford Dean, were ordained by the Pilgrim Holiness Church in 1957. They pastored four churches in Michigan: Midland, Lansing, Luther, and Muskegon North. They also pastored Wabash, Indiana Middle Street, and Beech Grove in Carey, Ohio. Donna Dean's ministry was viewed as encouraging and filling in wherever needed—teaching Sunday school, directing children's church and vacation Bible school, and being active in women's ministries.[42]

Dorothy A. K. Peters
de Freitas

Dorothy A. K. Peters was born in Swete Village, Antigua, West Indies, February 11, 1932. She attended the Faith, Hope and Charity High School and the Cana and Antigua Girls' School. Her parents separated, leaving her sad and lonely and humiliated because of the riches-to-rags result. She married her teenage sweetheart, a man by the name of de Freitas. Her marriage was a troubled one, at least in the early years. But she met a teacher and a neighbor who were Pilgrim Holiness ladies. Dorothy had a dream that one Sunday morning became a reality through the insistent invitation of one of these ladies to go to church with her. Dorothy was converted May 5, 1955, at the Grays Farm Pilgrim Holiness church, St. John's, Antigua. She was baptized in August 1955.

Dorothy de Freitas's husband and family forsook her because she had joined "a way-side church." One lady in the church was migrating to England, and Dorothy went with her, hoping to work as a nurse. Her friend located in Birmingham, and Dorothy located in London. They arrived in December 1955, and she did odd jobs until employed by a hospital in February 1956. The Pilgrim Holiness Church was not yet in operation in England, so she attended the Salvation Army.

In the latter part of 1957, Rev. Dennis Sampson arrived in England from the Caribbean and began to gather Pilgrim Holiness people into congregations, particularly in Manchester and Birmingham. Rev. Sampson challenged Dorothy with Esther 4:14. She quit her job and started making contacts to begin a church in London. She was asked to meet a Mr. H. Sealy, from Barbados, who was coming in on the train and who was looking for Pilgrim Holiness fellowship. She did. They started prayer meetings in Sealy's home and then Sunday school and church services. Then they got a hall called Busby's Place.

Dorothy de Freitas's husband arrived in England in 1958. They located at a distance from the new church. Dorothy got a job and a year or so later started a church in her home. This was at Forest Gate. Eventually this congregation bought a property, now known as Harrow Green.

Dorothy de Freitas began studying for the ministry. It took six years for her to complete the studies for ordination. She was listed by the British Isles District 1962–67. She served as district secretary during this time and was listed as a deaconess. At some point she achieved recognition as an ordained minister.

Once again Dorothy felt impressed to quit her well-paying job and go to Slough to start another church. She left the children in bed, in the care of her husband. She went for a walk and to get a paper called the *Christian Herald*. Coming out of the paper shop, she was praying. By a fence she saw something wrapped up in a paper. She picked it up, found it contained money and written on the paper was "Go to Slough." The next morning she used the money to buy her train ticket and traveled to Slough. She was looking

for an acquaintance, a Mr. Wade. She encountered him shortly after getting off the train. He took her home to his wife and children. Dorothy lived in Slough for three months and another church was started. The district listed her as pastor at Slough in 1966.

In June 1976, Dorothy came to America to attend the General Conference of The Wesleyan Church, filling in as an alternate delegate. She visited a relative of her husband in New York. Her husband was by now working in London for an American firm. He was encouraged by wife, relatives, and employers to go to America. He did in June 1977 and became an American citizen. Two and one-half years later Dorothy de Freitas joined him.

Dorothy went looking for a holiness church in Brooklyn. Walking down Flatbush she saw a little board outside a house with the name "Rev. Louis Goodman" on it. She knew him, went in, found ten Wesleyan worshipers, five of whom she knew. A few ladies began traveling with Dorothy to Brooklyn. They were getting home in the early morning hours and they believed the Lord was saying that they would have a church at Queens, where they lived. Dorothy de Freitas had acquired a job as an outpatient clerk at Memorial Sloan-Kettering Hospital. One morning in May 1983, as she got off the train the Lord told her she must give up her job and be about the Lord's business. The result, with the assistance of Louis Goodman, was a church in Queens. She invited people from the Bronx to visit the church in Queens. But they soon asked her to come and teach and preach to them in the Bronx. So on Christmas morning 1984, with seven adults and fifteen children, the Bronx Sunday school was started. It developed into a church in the home of one of the ladies. Eventually a property was purchased for the South Bronx Wesleyan Church. Dorothy served as pastor for fifteen years, 1984–99. She and her husband then decided, due to her health problems, that they would sell their house in England, buy one in Antigua, and live there in the winter and in New York in the summer.

Harry F. Wood, superintendent of the Pennsylvania and New Jersey District of The

Wesleyan Church, had this to say about Dorothy de Freitas in her pastorate at South Bronx:

> Her courage displayed in the face of tremendous vulnerability in such a drug and crime-infested area was remarkable. As a woman, she achieved a ministry that no man could have ever experienced. As urban ministers have often discovered, a woman can do what men sometimes are unable to do because the male presence often becomes too great a threat to crime/gang infrastructure.[43]

Edith Dowden

The records of the Florida District of the Pilgrim Holiness Church listed Edith Dowden among the ministers in 1957 and 1960–67. In 1960 and 1961 she was designated as unstationed.

Mrs. Mary Hargett

Mary Hargett was listed among the ministers in the records of the Southern Indiana District of the Pilgrim Holiness Church 1957–66. She was born in 1905 and died as a result of an automobile accident on November 2, 1965. She was living at College Corner at the time and was the pastor of the Milton, Indiana, church.

Estella Henderson

The records of the Northern Indiana District of the Pilgrim Holiness Church listed Estella Henderson among the ministers 1957–61. She was an ordained minister. She spent her last days in Wisconsin. She died in 1961.

Mattie McCoy

Mattie McCoy served in the California District of the Pilgrim Holiness Church as a minister 1957–58 and 1960–68. She pastored Lynwood Gardens June 1957 to June 1958. She pastored South San Gabriel 1966–68.[44]

Elsie R. Welch

Elsie R. Welch transferred into the Florida District of the Pilgrim Holiness Church in 1957. According to district records, she continued to be listed among the ministers 1957–67. She was listed in 1959 as retired.

Mary Maness Wesley

Mary Maness Wesley was received as an ordained minister on trial by the North Carolina Conference of the Wesleyan Methodist Church in 1957. She had been in the People's Methodist Church. According to conference records, she continued to be listed until 1967. She was received in full standing in 1958. From 1957 to 1958 she served as a conference evangelist. From 1958 to 1959, she served as assistant pastor with her husband, Arthur L. Wesley, Jr., at Nebo and People's Chapel at Laurel Hill. At the 1959 conference Mary was placed on reserve, but on September 9, 1969, she was appointed assistant pastor at Durham. From 1960 through 1964 she was appointed on reserve. Again she was appointed to reserve in 1965, but on August 10, 1965, she was appointed assistant pastor at the Ridgewood church in Raleigh. Arthur and Mary Wesley served at Raleigh until July 27, 1967, when they took letters of withdrawal to leave the denomination.

Dora Abel

Dora Abel was converted at age seventeen. She began home missionary labors when she was eighteen. She became the second wife of Rev. Fred Abel in 1911. They had one daughter and two sons. She spent her ministerial life in the service of the Missionary Bands of the World. When the Missionary Bands merged into the Wesleyan Methodist Church in 1958, she was received by the Kentucky Conference as a superannuated (retired) elder (ordained minister). She continued on the retired list until she died July 16, 1960.[45]

Ophelia Bach

Ophelia Bach was listed among the ordained ministers in the records of the Northern Indiana District of the Pilgrim Holiness Church 1958–67.

Thelma Bartley

The Kentucky District of the Pilgrim Holiness Church listed Thelma Bartley among the ministers 1958–67. She was ordained in 1958. From 1962 on she was listed as inactive.

Thelma Davidson

According to the records of the Kentucky Conference of the Wesleyan Methodist Church, Thelma Davidson was on the list of ministers 1958–67. At first she was pursuing the course of study and was licensed as a conference preacher (licensed minister). From 1959 to 1965 she served as a pastor in mountain mission work. From 1965 to 1967 she was listed as a conference evangelist. In 1967 she was ordained.

Elizabeth B. Evans

Elizabeth Evans first served in the Idaho-Washington District of the Pilgrim Holiness Church 1958–62. She had been converted as a girl. She graduated from Pasadena College and later earned a master's degree in education from Walla Walla College in Washington State and the Ontario College of Education in Toronto. She married Rev. Frank Evans, who was pastoring at that time in Canada. She served under the Ontario District of the Pilgrim Holiness Church 1963–67. Frank and Elizabeth continued as co-pastors of the Oakwood church in Toronto until retirement in 1968. Elizabeth Evans died August 24, 1983.[46]

Iris Eversole

The records of the Indiana Conference of the Wesleyan Methodist Church indicated that Iris Eversole was received in 1958 as an elder (ordained minister) in the merger of the Missionary Bands of the World with the Wesleyan Methodist Church. She was listed in 1958 as a retired missionary. In 1959 she requested that she not be continued as an elder.

Wilma Jean Jackson George

Wilma Jean Jackson George was listed in the records of the Michigan District of the Pilgrim Holiness Church 1958–67. She was ordained in 1958. She served 1958–61 as a medical missionary. From 1962 on, she served in higher education.

Mrs. H. J. Lewis

The records of the South Georgia Conference of the Wesleyan Methodist Church indicated that in 1958 Mrs. H. J. Lewis was received as an ordained minister on probation from the Pilgrim Holiness Church. She and her husband, H. J. Lewis, were appointed pastors at Waycross, Georgia, 1958–59. From 1959 to 1960 they pastored Bethlehem and Jesup. In December 1959, the South Georgia Conference and North Georgia Conference merged to form the Georgia Conference. The records of the Georgia Conference show that from 1960 to 1962 Mrs. Lewis was assistant pastor with her husband at the Crossroads charge. In 1963 the Lewises joined another denomination.

Mrs. Glenn Slater

Mrs. Glenn Slater was ordained in 1958 by the Kansas District of the Pilgrim Holiness Church, according to district records. The records also listed her in 1958 and 1959 as co-pastor of the Osawatomie church. In 1960 she transferred to the Church of the Nazarene.

Mrs. Joyce Morey Smith

Joyce Morey Smith (known by many simply as "Joy") was a graduate of Churchville-Chili High School in Rochester, New York. She attended Roberts Wesleyan College (a Free Methodist school) in Rochester for two years. She went on to receive her A.B. degree in psychology, religion, and sociology from Seattle Pacific University. She later received a bachelor of sacred theology from Biblical Seminary in New York, and an M. S. degree in counseling from the State University College at Brockport, New York. In 1988 she received her doctorate from Colgate Divinity School.

From 1958 to 1967, Joyce Smith was listed by the Lockport Conference of the Wesleyan Methodist Church (now Western New York District). In 1958 she was appointed as supply pastor at North Pembroke. On July 14, 1959, she received her letter of standing from the Genesee Conference of the Free Methodist Church, and that same year she was ordained by the Lockport Conference. She continued as pastor at North Pembroke until 1965. The North Pembroke church had been started by Rev. Alton J. Shea with nine charter members with a few others joining afterward. The church was pastored by student ministers from 1951 to 1958. Joyce Smith was the first resident pastor. In 1960 most of the members moved out of town and she had to start over. By one year later, nearly fifty families counted this as their church home.

Joyce resigned from North Pembroke, January 10, 1965, and was appointed as a conference evangelist. In 1966, 1967, and 1968 she was listed as a missionary, a representative to International Students. She led devotions at the conference sessions of 1959, 1963, and 1964. She was elected conference tithing secretary in 1962 and 1963.

Joyce Smith served as a pastor of local churches in New York for a total of seventeen years. Then she developed and led workshops for churches, colleges, community agencies, public schools, and business organizations. She established her own counseling service, "The People Place," in 1979.

Joyce served The Wesleyan Church in many ways—writing Sunday school curriculum, serving on the council for women in ministry, chairing the district social concerns committee, and serving on the district board of ministerial development.

Joyce Morey Smith passed away, January 8, 1996, at the age of seventy.[47]

Flora Weedman

The records of the Florida District of the Pilgrim Holiness Church list Flora Weedman as ordained in 1958. She was listed among the ministers 1961–64. In 1964 she was listed as inactive.

Mrs. Ted Wilson

According to the records of the Kentucky District of the Pilgrim Holiness Church, Mrs. Ted Wilson was ordained in 1958.

Marie Young

The records of the Northern Indiana District of the Pilgrim Holiness Church listed Marie Young among the ministers 1953–67. She transferred in 1953 from the Hephzibah Faith Missionary Association. From 1962 on she was listed as serving in denominational work.

Virginia Ruth Miller Anderson

Virginia Ruth Miller, more commonly known as Ruth, began her walk with the Lord with a simple prayer for forgiveness of her sins and inviting Jesus to live within. She spoke of the years that followed as times when tears drenched the altar of the Pleasant View Community Church, a little white frame building north of Zionsville, Indiana, as battles were fought over the lordship of her life. But eventually the "Miller will" crumbled, and she answered, "Yes," to the call and will of God.

Ruth Miller married Bob K. Anderson May 27, 1955. He had already said yes to God's call into the ministry, but his preparation for ministry had been on hold. The Lord had a "schedule that included a companion for life and ministerial service." In the summer of 1955 the Andersons joined the Westfield, Indiana, Wesleyan Methodist church. Rev. Orval and Rev. Vivian Bardsley were the pastoral team, and they and their congregation saw something in this young couple that they believed God could use. They lovingly yet firmly admonished the Andersons to "get serious" about preparing for the Lord's service. That winter, when Marion College, Marion, Indiana (now Indiana Wesleyan University) offered two weeks of night classes for those pursuing the course of study, the Bardsleys took the Andersons to the college, enrolled them, and got them started.

During this period of time, Ruth Anderson sensed that the Lord was dealing with her about preparing for the ministry.

Obedience to God's call had been settled when a teenager. However, the thought of serving the Lord in this manner was something I had not considered. A woman minister? What were the options for women in ministry? How would the call of God affect us individually and as a couple? As I prayed about serving the Lord in this capacity, He reminded me that He already knew the plans He had for me (Jeremiah 29:11) and that He would be with me (Joshua 1:5). That was good enough for me. Having settled His call, I joined Bob in preparing for ordination.

From 1956 to 1958, Bob and Ruth were appointed as supply pastors of the Eagle Creek Friends Church. The Bardsleys mentored them. Ruth had a new baby boy, was caring for her invalid mother, and was being a wife to her pastor husband. She was especially concerned for young women. She focused on listening, loving, and praying with them.

From 1958 to 1963, the Andersons served the Thorntown, Indiana, Wesleyan Methodist church. They made progress slowly toward ordination, with the help of faculty members at Marion College and at Frankfort Pilgrim College, Frankfort, Indiana, (later merged into United Wesleyan College, Allentown, Pennsylvania). In August 1961 the Indiana Conference of the Wesleyan Methodist Church ordained Bob K. and Virginia Ruth Anderson. She served at this time with children, youth and young women.

From 1963 to 1970, the Andersons served the Gas City Eastview church. Ruth was now able at last to fulfill her lifelong dream of going to college. She earned a bachelor's degree in education at Marion College and a master's degree in education at Ball State University, Muncie, Indiana. She began to teach in the public schools. She also taught at youth camps, vacation Bible schools, and ladies' groups. She also taught a college student Sunday school class, from which came future pastors, pastors' wives, and strong church leaders on both local and district levels.

From 1970 to 1992, Bob and Ruth served the Eastlawn Wesleyan Church in Indianapolis, succeeding the pastoral team of Lee and Maxine Haines. Besides teaching in public schools, Ruth taught an adult Sunday school class, worked in children's church, and had Bible studies with the youth. Occasionally she taught the midweek Bible study and filled the pulpit. She served as local church director of Wesleyan Women, also for a time as district director of Wesleyan women and also for a time as area director of Wesleyan Women. The latter post put her on the general executive committee for Wesleyan Women for the entire denomination.

In the fall of 1983, Ruth's rewarding life of service was invaded by Parkinson's Syndrome. She wondered whether she would be "put on the shelf." The Lord spoke to her through Amy Carmichael's pen: "A soldier in the spiritual army is never off his battlefield. He is only removed to another part of the field. No soldier on service is ever laid aside; he is only given another commission. . . . Soldiers are not shelved." She believed that the Lord designed a ministry for her now that would use her physical limitations to reach another circle of hurting people. As the volume and clarity of her speech deteriorated, she concentrated on working with small groups in discipleship and mentoring. She also had opportunities to witness through the written word.

In 1992, Bob K. and Virginia Ruth Anderson retired from full-time service, only to find other reassignments. From 1992 to 1993 they served as ministers of pastoral care at the Memorial Circle Wesleyan church in Anderson, Indiana, pastored by the husband of their daughter Rebecca, William T. Rose. From 1993 to 2001 they served in the same way at the Fountain City, Indiana, Wesleyan church, pastored by their son, David Anderson. This 150-year old congregation was experiencing breathtaking growth from the nineties to over eight hundred in attendance.[48]

Ella Voight Cawthon

The records of the North Georgia Conference of the Wesleyan Methodist Church first mentioned Ella Cawthon in 1953 as a delegate to the district Woman's Missionary Society meeting. Her husband, Clarence Cawthon, was listed in 1954 as pastor at Wesley Chapel. In 1955 Ella was now listed as co-pastor with her husband at Wesley Chapel. In 1956 they were ordained together. From 1956 to 1960 she served as associate pastor with her husband at Wesley Chapel. Ella served on the conference resolutions committee and the missionary board in 1957, 1958, and 1959. In December 1959 the North Georgia and South Georgia Conferences merged into the Georgia Conference. The records of the Georgia Conference listed Ella as assistant to her husband at Wesley Chapel 1960–62. At Wesley Chapel, Ella taught Sunday school, helped with youth work and the Young Missionary Workers Band (now Wesleyan Kids for Missions), and in singing, but did not preach. From 1962 to 1963, she was assistant to her husband at Cordele. In 1963 she was listed as "unstationed" (without appointment) at her own request.

Mrs. George E. Culver

The records of the Pittsburgh District of the Pilgrim Holiness Church listed Mrs. George E. Culver in 1959 as inactive.

Sheila Graham McCrea-MacCallum

Sheila Graham was born in the rural community of Maple Ridge, New Brunswick, on August 23, 1938. She was the fourth of nine children. Her parents were devout Christians in the Alliance of the Reformed Baptist Church of Canada. Before Sheila was born, the Lord assured her mother that her fourth child would be a minister. When Sheila was  born, her mother thought that she had misinterpreted God's message, since she was a girl. Her mother never told Sheila this until she became a minister.

Regular family altar was practiced in the home, and the family regularly attended Sunday school and Sunday morning worship. Sheila gave her heart to the Lord when she was eight. She often played church with other children, and she was always the preacher. She even preached to the cows and the hens while doing farm work. Her mother would come to see why she was taking so long. On hearing her preaching, her mother would return to the house without saying a word. Sheila wrote her first sermon when she was twelve. One night when Sheila was about fourteen, while her parents were at prayer meeting, she and her younger sisters had church at home. At the close, her six-year-old sister gave her life to the Lord. She later became a pastor's wife. Sheila was the youth president when she was fifteen, and at some youth services she would give a devotional. A visiting pastor heard her in the youth service, and as a result she was asked to preach her first message away from home at his church when she was sixteen. Once her pastor asked her to supply his circuit of three churches.

When Sheila graduated from high school shortly before her seventeenth birthday, she wanted to attend Bethany Bible College. But her older brother wanted to go, so she said nothing. Instead, she attended a teacher's college for one year. The next summer she directed a vacation Bible school and at night served as a youth evangelist in one of the churches. In the fall she began teaching school and serving as a youth evangelist on some weekends. She had a growing conviction that God wanted her to be an evangelist. In her second year of teaching, during the Christmas holidays she traveled to a church for youth services. The second night she excused herself from supper to go and pray. "How would I be able, as a woman, to be a full-time evangelist? Would I be accepted? Would I get any services? Finally, I yielded to the Lord and in total dependence on Him, took the leap of faith. What peace flooded my heart!" She placed her name in the Reformed Baptist paper, and by June, when her teaching was over, her schedule was full. In the fall of 1958, when she was twenty, she began to travel to Reformed Baptist, Nazarene, and Christian and Missionary Alliance churches in central and eastern Canada, the New England states, and New York state. In October 1959, she held revival services in the Free Will Baptist church at Linnaeus, Maine. Shortly before she arrived, the pastor resigned and moved elsewhere. Sheila was invited after the services to remain as pastor, and she stayed until June 1960. A number of families from that church became members of the Houlton, Maine, Reformed Baptist church when it was organized.

In 1963 Sheila went before the committee for ordination. She was asked, "Do you plan to marry?" Her response was "I hope so." She was told that if she married she would be expected to surrender her credentials. She was ordained in July that year.

After eight years of evangelism, Sheila "felt a hunger to learn more." In 1966 the year that the Reformed Baptists merged into the Wesleyan Methodist Church, Sheila enrolled at

Houghton College, Houghton, New York. While a student there, she served as assistant director of East Hall. In 1969 she received an A. B. degree in religion. Then she earned an M. S. in guidance counseling at Alfred University, Alfred, New York. From 1970 to 1973, she served as counselor for women at Malone College, Canton, Ohio, and in 1973–74 she served there as assistant dean of students. During these years at the colleges, she was still occasionally involved in evangelism.

In August 1974, Sheila married Glen McCrea, a widower with a daughter aged eleven and a son aged nine. He was an electrical engineer and a very active member of a Wesleyan church. They prayed until they were certain this was God's will for that time for Sheila. She then surrendered her ordination credentials.

In the years that followed, she started and led Bible studies for women in her local church—these groups continue to the present. She directed junior church for six years and served as district director of the Young Missionary Workers Band (now Wesleyan Kids for Missions), and later as district director of Wesleyan Women. In 1983 she began to speak at women's conventions.

On April 11, 1998, Glen became critically ill and within a week was diagnosed with terminal cancer. He died June 30, 1998. Three months later Sheila's mother died after a very brief illness. It was a very difficult time for Sheila. She cried out to the Lord again and again. Then she heard a still small voice, "When you are ready, I will show you the way." On July 1, 1999, David Medders called her to ask if she would serve as interim dean of discipleship at Bethany Bible College in Sussex, New Brunswick. She accepted and began to serve.

In the summer of 1999, H. C. Wilson, superintendent of the Atlantic District, initiated the restoration of Sheila McCrea's ministerial credentials. Her original certificate was restored to her at the ordination service at district conference that year. In 2000, Sheila married Kenneth MacCallum and has been known from then on as Sheila McCrea-MacCallum.[49]

Elvie Turner

Elvie Turner was listed in the records of the Dakota Conference of the Wesleyan Methodist Church among the ministers 1959–68. She had taught at Miltonvale Wesleyan College, Miltonvale, Kansas, many years before seeking ordination. She was ordained in 1959 and was listed that year as choosing her own field of labor. From 1960 on, she was listed as teaching at Miltonvale. In 1968 she was so listed but as being on a two-year leave of absence. At some point she was apparently involved in a house church at Artesian.

Nettie Waggoner

The records of the Southern Indiana District of the Pilgrim Holiness Church listed Nettie Waggoner among the ordained ministers 1959–67. She was ordained in 1959 after pastoring many years as a licensed minister. From 1959 to 1967 she was listed as pastor at Harvey Flats, Alton, Indiana.

Letha Wood

According to the records of the Kansas District of the Pilgrim Holiness Church, Letha Wood was listed among the ministers 1959–68. She was ordained in 1959. In 1959 and 1960 she was living in Eldorado, Kansas. In 1962, 1963, and 1964 she was listed as inactive. From 1965 on, she was released to work outside the denomination.

A Decade of Sweeping Change

The decade of the 1960s was a time of sweeping change in North American culture, in the Church, and for women called to ministry. In American society the 1960s saw the ascendancy of rock 'n' roll on the popular music scene; the sexual revolution, which claimed to bring "liberation"; "hippies," who broke all social conventions; and "Jesus people," who shared part of that lifestyle but who also talked of a Savior. It was the decade that saw the escalation of the divisive Vietnam War, the climax of the civil rights movement, and the charismatic revival.

For the denominations served by the women whose stories appear in this book, it was a time of both schism and merger. In 1962 the Africa Evangelistic Mission merged into the Pilgrim Holiness Church. In 1966 the Alliance of the Reformed Baptist Church of Canada merged into the Wesleyan Methodist Church and became its Atlantic Conference (District). As the Wesleyan Methodist and Pilgrim Holiness Churches began seriously to pursue merger, this possibility heightened tensions that were already evident in both bodies between those inclined toward some latitude in Christian lifestyle and those inclined toward a more legalistic demand for uniformity. The more legalistic group tended also to resist centralization of leadership and increasingly had reservations about church merger. In 1963 some thirty of the churches in the New York District of the Pilgrim Holiness Church, the carryover from what had been four decades earlier the Pentecostal Rescue

Mission, withdrew. Following the 1966 General Conference of the Wesleyan Methodist Church, most of the churches in the Allegheny, Tennessee, and Alabama Conferences and a significant number of churches in the Ohio Conference withdrew. The losses for the Wesleyan Methodists included thirteen percent of the denomination's churches and almost eleven percent of its members. In spite of the withdrawals, both denominations were experiencing remarkable growth. In 1966 they both voted to merge. The consummation took place in Anderson, Indiana, June 26 through July 1, 1968, with the birth of The Wesleyan Church.

The 1960s also saw a continued decline in the number of women entering Wesleyan ministry. The reasons for the decline in the 1950s as described in chapter 6 continued, and in some cases intensified, in the 1960s. There was also a decrease in the high respect for the ministry as the ideal area of service for the children of church families. In earlier generations many parents had thought that God had blessed them beyond measure when He called one of their children into the ministry. Now families began to dream of careers in medicine, law, engineering, or education. This affected the recruiting of both men and women for ministry. Also, the schisms removed from the church many women whose stories have been included in earlier chapters of this book and others who would have followed their lead into the ministry. This decade also saw the beginning of radical feminism, which would bring a backlash against women in leadership in holiness circles. Those new to the holiness churches did not know the long history of women in ministry and would label the ordination of women as collaboration with radical feminism. From the 1950s to the 1960s, there was a decline of more than 60 percent in the number of women entering the ministry in what became The Wesleyan Church. There were only about one-fourth as many women entering the ministry in Wesleyan churches in the 1960s as had entered in the 1940s. Here are stories of some who did enter.

Vallie Boston

According to the records of the Kentucky Conference of the Wesleyan Methodist Church, Vallie Boston was listed with the ministers 1961–67. On September 12, 1960, she was accepted as a conference preacher (licensed minister) and appointed co-pastor with her husband, O. C. Boston, at Mt. Calvary and Mt. Zion. They were continued in that appointment until 1962. From 1962 on, they were listed as co-pastors at Hope.

Velma Butts

The records of the Illinois District of the Pilgrim Holiness Church listed Velma Butts as a minister in 1960. Her service covered a longer period as she pastored at Martinsville, Jerseyville, and Ottawa.

Eva Dearinger

Eva Dearinger was listed in the records of the Illinois District of the Pilgrim Holiness Church 1960–67. She was ordained in 1960.

Ann Lenheiser Eagle

Ann Lenheiser was a nurse and a deaconess in the Pilgrim Holiness Church prior to the 1968 merger with the Wesleyan Methodists. She became a part of the North Michigan District of The Wesleyan Church. As a deaconess, Ann had had

voting privileges in the district conference prior to the merger but not after the merger. The Basis for Merger indicated that persons were to retain their previous status. Ann appealed on both the district and denominational levels. As a result, at the annual North Michigan District Ministers Convention at the Traverse City Bayview Wesleyan Church, in the 1970–71 district year, with a General Superintendent present, Ann was ordained as a minister. During that year Ann also married Rev. Howard Eagle, a retired minister from the Missionary Church. They supplied the Loomis, Michigan Missionary church together until his health forced retirement at Evart, Michigan. Ann Lenheiser Eagle died in 1982.[1]

Mrs. Lloyd Fitch

Mrs. Lloyd Fitch was listed as a minister by the California District of the Pilgrim Holiness Church 1960–67.

Pauline Karns

Records of the Southern Indiana District of the Pilgrim Holiness Church listed Pauline Karns as a minister 1960–67. She apparently served the first year in some manner at Frankfort Pilgrim College, Frankfort, Indiana (later merged into United Wesleyan College, Allentown, Pennsylvania). From 1964 on she was listed as pastor at Clarksburg, Indiana.

Mae Newton

Mae Newton was listed on the records of the Florida Conference of the Wesleyan Methodist Church 1960–67. She and her husband, Edward Newton, had moved to Vero Beach, Florida, as retired schoolteachers. When they realized there was no Wesleyan Methodist church there, they requested the district for permission to start services in their home. They received such permission and started a church. Mae Newton was appointed pastor at Vero Beach July 16, 1959. The Newtons went back to teaching so they could have more money to put into a new church building. Through their sacrificial giving of themselves and their finances, the church was erected. Apparently Mae Newton had had some ministerial preparation in Indiana. In 1961 she transferred from the Indiana Conference and was ordained by the Florida Conference. She was still pastoring Vero Beach in 1967. During these years they also added a parsonage. Edward Newton as a layman was a strong partner in the work. He also helped with the almost constant Sunday noon entertainment at the Newton dinner table.

Evon Pulliam

Evon Pulliam grew up on a farm in the mountains of western North Carolina, in a small town called West Jefferson in Ashe County. Her parents did not come from Christian homes, but her mother had been converted at a young age at the Bethel Baptist church. The first year her parents were married, they attended a "protracted meeting" at Bethel, and her father was converted. From then on their lives revolved around church and serving the Lord. They had four daughters and one son, with Evon next to the oldest.

Evon was converted at the age of twelve, July 4, 1954, in a tent meeting, under the preaching of her uncle, an itinerant preacher. As a teenager she conducted prayer meetings in the church and cottage prayer meetings in the home. She taught Sunday school and directed the Christmas program. Eventually her uncle began to take Evon along with his daughter on his summer forays in tent meetings in some of the rough mountainous areas where no one else would go. Evon led the singing, sang specials, accompanied herself on the accordion. Usually Thursday night would be youth night and her uncle would turn the entire service over to Evon. At first she found this frightening, but it seems that it was God's way of preparing her for a life of ministry.

Evon spent a total of ten years in full-time evangelism. She worked with Pilgrim Holiness, Wesleyan Methodist, Evangelical Methodist, and Nazarene churches. She sang and conducted the youth service in the Todd Camp Meeting, located near her home, for eight consecutive years.

In 1972 Evon married Robert Pulliam, the son of a Wesleyan pastor. Robert was a guidance counselor at a senior high school. They had two daughters. Three to four years after their marriage, they faced a time of financial stress. Their rent was raised and their budget was already tight. It was in August that Evon prayed and believed that the Lord assured her they would soon have their own home. They secured boxes for packing, ready to move. The boxes gathered dust for a while, and Satan would tell her she was foolish. But on November 9, they moved into their own house for only twenty-five dollars.

Evon Pulliam pastored two Wesleyan churches. She pastored the Staley Wesleyan church for four years. By July 1998 she had been the pastor at the Hopewell, North Carolina, Wesleyan church for ten years. With Robert's input and efforts, they had built fellowship halls at both churches. At Hopewell an older husband and wife were converted. He had been an alcoholic and she was a church dropout. Both became members and she taught the adult Sunday school class and he served as Sunday school superintendent and usher. Their grandson and his wife and their children also began to come to Sunday school and worship.

The Lord seemed to develop a special healing ministry in Evon's service. Answers to prayer came for the common cold and for a little baby born with an abnormality on his head. Evon encountered a lady at the grocery store who was having trouble breathing. She prayed for her there. Later on the parking lot at the same store, the lady knocked on her car window to tell her the Lord had healed her.

Evon Pulliam is now retired at Greensboro, North Carolina.[2]

Jeanne Lou Schwartz

Jeanne Lou Schwartz was born May 26, 1936, in Baltimore, Maryland. She was saved at the age of seven, joined the Pilgrim Holiness Church at twelve, and was sanctified at twenty-two. She graduated with a bachelor's degree in Christian education from Eastern Pilgrim College, Allentown, Pennsylvania (later United

Wesleyan College), and a B. S. in education from Coppin State Teacher's College in Maryland. The records of the Eastern District of the Pilgrim Holiness Church listed her among the ministers 1960–67. She pastored at Ridgley, Maryland for four years, in the 1960s. She entered upon her first term of service as a teacher on Antigua in the Caribbean, September 8, 1965. She taught for at least five years.

Margaret E. Zachary Wallace

Margaret Zachary married George T. Wallace in 1943. She began her ministry in the Northern Indiana District of the Pilgrim Holiness Church. She served as associate pastor at the Anderson, Indiana South Wesleyan church until 1987. The Wallaces had two sons, Thomas (a minister), John (an accountant), and one daughter, Rita (a school teacher). Margaret Wallace believed her mission was to help those in need. Often she would fill a grocery sack from her own pantry for someone in need. Her home was always open on Sunday as a place for the church to eat together or just to fellowship until the evening service.[3]

Mrs. Minnie Barnes

The records for Minnie Barnes are incomplete. The Rocky Mountain District of the Pilgrim Holiness Church listed her in its records as an ordained minister 1961–63. But she was already retired in 1961 when she was first listed. The Kansas District's records listed her from 1962 to 1964. She transferred to the Kansas District in 1962 and was living in Holly. She was listed by Kansas as retired in 1964 and she died in August 1964.

Magdalene Blank

Magdalene Blank was listed in the records of the Eastern District of the Pilgrim Holiness Church from 1961 to 1967 among the ministers.

Ruth K. Lanker Brewer

Ruth Lanker was listed in the records of the Ohio Conference of the Wesleyan Methodist Church 1961–68. In 1961 she had achieved status as a fourth-year ministerial student, based at least partially on credits from God's Bible School, Cincinnati, Ohio. She served as a conference evangelist 1961–64. She was ordained in 1963. She was listed as on reserve in 1964, and she was doing missionary work. She was listed on reserve in 1966, as a conference evangelist in 1967 and on reserve again in 1968. She married a Mr. Brewer in 1968.

Martha Browning

The records of the Eastern Ohio District of the Pilgrim Holiness Church listed Martha Browning among the ministers 1961–67. She was ordained in 1961 and was listed as unstationed or retired in 1966 and 1967.

Florence Cain

Florence Cain, according to the records of the Indiana Conference of the Wesleyan Methodist Church, was listed among the ministers 1961–68. She was received as an elder (ordained minister) on probation in 1961. On March 1, 1962, she was placed on the superannuated (retired) list and continued there through 1968.

Eva H. Carpenter

The records of the Rocky Mountain District of the Pilgrim Holiness Church listed Eva H. Carpenter 1961–67 among the ministers. She was listed as inactive the entire period.

Hattie Croft

Hattie Croft was listed among the ministers in the records of the Eastern Ohio District of the

Pilgrim Holiness Church 1961–67. She was ordained in 1961 and was listed as pastor of Wheelersburg that year.

Helen Doll

Helen Doll was listed in the records of the Rocky Mountain District of the Pilgrim Holiness Church among the ministers 1961–67.

Miriam Douglas

The records of the Kentucky Conference of the Wesleyan Methodist Church listed Miriam (Mrs. C. D.) Douglas among the ministers 1961–67. She was ordained in 1961 and was appointed as co-pastor at Clear Fork that year. From 1962 to 1963 she served as a conference evangelist. From 1963 to 1964 she was listed as supplying in Indiana. The Indiana Conference records for that year indicated that she was co-pastor at the Carthage, Indiana church. From 1964 on, the Kentucky Conference listed her as a conference evangelist.

Mrs. W. A. Elkins

The records for Mrs. W. A. Elkins appear to be incomplete. She was listed among the ministers in the records of the Rocky Mountain District of the Pilgrim Holiness Church 1961–63. In both 1962 and 1963 she was shown to be retired. She then transferred to the Arizona-New Mexico District. This district's records listed her in 1964 and 1965 as retired.

Dorothy Jean Hall

Dorothy Jean Hall was born at Scotland, Arkansas, January 24, 1931. She was saved at the age of twelve and sanctified a few months later. Early in life she chose the nursing profession and pursued it with dedication. After high school, she earned an associate of arts degree from Chaffey Junior College in 1949. She completed her nurse's

training at Orange County General Hospital in 1952. As she considered various fields of specialization in nursing, missionary nursing began to tug at her conscience. She tried to evade this impression for a time and then surrendered to the call of God. She spent eight years in general nursing. During this time she attended Pasadena College in Pasadena, California, completing her A.B. degree in 1955.

In 1961 she went to the Pilgrim Holiness mission field in Zambia, Africa, and served there several years in various mission stations. Her emphasis was on meeting physical needs not only in the hospital but also in village clinical work. She seized every opportunity to present the gospel to her patients. And many times God's healing power was manifest where medical treatment failed.

In 1966 Dorothy Jean Hall was ordained by the California District of the Pilgrim Holiness Church. After this she interrupted her work in Zambia for a two-year term in Guyana, South America.[4]

Martha Hansen

According to the records of the Indiana Conference of the Wesleyan Methodist Church, Martha Hansen was received in 1961 as an elder (ordained minister) on probation.

Evelee Doris Mason and Genevie Fern Mason

On July 15, 1923, in Tecumseh, Nebraska, triplets were born. One was a little boy who died. The two who lived were identical twin girls, Evelee Doris and Genevie Fern Mason. Their identical status caused no end of amusement in their childhood. Evelee was the first to be converted, in April 1939. The radical change in her life soon prompted Genevie to follow, and she did so a few months later.

Evelee and Genevie attended Hephzibah Faith School, Mitchell, South Dakota, and Colorado Springs Bible College, Colorado

Springs. They were granted local ministers' licenses in 1944, district licenses in 1948. and they were ordained to the ministry in June 1951. They pastored several churches in the Rocky Mountain District of the Pilgrim Holiness Church, including McCook, Nebraska; Pueblo, Colorado; Omaha, Nebraska; and Bladen, Nebraska. Their pastoral service was considered effective and they were held in the highest respect in the communities where they served.

On April 1, 1959, the Mason twins flew out of Indianapolis to become resident missionaries in what is now Guyana, South America. They pastored the New Amsterdam church and oversaw a number of outstations and branch Sunday schools. Between them they held thirty-two services each week. They served there until 1964. From 1964 on they were listed in Indianapolis, Indiana.[5]

Mrs. Gordon E. Miller

The records of the North Carolina District of the Pilgrim Holiness Church listed Mrs. Gordon E. Miller among the ministers 1961–68. She was ordained in 1961.

Mrs. L. M. Sanders

Mrs. L. M. Sanders was listed in the records of the Rocky Mountain District of the Pilgrim Holiness Church among the ministers 1961–67.

Rachel Vega

Rachel Vega was listed in the records of the Rocky Mountain District of the Pilgrim Holiness Church 1961–67. She was listed in Laredo, Texas, for this entire period.

Marion L. Walker

The Eastern District of the Pilgrim Holiness Church listed Marion L. Walker among the ministers 1961–67.

Mrs. Beulah Hicks

For Beulah Hicks, her experience of holiness and her call to the ministry came at the same time in 1931. Her first service was with the Interdenominational Ministerial Association. Then she served beginning in 1941 with the Free Methodists, alternating with a pastor on his circuit. She also held street meetings and revivals in various places. In 1952 she went to the Defiance, Ohio, Pilgrim Holiness Church, was granted a license, and filled in at different places along with street meetings and nursing homes. In 1962 she began a nine-year pastorate at the Hicksville, Ohio, Pilgrim Holiness Church. She was ordained by the Western Ohio District of The Wesleyan Church in 1969 at Victory Camp at Galena, Ohio. She later pastored at Celina, Ohio, 1979–81 and 1988–91. She retired in 1991 and subsequently filled in at different churches and also taught Sunday school classes.[6]

Mrs. Marion King

Marion King was listed in the records of the Idaho-Washington District of the Pilgrim Holiness Church among the ministers 1962–67.

Mrs. Edwin Mayes

The records of the Pennsylvania and New Jersey District of the Pilgrim Holiness Church listed Mrs. Edwin Mayes among the ministers 1962–67. She was listed as pastor at Millmont, Pennsylvania, in 1966, and as in education at Hobe Sound, Florida, in 1967.

Dorothy Staley

Dorothy (Mrs. Donald) Staley was listed in the records of the Kentucky Conference of the Wesleyan Methodist Church among the ministers 1962–67. She was listed as a conference preacher (licensed minister) pursuing the course of study in 1962 and 1963. She was ordained in 1964 and appointed co-pastor at Brooksburg. In 1966 and 1967 she was listed as pastor at the Franklin Avenue pioneer work (church plant).

Juanita Blue Epling

Juanita Blue was born on March 30, 1918, in Marion, Ohio. She was converted at the Coolville Camp as a teenager. On July 16, 1936, she married Gerald Epling. In their early years of marriage they were members of White's Chapel Wesleyan Methodist Church. Sensing the call of God, Juanita enrolled in the ministerial course of study. Her pastoral ministry began in 1963 at the Joy Church, an independent congregation in rural southeastern Ohio. She pastored the Dunkirk, Ohio, Wesleyan Methodist (Wesleyan) church 1964–70, 1972–96. In 1971–72 she served as supply pastor of Beech Grove Wesleyan Church near Carey, Ohio. She was ordained by the Ohio Conference of the Wesleyan Methodist Church in 1966 at Victory Camp in Galeena, Ohio. Her husband faithfully supported his wife in her ministry. They had three children of their own and adopted five of their grandchildren when that home was broken. Gerald Epling died in 1996 at the age of eighty-eight. Juanita Epling pastored to the end, dying December 17, 1996, at the age of seventy-eight.[7]

Phyllis Russell

Phyllis Russell was listed in the records of the Illinois District of the Pilgrim Holiness Church among the ministers 1963–68. She was ordained in 1963. She and her husband, Roger Russell, served as missionaries in Zambia, Africa.[8]

Mrs. Leavinia E. Walston

Leavinia Walston was listed in the records of the Western Ohio District of the Pilgrim Holiness Church among the ministers 1962–67. She lived in Batavia, Ohio in 1962 and 1963. She was ordained in 1962. In 1965 she was in Cincinnati, Ohio. By 1967 she was a missionary in Zambia, Africa.[9]

Mrs. Cornettia Webster

The records of the Kentucky District of the Pilgrim Holiness Church listed Cornettia Webster among the ordained ministers in 1963, 1964, and 1965. The latter two years she was listed as inactive.

Marie Browning

Marie Browning was listed in the records of the Southern Indiana District of the Pilgrim Holiness Church among the ministers 1964–67. She was the pastor at Milton in 1964–67 and was ordained in 1965. She was appointed as pastor of Centerville North Church in 1967.

Mrs. C. Gilbert Baker

Mrs. C. Gilbert Baker was listed among the ordained ministers in the records of the Eastern District of the Pilgrim Holiness Church in 1965 and 1966.

Mrs. Warren Howell

Mrs. Warren Howell was listed among the ministers in the records of the Tennessee District of the Pilgrim Holiness Church 1964–67. In the records of that district and the records of the Tennessee Conference of the Wesleyan Methodist Church when they met in 1968, it is indicated that Mrs. Howell was ordained that year.

Frances Ray Allred Mason

Frances Ray married George H. Allred back in the period of World War II. George Allred served in six major battles in the South Pacific and subsequently died in a plane crash at a U. S. naval base in California. Frances Allred established a scholarship fund in his honor at Central Wesleyan College, Central, South Carolina (now Southern Wesleyan University). The first recipient of the scholarship was James E. Wiggins, who was later to serve as a Wesleyan missionary in Sierra Leone, West Africa, a pastor of Wesleyan churches in South Carolina, and as superintendent of the Georgia and South Coastal Districts of The Wesleyan Church. Many other ministerial students were the beneficiaries of the fund.

At some point, Frances married a Mr. Mason. She was listed by the Georgia Conference of the Wesleyan Methodist Church 1964–67. She was a conference preacher in 1964, on the deaconess's course of study in 1965, and back on the conference preacher's list in 1966. At some point she pastored the Springdale Wesleyan Methodist church in Alabama, and perhaps one other in Alabama.

In the mid-1960s, Frances Mason was serving as the administrative secretary of the head of The Trust Company of Georgia in Atlanta. She was teaching an adult Sunday school class at the First Wesleyan Methodist Church in Atlanta. She had a dream of planting a church in Decatur, a suburb of Atlanta. She began to talk more and more about this in her Sunday school class, and with the pastor's permission to recruit some members of her class for the venture. On January 30, 1966 she was appointed pastor of the newly organized Decatur church. It met at first in a branch bank of the company she worked for. Don Wood, future faculty member at Southern Wesleyan University, was a member of Frances Mason's class and also a student at Columbia Theological Seminary. When the Decatur church outgrew the branch bank, Frances asked Don to seek permission from the president of Columbia for them to meet in the seminary chapel. Her boss at the trust company was a member of the seminary board and may also have been recruited to aid in securing permission. Permission was given, and they met there for several years, paying only a nominal amount for the utilities.

Don Wood had previously had what he called "cultural," not biblical reservations about women ministers. This soon changed.

The relationship I had with Frances over the three years I was at Columbia assured me that God was pleased to have women, at least this woman,

to serve him as pastor. She preached radiantly, administered wisely, counseled compassionately, and trusted God implicitly for the needs of the congregation. She was one of the best pastors I've ever known at helping people discover and use their spiritual gifts. The last two years I was there two other Wesleyan seminarians came to Columbia, and she made all three of us her assistant pastors with responsibilities commensurate with our gifts. Lay people found their niches at her invitation, and we all caught her vision.

Later Frances Mason served on the board of trustees of what became Southern Wesleyan University, and the school conferred an honorary doctorate on her. On Thursday, April 27, 1995, the Georgia District honored her with a special tribute. In her later years, Frances Mason ministered through teaching, counseling and writing.[10]

Mae Palmer

Miss Mae Palmer served as a missionary for the Wesleyan Methodists in Haiti 1953–69. She was listed in the records of the Dakota Conference of the Wesleyan Methodist Church 1964–68. Her home church was at Richland. At some point she became a conference preacher (licensed minister). She completed requirements for ordination in 1964.[11]

Frances Clark

The records of the Southern Indiana District of the Pilgrim Holiness Church listed Frances Clark among the ministers 1965–67. She was ordained in 1965 and was appointed as an evangelist in 1966 and 1967.

Catherine Hopper

Catherine Hopper was listed in the records of the Kentucky Conference of the Wesleyan Methodist Church among the ministers in 1965. She was received as an elder (ordained minister) that year from the Church of the Nazarene and was appointed as a conference evangelist.

Minnie M. Hale

Minnie (Mrs. Alfred) Hale was listed in the records of the Allegheny Conference of the Wesleyan Methodist Church in 1966. She transferred in from the Wesleyan Holiness Church and was listed as "superannuated" (retired).

Mrs. Elva M. Anderson Johnson

Elva Anderson Johnson was born in 1907. She was a member of the First Wesleyan Methodist Church of Dayton, Ohio, beginning in September 1922. She served in the missionary society, in the Prayer Band, on the usher board and stewardess board, and as a deaconess, exhorter, minister, and Sunday school superintendent.

Elva was licensed as a conference preacher (licensed minister) by the South Ohio Conference of the Wesleyan Methodist Church in 1966, 1967, and 1968. This conference was an all-black jurisdiction incorporating churches in Ohio and adjoining states, some of which had existed since prior to the Civil War. Following the 1968 merger, the churches were eventually absorbed in the districts of their geographical location. On Friday, August 29, 1969, she was ordained. She served as pastor of the Hillsboro, Ohio, church from 1968 through at least 1971. She was president of the conference Woman's Missionary Society, 1968 and 1969, and led devotions at conference in 1968. In 1969 and 1970 she served on the moral reform committee and in 1970 and 1971 as district secretary of world missions. She passed away February 6, 1972, at the age of sixty-five.[12]

Elizabeth Schott

Elizabeth "Betsy" Schott was listed by the Michigan Conference of the Wesleyan Methodist Church in 1966 and 1967. The Detroit Avenue Church recommended her as a special worker in 1966. In 1967 she was so listed and related to evangelism, Christian education, children's work, music, and chalk artistry. She later pastored in Florida and was ordained in the mid-1990s. She was retired in 2002.

Mrs. Ruth V. Brown

The records of the Eastern Ohio District of the Pilgrim Holiness Church listed Ruth V. Brown in 1966 and 1967 as an unstationed or retired minister.

Mary Hall

The records of the South Ohio Conference of the Wesleyan Methodist Church and the records of the South Ohio District of The Wesleyan Church (a former all-black district made up of churches in Ohio and adjacent states) listed Mary Hall among the ministers 1968–77. She was listed as pastor of the Parkersburg, West Virginia, and Cutter, Ohio, churches. She was listed as pastor at Parkersburg 1969 and 1971 and as assistant pastor there in 1976. She was apparently ordained in 1971. From 1972 to 1976, she was "on leave." And in 1977 she was listed as a reserve elder (ordained minister).

Mrs. C. Bonnie Henschen Sanders

C. Bonnie Sanders was born in 1923, the daughter of Rev. Walter G. and Rev. Fern Henschen, who served in the Midwest in the Pilgrim Holiness Church in the 1920s through the 1960s. Bonnie was converted in 1957. For two years she attended Frankfort Pilgrim College, Frankfort, Indiana (later merged into United Wesleyan College, Allentown, Pennsylvania). She completed the course of study in 1971. She pastored the North Fairmount church in Cincinnati, Ohio, for a time, and in 2002 was pastoring the First Wesleyan Church in St. Mary's, Ohio.[13]

Conclusion

This study of Wesleyan women in ministry has covered the period up to the 1968 merger that formed The Wesleyan Church. There are some details in the individual stories that reach to the early years of the twenty-first century, but a serious analysis of trends over the past thirty-five years is not within the scope of this work. It appears to the present writer, however, that the decline in the number of women entering the ministry in the 1950s and 1960s continued through the 1970s and 1980s. In the 1990s this decline appears to have given way to a strong upsurge in the number of women candidates for the ministry. In 2003 there were more than 200 women preparing for ministry in the Church's educational institutions and its non-traditional programs.

Yet it is still difficult for a woman minister to secure assignment as a solo or senior pastor. Women ministers serve in a limited manner on pastoral staffs and in educational, administrative, and mission ministries. But the role of primary preacher and pastor is seldom afforded to them. The reasons are probably the same as those listed in the introductory sections of chapters 6 and 7. The emergence of the radical feminist movement that was just beginning in the 1960s has no doubt had a significant backlash effect. Women from more liberal theological backgrounds have gone to extremes, with some becoming agnostic or atheistic or even pagan in their positions. Paganism is evident in the worship by some of a female goddess called Sophia (Greek for *wisdom*) a take-off on the personification of wisdom in the Book of Proverbs (1:20–33; 3:13–20; 4:5–9; 8:1–9:12). Their support of the ordination of both women and homosexuals has caused some to see Wesleyan ordination of women as due to such a movement and has held us "guilty by association." Of course, nothing could be farther from the truth.

Official actions of the Church's General Conference, ratified in turn by the districts, have clearly stated the right of women to be considered for the ministry. Prior to the 1968 merger, the Wesleyan Methodist Church adopted in 1959 a new Constitution (published for the first time in its 1963 *Discipline*). Included in this Constitution were statements that any full member was eligible to be elected to any office for which persons in full membership were eligible, and that any ordained minister was eligible to be elected to any office for which ordained ministers were eligible. These statements were incorporated into the Constitution of The Wesleyan Church in 1968 and were sufficient to provide women members with eligibility for ordination and to make ordained women ministers eligible for any and all ministerial roles. But to make the matter absolutely clear, in 1984 The Wesleyan Church added to its constitutional statement on non-discrimination by prohibiting discrimination against any member or minister on account of sex (*Discipline* 360:3d).

However, the adoption of statements in even the Church's governing document does not bring immediate change in human attitudes and choices. Local churches exercise the major role in ministerial employment, and the Church's historic acceptance of and wonderful experience with women in the ministry has not been known by many of our people, nor has its validity and reasonableness been widely published.

This book contains some lessons for women who believe God is calling them to ministry.

Women candidates for ministry need to recognize that even though hundreds of women have served the Church in the ministry and have served effectively, there has never been a time in the history of The Wesleyan Church when they have been able to enter "on a level floor." There have always been reservations on the part of some about women ministers and a preference on the part of many for men. This has not prevented women from serving and serving well, although it has no doubt driven some away. Women candidates today should not wait for equal opportunities any more than did those who went before them.

Time and time again the stories in this book reveal that women ministers did not go about defending their call or demanding a place of service. They simply obeyed God's call and ministered as He opened the door, often in a creative and innovative fashion. A woman minister will probably have to be better skilled than most men ministers and work harder than they in order to be accepted. That must not be undertaken in human strength but must be the result of empowerment by the Holy Spirit.

It is obvious that the women who succeeded in the past did not start out to make a career of the ministry. They were in the ministry because of an inescapable call from God and a compassion for the lost and needy, which could not be silenced. They found ways around opposition and over obstacles. They started churches on their own in places where they were needed, often supporting themselves with secular employment while spending the rest of their time in ministry. Under God they found ways to serve.

It is also obvious that they took advantage of little opportunities that led to great achievements.

Ministry is simply *serving*. If women candidates for ministry look for opportunities to *serve*, they will find them. And the Lord has promised that faithfulness and excellence in service in small matters will lead to ever larger opportunities.

Women who have succeeded in ministry in the past have developed patience, humility, persistence, and faithfulness, and they have demonstrated love for others—love will always make a way for itself. Women in the past found places of ministry where needs were greatest—in ghettos, red-light districts, among the derelicts and prostitutes, among the poor and deprived, in strange and foreign lands. Those needs are still present in our society, and candidates today need also to be prepared to find places of service outside their comfort zones.

Women whom God calls into ministry are called *because* they are women and have the unique traits and strengths and weaknesses of women. They should not assume masculine "macho" or anything else that is unnatural to them. God graces those He calls in ways unique to each, and it is who you are and what you have to give that He wants in His service.

This book also contains some lessons for the Church, and particularly for those in its leadership.

In the Old Testament, God called, worked through, and blessed the ministry of Miriam (Exod. 15:20–21; Mic. 6:4), Deborah (Judg. 3—4), Isaiah's wife (Isa. 8:3), and Huldah (2 Chron. 34:19–33). In the New Testament He likewise called, worked through, and blessed the ministry of Priscilla (Acts 18:24–26; Rom. 16:3), Philip's four daughters (Acts 21:8–9), Phoebe (Rom. 16:1–2), and Junias (Rom. 16:7). And the stories in this book provide adequate evidence that His promise that in the age of the Holy Spirit He would multiply ministry by both "sons and daughters," "men and women" (Joel 2:28–29; Acts 2:16–18) is still in effect. God still calls and uses women.

The Wesleyan Church asks for four "marks" to concur in the person God calls to ministry: grace, gifts, fruit, and an abiding sense of a divine call (*Discipline* 3006). As to fruit, it defines this as people having been truly convicted of sin and converted to God through their ministry as well as believers having been edified. The stories make it clear that all of these marks can and do concur in women ministers. And if the validation depends on evidence of fruit, it must be noted that many of the women ministers have won numerous persons, male and female, great and not-so-great, to the Lord.

Jesus asked us to pray that the Lord would send laborers into the harvest. How can we ignore many of those He calls and wants to send into the harvest, simply because they are women rather than men? If we ignore between one-half and two-thirds of our members in recruiting, preparing and deploying ministers to meet the staggering needs of our time, are we not frustrating His purpose and crippling our own vision and plans?

Finally, *leaders must be leaders* on this issue. This does not require an effort to force local churches to accept ministers they do not want. It does mean that leaders must develop a climate that will make it easier for local churches to consider *all* those whom God has called.

This involves referring to ministers as both men and women; suggesting highly qualified women for empty pulpits (both for temporary supply and ongoing assignment); making use of women ministers in camps and conferences by inviting them to pray in public, lead devotions, and preach; and recognizing women ministers with special awards for their accomplishments. It involves calling for both men and women candidates when preaching on the call to ministry. It would be good for each district to appoint at least one ordained woman minister to the district board of ministerial development in order to identify with and encourage women candidates.

Leaders need also to be responsible to clarify this issue, to help people recognize the biblical support for women in the ministry, to inform people of our rich heritage in women in the ministry, to make it clear that this is not the result of atheistic or pagan radical feminism but that we ordained women ministers for sound reasons *long before* the radical feminists came along.

Leaders need to *sponsor* individual women for ministry, to recognize their potential, to encourage others to receive their ministry, to introduce them broadly to the Church, particularly to those looking for pastors. In other words they need to save these women for and to the ministry as Barnabas rescued Saul (Paul) from obscurity and John Mark from premature rejection.

We have a wonderful heritage. Let us celebrate our daughters of the past and present, and let us open doors for our daughters (and granddaughters) for the challenging days ahead.

Notes

Chapter 1

1. Ira Ford McLeister and Roy Stephen Nicholson, *Conscience and Commitment*, Lee M. Haines, Jr. and Melvin E. Dieter, eds. fourth revised edition of *The History of the Wesleyan Methodist Church of America* (Marion, Ind.: The Wesley Press, 1976), 27.

2. Wayne E. Caldwell; ed., *Reformers and Revivalists, History of The Wesleyan Church,* (Marion, Ind.: The Wesley Press, 1992), 56, 57.

3. McLeister and Nicholson, *Conscience and Commitment,* 81.

4. Ibid., 93.

5. Ibid., 106.

6. Ibid., 603.

7. Ibid., 41.

8. Lee Haines, "Laura Smith Haviland: A Woman's Life Work," the second in a series of eight heritage brochures published by The Wesleyan Church. See also *A Woman's Life-Work: Labors and Experiences of Laura S. Haviland*, 4th ed. (Chicago: Publishing Association of Friends, 1889); Mildred E. Danforth, *A Quaker Pioneer: Laura Haviland, Superintendent of the Underground* (New York: Exposition Press, 1961).

9. *The Wesleyan*, October 10, 1860, 310; *American Wesleyan*, January 23, 1861, 15; February 20, 1861, 30; May 15, 1861, 78; June 12, 1861, 94; "Wesleyan Methodist Connection: Book of Minutes," 1864, hand-written, 189, 208, 283; *American Wesleyan*, October 5, 1870, 114; "Book of Minutes," 1879, 351; *American Wesleyan*, October 1, 1876, 1.

10. "Wesleyan Methodist Connection: Book of Minutes," 1864, handwritten,189; *American Wesleyan*, October 5, 1870, 114; June 14, 1871, 95; November 1, 1876, 1; September 24, 1879,2; December 24, 1879, 7.

11. Lee Haines, "Mary E. Depew: The Holy Spirit's Evangelist," the fourth in a series of eight heritage brochures published by The Wesleyan Church.

12. *The Wesleyan Methodist*, October 23, 1935.

13. *Indiana Conference Record: Indiana Annual Conference of the Wesleyan Methodist Connection of America*, 1876,212. (Typewritten copy of the handwritten minutes 1876.)

14. *The Wesleyan Methodist*, August 12, 1931, 14.

15. *Minutes of the Annual Session of the Michigan Conference of the Wesleyan Methodist Connection of America*, 1895–1908, 1910–1916; *Wesleyan Methodist Journal of the Michigan Conference*, containing the Minutes of the Annual Sessions, 1917–18.

16. Gipsie Miller, *History Woman's Missionary Society* (Marion, Ind.: Wesleyan Publishing House, 1968), 14.

17. T. J. Pomeroy, *A History of the Kansas Conference of the Wesleyan Methodist Church of America* (Miltonvale, Kans.: no publisher, 1935), 15, 29, 38; Miller, *History Woman's Missionary Society*, 14; McLeister and Nicholson, Conscience and Commitment, 345.

18. *American Wesleyan*, February 5, 1879, 3.

19. *Minutes of the Annual Session of the Allegheny Conference of the Wesleyan Methodist Connection (or Church) of America*, 1909–37; *The Wesleyan Methodist*, February 3, 1937, 14.

20. Miller, *History Woman's Missionary Society*, 32.

21. Paul L. Wilcox, *The Wesleyan Church: A Century of History in South Carolina 1893–1993* (Easley, S.C.: no publisher, 1994), 128.

22. Roy S. Nicholson, *Wesleyan Methodism in the South: Being the Story of Eighty-six Years of Reform and Religious Activities in the South as Conducted by the American Wesleyans* (Syracuse, N. Y.: The Wesleyan Methodist Publishing House, 1933), 122.

23. Miller, *History Woman's Missionary Society,* 32.

24. Wilcox, *The Wesleyan Church: A Century of History in South Carolina*, 83.

25. *Minutes of the Annual Sessions of the Ohio Conference of Wesleyan Methodist Connection, or Church, of America*, 1909, 1912, 1922–26.

26. Wilcox, *The Wesleyan Church: A Century of History in South Carolina*, 127–28.

27. *Minutes of the Annual Sessions of the Indiana Conference of the Wesleyan Methodist Connection, or Church, of America*, 1920–22.

28. *Minutes of the Annual Sessions of the Ohio Conference*, 1922–26.

29. *Minutes of the Annual Sessions of the Indiana Conference*, 1927–30.

30. Miller, *History Woman's Missionary Society,* 33.

31. *The Wesleyan Methodist*, March 25, 1931, 15.

32. Wilcox, *The Wesleyan Church: A Century of History in South Carolina*, 6–11.

33. Wilcox, *The Wesleyan Church: A Century of History in South Carolina*, 14.

34. *The Wesleyan Methodist*, May 14, 1947, 14.

35. Bulletin for the One Hundred Anniversary of The First Wesleyan Church, Gastonia, North Carolina, May 21, 2000.

36. *Minutes of the Annual Sessions of the Indiana Conference of the Wesleyan Methodist Connection of America*, 1906–09.

37. *The Wesleyan Methodist*, May 14, 1947, 14.

38. Clara Tear Williams's story is based on her handwritten memoirs typed and edited by her grandson, Harold C. McKinney, Jr.

39. Lee Haines, "A History of the Indiana Conference of the Wesleyan Methodist Church, 1867–1971" (M. of Theology thesis, Christian Theological Seminary, Indianapolis, Ind., 1973), 58.

40. McLeister and Nicholson, *Conscience and Commitment*, 116.

41. *The Wesleyan Methodist,* July 28, 1937, 14.

42. Personal letter from Rev. James Bence, January 31, 1998.

43. Olson W. Clark, "Well of Water Vignettes and Memoirs of Clara Tear Williams." Presented on April 25, 1999, at the placing of a Memorial Plaque of Clara Tear Williams on the wall of the Houghton Church Narthex.

44. *The Wesleyan Methodist*, July 28, 1937, 14.

45. Josephine M. Washburn, *History and Reminiscences of the Holiness Church Work in Southern California and Arizona* (Record Press, no date), 60, 66, 67, 279. All her ministerial activities are recorded by Mrs. Washburn.

46. The Historian Committee of the Pacific Southwest District of The Wesleyan Church, "History of the Holiness, Pilgrim and Pilgrim Holiness Churches in California" (January 1999), 7. (Computer typed looseleaf notebook.)

47. The Historian Committee, "History of the Holiness Churches in California," 77.

48. Ibid., 72

49. Ibid., 50.

50. Ibid., 156.

51. Washburn, *History and Reminiscences,* 181.

52. Ibid., 163.

53. Ibid., 457.

54. Ibid., 21.

55. Ibid., 20–22.

56. Ibid., 458.

57. Ibid., 216–17.

58. Ibid., 77.

59. Ibid., 140.

60. Ibid., 216–17.

61. Ibid., 304.

62. Ibid., 200.

63. Ibid., 193.

64. Historian Committee, "History of the Pilgrim Churches in California," 54.

65. Washburn, *History and Reminiscences,* 145.

66. Ibid., 95.

67. Ibid., 101.

68. Ibid., 105.

69. Ibid., 76.

70. Ibid., 76–77.

71. Ibid., 188.

72. Ibid., 205–07.

73. Ibid., 221.

74. Ibid., 238–40.

75. Ibid., 253–58.

76. Ibid., 265.

77. Ibid., 301.

78. Ibid., 308.

79. Ibid., 309.

80. Ibid., 310.

81. *The Pilgrim Holiness Advocate,* December 28, 1922, 2.

82. A. O. Northup, W. F. Lewis and L. C. Matton, *One Hundred Years for Christ 1842–1942* (published by the Champlain Conference, 1943), 53.

83. Aldis M. Lamos, ed., *One Hundred and Twenty-five Years for Christ, 1843–1968* (published by the Conference Historical Committee, 1968), 46, 53.

84. Materials provided by Rev. John Heavilin, a former District Superintendent of the Wesleyan Methodist Church of America, Wisconsin Conference (District). Materials were gleaned from *100 Years 1867–1967 Wisconsin Conference Centennial* (no publisher, no date [1967]).

85. Interview with Mrs. Vesta (Lawrence) Mullen at Beulah Camp, July 1998, and from newspaper and church periodical clippings which she provided from their historical collections of the Reformed Baptist Church in Canada.

86. *Minutes of the Annual Sessions of the Michigan Conference of the Wesleyan Methodist Connection of America,* 1891–1903.

87. Pomeroy, *History of Kansas Conference of the Wesleyan Methodist Church,* 16.

88. Ibid., 40.

89. Ibid., 39.

90. Ibid., 42.

91. Ibid., 61.

92. *Minutes of the Annual Sessions of the Kansas Conference of the Wesleyan Methodist Connection (or Church),* 1900–1907.

93. *The Wesleyan Methodist,* August 12, 1936, 14.

94. Facts for her story were taken from a booklet she wrote, *Sketches of My Life Story, Evangelist Sally Carter* (printed by Ralph Carter, 1988), and a newspaper clipping dated November 5, 1959 written by Ann Coffee and submitted by Rev. Melvin Gentry.

95. *Minutes of the Annual Sessions of the North Carolina Conference of the Wesleyan Methodist Connection (or Church) of America,* 1936–61.

96. *The Wesleyan Methodist,* June 28, 1961, 14.

97. *The Pilgrim Holiness Advocate,* October 12, 1939, 12.

98. Roy S. Nicholson, *Wesleyan Methodism in the South* (Syracuse, N.Y.: The Wesleyan Publishing House, 1933), 63.

99. Wilcox, *A Century of History in South Carolina,* 163.

100. *Minutes of the Annual Sessions of the South Carolina Conference of the Wesleyan Methodist Connection, or Church, of America,* 1913–1920.

101. *The Wesleyan Methodist,* May 29, 1935, 14.

102. Nicholson, *Wesleyan Methodism in the South,* 126–28.

103. Centennial Committee, "Centennial Celebration 1879–1979 North Carolina (Colfax) District (published by the Centennial Committee, no date).

104. *The Wesleyan Methodist,* May 29, 1935, 14.

105. *Minutes of the Annual Sessions of the Indiana Conference of the Wesleyan Methodist Connection (or Church) of America,* 1903–35.

106. *The Wesleyan Methodist,* May 29, 1935, 14.

107. *The Wesleyan Methodist,* August 5, 1936, 11.

108. *Minutes of the Annual Sessions of the Iowa Conference of the Wesleyan Methodist Connection (or Church) of America,* 1897, 1900–10, 1915–16, 1919–35.

109. Her service record was found in the *Minutes of*

the Annual Sessions of the Kansas Conference of the Wesleyan Methodist Connection (or Church) of America, 1903–17.

110. Pomeroy, *History of the Kansas Conference of the Wesleyan Methodist Church,* 59.

111. Ibid., 66.

112. Mary E. Bennett, ed., *Our Heritage Lockport Conference Centennial 1861–1961* (Houghton, N.Y.: Lockport Conference of The Wesleyan Methodist Church of America, 1961).

113. *Minutes of the Annual Sessions of the Iowa Conference of the Wesleyan Methodist Connection (or Church) of America,* 1907–08.

114. *Minutes of the Annual Sessions of the Lockport Conference of the Wesleyan Methodist Connection (or Church) of America,* 1906–07, 1915–20, 1928–32.

115. *The Wesleyan Methodist,* March 10, 1954, 15.

116. Facts about her life and work were found in the *Journal of Proceedings of the Annual Session of the Indiana Conference and the First Annual Session of the Southern Indiana Conference of the Pilgrim Holiness Church, 1951,* and *The Pilgrim Holiness Advocate,* January 6, 1951, 11.

117. Her life and ministerial work were supplied in her obituary found in *The Pilgrim Holiness Advocate,* June 15, 1963, 15.

118. *Minutes of the Annual Conference of the Indiana North District Pilgrim Holiness Church,* 1963.

119. Paul Westphal Thomas and Paul William Thomas, *The Days of Our Pilgrimage: the History of the Pilgrim Holiness Church,* edited by Melvin E. Dieter and Lee M. Haines, Jr. (Marion, Ind.: The Wesley Press, 1976), 65, 89–90, 260, 334.

120. William E. Hall, *History Sketches of the Pilgrim Holiness Church Illinois District* (no publisher, no date), 6.

121. *Minutes of the Indiana Holiness Christian Assembly,* 1902–15; *Minutes of the State Assembly International Holiness Church Kentucky,* 1920–21; *Minutes of the Kentucky District Pilgrim Holiness Church,* 1922–33; *Minutes of the Assembly Tennessee-Alabama Pilgrim Holiness Church,* 1934–41; *Minutes of Conference Tennessee Pilgrim Holiness Church,* 1942–44; *Minutes of Pilgrim Holiness Church Louisiana-Mississippi,* 1943–45; *Minutes of the Pilgrim Holiness Church Indiana Conference,* 1948–50; and *Minutes of the Annual Conference of Indiana North District Pilgrim Holiness Church,* 1951–63.

122. *Minutes of the Annual Sessions of the North Michigan Conference of the Wesleyan Methodist Connection of America,* 1898–1916.

123. *Minutes of the Annual Sessions of the Michigan Conference of the Wesleyan Methodist Connection of America,* 1899–1903.

124. *Minutes of the Annual Sessions of the Iowa Conference of the Wesleyan Methodist Connection of America,* 1901–14.

125. The Historian Committee, "History of the Holiness Churches in California, 58, 103.

126. Paul S. Rees, *Seth Cook Rees, the Warrior-Saint* (Indianapolis, Ind.: The Pilgrim Book Room, 1934), p 12–43.

127. Rees, *Seth Cook Rees,* 52–53.

128. Ibid., 134.

129. The Historian Committee, "History of the Holiness Churches in California," 135.

130. Rees, *Seth Cook Rees,* 98–108.

131. Ibid., 109.

132. Ibid., 134.

133. *Proceedings of the Annual California District Assembly of the Pilgrim Holiness Church,* 1924–59.

134. The Historian Committee, "History of the Holiness Churches in California," 75.

135. Washburn, *History and Reminiscences,* 258.

136. The Historian Committee, "History of the Holiness Churches in California," 50.

137. *The Pilgrim Holiness Advocate,* December 4, 1965, 17.

138. *Minutes of the Annual Assembly of the Pilgrim Holiness Church Indiana Conference,* 1940–50; *Minutes of the Annual Conference of the Indiana North District Pilgrim Holiness Church,* 1951–66.

Chapter 2

1. *The Wesleyan Methodist,* April 18, 1934, 14.

2. *Minutes of the Annual Assembly of the Oklahoma District of the Pilgrim Holiness Church,* 1927–32; *Minutes of the Annual Assembly of the Oklahoma and Texas District Pilgrim Holiness Church,* 1935–37; *Minutes of the Annual Assembly of the Oklahoma-Texas-Louisiana District of Pilgrim Holiness Church,* 1938–40; *Minutes of the Annual Conference Pilgrim Holiness Church Oklahoma District,* 1941–57; *Pilgrim Holiness Advocate,* July 18, 1953, 17.

3. *The Wesleyan Methodist,* May 22, 1935, 14.

4. *Minutes of the Annual Sessions of the Champlain Conference of the Wesleyan Methodist Connection, or Church, of America,* 1901–34.

5. *Wesleyan Methodist,* January 31, 1934, 14.

6. *Minutes of the Annual Assembly Indiana District of the International Holiness Church,* 1922; *Minutes of the Annual Assembly of the Pilgrim Holiness Church and First Annual Conference Northern Indiana Conference,* 1923–62.

7. Chapters I–IV of the personally typed diary of Mrs. Ella Kinney Sanders; an interview with Mrs. Lawrence (Vesta) Mullins, July 1998 at Beulah Camp; and a newspaper clipping dated Wednesday, April 25, 1962 from their collection of Reformed Baptist Church in Canada history.

8. *Minutes of the Alliance of the Reformed Baptist Church of Canada,* 1917–61.

9. Josephine M. Washburn, *History and Reminiscences of the Holiness Church Work in Southern California and Arizona* (South Pasadena: Record Press, no date), 294, 303; The Historian Committee, "History of the Holiness, Pilgrim and Pilgrim Holiness Churches of the Pacific Southwest District of the Wesleyan Church" (computer typed loose leaf notebook, 1999), 21.

10. Her service record was found in the *Pentecostal Rescue Mission Yearly Meeting Minutes,* 1910, 1913, 1915–16, 1918–23; *District Assembly International Holiness Church,* 1924, 1926; *Official Record of the Annual Assembly of the Pilgrim Holiness Church New York District,* 1928–48, 1950–59.

11. Paul Pierpoint, "The Pentecostal Rescue Mission/Pilgrim Holiness Church of New York Seventy-fifth Anniversary July 10, 1972."

12. *Minutes of the International Holiness Churches, Michigan District*, 1924 and *Minutes of the Annual Sessions of the Michigan District Pilgrim Holiness Church*, 1926–31.

13. *The Pilgrim Holiness Advocate*, February 27, 1947, 15.

14. The record of her ministerial work is found in *Minutes of the Annual Sessions of the Indiana Conference of the Holiness Christian Church*, 1901–15; *Minutes of the Annual Assembly of the Illinois and Missouri District Pilgrim Holiness Church*, 1923–30; *Minutes of the Annual Assembly of the Ohio District Pilgrim Holiness Church*, 1931–54; *Minutes of the Annual Conference of the Eastern Ohio District of the Pilgrim Holiness Church*, 1955–64.

15. *The Pilgrim Holiness Advocate*, September 19, 1964, 15.

16. W. W. Hall, *History Sketches of the Pilgrim Holiness Church Illinois District now Southern Illinois District of The Wesleyan Church* (no publisher, no date), 31.

17. *Minutes of the Oklahoma Conference of the Wesleyan Methodist Connection (or Church) of America*, 1902–07.

18. Washburn, *History and Reminiscences*, 320, 337, 353, 357.

19. *Minutes of the Annual Session of the Indiana Conference of the Wesleyan Methodist Connection, or Church, of America*, 1904–16.

20. Ibid., 1903–12.

21. Washburn, *History and Reminiscences*, 320.

22. Materials provided by the Rev. Etta M. Clough, an ordained minister in the Eastern District of the Pilgrim Holiness Church beginning in 1925, and Mrs. Beatrice Joseph, also of the Eastern District.

23. *The Pilgrim Holiness Advocate*, May 31, 1952, 15.

24. *Minutes of the Eastern District Pilgrim Holiness Church*, 1925–51.

25. "History of the Fairmount Bible School," 12.

26. *Minutes of the Annual Session of the Indiana Conference of the Wesleyan Methodist Connection, or Church, of America*, 1909–14.

27. *Minutes of the Annual Session of the Kansas Conference of the Wesleyan Methodist Connection, or Church, of America*, 1903–49.

28. Timothy J. Pomeroy, "History of the Kansas Conference of the Wesleyan Methodist Church of America," typewritten carbon copy, 1950, 66.

29. *The Wesleyan Methodist*, November 16, 1949,12.

30. *Minutes of the Annual Session of the Indiana Conference of the Wesleyan Methodist Connection, or Church, of America*, 1903–52.

31. Roy S. Nicholson, *Wesleyan Methodism in the South* (Syracuse, N.Y.: The Wesleyan Methodist Publishing House, 1933), 259–60.

32. *Minutes of the Annual Session of the Indiana Conference of the Wesleyan Methodist Connection, or Church of America*, 1903–43.

33. *The Wesleyan Methodist*, May 14, 1941, 14.

34. *Minutes of the Indiana Conference of the Wesleyan Methodist Connection, or Church, of America*, 1903–13; 1915–18, 1920–24, 1930–41; *Minutes of the Annual Session of the North Michigan Conference of the Wesleyan Methodist Connection, or Church, of America*, 1914.

35. Lancaster Wesleyan Church Centennial Album 1887–1987.

36. Washburn, *History and Reminiscences*,325; The Historian Committee, "History of the Holiness Churches of California," 65.

37. *Minutes of the Annual Session of the Indiana Conference of the Wesleyan Methodist Connection, or Church, of America*, 1904–09.

38. Facts gleaned from materials sent by Ethel Lundy, a longtime member of Wesley Chapel Church; materials sent by Betty Cummins, granddaughter of Ella Roof Graham; and a history and life sketch of Ella Roof Graham by her daughter, Edith Graham Hudnall.

39. Nicholson, *Wesleyan Methodism in the South*, 256.

40. *The Wesleyan Methodist*, July 9, 1952, 13.

41. *Minutes of the Annual Session of the North Georgia Conference of the Wesleyan Methodist Connection, or Church, of America*, 1907–52.

42. Her service record was found in the *Minutes of the Annual Session of the Indiana Conference of the Holiness Christian Church*, 1904–15; *Minutes of the Annual Session of the Eastern Kansas and Oklahoma District of the Pilgrim Holiness Church*, 1923–26; *Minutes of the Annual Assembly of the Oklahoma District of the Pilgrim Holiness Church*, 1927–33; 1942–46; *Minutes of the Annual Assembly of the Oklahoma and Texas District of the Pilgrim Holiness Church*, 1934–37; *Minutes of the Annual Assembly of the Oklahoma/Texas/Louisiana District of the Pilgrim Holiness Church*, 1938–40.

43. Her life story was written by her niece, Norma L. Clawson Stuve.

44. *Minutes of the Annual Session of the Kansas Conference of the Wesleyan Methodist Connection, or Church, of America*, 1904–14.

45. Pomeroy, "A History of the Kansas Conference of the Wesleyan Methodist Church," 85.

46. *Minutes of the Annual Session of the Wisconsin Conference of the Wesleyan Methodist Church of America*, 1933–39.

47. Materials of her life were given by the Rev. Donald and Mildred Fisher, son-in-law and daughter of Arthur and Della Osborne.

48. *Minutes of the Annual Session of the Kansas Conference of the Wesleyan Methodist Connection, or Church of America*, 1904–09.

49. Pomeroy, "History of the Kansas Conference of the Wesleyan Methodist Church," 58.

50. *Minutes of the Annual Session of the Ohio Conference of the Wesleyan Methodist Connection, or Church, of America*, 1908–68.

51. *Minutes of the Annual Session of the Kansas Conference of the Wesleyan Methodist Connection, or Church, of America*, 1900–02.

52. *Minutes of the Oklahoma Mission Conference*, 1904, printed in the *Minutes of the Kansas Conference of the Wesleyan Methodist Connection, or Church, of America*, 1904.

53. *Pilgrim Holiness Advocate*, December 28, 1963.

54. Ibid., 1963.

55. Materials provided by the Rev. Earnest Batman, former District Superintendent of the Indiana Central District of The Wesleyan Church.

56. Thomas and Thomas, *The Days of Our Pilgrimage*, 72, 73, 79, 335, 352.

57. *The Pilgrim Holiness Advocate*, July 27, 1950, 15; *The Wesleyan Advocate*, April 30, 1973, 18.

58. "History of the Fairmount Bible School," 12.

59. *Minutes of the Indiana Conference of the Wesleyan Methodist Connection, or Church, of America*, 1905–33.

60. *The Wesleyan Methodist*, May 23, 1951, 13.

61. *The Wesleyan Advocate*, January 13, 1969.

62. Gerald A. Wolter, ed., "The Iowa Conference Centennial 1853–1953" (Iowa Conference of the Wesleyan Methodist Church of America, no date).

63. *Minutes of the Annual Session of the Iowa Conference of the Wesleyan Methodist Connection, or Church, of America*, 1905–67.

64. *Minutes of the Annual Assembly of the International Holiness Church Michigan District*, 1924, 1925; *Minutes of the Annual Assembly of the Michigan District Pilgrim Holiness Church*, 1926–56.

65. *Minutes of the Annual Session of the Indiana Conference of the Wesleyan Methodist Connection, or Church, of America*, 1905–26.

66. *Minutes of the Annual Session of the Iowa Conference of the Wesleyan Methodist Connection, or Church, of America*, 1905–35.

67. *Minutes of the Annual Session of the Lockport Conference of the Wesleyan Methodist Connection, or Church*, 1906–15, 1934–53.

68. David L. Gowan, ed., "A Century in Dakota Territory 1881–1981, Historical Sketch of the Dakota District of The Wesleyan Church, June 21, 1981," 40.

69. Gowan, "A Century in Dakota Territory," 29.

70. *Minutes of the Annual Session of the Kansas Conference of the Wesleyan Methodist Connection, or Church, of America*, 1906–21.

71. *Minutes of the Annual Session of the Indiana Conference of the Holiness Christian Church*, 1906, 1909–16, 1919; *Minutes of the Annual Assembly of the Indiana District of the International Holiness Church*, 1921–22; *Minutes of the Annual Assembly of the Pilgrim Holiness Church Indiana Conference*, 1926–50; *Minutes of the Annual Conference of the Northern Indiana District Pilgrim Holiness Church*, 1951–61.

72. *Minutes of the Annual Session of the Indiana Conference of the Wesleyan Methodist Connection, or Church, of America*, 1907–37

73. *The Wesleyan Methodist*, March 30, 1938, 14.

74. "History of the Fairmount Bible School," 12.

75. *Minutes of the Annual Session of the Indiana Conference of the Wesleyan Methodist Connection, or Church, of America*, 1906–13.

76. Ibid., 1906–19.

77. *The Wesleyan Methodist*, September 16, 1936, 14.

78. *Pilgrim Holiness Advocate*, May 23, 1938, 14.

79. *Minutes of the Eastern District Pilgrim Holiness Church*, 1925–45.

80. Ibid., 1925–45.

81. *The Wesleyan Methodist*, July 27, 1938, 14.

82. *Minutes of the Annual Session of the Lockport Conference of the Wesleyan Methodist Connection, or Church, of America*, 1907–09.

83. *Minutes of the Annual Session of the Allegheny Conference of the Wesleyan Methodist Connection, or Church, of America*, 1909.

84. *Minutes of the Annual Session of the Kansas Conference of the Wesleyan Methodist Connection, or Church, of America*, 1907–22.

85. *Minutes of the Annual Session of the Indiana Conference of the Wesleyan Methodist Connection, or Church, of America*, 1907–68.

86. *The Wesleyan Advocate*, January 16, 1984, 17.

87. "History of the Fairmount Bible School," 12.

88. *The Wesleyan Advocate*, January 16, 1984, 17.

89. Nicholson, *Wesleyan Methodism in the South*, 262–64.

90. McLeister and Nicholson, *Conscience and Commitment*, 629.

91. *Minutes of the Annual Session of the Alabama Conference of the Wesleyan Methodist Connection, or Church, of America*, 1910–11.

92. A partial record of her ministerial service may be found in *Minutes of the Annual Session of the Syracuse Conference of the Wesleyan Methodist Connection, or Church, of America*, 1909–11; *Minutes of the Annual Session of the Iowa Conference of the Wesleyan Methodist Connection, or Church, of America*, 1912–13; *Minutes of the Annual Session of the Middle Atlantic States Mission Conference of the Wesleyan Methodist Connection, or Church, of America*, 1930–53.

93. Newspaper clippings sent by her son-in-law, A. J. Shea (no headings or dates).

94. Harland Worden, "A Local Church History of the Shawville Wesleyan Methodist Church"; Henry Kielty, "The Wesleyan Methodist Church of America in Canada, 1894–1968" (H. Kielty, August 1984, typescript manuscript), 87.

95. Kielty, "The Wesleyan Methodist Church of America in Canada," 33.

96. Newspaper clipping from Rev. A. J. Shea.

97. Wolter, "The Iowa Conference Centennial."

98. *The Wesleyan Methodist*, June 23, 1954, 13.

99. Newspaper clippings from Rev. A. J. Shea.

100. Various newspaper clippings from Rev. A. J. Shea.

101. "History of the Fairmount Bible School," 12.

102. *Minutes of the Annual Session of the Indiana Conference of the Wesleyan Methodist Connection, or Church, of America*, 1908–53.

103. *Minutes of the Annual Session of the Iowa Conference of the Wesleyan Methodist Connection, or Church, of America*, 1909–16.

104. "History of the Fairmount Bible School," 12.

105. *Minutes of the Annual Session of the Indiana Conference of the Wesleyan Methodist Connection, or Church, of America*, 1909–73.

106. *The Wesleyan Advocate*, October 20, 1980.

107. *The Wesleyan Methodist*, June 11, 1952, 13.

108. *The Wesleyan Methodist*, December 2, 1953, 16.

109. *Minutes of the Annual Session of the Iowa Conference of the Wesleyan Methodist Connection, or Church, of America*, 1911–51.

110. *Minutes of the Annual Session of the Indiana Conference of the Holiness Christian Church*, 1908–19; *Minutes of the Annual Assembly Indiana District of the International Holiness Church*, 1919–22.

111. *The Pilgrim Holiness Advocate*, May 10, 1928, 6.

112. *The Pilgrim Holiness Advocate*, August 29, 1953.

113. *The Wesleyan Methodist*, February 27, 1957, 14.

114. *The Wesleyan Methodist*, September 29, 1965, 14.

115. Ibid., 14.

116. *Minutes of the Annual Session of the Allegheny Conference of the Wesleyan Methodist Connection, or Church, of America*, 1909.

117. McLeister and Nicholson, *Conscience and Commitment*, 408.

118. *Minutes of the Annual Conference Holiness Christian Church (Indiana)*, 1908–1919.

119. *Minutes of the Annual Assembly Indiana District of the International Holiness Church*, 1920–22.

120. *Minutes of the Annual Assembly of the Pilgrim Holiness Church Indiana Conference*, 1923–50; *Minutes of the Annual Conference of the Indiana North District Pilgrim Holiness Church*, 1951–61.

121. Thomas and Thomas, *The Days of Our Pilgrimage*, 70–71.

122. *Minutes of the Annual Session of the Indiana Conference of the Wesleyan Methodist Connection, or Church, of America*, 1917–55.

123. Rosa Crosby Visser, compiler, "From Darkness to Light: Sketches from the Life of Hattie Crosby Manyon, Missionary to Sierra Leone, West Africa" (Coldwater, Mich.: no publisher, 1960).

124. *Minutes of the Annual Session of the Dakota Conference of the Wesleyan Methodist Connection, or Church, of America*, 1909–15.

125. *Minutes of the Annual Session of the Kansas Conference of the Wesleyan Methodist Church*, 1949–67.

126. *Minutes of the Session of the Annual Conference Virginia District of the Pilgrim Holiness Church*, 1954–55; *Pilgrim Holiness Advocate*, August 18, 1956, 14.

127 *Minutes of the Annual Session of the Syracuse Conference of the Wesleyan Methodist Connection, or Church, of America*, 1909–11; *The Wesleyan Methodist*, December 18, 1935, 15.

128. *Minutes of the Indiana Holiness Christian Church*, 1909–19; *Minutes of the International Holiness Church*, 1920–22; *Minutes of the Pilgrim Holiness Indiana Conference*, 1923–51; *Minutes of the Annual Session of the Southern Indiana Conference of the Pilgrim Holiness Church*, 1952–54.

129. *The Wesleyan Methodist*, July 14, 1943, 14.

130. *Minutes of the Annual Session of the Oklahoma Conference of the Wesleyan Methodist Connection, or Church, of America*, 1909, 1923, 1930–43, 1968; McLeister and Nicholson, *Conscience and Commitment*, 603–04.

131. *The Wesleyan Methodist*, July 14, 1943, 14.

132. Most of the facts about Francene McMillan were found in Gipsie M. Miller, *History Woman's Missionary Society* (Marion, Ind.: Wesleyan Publishing House, no date), 23.

133. *Minutes of the Annual Session of the Ohio Conference, Wesleyan Methodist Connection, or Church, of America*, 1909–1912, 1919.

134. *The Pilgrim Holiness Advocate*, September 28, 1950, 13.

135. Most of the material on Grace Nelson came from her daughter, Caroline Nelson Lewis, as a tribute to her mother.

136. Her service records were found in the *Minutes of the Indiana Holiness Christian Church*, 1909–14; *Minutes of the Kansas and Oklahoma District of the International Holiness Church*, 1920–23; *Minutes of the Kansas, Oklahoma and Texas District of the Pilgrim Holiness Church*, 1923–37; *Minutes of the Oklahoma/Texas/Louisiana District of the Pilgrim Holiness Church*, 1938–40; *Minutes of the Oklahoma District of the Pilgrim Holiness Church*, 1941–53.

137. *Minutes of the Annual Session of the Indiana Conference of the Holiness Christian Church*, 1909–15 and *Minutes of the Annual Assembly of the Illinois and Missouri District Pilgrim Holiness Church*, 1923, 1934.

138. Mabel Perrine, "A Brief History of the Woman's Home and Foreign Missionary Society of the Wesleyan Methodist Church, 1903–43," 86–88.

139. *Minutes of the Annual Session of the Michigan Conference of the Wesleyan Methodist Connection, or Church, of America*, 1909–20.

140. *Minutes of the Annual Session of the Lockport Conference of the Wesleyan Methodist Connection, or Church, of America*, 1909, 1916–29, 1936–59; *Minutes of the Annual Session of the Allegheny Conference of the Wesleyan Methodist Connection, or Church, of America*, 1933–35.

141. *The Wesleyan Methodist*, November 25, 1959, 14.

142. Materials were provided by a grandson, Ivan Kellogg; a granddaughter, Carolyn Pocock Kindley; and former District Superintendent James Bence.

143. Paul H. Yager, Jr., "A Flame Burning A History of the Central New York District of the Wesleyan Church 1843–1993," 19.

144. Service record was found in the *Minutes of the Annual Session of the Syracuse Conference of the Wesleyan Methodist Connection, or Church of America*, 1912; *First Annual Session of the Central New York and Pennsylvania Conference (union of Syracuse and Rochester Conference)*, 1912; *Minutes of the Annual Session of the Lockport Conference of the Wesleyan Methodist Connection, or Church, of America*, 1913–16; *Minutes of the Annual Session of the Rochester Conference of the Wesleyan Methodist Connection, or Church, of America*, 1917–67; Mary E. Bennett, ed., "Our Heritage: Lockport Conference Centennial 1861–1951" (Houghton, New York: Lockport Conference of the Wesleyan Methodist Church of America, no date).

145. Yager, "A Flame Burning," 103.

146. *The Wesleyan Methodist*, June 7, 1944, 11; *The Wesleyan Methodist*, February 14, 1968.

147. *The Wesleyan Methodist*, April 23, 1947, 10.

148. *Minutes of the Annual Session of the Ohio Conference of the Wesleyan Methodist Connection, or Church, of America*, 1909–13, 1939–46.

149. *Minutes* of the Pentecostal Rescue Mission were incomplete but her service records as stated here were found in *The Pentecostal Rescue Mission Yearly Meeting*

Minutes of 1910 (New York); Minutes of the Yearly Meeting of the Pentecostal Rescue Mission (New York), 1913, 1918; *Minutes of the Yearly Meeting of the Pentecostal Mission Association (New York),* 1915; *Pentecostal Rescue Mission Association (New York),* 1916; *Minutes of the Yearly Meeting of the Pentecostal Rescue Mission Association (New York),* 1919–21.

150. Facts provided by her daughter, Mrs. Ronald (Rosalee) Brannon and the *Minutes of the Annual Session of the Kansas Conference of the Wesleyan Methodist Connection, or Church, of America,* 1921–67.

151. *The Wesleyan Methodist,* December 6, 1967, 18.

152. *Minutes of the Annual Assembly Indiana District of the International Holiness Church,* 1920–23; *Minutes of the Annual Assembly of the Pilgrim Holiness Church Indiana Conference,* 1923–50; *Minutes of the Annual Conference of the Indiana North District Pilgrim Holiness Church,* 1951–58.

153. *Minutes of the Annual Session of the Kansas Conference of the Wesleyan Methodist Connection, or Church, of America,* 1910–14; *Minutes of the Annual Session of the Iowa Conference of the Wesleyan Methodist Connection, or Church, of America,* 1913–21; *Minutes of the Annual Session of the South Georgia Conference of the Wesleyan Methodist Connection, or Church, of America,* 1942–59; *Minutes of the Annual Session of the Georgia Conference of the Wesleyan Methodist Church of America,* 1960–67.

154. *Minutes of the Annual Session of the North Michigan Conference of the Wesleyan Methodist Connection, or Church, of America,* 1911–19.

155. *The Wesleyan Methodist,* April 30, 1947, 14.

156. *Minutes of the Brethren in Christ Church Conference,* 1908–17; *Minutes of the Annual Conference of the Pentecostal Brethren in Christ,* 1918–23.

157. *The Pilgrim Holiness Advocate,* February 27, 1947, 12–13.

158. *Manual International Apostolic Holiness Union of Kentucky,* 1910; *Minutes of the Annual Assembly of the Pilgrim Holiness Church, Kentucky District,* 1929–53.

159. Facts for her story were gleaned from Bessie Mitchell, "My Story" (edited and compiled by Etta M. Mitchell, her daughter), materials provided by her son, Russell, and by Etta Clough and Mrs. Beatrice Joseph, who have been members of the Eastern District of the Pilgrim Holiness Church, and *Minutes of the Eastern District Pilgrim Holiness Church,* 1925–60.

160. Nicholson, *Wesleyan Methodism in the South,* 146.

161. Centennial Committee, "Centennial Celebration 1879–1979, North Carolina (Colfax) District The Wesleyan Church." (Published by the North Carolina Colfax District The Wesleyan Church, no date.)

162. *Minutes of the Annual Session of the North Carolina Conference of the Wesleyan Methodist Connection, or Church, of America,* 1936–46.

163. Her life's story was written by her daughter, Mrs. Norma L. Stuve and additional notes were added from "100 Years 1867–1967 Wisconsin Conference Centennial Wesleyan Methodist Church of America" (published by the Wisconsin Conference of the Wesleyan Methodist Church of America, no date).

164. Service record found in the *Minutes of the Annual Session of the Wisconsin Conference of the Wesleyan Methodist Connection, or Church, of America,* 1933–53, and in "Wisconsin Conference Centennial."

165. *Minutes of the Annual Convention Apostolic Holiness Union of Indiana,* 1911, 1913–15, 1917, 1919; *Minutes Annual Assembly Indiana District of the International Holiness Church,* 1920–22; *Minutes of Annual Assembly of the Pilgrim Holiness Church Indiana Conference,* 1923–35.

166. *Minutes of the Annual Indiana Conference Holiness Christian Church,* 1911–19; *Minutes Annual Assembly Indiana District of the International Holiness Church,* 1920–22; *Minutes of Annual Assembly of the Pilgrim Holiness Church Indiana Conference,* 1923–50; *Journal of Proceedings of the Annual Session of the Southern Indiana Conference of the Pilgrim Holiness Church,* 1952–63.

167. *Minutes of the Indiana Conference Holiness Christian Church,* 1919; *Minutes of the Annual Session of the International Holiness Churches Michigan District,* 1922–24; *Minutes of the Annual Assembly of the Michigan District Pilgrim Holiness Church,* 1926–55; *Minutes of the Annual Assembly of the East Michigan District Pilgrim Holiness Church,* 1956–57.

168. Her life story was written by her daughter, Mrs. Helen (George) Kilpatrick. Facts of her service record are recorded in the *Minutes of the Annual Session of the South Carolina Conference of the Wesleyan Methodist Connection, or Church, of America,* 1927–29; *Minutes of the Annual Session of the Allegheny Conference of the Wesleyan Methodist Connection, or Church, of America,* 1933–66; *Minutes of the Annual Session of the Lockport Conference of the Wesleyan Methodist Church,* 1967; I. F. McLeister and J. B. Markey, "The Allegheny Conference Centennial: The History of One Hundred Years of Conference Activities," (no publisher: [1943]); *Wesleyan Advocate,* December 9, 1979, 18.

169. *Minutes of the Annual Conference, Holiness Christian Church (Indiana),* 1911–19; *Minutes of the Annual Assembly Indiana District of the International Holiness Church,* 1920–22; *Minutes of Annual Assembly of the Pilgrim Holiness Church Indiana Conference,* 1923–50.

170. *Minutes of the Annual Session of the Indiana Conference of the Wesleyan Methodist Connection, or Church, of America,* 1911–1915.

171. "History of the Fairmount Bible School," 15.

172. *Minutes of the Annual Session of the Indiana Conference of the Wesleyan Methodist Connection, or Church, of America,* 1912–27.

173. *The Wesleyan Methodist,* May 26, 1965, 14.

174. "History of the Fairmount Bible School," 15.

175. Service record found in *Minutes of the Annual Session of the Indiana Conference of the Wesleyan Methodist Connection, or Church, of America,* 1912–68; *Minutes of the Annual Session of the Lockport Conference of the Wesleyan Methodist Connection, or Church, of America,* 1916.

176. Additional materials were provided by Miriam Jennings Watson's son, Lowell Jennings.

177. *Minutes of the Annual Session of the Lockport Conference of the Wesleyan Methodist Connection, or Church, of America,* 1912–13.

178. David L. Gowan, *A Century in Dakota Territory 1881–1981, Historical Sketch The Dakota District of The Wesleyan Church* (The Dakota District of The Wesleyan Church, 1981), 4.

179. *The Wesleyan Methodist*, September 15, 1965,15.

180. *The Pilgrim Holiness Advocate*, October 21, 1950, p, 11; *Minutes of the Annual Assembly of the Ohio District of the Pilgrim Holiness Church*, 1950.

181. *The Wesleyan Advocate*, March 1990, 30.

182. Ibid., 30.

183. *Minutes of the Holiness Christian Church*, 1919, 1.

184. "History of the Fairmount Bible School," 14.

185. *Minutes of the Annual Session of the Indiana Conference of the Wesleyan Methodist Connection, or Church, of America*, 1913–68.

186. *Minutes of the Indiana Conference Holiness Christian Church*, 1913–19; *Minutes of the Annual Session of the Indiana International Holiness Church*, 1921–22.

187. *Minutes of the Annual Conference Southern District International Apostolic Holiness Church*, 1916–18.

188. *Minutes of the Annual Conference Carolina District International Apostolic Holiness Church*, 1914; *Minutes of the Annual Conference Southern District International Apostolic Holiness Church*, 1916–18; *Minutes of the Annual Assembly of the Pilgrim Holiness Church, Southern District*, 1926–33; 1935–41; *Minutes of the North Carolina District Pilgrim Holiness Church*, 1942–68.

189. *Minutes of the Annual Convention of the Apostolic Holiness Church of Pennsylvania*, 1914–19.

190. *Minutes of the Annual Assembly of the Pilgrim Holiness Church of Pennsylvania and New Jersey*, 1922–51.

191. *The Pilgrim Holiness Advocate*, March 8, 1952, 15.

192. *Minutes of the Annual Session of the Indiana Conference of the Holiness Christian Church*, 1915–19; *Minutes of the Annual Session of the Indiana Assembly International Holiness Church*, 1921–22; *Minutes of the Annual Assembly of the Pilgrim Holiness Church Indiana Conference*, 1925–48.

193. "The Pentecostal Rescue Mission Pilgrim Holiness Church of New York, Seventy-fifth Anniversary, July 12, 1972."

194. The International Holiness Church and the Pentecostal Rescue Mission merged, and with the merger with the Pilgrim Church became the Pilgrim Holiness Church, New York District. Much of Ethel Wilson Carroll's service record is found in the *Minutes of the Annual Assembly of the Pilgrim Holiness Church (New York)*, 1924–63; *Minutes of the Annual Assembly of the Michigan District Pilgrim Holiness Church*, 1967; and *Wesleyan Advocate*, September 12, 1977, 18.

195. Centennial Committee, "Centennial Celebration 1879–1979, North Carolina (Colfax) District The Wesleyan Church."

196. *Minutes of the Fifth Annual Session of the Virginia Conference of the Wesleyan Methodist Church*, 1964, 12.

197. *The Wesleyan Methodist*, July 8, 1936, 15.

198. *The Wesleyan Methodist*, January 24, 1951, 14.

199. Pomeroy, "A History of the Kansas Conference of the Wesleyan Methodist Church of America,"84; *Minutes of the Annual Session of the Kansas Conference of the Wesleyan Methodist Connection, or Church, of America, 1919–44.*

200. *Minutes of the First Annual Conference of the Western Ohio District of the Pilgrim Holiness Church,* 1955.

201. *Minutes of the Annual Conference of the Pentecostal Brethren in Christ*, 1918–23.

202. *Minutes of the Annual Assembly of the Western Kansas District Pilgrim Holiness Church*, 1926–54.

203. "History of Fairmount Bible School," 17.

204. *Minutes of the Annual Session of the Indiana Conference of the Wesleyan Methodist Connection, or Church, of America*, 1916–60.

205. *Wesleyan Advocate*, April 7, 1980, 17.

206. Her life story facts were written by her daughter, Eunice Hansen; other information was gleaned from the *Minutes of the Annual Session of the Indiana Conference of the Wesleyan Methodist Connection, or Church, of America*, 1916, 1922–66.

207. Many of the personal notes of Mary Greene's life came from a video made the day her picture was placed in the Hall of Heroes at Marion College (now Indiana Wesleyan University). Persons who spoke or were represented by letters which they had written previously on that video were Marcille Bostic, Agnes Clapp, Dr. Charles Carter, Hazel Jones, Mrs. Kenneth Knapp, Alton E. Liddick, Floyd Banker and Marie Noggle. All these people knew Mary personally and several of them worked with her in India. Additional personal information was obtained from her niece, Reva Cockran.

208. "History of Fairmount Bible School," 16.

209. *Minutes of the Annual Session of the Indiana Conference of the Wesleyan Methodist Connection, or Church, of America*, 1912–56.

210. *Wesleyan Methodist*, October 9, 1957, 13.

211. *Wesleyan Methodist*, January 31, 1940, 14.

212. "History of Fairmount Bible School," 16.

213. *Minutes of the Annual Assembly of the Pilgrim Holiness Church Indiana Conference*, 1929–33.

214 *Minutes of the Annual Session of the Ohio Conference of the Wesleyan Methodist Connection, or Church, of America*, 1936.

215. *Minutes of the Annual Session of the Kentucky Conference of the Wesleyan Methodist Connection, or Church, of America*, 1941–43, 1945–47.

216. *The Wesleyan Methodist*, October 3, 1951, 15.

217. *The Wesleyan Methodist*, January 30, 1962, 14.

218. *Minutes of the Annual Conference of the Indiana Apostolic Holiness Church*, 1917, 1919; *Minutes of the Annual Convention of the International Apostolic Holiness Church Indiana*, 1920–22; *Minutes of the Annual Assembly of the Pilgrim Holiness Church Indiana Conference*, 1923–50.

219. *Minutes of the Annual Session of the Indiana Conference of the Wesleyan Methodist Connection, or Church, of America*, 1917–62.

220. "Lancaster Wesleyan Church Centennial Album, 1897–1997," 13.

221. *The Wesleyan Methodist*, May 22, 1963, 14.

222. "History of the Fairmount Bible School," 10, 17.

223. *Minutes of the Annual Session of the Indiana Conference of the Wesleyan Methodist Connection, or Church, of America,* 1917–68. These *Minutes* contain the record of her service appointments.

224. *The Wesleyan Advocate,* June 6, 1977, 18.

225. *Minutes of the Annual Session of the Rochester Conference of the Wesleyan Methodist Connection, or Church, of America,* 1917–33, 1961–67.

226. *Minutes of the Annual Session of the Lockport Conference of the Wesleyan Methodist Connection, or Church, of America,* 1931–60.

227. Facts about Chloie Meeks' personal life came from a telephone interview with her daughter, Virginia Wright, July 20, 1999, and from a book written by Virginia M. Wright, *God of Miracles,* (Marion, Ind.: Wesley Press, 1986).

228. W. E. Hall, *History Sketches of the Pilgrim Holiness Church Illinois District Now Southern Illinois District of The Wesleyan Church,* 36–37.

229. Her service record can be found in the *Minutes of the Annual Assembly of the Illinois and Missouri District Pilgrim Holiness Church,* 1923–37; *Minutes of the Annual Assembly of the Pilgrim Holiness Church Illinois District* 1938–67; and the *Wesleyan Advocate,* September 20, 1982.

230. *Minutes of the Alliance of the Reformed Baptist Church of Canada,* 1917–56; an interview with Mrs. Vesta (Lawrence) Mullens, July 1998.

231. *Wesleyan Advocate,* December 28, 1970, 18.

232. *Minutes of the Annual Session of the Kansas Conference of the Wesleyan Methodist Connection, or Church, of America,* 1917–37.

233. *Annual Conference Journal Oregon Conference of the Wesleyan Methodist Connection, or Church, of America,* 1937–67.

234. Alton J. Shea, *Who Will Go?* (Houghton, N.Y.: The Young Missionary Workers Band of the Wesleyan Methodist Church, 1945), 5.

235. McLeister and Nicholson, *Conscience and Commitment,* 412.

236. *Wesleyan Advocate,* July 20, 1982, 21–22.

237. Floyd and Hazel Banker, *From Famine to Fruitage* (Marion, Ind.: Wesley Press, 1960), 57–59.

238. McLeister and Nicholson, *Conscience and Commitment,* 409.

239. Banker, *From Famine to Fruitage,* 71–72.

240. Ibid., 64.

241. *Minutes of the Annual Session of the Wisconsin Conference of the Wesleyan Methodist Connection, or Church, of America,* 1930–35.

242. Wolter, *The Iowa Conference Centennial 1853–1953.*

243. Miller, *History of the Woman's Missionary Society,* 82.

244. *Wesleyan Methodist,* March 28, 1973, 17.

245. *Minutes of the Annual Session of the North Georgia Conference of the Wesleyan Methodist Church,* 1952–56.

246. *Wesleyan Methodist,* March 28, 1973, 17.

247. Materials provided by the Rev. William H. Richardson from her obituary read at her funeral.

248. *Wesleyan Advocate,* August 15, 1988; May 1993.

249. *Wesleyan Methodist,* September 5, 1962, 15.

250. *Minutes of the Annual Session of the Iowa Conference of the Wesleyan Methodist Connection, or Church, of America,* 1918–1962.

251. Personal letter written by Harold Crosser, a personal friend of Bessie Hatcher. He first met her at Beulah Park Camp Meeting at Allentown, Pennsylvania, in 1933. And a personal letter written by David Tonnessen whose father was the last camp president of Wesley Grove after he had served the camp for nearly twenty years as business manager and treasurer.

252. *Minutes of the Annual Session of the Middle Atlantic States Mission Conference of the Wesleyan Methodist Connection, or Church, of America,* 1923–25.

253. *Minutes of the Annual Conference of the International Holiness Church of Pennsylvania and New Jersey,* 1920–48; *The Conference Journal of the Pennsylvania and New Jersey District of the Pilgrim Holiness Church,* 1949–60.

254. "History of the Fairmount Bible School," 17.

255. *Minutes of the Annual Session of the Kentucky Conference of the Wesleyan Methodist Connection, or Church, of America,* 1930–33.

256. *Minutes of the Annual Session of the Indiana Conference of the Wesleyan Methodist Connection, or Church, of America,* 1919–27; 1933–68.

257. *Pilgrim Holiness Advocate,* July 6, 1957, 13; *Annual Conference of the California District of the Pilgrim Holiness Church,* 1957.

258. *Minutes of the Annual Session of the Indiana Conference of the Wesleyan Methodist Connection, or Church, of America,* 1919–20.

259. *Minutes of the Annual Session of the North Michigan Conference of the Wesleyan Methodist Connection, or Church, of America,* 1913–18, 1920–59.

260. Personal letter from Robert Cooper.

261. *Official Minutes of the Annual Wisconsin Conference of the Pilgrim Holiness Church,* 1957.

262. *Minutes of the Annual Session of the Ohio Conference of the Wesleyan Methodist Connection, or Church, of America,* 1919–68; *Wesleyan Advocate,* May 8, 1978, 22.

263. *Minutes of the Annual Session of the Michigan Conference of the Wesleyan Methodist Connection, or Church, of America,* 1919–67; *Wesleyan Advocate,* September 3, 1984, 18.

Chapter 3

1. Personal facts of her life were taken from a booklet by Alton J. Shea, *Who will Go?* (Houghton, N.Y.: 1945), 27.

2. *Minutes of the Annual Session of the Michigan Conference of the Wesleyan Methodist Connection of America,* 1920–46.

3. *Minutes of the Annual Session of the Michigan Conference of the Wesleyan Methodist Church of America,* 1947–59.

4. *Minutes of the Annual Session of the North Carolina West District of The Wesleyan Church,* 1994.

5. *The Pilgrim Holiness Advocate,* September 19, 1929.

6. *The Wesleyan Methodist,* December 17, 1958, 14.

7. *The Pilgrim Holiness Advocate*, November 6, 1924, 1–3.

8. Thomas and Thomas, *The Days of Our Pilgrimage*, 37–38.

9. *The Pilgrim Holiness Advocate*, May 7, 1960, 2.

10. *The Pilgrim Holiness Advocate*, December 4, 1947; August 27, 1966, 17.

11. *The Wesleyan Advocate*, December 4, 1978, 18.

12. *The Pilgrim Holiness Advocate*, January 11, 1945, 12.

13. The Minutes of the South Ohio District were not found in the Archives at the International Center. Materials on her life were provided by the Rev. Eugene Ramsey, former conference president/district superintendent and Mrs. Lucille Morrow.

14. Shea, *Who Will Go?* 18–19.

15. *The Wesleyan Advocate*, January 1996, 32.

16. *The Pilgrim Holiness Advocate*, February 5, 1955, 14.

17. Shea, *Who Will Go?* 13.

18. Ira Ford McLeister, *History of the Wesleyan Methodist Church of America*, (Syracuse, N.Y.: Wesleyan Methodist Publishing Association, 1934), 217.

19. *The Wesleyan Advocate*, April 21, 1986, 18; *Minutes of the Annual Session of the Allegheny Conference of the Wesleyan Methodist Connection, or Church, of America*, 1933–64.

20. *The Wesleyan Methodist*, August 17, 1949, 13.

21. *Minutes of the Annual Session of the North Michigan Conference of the Wesleyan Methodist Connection, or Church, of America*, 1920–46; personal letter from Robert Cooper.

22. The Historian Committee of the Pacific Southwest District of The Wesleyan Church, "History of the Holiness, Pilgrim and Pilgrim Holiness Churches of California" (January 1999), 59, 68, 88 (computer typed looseleaf notebook).

23. *The Pilgrim Holiness Advocate*, February 22, 1964, 15.

24. *Minutes of the Annual Assembly of the Pilgrim Holiness Church Indiana Conference*, 1943–50; *Journal of Proceedings of the Annual Session of the Southern Indiana Conference of the Pilgrim Holiness Church*, 1951–63.

25. *Minutes of the Annual Assembly Indiana District of the International Holiness Church*, 1921–22; *Pilgrim Holiness Church Indiana Conference Sessions*, 1923–29.

26. *Minutes of the Annual Assembly of the Illinois and Missouri District Pilgrim Holiness Church*, 1924–26.

27. *The Wesleyan Advocate*, April 20, 1981, 16; *Minutes of the Annual Conference of the Northern Indiana District Pilgrim Holiness Church.*

28. Personal notes from the Rev. W. M. Rampey, pastor and district leader in the South Carolina District and *Minutes of the Annual Session of the South Carolina Conference of the Wesleyan Methodist Connection, or Church, of America*, 1921–48.

29. *Minutes of the Annual Assembly of the Pilgrim Holiness Church Indiana Conference*, 1923–24.

30. *Minutes of the Annual Session of the Middle Atlantic States Mission Conference of the Wesleyan Methodist Connection, or Church, of America*, 1923–25.

31. *Minutes of the Annual Session of the West Virginia District Assembly of the International Holiness Church*, 1921–22; *Minutes of the Annual Session of the West Virginia Assembly of the Pilgrim Holiness Church*, 1923–41; *Minutes of the West Virginia District Conference Pilgrim Holiness Church*, 1942–67; *Wesleyan Advocate*, October 5, 1981, 18.

32. Thomas and Thomas, *Days of Our Pilgrimage*, 248, states that A. L. Luttrull led the Trinity Gospel Tabernacle Association, centered in Evansville, Indiana, into the Indiana District of the Pilgrim Holiness Church. A. L. Luttrull and one delegate from the Evansville work attended the 1950 General Conference of the Pilgrim Holiness Church at Frankfort, Indiana.

33. *The Pilgrim Holiness Advocate*, November 9, 1933, 12.

34. Her ministerial service record may be found in *Minutes of the Annual Convention of the International Apostolic Holiness Church of Ohio*, 1921–24; *Minutes of the Annual Assembly of the Ohio Pilgrim Holiness District*, 1926–54; *Minutes of the Annual Conference of the Eastern Ohio District and the Western Ohio District of the Pilgrim Holiness Church*, 1955; *Minutes of the Annual Conference of the Western Ohio District of the Pilgrim Holiness Church*, 1956–62; *Minutes of the Annual Conference of the Indiana North District Pilgrim Holiness Church*, 1963–64.

35. *Pilgrim Holiness Advocate*, May 15, 1965, 13.

36. *Minutes of the Annual Assembly Indiana District of the International Holiness Church*, 1921–22; *Minutes of the Annual Assembly of the Illinois and Missouri District Pilgrim Holiness Church*, 1924–25; *Minutes of the Annual Assembly of the Pilgrim Holiness Church Indiana Conference*, 1927–29, 1934.

37. Her ministerial record can be found in *Minutes of the Annual Assembly of the Pilgrim Holiness Church Illinois District*, 1938–51, 1962–68; *Minutes of the Annual Conference of the Oklahoma-Texas District Pilgrim Holiness Church*, 1954–55; *North Central District Pilgrim Holiness Church Annual Conference Journal*, 1957–61.

38. From a personal letter.

39. *The Wesleyan Advocate*, July/August, 1998, 31. Her service record is recorded in the *Minutes of the Annual Session of the Indiana Conference of the Wesleyan Methodist Connection, or Church, of America*, 1922–68.

40. Materials were provided by her grandson, Glendon Kierstead and *Minutes of the Alliance of the Reformed Baptist Church of Canada*, 1927–50.

41. *Minutes of the Annual Assembly Michigan District of the International Holiness Church*, 1922; *Minutes of the Annual Assembly Michigan District Pilgrim Holiness Church*, 1927–50.

42. *Minutes of the Annual Convention of the International Apostolic Holiness Church of Ohio*, 1920–24; *Minutes of the Annual Assembly of the Ohio District Pilgrim Holiness Church*, 1926–55; *Minutes of the Annual Conference of the Western Ohio District of the Pilgrim Holiness Church*, 1956–67; *The Wesleyan Advocate*, October 7, 1968, 42.

43. *Pentecostal Rescue Mission Yearly Meeting Minutes*, 1918–23; *Official Record of the Annual Assembly of the Pilgrim Holiness Church New York District*, 1928–67.

44. Materials provided by District Superintendent Marlin Hotle from the book, *History of the Tennessee Conference of the Pilgrim Holiness Church*, 2–4.

45. *The Pilgrim Holiness Advocate*, June 14, 1928, 7.

46. Service records found in the *Minutes of the Annual Assembly of the Pilgrim Holiness Church Kentucky District*, 1932; *Minutes of the Annual Session of the Tennessee-Alabama District Pilgrim Holiness Church*, 1934–39; *Minutes of the Annual Conference of the Tennessee District Pilgrim Holiness Church*, 1941–67.

47. *The Wesleyan Methodist*, September 30, 1933, 14. Her ministerial record can be found in the *Minutes of the Annual Session of the Indiana Conference of the Wesleyan Methodist Connection, or Church, of America*, 1923–25, 1930–33.

48. Shea, *Who Will Go?* 22–23, gives her early life and missionary activities.

49. *Minutes Of the Annual Session of the Kansas Conference of the Wesleyan Methodist Connection, or Church, of America*, 1923–55; *Minutes of the Annual Session of the Michigan Conference of the Wesleyan Methodist Church; The Wesleyan Advocate*, August 20, 1973, 17.

50. *Minutes of the Annual Session of the Iowa Conference of the Wesleyan Methodist Connection, or Church, of America*, 1922–40.

51. *St. Petersburg Times*, Saturday, August 11, 1990, 9.

52. *Minutes of the Annual Convention of the International Apostolic Holiness Church of Ohio*, 1920–24; *Minutes of the Annual Assembly of the Ohio District of the Pilgrim Holiness Church*, 1926–53.

53. *St. Petersburg Times*, Saturday, August 11, 1990, 9.

54. *Minutes of the Annual Assembly of the Illinois and Missouri District Pilgrim Holiness Church*, 1923–34; *Minutes of the Annual Assembly of the Kansas District of the Pilgrim Holiness Church*,1935–37; *Minutes of the Annual Assembly of the Pilgrim Holiness Church Illinois District*, 1938–68; *Pilgrim Holiness Advocate*, August 1, 1953.

55. *Minutes of the Annual Assembly of the West Virginia District of the Pilgrim Holiness Church*, 1923–41.

56. *Minutes of the Annual Assembly of the Pilgrim Holiness Church Indiana Conference*, 1923–40.

57. *Minutes of the Annual Assembly of the Pilgrim Holiness Church Indiana Conference*, 1923–29; *Minutes of the Annual Assembly of the Ohio District Pilgrim Holiness Church*, 1927–51.

58. *The Pilgrim Holiness Advocate*, August 16, 1952, 15.

59. *Official Record of the Annual Assembly of the Virginia District of the Pilgrim Holiness Church*, 1934–39.

60. *Minutes of the Annual Session of the West Virginia Assembly of the Pilgrim Holiness Church*, 1923–33; *Official Record of the Annual Assembly of the Pilgrim Holiness Church, New York District*, 1940–41; *Minutes of the Annual Conference of the Pittsburgh District*, 1942–53.

61. Historical Committee Pacific Southwest District, "History of the Holiness, Pilgrim and Pilgrim Holiness Churches of California," 162.

62. Ira Ford McLeister, *The Life and Work of Rev. Mrs. Clara McLeister* (no publisher, no date), 9–25.

63. Personal letter from James Bence, a former conference president.

64. *Minutes of the Annual Session of the Rochester Conference of the Wesleyan Methodist Connection, or Church, of America*, 1923–57.

65. *Minutes of the Annual Session of the Indiana Conference of the Wesleyan Methodist Connection, or Church, of America*, 1923–45.

66. *Minutes of the Pilgrim Holiness Church Indiana Conference*, 1923–37; *Proceedings of Annual California District Assembly of the Pilgrim Holiness Church*, 1926–32.

67. *Proceedings of Annual California District Assembly of the Pilgrim Holiness Church*, 1923–24.

68. *Proceedings of the Western Kansas District Assembly of the Pilgrim Holiness Church*, 1927.

69. Annie Eubanks (Thompson), compiler, *Pilgrim Missions in Latin America* (Indianapolis, Ind.: Pilgrim Holiness Church, 1958), 21–23.

70. *Proceedings of Annual California District Assembly of the Pilgrim Holiness Church*, 1923–37; *Minutes of the Annual Conference of the Pilgrim Holiness Church California District*, 1938–57.

71. Eubanks, *Pilgrim Missions in Latin America*, 24, 46.

72. Paul W. Thomas, compiler, *25 Years with Christ in Mexico* (Indianapolis, Ind.: Foreign Missionary Office Pilgrim Holiness Church, no date [1945]), 39.

73. *The Pilgrim Holiness Advocate*, May 2, 1928, 12–13.

74. *The Pilgrim Holiness Advocate*, April 13, 1939, 12; *Minutes of the Annual Assembly of the Michigan District Pilgrim Holiness Church*, 1926–37.

75. *Minutes of the Annual Session of the Pilgrim Holiness Church Texas District*, 1924.

76. *Minutes of the Annual Assembly of the Oklahoma District of the Pilgrim Holiness Church*, 1931; *Minutes of the Annual Assembly of the Oklahoma/Texas/Louisiana District Pilgrim Holiness Church*, 1938–40; *Minutes of the Annual Assembly of the Oklahoma District Pilgrim Holiness Church*, 1941–43.

77. *Annual Conference of the Brethren in Christ*, 1909–23.

78. *Minutes of the Annual Conference of the Pilgrim Holiness Church California District*, 1924–67.

79. *Minutes of the Annual Session of the Kansas Conference of the Wesleyan Methodist Connection, or Church, of America*, 1924–27.

80. Facts from a phone call with Fern Henschen's niece, Virginia (Meeks) Wright.

81. *The Pilgrim Holiness Advocate*, March 26, 1960, 15. Her service record may be found in *Minutes of the Annual Assembly of the Illinois and Missouri District Pilgrim Holiness Church*, 1924–27; *Minutes of Annual Assembly of the Pilgrim Holiness Church Indiana Conference*, 1929–34; *Minutes of the Annual Assembly of the Pilgrim Holiness Church Illinois District*, 1941–47; *Minutes of Annual Conference of the Ohio District Pilgrim Holiness Church*, 1949–55; *Minutes of the Annual Conference of the Western Ohio District of the Pilgrim Holiness Church*, 1956–59.

82. *Minutes of the Annual Assembly of the Illinois and Missouri District Pilgrim Holiness Church*, 1924–32;

Minutes of the Annual Assembly of the Pilgrim Holiness Church Illinois District, 1938–39.

83. *The Wesleyan Advocate,* December 13, 1971, 17; *Minutes of the Annual Convention of the International Apostolic Holiness Church of Ohio,* 1924.

84. *Minutes of the Annual Assembly of the Pilgrim Holiness Church Indiana Conference,* 1924–48.

85. *Minutes of the Annual Assembly of the Illinois and Missouri District Pilgrim Holiness Church,* 1924–37; *Minutes of the Annual Assembly of the Pilgrim Holiness Church Illinois District,* 1938–67.

86. Facts of her life story were gleaned from her book, Ruby Reisdorph, *Chores Around Father's House* (Shoals, Ind.: Old Paths Tract Society, 1990); *Minutes of the Annual Session of the Dakota Conference of the Wesleyan Methodist Church of America,* 1933–68.

87. *Minutes of the Annual Session of the North Michigan Conference of the Wesleyan Methodist Connection, or Church, of America,* 1924–29.

88. *Minutes of the Annual Assembly of the Pilgrim Holiness Church Indiana Conference,* 1924–50; *Journal of Proceedings of the Annual Session of the Indiana Conference and the First Annual Session of the Southern Indiana Conference of the Pilgrim Holiness Church,* 1951; *Journal of Proceedings of the Annual Session of the Southern Indiana Conference of the Pilgrim Holiness Church,* 1952–67.

89. *Minutes of the Annual Assembly of the Pilgrim Holiness Church Indiana Conference,* 1924–35; *The Pilgrim Holiness Advocate,* May 28, 1931, 13.

90. Materials were taken from a vita sheet prepared for the Eastern Ohio District celebration of those ministers celebrating fifty years of ministry and *Minutes of the Annual Assembly of the Ohio District Pilgrim Holiness Church,* 1942–52; *Minutes of the Annual Assembly of the Pilgrim Holiness Church Illinois District,* 1953–68.

91. A partial service record may be found in *Minutes of the Annual Session of the Dakota Conference of the Wesleyan Methodist Church of America,* 1933–45; *Minutes of the Annual Session of the Oklahoma Conference of the Wesleyan Methodist Connection, or Church, of America,* 1945–59, 1964–68; *Minutes of the Annual Session of the Kansas Conference of the Wesleyan Methodist Church of America,* 1959–1963; *The Wesleyan Advocate,* April 6, 1987, 18.

92. *Conference Journal of the Penn/New Jersey District of the Pilgrim Holiness Church,* 1953–66; *The Wesleyan Advocate,* December l, 1980, 17.

93. Among those young ladies who boarded with Etta Clough was Mrs. Dorothy Ammons. Dorothy supplied much of the materials on the planting of the Baltimore churches.

94. Materials supplied by Mrs. Lottie (Joseph) Neal, a convert of Etta Clough in the Greenwood, Maryland Church.

95. Etta Clough's sister, Margaret Lohr, provided materials on her book.

96. Dr. Ronald Kelly, former superintendent of the West Michigan District and currently the General Secretary of The Wesleyan Church. Dr. Kelly grew up in the Eastern District of the Pilgrim Holiness Church.

97. Centennial Committee of North Carolina (Colfax) District, *Centennial Celebration 1879–1979* (published by the North Carolina Colfax District The Wesleyan Church, no date); *Minutes of the Annual Session of the North Carolina Conference of the Wesleyan Methodist Connection, or Church, of America,* 1936, 1946–68; *Minutes of the Annual Session of the Virginia Conference of the Wesleyan Methodist Church of America,* 1964, 13.

98. *The Wesleyan Methodist,* June 18, 1958, 15.

99. *The Wesleyan Advocate,* February 5, 1973, 18.

100. *The Wesleyan Advocate,* April 1, 1985,18; *Minutes of the Eastern District Pilgrim Holiness Church,* 1929–30, 1934–67.

101. *Minutes of the Annual Session of the Lockport Conference of the Wesleyan Methodist Connection, or Church, of America,* 1925–32; Bennett, *Our Heritage Lockport Conference Centennial; Oregon Conference of the Wesleyan Methodist Connection, or Church, of America, Annual Conference Journal,* 1937–43; Gowan, "Oregon Country Wesleyan Methodism," 13.

102. Book on Pilgrim Holiness missionaries.

103. *The Wesleyan* Advocate, August 30, 1976, 17; Minutes *of the Annual Assembly of the Pilgrim Holiness Church of the Pennsylvania and New Jersey District,* 1923–30; *Official Record of the Annual Assembly of the Virginia District of the Pilgrim Holiness Church,* 1931–37; *Minutes of the Annual Assembly of the Pilgrim Holiness Church Indiana Conference,* 1938–50; *Minutes of the Annual Conference of the Northern Indiana District of the Pilgrim Holiness Church,* 1951–65; *Minutes of the Eastern District Pilgrim Holiness Church,* 1965–67.

104. *The Wesleyan Advocate,* November 1999, 33.

105. *The Pilgrim Holiness Advocate,* November 10, 1962, 15; *Minutes of the Annual Conference of the Kentucky District of the Pilgrim Holiness Church,* 1931–62.

106. *The Wesleyan Advocate,* August 15, 1983, 17.

107. *The Pilgrim Holiness Advocate,* April 16, 1942, 4.

108. *The Pilgrim Holiness Advocate,* October 30, 1954, 15; *Minutes of the Annual Assembly of the Illinois and Missouri District Pilgrim Holiness Church,* 1923–37; *Minutes of the Annual Assembly of the Pilgrim Holiness Church Illinois District,* 1938–54.

109. *The Wesleyan Advocate,* August 26, 1968, 17.

110. Conference Historical Committee (Champlain), *One Hundred and Twenty-Five Years for Christ, 1843–1968* (no publisher, 1968), 58, 93. Charles Dayton became the longtime president of the Champlain Conference.

111. *Minutes of the Annual Session of the Ohio Conference of the Wesleyan Methodist Connection, or Church, of America,* 1925–53.

112. *Minutes of the Annual Session of the Middle Atlantic States Mission Conference of the Wesleyan Methodist Connection, or Church, of America,* 1930–46; *Minutes of the Annual Session of the Middle Atlantic States Mission Conference of the Wesleyan Methodist Church of America,* 1947–67; *The Wesleyan Advocate,* December 21, 1981, 18.

113. *Minutes of the Annual Assembly of the Michigan District Pilgrim Holiness Church,* 1924, 1926; *Minutes of the Twenty-second Annual Assembly of the Ohio District of the Pilgrim Holiness Church,* 1926; *Minutes of the Annual Assembly of the Ohio District Pilgrim Holiness Church,* 1927.

114. *The Wesleyan Methodist,* March 25, 1953; *Minutes of the Annual Session of the Allegheny Conference of the Wesleyan Methodist Church of America,* 1948–52.

115. *Proceedings of the Western Kansas District Assembly of the Pilgrim Holiness Church,* 1927–29; 1931–34. *Minutes of the Thirteenth Annual Assembly of the Eastern Kansas and Oklahoma District of the Pilgrim Holiness Church,* 1926.

116. *The Pilgrim Holiness Advocate,* February 4, 1956, 16. No service record could be found before 1926. *Minutes of the Annual Assembly of the Ohio District Pilgrim Holiness Church,* 1926–55.

117. *Minutes of the Annual Conference Carolina District International Apostolic Holiness Church,* 1914; *Minutes of the Annual Conference Southern District International Apostolic Holiness Church,* 1916–18.

118. *Minutes of the Annual Assembly of Virginia District of the Pilgrim Holiness Church,* 1926–29; *Official Record of the Annual Assembly of the Virginia District of the Pilgrim Holiness Church,* 1930–52; *Minutes of the Session of the Annual Conference Virginia District Pilgrim Holiness Church,* 1953–62; History of the Christiansburg Wesleyan Church written for the dedication of the new building in 1986; *The Pilgrim Holiness Advocate,* January 12, 1963, 15.

119. *Minutes of the Annual Session of the South Carolina Conference of the Wesleyan Methodist Connection, or Church, of America,* 1926–31, 1941–51; *Minutes of the Annual Session of the Kentucky Conference of the Wesleyan Methodist Church of America,* 1952–67; a personal note from Rev. W. M. Rampey, a pastor in the South Carolina District of The Wesleyan Church.

120. Wayne Plummer, District Secretary, "History of the Kansas District of the Pilgrim Holiness Church." History is found in the minutes of the *Fortieth Annual Conference of the Kansas District Pilgrim Holiness Church,* 1953.

121. *Minutes of the Annual Session of the Kentucky Conference of the Wesleyan Methodist Connection, or Church, of America,* 1926, 1930.

122. *Minutes of the Annual Assembly of the Pilgrim Holiness Church Southern District,* 1926, 1930–41; *Minutes of the North Carolina District Pilgrim Holiness Church,* 1942–68.

123. *Minutes of the Annual Assembly of the Idaho-Washington District Pilgrim Holiness Church,* 1926–62.

124. *The Wesleyan Methodist,* October 11, 1967, 18.

125. From a personal note from Dr. Ronald Kelly, General Secretary of The Wesleyan Church.

126. *The Wesleyan Advocate,* September 1992; *Minutes of the Annual Assembly of the Michigan District Pilgrim Holiness Church,* 1926–34, 1958–67; *Minutes of the Annual Assembly of the Ohio District Pilgrim Holiness Church,* 1935–55; *Minutes of the Annual Conference of the Western Ohio District of the Pilgrim Holiness Church,* 1956–57.

127. Written by former district superintendent, Ernest R. Batman, from the Indiana Central District. Quotes were excepts from his funeral message.

128. *Minutes of the Annual Session of the South Carolina Conference of the Wesleyan Methodist Connection, or Church, of America,* 1926–63.

129. *Minutes of the Annual Session of the Indiana Conference of the Wesleyan Methodist Connection, or Church, of America,* 1928–39.

130. *Minutes of the Annual Assembly of the Ohio District of the Pilgrim Holiness Church,* 1929–53.

131. *Minutes of the Pilgrim Holiness Louisiana and Alabama District,* 1954–56; *Minutes of the Florida District Pilgrim Holiness Church,* 1956–67.

132. *The Wesleyan Advocate,* February 20, 1984, 17.

133. *Minutes of the Annual Session of the Champlain Conference of the Wesleyan Methodist Connection, or Church, of America,* 1926–42. Personal letter from Kathleen Edwards, member of the Northwest District.

134. *The Wesleyan Advocate,* April 15, 1974, 18; *Minutes of the Annual Assembly of the Pilgrim Holiness Church Southern District,* 1926–32; *Minutes of the Annual Conference of the Pilgrim Holiness Church Rocky Mountain District,* 1961–67.

135. *The Pilgrim Holiness Advocate,* December 24, 1942, 12; *Minutes of the Annual Assembly of the Pilgrim Holiness Church Southern District* 1926–41.

136. *Minutes of the Annual Session of the Iowa Conference of the Wesleyan Methodist Connection, or Church, of America,* 1926–61.

137. *Minutes of the Annual Session of the Nebraska Conference of the Wesleyan Methodist Church of America,* 1945–53.

138. *Minutes of the Annual Session of the North Michigan Conference of the Wesleyan Methodist Connection, or Church, of America,* 1926–41, 1954–66.

139. *The Wesleyan Advocate,* April 1991; *Minutes of the Annual Assembly of the Michigan District Pilgrim Holiness Church,* 1927–36; *Minutes of the Annual Assembly of the Pilgrim Holiness Church of Pennsylvania and New Jersey District,* 1933, 1937–45; *Minutes of the Annual Assembly of the Pilgrim Holiness Church Indiana Conference,* 1946–50; *Minutes of the Annual Conference of the Indiana North District Pilgrim Holiness Church,* 1951–67.

140. *Proceedings of the Western Kansas District Assembly of the Pilgrim Holiness Church,* 1927–42; *Minutes of the Annual Conference of the Kansas District of the Pilgrim Holiness Church,* 1943–51.

141. *Minutes of the Annual Session of the Indiana Conference of the Wesleyan Methodist Connection, or Church, of America,* 1927–28.

142. *Minutes of the Annual Assembly of the Pilgrim Holiness Church Kentucky District,* 1927–29; *Minutes of the Annual Assembly of the Pilgrim Holiness Church of Pennsylvania and New Jersey,* 1930–46; *Minutes of the Annual Assembly of the Ohio District Pilgrim Holiness Church,* 1947–50; *Minutes of the Annual Conference of the Oklahoma/Texas District Pilgrim Holiness Church,* 1950–62; *Minutes of the Central District of the Pilgrim Holiness Church,* 1963–67; *The Pilgrim Holiness Advocate,* September 23, 1967, 18.

143. *Minutes of the Annual Session of the Champlain Conference of the Wesleyan Methodist Connection, or Church, of America,* 1927–29; *Minutes of the Annual Session of the Rochester Conference of the Wesleyan Methodist Connection, or Church, of America,* 1929–36; *Minutes of the Annual Session of the Allegheny*

Conference of the Wesleyan Methodist Connection, or Church of America, 1937–66.

144. Paul Yager, Rome Historian, *Actionline*, Central New York District The Wesleyan Church, June 1999, 9.

145. Yager, *A Flame Burning*, 81.

146. *Minutes of the Annual Session of the Rochester Conference of the Wesleyan Methodist Connection, or Church, of America*, 1925–55.

147. *The Pilgrim Holiness Advocate*, May 17, 1952, 15; *Minutes of the Annual Assembly of the Oklahoma District of the Pilgrim Holiness Church*, 1927–31.

148. *Minutes of the Annual Convention of the International Apostolic Holiness Church of Ohio*, 1921–24; *Minutes of the Annual Assembly of the Ohio Pilgrim Holiness District*, 1926–27.

149. *Minutes of the Annual Assembly of the Virginia District of the Pilgrim Holiness Church*, 1927–30.

150. *Minutes of the Annual Assembly of the Michigan District Pilgrim Holiness Church*, 1942–45.

151. *Minutes of the Annual Session of the Champlain Conference of the Wesleyan Methodist Connection, or Church, of America*, 1927–33.

152. *Minutes of the Annual Session of the Lockport Conference of the Wesleyan Methodist Connection, or Church, of America*, 1933–41.

153. From a personal letter from her sister-in-law, Doris Ferns.

154. *Minutes of the Annual Assembly of the Oklahoma District of the Pilgrim Holiness Church*, 1928–31; *Minutes of the Annual Assembly of the Oklahoma/Texas District of the Pilgrim Holiness Church*, 1933–37; *Minutes of the Annual Assembly of the Oklahoma-Texas-Louisiana District of the Pilgrim Holiness Church*, 1938–40; *Minutes of the Annual Assembly of the Oklahoma District of the Pilgrim Holiness Church*, 1941; *Minutes of the Annual Conference of the Pilgrim Holiness Church Oklahoma District*, 1942–43; *Minutes of the Annual Conference of the Oklahoma-Texas District of the Pilgrim Holiness Church*, 1944–48.

155. History of Fairmount Bible School, 14.

156. *Minutes of the Annual Session of the Indiana Conference of the Wesleyan Methodist Connection, or Church, of America*, 1928–51, 1959–68; *Minutes of the Annual Session of the Florida Conference of the Wesleyan Methodist Church of America*, 1952–59.

157. *Minutes of the Annual Conference of the Kentucky District Pilgrim Holiness Church*, 1928–29; *Proceedings of Annual California District Assembly of the Pilgrim Holiness Church*, 1929–30.

158. *Minutes of the Annual Session of the Indiana Conference of the Wesleyan Methodist Connection, or Church, of America*, 1928–36.

159. *The Wesleyan Methodist*, June 8, 1932, 13–14.

160. *Minutes of the Annual Session of the Indiana Conference of the Wesleyan Methodist Connection, or Church, of America*, 1928–40.

161. *Minutes of the Annual Assembly of the Ohio District Pilgrim Holiness Church*, 1928–54; *Minutes of the Annual Conference of the Eastern Ohio District and the Western Ohio District of the Pilgrim Holiness Church*, 1955; *Minutes of the Annual Conference of the Western Ohio District of the Pilgrim Holiness Church*, 1956–67.

162. *Minutes of the Annual Conference of the Kentucky District Pilgrim Holiness Church*, 1928–30.

163. *Minutes of the Eastern District Pilgrim Holiness Church*, 1935–37.

164. *Minutes of the Annual Assembly of the Pilgrim Holiness Church of the Pennsylvania and New Jersey District*, 1939–46.

165. *Minutes of the Annual Conference of the Western Ohio District of the Pilgrim Holiness Church*, 1959–67.

166. *Wesleyan Advocate*, April 26, 1976, 22.

167. *Minutes of the Annual Assembly of Canada Pilgrim Holiness Church Ontario District*, 1934–67.

168. *Minutes of the Annual Session of the North Michigan Conference of the Wesleyan Methodist Connection, or Church, of America*, 1934–37.

169. *Annual Assembly California District Pilgrim Holiness Church*, 1929–41.

170. "Rev. Mrs. Berg Honored," *Actionline of the Central New York District of The Wesleyan Church*, June 1998, 11.

171. Annie Eubanks, ed., *These Went Forth* (Indianapolis, Ind.: Foreign Missions Department Pilgrim Holiness Church, no date), no page number.

172. *Actionline*, 11; *Minutes of the Annual Conference of the Pilgrim Holiness Church New York District*, 1946–67.

173. Paul H. Yager, Jr. *A Flame Burning A History of the Central New York District of The Wesleyan Church 1843–1993* (no date, no publisher), 50.

174. *Minutes of the First Annual Conference of the Eastern Ohio District and the Western Ohio District of the Pilgrim Holiness Church*, 1955; *Minutes of the Annual Conference of the Eastern Ohio District of the Pilgrim Holiness Church*, 1956–65.

175. *Official Record of the Annual Assembly of the Pilgrim Holiness Church New York District 1937–42*; *Minutes of the Annual Conference of the Pilgrim Holiness Church New York District*, 1943–53.

176. *Minutes of the Annual Session of the Ohio Conference of the Wesleyan Methodist Connection, or Church, of America*, 1929–31.

177. *Minutes of the Annual Assembly of the Pilgrim Holiness Church Indiana Conference*, 1929–30; *Minutes of the Annual Assembly of the Illinois and Missouri District Pilgrim Holiness Church*, 1930–36; *The Pilgrim Holiness Advocate*, July 16, 1936, 461.

178. *Minutes of the Middle Atlantic States Mission Conference of the Wesleyan Methodist Connection, or Church, of America*, 1929–1946; *Minutes of the Middle Atlantic States Conference of the Wesleyan Methodist Church of America*, 1948–67.

179. *The Wesleyan Advocate*, September 20, 1982, 21.

180. Many persons wrote notes about Lois E. Richardson and Carrie M. Hazzard. Among them were David Tonnesson, a layman from the Chesapeake District; Dr. Harry F. Wood, current district superintendent Pennsylvania and New Jersey; Rev. Charles Williams, former district superintendent Western Pennsylvania. Rev. Williams' wife, Edna, was a convert of these women. She remembers them as women of prayer.

181. *Minutes of the Annual Session of the Kansas Conference of the Wesleyan Methodist Connection, or Church, of America*, 1924–67.

182. *The Minutes of the Annual Assembly of the Pilgrim Holiness Church Indiana Conference, 1929–35; 1938–46; Proceedings of the Annual Assembly California District of the Pilgrim Holiness Church, 1936–38; Minutes of the Annual Session of the Wisconsin Conference of the Wesleyan Methodist Church of America,* 1947–49; records of the *Annual Conference California-Arizona District of the Pilgrim Holiness Church,* 1949–60; *Minutes of the Annual Assembly of the Idaho-Washington District Pilgrim Holiness Church,* 1961–65; *Minutes of the Annual Assembly of the Michigan District Pilgrim Holiness Church,* 1966–67; *Minutes of the Annual Assembly of the East Michigan District Pilgrim Holiness Church,* 1968.

183. *Wesleyan* Advocate, June 7, 1976,18; *Pilgrim Holiness Advocate,* November 3, 1932, 12.

184. Historical Committee Pacific Southwest District, "History of the Holiness, Pilgrim and Pilgrim Holiness Churches of California," 158.

185. *Minutes of the Annual Assembly of the Ohio District Pilgrim Holiness Church,* 1929–30.

186. *Minutes of the Annual Conference of the Kentucky District Pilgrim Holiness Church,* 1930–67; biographical file on Rev. L. S. Houston in the Archives and Historical Library of The Wesleyan Church; *Wesleyan Advocate,* April 19, 1971,17.

187. *The Encyclopedia of World Methodism,* 1974 edition, "Dr. Mary Stone."

188. *Pilgrim Holiness Advocate,* January 12, 1952, 15.

189. Paul S. Rees, *Seth Cook Rees The Warrior-Saint* (Indianapolis, Ind.: The Pilgrim Book Room, 1934), 105.

190. *Pilgrim Holiness Advocate,* January 12, 1952,15.

191. *Minutes of the Annual Conference of California-Arizona District Pilgrim Holiness Church,* 1955.

192. *Pilgrim Holiness Advocate,* June 10, 1960, 13.

193. Viola Leyh's story was written by her daughter, Erma Jean Johnson. Other facts were from the *Wesleyan Advocate,* October 6, 1986, 18; and *Minutes of the Annual Session of the Dakota Conference of the Wesleyan Methodist Church of America,* 1933–68.

194. *Minutes of the Annual Conference of the Northern Indiana District Pilgrim Holiness Church,* 1951–67.

195. *Wesleyan Advocate,* May 4, 1970, 17.

196. David L. Gowan, ed., "A Century in Dakota Territory 1881–1981, 8.

197. *Minutes of the Annual Session of the Dakota Conference of the Wesleyan Methodist Church of America,* 1933–68.

198. Gowan, "A Century in Dakota Territory 1881–1981, 20.

199. *Minutes of the Annual Session of the South Georgia Conference of the Wesleyan Methodist Connection, or Church of America,* 1942–47; *Minutes of the Annual Session of the South Georgia Conference of the Wesleyan Methodist Church,* 1948–50; *Minutes of the Annual Session of the Florida Conference of the Wesleyan Methodist Church of America,* 1950–67; and a personal letter from Rev. W. M. Rampey.

200. *Minutes of the Annual Assembly of the Kentucky/Tennessee District Pilgrim Holiness Church,* 1929–31, 1933; *Minutes Louisiana/Mississippi District Pilgrim Holiness Church,* 1940; *Minutes of the Annual Assembly of the Pilgrim Holiness Church Southern District,* 1935–39, 1941; *Minutes of the Annual Conference Tennessee District Pilgrim Holiness Church,* 1948–49; *Minutes of the Annual Assembly of the North Carolina District Pilgrim Holiness Church,* 1942–47, 1950–68.

201. *Proceedings of the Annual California District Assembly of the Pilgrim Holiness Church,* 1929–31.

202. Martha Stratton sent all the facts about her life and ministry. Other materials were gathered from *Minutes of the Annual Session of the Ohio Conference of the Wesleyan Methodist Connection, or Church, of America,* 1929–47; *Minutes of the Annual Session of the Ohio Conference of the Wesleyan Methodist Church of America,* 1948–68.

203. *Proceedings of the Annual California District Assembly of the Pilgrim Holiness Church,* 1929–62.

204. Grace E. M. Sanders, "A Sketch of My Life," a typed, unpublished manuscript of her life ending around 1950; *Wesleyan Advocate,* October 6, 1980, p 17–18; *Minutes of the Alliance of the Reformed Baptist Church of Canada,* 1935–66; *Minutes of the Atlantic Conference of the Wesleyan Methodist Church of America,* 1967.

Chapter 4

1. *Minutes of the Annual Assembly of the Pilgrim Holiness Church Southern District,* 1930–41; *Minutes of the North Carolina District Pilgrim Holiness Church,* 1942–66.

2. *Minutes of the Annual Assembly of the Pilgrim Holiness Church Indiana Conference,* 1930–38, 1948–50; *Journal of Proceedings of the Annual Sessions of the Indiana Conference and the First Annual Session of the Southern Indiana Conference of the Pilgrim Holiness Church,* 1951; *Journal of Proceedings of the Annual Session of the Southern Indiana Conference of the Pilgrim Holiness Church,* 1952–62.

3. *Wesleyan Advocate,* February 1991.

4. *Minutes of the Annual Session of the South Carolina Conference of the Wesleyan Methodist Connection, or Church, of America,* 1931–63.

5. Ibid.

6. *Minutes of Annual Assembly of the Pilgrim Holiness Church Indiana Conference,* 1930–36; *Pilgrim Holiness Advocate,* August 5, 1937.

7. *Minutes of Annual Assembly of the Pilgrim Holiness Church Indiana Conference,* 1930–50; *Minutes of the Annual Conference of the Indiana North District Pilgrim Holiness Church,* 1951–67.

8. *Minutes of the Annual Session of the North Carolina Conference of the Wesleyan Methodist Connection, or Church, of America,* 1936–41; *Minutes of the Annual Session of the North Carolina Conference of the Wesleyan Methodist Church of America,* 1948–68; *Wesleyan Advocate,* September 16, 1985, 17.

9. *Minutes of the Annual Session of the Oklahoma Conference of the Wesleyan Methodist Connection, or Church, of America,* 1930–40; *Minutes of the California Conference of the Wesleyan Methodist Connection, or Church, of America,* 1942–46; *Minutes of the California Conference of the Wesleyan Methodist Church of America,* 1947–68.

10. *Wesleyan Advocate*, March, 1992; *Annual Assembly Kentucky District Pilgrim Holiness Church, 1930–33; Minutes of the Annual Assembly Tennessee-Alabama District Pilgrim Holiness Church, 1934–40; Minutes of Annual Assembly of the Pilgrim Holiness Church Indiana Conference, 1946–50; Minutes of the Annual Conference of the Northern Indiana District Pilgrim Holiness Church, 1951–56; Minutes of the Louisiana-Mississippi District Pilgrim Holiness Church, 1944–45; Conference Journal Alabama/North-West Florida Conference Pilgrim Holiness Church, 1957–61; Minutes of the Annual Assembly of Illinois District Pilgrim Holiness Church, 1962–68*.

11. *Minutes of the Kentucky Conference of the Wesleyan Methodist Connection, or Church, of America, 1930–46; Minutes of the Kentucky Conference of the Wesleyan Methodist Church of America, 1947–48, 1949–54; Minutes of the Annual Session of the South Georgia Conference of the Wesleyan Methodist Church of America, 1948–49; Minutes of the Indiana Conference of the Wesleyan Methodist Church of America, 1955–57*.

12. *Pilgrim Holiness Advocate*, May 17, 1958; *Minutes of the Annual Assembly of the Ohio District Pilgrim Holiness Church, 1950–54; Minutes of the Annual Conference of the Eastern Ohio District Pilgrim Holiness Church, 1956–58*.

13. *Proceedings of the Annual Assembly California District of the Pilgrim Holiness Church, 1936–41; Minutes of the Annual Conference of the Pilgrim Holiness Church California District, 1942–58*.

14. *Wesleyan Advocate*, March 2, 1981, 18.

15. Bulletin printed for her funeral, November 3, 1980.

16. *Wesleyan Advocate*, March 1993, 32; remarks made by her district superintendent, Rev. Ernest R. Batman.

17. *Minutes of the Annual Session of the Rochester Conference of the Wesleyan Methodist Connection, or Church, of America, 1930–46; Minutes of the Annual Session of the Rochester Conference of the Wesleyan Methodist Church of America, 1947–67; Wesleyan Methodist*, November 22, 1967, 18.

18. *Minutes of the Annual Assembly of the Pilgrim Holiness Church of the Pennsylvania and New Jersey District, 1930–48; Conference Journal Pennsylvania and New Jersey District of the Pilgrim Holiness Church, 1949–50*.

19. *Minutes of the Annual Conference of the Kentucky District Pilgrim Holiness Church, 1937–41; Minutes of the Annual Conference of the Kentucky District Pilgrim Holiness Church, 1942–53*.

20. *Journal of Proceedings of the Annual Session of the Southern Indiana Conference of the Pilgrim Holiness Church*, 1965–67.

21. *Minutes of the Annual Assembly of the Pilgrim Holiness Church of the Pennsylvania and New Jersey District, 1934–48; Conference Journal of the Pennsylvania and New Jersey District of the Pilgrim Holiness Church, 1949–52; Journal of Proceedings of the Annual Session of the Southern Indiana Conference of the Pilgrim Holiness Church, 1953–60; Minutes of the Annual Conference of the Eastern District of the Pilgrim Holiness Church, 1960–67; Pilgrim Holiness Advocate*, July 15, 1967, 18.

22. *Minutes of the Annual Session of the Rochester Conference of the Wesleyan Methodist Connection, or Church, of America, 1930–46; Minutes of the Annual Session of the Rochester Conference of the Wesleyan Methodist Church of America, 1947–67*.

23. Ethel Goldie Skinner wrote the facts about her own story and additional information was gathered from the *Minutes of the Annual Assembly of the Michigan District Pilgrim Holiness Church, 1940–54; Minutes of the Annual Assembly of the East Michigan District Pilgrim Holiness Church, 1955–67*.

24. *Minutes of the Annual Assembly of the Pilgrim Holiness Church Indiana Conference, 1930–38*.

25. *Wesleyan Methodist*, May 8, 1940, 14.

26. *Wesleyan Methodist*, February 8, 1961, 15; *The Wesleyan Methodist*, February 22, 1961, 14; *Allegheny Conference of the Wesleyan Methodist Church Annual Journal*, 1953–61.

27. *Minutes of the Annual Assembly of the Illinois and Missouri District of the Pilgrim Holiness Church*, 1930.

28. *Minutes of the Annual Assembly of the Pilgrim Holiness Church Illinois District, 1943–68*.

29. *Minutes of the Kentucky Conference of the Wesleyan Methodist Connection, or Church, of America, 1930–37*.

30. *Minutes of the Annual Session of the Ohio Conference of the Wesleyan Methodist Connection, or Church, of America, 1938–49*.

31. *The Wesleyan Methodist*, June 11, 1958, 14.

32. *God's Revivalist and Bible Advocate*, October 1999, 14.

33. *The Wesleyan Advocate*, April 1991, 31.

34. Records (minutes) of the Ohio Conference of the Wesleyan Methodist Church, 1931–68.

35. *Minutes of the Annual Session of the Kansas Conference of the Wesleyan Methodist Connection, or Church, of America, 1931–49*.

36. *Minutes of the California Conference of the Wesleyan Methodist Church of America, 1949–61*.

37. *Minutes of the Annual Session of the Lockport Conference of the Wesleyan Methodist Connection, or Church, of America, 1931–42*.

38. Mary E. Bennett, ed., "Our Heritage Lockport Conference Centennial 1851–1961."

39. *Minutes of the Annual Session of the Ohio Conference of the Wesleyan Methodist Connection, or Church, of America, 1943–50*.

40. *Minutes of the Ohio Conference, 1954–60*.

41. *Minutes of the Annual Session of the Allegheny Conference of the Wesleyan Methodist Church of America, 1961–66*.

42. *Minutes of the Annual Assembly of the Ohio District Pilgrim Holiness Church, 1931–43; Wesleyan Advocate*, June 21, 1976, 18.

43. Shea, *Who Will Go?* p 15–16; Gipsie M. Miller, *History Woman's Missionary Society* (Marion, Ind.: Wesleyan Publishing House, no date), 64.

44. *Minutes of the Annual Session of the Champlain Conference of the Wesleyan Methodist Connection, or Church of America, 1942–47; Minutes of the Annual Session of the Champlain Conference of the Wesleyan Methodist Church of America, 1948–50*.

45. *Minutes of the Annual Session of the Lockport*

Conference of the Wesleyan Methodist Church of America, 1950–67.

46. *Pilgrim Holiness Advocate,* June 3, 1967, 16, 17.

47. Annie Eubanks, *These Went Forth* (Indianapolis, Ind.: Foreign Missions Department Pilgrim Holiness Church, no date), no page number.

48. *Kansas District Pilgrim Holiness Church Annual Conference,* 1955–58, 1963–66; *Minutes of the Annual Conference of the Texas District of the Pilgrim Holiness Church,* 1956–57; *Minutes of the Annual Conference Tennessee District Pilgrim Holiness Church,* 1962–63; *North Central District Pilgrim Holiness Church Annual Conference Journal,* 1958–61.

49. *Minutes of the Annual Session of the Lockport Conference of the Wesleyan Methodist Connection, or Church, of America,* 1932–67; *Minutes of the Annual Session of the Western New York District Incorporated of The Wesleyan Church,* 1968.

50. Gipsie M. Miller, *History Woman's Missionary Society* (Marion, Ind.: Wesleyan Publishing House, no date), 104.

51. *Wesleyan Advocate,* August 14, 1970, 16.

52. *Minutes of the Annual Assembly of the Pilgrim Holiness Church Southern District,* 1932–38; *Minutes of the Annual Assembly of the Pilgrim Holiness Church Illinois District,* 1938–40.

53. *Minutes of the Annual Conference of the Pilgrim Holiness Church California District,* 1941–43; *Minutes of the North Carolina District Pilgrim Holiness Church,* 1945–47.

54. Esther Close with Ed Erny, *To India With Love,* (Greenwood, Ind.: OMS International, 1999); *Minutes of the Annual Assembly of the Kentucky District Pilgrim Holiness Church,* 1934–36; *Minutes of the Annual Assembly of the Tennessee/Alabama District Pilgrim Holiness Church,* 1936–41; *Minutes of the Annual Conference Tennessee District Pilgrim Holiness Church,* 1942–57; *Minutes of the Annual Conference of the Pilgrim Holiness Church Rocky Mountain District,* 1963–67.

55. *Minutes of the Annual Session of the Iowa Conference of the Wesleyan Methodist Connection, or Church, of America,* 1932–47.

56. *Minutes of the Annual Session of the Middle Atlantic States Mission Conference of the Wesleyan Methodist Church of America,* 1947–67.

57. *Wesleyan Advocate,* February 3, 1975, 18.

58. *Minutes of the Annual Assembly of the Michigan District Pilgrim Holiness Church,* 1932–34, 1937–55; *Minutes of the Annual Assembly of the East Michigan District Pilgrim Holiness Church,* 1955–65.

59. *Minutes of the Annual Session of the Iowa Conference of the Wesleyan Methodist Connection, or Church, of America,* 1932–37.

60. *Minutes of the Annual Assembly of the Kentucky/Tennessee District Pilgrim Holiness Church,* 1932–33.

61. *Minutes of the Annual Session of the West Virginia District Assembly of the Pilgrim Holiness Church,* 1934–41; *Minutes of the Annual Session of the West Virginia District Conference of the Pilgrim Holiness Church,* 1942–53; *Minutes of the West Virginia District Pilgrim Holiness Church,* 1954–65.

62. Florabel McCombs, "Is She Really Retired?" *The Wesleyan Advocate,* July 15, 1985, 6.

63. McCombs, "Is She Really Retired?"

64. Additional information in her story was given by Rev. Foster Piatt, former president of the Florida Conference of the Wesleyan Methodist Church, and Mrs. Raymond (Marcella) Kensell. Rev. Raymond Kensell is a former superintendent of the Florida District of The Wesleyan Church.

65. *The Wesleyan Advocate,* May 4, 1981, 17; *Minutes of the Annual Assembly of the Ohio District Pilgrim Holiness Church,* 1939–55; *Minutes of the Annual Conference of the Western Ohio District of the Pilgrim Holiness Church,* 1956–67.

66. *Minutes of the Annual Session of the Champlain Conference of the Wesleyan Methodist Connection, or Church, of America,* 1932–68.

67. *The Wesleyan Advocate,* March 1, 1976, 18.

68. *Minutes of the Annual Session of the Middle Atlantic States Mission Conference of the Wesleyan Methodist Connection, or Church, of America,* 1946–47; *Minutes of the Annual Session of the Middle Atlantic States Mission Conference of the Wesleyan Methodist Church of America,* 1948–67.

69. David L. Gowan, editor, *A Century in Dakota Territory 1881–1981 Historical Sketch The Dakota District of The Wesleyan Church* (published by the Dakota District of The Wesleyan Church, June 21, 1981), 1; *Minutes of the Annual Session of the Dakota Conference of the Wesleyan Methodist Connection, or Church, of America,* 1933–47; *Minutes of the Annual Session of the Dakota Conference of the Wesleyan Methodist Church of America,* 1948–56.

70. *Minutes of the Annual Session of the Wisconsin Conference of the Wesleyan Methodist Church of America,* 1957–62.

71. *The Wesleyan Advocate,* April 1991, 32.

72. *Minutes of the Annual Session of the Wisconsin Conference of the Wesleyan Methodist Connection, or Church, of America,* 1933–47; *Minutes of the Annual Session of the Wisconsin Conference of the Wesleyan Methodist Church of America,* 1947–53.

73. *Minutes of the California Conference of the Wesleyan Methodist Church of America* 1954–61; *The Wesleyan Methodist,* December 13, 1961, 14.

74. *Minutes of the Annual Session Allegheny Conference of the Wesleyan Methodist Connection, or Church, of America,* 1933–47; *Minutes of the Annual Conference of the Allegheny Conference of the Wesleyan Methodist Church of America,* 1947–51; *Minutes of the Annual Conference of the Allegheny Conference of the Wesleyan Methodist Church,* 1952–66.

75. *The Wesleyan Advocate,* January 2, 1984, 17, 18.

76. *Minutes of the Annual Session of the Iowa Conference of the Wesleyan Methodist Connection, or Church, of America,* 1938–46; *Minutes of the Annual Session of the Iowa Conference of the Wesleyan Methodist Church of America,* 1947–52.

77. *Minutes of the Annual Session of the Dakota Conference of the Wesleyan Methodist Church,* 1951–68.

78. Miller, *History Woman's Missionary Society,* 44, 45.

79. Shea, *Who Will Go?* 23, 24.

80. *Minutes of the Annual Session of the Michigan*

Conference of the Wesleyan Methodist Connection, or Church, of America, 1933–47; *Minutes of the Annual Session of the Michigan Conference of the Wesleyan Methodist Church of America*, 1948–67.

81. *The Wesleyan Advocate*, September 1998, 33.

82. *Minutes of the Annual Session of the Middle Atlantic States Mission Conference of the Wesleyan Methodist Connection, or Church, of America*, 1933–47; *Minutes of the Annual Session of the Middle Atlantic States Mission Conference of the Wesleyan Methodist Church of America*, 1947–67.

83. *Minutes of the Annual Assembly of the Kansas District of the Pilgrim Holiness Church*, 1933–37.

84. *Official Record of the Annual Assembly of the Virginia District of the Pilgrim Holiness Church*, 1933–34.

85. *Minutes of the Annual Assembly of the Ohio District Pilgrim Holiness Church*, 1933–46.

86. *Minutes of the Annual Conference Indiana North District Pilgrim Holiness Church*, 1953.

87. *Pilgrim Holiness Advocate*, August 1, 1953, 17.

88. *Pilgrim Holiness Advocate*, January 24, 1946, 14.

89. Facts and information about Leah Isgrigg's life and ministry were provided by her daughter, Mrs. David (Ruth) Smith. Her service record may be found in the *Minutes of the Annual Assembly Kansas District of the Pilgrim Holiness Church*, 1935–44; *Minutes of the Annual Assembly of the Pilgrim Holiness Church Indiana Conference*, 1945–50; *Minutes Of the Annual Conference of the Indiana North District Pilgrim Holiness Church*, 1951–67.

90. This part of Grace Kauffman's story was written by Norma L. Stuve, daughter of Rev. J. B. Clawson. Norma roomed and boarded in the Kauffman home while she taught school in Hillsboro.

91. *Minutes of the Annual Session of the Wisconsin Conference of the Wesleyan Methodist Connection, or Church, of America*, 1933–46; *Minutes of the Annual Session of the Wisconsin Conference of the Wesleyan Methodist Church of America*, 1947–54; *Minutes of the Annual Session of the Dakota Conference of the Wesleyan Methodist Church of America*, 1955–68.

92. *Minutes of the Annual Session of the Lockport Conference of the Wesleyan Methodist Connection, or Church, of America*, 1933–45.

93. *Minutes of the Annual Session of the North Georgia Conference of the Wesleyan Methodist Connection, or Church, of America*, 1945–47; *Minutes of the Annual Session of the North Georgia Conference of the Wesleyan Methodist Church of America*, 1948–59; *Minutes of the Annual Session of the Georgia Conference of the Wesleyan Methodist Church of America*, 1960–67.

94. *The Wesleyan Advocate*, December 1996, 27.

95. *Minutes of the Annual Session of the Dakota Conference of the Wesleyan Methodist Connection, or Church, of America*, 1933–47; *Minutes of the Annual Session of the Dakota Conference of the Wesleyan Methodist Church of America*, 1948–68.

96. *Minutes of the Annual Session of the Allegheny Conference of the Wesleyan Methodist Connection, or Church, of America*, 1933–46; *Minutes of the Annual Session of the Allegheny Conference of the Wesleyan Methodist Church of America*, 1947–51; *Minutes of the*

Annual Session of the Allegheny Conference of the Wesleyan Methodist Church, 1952–66.

97. From materials supplied by Mrs. Dorothy Ammons and Mrs. Lottie Neal for Etta Clough's story.

98. Materials provided by her brother, Rev. E. R. Mitchell; and *The Wesleyan Advocate*, October 1994, 32.

99. *Minutes of the Annual Session of the Rochester Conference of the Wesleyan Methodist Connection, or Church, of America*, 1933–46.

100. *Minutes of the Annual Session of the Champlain Conference of the Wesleyan Methodist Connection, or Church, of America*, 1946–47; *Minutes of the Annual Session of the Champlain Conference of the Wesleyan Methodist Church of America*, 1948–67.

101. *The Wesleyan Advocate*, July 17, 1978, 17.

102. Centennial Committee, *Centennial Celebration 1879–1979* (North Carolina Colfax District The Wesleyan Church, no date).

103. *Minutes of the Annual Session of the North Carolina Conference of the Wesleyan Methodist Connection, or Church, of America*, 1936, 1939; *Minutes of the Annual Session of the Tennessee Conference of the Wesleyan Methodist Connection, or Church, of America*, 1942, 1944, 1946.

104. *Minutes of the Annual Session of the Allegheny Conference of the Wesleyan Methodist Connection, or Church, of America*, 1933–46; *Minutes of the Annual Session of the Allegheny Conference of the Wesleyan Methodist Church of America*, 1947–51; *Minutes of the Annual Session of the Allegheny Conference of the Wesleyan Methodist Church*, 1952–66.

105. *Minutes of the Annual Session of the Oklahoma Conference of the Wesleyan Methodist Connection, or Church of America*, 1933–46; *Minutes of the Annual Session of the Oklahoma Conference of the Wesleyan Methodist Church of America*, 1947–51; *Minutes of the Annual Session of the Oklahoma Conference of the Wesleyan Methodist Church*, 1952–68.

106. *Minutes of the Annual Session of the Middle Atlantic States Mission Conference of the Wesleyan Methodist Connection, or Church, of America*, 1933–34.

107. *The Wesleyan Advocate*, March 16, 1981, 17.

108. *Minutes of the Annual Session of the Kentucky Conference of the Wesleyan Methodist Church*, 1954–67.

109. *Minutes of the Annual Session of the Kansas Conference of the Wesleyan Methodist Connection, or Church, of America*, 1933–46; *Minutes of the Annual Session of the Kansas Conference of the Wesleyan Methodist Church of America*, 1947–51; *Minutes of the Annual Session of the Kansas Conference of the Wesleyan Methodist Church*, 1952.

110. *California District Journal and Minutes of the Annual Conference Pilgrim Holiness Church*, 1960–67.

111. *Minutes of the Annual Assembly Kansas District of the Pilgrim Holiness Church*, 1933–35, 1939–47.

112. *Proceedings of the Annual Assembly California District of the Pilgrim Holiness Church*, 1933–37; *Annual Assembly California District Pilgrim Holiness Church*, 1938–41; *Minutes of the Annual Conference of the Pilgrim Holiness Church California District*, 1942–43; *Annual Conference California District Pilgrim Holiness Church*, 1944–46; *Annual Conference California-Arizona Conference of the Pilgrim Holiness*

Church, 1947–56; *Annual Conference of the California District of the Pilgrim Holiness Church*, 1957; *California District Journal and Minutes of the Annual Conference*, 1958–68.

113. Rev. Morris Davis tracked down the information on the Cheney family and reported it to me. A partial record of her ministry may be found in *Minutes of the Annual Conference of the Pilgrim Holiness Church Rocky Mountain District*, 1961; *Kansas District Pilgrim Holiness Annual Conference*, 1962–67.

114. *The Wesleyan Advocate*, December 1999, 391.

115. *Minutes of the Annual Session of the Dakota Conference of the Wesleyan Methodist Connection, or Church, of America*, 1933–46; *Minutes of the Annual Session of the Dakota Conference of the Wesleyan Methodist Church of America*, 1947–51; *Minutes of the Annual Session of the Wesleyan Methodist Church*, 1952–68.

116. *Minutes of the Annual Assembly of the Pilgrim Holiness Church Indiana Conference*, 1934–53.

117. *Minutes of the Annual Conference of the Northwest District Pilgrim Holiness Church*, 1954–60.

118. *Minutes of the Annual Session of the Wisconsin Conference of the Wesleyan Methodist Connection, or Church, of America*, 1934–46; *Minutes of the Annual Session of the Wisconsin Conference of the Wesleyan Methodist Church of America*, 1947–56.

119. *Minutes of the Annual Session of the Indiana Conference of the Wesleyan Methodist Connection, or Church, of America*, 1932–45.

120. *Minutes of the Annual Assembly of the Pilgrim Holiness Church of Canada (Ontario)*, 1934–35.

121. *Minutes of the Annual Assembly of the Ontario District Pilgrim Holiness Church*, 1939–52.

122. *The Wesleyan Advocate*, September 1990, 31.

123. *Minutes of the Annual Conference of the Oklahoma/Texas District Pilgrim Holiness Church*, 1950–52; *North Central District Pilgrim Holiness Church Annual Conference Journal*, 1952–58; *Minutes of the Annual Conference Texas District Pilgrim Church*, 1959–67.

124. *Minutes of the Annual Conference of the Kentucky District Pilgrim Holiness Church*, 1937–46.

125 *Minutes of the Annual Assembly of the Pilgrim Holiness Church of the Pennsylvania and New Jersey District*, 1948; *Conference Journal Pennsylvania New Jersey District of the Pilgrim Holiness Church*, 1949–59.

126. *Minutes of the Annual Assembly of the Pilgrim Holiness Church Indiana Conference*, 1934–50; *Minutes of the Annual Conference of the Indiana North District Pilgrim Holiness Church*, 1951–67.

127. *Minutes of the Annual Session of the Middle Atlantic States Mission Conference of the Wesleyan Methodist Connection, or Church, of America*, 1934–37; *Minutes of the Annual Session of the Rochester Conference of the Wesleyan Methodist Connection, or Church, of America*, 1937–39; *Minutes of the Annual Session of the Middle Atlantic States Mission Conference of the Wesleyan Methodist Church*, 1947–67.

128. *The Wesleyan Advocate*, February 21, 1983, 17.

129. *Minutes of the Annual Session of the Kansas Conference of the Wesleyan Methodist Connection, or Church, of America*, 1934–46; *Minutes of the Annual Session of the Kansas Conference of the Wesleyan Methodist Church of America*, 1947–51; *Minutes of the Annual Session of the Kansas Conference of the Wesleyan Methodist Church*, 1952–67; *The Wesleyan Advocate*, April 2, 1984, 18.

130. Ibid.

131. *Minutes of the Annual Assembly of the Pilgrim Holiness Church Pennsylvania and New Jersey District*, 1939–43.

132. *Minutes of the Annual Conference of the Western Ohio District of the Pilgrim Holiness Church*, 1956–62.

133. *Minutes of the Annual Session of the Middle Atlantic States Mission Conference of the Wesleyan Methodist Connection, or Church, of America*, 1933–46; *Minutes of the Annual Session of the Middle Atlantic States Mission Conference of the Wesleyan Methodist Church of America*, 1947–49, 1951–67.

134. *The Wesleyan Methodist*, October 18, 1961, 13.

135. *Minutes of the Annual Session of the Iowa Conference of the Wesleyan Methodist Connection, or Church, of America*, 1934–46; *Minutes of the Annual Session of the Iowa Conference of the Wesleyan Methodist Church of America*, 1947–51; *Minutes of the Annual Session of the Iowa Conference of the Wesleyan Methodist Church*, 1952–62; *Minutes of the Annual Session of the Kansas Conference of the Wesleyan Methodist Church*, 1962–67; *The Wesleyan Advocate*, December 2000, 16.

136. *Minutes of the Annual Session of the Kansas Conference of the Wesleyan Methodist Connection, or Church, of America*, 1932–37, 1946; *Minutes of the Annual Session of the Kansas Conference of the Wesleyan Methodist Church of America*, 1947–51; *Minutes of the Annual Session of the Kansas Conference of the Wesleyan Methodist Church*, 1952–58.

137. *Minutes of the Annual Session of the Kansas Conference of the Wesleyan Methodist Connection, or Church, of America*, 1940–42.

138. *The Wesleyan Advocate*, July–August 1996, 30; *Minutes of the Annual Conference of the Pilgrim Holiness Church California District*, 1933–67.

139. *Minutes of the Annual Assembly Kansas District of the Pilgrim Holiness Church*, 1934–35.

140. Facts taken from a letter from her daughter, Ruth Smith, dated September 9, 1999; *The Wesleyan Advocate*, March 1993, 32.

141. *Minutes of the Annual Conference of the Western Ohio District of the Pilgrim Holiness Church*, 1956–67.

142. *Minutes of the Annual Session of the Middle Atlantic States Mission Conference of the Wesleyan Methodist Connection, or Church, of America*, 1934–46; *Minutes of the Annual Session of the Middle Atlantic States Mission Conference of the Wesleyan Methodist Church of America*, 1947–51; *Minutes of the Annual Session of the Middle Atlantic States Mission Conference of the Wesleyan Methodist Church*, 1952–67.

143. *The Wesleyan Advocate*, November 1997, 33.

144. *Minutes of the Annual Assembly of the Ohio District Pilgrim Holiness Church*, 1934–46.

145. *Minutes of the Annual Assembly of the Pilgrim Holiness Church Indiana Conference*, 1935–50.

146. *Journal of Proceedings of the Annual Sessions of the Indiana Conference and the Southern Indiana*

Conference of the Pilgrim Holiness Church, 1951; *Journal of Proceedings of the Annual Session of the Southern Indiana Conference of the Pilgrim Holiness Church*, 1952–67.

147. *Minutes of the Annual Session of the Indiana Conference of the Wesleyan Methodist Connection, or Church, of America*, 1935–46; *Minutes of the Annual Session of the Indiana Conference of the Wesleyan Methodist Church of America*, 1947–51; *Minutes of the Annual Session of the Indiana Conference of the Wesleyan Methodist Church*, 1952–68.

148. *Annual Conference California District Pilgrim Holiness Church*, 1946; *Annual Conference California/Arizona Conference of the Pilgrim Holiness Church*, 1947–48; *Minutes of the Annual Assembly of the Michigan District Pilgrim Holiness Church*, 1948–55; *Minutes of the Annual Assembly of the East Michigan District Pilgrim Holiness Church*, 1955–67; *The Wesleyan Advocate*, May 1994, 29.

149. From materials sent by her stepdaughter, Elizabeth Ortli She had contacted Catharine's sister, Helen Bard, and talked with her by phone to obtain more information. Her service record was found in the *Minutes of the Annual Session of the Allegheny Conference of the Wesleyan Methodist Connection, or Church, of America, 1935–46; Minutes of the Annual Session of the Allegheny Conference of the Wesleyan Methodist Church of America, 1947–51; Minutes of the Annual Session of the Allegheny Conference of the Wesleyan Methodist Church*, 1952–66.

150. *Minutes of the Annual Session of the Indiana Conference of the Wesleyan Methodist Connection, or Church, of America*, 1935–46; *Minutes of the Annual Session of the Indiana Conference of the Wesleyan Methodist Church of America*, 1947–51; *Minutes of the Annual Session of the Indiana Conference of the Wesleyan Methodist Church*, 1952–68.

151. *Minutes of the Annual Session of the Kansas Conference of the Wesleyan Methodist Connection, or Church of America*, 1935–46; *Minutes of the Annual Session of the Kansas Conference of the Wesleyan Methodist Church of America*, 1947–51; *Minutes of the Annual Session of the Kansas Conference of the Wesleyan Methodist Church*, 1952–67.

152. *Minutes of the Annual Assembly of the Pilgrim Holiness Church Southern District*, 1935–41; *Minutes of the Annual Conference of the Northwest District Pilgrim Holiness Church*, 1950–61; *California District Journal and Minutes of the Annual Conference*, 1962–68.

153. *The Wesleyan Advocate*, January 1999, 33.

154. Joy Bray, editor, *Of Noble Character*, article written by Jo Anne Lyon "Myrtle Carter," 106–07.

155. Much of the information in Vera Close's story was found in the bulletin and tapes of her funeral which were provided by her daughter, Dr. Jo Anne Lyon.

156. *Minutes of the Annual Assembly of the Pilgrim Holiness Church Southern District*, 1935–36, 1940.

157. *Minutes of the Annual Assembly of the Pilgrim Holiness Church Indiana Conference*, 1940–44; *Minutes of the North Carolina District Pilgrim Holiness Church*, 1946–68.

158. *Minutes of the Annual Session of the Allegheny Conference of the Wesleyan Methodist Connection, or Church, of America*, 1936–46; *Minutes of the Annual Session of the Allegheny Conference of the Wesleyan Methodist Church of America*, 1947–51; *Minutes of the Annual Session of the Allegheny Conference of the Wesleyan Methodist Church*, 1952–58.

159. Letter from Dr. Ronald Kelly, April 9, 1998.

160. *Minutes of the Eastern District Pilgrim Holiness Church*, 1935–68.

161. *Minutes of the North Carolina District Pilgrim Holiness Church*, 1947–68.

162. *Minutes of the Annual Assembly of the Pilgrim Holiness Church Indiana Conference*, 1935–36, 1941–50; *Minutes of the Annual Conference of the Indiana North District Pilgrim Holiness Church*, 1951–53.

163. *Minutes of the Annual Session of the Indiana Conference of the Wesleyan Methodist Connection, or Church, of America*, 1937–46; *Minutes of the Annual Session of the Indiana Conference of the Wesleyan Methodist Church of America*, 1947–51. Marie provided her life story as she told it in Rio Negro January 9, 1999 at the Fiftieth Anniversary Celebration of our work in Colombia, South America. She made the trip by air and the aid of wheelchairs in the airports at the age of eighty-six.

164. The *Minutes* of the California District changed names almost every year but are listed here simply as *Minutes of the Annual Conference of the Pilgrim Holiness Church California District*, 1935–68.

165. *Minutes of the Annual Assembly of the Pilgrim Holiness Church of Canada Ontario District*, 1935–37; *Minutes of the Annual Assembly of the Ontario District Pilgrim Holiness Church*, 1938–56.

166. *Minutes of the Annual Session of the Iowa Conference of the Wesleyan Methodist Church of America*, 1936–44, 1946, 1961–67; *Minutes of the Organizing* and *Annual Sessions of the Nebraska Conference of the Wesleyan Methodist Church of America*, 1944–61; *Wesleyan Advocate*, March 17, 1971,18; personal information supplied by Elsie Spain Mason.

167. *Minutes of the Annual Assembly of the Pilgrim Holiness Church of Canada Ontario District*, 1935–37; *Minutes of the Annual Assembly of the Ontario District of the Pilgrim Holiness Church*, 1938–67; *The Wesleyan Advocate*, January 2, 1984,18.

168. *Minutes of the Annual Assembly of the Illinois and Missouri District Pilgrim Holiness Church*, 1936; *Minutes of the Pilgrim Holiness Church Iowa/Missouri/Arkansas District*, 1937–45; *Minutes of the Annual Assembly of the Pilgrim Holiness Church Illinois District*, 1946–67.

169. *Minutes of the Annual Assembly of the Ohio District Pilgrim Holiness Church*, 1936–37; *Wesleyan Advocate*, July 22, 1974, 18.

170. Paul H. Yager, Jr., general editor, "A Flame Burning A History of the Central New York District of The Wesleyan Church 1845–1993." A booklet published for their sesquicentennial anniversary.

171. From the notes sent by her stepson, Rev. Edward A. Crandall, pastor of the Wesleyan church in Elmira, New York.

172. *The Wesleyan Methodist*, November 9, 1938, 12.

173. Yager, "A Flame Burning," 51.

174. Additional facts about her life were gleaned from *Minutes of the Annual Session of the Rochester Conference of the Wesleyan Methodist Connection, or Church, of America*, 1936–46; *Minutes of the Annual Session of the Rochester Conference of the Wesleyan Methodist Church of America*, 1947–51; *Minutes of the Annual Session of the Rochester Conference of the Wesleyan Methodist Church*, 1952–67; and notes sent by her stepson, Rev. Edward Crandall.

175. Her facts for her story were gleaned from a tape she recorded January 26, 1998 and the *Minutes of the Annual Assembly of the Ohio District Pilgrim Holiness Church*, 1936–55; *Minutes of the Annual Conference of the Western Ohio District of the Pilgrim Holiness Church*, 1956–57; *Minutes of the Annual Assembly of the East Michigan District Pilgrim Holiness Church*, 1958–67.

176. *The Daily Press*, Newport News, Section D, pages 1 and 7, Thursday, June 15, 2000. Elma Honeycutt was eighty-six years old at the time. Article was entitled, "Lifetime ministering."

177. *Minutes of the Annual Assembly of the Kentucky District of the Pilgrim Holiness Church*, 1934–36; *Minutes of the Annual Assembly Tennessee-Alabama District Pilgrim Holiness Church*, 1936–37; *Minutes of the Annual Assembly of the Oklahoma-Texas-Louisiana District Pilgrim Holiness Church*, 1938–39; *Minutes of the Annual Assembly of the Louisiana-Mississippi District Pilgrim Holiness Church*, 1940; *Minutes of the Annual Conference Tennessee District Pilgrim Holiness Church*, 1944–46; *Minutes of the Annual Assembly of the Pilgrim Holiness Church Indiana Conference*, 1947; *Minutes of the Annual Assembly of the Pilgrim Holiness Church Illinois District*, 1948–55; *Minutes of the Annual Conference of the Eastern Ohio District of the Pilgrim Holiness Church*, 1959–63; *Conference Journal of the Pennsylvania and New Jersey District of the Pilgrim Holiness Church*, 1954–57, 1966.

178. *The Wesleyan Methodist*, January 30, 1963,14; *Minutes of the Annual Session of the Kansas Conference of the Wesleyan Methodist Connection, or* Church, *of America*, 1936–46; *Minutes of the Annual Session of the Kansas Conference of the Wesleyan Methodist Church of America*, 1947–51; *Minutes of the Annual Session of the Kansas Conference of the Wesleyan Methodist Church*, 1952–62.

179. *Official Record of the Annual Assembly of the Virginia District of the Pilgrim Holiness Church*, 1936–43; *Minutes of the Session of the Virginia District of the Pilgrim Holiness Church Annual Conference*, 1944–52; *Minutes of the Session of the Annual Conference Virginia District of Pilgrim Holiness Church*, 1953–64.

180. *Minutes of the North Carolina District Pilgrim Holiness Church*, 1942–68.

181. *The Wesleyan Advocate*, June 3, 1985, 18.

182. *Minutes of the Annual Session of the South Carolina Conference of the Wesleyan Methodist Connection, or Church, of America*, 1936–46; *Minutes of the Annual Session of the South Carolina Conference of the Wesleyan Methodist Church of America*, 1947–51; *Minutes of the Annual Session of the South Carolina Conference of the Wesleyan Methodist Church*, 1952–68;

Bulletin for the Thirty-First Annual Conference Day of Remembrance, July 13, 1998.

183. *Minutes of the Annual Session of the Indiana Conference of the Wesleyan Methodist Connection, or Church, of America*, 1936–46; *Minutes of the Annual Session of the Indiana Conference of the Wesleyan Methodist Church of America*, 1947–51; *Minutes of the Annual Session of the Indiana Conference of the Wesleyan Methodist Church*, 1952–68; *The Wesleyan Advocate*, March 1990, 31.

184. *Minutes of the Annual Session of the Middle Atlantic States Mission Conference of the Wesleyan Methodist Connection, or Church, of America*, 1936–38.

185. *Minutes of the Annual Assembly of the Pilgrim Holiness Church Indiana Conference*, 1943–50; *Minutes of the Annual Conference of the Indiana North District Pilgrim Holiness Church*, 1951–56; *The Pilgrim Holiness Advocate*, March 31, 1956, 19.

186. *The Pilgrim Holiness Advocate*, March 4, 1963, 14.

187. *Minutes of the Annual Assembly of the Pilgrim Holiness Church Indiana Conference*, 1936–50; *Journal of Proceedings of the Annual Sessions of the Southern Indiana Conference of the Pilgrim Holiness Church*, 1951–63.

188. *Proceedings of the Annual Assembly California District of the Pilgrim Holiness Church*, 1936–37; *Annual Assembly California District Pilgrim Holiness Church*, 1938–41.

189. *Minutes of the Annual Session of the Tennessee Conference of the Wesleyan Methodist Connection, or Church, of America*, 1942–46; *Minutes of the Annual Session of the Tennessee Conference of the Wesleyan Methodist Church of America*, 1947–51; *Minutes of the Annual Session of the Tennessee Conference of the Wesleyan Methodist Church*, 1952–59.

190. Most of the information was received from talking with Augusta in Brooksville, Florida, where she was living at the time, and from her son, Jerry Brecheisen. Her ministerial records were from the *Official Record of the Annual Assembly of the Pilgrim Holiness Church, New York District*, 1937–42; *Minutes of the Annual Conference of the Pilgrim Holiness Church New York District*, 1943–44; *Minutes of the Annual Assembly of the East Michigan District Pilgrim Holiness Church*, 1955; *Minutes of the Annual Assembly of the Michigan District Pilgrim Holiness Church*, 1952–67.

191. *Minutes of the Annual Session of the Kentucky Conference of the Wesleyan Methodist Connection, or Church, of America*, 1936–46; *Minutes of the Annual Session of the Kentucky Conference of the Wesleyan Methodist Church of America*, 1947–51; *Minutes of the Annual Session of the Kentucky Conference of the Wesleyan Methodist Church*, 1952–58.

192. *Minutes of the Annual Assembly of the Pilgrim Holiness Church Indiana Conference*, 1937–43.

193. *Minutes of Annual Assembly of the Kansas District of the Pilgrim Holiness Church*, 1936–49; *Kansas District Pilgrim Holiness Church Annual Conference*, 1950–68.

194. *Official Record of the Annual Assembly of the Pilgrim Holiness Church New York District*, 1937–42; *Minutes of the Annual Conference of the Pilgrim*

Holiness Church New York District, 1943–63; Thomas and Thomas, *The Days of Our Pilgrimage*, 348.

195. *Minutes of the Annual Session of the Kentucky Conference of the Wesleyan Methodist Connection, or Church, of America*, 1937–41, 1945–46; *Minutes of the Annual Session of the Kentucky Conference of the Wesleyan Methodist Church of America*, 1947–51; *Minutes of the Annual Session of the Kentucky Conference of the Wesleyan Methodist Church*, 1952–67.

196. *Minutes of the Annual Session of the Tennessee Conference of the Wesleyan Methodist Connection, or Church, of America*, 1942–44.

197. *Minutes of the Annual Session of the Kentucky Conference of the Wesleyan Methodist Connection, or Church, of America*, 1937–46; *Minutes of the Annual Session of the Kentucky Conference of the Wesleyan Methodist Church of America*, 1947–51; *Minutes of the Annual Session of the Kentucky Conference of the Wesleyan Methodist Church*, 1952–67.

198. *Minutes of the Annual Assembly of the Pilgrim Holiness Church of the Pennsylvania and New Jersey District*, 1937–48; *Conference Journal of the Pennsylvania and New Jersey District of the Pilgrim Holiness Church*, 1949–67.

199. Eunice Hansen provided her own story. Additional facts were taken from the *Minutes of the Annual Session of the Indiana Conference of the Wesleyan Methodist Connection, or Church, of America*, 1937–46; *Minutes of the Annual Session of the Indiana Conference of the Wesleyan Methodist Church of America*, 1947–51; *Minutes of the Annual Session of the Indiana Conference of the Wesleyan Methodist Church*, 1952–68.

200. *Oregon Conference of the Wesleyan Methodist Connection, or Church, of America Annual Conference Journal*, 1937–42; Ira Ford McLeister and Roy S. Nicholson, *Conscience and Commitment: The History of the Wesleyan Methodist Church of America*, 4th rev. ed., Wesleyan History Series, vol. 1; Lee M. Haines, Jr. and Melvin E. Dieter, eds. (Marion, Ind.: The Wesley Press, 1976), 406.

201. *Minutes of the Annual Session of the Indiana Conference of the Wesleyan Methodist Connection, or Church, of America*, 1937–46; *Minutes of the Annual Session of the Indiana Conference of the Wesleyan Methodist Church of America*, 1947–51; *Minutes of the Annual Session of the Indiana Conference of the Wesleyan Methodist Church*, 1952–68; *The Wesleyan Advocate*, September, 2000, 16.

202. *Minutes of the Annual Session of the Ohio Conference of the Wesleyan Methodist Connection, or Church, of America*, 1937–46; *Minutes of the Annual Session of the Ohio Conference of the Wesleyan Methodist Church of America*, 1947–49; *The Wesleyan Methodist*, December 21, 1949, 13.

203. *Pilgrim Holiness Advocate*, August 28, 1965, 18; *Minutes of the Annual Assembly of the Kansas District of the Pilgrim Holiness Church*, 1937–39; *Minutes of the Annual Assembly of the Louisiana-Mississippi District Pilgrim Holiness Church*, 1940–45; *Minutes Gulf States District Pilgrim Holiness Church Annual Conference*, 1945–48; *Minutes of the Louisiana District Pilgrim Holiness Church Annual Conference*, 1949–62; *Minutes Gulf States District Pilgrim Holiness Church Annual Conference*, 1962–64.

204. *Pilgrim Holiness Advocate*, May 9, 1964, 15.

205. *Minutes of the Annual Assembly of the Pilgrim Holiness Church of the Pennsylvania and New Jersey District*, 1937–48; *Conference Journal of the Pennsylvania and New Jersey District of the Pilgrim Holiness Church*, 1949–64.

206. *Minutes of the Annual Session of the Middle Atlantic States Mission Conference of the Wesleyan Methodist Connection, or Church, of America*, 1937–39, 1943–45.

207. *Oregon Conference of the Wesleyan Methodist Connection, or Church, of America*, 1940–41.

208. *Minutes of the Annual Assembly of the Pilgrim Holiness Church of the Pennsylvania and New Jersey District*, 1937–38, 1952–63.

209. *Minutes of the Annual Assembly of the Pilgrim Holiness Church Illinois District*, 1948–51.

210. *Minutes of the Annual Conference of the Eastern Ohio District of the Pilgrim Holiness Church*, 1965–67.

211. Ruth Alexander, *The Parson Was a Lady* (written and published by her; no date.); *Minutes of the Annual Assembly of the Michigan District Pilgrim Holiness Church*, 1942–55; *Minutes of the East Michigan District Pilgrim Holiness Church*, 1955–67; *The Wesleyan Advocate*, May 1991.

212. *Minutes of the Annual Session of the Oklahoma Conference of the Wesleyan Methodist Connection, or Church, of America*, 1938–46; *Minutes of the Annual Session of the Oklahoma Conference of the Wesleyan Methodist Church of America*, 1947–63.

213. *Minutes of the Annual Session of the Kentucky Conference of the Wesleyan Methodist Connection, or Church, of America*, 1938–46; *Minutes of the Annual Session of the Kentucky Conference of the Wesleyan Methodist Church of America*, 1947–67.

214. *The Wesleyan Advocate*, November 7, 1983, 17.

215. *Minutes of the Annual Session of the South Carolina Conference of the Wesleyan Methodist Church of America*, 1947–48.

216. *Minutes of the Annual Assembly of the Pilgrim Holiness Church Indiana Conference*, 1938–41.

217. *Minutes of the Annual Session of the Kentucky Conference of the Wesleyan Methodist Connection, or Church, of America*, 1938–46.

218. *Minutes of the Annual Session of the Kentucky Conference of the Wesleyan Methodist Church of America*, 1947–67.

219. *Minutes of the Annual Session of the South Carolina Conference of the Wesleyan Methodist Church of America*, 1947–48.

220. *Minutes of the Annual Assembly of the Ohio District Pilgrim Holiness Church*, 1938–42.

221. *Minutes of the Annual Assembly of the Ontario District Pilgrim Holiness Church*, 1938–50, 1954.

222. Dates and other facts were obtained from the *Minutes of the Annual Session of the Middle Atlantic States Mission Conference of the Wesleyan Methodist Connection, or Church, of America*, 1937, 1940–46; *Minutes of the Annual Session of the Middle Atlantic States Mission Conference of the Wesleyan Methodist Church of America*, 1947–51; *Minutes of the Annual*

Session of the Middle Atlantic States Mission Conference of the Wesleyan Methodist Church, 1952–67; Minutes of the Annual Session of the Rochester Conference of the Wesleyan Methodist Connection, or Church, of America, 1938–39.

223. *Minutes of the Annual Session of the Indiana Conference of the Wesleyan Methodist Connection, or Church, of America, 1938; 1941–43; Minutes of the Annual Session of the North Michigan Conference of the Wesleyan Methodist Connection, or Church, of America, 1939–40.*

224. Norma L. Stuve, daughter of a former president of the Wisconsin Conference, provided the personal data on Miss Johnson. *Minutes of the Annual Session of the Wisconsin Conference of the Wesleyan Methodist Connection, or Church, of America, 1938–46; Minutes of the Annual Session of the Wisconsin Conference of the Wesleyan Methodist Church of America, 1947–51; Minutes of the Annual Session of the Wisconsin Conference of the Wesleyan Methodist Church, 1952–64.*

225. *Minutes of the Eastern District Pilgrim Holiness Church, 1938–52; The Pilgrim Holiness Advocate, April 20, 1951, 13.*

226. *Minutes of the Annual Assembly of the California District of the Pilgrim Holiness Church, 1938–56.*

227. *Minutes of the Annual Session of the Eastern District Pilgrim Holiness Church, 1947–60; Minutes of the Annual Conference Tennessee District Pilgrim Holiness Church, 1961–67.*

228. *Official Record of the Annual Assembly of the Pilgrim Holiness Church, New York District, 1938–42; Minutes of the Annual Conference of the Pilgrim Holiness Church New York District, 1943–63.*

229. *Proceedings of the Annual Assembly California District of the Pilgrim Holiness Church, 1938–68.*

230. *The Wesleyan Advocate,* July 13, 1987, 17.

231. *The Wesleyan Methodist,* April 19, 1950, 14.

232. *Minutes of the Annual Session of the Champlain Conference of the Wesleyan Methodist Connection, or Church, of America, 1938–46; Minutes of the Annual Session of the Champlain Conference of the Wesleyan Methodist Church of America, 1947–50.*

233. Gertrude Hooth Shaw, *Echoes of the Past* (Fort Erie, Ontario, Canada: Ann Marie Shaw, publisher, by Pony Printing Services, 1993).

234. Additional information was gathered from *Minutes of the Annual Assembly of the Ontario District Pilgrim Holiness Church, 1938–67.*

235. *Minutes of the Alabama Conference of the Wesleyan Methodist Connection (or Church) of America, 1938–44; Minutes of the Annual Session of the Alabama Conference of the Wesleyan Methodist Church of America, 1945–67.*

236. *Wesleyan Methodist,* June 28, 1939, 14.

237. *Minutes of the Annual Session of the Dakota Conference of the Wesleyan Methodist Church of America, 1938–39; Minutes of the Annual Session of the Kansas Conference of the Wesleyan Methodist Connection (or Church) of America, 1939–40, 1943–58; Minutes of the Annual Session of the Oklahoma Conference of the Wesleyan Methodist Connection (or Church) of America, 1941–43; Minutes of the Annual Session of the Lockport Conference of the Wesleyan*

Methodist Church of America, 1958–67; Minutes of the Annual Session of the Western New York District of The Wesleyan Church, 1968; personal information supplied by Loretta Wilson.

238. *Minutes of the Annual Session of the Indiana Conference of the Wesleyan Methodist Church of America, 1940–60; Minutes of the California Conference of the Wesleyan Methodist Church of America, 1953; Minutes of the Annual Session of the South Carolina Conference of the Wesleyan Methodist Church of America, 1961–68; Wesleyan Advocate,* July 29, 1968, 16 (40); September 23, 1968, 121.

239. *Minutes of the Annual Conference of the Pilgrim Holiness Church of the Pittsburgh District, 1940–47; Minutes of the Annual Session of the Pilgrim Holiness Church of Pennsylvania and New Jersey District, 1948–53; Minutes of the Eastern District of the Pilgrim Holiness Church, 1953–67; Wesleyan Advocate,* February 2000, 32.

240. *Minutes of the Annual Assembly of the Michigan District, Pilgrim Holiness Church, 1939–52.*

241. *Minutes of the Annual Session of the Kansas Conference of the Wesleyan Methodist Connection (or Church) of America, 1939–51; Minutes of the Annual Session of the Kansas Conference of the Wesleyan Methodist Church of America, 1952–67; Wesleyan Advocate,* April 4, 1988.

242. *Journal of Proceedings of the Annual Session of the Indiana Conference of the Pilgrim Holiness Church, 1939–50; Journal of Proceedings of the Annual Session of the Southern Indiana Conference of the Pilgrim Holiness Church, 1951–65; Pilgrim Holiness Advocate,* November 6, 1965, 17.

243. *Minutes of the Annual Assembly of the Ohio District of the Pilgrim Holiness Church, 1939–47; Pilgrim Holiness Advocate,* February 27, 1947, 15.

244. *Journal of Proceedings of the Annual Session of the Indiana Conference of the Pilgrim Holiness Church, 1939–41; Minutes of the Annual Assembly of the Pilgrim Holiness Church, Illinois District, 1942–50; Journal of Proceedings of the Southern Indiana Conference of the Pilgrim Holiness Church, 1951–66; Pilgrim Holiness Advocate,* June 1, 1968, 18.

245. *Minutes of the Annual Session of the Wisconsin Conference of the Wesleyan Methodist Church of America, 1939–67;* an undated clipping from the Clay Center *Dispatch,* entitled, "Woman sees over century of change."

246. *Minutes of the Annual Assembly of the Ohio District, Pilgrim Holiness Church, 1939–41, 1946–54; Minutes of the Annual Assembly of the Pilgrim Holiness Church, Illinois District, 1942–45; Minutes of the First Annual Conference of the Eastern Ohio District and Western Ohio District of the Pilgrim Holiness Church, 1955; Minutes of the Annual Conference of the Western Ohio District of the Pilgrim Holiness Church, 1959–67.*

247. *Minutes of the Annual Session of the Kansas Conference of the Wesleyan Methodist Connection (or Church) of America, 1939–46; Minutes of the Annual Session of the Kansas Conference of the Wesleyan Methodist Church of America, 1947–67;* T. J. Pomeroy, *A History of the Kansas Conference of the Wesleyan Methodist Church of America* (Miltonvale, Kansas, 1950), 125.

248. *Journal of the Proceedings of the Annual Session of the Indiana Conference of the Pilgrim Holiness Church*, 1939–49; *Pilgrim Holiness Advocate*, May 4, 1950, 12.

249. *Minutes of the Annual Assembly of the Ohio District, Pilgrim Holiness Church*, 1939–54; *Minutes of the 1st Annual Conference of the Eastern Ohio District and the Western Ohio District of the Pilgrim Holiness Church*, 1955; *Minutes of the Annual Conference of the Western Ohio District of the Pilgrim Holiness Church*, 1956–67; a clipping entitled "Retired Workers" from a book on missionaries; an anonymous tribute to Ethel Jordan, entitled, "Not Forgotten."

250. *Minutes of the Annual Assembly of the Ohio District, Pilgrim Holiness Church*, 1940–53; *Pilgrim Holiness Advocate*, January 9, 1954, 19.

251. *Minutes of the Annual Session of the Oklahoma Conference of the Wesleyan Methodist Connection (or Church) of America*, 1939–41; *Minutes of the Annual Session of the Dakota Conference of the Wesleyan Methodist Church of America*, 1942–44; *Minutes of the Annual Session of the Iowa Conference of the Wesleyan Methodist Church of America*, 1944–67.

252. *Minutes of the Annual Session of the Wisconsin Conference of the Wesleyan Methodist Connection (or Church) of America*, 1938–67; *Wesleyan Advocate*, November 20, 1978, 17.

253. W. E. Hall, *History Sketches of the Pilgrim Holiness Church, Illinois District*.

254. *Minutes of the Annual Assembly of the Pilgrim Holiness Church, Illinois District*, 1938–67.

255. *Minutes of the Wisconsin Conference of the Wesleyan Methodist Church of America*, 1934, 1939–67; *Wesleyan Advocate*, August 6, 1973; a letter from her friend, Norma L. Stuve.

256. *Journal of Proceedings of the Annual Session of the Indiana Conference of the Pilgrim Holiness Church*, 1939–51; *Journal of Proceedings of the Annual Session of the Southern Indiana Conference of the Pilgrim Holiness Church*, 1951–58; *Minutes of the Annual Session of the Kentucky Conference of the Wesleyan Methodist Church of America*, 1959–63.

257. *Minutes of the Annual Session of the North Carolina Conference of the Wesleyan Methodist Connection (or Church) of America*, 1939–46; *Minutes of the Annual Session of the North Carolina Conference of the Wesleyan Methodist Church of America*, 1947–68.

258. *Minutes of the Annual Session of the Iowa Conference of the Wesleyan Methodist Connection (or Church) of America*, 1939–47.

259. *Minutes of the Annual Session of the Wisconsin Conference of the Wesleyan Methodist Connection (or Church) of America*, 1943–45; *Minutes of the Annual Session of the Iowa Conference of the Wesleyan Methodist Church of America*, 1945–53; *Wesleyan Advocate*, December 1991.

260. John Henley, *Missionary Work Among the Mexicans*; *Minutes of the Annual Session of the Oklahoma Conference of the Wesleyan Methodist Connection (or Church) of America*, 1939–47; *Minutes of the California Conference of the Wesleyan Methodist Church of America*, 1947–68.

261. Clipped article by Rev. J. R. Swauger, entitled, "Ruth Patterson Saunders," written just before their first departure for Africa; *Minutes of the Annual Session of the Allegheny Conference of the Wesleyan Methodist Connection (or Church) of America*, 1939–46; *Minutes of the Annual Session of the Allegheny Conference of the Wesleyan Methodist Church of America*, 1947–66; Wesleyan Medical Fellowship "Newsletter," January 2000.

262. Conference records (minutes) cited above; *Pilgrim Holiness Advocate*, May 31, 1952, 15.

263. *Minutes of the Annual Session of the Michigan Conference of the Wesleyan Methodist Church of America*, 1939–41.

264. Helen Strong's name appears in the district conference minutes of the Tennessee-Alabama District, 1939–40; Louisiana-Mississippi District, 1944–45; Gulf States District, 1945–47; Alabama District, 1948–49; Alabama-Northwest Florida District, 1951–53, 1956–57, 1961; Louisiana-Alabama District, 1961; Gulf States District, 1962–67; *Wesleyan Advocate*, July/August 1999, 32.

265. An article on, "Rev. and Mrs. Ermal Leroy Wilson," in *Know Your Missionaries*; *Journal of Proceedings of the Annual Session of the Indiana Conference of the Pilgrim Holiness Church*, 1939–50; *Journal of Proceedings of the Annual Session of the Indiana Conference and the First Annual Session of the Southern Indiana Conference of the Pilgrim Holiness Church*, 1951; *Journal of Proceedings of the Southern Indiana Conference of the Pilgrim Holiness Church*, 1952–66.

266. Paul Shea, *Who Will Go?* 9–10; *Minutes of the Annual Session of the North Carolina Conference of the Wesleyan Methodist Connection (or Church) of America*, 1930, 1939–46; *Minutes of the Annual Session of the North Carolina Conference of the Wesleyan Methodist Church of America*, 1947–68.

267. Pittsburgh District Conference Journal, Pilgrim Holiness Church, 1939–44.

Chapter 5

1. *Minutes of the Annual Session of the Lockport Conference of the Wesleyan Methodist Connection (or Church) of America*, 1942–49; "Our Heritage: Lockport Conference Centennial, 1861–1961," Mary E. Bennett, ed.; *Minutes of the California Conference of the Wesleyan Methodist Church of America*," 1949–68; John Henley, *Mission Work Among the Mexicans*, 7–9; *Pacific Southwest District Journal*, 1997 (obituary).

2. *Minutes of the Annual Session of the Allegheny Conference of the Wesleyan Methodist Connection (or Church) of America*, 1940–46; *Minutes of the Allegheny Conference of the Wesleyan Methodist Church of America*, 1947–67; Gipsie M. Miller, *History of the Woman's Missionary Society of the Wesleyan Methodist Church*, Marion, Indiana: Wesleyan Publishing House, no date, 83; *Wesleyan Advocate*, March 1992.

3. *Minutes of the Annual Assembly of the Ohio District, Pilgrim Holiness Church*, 1940–55; *Minutes of the Annual Conference of the Western Ohio District of the Pilgrim Holiness Church*, 1955–59.

4. *Minutes of the Annual Session of the Kansas Conference of the Wesleyan Methodist Connection (or*

Church) of America, 1939–46; *Minutes of the Annual Session of the Kansas Conference of the Wesleyan Methodist Church of America*, 1947–67; Gipsie M. Miller, *History of the Women's Missionary Society of the Wesleyan Methodist Church*, 88.

5. *Minutes of the Eastern District Conference of the Pilgrim Holiness Church*, 1959–65; *Wesleyan Advocate*, February 18, 1985, 16–17.

6. *Minutes of the Annual Session of the Champlain Conference of the Wesleyan Methodist Connection (or Church) of America*, 1940–47; *Minutes of the Annual Session of the Champlain Conference of the Wesleyan Methodist Church of America*, 1948–68; personal correspondence with Marjean Dayton.

7. *Minutes of the Annual Session of the Dakota Conference of the Wesleyan Methodist Church of America*, 1940–51, 1957–68; *Minutes of the Annual Session of the Nebraska Conference of the Wesleyan Methodist Church of America*, 1951–57; *A Century in Dakota Territory 1881–1981, Historical Sketch, The Dakota District of The Wesleyan Church*, David L. Gowan, historian and editor, June 21, 1981, The Dakota District of The Wesleyan Church, 5, 45; personal letter from Louise Goodsell, April 14, 1998; *Tower*, Bartlesville Wesleyan College, Winter 1998, 6.

8. *Minutes of the Annual Session of the Iowa Conference of the Wesleyan Methodist Connection (or Church) of America*, 1940–44; *Minutes of the Annual Session of the Nebraska Conference of the Wesleyan Methodist Church of America*, 1944–54; *Minutes of the Annual Session of the Iowa Conference of the Wesleyan Methodist Church of America*, 1955–67; *The Iowa Conference Centennial, 1853–1953*, Gerald A. Wolter, ed., published by the Iowa Conference of the Wesleyan Methodist Church; Gipsie M. Miller, *History of the Woman's Missionary Society of the Wesleyan Methodist Church*, Marion, Indiana: Wesleyan Publishing House, no date, p 68–69; *Wesleyan Advocate*, January 18, 1988.

9. *Minutes of the Annual Session of the Dakota Conference of the Wesleyan Methodist Church of America*, 1940–42; *Oregon Conference of the Wesleyan Methodist Church of America Annual Conference Journal*, 1943–67; personal letter from Kathleen Kelsven Edwards.

10. *Journal of Proceedings of the Annual Session of the Indiana Conference of the Pilgrim Holiness Church*, 1940–51; *Journal of Proceedings of the Annual Session of the Southern Indiana Conference of the Pilgrim Holiness Church*, 1951–67; *Pilgrim Holiness Advocate*, June 1, 1957, 18.

11. *Minutes of the Annual Session of the Kentucky Conference of the Wesleyan Methodist Connection (or Church) of America*, 1940–46; *Minutes of the Annual Session of the South Carolina Conference of the Wesleyan Methodist Connection (or Church) of America*, 1947; *Minutes of the Annual Session of the Kentucky Conference of the Wesleyan Methodist Church of America*, 1947–62; *Minutes of the Annual Session of the Alabama Conference of the Wesleyan Methodist Church of America*, 1962–63; *Wesleyan Methodist*, March 18, 1964, 13–14.

12. Records of the Michigan District of the Pilgrim Holiness Church, 1940–67; personal correspondence collected and compiled by Mrs. Edna Johnson, former missionary to Japan and a longtime friend of Mrs. Lila Cairns Manker; *Pilgrim Holiness Advocate*, November 12, 1960, 13; *Wesleyan Advocate*, May 5, 1986, 18.

13. Records cited above; *Wesleyan Methodist*, March 15, 1967, 18.

14. *Minutes of the Eastern District Conference of the Pilgrim Holiness Church*, 1925–67; *Wesleyan Advocate*, October 1999; personal correspondence with the Rev. Elizabeth Thompson Reed.

15. *Journal of Proceedings of the Annual Session of the Southern Indiana Conference of the Pilgrim Holiness Church*, 1962–67; *Wesleyan Advocate*, September 1997.

16. *Minutes of the Annual Session of the Allegheny Conference of the Wesleyan Methodist Connection (or Church) of America*, 1940–46; *Minutes of the Annual Session of the Allegheny Conference of the Wesleyan Methodist Church of America*, 1947–66.

17. *Minutes of the Annual Assembly of the Ohio District of the Pilgrim Holiness Church*, 1940–54; *Minutes of the Annual Conference of the Eastern Ohio District of the Pilgrim Holiness Church*, 1955–62.

18. *Minutes of the Annual Assembly of the Pilgrim Holiness Church, Indiana Conference*, 1941–46; *Minutes of the Annual Conference of the Oklahoma-Texas District, Pilgrim Holiness Church*, 1947–50; *Minutes of the Annual Conference of the Oklahoma District, Pilgrim Holiness Church*, 1951; *Minutes of the Annual Conference of the Texas District of the Pilgrim Holiness Church*, 1954; *Minutes of the Annual Conference of the Northern Indiana District, Pilgrim Holiness Church*, 1955–67; "A Celebration of the life of Rev. Ellen Atkinson," funeral bulletin, April 16, 1998, Brooksville Wesleyan Church, Brooksville, Florida; Rachel J. Satterfield, "Memories of Aunt Ellen, April 1998."

19. *Minutes of the Annual Assembly of the Ohio District of the Pilgrim Holiness Church*, 1941–54; *Minutes of the Annual Assembly of the Eastern Ohio District of the Pilgrim Holiness Church*, 1955–67.

20. *Minutes of the Annual Session of the Indiana Conference of the Wesleyan Methodist Church of America*, 1941–68; *Wesleyan Advocate*, December 2, 1968, 22.

21. *Minutes of the Annual Session of the Middle Atlantic States Mission Conference of the Wesleyan Methodist Connection (or Church) of America*, 1943–46; *Minutes of the Annual Session of the Middle Atlantic States Mission Conference of the Wesleyan Methodist Church of America*, 1947–67; David E. Tonnessen, letter, August 11, 1999.

22. *Minutes of the Annual Conference of the Pilgrim Holiness Church of the Pittsburgh District/Pittsburgh District Conference Journal, Pilgrim Holiness Church*, 1941–43, 1958–63; *Minutes of the Eastern District Conference of the Pilgrim Holiness Church*, 1963–67.

23. *Minutes of the Annual Session of the Kansas Conference of the Wesleyan Methodist Connection (or Church) of America*, 1941–47; *Wesleyan Methodist*, May 7, 1947, 10, 12.

24. *Minutes of the Annual Session of the Indiana Conference of the Wesleyan Methodist Connection (or Church) of America*, 1940–46; *Minutes of the Annual Session of the Indiana Conference of the Wesleyan*

Methodist Church of America, 1947–64; *Wesleyan Methodist*, May 26, 1948, 12.

25. *Wesleyan Methodist*, July 30, 1941,12; *Minutes of the Annual Session of the Tennessee Conference of the Wesleyan Methodist Connection (or Church) of America*, 1942–46; *Minutes of the Annual Session of the Tennessee Conference of the Wesleyan Methodist Church of America*, 1947–68; *Wesleyan Advocate*, May 13, 1974, 18; May 6, 1985, 18.

26. Records for the conference and years cited above.

27. Records cited above; information supplied by Dr. John A. Dunn, former district superintendent in Arizona and New Mexico.

28. North Michigan conference records, 1943, 1945, 1948–57; *Wesleyan Advocate*, May 4, 1987, 18; May 1994; information supplied by Flossie Manker Peterson and the Rev. Robert Cooper, former leader in North Michigan.

29. *Wesleyan Advocate*, May 4, 1981, 17.

30. *Journal of Proceedings of the Annual Session of the Indiana Conference of the Pilgrim Holiness Church*, 1941–51; *Minutes of the Annual Conference of the Northern Indiana District, Pilgrim Holiness Church*, 1951–67; *Wesleyan Advocate*, November 2000, 16; *Indiana South Wesleyan*, October 2000,4; "Embracing Holiday Memories," a feature dealing with the Ragsdale family in the *Indianapolis Star*, November 2000, "Seniority Counts" section, 9–10; article from missionary booklet.

31. *Minutes of the Annual Session of the Oklahoma Conference of the Wesleyan Methodist Connection (or Church) of America*, 1939, 1941, 1943–47; *Minutes of the Annual Session of the Dakota Conference of the Wesleyan Methodist Church of America*, 1947–57; *Minutes of the Iowa Conference of the Wesleyan Methodist Church of America*, 1954–56; *Wesleyan Methodist*, June 16, 1943, 12.

32. Some of the above information was supplied by the Rev. Ernest R. Batman, former superintendent of the Indiana Central District of The Wesleyan Church.

33. Correspondence with Mrs. Gertrude Bonner.

34. Historian Committee of the Pacific Southwest District of The Wesleyan Church, "A History of the Holiness, Pilgrim and Pilgrim Holiness Churches in California," computer-typed looseleaf notebook (January 1999), 103.

35. *Journal of Proceedings of the Annual Session of the Indiana Conference of the Pilgrim Holiness Church*, 1942–51; *Journal of Proceedings of the Annual Session of the Southern Indiana Conference of the Pilgrim Holiness Church*, 1951–52; *Minutes of the Annual Conference of the Indiana North District of the Pilgrim Holiness Church*, 1951–67; *Pilgrim Holiness Advocate*, July 12, 1952, 12; *Wesleyan Advocate*, June 16, 1986, 17; information supplied by the Rev. Ernest R. Batman, former superintendent of the Central Indiana District of The Wesleyan Church.

36. Information supplied by the Rev. Henrietta M. Griffith; *Kentucky Messenger*, July 1999.

37. *Minutes of the Annual Conference of the Tennessee Conference of the Wesleyan Methodist Connection (or Church) of America*, 1942–46; *Minutes of the Annual Conference of the Tennessee Conference of the Wesleyan Methodist Church*, 1947–54.

38. *Minutes of the Annual Session of the Wisconsin Conference of the Wesleyan Methodist Connection (or Church) of America*, 1942–46; *Minutes of the Annual Session of the Wisconsin Conference of the Wesleyan Methodist Church of America*, 1947–56; *Minutes of the California Conference of the Wesleyan Methodist Church of America*, 1956–68; information supplied by the Rev. Alice Mae Heavilin.

39. *Minutes of the Annual Session of the Dakota Conference of the Wesleyan Methodist Church of America*, 1942–66.

40. Records of the Western Kansas District of the Pilgrim Holiness Church, 1942–45; *Minutes of the Annual Conference of the Pilgrim Holiness Church, Rocky Mountain District*, 1961–65; *Pilgrim Holiness Advocate*, January 28, 1967.

41. Records of the Western Kansas District of the Pilgrim Holiness Church, 1942–63; *Wesleyan Advocate*, October 20, 1980,18; September 1994, 31.

42. *Minutes of the Annual Session of the Michigan Conference of the Wesleyan Methodist Church of America*, 1945–67; John Henley, *Mission Work Among the Mexicans*, 8–9; *Wesleyan Advocate*, February 1998, 32.

43. *Minutes of the Annual Session of the Kansas Conference of the Wesleyan Methodist Connection (or Church) of America*, 1942–46; *Minutes of the Annual Session of the Kansas Conference of the Wesleyan Methodist Church of America*, 1946–67.

44. *Minutes of the Annual Session of the Dakota Conference of the Wesleyan Methodist Church of America*, 1950–58; *District Journal of the Dakota District of The Wesleyan Church*, 1997.

45. *Minutes of the Annual Session of the Tennessee Conference of the Wesleyan Methodist Connection (or Church) of America*, 1942–49; *Wesleyan Methodist*, July 30, 1941, 12; December 21, 1949, 13.

46. *Minutes of the South Georgia Conference of the Wesleyan Methodist Connection (or Church) of America*, 1942, 1944–46; *Minutes of the South Georgia Conference of the Wesleyan Methodist Church of America*, 1947–50; *Minutes of the Annual Session of the Florida Conference of the Wesleyan Methodist Church of America*, 1950–58.

47. *Minutes of the Annual Session of the North Georgia Conference of the Wesleyan Methodist Connection (or Church) of America*, 1942; *Minutes of the Annual Session of the South Georgia Conference of the Wesleyan Methodist Connection (or Church) of America*, 1942–48; *Minutes of the Annual Session of the South Carolina Conference of the Wesleyan Methodist Church of America*, 1948–54; *Minutes of the Annual Session of the Florida Conference of the Wesleyan Methodist Church of America*, 1954–56; *Minutes of the Annual Session of the South Georgia Conference of the Wesleyan Methodist Church of America*, 1957–59.

48. Conference/district records for the places and years cited above; *Wesleyan Advocate*, January 13, 1969, 17.

49. *Pilgrim Holiness Advocate*, December 23, 1961, 15; *Conference Journal of the Pennsylvania and New Jersey District of the Pilgrim Holiness Church*, 1962.

50. *Journal of Proceedings of the Annual Session of the Indiana Conference of the Pilgrim Holiness Church*, 1942–51; *Journal of Proceedings of the Annual Session of the Southern Indiana Conference of the Pilgrim Holiness Church*, 1951–67; information supplied by the Rev. Edith Rose Smith.

51. Conference records for the places and years cited above.

52. *Minutes of the Annual Session of the Indiana Conference of the Wesleyan Methodist Connection (or Church) of America*, 1942–47; *Minutes of the Annual Session of the Indiana Conference of the Wesleyan Methodist Church of America*, 1948–52, 1955–68; *Minutes of the Annual Session of the Wisconsin Conference of the Wesleyan Methodist Church of America*, 1952–55; *Wesleyan Advocate*, October 18, 1982, 17.

53. Personal information supplied by Sybil Yoder; *Wesleyan Advocate*, March 1993, 33.

54. District conference minutes, North Carolina District of the Pilgrim Holiness Church, 1942–68; personal information supplied by Junia Apple.

55. District conference minutes, Kentucky District of the Pilgrim Holiness Church, 1943–67; district conference minutes, Eastern District of the Pilgrim Holiness Church, 1960; *Pilgrim Holiness Advocate*, August 12, 1948, 15; *Wesleyan Advocate*, July 23, 1984, 17.

56. *Minutes of the Annual Session of the Iowa Conference of the Wesleyan Methodist Connection (or Church) of America*, 1942–49; *Minutes of the Annual Session of the North Michigan Conference of the Wesleyan Methodist Church of America*, 1950–66; *Wesleyan Advocate*, April 17, 1972; information supplied by Rev. Robert W. Cooper, former superintendent of the North Michigan District of The Wesleyan Church.

57. *Minutes of the Annual Session of the Oklahoma Conference of the Wesleyan Methodist Connection (or Church) of America*, 1943–50; *Wesleyan Methodist*, October 31, 1945.

58. District records cited above, supplemented by information supplied by Rev. Ernest R. Batman, former superintendent of the Indiana Central District of The Wesleyan Church.

59. *Wesleyan Advocate*, September 1993, 32.

60. *Minutes of the Annual Session of the Dakota Conference of the Wesleyan Methodist Church of America*, 1943–56.

61. *Minutes of the Annual Session of the Kansas Conference of the Wesleyan Methodist Connection (or Church) of America*, 1943–46; *Minutes of the Annual Session of the Kansas Conference of the Wesleyan Methodist Church of America*, 1947–58.

62. *Minutes of the Annual Session of the Nebraska Conference of the Wesleyan Methodist Church of America*, 1959–60; *Minutes of the Annual Session of the Kansas Conference of the Wesleyan Methodist Church of America*, 1960–67.

63. *Minutes of the Annual Session of the Allegheny Conference of the Wesleyan Methodist Connection (or Church) of America*, 1943–46; *Minutes of the Annual Session of the Allegheny Conference of the Wesleyan Methodist Church of America*, 1947–67; *Minutes of the Annual Session of the Kansas Conference of the Wesleyan Methodist Church of America*, 1951–67; information supplied by Mrs. Herbert H. Dongell, Mrs. Ruby Stonebraker (niece of Anna Martin) and Rev. Philip Birchall.

64. *Minutes of the Annual Session of the Tennessee District of the Pilgrim Holiness Church*, 1943–60; *Pilgrim Holiness Advocate*, January 10, 1946, 12; September 25, 1965, 19.

65. *Minutes of the Annual Session of the Pennsylvania and New Jersey District of the Pilgrim Holiness Church*, 1943–45, 1966–67; *Minutes of the Annual Session of the New York District of the Pilgrim Holiness Church*, 1945–48, 1953–55; *Minutes of the Eastern District of the Pilgrim Holiness Church*, 1957–65; *Wesleyan Advocate*, August 15, 1988, 15; June 1998; information supplied by Mrs. Beatrice Joseph, Rev. Harold Crosser and Dr. Harry F. Wood, superintendent of the Pennsylvania and New Jersey District of The Wesleyan Church.

66. *Minutes of the Annual Session of the Indiana Conference of the Wesleyan Methodist Church of America*, 1948–68; *Wesleyan Advocate*, February 17, 1975, 17; August 17, 1981, 21; Surface family tree, compiled by grandson, Keith Smith; information from "Memories," written by Rose Surface; information supplied by daughter, Norma Surface Krieg.

67. *Minutes of the Annual Session of the Oklahoma Conference of the Wesleyan Methodist Connection (or Church) of America*, 1944–47; *Minutes of the Annual Session of the Oklahoma Conference of the Wesleyan Methodist Church of America*, 1948–49.

68. *Minutes of the Annual Session of the West Virginia Conference of the Pilgrim Holiness Church*, 1944–45; *Minutes of the Annual Conference of the Pilgrim Holiness Church New York District*, 1947; *Days of Our Pilgrimage*, 347.

69. Records of the Rocky Mountain and Michigan Districts of the Pilgrim Holiness Church; book on missionaries; personal information supplied by Madge Bursch; *Days of Our Pilgrimage*, 274.

70. District conference records cited above; *Wesleyan Advocate*, January 1990, 33; information supplied by Rev. Ernest R. Batman, former superintendent of the Indiana Central District of The Wesleyan Church.

71. *Minutes of the Middle Atlantic States Mission Conference of the Wesleyan Methodist Connection (or Church) of America*, 1944–46; *Minutes of the Middle Atlantic States Mission Conference of the Wesleyan Methodist Church of America*, 1947–67; *Conscience and Commitment*, 374; *Wesleyan Advocate*, February 5, 1979, 18.

72. District records cited above; *Days of Our Pilgrimage*, 349; information supplied by Mrs. Beatrice Joseph.

73. This story was written by Lee M. Haines, using a few brief notes Maxine left in her file along with his own memories and records.

74. District records cited; information supplied by Rev. Ernest R. Batman, former superintendent of the Indiana Central District of the Pilgrim Holiness Church.

75. District records cited above; *Days of Our Pilgrimage*, 114.

76. Conference records cited above; *A Flame Burning, A History of the Central New York District of The Wesleyan Church*, 20.

77. District records cited above; *Wesleyan Advocate*, March 14, 1977, 18.

78. District records cited above; information supplied by Ruby Sida of First Wesleyan Church, Mooresville; a paper apparently read by her pastor at Bertha Lapish Nation's funeral.

79. Oregon Conference records cited above; *Wesleyan Advocate*, December 1995, 30.

80. District records cited above; a book on missionaries; "Siftings," May 2003, published by the Office of the General Secretary of The Wesleyan Church.

81. Conference records cited above; *Wesleyan Methodist*, March 29, 1967, 18.

82. *Minutes of the Annual Session of the Allegheny Conference of the Wesleyan Methodist Connection (or Church) of America*, 1944–46; *Minutes of the Annual Session of the Allegheny Conference of the Wesleyan Methodist Church of America*, 1947–66.

83. Indiana District conference records, 1944–48.

84. Conference records cited above.

85. *Minutes of the Annual Session of the Indiana Conference of the Wesleyan Methodist Church of America*, 1945–50.

86. Conference records for the years cited.

87. *Minutes of the Annual Conference of the Pilgrim Holiness Church Rocky Mountain District*, 1964–67; personal information supplied by Ruth Brizendine, May 15, 1998.

88. District conference records cited; information supplied by Rev. Robert W. Cooper, former superintendent of the North Michigan District of The Wesleyan Church.

89. Records of the North Carolina District of the Pilgrim Holiness church, 1945, 1955–68; Journal of the North Carolina District of The Wesleyan Church, 1996.

90. Conference records cited; *Wesleyan Advocate*, July 18, 1977, 18.

91. Nebraska conference records cited; information supplied by George Francis, April 6, 1998.

92. Kansas Conference records for the years cited; *Conscience and Commitment*, 406.

93. Nebraska Conference records for years cited; *Wesleyan Advocate*, September 20, 1971, 17.

94. Ohio Conference records, 1947–68; personal information supplied by Ruth Nicholson Huff.

95. Records of the New York District of the Pilgrim Holiness Church, 1945–54; records of the Pittsburgh District, 1953–66; book on Pilgrim Holiness missionaries.

96. Records of the Dakota Conference, 1945; records of the Ohio Conference, 1945–53.

97. Records of the Kansas District of the Pilgrim Holiness Church, 1954–57; records of the Pacific Northwest District of the Pilgrim Holiness Church, 1958–68; *Wesleyan Advocate*, August 16, 1982, 17.

98. Records of the Idaho-Washington District of the Pilgrim Holiness Church, 1945–49, 1957–59; records of the California District 1950–53; records of the Northwest District, 1952–56; records of the Texas District, 1960–68; *Wesleyan Advocate*, April 1993; information supplied by Herman D. Nettleton.

99. *Journal of Proceedings of the Annual Session of the Indiana Conference of the Pilgrim Holiness Church,* 1945–49; *Journal of Proceedings of the Annual Session of the Indiana Conference and the First Annual Session of the Southern Indiana Conference of the Pilgrim Holiness Church*, 1951; *Minutes of the Annual Conference of the Northern Indiana District of the Pilgrim Holiness Church*, 1951–52; *Journal of Proceedings of the Annual Session of the Southern Indiana Conference of the Pilgrim Holiness Church*, 1952–53.

100. *Pilgrim Holiness Advocate*, July 27, 1950, 15.

101. *Minutes of the Annual Conference of the Oklahoma District of the Pilgrim Holiness Church*, 1953–58; *Pilgrim Holiness Advocate*, January 10, 1959, 15; *Minutes of the Annual Conference of the Texas District of the Pilgrim Holiness Church*, 1959–62; *Minutes of the Annual Conference of the Western Ohio District of the Pilgrim Holiness Church*, 1963–67; records of the Central District of the Pilgrim Holiness Church, 1968.

102. Records of the Eastern District of the Pilgrim Holiness Church, 1954–67; one book on Pilgrim Holiness missionaries and one on missionaries of The Wesleyan Church after the 1968 merger; personal information supplied by Elizabeth Phillips.

103. Records of the Eastern District of the Pilgrim Holiness Church, 1945–67; records of the Louisiana and Alabama District, 1951; *Wesleyan Advocate*, December 1998, 30.

104. District conference records for the years indicated.

105. District conference records for the years indicated.

106. *Minutes of the Annual Session of the Canada Conference of the Wesleyan Methodist Church*, 1945–67; *The Wesleyan Methodist Church of America in Canada, 1894–1968*.

107. Records of the Kentucky District of the Pilgrim Holiness Church, 1928, 1948, 1955–56, 1961–64; Records of the Tennessee District of the Pilgrim Holiness Church, 1956–60; personal information supplied by Jenny V. Vincent.

108. *Wesleyan Advocate*, January 1997.

109. Records of the Indiana District of the Pilgrim Holiness Church, 1945–50; *Pilgrim Holiness Advocate*, May 13, 1948,12; records of the Northern Indiana District, 1951–52; *Pilgrim Holiness Advocate*, December 29, 1956, 912; records of the New York District, 1953–57.

110. District conference records cited; *Days of Our Pilgrimage*, 347.

111. Records of the Kansas Conference of the Wesleyan Methodist Church, 1946–54; records of the Dakota Conference of the Wesleyan Methodist Church and of the Dakota District of The Wesleyan Church, 1955–68, 1995; *Wesleyan Advocate*, February 1995; personal memories of Larry Johnson, former superintendent of the Dakota District of The Wesleyan Church—the Bingamans were among his early pastors.

112. Conference records for years indicated.

113. *Minutes of the Annual Conference of the Pilgrim Holiness Church of the Pittsburgh District*, 1948–56; *Minutes of the Annual Conference of the Pilgrim Holiness Church, Rocky Mountain District*, 1961–67;

book on Pilgrim Holiness missionaries; *Wesleyan Advocate*, December 3, 1984, 18.

114. District records for the years cited; information supplied by Rev. Ernest R. Batman, former superintendent of the Indiana Central District of The Wesleyan Church.

115. Conference records of the Eastern District of the Pilgrim Holiness Church, 1946–57; *Pilgrim Holiness Advocate*, January 4, 1958, 12.

116. *Minutes of the Annual Session of the North Carolina Conference of the Wesleyan Methodist Church of America*, 1946–64.

117. *Minutes of the Annual Session of the Lockport Conference of the Wesleyan Methodist Church*, 1946–67; *Minutes of the 107th Annual Session of the Western New York District, Inc. of The Wesleyan Church (formerly Lockport Annual Conference Inc. of the Wesleyan Methodist Church of America*, 1968; *Our Heritage: Lockport Conference Centennial 1861–1961*, published by the Lockport Conference of the Wesleyan Methodist Church of America, Houghton, New York, Mary E. Bennett, Editor; *Our Heritage: Ten Years Supplement 1960–1970*, Western New York District, Dr. Josephine Rickard, mimeographed booklet; *Wesleyan Advocate*, May 4, 1987, 18.

118. Pilgrim Holiness district conference records for the years cited; personal information provided by E. Louise Van Matre.

119. *Minutes of the Annual Session of the Middle Atlantic States Mission Conference of the Wesleyan Methodist Church of America*, 1946–67; *Conscience and Commitment*, 213, 231, 424–25, 427, 433, 435–36.

120. *Minutes of the Annual Session of the Indiana Conference of the Wesleyan Methodist Church of America*, 1947–68; Gipsie M. Miller, *History Woman's Missionary Society Wesleyan Methodist Church*, 68; *Wesleyan Advocate*, September 5, 1988, 14; personal information supplied by Olive Coleson.

121. *Minutes of the Annual Session of the Indiana Conference of the Wesleyan Methodist Church of America*, 1958–59; *Conscience and Commitment*, 451.

122. *Minutes of the Annual Session of the Kansas Conference of the Wesleyan Methodist Church of America*, 1947, 1951–57; *Minutes of the Annual Session of the Oklahoma Conference of the Wesleyan Methodist Church of America*, 1958–68.

123. *A Century in Dakota Territory 1881–1981, Historical Sketch of the Dakota District of The Wesleyan Church*, David L. Gowan, historian and editor, June 21, 1981, the Dakota District of The Wesleyan Church; *Minutes of the Annual Session of the Oregon Conference of the Wesleyan Methodist Church of America*, 1947, 1951; *Tri-State District Journal*, 1997; *Minutes of the Annual Session of the Oklahoma Conference of the Wesleyan Methodist Church of America*, 1951–68; *Wesleyan Advocate*, December 1990; June 1997,32.

124. Records of the Eastern District of the Pilgrim Holiness Church, 1947, 1951; information supplied by Mrs. Beatrice Joseph; information supplied by Dr. Ronald D. Kelly, General Secretary of The Wesleyan Church, who grew up in the Eastern District.

125. District conference records cited above; book on Pilgrim Holiness missionaries; information supplied by

Beulah M. Tackett; funeral notice distributed by the office of the General Secretary of The Wesleyan Church.

126. *Minutes of the Annual Session of the Ohio Conference of the Wesleyan Methodist Church of America*, 1947–68.

127. *Minutes of the Annual Session of the Nebraska Conference of the Wesleyan Methodist Church of America*, 1951–64; *Conscience and Commitment*, 439–40; *Wesleyan Advocate*, October 5, 1987, 18.

128. *Minutes of the Annual Session of the Kentucky Conference of the Wesleyan Methodist Church of America*, 1947–52; *Minutes of the Annual Session of the Ohio Conference of the Wesleyan Methodist Church of America*, 1952–66.

129. *Minutes of the Annual Session of the Indiana Conference of the Wesleyan Methodist Church of America*, 1948–68; *Wesleyan Advocate*, June 19, 1978, 17; information supplied by Richard Abraham Shirley Tharp Abraham, and Roger Abraham.

130. *Minutes of the Annual Session of the Ohio Conference of the Wesleyan Methodist Church*, 1947; *Minutes of the Annual Session of the Allegheny Conference of the Wesleyan Methodist Church*, 1948–49; records of the Kentucky District of the Pilgrim Holiness Church, 1949–51; *Minutes of the Annual Session of the Indiana Conference of the Wesleyan Methodist Church*, 1942–48; information supplied by Louise Hamilton Harrell Close.

131. *Minutes of the Annual Session of the Champlain Conference of the Wesleyan Methodist Church of America*, 1948–68.

132. *Minutes of the Annual Session of the Indiana Conference of the Wesleyan Methodist Church of America*, 1948–68; personal information supplied by Edna M. Wildey.

133. Records of the Pilgrim Holiness Church, Louisiana-Alabama District, 1949–50; *Minutes of the Annual Conference of the Pilgrim Holiness Church of the Pittsburgh District*, 1950–58; *Minutes of the Annual Conference of the Western Ohio District of the Pilgrim Holiness Church*, 1959–62; *Minutes of the Eastern District of the Pilgrim Holiness Church*, 1963–67; *Wesleyan Advocate*, December 2000,12; March 2002,16.

134. *Minutes of the Annual Assembly of the Pilgrim Holiness Church, Illinois District*, 1960–68; W. E. Hall, "History Sketches of the Pilgrim Holiness Illinois District," 50.

135. *Conference Journal of the Pennsylvania and New Jersey District of the Pilgrim Holiness Church*, 1948–62; *Pilgrim Holiness Advocate*, January 4, 1964, 13.

136. Records of the Eastern District, 1949–62; information supplied by Kathryn Savage Johnson.

137. Records of the Michigan District of the Pilgrim Holiness Church, 1955–67; two books on Pilgrim Holiness missionaries; information supplied by Orpha Case Lehman; *Wesleyan Advocate*, June 1999, 32.

138. Records of the Eastern District of the Pilgrim Holiness Church, 1949–67; information supplied by Dr. Ronald D. Kelly, originally from the Eastern (Delmarva/Chesapeake) District and later General Secretary of The Wesleyan Church; information supplied by Mrs. Beatrice Joseph; *Wesleyan Advocate*, April 1990, 28.

139. Records of the Kentucky District of the Pilgrim

Holiness Church, 1949–67; book on Pilgrim Holiness missionaries.

140. Records of the Alabama District of the Pilgrim Holiness Church, 1949; the Alabama-Northwest Florida District, 1951–54; Northern Indiana District, 1955–63; *Pilgrim Holiness Advocate*, April 21, 1962, 13; personal information supplied by Annie Eubanks Carlson Thompson.

141. *Minutes of the Annual Session of the Dakota Conference of the Wesleyan Methodist Church of America*, 1949–64; records of the Oregon Conference, 1964–67; *Wesleyan Advocate*, February 14, 1977, 18; January 1998, 33.

142. *Journal of Proceedings of the Annual Session of the Indiana Conference of the Pilgrim Holiness Church*, 1948–51; *Journal of Proceedings of the Annual Session of the Southern Indiana Conference of the Pilgrim Holiness Church*, 1951–67; *Wesleyan Advocate*, September 1996, 33; information supplied by Rev. Ernest R. Batman, former superintendent of the Indiana Central District of The Wesleyan Church; information supplied by Rev. Jesse Tewell, former superintendent of the Southern Illinois District of The Wesleyan Church.

Chapter 6

1. *Minutes of the Annual Session of the Dakota Conference of the Wesleyan Methodist Church of America*, 1950–68; *Conscience and Commitment*, 400, 407; *Know Your Missionaries*; *A Century in Dakota Territory 1881–1981, Historical Sketch, The Dakota District of The Wesleyan Church*, David L. Gowan, historian and editor, June 21, 1981, 47.

2. *Minutes of the Annual Session of the Alabama Conference of the Wesleyan Methodist Church of America*, 1950–59; *Minutes of the Annual Session of the Allegheny Conference of the Wesleyan Methodist Church of America*, 1960–66.

3. *Minutes of the Annual Session of the Dakota Conference of the Wesleyan Methodist Church of America*, 1950–68; *Conscience and Commitment*,406; *Wesleyan Advocate*, September 3, 1984, 18.

4. *Wesleyan Advocate*, December 10, 1973, 17.

5. *Minutes of the Annual Session of the Nebraska Conference of the Wesleyan Methodist Church of America*, 1950–64; *Minutes of the Annual Session of the Dakota Conference of the Wesleyan Methodist Church of America*, 1966–68.

6. Information supplied by Hazel Thomas Leatherman.

7. *Minutes of the Annual Session of the Illinois Conference of the Wesleyan Methodist Church of America*, 1951–58, 1960–66.

8. Information supplied by Carrie N. Hancock, who had co-pastored with Henrietta News for fifteen years.

9. Records of the Eastern Ohio District of the Pilgrim Holiness Church, 1956–57, 1959–67; book on Pilgrim Holiness missionaries; *Wesleyan Advocate*, October 20, 1986, 17.

10. *Minutes of the Annual Session of the Nebraska Conference of the Wesleyan Methodist Church of America*, 1950–64; *Conscience and Commitment*, 441.

11. Personal information supplied by Ruth Willingham, and by her son, Rev. Steven R. Willingham,

campus director of the Wesleyan Seminary Foundation at Asbury Theological Seminary, Wilmore, Kentucky.

12. *Minutes of the Annual Assembly of the Pilgrim Holiness Church Illinois District*, 1950–52; *Minutes of the Annual Conference of the Tennessee District Pilgrim Holiness Church*, 1954–57.

13 *Minutes of the Annual Conference of the Indiana District, Pilgrim Holiness Church*, 1950; *Minutes of the Annual Conference of the Northern Indiana District, Pilgrim Holiness Church*, 1951–67; *Wesleyan Advocate*, July 17, 18; information supplied by Rev. Ernest R. Batman, former superintendent of the Indiana Central District of The Wesleyan Church.

14. *Know Your Missionaries*.

15. *Minutes of the Annual Session of the Nebraska Conference of the Wesleyan Methodist Church of America*, 1951–58, 1960–64.

16. *Minutes of the Annual Session of the North Carolina Conference of the Wesleyan Methodist Church of America*, 1942, 1945–68; personal information supplied by Ruth Hames Sparks.

17. *Minutes of the Annual Session of the Ohio Conference of the Wesleyan Methodist Church of America*, 1952–59.

18. *Minutes of the Annual Session of the North Carolina Conference of the Wesleyan Methodist Church of America*, 1952–68; *Centennial Celebration 1879–1979, North Carolina (Colfax) District, The Wesleyan Church*, published by the North Carolina Colfax District of The Wesleyan Church, Centennial Committee: Dr. B. H. Phaup, Rev. Dewey Miller and Rev. A. Dixon Wood.

19. *Minutes of the Annual Session of the Florida Conference of the Wesleyan Methodist Church of America*, 1952–67.

20. Records of the Michigan District of the Pilgrim Holiness Church, 1956–63, 1966–67; information supplied by Rev. Robert Cooper, former superintendent of the North Michigan District of The Wesleyan Church.

21. *Minutes of the Annual Session of the Lockport Conference Inc. of the Wesleyan Methodist Church of America*, 1950, 1953–57; *Minutes of the Annual Session of the Ohio Conference of the Wesleyan Methodist Church of America*, 1957–68.

22. *Minutes of the Annual Session of the Ohio Conference of the Wesleyan Methodist Church of America*, 1953–68; book on Wesleyan Methodist missionaries; books on missionaries of The Wesleyan Church; *Conscience and Commitment*, 435–436; personal information supplied by Freda Farmer.

23. *Minutes of the Annual Conference of the Indiana North District Pilgrim Holiness Church*, 1963–67; book on Pilgrim Holiness missionaries; *Journal of the North Carolina East District of The Wesleyan Church*, 1997; *Wesleyan Advocate*, May 1997, 32.

24. Records of the Idaho-Washington District of the Pilgrim Holiness Church, 1953–55; *Conference Journal of the Pennsylvania and New Jersey District of the Pilgrim Holiness Church*, 1956–67; *Wesleyan Advocate*, May 1991; personal information supplied by Betty Lou Washburn.

25. *Minutes of the Annual Session of the Wisconsin Conference of the Wesleyan Methodist Church of America*, 1954–67.

26. *Minutes of the Annual Session of the Ohio Conference of the Wesleyan Methodist Church of America*, 1954–68.

27. Records of the Idaho-Washington District of the Pilgrim Holiness Church, 1954–57; records of the California District of the Pilgrim Holiness Church, 1960–61; records of the Kansas District of the Pilgrim Holiness Church, 1962–68; *Wesleyan Advocate*, October 7, 1985, 18.

28. *Minutes of the Annual Session of the Iowa Conference of the Wesleyan Methodist Church of America*, 1954–55; *Minutes of the Annual Session of the Wisconsin Conference of the Wesleyan Methodist Church of America*, 1955–65; *100 Years 1867–1967 Wisconsin Conference Centennial*; personal information supplied by Dorothy Johnson Clark.

29. Records of the South Central District of the Pilgrim Holiness Church, 1954; records of the California District of the Pilgrim Holiness Church, 1963; The Historian Committee, "History of the Holiness Churches of California."

30. *Minutes of the Annual Session of the Illinois Conference of the Wesleyan Methodist Church of America*, 1954; *Minutes of the Annual Session of the Middle Atlantic States Mission Conference of the Wesleyan Methodist Church of America*, 1954–67.

31. Records of the Eastern District of the Pilgrim Holiness Church, 1954–55; *Conference Journal of the Pennsylvania and New Jersey District of the Pilgrim Holiness Church*, 1956–67; personal information supplied by Margie F. Morris.

32. *Journal of Proceedings of the Annual Session of the Southern Indiana Conference of the Pilgrim Holiness Church*, 1954–67; *Wesleyan Advocate*, February 1995.

33. *Minutes of the Annual Session of the Kentucky Conference of the Wesleyan Methodist Church of America*, 1955–67; *Wesleyan Advocate*, September 7, 1987.

34. *Minutes of the Annual Session of the Champlain Conference of the Wesleyan Methodist Church of America*, 1955–68; *Wesleyan Advocate*, May 28, 1973, 17.

35. *Minutes of the Annual Conference of the Pilgrim Holiness Church Rocky Mountain District*, 1961–67; *Wesleyan Advocate*, March 2000, 32.

36. *Minutes of the Annual Session of the North Carolina Conference of the Wesleyan Methodist Church of America*, 1956–68.

37. Records of the three districts for the years indicated; information supplied by Dr. James Vermilya, former superintendent of the Western Ohio District of The Wesleyan Church.

38. Records of the Eastern District of the Pilgrim Holiness Church, 1956–67; information supplied by Dr. Ronald D. Kelly, General Secretary of The Wesleyan Church, who grew up in the Eastern District.

39. *Minutes of the Annual Session of the Nebraska Conference of the Wesleyan Methodist Church of America*, 1956–64.

40. *Minutes of the Annual Session of the Lockport Conference Inc. of the Wesleyan Methodist Church of America*, 1956–60; *Minutes of the Annual Session of the Canada Conference of the Wesleyan Methodist Church*, 1960–66; *Our Heritage, Lockport Conference Centennial 1861–1961*, published by the Lockport Conference of the Wesleyan Methodist Church of America, Houghton, New York, Mary E. Bennett, editor; "A History of the Wesleyan Methodist Church of America in Canada, 1894–1968," H. Kielty, August 1984, typewritten manuscript.

41. Records of the Kentucky District of the Pilgrim Holiness Church, 1956–57; an unidentified newspaper feature about Helen Winchester's ministry; personal information supplied by Helen Winchester.

42. Personal information supplied by Donna Dean; information supplied by Dr. James Vermilya, former superintendent of the Western Ohio District of The Wesleyan Church.

43. Records of the British Isles District, 1962–67; personal information supplied by Dorothy de Freitas; information supplied by Dr. Harry F. Wood.

44. Records of the California District of the Pilgrim Holiness Church, 1960–68; The Historian Committee, "History of the Holiness Churches in California," 160.

45. *Minutes of the Annual Session of the Kentucky Conference of the Wesleyan Methodist Church of America*, 1958–59; *Wesleyan Methodist*, September 28, 1960, 15.

46. Records of the Idaho-Washington District of the Pilgrim Holiness Church, 1958–62; *Minutes of the Annual Assembly of the Ontario District of the Pilgrim Holiness Church*, 1963–67; *Wesleyan Advocate*, January 2, 1984, 18.

47. *Minutes of the Annual Session of the Lockport Annual Conference Inc. of the Wesleyan Methodist Church of America*, 1958–67; *Our Heritage Lockport Conference Centennial 1861–1961*, published by the Lockport Conference of the Wesleyan Methodist Church of America, Houghton, New York, Mary E. Bennett, editor; *Wesleyan Advocate*, May 1996, 31.

48. *Minutes of the Annual Session of the Indiana Conference of the Wesleyan Methodist Church of America*, 1959–68; personal information supplied by Virginia Ruth Anderson.

49. *Minutes of the Alliance of the Reformed Baptist Church of Canada*, 1959–66; *Minutes of the Atlantic Conference of the Wesleyan Methodist Church of America*, 1967; personal information supplied by Sheila McCrea-MacCallum.

Chapter 7

1. Information supplied by Rev. Robert W. Cooper, former superintendent of the North Michigan District of The Wesleyan Church.

2. Information supplied by Evon Pulliam.

3. Information supplied by Rev. Ernest R. Batman, former superintendent of the Indiana Central District of The Wesleyan Church; *Wesleyan Advocate*, August 15, 1988.

4. Records of the California District of the Pilgrim Holiness Church, 1966–67; books on Wesleyan Church missionaries.

5. *Minutes of the Annual Conference of the Pilgrim Holiness Church Rocky Mountain District*, 1961–67; book on Pilgrim Holiness missionaries.

6. *Minutes of the Annual Conference of the Western Ohio District of the Pilgrim Holiness Church*, 1962–67;

personal information supplied by Mrs. Beulah Hicks.

7. *Minutes of the Annual Session of the Ohio Conference of the Wesleyan Methodist Church of America*, 1963–68; information supplied by Dr. James Vermilya, former superintendent of the Western Ohio District of The Wesleyan Church; *Wesleyan Advocate*, May 1997, 31.

8. *Minutes of the Annual Assembly of the Pilgrim Holiness Church Illinois District*, 1963–68; *Days of Our Pilgrimage*, 352.

9. *Minutes of the Annual Conference of the Western Ohio District of the Pilgrim Holiness Church*, 1962–67; *Days of Our Pilgrimage*, 353.

10. *Minutes of the Annual Session of the Georgia Conference of the Wesleyan Methodist Church*, 1964–67; information supplied by Rev. Hugh C. Pope, former superintendent of the Georgia District of The Wesleyan Church; letter from Dr. Donald Wood, faculty member, Southern Wesleyan University; copy of the tribute given by the Georgia District in 1995.

11. *Minutes of the Annual Session of the Dakota Conference of the Wesleyan Methodist Church of America*, 1964–68; *Conscience and Commitment*, 441.

12. Records of the South Ohio Conference of the Wesleyan Methodist Church/South Ohio District of The Wesleyan Church, 1968–71; "A Story of One Hundred Years 1842–1942 of the First Wesleyan Methodist Church at Dayton, Ohio," compiled and edited by Charles R. H. Johnson; a handwritten obituary.

13. Information supplied by Dr. James Vermilya, former superintendent of the Western Ohio District of The Wesleyan Church.

Index

*I*n the Index, an attempt has been made to include all possible forms of each lady's name (pre-marriage, married, multiple marriages) so readers can find a woman's story regardless of which form of her name they know. Also, there are instances in which two persons have identical names. Both are listed in the same entry in the Index by appropriate page numbers. There may be instances in which, because of marriage, change of district, or different phase of life, there are two stories that relate to the same person, but the available evidence is insufficient to be sure.

Harris, Florence 120-121
Harris, Gertrude 116-117
Harris, Mrs. James B. 116-117
Harris, Verna 195, 249-250
Harrold, Mrs. H. S. 195
Hart, Alice M. 72-73
Hart, Cora Hathaway 188
Hart, Mrs. William J. 72-73
Hartley, Anna 339
Hartley, Mrs. Kenneth J. 339
Hartnal, Lorena E. 43
Harvey, Mary 175
Harvey, Mary E. Powers 175
Harvey, Mrs. Charles 157
Harvey, Mrs. Harrison A. 270-271
Harvey, Mrs. Lorenzo A. 175
Harvey, Mrs. Mills A. 46-47
Harvey, Sarah 46-47
Harvey, Willa E. Nelson 270-271
Hatcher, Bessie 107-108, 377
Hatcher, Bessie F. 107-108, 377
Hathaway, Cora 188
Hathaway, Jessie 251
Haun, Vivian 249, 251
Haviland, Laura Smith 16-17, 369
Haviland, Mrs. Charles 16-17, 369
Hawk, Irene 331
Hawk, Irene Frances 331
Hayden, Mrs. H. E. 18
Haymond, Bertha 84
Hazeltine, Elsie M. 34
Hazelwood, Dorotha Shook 276
Hazewinkle, Cathrine 161
Hazzard, Carrie 164-165, 241, 382
Hazzard, Carrie M. 164-165, 241, 382
Headley, Aldene 261
Heath, Florence 99
Heath, Florence E. 99
Heavilin, Alice Mae 192, 276, 394
Heavilin, Mrs. Ronald A. 192, 276, 394
Heck, May S. 305
Heckart, Alice 143
Heckart, Alice Pearl Hoover Lutz 143

Heckart, Mrs. Robert 143
Heim, Ruth 301-302
Henderson, Estella 348
Henderson, Louise 142
Henderson, Louise J. Gifford 142
Henderson, Norma 249
Henry, Mrs. F. W. 221
Henry, Mrs. Frank W. 221
Henschen, C. Bonnie 363
Henschen, Fern Neely 135-136
Henschen, Mrs. Walter G. 135-136
Hensley, Martha 143
Hertel, Velma H. 306
Heslop, Mrs. William 130
Heslop, Norah 130
Hickman, Hattie 121
Hicks, Beulah 360, 400
Higgs, Fannie 136
Higgs, Mrs. A. R. 136
Hildenbrand, Marie 237
Hiles, Mrs. Lewis C. 157
Hiles, Vera Anna 157
Hiles, Vera Anna Hunter 157
Hines, Anna E. 63
Hitesman, Nora 210
Hobbs, Christina 240
Hobbs, Florence 161
Hodge, Mrs. Paul 175-176
Hodge, Olive 175-176
Hodge, Olive Lucinda 175-176
Hodgin, Jennie 130
Hodson, Ada Scott 263
Hodson, Belle 23-24
Hodson, Mrs. Harley 23-24
Hofen, Judith 317
Hofen, Mrs. O. R. 317
Hoffman, Etta 51-52, 84
Hoffman, Mrs. Harley 233
Hoffman, Mrs. Jacob 51-52, 84
Hogarth, Mrs. Virgil 339
Hogarth, Ruth 339
Hoien, Grace Miller 277
Hoien, Mrs. Clifford 271
Hoien, Mrs. John 277
Hoien, Ruth E. 271
Holden, Louella 220-221
Holden, Luella 220-221
Holden, Nellie 220-221

Holgate, Margaret 189-190
Hollenback, Alma G. 244
Hollenback, Mrs. U. T. 244
Hollowell, Katherine 110, 166
Holstein, Billie 187
Holycross, Viola 296
Holycross, Viola M. 296
Honeycutt, Elma 226-227, 389
Honeycutt, Mrs. W. E. 226-227, 389
Hood, Mrs. Albert M. 344
Hooker, Reba 216
Hoos, Carrie Mae Crumpton 60-61
Hoos, Carrie 60-61
Hoos, Mrs. Thomas H. 60-61
Hooth, Gertrude 246-247, 391
Hoover, Alice Pearl 143
Hoover, Deborah 317
Hopper, Catherine 362
Horst, Helen 258
Hotle, Della 195-196
Hotle, Della J. Turner 195-196
Hotle, Mrs. Frank C. 195
Houch, Laura 342
Houch, Mrs. W. C. 342
Houston, Edith 166
Houston, Edith Downs Wenz 166
Houston, Mrs. Laurence S. 166
Hovland, Elvina Anna 254-255
Howard, Deborah 317
Howard, Madge 257, 392
Howard, Mrs. Alonzo 317
Howell, Mrs. E. O. 40, 176
Howell, Mrs. Warren 361
Howell, Rachel 176
Howerton, Vera 218
Howlett, Cordelia Rebecca "Delia" 68-69
Howlett, Delia 68-69
Hu, Betty 328
Hubby, Bernice 298
Hubby, Marie 263-264
Hubby, Mrs. G. M. 263-264
Hubby, Mrs. William 298
Huddleston, Callie 305
Huff, Eunice May 211-212
Huff, Mrs. Carl W. 298, 396
Huff, Ruth 298, 396
Huffine, Bernice 344